SEPARATISM AND SUBCULTURE

SEPARATISM

Boston

Catholicism,

1900–1920

PAULA M. KANE

The

University

of North

Carolina

Press

Chapel Hill

& London

AND SUBCULTURE

Library of Congress Cataloging-in-Publication Data
Kane, Paula M.
    Separatism and subculture : Boston
Catholicism, 1900–1920 / by Paula M. Kane.
        p. cm.
    Includes bibliographical references
and index.
    ISBN 0-8078-2128-4 (alk. paper)
    1. Catholics—Massachusetts—Boston—
Cultural assimilation. 2. Catholics—
Massachusetts—Boston—History—20th
century. 3. Boston (Mass.)—Social
conditions. 4. Boston (Mass.)—Church
history. I. Title.
F73.9.C3K36 1994
305.6'2074461—dc20   93-32053
                                        CIP

98 97 96 95 94   5 4 3 2 1

To my parents, Joseph and Annette

CONTENTS

Acknowledgments   xi

1   Chapter 1. The Dilemma of Catholic Separatism

Introduction   1
Boston and the Vatican   8
Social Catholicism and Institutionalism   10
Archbishop William O'Connell   13

22   Chapter 2. The Limits of Americanization

The 1908 Catholic Centenary   22
Catholics and "Boston, 1915"   31
Ford Hall Forum and Democratization   36
Social Work and Immigrant Americanization   38
The Catholic Common Cause Society   42
"Cross and Flag Aloft"   45

48   Chapter 3. Class, Manhood, and Material Success

Religion and Ethnic Assimilation   48
The Boston Catholic Elite   51
"Ishmaelites in America": Defining Catholic Manhood   75
Catholic Education and Material Success   89
Lay Associations and Fraternalism   95
A Catholic Critique of Individualism   104

108   Chapter 4. The Functions of Catholic Architecture

A Catholic Antiurban Tradition   108
Architecture as Apologetic   114
The Gothic Ideal   120
The Financing of Churches   128
Catholic Architects and Builders in Boston   132
Growth of Related Industries   139
Architecture as Tradition   143

145   Chapter 5. The Ideology of Catholic Womanhood

The Church's View of Woman   145
Home and the Moral Order   153
From Daughters of Eve to Children of Mary   157
Women and Education   167
"A Properly Guarded Youth": Female Advice Literature   176
Female Converts to Catholicism   180
The Ideal Catholic Woman   196

200   Chapter 6. Organizing Catholic Women

Clubwomen and Middle-Class Formation   200
Catholic Women's Societies   205
Professional Laywomen: Two Examples   221
Toward Women's Autonomy:
   Suffrage, Work, and Social Feminism   239

253   Chapter 7. The Control of Culture

Situating Catholic Culture   253
The Anti-Ugly Crusade in Catholic Aesthetics   262
Against Modernism   268
Production of a Catholic Subculture   274
The Catholic Writer and Publisher   282
Catholic Books and the Market   289
Babylon or Israel?: The Politics of Popular Entertainment   293
Censorship and Culture   298

314   Chapter 8. The Achievement of Separatist Integration

"The Puritan has passed; the Catholic remains"   314

Notes   325

References   377

Index   405

ILLUSTRATIONS

16 William Cardinal O'Connell and James P. E. O'Connell, 1918

23 Catholic parade pageantry, Worcester, Massachusetts, 1907

31 Second Catholic Missionary Congress, 1913

35 "Boston, 1915" exhibition in Copley Square

64 James Jeffrey Roche

67 Joseph Pelletier

77 Seminarians at St. John's, 1922–23

80 Michael Earls as a Jesuit novice

90 St. Agnes School

93 Male student playing Hecuba at Holy Cross College, 1926

101 Cardinal O'Connell and Rev. Michael Splaine, 1924

119 Neo-Gothic at Boston College

120 St. Joseph's Chapel at Holy Cross College

123 Charles Maginnis

131 Ready-made church architectural plan, 1907

135 Church of St. Catherine of Genoa, Somerville

140 Eleanor Manning O'Connor

142 Fish flake advertisement in the Catholic press

167 Backyard theatricals at Guiney's Longwall Cottage, 1918

169 Sisters of St. Joseph in the St. Regis Orchestra

183 Martha Moore Avery

189 Rose Hawthorne Lathrop (Mother Mary Alphonsa)

210   Cardinal Gibbons at Catholic Summer School, 1910

226   Katherine Conway

233   Louise Imogen Guiney

237   J. J. Roche cartoon of himself and Louise Guniey

238   Household of Guiney women

240   Mary Boyle O'Reilly

279   Michael Earls and G. K. Chesterton at Holy Cross College

280   The senior debating team, Holy Cross College, 1907–8

300   Eamon De Valera at Holy Cross College, 1920

316   Martha Moore Avery and David Goldstein

318   David Goldstein

ACKNOWLEDGMENTS

I would like to express my appreciation to the many persons and institutions who have helped me since this book's first appearance as a dissertation. For those friends who had presumed that my subject was the Fitzgeralds and the Kennedys, I hope they are not disappointed. For my college friends who have wondered if their Irish Catholic ancestors would appear in these pages, even if they do not agree entirely with my interpretation, they will surely recognize traces of early twentieth-century Catholicism in their own experience, no matter how faint or quaint.

Sydney Ahlstrom, my initial dissertation advisor at Yale University, did not live to see the final product. David Montgomery took up the task of dissertation advisor thereafter, and I am grateful for his continued interest in a project that, although not focused on labor history, has implications for the study of intersections between religion, labor, and class formation. Among the other professional debts I have accumulated are those to David O'Brien of the College of the Holy Cross, who first introduced me to the historical study of Catholicism; James O'Toole of the University of Massachusetts-Boston; Mary Oates of Regis College; and Debra Campbell of Colby College. Each has provided inspiration, advice, and a scholarly network for the study of Boston and of American Catholicism. The late Monsignor Francis J. Lally of Boston offered anecdotal evidence in abundance when I interviewed him at this project's beginning. I am especially grateful to Robert Resch for his suggestions, for his insights into social theory, and for his emotional support. In his capacity as reader, James Fisher provided helpful suggestions for the final stage of manuscript preparation. Jim Ford helped locate photographs in the Boston Public Library. Dana Polan volunteered comments on my discussion of Catholics and film in Chapter 7. The Cushwa Center for the Study of American Catholicism at the University of Notre Dame distributed a portion of Chapter 7 in its Working Paper Series, and I thank the center staff and affiliated members of the university, especially Jay Dolan and Philip Gleason, for their gracious interest in the progress of this book over the years.

In terms of institutional support, I gratefully acknowledge reception of a grant from the Central Research Fund of the Faculty of Arts and Sciences,

University of Pittsburgh, as well as a Third Term Faculty Research Grant. My research was also supported by a faculty development grant from Texas A&M University. The National Endowment for the Humanities provided a travel to collections grant that partially funded research in Rome at the Vatican Archives. Finally, I thank the staffs at each of the archives and libraries listed at the end of this volume. Among these, James Mahoney, curator of rare books at Holy Cross College, deserves special thanks for his extraordinary accommodations to my research schedule and for his beguiling treasury of reminiscences of Catholic New England.

SEPARATISM AND SUBCULTURE

1

THE DILEMMA OF CATHOLIC SEPARATISM

That the Church had been in a State of Siege for three centuries, was no longer so, yet had not completely adapted herself to the new situation and to Protestantism and Secularism, she had drawn within her entrenchments, refused intellectual parley with a hostile world, and concentrated on arming and drilling her own subjects for the defence of the City to the comparative neglect of its normal development.
—Maisie Ward, *The Wilfrid Wards and the Transition*

It will be a mighty interesting thing, I grant you, to watch Catholicism in America[,] . . . and a mighty dramatic thing too. Personally, I stand outside of all religions. But I hope the Roman Church won't lose sight of its real opportunity in the effort to get control of secular affairs.—"Ferguson" in Vida Scudder, *A Listener in Babel*

Fifty years ago, Catholics were suspected of being incapable of patriotism. Today real patriotism finds its chief maintenance and nourishment in the Catholic heart . . . which pulsates in the very heart of Christendom, the center of the Church's life—Rome, Eternal Rome, where Christ's own Vicar reigns, and where the immutable principles of God's revelation are conserved and faithfully guarded.
—Archbishop William O'Connell, "The Nation's Manhood"

Introduction

Between 1900 and 1920 the Catholic community of Boston experienced a cultural transition from the ethnic enclaves of nineteenth-century immigrants toward the acculturated but ghettoized Catholic America of the 1950s. A distinct Catholic subculture may have intervened somewhere in this passage from immigrant to American, marked by a new form of religious identity hoping to unite ethnic factions and to maintain Catholic autonomy against perceived oppressors. The unique divisions in Boston between Irish Catholics and Yankee Protestants were described by Katherine Conway, who moved there in the 1880s: "To a young journalist coming to the capital of New England from Western New York, it was like coming to another world. . . . The whole aspect and outlook were radically different. There was a line of cleavage in Boston that she had not encountered before in the few cities in which she had dwelt. It was a frankly racial and religious line—a little more religious than racial."[1]

This noticeable barrier separating Catholics from Protestants, which shaped the perspective of Massachusetts Catholics, had been hardened by their memories of antebellum convent-burnings, street riots, the sensationalist *Maria Monk* novels, Know-Nothingism, and the housing, school, and job discrimination perpetuated by Protestants. However, the religious bias that Conway felt had just as often taken the form of racial prejudice. New Englanders typically charged Irish immigrants with antirepublicanism, rather than attacking their theology or religious practices. From the Gilded Age through the Progressive era, Americans continued to couch debates about ownership of democratic ideals of freedom in political rather than religious terms. Still, in Massachusetts, such debates frequently had undeniable religious implications, as in the defeat of funding for parochial schools in 1889, the rise of the American Protective Association and other anti-Catholic groups in the 1890s, and the passage of the "Anti-Aid" or sectarian amendment in 1917, which, by denying state aid to parochial schools, rejected the legitimacy of Catholic private education. These events perhaps convinced Irish Catholics that they were destined to permanent outsiderness.

Around 1900, the archdiocese of Boston comprised some 1 million Catholics who were struggling for acceptance as Americans, but who would soon be urged to cultivate a Catholic identity distinct from the Yankee Protestant environment and from secular influences. As described by Kerby Miller, the role of the Catholic Church had become one of preaching "the twin gospels of respectability and resignation."[2] These tensions between individual ambition and group powerlessness took the form of contradictory tendencies toward assimilation and separatism as represented by "insider" and "outsider" mentalities. The presence of an insider-outsider mentality in Catholicism is defined by distinctions made by historians and by historical actors themselves about the relationship between some cultural and economic mainstream and themselves as a deviant group.[3] Religious historians have often described America as dominated by Protestant insiders who have ideologically constructed American identity. While this overstates the case, in Massachusetts, state and local power did reflect sharp ethnic and religious divisions. Over time, as the Irish developed a viable middle class and an organized political clique, they became receptive to assimilationist pressures and to mainstream values as well as to the Church's strategies to promote and isolate them. However, a sense of being excluded remained a useful stimulus for the formation of an autonomous, separatist subculture, providing Catholics with an outgroup communal identity.[4] Indeed, since insider and outsider identities seldom appear independently of each other, Catholics could continue to protest anti-Catholic discrimination when it was useful to do so, while at the same time growing to resemble insiders by gaining control of institutions that Protestants had long manipulated: city government, public schools, public libraries, and the press.[5]

As a study of a historical moment in the life of one Catholic archdiocese, this book explores how power is exerted by and within an American religious community that was itself shaped by local, national, and transnational factors. The Church's role went well beyond defining doctrinal orthodoxy to affect many aspects of lay experience, including individual and group religious identity, attitudes toward material success, culture, and gender relations. In selecting these four areas, I do not mean to undervalue or ignore the significance of the ritualistic component of Roman Catholicism—going to Mass, participating in the sacraments, saints' festivals, weddings, wakes, burials, and so forth—but in the interest of describing the interplay between Catholic insider and outsider attitudes and between clergy and laity, I have emphasized instead the effects of what I will call the Church's strategy of separatist integration.

The conflict between integration and separatism, between insider and outsider strategies, was complicated by authoritarian strategies of the American hierarchy, as it underwent a major transition from the parish-centered immigrant Church of the nineteenth century to the bishop-centered dioceses of the pre–Vatican II era. Led by Archbishop William O'Connell (1859–1944) for thirty-seven years, the archdiocese of Boston epitomized the centralizing, aggressively separatist tendencies of this ecclesiology. Still, the Boston community was not a mirror of the archbishop's views. In fact, tensions between Catholic culture and American culture were heightened by competing factions within Catholicism over three areas: clerical culture versus lay culture, parochial autonomy versus diocesan leadership, and an immigrant lower class versus an assimilated Catholic middle class.[6]

The ability of the clergy to speak for the Catholic community was decisively shaped by the character and longevity of the administration of Archbishop O'Connell between 1907 and 1944.[7] One cannot deny O'Connell's arrogance, but it is likewise unfair to dismiss his critiques of American culture as mindlessly destructive or callous gestures, as some have done.[8] In fact, in many ways his opinions expressed exactly those of the upwardly mobile Irish. We should, however, distinguish briefly between the Church's hostility to social and political change (antimodernism) and its theological anti-Modernism. The doctrinal propositions and methods condemned as heresies by the Church in 1907 were not synonymous with those aspects of American society to which the Church objected, although the same fear of "innovation" and "subversion" of Church authority underlay both. O'Connell's 1907 pastoral letter against Modernism in fact implied close affinities between American mainstream values and the Modernist creed: "The American people are not given to religious speculation as those more idealistic," he wrote, "but in practical life their characteristics are precisely those by which the Modernist was influenced in framing his scheme of doctrine and apologetics."[9] O'Connell's harangues against modern civilization meant to "build up" Roman Catholicism as the pinnacle of American republican institutions. Although he never intended to place nationalism above the Catholic religion, O'Connell's vision of the common destiny of church and republic seized an old Yankee Protestant theme of a harmonious citizenry and made it a unique form of separatist, sectarian power. By the end of World War I, he even suggested that Catholics alone were the bearers of American values. By this mixture of aggressive patriotism and righteous sectarianism, he attempted to unite clerical and lay goals.

As noted above, the locus of power within the Catholic Church was changing at the end of the nineteenth century, which gave rise to a second kind of factionalism. There was a growing distinction between the parish-centered life of immigrants and the diocesan focus and nationally organized church born from a recent organizational revolution. The movement to bureaucratize and centralize Catholic charities, schools, seminaries, colleges, and even the diocesan press affected Boston. While he did not intend to undermine parish loyalty, Archbishop O'Connell's attempt to consolidate power made it unacceptable (at least in theory) for clergy or laity to offer rival initiatives from the parish level or from outside the parish structure that conflicted with diocesan goals. O'Connell announced his plan for standardizing liturgy and the financial administration of parishes as early as 1909 and relied on a circle of priest-bureaucrats subservient to himself for its enforcement.[10] He only partially achieved these goals, however, checked by continuing challenges from antagonistic pastors and nuns, the demands of ethnic parishes, and the complex infrastructure of the chancery offices and bureaus.[11]

A third conflict among Boston Catholics derived from class tensions within the Irish population, between a lower class with strong ethnic ties and a post-immigrant middle-class community, not lacking ethnic consciousness but now an influential cohort with economic interests to defend. Irish Catholics nonetheless retained a disproportionately large underclass over time, in contrast to their mobility in other U.S. cities and the pattern of other ethnic groups. In some ways Boston represented a swamp of Irish underachievement, while giving the appearance of a thriving community. Nonetheless, a Catholic middle class emerged primarily from those Irish who had arrived in New England well before the southern Europeans who came between 1880 and 1924.[12]

A focus on Boston's Irish Catholics is also justified by the disproportionate impact of the Irish on American Catholicism. The religious influence of the Irish extended well beyond the Northeast to the style and leadership of most American dioceses. Even in New York City, where after 1880 Italians outnumbered all other immigrant groups, the form of parish organization remained Irish.[13] Throughout the United States, complaints about a "Hibernarchy" were heard as early as the 1860s, and most bishops, priests, and nuns continued to be of Irish descent until at least the 1950s. Boston's Catholic character was additionally influenced by Irish attitudes toward Irish politics and Vatican authority. A revitalized loyalty of Irish Catholics to the Roman Church had been achieved in Ireland during its so-called devotional revolution of the mid-nineteenth century.[14] Irish immigrants to America were predisposed toward social conservatism and clericalism, and to a romantic identification between the Church and Irish nationalist claims against Great Britain. Irish immigrants came to dominate the American hierarchy and priesthood simultaneously, many of them products of Maynooth Seminary near Dublin, of Rome, or of Boston's diocesan seminary. Succeeding generations of Irish Catholics were predisposed to favor the institutional Church and their own clergy. In Boston, the Irish, dominant clerically, numerically, and economically, controlled the basic units of religious and political culture.

This observation by no means suggests a lack of ethnic diversity of Boston's parishes. Selecting one random example, we find that the 1909 parish census at Sacred Heart Parish, Cambridge, recorded a total of 1,360 families and 7,050 members, mostly Irish. However, Sunday school records note the presence of "foreigners": 39 Italian, 28 French, 25 Portuguese, 15 Polish, 6 German, 3 Swedish, 1 Armenian, and 1 Lithuanian.[15] To accommodate ethnic pluralism, about 30 percent of new parishes founded in New England between 1880 and 1930 were ethnic (national) parishes, compared with a mere 9 percent between 1850 and 1880.[16] Nonetheless, it is estimated that even by the time of Cardinal O'Connell's death in 1944, 85 percent of Boston's parishes and about 80 percent of Boston's urban population from downtown to within a ten-mile radius were Irish.[17] Although the Irish dominated clerical and class leadership, giving the illusion of ethnic solidarity, class awareness did emerge in the often repeated distinctions between "lace curtain" and "shanty" Irish.

In Boston's inhospitable social environment, Catholic laymen gained some footholds through politics and military service, aided by cooperative Yankee liberals. The first Catholic mayor of Boston, Hugh O'Brien, served four successive terms, from 1885 to 1889. His victory was possible because of Yankee-Irish bonding, which lasted through the 1906–8 term of Boston's third Irish Catholic mayor, John ("Honey Fitz") Fitzgerald, but which collapsed in the bitter mayoral election that put George Hibbard in City Hall. Fitzgerald, however, returned as mayor from 1910 to 1913, before he was defeated by another Irish Catholic, the boisterous "rascal king," James Michael Curley. While Curley was just beginning his flamboyant and often illegal maneuvers as mayor of Boston, what was perhaps the most honorable and sustained Catholic career in politics was being undertaken by David I. Walsh of Worcester, who was elected lieutenant governor in 1912, governor in 1914, and senator in

1918 and 1926. But in municipal politics, Martin "Mahatma" Lomasney, perhaps the most powerful of the Irish ward bosses, held sway in the West End of Boston, while others held lesser fiefdoms around the city—Patrick Kennedy in the East End, Joe Corbett in Charlestown, Joe O'Connell in Dorchester, and James Donovan in the South End.[18]

In addition to political machines, wars had an assimilationist effect on Irish Catholics. Their military service in the Civil War was their first chance to prove loyalty to the Union. World War I provided the same opportunity on a larger scale and also handed Catholics an ideological victory: 1921 found Catholics "untouched by postwar disillusionment" and able to preside over the idealism that other Americans had allegedly lost. Catholics reputedly maintained this "innocent" sensibility until after the Second World War. Reflecting the late nineteenth-century Thomistic revival, buoyed by intellectual and philosophical optimism, and shaped by American imperialist attempts to democratize the world, the Church claimed that there existed "a uniquely Catholic view of things."[19] By sharpening their political pressure tactics, by the 1920s Catholic Church leaders acquired a reputation for moral puritanism. Their opposition to woman suffrage reflected widespread conservative attitudes about woman's proper domain in society, while the rejection of child labor regulation reflected the suspicion of many Americans toward social change engineered by government intervention. But the Progressive era saw rising misunderstanding and intolerance of the Catholic Church. The Church's opposition to the Nineteenth Amendment in 1920, and its role in defeating a proposed federal constitutional amendment protecting minors from the abuses of child labor in 1924, gave the Progressives, for example, an impression of Roman Catholics as inexplicably opposing the enfranchisement of women and the protection of children.[20] By the 1930s, Catholic puritanism had organized national theater and film censorship campaigns, crusades against birth control and divorce, and related denouncements of modern culture.

By 1900 an informal variety of Catholic social and benevolent associations, clubs, and publications existed, generally anchored around the parish. In the next half-century the Church lost its survivalist ethic and became patterned on bourgeois norms and social institutions. As Catholicism began to lose its foreign flavor by the 1910s, and as the number of Irish Americans with foreign-born parents declined sharply after the restrictionist legislation of the 1920s, the Church rechanneled the lay campaigns of the 1890s to indoctrinate American-born Catholics against socialism, in order to prevent the radicalization and secularization of the working class. What forms and functions, then, did a separatist Catholic subculture serve in Boston in the transitional decades between the Gilded Age and the Jazz Age?

While this book is not the place to resolve extensive scholarly debate over the definitions of culture and subculture, some parameters are useful. In examining culture, I bear in mind the ongoing reflections of a circle of cultural studies practitioners interested in a materialist theory of culture, who have identified and developed two opposing factions: those who see culture as lived experience affected by material life, and those who stress ideology or the ways in which mental life is determined.[21] In agreement with the assumption that culture reflects both material conditions and consciousness, in my usage culture therefore implies a traditional definition of the unity of the experience of symbols, rituals, beliefs, and ideologies shared by a people, but it also includes the ways in which individual consciousness has a social formation. In this case, ideology may in fact be economic in the last instance, although it is not understood crudely as a direct result of material practices. Religion, then, can be studied as an inseparable part of culture that is both deeply embedded in and reflective of local and national cultures and economies, yet which is not some inevitably determined product of them. Religions have, for example, mobilized resistance to their host environment.

My description of a religious subculture implies "a group—or its beliefs and practices—existing within a broader society and culture, but deviating from the norms of that culture in a significant fashion."[22] *Subculture* has been generally used by students of immigration history without reference to these theoretical debates about culture. Ethnic subcultures, as they have been viewed, emerged as survival mechanisms for immigrants. Though by 1910 the relatively unplanned ghetto of Boston Catholicism had already absorbed many elements of the American way of life, including capitalism, pragmatism, and patriotic identification, the Church now began to deliberately construct a discourse of Catholic difference and even of superiority.

The assimilation or "Americanization" of American-born Catholics followed "the processes by which individuals and identifiable social groups shed the characteristics that mark them as foreign, adopt the cultural norms of American society, become fully integrated into American life, and come to think of themselves simply as Americans."[23] Assimilation acts upon groups and individuals in recognizable phases: first comes the disappearance of language distinctions and the adoption of English, followed by increasing differences between generations, upward social mobility, exogamous marriage, and finally, an identity crisis about the loss of ethnic roots. Catholicism helped to define a subculture in Boston partly because it took the place of other aspects of Irishness that had to be abandoned, such as language, and because it developed comprehensive strategies to resist conflicted aspects of American life.[24] Some Irish escaped the severe language dislocation of other immigrants, since their native Gaelic had been suppressed already by English colonization of Ireland. Yet despite the colonized status Catholics had endured in Ireland for seven centuries prior to migration, Irish Americans were unprepared for the religious, racial, and economic discrimination that faced them in Anglo-Protestant New England. One form that their resistance took was a tribal sensibility that protected endogamy and focused upon limited, localized political clans. Another related strategy was the Church's invocation of its global authority to contribute to a strong subcultural identity.

Boston and the Vatican

The world-rejection of the Catholic Church apparent in its refusal to accept modern materialist and rationalist philosophies was a defensive response to the loss of its monopoly over the value systems of European Catholics. Antimodernism was perhaps more acute in Europe, where 1,200 years of papal political and social sovereignty were ending, despite the fierce attempt of Vatican I to forestall it. From the 1860s on, signaled by the Syllabus of Errors, Roman Catholicism became an intractable opponent of secularism and liberalism. In response to political and philosophical challenges, Vatican I promulgated two controversial, landmark Catholic doctrines in 1870—papal jurisdiction and papal infallibility—that extended the power of the pope. In the United States, the response to the declaration of papal infallibility was somewhat delayed by the aftermath of the Civil War. Nonetheless it made American Catholics fear a resurgence of the nativist persecution that had characterized the antebellum era and reminded them that Vatican Eurocentrism had little regard for the democratic, pluralist environment of the United States.

Some have argued that the Church, having already lost the support of the working class, fiercely waged this battle for control of a faithful remnant. While European Catholicism was no longer the uncontested source of common meaning and vision in the lives of its own members after several centuries of secular national integration, in the United States such a loss of political and social status was not the case. In fact, there is evidence that immigrants became stronger supporters of Catholicism as they prospered. Although the Church began as an alien institution with distinct disadvantages, after a half-century of nativist discrimination, Boston Catholics were beginning to achieve social acceptance and economic security. Some liberal bishops had endeavored to demonstrate that the Church's hierarchical structure was compatible with democratic republicanism, a debate that began before the Civil War and continued through John Courtney Murray in the 1960s.

The American Church experienced new difficulties in its relationship with Rome after 1890, however, because of its perceived willingness to embrace and reconcile itself to the very democratic pluralism and national identification condemned by the papacy in continental Europe. Two events in the early twentieth century indicate the fragile nature of the relationship between American Church leaders and Roman authorities. In 1908 the Vatican removed the United States from its "mission territory" status, which implied acceptance of the American hierarchy as equal participants in Curial matters. However, in 1899, the papal condemnation of "Americanism" as a heresy, and subsequent Vatican rejection of Modernism in 1907, halted the growth of independent initiative, intellectualism, and theological dialogue within the American Church until Vatican II. Roman-educated prelates like William O'Connell encouraged Catholics to respond to creeping secularism by building a separatist subculture via institutions he referred to, somewhat vaguely, as "the Catholic equivalent" to their secular counterparts. These separatist tendencies have been described picturesquely as a "siege mentality," a regal but irrelevant aloofness, and a self-imposed exile of "withdrawn entrenchment."[25] However, such generalizations miss the central point: the existence of an aggressive counteroffensive by the Church itself that was directed against identification of its members with secular values, not their ostracism from the nation. Catholics were encouraged to avoid secularism in order to maintain a purified version of American culture within their Catholic organizations. Hence, from America's upgraded status at the Vatican came a tremendous expansion of domestic lay evangelization societies and worldwide Catholic missionary efforts to the unchurched as well as significant growth in didactic programs for the already churched.

One may argue, as I do, that the Church attempted to achieve all-encompassing control of the experience of the laity by setting boundaries to lay involvement in society, exerting control through parish and diocesan institutions, by prescribing individual moral responses that fit Rome's interpretation of Christian doctrine. Debating whether or not the Church should have sought to modernize itself overlooks the unitive achievements and functions of a separatist subculture as well as the many gradations of secular accommodation that did occur among Catholics. In Boston, Catholicity more or less successfully transcended the divisions of ethnicity between parishes otherwise unrelated to each other by encouraging Catholics to understand themselves as distinctive, but loyal, Americans. Furthermore, the presence of a strong Catholic subculture formed an ideological tool to create identity through a comprehensive moral system that overrode ethnic barriers.

The Church tried to avoid Catholic disintegration by eschewing theories of class conflict and by using middle-class Catholics to teach and manage the poor. As we shall see in the following chapters, such tactics conveyed conflicting messages about the relative merits of success and poverty. Failing to generate a positive platform to unite Catholics, the Church relied on negative

strategies of condemning common enemies—radicals, socialists, atheists—
which provided the only way to link its assimilationist and separatist tendencies. Although it is futile to pinpoint precisely when Catholics entered an
American "mainstream," scholars need to consider the ways in which Catholics and non-Catholics defined Catholic identities by association with the
center or the periphery of real (economic) or perceived (ideological) power.
The strength of Catholic anticommunism during the Cold War, for example,
is a classic example of a group portraying itself as the defender of American
insider ideals: by the 1950s Catholics had become mainstream and thus had
no need to play the outsider. Between 1900 and 1920, however, Catholics
portrayed themselves simultaneously as victors (assimilated and empowered)
and as martyrs (persecuted and marginalized). In those two decades this in-
triguing blend failed to resolve the ambiguities that it posed for Catholics
living in a competitive, individualist, capitalist culture.

Social Catholicism
and Institutionalism

An "institutional model" of the Catholic Church that was epitomized by the
decrees of the Council of Trent in the sixteenth century aptly describes Boston
under O'Connell's leadership. Characterized by a hierarchical concept of authority that was only reinforced by Vatican I, the institutional model is defined
by clericalism, juridicism, and triumphalism.[26] It strengthened Catholicism in
several ways. First, it preserved orthodoxy based on faithfulness to Church
documents; next, it portrayed the Church as "a zone of stability" in an uncertain present. Finally, institutionalism fostered a strong sense of corporate
identity among Catholics. In practice, these attitudes also produced three corresponding defects: a reduction of the role of the laity to a passive one of "a
mere appendage of the hierarchy," an overemphasis on human authority embodied in the hierarchy, and finally, a monopolistic outlook upon salvation by
the Catholic Church.

In Europe, the Catholic Church reacted to political pressures that furthered
its separatist course after Vatican I. *Rerum Novarum,* the 1891 encyclical of
Leo XIII, and subsequent "social encyclicals" by Pope Leo and his successors,
proposed a program for Christian social reform derived in part from reactionary impulses. The structural analysis of political economy advanced by
Leo XIII was quite conservative: it continued to assert an organic model of
society and described social inequality as a residue from original sin. On the
other hand, *Rerum* tried to find a middle ground between capitalism and socialism by recognizing the dignity of human labor. In practice, this meant
allying with the middle class to circumvent socialism.[27] While *Rerum Nova-*

rum recognized the legitimacy of nonmilitant labor unions, and even conceded the duty of state intervention to help the working poor, it also endorsed
private property as a natural right and opposed socialism, materialism, and
moral relativism, although in a less categorical way than *Mirari Vos* of 1832
and the Syllabus of Errors of 1864. As the Church in Europe was facing the
loss of its authority over the working classes, one might interpret the conservative core and modest liberal concessions of *Rerum Novarum* as a desperate
effort to stem the tide. In the United States, where Catholics had not defected
in large numbers from the Church, Catholic "social teaching" became primarily a means to oppose such phenomena as socialism and feminism. For
cities like Boston where Catholic Church attendance and parish growth suggested health rather than decay, there are obvious limits to pursuing parallels
to European Catholicism because the Church did not "lose" the immigrant
working classes in the century following the French Revolution. What did
become significant to American Catholics was the Vatican's ambivalence toward capitalism and private property created by its antimodernist outlook.

Political factors aside, the emergence of a Catholic progressive social, economic, and political strategy was unlikely in 1900 given the concept of religious faith as a set of immutable a priori principles. Truth corresponded to
divine revelation, not to a process of discovery. The discipline of theology was
therefore not conceived as an ongoing discussion among lay and clerical scholars, but as a replication and repetition of ahistorical propositions by the
hierarchy and priesthood. With the declaration of papal infallibility thirty
years earlier, and the establishment of Thomism as Catholicism's official theology and method in 1878, the papacy had begun a process of reasserting the
primacy of tradition and Roman authority. This primacy was further expressed by several papal interventions in America in the 1890s. An apostolic
delegate to the United States was appointed in 1893, and an encyclical of 1895
warned against idealizing American separation of church and state. A death
blow to liberalism in the Church came from the pope's condemnations of
Americanism and Modernism. When both liberal and conservative American
bishops sided with the pope against the European Modernists in 1907, they
decisively aligned the American Church for the next several decades with the
ultramontanism of the popes and the Curia. They also determined a path that
turned from pursuit of historical and biblical critical problems to an increased
attention to social reform.

Despite Vatican resistance to modernity, Catholic institutionalism had
some potential to increase Catholic unity in Boston. First, Catholic separatism
prevented Church fragmentation into numerous ethnic groups loyal to national parishes, by encouraging Catholics to understand themselves as loyal
Americans, albeit with a universal religious and cultural heritage. Catholic

over-identification with nationalism was a phenomenon the Vatican hoped to avoid, despite its success as an anti-Protestant device in Ireland. Second, the effects of institutional ecclesiology carried over into popular piety and social programs. The emotional and intellectual appeal of Leo XIII's call, "Let the faithful unite," and Pius X's motto, "To restore all things in Christ," inspired numerous lay organizations born in the early 1900s and offered lay people a possibility to infuse faith into their secular lives by feeling involved in a momentous undertaking to save Christian civilization.

These appeals, however, also worked against the initiatives of the American laity in the 1880s. The lay renaissance of 1885–93, not more than two national lay congresses held in 1889 and 1893 in Baltimore and Chicago, suffered from lack of sustained support from bishops when other national issues polarized the American hierarchy, such as parochial school controversies, national parish dilemmas, and renewed debates on the threats of secularization and Protestantization.[28] Even conservative lay associations like the American Federation of Catholic Societies (AFCS) that emerged in following decades were not viable sequels to the lay congresses and, in fact, supported the hierarchy's agenda of insulating the laity within a completely Catholic environment. Following Rome's calls for unity, churchmen molded lay initiatives into devotional, charitable, and social associations that they controlled. Since Vatican I, the American Catholic hierarchy had been striving to consolidate its power over the laity, an effort given new urgency by papal struggles against European anticlericalism. But American Catholics had no ancient tradition of indigenous anticlericalism, and in fact, lay devotionalism and regular Church attendance in Boston peaked between 1920 and 1950. One might therefore conclude that the laity found ways to be assimilated Americans and good Catholics at the same time, and that assimilation actually increased their religious identification. The episcopacy often seemed to draw the opposite conclusion, as it embarked upon a policy of drawing lay activities under Church supervision. Bishops' control of lay initiatives ostensibly also preserved the Church's power as an independent social force in a secular national culture. Ghetto Catholicism, usually associated with the thirty years before Vatican II, was intimated in Boston well before 1920. A Catholic subculture conflated institutional with spiritual elements in order to build communal solidarity.

What was, finally, the milieu in which a subculture for Boston Catholics emerged? Locally, it defined itself against Protestants and secularists, terms that were often used interchangeably as marks of the flaws of American society. Despite the archbishop's attempts to portray his flock as "menaced by the contagion of a thousand sophistries," Catholic Bostonians would nonetheless embrace a middle-class ethos. Middle-class status may have contributed to waning ethnic identity as well. While folk piety may have served certain immigrant groups as progressive forces and as "powerful impulses to accommodation and innovation," as Timothy Smith has claimed, this may not have been true of the Irish. Their ancient Celtic customs were especially troublesome to the Church, which at this moment preferred to stress the Christian unity of Ireland, not its pagan past.[29] A symbiotic relationship between Irishness and Roman Catholicism had been fostered during the days of Daniel O'Connell because of his deliberate involvement of priests in his popular nationalist campaigns. Therefore, as Irish American culture became identified with Catholic Ireland in nationalist rhetoric of the 1910s, it both fed and fed upon the Church's legitimacy. As for other ethnic groups in the Hub, the percentage of new national parishes rose between 1900 and 1920, and some ethnic festivals and processions were tolerated. Still, as in other cities, the rapid multiplication of national parishes constituted "an emergency measure," not concessions to other nationalities.[30]

Ironically, while the Church proved to be an agent and promoter of Catholic assimilation, it failed to evolve an ecclesiology or a theology derived from the laity's experience of America. When the Church stridently opposed socialism, for example, its muted criticisms of capitalism scarcely made a ripple in the lives of increasingly affluent Catholics since the ethic of competitive capitalism supported the American Church's base of economic and denominational power. Further, the image of America as a harmonious classless society (which the relative hegemony of capitalism certainly endorsed), was akin to Catholic doctrines rejecting theories of society based on class antagonism. Catholic dogma permitted lay people few reasons to embrace America's secular culture, but at the same time, the American hierarchy demanded their unquestioning allegiance to the nation and its democratic (and, by implication, economic) institutions. Catholic capitulation to the "American way of life," which Will Herberg and others have characterized as a phenomenon of the 1950s, was anticipated in Boston soon after 1900, where a Catholic faith compatible with capitalism and nationalism was prepared to replace ethnicity as a leading category of self- and group identification.

Archbishop William O'Connell

William O'Connell's meteoric rise to power in the early twentieth century remains somewhat mysterious, partly because he tried to obscure his self-serving behavior and partly because certain crucial documents are unavailable. Called "that fabulous churchman" by church historian John Tracy Ellis and considered "eager and calculating in seizing opportunities for promotion" by historian Donna Merwick, O'Connell has been judged a status seeker and an opportunist.[31] He exercised power disproportionate to his experience because of Vatican patronage during his early career, which accounted for his rapid ascent and his equally swift decline in subsequent decades. A listing of his clergy appointments indicates the unusual speed of his advancement. After serving as a parish assistant and curate in Massachusetts from 1885 to 1895, O'Connell suddenly was named rector of the North American College in Rome, where he had been a student from 1881 to 1884. He replaced Denis O'Connell, who had fallen out of favor with the Curia because of his alleged Americanist leanings. The North American College, founded in 1859, molded American seminarians into conservative priests loyal to the ultramontane politics of the Vatican. Returning from Rome in 1901, O'Connell was promoted to bishop of Portland, Maine, without any recommendation from local clergy and without ever having been pastor of his own parish. Pope Pius X sent him on a mission to Japan in 1905 at the end of the Russo-Japanese war as a special papal legate to the emperor of Japan. While O'Connell was en route back to the United States, the pope announced, again in disregard of episcopal recommendations, that O'Connell would become coadjutor bishop in Boston, with rights to succession upon the death of John Williams (1851–1907).

In 1907, at the age of forty-seven, O'Connell assumed the see of Boston, the third largest American diocese, without ever having been listed on the customary *terna* for the selection of bishops, once again to the outrage of more likely contenders. His advancement under Pius X's favor continued, and in 1911 he was named a cardinal. In these promising early years, Cardinal O'Connell capitalized on the chance to promote himself as a heroic reformer of the administrative chaos purportedly left by Williams, the first archbishop of Boston, who had turned down a red hat in order not to offend local Protestants. Not troubled by any such modesty, O'Connell claimed that he was turning the "haphazard" growth of the archdiocese during the previous forty years into something purposeful and profitable. He increased the number of parishes by 40 percent, and he more than doubled the number of priests and quadrupled the ranks of religious sisters. Elementary parochial schools grew from 75 to 158 in number. Parochial high schools increased from 22 to 67; private academies and prep schools, from 10 to 24.[32] Boston College and St. John's Seminary expanded. Three women's colleges opened. O'Connell centralized charities under the Catholic Charitable Bureau (CCB) in 1910 and liquidated the large diocesan debt.

Yet O'Connell never achieved complete control over the running of the archdiocese, and despite his pride in Catholic school expansion, "the relative net results were less than spectacular."[33] Moreover, O'Connell's strong support for private and convent academies (as against parochial schools) seemed to manifest an elitist outlook on education hardly compatible with the pressing needs of an assimilating population. That O'Connell's control of Boston was never as complete as he himself maintained is shown also in ethnic relations and clerical control. O'Connell never actively encouraged the formation of national/ethnic parishes and endured ongoing turf wars with certain diocesan priests who were critical of his policies, such as John Mullen and John O'Brien. O'Connell lost a long-term struggle to wrest control of the *Sacred Heart Review* from the editorial control of Father O'Brien, pastor at Sacred Heart. The issue was only resolved upon O'Brien's death in 1917, when O'Connell appointed the dutiful Hugh Blunt as pastor. In a wrangle with his own alma mater, Boston College, O'Connell was outwitted by President Thomas Gasson in 1908 by a maneuver that kept the college in the hands of the Jesuits. Even religious orders of women, usually portrayed as passive victims of the episcopacy, were able to circumvent the archbishop in some cases to retain their control of hospitals and similar institutions.[34]

In the 1910s, several factors combined to diminish O'Connell's reputation and power. First, the death of Pius X in 1914 meant the loss of his greatest patron. Second, the removal of his close friend Merry del Val as cardinal secretary of state at the Vatican put an end to O'Connell's insider status. Third, a scandal involving his nephew and another diocesan priest damaged O'Connell's reputation and gave his clerical enemies a chance to try to unseat him as archbishop. The facts of this notorious case are, briefly, as follows.[35] The archbishop's nephew, James P. E. O'Connell, a Boston priest and chancellor of the archdiocese, secretly married a divorcée (who knew he was a priest) in 1912. For over seven years, James O'Connell made weekly visits to his wife and mother-in-law in New York City, using the name Roe. Having served as his uncle's private secretary for six years, and chancellor for eight, James managed the archdiocesan account books, from which he embezzled archdiocesan money for his wife, their European honeymoon, and his real estate speculations. His marriage and thefts, allegedly discovered by O'Connell at some point prior to 1918, were concealed from the local press and denied by O'Connell in Church circles. It is unclear when the cardinal actually learned of his nephew's marriage, but since James lived in the archbishop's residence, it is hard to imagine that O'Connell did not notice his frequent absences or financial irregularities in the diocesan accounts. A third priest in O'Connell's ménage was David J. Toomey, a friend of James O'Connell from the American College in Rome, who became personal chaplain to the cardinal in 1912. O'Connell had also made him the editor of the Boston *Pilot*. While editor, Father Toomey dallied with a woman who interpreted his interest as a marriage proposal and then sued him for breach of promise. O'Connell's lawyer handled the problem by trying to buy the silence of the woman with an out-of-court settlement. Through "Mr. and Mrs. Roe," Toomey met another

William Cardinal O'Connell kneeling at prayer at Fort Devens, Massachusetts, in 1918 with his soon-to-be-infamous nephew, Father James P. E. O'Connell. (Archives of the Archdiocese of Boston)

woman in New York and married her in 1914, choosing the alias of Fossa ("tomb"), an Italian pun on his name. Curious about his alleged career as a secret service agent in Boston, "Mrs. Fossa" followed him to Massachusetts one weekend, to surprise him with yet another woman in Cambridge, who was his secretary at the *Pilot*. Father Toomey was excommunicated by the Church, and his editorship at the *Pilot* was terminated. However, he went on to imply to Vatican investigators that Cardinal O'Connell was avoiding inquiries about his own nephew because he was being blackmailed by James, who threatened to expose O'Connell's alleged homosexuality. Meanwhile, independent inquiries conducted by Archbishop John Bonzano, the apostolic delegate in Washington, D.C., had produced enough evidence from credible witnesses to inform Vatican officials about the marriage of James O'Connell. O'Connell was confronted about the matter of his nephew in a May 1920 meeting before Pope Benedict XV, who produced a copy of James's marriage license. James O'Connell was dismissed and excommunicated. Rumors about the cardinal's sexual life were not investigated.

Before 1921 O'Connell had suffered virtually no setbacks in terms of aggrandizing himself through the aid of his Vatican cronies. He had actively insinuated himself by giving monies to the pope's favorite causes and to the annual Peter's Pence collection. Thereafter, however, his power was abruptly curtailed and confined to Boston. Even regionally, O'Connell now found himself the object of episcopal contempt. In 1922 an annual conference of New England bishops formally denounced him, although a similar plan for censure at a national meeting never materialized, despite a personal visit to the pope by Bishop Louis Walsh of Portland.[36] Loss of face among suffragan bishops might be one reason why O'Connell became more strident about maintaining control over local affairs and why he sought the adulation of Bostonians to an almost embarrassing degree. Never missing a publicity opportunity, he recovered a national presence in the 1930s by offering his negative opinions about modern morality. On one occasion in 1932 he condemned male singers and their "immoral slush," bringing a wave of editorial backlash from around the country. The defense of popular songs was led by Bing Crosby, Rudy Vallee, and others. On more significant issues, such as the value of psychoanalysis or the theory of relativity, O'Connell also succeeded in looking absurdly ignorant when he sounded forth. When he died in 1944, he was succeeded by Richard Cardinal Cushing (1895–1970), who despite his own peculiarities was generally respected.

Boston's Catholic public remained uninformed of the James O'Connell and David Toomey affairs. Perhaps they continued to think of the archbishop in the enthusiastic terms that greeted him in 1908, when Felix McGettrick had praised O'Connell's virtues to the Knights of Columbus: "A brilliant scholar, he possesses rare talent for the practical handling of great problems; favored with extraordinary opportunity for observation of and dealing with world conditions, his profound religious thought and sentiment have developed with his learning and experience until he stands before the Christian world as a virile exemplifier of the living faith that has nothing to fear, but everything to gain from the teaching and learning of basic and structural truth in every field of human research."[37] Undeniably able in several disciplines, O'Connell was a hymnist, was conversant in several languages, and had been an excellent college student. His strength lay in the ability to make forceful speeches that sounded inspiring and struck the right notes of Catholic triumphalism. As a theologian, however, he was neither original nor exceptional. It is a striking sign of O'Connell's insecurity and his nonspiritual bent that he rarely generated spiritual reflections or offered Mass for his own priestly community. Moreover, O'Connell has a mixed record as a spokesman and advocate for Irish Americans. When Irish nationalism became a heated issue in the 1910s, the cardinal showed himself to be a double-dealer. Having appeared in public on several occasions with Eamon De Valera and having made stirring speeches before pro-Irish nationalist conventions in New York City, O'Connell simultaneously contacted British diplomats to reassure them that he was only placating his constituency.[38] As a prominent archbishop, he neither boosted Irish Catholicism to the exclusion of other ethnic groups nor proposed a "strictly Catholic culture," as one account has claimed. Instead of playing ethnic politics, he spent much of his life in New England cultivating powerful elites to enhance his local image as well as his reputation with Curial allies in Rome.

O'Connell's ultramontanist bent was shaped by his Roman education, the promulgation of *Rerum Novarum,* and the condemnation of Modernism, each of which occurred at crucial points in his early career. He slavishly "studied every sentence" of Leo XIII's encyclicals in order to align his policies with Vatican pronouncements. His thinking on socioeconomic issues remained undeveloped, however, reflecting the general inability of his episcopal peers to distinguish between economic and philosophical principles associated with Marxism and materialism. O'Connell's 1921 pastoral letter on industrial relations discussed the opposition of capital and labor solely in moral, not economic, terms. His most extended statement on the role of government in family issues, "The Reasonable Limits of State Activity," had been written by a professor at St. John's, Rev. Patrick J. Waters, and was delivered only after the controversial Lawrence textile mill strike of 1919 had ended.[39] Furthermore, O'Connell offered no enlightenment about two economic events affecting American Catholics: the Great Depression of 1929–39 and Pius XI's publication of *Quadragesimo Anno* in 1931.

Under O'Connell's administration, the hopes of the liberal Catholic minority of the 1880s and 1890s, the generation of the alliance between Father Edward McGlynn and Henry George, were snuffed out. Unwittingly, the liberals' social critique of American society was taken up by the victorious conservative bishops, including O'Connell, and repeated with violent force in the early 1900s. O'Connell, for example, refused to acknowledge that class conflict existed, and condemned all forms of labor agitation as a sign of the encroachment of socialists and radicals. He used occasions such as the Lawrence strikes as vehicles to address social unrest, but from a didactic position of moral superiority rather than one of dialogue with the strikers or mill owners.

Nor did O'Connell support the brand of "share the wealth" populism espoused in the 1930s by Father Charles Coughlin. The "radio priest" had dared to publicly chastise O'Connell (who had previously attacked Coughlin) for his silence on social justice issues and for remaining uncritical of acquisitive capitalism, which had created America's glaring disparities between the haves and the have-nots.[40] Rather, O'Connell attacked big capitalism, plutocrats, and the exploitation of workers in a negative fashion, that is, by blaming them upon the degeneracy of the WASP population or upon the general spread of atheism. His tactic further represented the Catholic community's outsider sensibility as an emblem of its purity against the morally bankrupt insiders of Boston.

O'Connell's biography may be read as a comic-pathetic narrative of a man who attempted to overcome his working-class Lowell roots by carefully constructing the self-image he wished the public to see. Though he occasionally played up his humble origins as a "son of the Spindle City," he also stressed the royal ancestry of the O'Connell name and falsely claimed a family relationship to the Irish nationalist hero Daniel O'Connell. He used his position as a "prince of the Church" to support an extravagant and self-indulgent lifestyle, including purchasing well-situated real estate for his family and his vacations, and traveling extensively in Europe and to the Caribbean for winter vacations. Eventually, O'Connell's extraordinary capacity for self-deception caught up with him, although indications of his talent for ingenuousness were present all along. As a young monsignor, he feigned surprise in 1906 when learning of his appointment as successor to Archbishop Williams of Boston, after having campaigned secretly by having friends deluge the Vatican with commendations on his behalf. Further, the publication of volume one of his *Letters* in 1915, covering his seminary years, was marred by rumors about their validity. It seems clear now that O'Connell fabricated the letters and even some of the correspondents at the time of publication.[41] By the late 1910s, among the American hierarchy and in certain Vatican circles O'Connell began to look incompetent rather than omnipotent. After being named a cardinal in 1911, the highest ecclesiastical honor he could achieve, O'Connell missed two papal conclaves in Rome, arriving too late in both instances to vote upon a papal candidate. The unexpected accession of Benedict XV in 1914 led to the departure of his former patrons from the Curia, and subsequent revelations about married priests and embezzled funds in his diocese made him look unprincipled and dishonest, or incapable of leadership. In American government, nearly all of the legislation that O'Connell had opposed was enacted into law.

All in all, O'Connell's power crested too early in his career to keep him on the international stage. Following the Vatican investigation of James O'Connell, the cardinal's power became increasingly localized, severed from even the New England bishops. In 1921–22 he and Archbishop Dennis Dougherty of Philadelphia led a failed campaign to suppress the new National Catholic Welfare Council. By the 1930s, O'Connell's authority was eclipsed by younger "builder bishops" including his former subordinate Francis Spellman as well as Fulton J. Sheen, Chicago's George Mundelein, and Cincinnati's John McNicholas.[42] O'Connell's aggressive qualities led to inconsistencies in his leadership: he believed strongly in the local church, unencumbered by national control, but he objected to parish autonomy or powerful pastors who threatened his supremacy. He projected an image of the archdiocese as an efficiently run, financially solid institution when in fact it was undermined by corruption and by his often fruitless maneuvering against individual parishes to gain control of some valuable asset. He ostentatiously promoted the federation of Catholic lay societies, yet he viciously opposed the formation of the National Catholic Welfare Council after World War I. His policies were ambivalent toward parochial education, which he defended as the solution to encroaching statism but which he did not successfully translate to Massachusetts parishes. He failed to create a united front with local Irish politicians because of his personal prejudices. Whether swamped by his own shortcomings, outmaneuvered by the dynamics of his rapid mobility, crushed by loss of Vatican confidence, or hemmed in by local politics, O'Connell could have institutionalized a Catholic subculture much more thoroughly. He presided over a decentralized Church that remained stubbornly led by its priests as much as by its archbishop.[43] As early as 1920 O'Connell's power and reputation were on the verge of dramatic decline, although the Boston laity remained unaware. As a prelate who presided over an expansionist phase in diocesan history, O'Connell's legacy of an administrative style and a repressive moralism in many ways exceeded his personal mark on Boston. It would be a mistake, however, to interpret him as an omnipotent archbishop. Rather, William O'Connell seems to have been overcome by the doctrinal and socioeconomic contradictions that had produced him.

The implications of this study extend beyond 1920, posing questions that are significant to the study of American religion today. At the outset, one might assume that there are major differences between the American Catholic Church of 1890 and of the 1990s. Especially since the end of World War II, assimilation, changing socioeconomic status, the doctrinal innovations of Vatican II, and cultural change external to Catholicism have wiped away many of the differences between Catholics and other Americans, thus undercutting the need for a distinctive and defensive subculture. There is ample evidence that Catholics have assimilated to such a degree that Catholic schools and colleges feel compelled to define what makes them Catholic anymore, while the declining numbers of men and women religious foretell a serious vocational shortage for the twenty-first century. With the loss of such traditional hallmarks of Roman Catholicism—education and clergy—one might claim that the heyday of a unique Catholic identity has passed.

2

THE LIMITS OF AMERICANIZATION

Well, it is high time to give Boston a reputation for other than a centre of ancestor-worship or a paradise of faddists.—Mayor John Fitzgerald, on the founding of Boston High School of Commerce, May 15, 1909.

Three millions of Catholics occupy the limits where then one hundred lived. And the needs have grown with the number and altered with the conditions. To train the docile mind and heart of a few scattered immigrants was a task infinitely more easy than to preserve the purity of the Faith in the denizens of crowded cities, menaced by the contagion of a thousand sophistries, and to keep untainted souls beckoned on all sides to a thousand seductions. Poverty and the humiliations of a cold welcome have their hard features. But the pride of life and the corruption of luxury are infinitely more to be feared. —William Cardinal O'Connell, "In the Beginning"

They are men who by their private lives of dishonor and their public lives of dishonesty bring shame upon the church—cowardly traitors who betray Catholic interests. They are selfish men who cannot leave personal considerations out of any calculation. They are always finding fault with the church; with her visible head, with their bishops and their pastors.—Rev. David Toomey, *Boston Globe,* May 9, 1910.

The 1908 Catholic Centenary

The unevenness of Catholic social and economic integration was apparent in the varying degrees of Catholic involvement in urban life. I have chosen five components of civic life in Boston to display the spectrum of Catholic participation: the celebration of the archdiocesan centennial in 1908; Catholic involvement in the "Boston, 1915" movement; Catholic speakers and topics in the Ford Hall Forum; and Catholic relations with two secular immigrant aid societies. A sixth element, the Catholic Common Cause Society, fully approved by the Church, serves as an example of the Church's ideal lay association.

In October 1808, Boston became a Roman Catholic diocese. In October 1908, Catholics inaugurated their second century with a Mass in Holy Cross Cathedral, celebrated by the papal apostolic delegate to America. After the solemn liturgy, the Catholic fraternal and devotional organizations held a massive meeting in Symphony Hall, including the AFCS, the Knights of Columbus,

Catholic parade pageantry: Cardinal Gibbons in carriage parade through Main Street, Worcester, Massachusetts, June 17, 1907. Note the prominent display of American flag bunting and the photographer on the roof at top left. (Holy Cross College Archives)

the Ancient Order of Hibernians, the Catholic Order of Foresters, and the Holy Name Society.[1] The significance of the centenary as a conscious expression of Catholic power in Boston cannot be overstated. Archbishop O'Connell's often-quoted sermon, "In the Beginning," set the tone for Catholic liberation from Protestant domination: "The Puritan has passed; the Catholic remains."[2] The day's festivities culminated in the Holy Name Society parade involving 44,000 participants and 300,000 spectators and lasting nearly five hours.[3]

The centenary provided the public forum for Catholics to display religious unity and racial pride before a huge, largely partisan audience, much as had the initial dedication of the cathedral in 1875. A Boston lawyer applauded Archbishop O'Connell for instilling loyalty in the rising generation of American-born Catholics: "Your militant stand has made kow-towing unpopular. They [Catholics] are shamed into reformation. Your splendid work is infusing into the younger set who have been taught by the elders to 'uncover,' a pride and a glory in religion and race which they are evincing in mixed company."[4] Massachusetts's political dignitaries attended the parade, which unfurled like an immense banner before the onlookers, who took pride in the contributions and expansion of Catholic organizations. In an era when even nonliturgical rituals such as a Marian procession could draw 1,400 participants, the 44,000 costumed marchers carrying flags and musical instruments could not fail to impress the throngs along the parade route.[5]

The 1908 event exceeded the "monster parade" of 1892, which had marked the quadricentennial of American Catholicism since Columbus's landing at San Salvador. The role of one parish in the Columbian anniversary suggests that nationalist displays by the Catholic Church were already maturing at the end of the nineteenth century. At the culmination of a month of preparatory historical lectures about the importance of 1492, the Roxbury Mission Church of the Redemptorists assembled 1,000 paraders: a marching band, 475 men of the Holy Family Association, 350 men stepping in columns of four, 150 boys carrying the American flag, 6 carriages carrying the pastor and representative men, 6 drummers with tambourines, standard bearers on horseback, a float with an "angel choir" floating beneath a large American eagle, and tableaux of Columbus, Indians, Washington, Franklin, and other American heroes.[6] Sixteen years later the emotional chord struck by the even grander centenary was summed up by a Boston police captain who helped control crowds and traffic. When he received a commemorative medal as a gift from the archbishop, he wrote in response: "I will cherish and remem-'ber this gift of yours for just as long a time. . . . Let me assure you that to have you appreciate my humble efforts in this recent celebration, will always be considered by me as one of the greatest credits of my career as a police officer."[7]

The vibrancy of public Roman Catholicism that these spectacles illustrated also expressed a rising sectarianism by Catholics. While the program included prominent non-Catholics, the centenary displayed Catholic charity as a badge of identity and superior generosity. Catholic charitable and benevolent societies, originally chartered to serve Irish immigrants, now boasted that they served all creeds, while "Puritans" persisted in helping only Protestants.[8] Local Protestant societies, especially the YMCA and the Christian Endeavor Society, which still refused to admit or assist Catholics, became targets of Church criticism.[9] Underlying Catholics' justifiable pride was an ideological duel being waged by the hierarchy against Protestant and professional reformers. The Church objected that the new social workers treated the body but not the soul. In opposition to the tenets of Progressivism, the Church insisted that reform must be guided by spiritual ideals rather than by social engineering, as O'Connell insisted in a sermon to diocesan charities in 1909: "Today there is a movement abroad the obvious motive of which is to elevate Philanthropy to the status of a religion, with the scarcely concealed corollary, that work in the social order is the affair of scientific experts only, and that eventually scientific social work must supplant the Church."[10]

Two related anxieties underlay the archbishop's remarks. First was the Church's fear that philanthropic experts would displace and replace the Church's institutions; second was the concern that scientized charity would undermine the family as the primary sacred unit of society. In response to the creation of European nation-states in the nineteenth century, the Church had denied that the state was the optimal administrator of charity to the poor because of the threat posed by those governments to its own dominant position in European culture. Inheritors of this debate, American Catholics were being torn between the Vatican's antistatism, the American hierarchy's support for republican government, and the slightly enlarged role for government in labor relations and poor relief finally conceded by the papacy in *Rerum Novarum* of 1891.[11] Nevertheless, hostility remained endemic to the Church's pronouncements about charity work that professed a Protestant or rational-scientific bias.

Despite the Church's negative response to European secular politics, democratic movements, and autonomous labor unions, Catholics were not immune to the theoretical and practical changes occurring in American social reform, including the Progressives' commitment to the application of social science. Catholics had begun to cooperate with some Protestant and Jewish philanthropies as well as with government agencies in Massachusetts and had begun centralizing and rationalizing Catholic charities as well. The Church, however, taught its own version of the "new sociology" in its seminaries and its new schools for social service. Scientized reform, however, never became integral to the Catholic view for several reasons. Initially, Catholics argued that in maintaining their separate charities, they could copy the methods of others without imitating their philosophies and thus preserve a distinctive Catholic identity. "No, we do not need to borrow methods from our Protestant friends," wrote a Catholic journalist. "We can study the vital principles of their philanthropic work, where they originated under the influence of the Church."[12] Ironically, over time, clergy and lay scholars unwittingly absorbed the "categories of inquiry set by the socialists and laissez-faire theorists whom they opposed," while devising their own ostensibly Catholic solutions.[13] Nonetheless, the Church maintained it was preserving its uniqueness through the formation of a network of local agencies that expressed Catholic consolidation in tandem with American patriotism. Unlike liberal reformers, among whom social work emerged as a paid profession dominated by women, Catholic women prior to World War I were generally isolated from training programs in housing, sanitation, and nutrition. They were even excluded from

Victorian definitions of charity as home visitation of the poor by the presence of sisters in this ministry. Catholic resistance to academic social science and its applications hampered modernized social reform, particularly when it challenged Catholic interpretations of gender roles and when it required secular professional training and state certification. In some ways, however, the archbishop's caution mirrored the conservativism of local elitists like Charles Eliot, president of Harvard, who also opposed social science.

Historically, the Catholic Church had been slow to concede the legitimacy of state intervention in social welfare. In America, Catholicism now faced an identity crisis, caught between its loss of dominance in European society and uncertainty about the limits of "reform Catholicism" during the pre–World War I era. The Church's official position was that it "consistently opposed modern sociological uplifters who seek to foist upon the home 'reforms' and 'system' that spell domestic infelicity and national ruin."[14] Cardinal O'Connell claimed that "without the Christian standpoint, all altruism is essentially defective, and must, whatever its external appearances or pretence, finally resolve itself into another form of egotism."[15] By alleging their sectarian superiority, the Church hierarchy and clergy refused to admit potential benefits to cooperating with secular reform and ran the danger of professing a narrowly focused faith that accepted no social duties or civic responsibilities for the laity except to issues directly affecting the Church. The *Pilot* expressed the Church's antimodernism in an editorial against the "So-So Age," of "socialism and sociology and sociability and social settlements."[16] The So-So Age suffered from faddish, false philosophies that would destroy the family and the Catholic Church. By conflating these distinct modern movements, the newspaper presented them as an undifferentiated menace to Catholics. During World War I Boston's archbishop stated more floridly, "If only all the parlor philosophers and the parlor sociologists could be ordered to go to the front and stay there long enough to become genuine and sincere, and lose their halos in the blaze of artillery, the world would be rid, at least for the rest of this generation, of some up-to-date fallacies and cure-all sociologies."[17] In the postwar era, O'Connell extended his polemics against materialist philosophies that he now regarded as attacks on individual liberty at the heart of American existence.[18] In one generation, then, Boston Catholics went from opposition to social engineering, to rejection of socialism, to the defense of individualism—a clear indication of the intertwined threads of separatist and integrationist strategies.

On the whole, Boston Catholics remained aloof from the Progressive movement in its philosophical and civic manifestations, although each group sought social harmony without advocating destroying the foundations of private property or family life. Church leaders disagreed with Progressive attempts to increase state power over corrupt corporations and exploitative labor practices out of fear of a loss of Church influence in these spheres. Progressives saw Catholics as enemies of their plans for social improvement based on regulating predatory interests, while Catholics saw themselves defending the family from encroaching statism and its successor, socialism. From the standpoint of the Catholic hierarchy, in practice Progressivism was preferable to socialism, even though the Church continued to disdain scientized reform. What limited Protestant-Catholic interaction that had been achieved in Boston by 1920 affirmed that some cooperation did occur but that mutual coexistence of charitable and reform societies based on Victorian models continued to be the norm. Further research on Church cooperation with the state board of charities, municipal boards, juvenile agencies, and the prison commission, for example, would most likely revise the thesis of strict Catholic separation.[19]

As internal debates on social work and the professionalization of charity indicated, Catholics were facing the same dilemmas about the social interpretation of Christianity that inspired Protestants to join the Social Gospel movement. Further, the dynamism behind Progressive reforms, especially the settlement house movement, actually derived from the crisis in Protestantism in both England and America. Protestant reformers could no longer believably preach personal conversion to Christ as a solution to the widespread social ills of poverty, political corruption, alcoholism, and crime. As social policy evolved from explaining poverty and its results as a personal failing, environmental factors were increasingly invoked in Protestant and Progressive approaches to charity. Despite that fact, Catholic attacks on social engineering implicitly criticized Protestantism as well for judging Catholic immigrants by the yardstick of the Protestant work ethic.

Catholic models for Christian social reform, however, were complicated by dependence on the model of medieval corporatism, by ethnic tensions between Catholics, and by antagonism toward the perceived condescension of social workers and Protestant evangelists toward the Catholic poor. Settlement houses did not emerge among Catholics in Boston for quite a while; the first was founded in 1930 after the archdiocese received a house in the West End as a donation from the Episcopal church. As early as 1909 Archbishop O'Connell expressed doubts about whether Protestants were genuine in their invitation for cooperation from Catholics for settlements in the South End, and he apparently took no action on their overtures.[20] Catholic women, however, seemed desirous of a South End settlement as early as 1910.[21] Apparently O'Connell's suspicion of "new-fangled" reform retarded the development of settlement houses in Boston, unlike dioceses such as Brooklyn, Chicago, Detroit, or Los Angeles, which developed viable Catholic settlement houses be-

ة

tween 1898 and 1910.[22] On the other hand, some programs run by the Boston
League of Catholic Women after its founding in 1910 duplicated settlement
work, though not centered in residential houses or with full-time staffs.
Women seemed to be able to justify such work when it was related to preventing loss of faith among the new immigrants, but when projects like settlement houses gained too much autonomy, the hierarchy either took them
over, as happened at Brownson House in Los Angeles, or made it unpleasant
for the foundress and staff to remain.

Aside from reflecting tensions over differing notions of the roots of poverty
and social deviance, and competing strategies for amelioration, the administration of Catholic charities in Boston reflected a Church in transition from
the parish-centered milieu of the immigrant to the structured bureaucracy of
the emerging national, state-run federations and associations that undermined
the localism of the parish base and subordinated individual initiatives to centralized aims. The changes in administration of Boston's charities between
1907 and 1923 illustrate this point: although the budget for the CCB, established in 1903, increased twentyfold during these years, the attempt to coordinate all Catholic social welfare work in one bureau still left dozens of
societies performing overlapping functions.[23] While O'Connell championed
"federation" among Catholics as a way to ward off labor violence, his creation
of the CCB led to a corresponding loss of autonomy for many of the lay charities incorporated into it, especially organizations run by laywomen and
women religious.[24] Calls for Catholic unity, combined with insistence that the
only solutions to social problems came from the Catholic tradition, led
O'Connell to suggest to some 200 representatives of Catholic charitable societies that their participation in his plan would overcome the fallacies of state-
sponsored reform: "What is needed today among all classes of Catholics here
in America is more confidence in themselves and less weakly imitation and
spineless subservience to what is called the spirit of the age, this up-to-
dateness, this yesterday civilization with its cocksure methods and its empty
boastfulness. By this time the world ought to realize that what is most needed
today is not a new batch of fads but a glance backward to the ages of faith."[25]
Because of O'Connell's negative outlook on secular social reform, parish-
based charities continued long after a centralized diocesan focus had been
initiated, indicating the survival of a tradition of Catholic localism and separatism. However, as class stratification increased among Catholics, so did
the differences between wealthy and poor parishes. The hierarchy's attempts
to coordinate parish and diocesan charitable organizations spanned the next
several decades; attempts to cooperate with secular charity were inconsistently supported and often explicitly discouraged.

In addition to the Columbian centenary, which gave rise to public reflection on Catholic philanthropy, two other conventions held in Boston contributed to the conflicting image of outsider Catholicism forced to care for its own versus the Church as an insider institution. Two months prior to the centenary, the archdiocese hosted the annual meeting of the AFCS. The *Boston Globe* ran a banner headline that suggested its patriotic thrust: "O'Connell Calls on FCS to Cultivate a Civic Conscience and Thus Ward Off Dangers to the Republic."[26] After the lieutenant governor and the mayor spoke, Archbishop O'Connell, frequently interrupted by applause, announced like a military general addressing troops before battle that the federation had become "the most potent barrier in all this broad country to the awful social evils which already threaten its prosperity." Such transparent appeals to God and Country against social chaos made the meaning clear to his audience: bad Catholics were double traitors, to their faith and to their nation.

The AFCS performed a second function that served O'Connell's local aims: it helped eliminate ethnic squabbling between Catholic societies.[27] O'Connell was pleased that the AFCS drew together the various Irish American, German American, Italian American, and French Canadian societies. Seen as a forerunner to the centenary, the AFCS convention set a precedent for grand-scale publicity that presented Catholics as devoted citizens, organized and modernized.[28] In fact, O'Connell spoke ardently of making the nation indebted to Catholicism because of groups like the AFCS that labored for the common good.[29]

Following the centenary was a second occasion for triumphal display: the Second Catholic Missionary Congress in 1913. International missions took on an increasing role in American Catholicism as the United States was released by the Vatican from its status as a mission territory in 1908. In that year Chicago had hosted the first missionary congress. O'Connell, absent but able to have his prepared speech read to the delegates, maneuvered to schedule the next congress on his own turf. As a new archbishop, O'Connell was courting his peers and Boston's WASP elites, who each received a challenge in his address, which overflowed with imperialist rhetoric: "All indications point to our vocation as a great missionary nation. . . . Our country has already reached out beyond her boundaries and is striving to do a work of extension of American civic ideals for other peoples. Shall it be said that the Church in this land has been outstripped in zeal by the civil power under which we live?"[30]

For the opening Mass of the 1913 congress, 50,000 persons surged into the plaza before Holy Cross Cathedral in South Boston on Sunday morning, October 19. The lengthy procession featured cross bearers, thurifers and acolytes, the Knights of Columbus honor guard, a seventy-five-voice choir, the seminarians from St. John's, all of Boston's clergy, and visiting priests.

Abbots, bishops, and archbishops in copes and miters were followed by the
Cathedral Guild, the Diocesan Council, the papal delegate, O'Connell and his
entourage, notable laymen in the full regalia of their papal honors, and more
Knights of Columbus. Church hierarchy was patently visible in the marching
order and by the garb of the processors. O'Connell missed no opportunity to
enhance his own image. He gave the inaugural sermon, delivered the opening
and closing remarks of each day's sessions, and chose selections from his own
hymnal to be sung at the High Mass.[31] O'Connell's opening sermon reflected
the same triumphal story he had presented five years earlier at the centenary:
"The Church in Boston, which 100 years ago counted so few that they could
be shepherded by those two apostolic sons of France, Cheverus and Matignon,
. . . now numbers 1,000,000 souls."[32] O'Connell was clearly delighted to
show Yankee Boston, as well as his fellow prelates and Vatican allies, that
Boston had seized a leadership role in the American Church. The missionary
congress was reportedly the largest gathering of American Catholics ever
held.[33] Its emphasis on home missions reflected growing concern to evangelize
Indians, blacks, and Mexicans within the United States, while American Catholic participants in foreign missions hoped to end Vatican perceptions of
American inferiority.

O'Connell's image of a competition between civil and religious conquest
of the globe suggests that despite the fact that separation of church and state
was well established in the United States, conservatives like himself maintained ambivalent opinions about whether religion should be primarily a private affair. Indeed, the modern Western political model of privatized religion
did not "fit" well with European Catholicism, rededicated to Thomism and
an infallibilist papacy. Moreover, American Catholicism had shown itself capable of exhibiting a "republican style" at previous points in its history, in
marked contrast to European feudal paternalism.[34] In the United States, the
Church still struggled against anti-Catholic bigotry in a society dominated
ideologically by Protestants, although Catholics had been the largest single
denomination since 1850. The aggressive but insecure public Catholicism that
evolved in Boston after 1900 defined the parameters for debates on the formation of "Catholic identity." The pageants, conventions, and congresses
epitomized the deliberate attempt of Roman Catholics to construct an identity
of respectability and of power and to sustain, among themselves, the codes
of a shared symbolic world. Parades and choreographed ceremonies, as opposed to the personal or familial symbolic world of household shrines, wakes,
and prayers, framed and universalized the community's "inherited tradition
and moral wisdom."[35] Unlike ethnic folk religious festivals, however, the diocesan and federation parades sought to transcend racial and ethnic bound-

On the cathedral steps, Cardinal O'Connell presides over the opening Mass of the Second Catholic Missionary Congress in 1913. Boston laymen of the cardinal's suite, wearing the knightly regalia of their papal orders, are arranged on the steps. (From Kelley, *Great American Catholic Missionary Congresses*)

aries by highlighting the unifying elements of Catholicism and its allegiance, but not subservience, to American ideals.

Antebellum American Catholics have been characterized as a necessarily inward-looking community because of the Church's immigrant composition. As assimilation increased, the Church's public style in local, state, and national affairs reflected both a defensive and an aggressive program expressive of the insider-outsider mentality at a transitional stage. Regarding the civic responsibility of Catholics, the Church was hostile to programs that lacked a purely spiritual basis. Church involvement in community affairs, therefore, provides one index of the seriousness of its commitment to social reform and to the preservation of communalism. The examples below indicate that the smaller the religious component of a program, and the less prominent the role of Catholic leaders, the lower the Church's enthusiasm to participate or even to pledge nominal support.

Catholics and "Boston, 1915"

Archbishop O'Connell encouraged Catholics to embrace civic responsibility, even through confrontation: "The time has come when every Catholic must stand up and be counted for the faith or against it. It is time for Catholic manhood to stand erect, square its shoulders, look the whole world in the eye and say, 'I am a Roman Catholic citizen; what about it?'"[36] The archbishop showed little flexibility, however, when approached by city leaders seeking Catholic support, which hampered even the simplest attempts at civic cooperation. O'Connell manipulated the insider-outsider mentality in his guidelines for Catholic participation in a program for urban development.

"Boston, 1915," heretofore studied by political historians as part of the Good Government thrust of urban Progressive reform, reveals how Catholicism attempted to maintain its theological superiority and moral high ground while accommodating itself to capitalism. Called a "noble experiment" by a modern historian of city planning, "Boston, 1915" was essentially an enterprising six-year plan that disintegrated after three years. The plan was designed to draw new business to the city by touting the opportunities for investors and businessmen in Boston, while minimizing the city's socioeconomic problems. Hence, the project became an effort to rescue the ailing local economy, packaged as reform. Edward A. Filene (1860–1937), son of a Prussian Jewish father and Bavarian mother, and heir to his father's prospering Boston department store in 1891, brought Lincoln Steffens to Boston in 1909 to organize an urban uplift program spanning the next six years. Numerous Yankee Progressive reformers of Boston, including James J. Storrow, Robert A. Woods, Robert Treat Paine, and others, held a series of meetings to plan the campaign.[37] Initiated and chaired by Filene, a native of nearby Salem, "Boston, 1915" was intended to "unite all the interests of the city over a five-year period to plan for future growth and development."[38] A concentrated publicity campaign, beginning with publication of *New Boston* in 1910 and combined with numerous public education programs, gave the directors of "Boston, 1915" high hopes. Ultimately, despite Filene's ever-optimistic faith in human rational behavior, "Boston, 1915" was unsuccessful in drawing Boston's thirty-seven surrounding towns into the cooperative effort, and the movement folded in 1912.

The committee did not perform a comprehensive survey of Boston on the model of the recent Pittsburgh Survey of 1909, although it did draw upon the observations of Robert Woods, Lincoln Steffens, and the expertise of leading businessmen and professionals. In seeking proposals for redesigning portions of the city, the committee appealed, for example, to the Catholic architectural partners, Charles Maginnis and Timothy Walsh.[39] By spring of 1911, the committee received news that seemed to predict a bright future for the movement: the state legislature authorized Governor Eugene Foss to appoint a temporary commission to investigate the need for a metropolitan plan. Foss chose the trio of Edward Filene; J. Randolph Coolidge, Jr., an architect; and John Nolen, a landscape architect and city planner.

Unfortunately, the towns surrounding Boston remained unconvinced of the benefits of federating with Boston and opposed having all their improvement plans overseen by a commonwealth commission. Mayor John Fitzgerald, who supported "Boston, 1915," criticized Newton, Brookline, and other elite suburbs for their "parochial shortsightedness," which doomed Boston to piecemeal planning efforts. In 1873, local suburbs had first rejected an annexation movement; now, forty years later, annexation again failed. The state legislature never approved Foss's metropolitan planning board as a permanent commission, and "Boston, 1915" dissolved in April 1912.[40] It probably would not have survived Mayor James Curley's first term in 1914, anyway: among his favorite political targets were the Brahmin banking elite who backed "Boston, 1915" and the "Goo-Goos" (the Good Government Association).[41]

Besides linking Boston with the City Beautiful Movement and the nascent profession of city planning, "Boston, 1915" tapped the forces within Progressive reform aimed at improving the quality of life in the city. Following upon the overhaul of the public school system, "Boston, 1915" attempted to revive the city's former commercial prominence by allying the business community with City Hall. Although Mayor Fitzgerald was put out of office by such reformers, namely the Boston Finance Commission of 1907–8, and although Mayor Curley began and ended his political career in jail for various alleged acts of municipal corruption, nonetheless, each mayor won praise for boosting Boston. Honey Fitz's first-term slogan was A Bigger, Better and Busier Boston; Curley chose Boom Boston, hastening to reassure businessmen that campaign materials would tastefully promote the city.[42] In some ways, as both Boston's Catholic and secular presses observed, the "Boston, 1915" campaign simply copied strategies proposed as early as 1902 as part of a plan for renewal of Boston's harbor by John Fitzgerald. Reiterated during his mayoral administration in a program he called "Boston Old Home Week," Fitzgerald's folksy style was criticized by Brahmins as undignified. Catholics, however, remained proud that one of their own had led the way in urban reform, pointing out that Progressives later tried to steal his thunder.[43] The Church did not comment on the blatant business interests underlying the project that had proposed for the next decade to restrict immigration of unskilled labor to Boston as a way to protect local entrepreneurs.

Catholics participated in "Boston, 1915" as members of the board of directors and various committees. Archbishop O'Connell (who never appeared in person at these meetings and later stopped answering correspondence, citing his other obligations) designated Chancellor Michael Splaine to represent the Catholic chancery along with Auxiliary Bishop Joseph Anderson. Thomas Bernard Fitzpatrick, owner of the Brown-Durrell Company, a dry goods enterprise, and Bernard Rothwell, an Irish immigrant who was now a successful

manufacturer, worked with the planning committee. Joseph C. Pelletier, the
district attorney, and Father Thomas Gasson, president of Boston College,
were listed on the letterhead of the board of directors along with a Mr. Fahey
and a Mr. Sullivan. Numerous other Catholics in civil service positions were
named to committees on education, health, labor, charities, and contributions.
Invitations for Catholic participation symbolized gestures of goodwill toward
the Catholic mayor and his administration even though Fitzgerald's term was
soon interrupted by charges of corruption. Catholics, however, had strong
reasons to be wary of Honey Fitz's opponents, especially members of the Immigration Restriction League (IRL) whose activities were largely directed
against Catholics and Jews.[44] "Boston, 1915," after all, was intended to offer
investment opportunities, achieved by city planning and finally by immigration restriction. Perhaps an inkling of the anti-Catholic potential of the movement led O'Connell to keep Catholics fairly distant from the project, but there
is no evidence that he acted this subtly. He permitted all parishes to submit
posters depicting church activities in Boston for a public exhibition in the art
museum (then in Copley Square), boasting that "the Archbishop desires that
the Catholic Church of Boston be adequately represented as it is doing much
more work in the city and for its people than any other institution within its
limits." But O'Connell inexplicably forbid Church participation in the Religious Day of the "Boston, 1915" exhibition, the one event that would have
given Catholics a chance to publicize their undertakings to a wide audience.[45]

What explains the Church's limited participation in civic programs like
"Boston, 1915"? Perhaps it was the sentiment that, as the Boston *Pilot* maintained, the Church, not social engineering, possessed the solutions to all social
problems: "A fact that has become most patent of late is that there are moral
problems involved in the social question. Hence the Catholic Church, the historic teacher of Christian truth, and the source of Christian morality, cannot
help being interested in them."[46] O'Connell's noteworthy 1908 sermon, "The
Church—the Strong Safeguard of the Republic," had stated that "there is not
a single condition existing to-day in the whole world, civilized or uncivilized,
which the Church of Christ has not faced one hundred times before and settled
with the same identical principle." Further, O'Connell asserted that the
Church's claim to moral authority was in fact protected by the institutions of
America's democratic government: "If there is any form of government which
needs for its permanence and prosperity the conserving force of right moral
Christian sentiment it is a republic."[47] Although he undercut the Church's
opportunities to be represented in municipal reform, O'Connell carefully
maintained the relevance of Christian moral principles to civic culture.

The Church's self-proclaimed role, therefore, in the midst of political dis-
cord, social diversity, and urban economic decline, was an imperialistic pos-

"Boston, 1915" exhibition in Copley Square. (Boston Public Library)

ture of stating, "We have the answers." Catholic commitments to pluralism
often became occasions for the Church to exhibit arrogance about its own
invincibility and to display an embarrassing petulance about "joining the
group." Among Catholics themselves, a noticeable split between what the
Church said and what the laity did in public life manifested itself in extreme
form in the venality of the Irish political machines, which rivaled the Church
in attempting to subvert or expand the system to give advantages to outsiders.

Although the Church had undoubtedly impressed many upright public servants by preaching civic virtue and good citizenship, there was no structural
mechanism within Catholicism that correlated private and public morality,
condemned political immorality, or demanded a reform of the political patronage game. If ethnic machines represented more than warts on the political
system, namely a logical extension of ways in which various groups sought
economic advantages within capitalism, then the Church's silence about them
represented another instance of its unwillingness to acknowledge capitalism's
impact on its assumptions. O'Connell's snubbings of Mayor Curley and other
ward politicians of whom he disapproved were largely motivated by his fear
of rivals, not by a religious critique of their behavior. O'Connell was not universally effective in changing popular support for even the most corrupt Irish
politicians because his power did not necessarily supersede ethnic and partisan loyalty. Moreover, the Church enveloped the faithful in democratic rhetoric designed to justify its own influence over public morality without helping

develop the private consciences of the laity. Ultimately, the Church continued its policy of discouraging average Catholics from mingling fully in events not directed by the Church.

Ford Hall Forum and Democratization

"Boston, 1915" was not the rousing success hoped for by urban planners, entrepreneurs, and religious participants. Catholic involvement in the Ford Hall Forum, by contrast, revealed a slightly increased willingness of the Church to participate in non-Catholic events. The Ford Hall Forum and meetings were founded and funded through the Boston Baptist Social Union and were held Sunday evenings from 1908 until 1928, when Ford Hall became independent of the Baptists. The founder, president, and moderator of the programs, George Coleman, called the project "democracy in the making."[48] Coleman, an advertising agent, modeled the program on the Cooper Union of New York City, which used public debates to foster adult education and Americanization. In a lecture-saturated city, the enduring popularity of public forums like Ford Hall marked a continuation of the nineteenth-century lyceum circuits and of Boston's tolerance of free speech, self-education, and faddists of all sorts. Ford Hall expressed contemporary, Progressive concerns to provide public information about the latest social research.

Debate topics were nonsectarian but frequently religious, since its directors believed that "Man is 'incurably religious.'"[49] In 180 evenings, for example, 68 religious leaders appeared, including 21 Baptists, 17 Jews, and 12 Congregationalists. Roman Catholics were represented by only 5 speakers, ranking seventh of ten denominations. By occupation, the speakers came from the ranks of college professors, businessmen, social workers, journalists, and laborers.[50] At least one Catholic, Mary Boyle O'Reilly, served on the Committee of Citizens for a time with social reformer Robert Woods and with several other "representative" citizens who helped select the speakers. A Jesuit priest, Michael Ahern, sometimes substituted for George Coleman as moderator. On one occasion, he amused the audience by mistakenly addressing well-known Professor Harry Overstreet as "Professor Crabtree."[51] Catholic writers such as poet Denis McCarthy and journalist A. J. Philpott, among others, were endorsed by Ford Hall as public speakers sponsored by the New England Congress of Forums.

A sample of Ford Hall programs from 1908 to 1915 reveals that popular speakers returned more than once: Baptist Social Gospel minister Walter Rauschenbusch gave six lectures, and Reformed Rabbi Stephen Wise delivered five. Father John A. Ryan, a rising Catholic reformer, also spoke to five Forum audiences.[52] The relative prominence of Ivy League professors, liberal Protestants, and Reform Jews in the forum perhaps explains the hesitancy of the Catholic hierarchy to aggressively promote Catholic speakers. A second factor in the low level of publicity for Catholic clergy who appeared was probably the policy of Archbishop O'Connell, who claimed the right to approve all public statements by priests.

A contemporary analyst compared the Ford Hall assemblies to "the curriculum of a sociological course," although it recalled its Baptist roots in such gestures as an opening prayer and opening and closing hymns. The guest speaker was allotted an hour, followed by a question period in which any member of the audience could address the speaker. The forum was particularly proud of its open discussion feature. Certain types of questions (and responses) were predictable: "An evening without Socialism, woman suffrage, and theological queries is almost unknown."[53] Any anti-Catholic remarks made by speakers or audience were invariably censured in the Catholic press and pulpit. When Episcopal Bishop William Lawrence criticized the imperialism of the emperor of Belgium and, by implication, the Catholic Church, the *Pilot* chided him: "This is the year 1910, and Ford Hall is situated in the city of Boston, 75 percent of which is Catholic. We advise you either to go back to England, to the Lambeth Congress, and stay there, where all this hypocritical jingoism against the Congo is accepted."[54]

Quasi-spiritual uplift seemed to attract many persons to the forum. An attendee said that "the meetings make me feel good." James Roberts reported that a Catholic couple "found themselves becoming better Catholics." "It is interesting," Roberts continued reassuringly, "that increasing their loyalty to their church did not lessen their loyalty to Ford Hall." This veneer of ecumenism disturbed Father Ryan from Minnesota, who helped popularize the concept of the "living wage" following the publication of his Catholic University dissertation in 1906. Ryan was glad to give "educational value" to audiences that had often never seen or met a Catholic priest. He sensed a warmer response each time he spoke, but he remained hostile to Catholic cooperation with the Ford forum, which made Protestant evangelical appeals to "the unchurched." "No Catholic can conscientiously become a part of any social or civic movement which is organized on a professedly religious basis, or purports to be a religious undertaking, even though the lines followed may be entirely undenominational," wrote Ryan. "For the Catholic there is only one religion, and there are not legitimate substitutes."[55] Further, the theories advocated at Ford Hall on "ethics of industry, education, civics, the family, feminism, eugenics" often conflicted with Catholic moral teaching. Ryan gave as one example the "high" percentage of socialist speakers at Ford Hall in 1914: six of the total of twenty-four. Ryan claimed that Catholics, who opposed socialism on moral grounds, denied the need to air false doctrines in public, just as they denied the necessity of discussing obvious truths like the multiplication tables.[56]

Ryan championed social separation based on a sense of moral superiority, which was the essence of Catholic cultural isolationism. Ironically, while his advocacy of Catholic separatism and strict denominational distinctions echoed O'Connell, the cardinal hesitated to allow Ryan to speak in Boston because he considered him a dangerous radical on social issues.[57] Through the 1920s O'Connell also remained wary about permitting priests from his own diocese to lecture at Ford Hall. In 1925 Father Ahern, then teaching chemistry at Holy Cross College in Worcester, reported that O'Connell had finally allowed him to accept engagements through the New England Speaker's Bureau, the agent for Ford Hall.[58]

Despite Ryan's impressions, Catholic speakers were in fact well represented: *Boston Globe* journalist A. J. Philpott spoke in 1913; Professor Frank O'Hara delivered an address in 1915 titled "What the Irish Immigrant Has Done for America," along with James J. Walsh on the Middle Ages and James P. Magenis on "Some Lessons Learned from the Law." As the number of Catholic speakers increased through the 1920s, Ford Hall heard Margaret Slattery on "The Power of Prejudice" and "What Shall We Do with the Reformer?," and Father Jones I. Corrigan on "The Social Menace of Divorce" and "The Church and Politics." In 1929 Father Ahern spoke on what must have been a perennial favorite, "What We Don't Know about the Jesuits."[59] In the end, although the forum was intended to Americanize immigrant audiences through demonstrating toleration of pluralism, Catholics were overly sensitive to the fact that other religious traditions were more visibly represented, and they reacted chauvinistically to any perceived insults to Roman Catholicism, thereby inhibiting its effectiveness.

Social Work and Immigrant Americanization

While Ford Hall represented the educational thrust of Progressivism, Progressives had also formed agencies to meet the everyday needs of immigrants. As a major port of entry since colonial times, Boston was the home of many immigrant aid societies, providing the national headquarters of the North American Civic League for Immigrants (NACLI), founded in 1908. The Catholic Church had a logical interest in Americanization agencies because of its extensive immigrant population. Its opposition to state-run social planning, however, and its tentative involvement in "Boston, 1915" and Ford Hall indicate the fledgling quality of Catholic self-confidence in Boston and the persistence of an insider-outsider sensibility that undermined Church participation in non-Catholic activities and intensified its sectarian priorities. Concerning the NACLI, the hierarchy and the laity approved the democratic goals of the undertaking and showed a certain willingness to help assimilate new immigrants at the group level. In the league, Catholics were represented by Bernard Rothwell (who later served "Boston, 1915"), here appearing as vice-president. Cardinal O'Connell was a member of the board of managers, which also included James Cardinal Gibbons of Baltimore. Administered nationally from Boston, the league represented a consciously interfaith effort among Protestants, Catholics, and Jews to aid immigrants in need of language skills, housing, and work.[60]

Representative of what has been called the "nervously nationalistic" first phase of Americanization efforts, the wide-ranging activities of the NACLI included assisting newcomers with naturalization papers, reuniting families, offering protection to women, and providing interpreters, fraud protection, employment, and legal advice.[61] The league worked with local churches and chambers of commerce, the YMCA, the National Federation of Women's Clubs, the Twentieth Century Club, the Sons and Daughters of the American Revolution, the Massachusetts Federation of Churches, and the Hebrew Immigrant Society. Presumably, the Catholic Church would have supported the NACLI's programs to the utmost, even though they undoubtedly duplicated efforts of groups like the Catholic Immigration Society, established in 1912 by the Catholic Alumni Sodality, and of other groups affiliated with the CCB.

In principle, O'Connell approved of the league's antisocialist spirit, which intensified among leaguers and Catholics following the ten-week strike among Italian textile mill workers in Lawrence, Massachusetts, in 1912.[62] Inklings of the hierarchy's lukewarm support for the NACLI, however, were soon apparent. When invited to submit a short written statement of his approbation of the league's "general work," O'Connell responded tersely that lending his name to the league's letterhead was sufficient.[63] Thus, when more than financial assistance to the poor was at issue, the Catholic Church questioned the secular thrust of Americanizers. Catholics claimed that their efforts provided better care for immigrants. Even though in theory Catholics upheld the values of Americanization and of pluralism, in practice they chose to justify separatism by claiming that superlative social programs were based on Catholic principles. O'Connell's clergy friends shared his suspicion of political motives behind attempts to involve Catholics in public philanthropy. Father Joseph Anderson, for example, then a pastor in Dorchester, had been invited in 1908 to join the Boston Finance Commission concerning improvement in city charitable institutions. He declined, stating to O'Connell that he feared "that there might be some political move in this having me to serve on this committee [namely, in having the Catholic clergy endorse the finance commission]. . . .

I will also see Mr. Sullivan . . . and find out definitely what is back of this movement and if it is advisable to serve."[64] Aside from the legitimate concern that priests avoid becoming tools of partisan politics, the episode evinced a by-now familiar anxiety of Catholics that centralized state-run charities would erase the Catholic identity of immigrants and, ultimately, destroy Church authority.

If the NACLI represented a nationalist yet benevolent form of Americanization, the IRL was its antithesis. IRL membership duplicated that of the NACLI in many cases, except that among the IRL leadership, anti-Catholic and anti-Irish sentiments were openly expressed and shared. By 1906, conservative forces in Massachusetts were reviving to rally around the IRL, founded in 1894 by Joseph Lee, Robert DeCourcy Ward, and others, to pressure the federal government to pass stricter immigration restriction laws. These included addition of an increased tax on each immigrant (up to as much as $50), a literacy test, educational tests, and special restrictions on Asians, Latins, Slavs, the diseased mentally deficient, anarchists, and those unable to work. Although contemptuous of recent immigrants, Joseph Lee (1862–1937), president of the IRL, had not lost his fear of the Irish Catholics: "I believe that the Catholic Church is becoming a great evil. I see it every day in Massachusetts. Its ideas are precisely the opposite of democracy, and I don't believe that the two can permanently get along together here any more than they can in France or Italy."[65] Lee, a Progressive who founded the Massachusetts Civic League, is often also remembered kindly as the father of the American playground movement. However, his published writings and personal correspondence suggest a dark side of Progressivism, which joined evolutionary theory to pseudoscientific biological and ethnological research, Anglo-Saxonism, and primitive genetic theory. Lee and his colleagues supported the idea that life represents a struggle between the higher and lower races as well as a struggle within the individual between one's higher, divine self and a lower nature. The IRL supported the view that heredity is destiny and that racial traits are permanent and indelible. Therefore, it feared the atavistic impact of inferior character traits and lower races upon Anglo-Saxon superiority.

Many of these racial fears took political form. Joseph Lee and his cohorts encouraged the to whip up anti-Catholic frenzy: "Can't you get after the Masonic crowd," he asked the IRL secretary, "through editorials in their paper? If they realized that it means the dominance of the Catholic Church in Massachusetts and elsewhere (as it can now choose the Mayor of Boston and will soon be able to choose the Governor) perhaps they would get busy."[66] For the next decade, the IRL's political activities focused on pressuring Massachusetts senator Henry Cabot Lodge to legislate a literacy test for immigrants, and on denouncing all non-Anglo-Saxons.

In light of this new wave of anti-Catholic and antiimmigrant prejudice, O'Connell's chauvinism toward non-Catholic projects seems somewhat more understandable by the 1910s. Even NACLI president Daniel Chauncey Brewer revealed his true colors as a militant Anglo-Saxonist who feared that his kind were being mongrelized by foreigners. He joined in the anti-Irish chorus, urging his readers "to take note of the part Boston is playing in this drama of dramas," having lost "its native characteristic because of the great influx of Irish who are in active control of its municipal housekeeping."[67] Fear about the loss of Protestant hegemony fueled Brewer's contention that Yankee control had been "reduced" to the banking realm in New England by the immigrant hordes.

Not satisfied with their legislative victory of 1917, the IRL played a part in increasing the antialien hysteria of the post–World War I years by playing to antialien and economic anxieties. By 1919 the IRL had increased its warnings against a glut of unskilled labor arriving in America in order to gain support for further exclusionary measures, noting that the "poor quality" of European candidates was likely to increase after the war. The IRL supported Americanization programs and stringent restriction laws in order to hasten the emergence of an optimal "national type," from which America's future leaders would emerge. Lee and others advocated eugenics, believing that the vacuum created by emigration from a country encouraged the undesirable breeding of the lower classes. Immigration restrictionists justified their belief in "world eugenics" as a plan to save Europe from becoming a genetic cesspool.

Joseph Lee defended the right to exclude undesirables from America by contending that its original Puritan immigration had been of "selected stock." He wrote that "the New England immigrant was not only selected but was selected for its pre-eminent democracy even in democratic England, and it is that part of our immigration that has given the general tone to the country."[68] Since the IRL believed that only Anglo-Saxons properly understood democracy, it renewed its attacks on Irish Americans following the creation of the Irish Free State in 1922. Lee stated, "The hatred of everything English or American that is preached every Sunday by Cardinal O'Connell gives some line on the real Americanism of one section of the Irish and also of the kind of a life they would lead Ulster if they had her in their power."[69] Shared by Boston's WASP elites, Lee's view merely reiterated nineteenth-century arguments condemning Catholics as antirepublican conspirators, while adding new "evidence" from fashionable social Darwinist and racialist theories. In the 1920s, when anti-Irish feeling returned to fever pitch because of the Anglo-Irish war, Lee hoped that restrictions in the proposed Johnson immigration act would exclude additional Irish arrivals as well. He confided to Robert Ward: "If it would get through, I should think it would be fine. It would keep out the Irish."[70]

Thus, the "Irish question" kept resurfacing in Boston politics and religion as domestic and international events prompted fresh outbreaks of anti-Irish prejudice. Between 1910 and 1920 Boston's Yankee elites protested the Sinn Fein movement, the 1916 uprising, Irish neutrality during the world war, the election of Eamon De Valera, and the creation of the Irish Free State. Even immigration restrictionists who had begun to concede that the Irish were preferable to Slavs, Latins, and Asians, revived antebellum rhetoric about how Irish Catholics would deform American democratic institutions into feudal pawns of the papacy.

To defend their patriotism, Irish Catholics attempted to show that their historical record was unimpeachably democratic. In the 1910s this was accomplished primarily through sponsoring an ongoing campaign against socialism in Massachusetts, which identified Catholics as insiders united against America's enemies. Both the Catholic hierarchy and the NACLI opposed the role of the Industrial Workers of the World (IWW) in the Lawrence textile strike of January 4–March 19, 1912. Marching under banners stating No God, No Master, the IWW radicals had stirred up (mostly Italian) Catholic millworkers enough to cast doubts upon the public image of the Catholic working class that O'Connell had tried so hard to achieve: conservative, stable, patriotic, and dependable. As a consequence, Catholic activists and clergy who went to Lawrence during and after the strike demonstrated the divisions between Catholic Irish elites and Italian newcomers, emphasizing that even though worker demands might be just, the strikers were destroying the fabric of family life and of national consensus. A lecturer in the Knights of Columbus antisocialist series, one month after the first Lawrence strike, defined class consciousness as "class hatred and organized envy, and aims to unite wage-earners against all the other elements of human society."[71] Fears of an "atheistic multitude" drowned out workers' demands for justice. Clerical Americanism thereby orchestrated the laity's class and social resentments against common enemies of Americanism to provide further support for its strategy of separatist integration.

The Catholic Common Cause Society

The animus of the Catholic Church against socialism was fully articulated in the Common Cause Society, established in 1912. When Cardinal O'Connell was not busy burying the last Puritan, he was fighting the rising socialist. When O'Connell became archbishop, the separation of church and state in France was the leading Catholic news event, because of the anticlericalism it generated and the feudal precedents it was destroying. Soon after, socialism became the Church's perennial target. Because O'Connell remained suspicious of Catholic immersion in Boston's secular life, he gladly welcomed the Common Cause Society, a Catholic equivalent to Ford Hall. Common Cause described the Ford Hall meetings as "the most attractive of Boston's public forums, and we think the most dangerous, because its attacks upon the faith are insidious, never open."[72] Although ostensibly established in Boston as part of the Church's strategy to combat socialism, Common Cause adopted a time-honored feature of Yankee culture, the urban forum, and even some Protestant evangelical tactics. Nonetheless, the society was part of an international pattern in Catholicism, which throughout western Europe was making use of organizational techniques to forge Catholic social action. In England, for example, the Catholic Evidence Guild, which sent zealous street evangelists to the speaker's corner in London's Hyde Park, similarly appropriated English customs of free speech and of Protestant street speaking to its own needs.

Conceived by its founders, converts Martha Moore Avery and David Goldstein, as the cornerstone of a lay evangelization movement, Common Cause met on Sunday nights at Franklin Union Hall during the winter, holding audiences of over 1,000 persons. During the summer, it held open air gatherings on the Boston Common on Sunday afternoons and in public squares on Saturday nights. Like Ford Hall, the speaker's opponents were allowed to make rebuttals; at Common Cause however, opponents actually took the platform following the main address.[73] Unlike Ford Hall, which portrayed itself simply as an agent of Americanization, Common Cause proposed a more sectarian intent: "In this way *we save and strengthen our own* and the alien Catholic coming to our shores has a fighting army for a friend."[74] Where Ford Hall invited participants of all religious and philosophical beliefs, Common Cause decided that while it would not restrict membership to adherents of "strictly Catholic principles," members should profess belief in the Catholic sociological principles of Leo XIII.[75] An early test of that clause came in a debate over the membership of Max Mason, a Jew, who was one of the charter members. The society's president, Charles Fay, described Mason as a young man who "defended the Church, often in public, against Socialists, Atheists, and others," and Fay urged Cardinal O'Connell to decide in Mason's favor. Rev. Patrick Waters, the spiritual advisor of Common Cause, appealed to O'Connell to restrict the society to Catholics. O'Connell eventually sustained Mason's membership as an exception, and Mason remained in Common Cause.[76] Although Common Cause claimed to be a lay-directed open forum, it was closely overseen by the clergy. In 1914, debates over the society's constitution led to an amendment stating that the elected president would be subject to the approval of the archbishop of Boston.[77] The society's chaplain, appointed in February 1914, was chosen not only because he could nimbly refute the socialist speakers, but also because of his obsequious loyalty to O'Connell. In a letter to the head of St. John's Seminary, O'Connell had specifically requested a priest "for the work of co-operating with the Common Cause Society by taking up and confuting the arguments advanced by Socialistic speakers at Ford Hall and elsewhere."[78] Father Waters, who customarily signed his letters to O'Connell, "Kissing the sacred purple, I am your most humble servant," was eventually retitled spiritual advisor in accord with Martha Moore Avery's request to Archbishop O'Connell. O'Connell continued to meddle in the affairs of Common Cause, warning it to choose speakers carefully and forbidding it to take political stands on "woman's suffrage or any other matter" without his instructions.[79] Thus circumscribed, Common Cause set forth to discredit both socialism and forces in Massachusetts that portrayed Catholics as anti-American.

Common Cause had a core membership of about twenty-five men and was about 80 percent Catholic in 1913, according to President Fay. Martha Moore Avery, who appeared to be the sole female member, later served as president from 1922 to 1929. The society's name came from a magazine published in New York by the Social Reform Press,[80] and its motto indicated that the society stood for "God and Country, and opposes Anarchy, Socialism and kindred evils." Despite Avery's presence, Common Cause's membership was probably deemed unsuitable for women because of its public apostolate. Avery was a useful exception because she was a convert from Protestantism and Marxism and because her Boston School of Political Economy, founded after her defection from the Socialist party, served similarly conservative aims by educating students about the flaws of socialism. There is evidence that O'Connell encouraged women to join Common Cause on at least one occasion. When Catholic women working at the statehouse in Boston tried to form an antisuffrage group, the cardinal pressured them to join Common Cause instead, exemplifying his distaste for lay initiative, especially from women.[81]

The "common cause" of the movement was antisocialism and antiradicalism. By endorsing the Church's political conservatism, Catholics could overcome their outsider defensiveness by proving their patriotism. Common Cause's founding followed on the heels of an antisocialist lecture series that O'Connell had sponsored from 1907 to 1910. These programs had been held simultaneously in four locations throughout the city on Sunday afternoons to coincide with wage earners' only free time.[82] Clerical and lay leaders addressed crowds on the condition of labor, explained Leo XIII's social teachings, and

LIMITS OF AMERICANIZATION

reiterated the Church's ultimate authority. They appealed to workers to "show forth in your lives as Catholic workingmen the constructive, and at the same time, the conservative power of the Church of God." Some of the priests giving lectures had come from local working-class communities: Monsignor Michael Splaine, for example, grew up in Watertown, although by then he had been rewarded with a pastorship in a more affluent community and later was appointed archdiocesan chancellor.

Cardinal O'Connell approved of Common Cause because it diverted Catholics from socialism and suffrage, which he believed would destroy their faith as well as their credibility as good citizens. As might be expected of an outsider group, Common Cause masked Catholic insecurity with triumphalism. It protested the meager and biased coverage it received in Boston newspapers but was optimistic about "creating a public opinion that shall be dominated by Catholic thought and feeling," as soon as it could overcome "the vast multitude still under the influence of Yankee psychology."[83]

"Cross and Flag Aloft"

The Boston hierarchy and clergy was hardly prophetic or radical in its social, economic, and political outlook. Led by a series of reactionary popes, the Church had responded to intellectual and practical challenges since 1789 by condemning materialism, socialism, and communism, largely ignoring the implications of papal criticisms of the fallacies of economic liberalism and capitalism. The failure of the Church to develop a searching critique of capitalism as a counterweight to its overwhelming rejection of socialism is a vital part of the narrative of middle-class formation among Catholics. The desire of Catholics to assimilate economically meant that their religious principles must not reject the dominant culture's work ethic nor the capitalist structures of its economy, which in turn gave extra force to the militancy of Catholic anti-socialism in Boston. Thus Archbishop O'Connell was able to define the Church as an "impregnable bulwark" and "an army against the growing dangers of anti-Christian socialism."[84] This negative construction of identity—describing what Catholicism is not—dissociated good Catholics from socialism, which was blamed for the destruction of family life and female purity. Assuredly, Catholic support became largely responsible for the failure of socialism and radicalism in Massachusetts and for the embrace of middle-class values among Catholics. The Church had unquestionably overreacted to the abortive socialism that had peaked in Massachusetts as early as 1903 and that had never captured large numbers of foreign-born workers in the first place. In fact, 71 percent of the national membership of the Socialist party in 1908 was made up of native-born Americans; only 19.5 percent were "old" immigrants, such as Irish and Germans, while a mere 9.5 percent were other foreigners.[85]

Catholic antisocialism continued to thrive nonetheless. Though even O'Connell had declared the threat of socialism in Boston over in 1910, he requested in 1914 that "a priest be set aside to meet Socialist propaganda."[86] After World War I, Father John Ryan lamented that "the majority of our Catholic men have restricted their beneficent activity in civic and social movements to the task of combating wrong views and measures."[87] However, this defensive strategy was unlikely to disappear in Boston, where after 1919 the Church simply added anti-Bolshevik arguments to its antisocialist platform. Common Cause was reinforced by another Avery and Goldstein collaboration, the Catholic Truth Guild. The *Pilot* and lay Catholic associations reiterated antisocialist propaganda through the Second World War. During the Cold War, Catholic anticommunist rhetoric repeated the same propaganda and employed the same tactics as the generation of the 1910s. Thus, the social agenda of the papacy had far-reaching effects on American Catholics in molding reactionary responses that remained largely unchanged between Vatican I and Vatican II.

Beginning with the centenary of 1908, we have traced a process showing how Catholics began to orchestrate public perception of Catholic identity in Boston. The crowded Mass and the massed crowds of the parade; the shimmering satin banners of the Catholic clubs mingled with American flags; the colorful uniforms, rosettes, baldrics, bugles, and swords of the fraternal orders; and the speeches about triumph over harsh prejudice seemed to affirm a limitless Catholic future. Catholic self-confidence engendered by "united Catholic action" spoke of the need for strenuous religious and civic service from the laity. "Lukewarm indorsements [*sic*] butter no parsnips," cried the AFCS president with a flourish. "We want the hearty, energetic recognition of every ecclesiastic and layman in the country for federation."[88] Yet, self-imposed constraints upon participation in projects like the Ford Hall Forum indicated how Catholic hopes were still tempered by suspicion of nativist Yankee Protestant culture. Catholics retreated into their own subculture when Ford Hall offerings contradicted their own doctrines, objecting to public discussion of such "absurdities" as socialism, eugenics, and birth control. Further responses to secularism such as the Common Cause Society were themselves curbed by the hierarchy when lay leaders showed tendencies toward too much independence. The archbishop's strong support of Common Cause indicates that it embodied the hierarchy's vision of the optimal lay association: a Church-directed society, promoting Catholic principles and ultimately responsive to papal direction.

The participation of Catholic clergy and businessmen in "Boston, 1915" demonstrated that Catholics were civic minded but, more importantly, high-lighted how the Catholic middle class had aligned itself with the conservative business and management elements of the community, who represented stability and social mobility. Bourgeois Catholics wanted to share the charmed position of Yankee Protestants, yet their growing prosperity potentially threatened Catholic outsider solidarity. The victim mentality of Catholics persisted, however, leaving them suspicious of Brahmins who reacted to their own waning power by renewing attempts to restrict "papist" immigration. In response to these attacks on Catholic citizenship, the Church emphasized "constructive conservatism," portraying Catholics as useful and patriotic Americans, determined to defeat leftist politics and to uphold republican institutions. In short, Catholics were no threat because they were just like the American middle class. The term *lay apostolate,* which is frequently applied to organized lay action from the 1930s through Vatican II, implies that lay persons had a mission to serve the Church by evangelizing the world. But as early as the 1910s, lay roles were linked to the building of a subculture, thereby defining the laity as servants of the clergy.

While debate between Catholic and American identities continued in the twentieth century, the cultural separatism associated with the emerging subculture served Boston's laity in both a positive and a negative fashion. Seeing itself as an oppressed majority in Boston, the Church promoted Catholicism via insider rhetoric—as custodian of culture, protector of the people, supreme moral authority over individuals, and even counselor to the democratic state. While the Church committed itself to an adversarial position toward secular social reform, social work, and social programs, ongoing interaction between its self-representation and the normal assimilative pressures of lay existence produced a recognizable pattern of Catholic religious and social life in Boston: confessional arrogance, conservative morality, manipulative politics, conditional encouragement for lay initiative, and limited support for secular integration of the laity. One crucial result of the pursuit of a separatist Catholic subculture was that the hierarchy was now convincing its members to defend Catholicism as the fullest revelation of American principles, and the very font of democracy. As Catholic men marched off to war in 1917, a priest's poem captured the tone: "Cross and flag aloft shall bless brave lads who went today."[89]

3

CLASS, MANHOOD, AND MATERIAL SUCCESS

"Blackleg" was the word used to classify the American-born offspring of Irish parents. It is difficult to understand or to justify the
feelings of native-born Irish-men toward so-called country-borns or
blacklegs. The accident of birth on any other than Irish soil was held
to dilute the blood or adulterate it. It was no longer the pure substance. Because the new generation had not suffered the same hardships as the older generation, they were considered to be physically
weaker, and because they were not sufficiently impressed by old
superstitions, banshees, ancestral curses, they were blasphemous.
—Joseph Dinneen, *Ward Eight*

Boston politics of this era was not unlike that in Ireland before the
Anglo-Norman conquest. The Irish had their local chieftains, who
often warred against one another for fancied glory and advantages
for themselves and their followers. They made unstable alliances that
could find one year's ally another year's foe. Yet they produced especially strong leaders, superchieftains who reigned as kings over large
regions, in turn allying and defecting and forming new constellations
as the winds blew.—Rose Kennedy, *Times to Remember*

The Catholic man who seeks for civil honors and then betrays the
public conscience is doubly guilty, guilty of his own crime against the
state and guilty of an awful crime against the church to which inevitably his treachery will be imputed.—Archbishop William O'Connell,
address to AFCS convention, August 10, 1908

Religion and Ethnic Assimilation

The citations above from Joseph Dinneen, Rose Kennedy, and
Archbishop O'Connell pinpoint three different facets of the crisis created by
Irish American assimilation: degeneration of Irish identity; political infighting
among Irish bosses, which restricted ethnic power to the local level; and rejection of religious unity as a way to transcend intraethnic and interethnic
division. The ability to preserve a separate ethnic, political, and religious identity was an essential tool of Irish solidarity against New England's Protestant
insiders, but the Catholic Church's aim was somewhat different: to inspire
loyalty to a subculture defined by religion.

Since the publication of Oscar Handlin's generally pessimistic portrayal of
Irish Americans as maladjusted peasants in *Boston's Immigrants, 1790–
1880: A Study in Acculturation* (1941), and from elaborations on this theme

by Handlin's followers, scholars have generally accepted the attribution of certain negative traits to the Irish (melancholy, despair, and alcoholism), which presumably fostered Irish resistance to regular work habits, antipathy toward American standards of success, and economic underachievement. As Kerby Miller reconsidered the transatlantic experience of the Irish, he subjected the native origins of these counterassimilative traits to Antonio Gramsci's model of "cultural hegemony" and to the cultural theories of Raymond Williams. Using extensive immigrant correspondence, Miller concluded that the famine Irish were predisposed to be antagonistic to bourgeois ideals and leadership and that they transformed this premigration sensibility into an exile mentality that fueled their anti-Anglo hostility in America.[1] In Miller's application of the theoretical matrix of Williams and Gramsci, emergent cultures, like that of the Irish Catholics in Boston, formed new ideological blocs, such as that between the Church and the bourgeoisie, which in the end articulated the values of the dominant culture in order to reconcile contradictions between residual values, such as those of feudal Catholicism and the Irish peasantry, and the new demands of capitalist individualism. Historians of American immigration have often sidestepped the concept of hegemony and have chosen to write of only those cultural traditions that aided immigrant survival. These consensus-minded historians have tended to minimize a group's "pathological" or separatist traits whose persistence would tend to discredit the melting pot model that had long served as the dominant paradigm for American assimilation. Unhealthy behaviors that did not contribute to the image of a successful ethnic subculture were conveniently overlooked. By contrast, conflict-minded historians point to evidence of ethnic resistance to assimilation. Among the Irish such resistance included enduring patterns of endogamy and clannish politics that foiled the expected trends toward intermarriage and political cooperation. Because of the facility of the Irish in mimicking Anglo-Saxon culture, their ethnic and class fissures with Yankee Americans were often obscured. But the contradictions between Irish and Yankee identity did not disappear. The postimmigrant Irish never completely abandoned their nostalgic, romantic identification with Ireland or their outsider resentment of Anglo-Saxon Boston. Miller's model shows us that while few Irish Americans returned to their "dear old mother land," eventually "bourgeois-defined traits and associations that characterized 'good Irish Americans' also enabled them to assert that they were 'good Americans' as well."[2] Thus, Irish integration joined a middle-class outlook with a fierce determination to locate the sources of loyal Americanism within Catholicism. As Francis Slattery of Brighton put it, "The bud of Catholic ideals of freedom, under the tender and ceaseless care of the Church, finally has matured into the peerless flower of liberty, true Americanism."[3] Boston's archbishop, as we have seen, affirmed civic ideals because patriotism, so defined, helped the Church assume responsibility for its members' interaction with the secular world.

The following group portrait of Boston Irishmen summarizes their salient features as a social group, following Miller's analysis of the formation of cultural hegemony and counterhegemony. First, Irish immigrants to New England during and after the famine were more likely to remain unskilled laborers and to be economically deprived than were immigrants in other regions, which contributed to their self-image of being exiled and marginalized. In Massachusetts, some Irish families even experienced downward mobility through generations. Nationwide, the Irish were absorbed into the class structure of America, even though ethnicity rather than class dominated the existence of workers from 1880 to 1930.[4] Second, the Boston Irish eventually stratified and produced middle-class elites, the so-called cut glass or lace curtain Irish, who aspired to and imitated the lifestyle and habits of genteel Yankee Protestants, but who were called upon to be leaders of Irish and Catholic solidarity. In Ireland, the emergence of a Catholic middle class in the late eighteenth century rehearsed this same dilemma as it sought the support of the masses in order to challenge the authority of British hegemony. By the nineteenth century the Irish bourgeois class formed the core of the nationalist cause. At the same time, its own counterhegemonic strategy led it to identify with bourgeois institutions of the English oppressors. While it could not overcome English dominance without popular support, its economic interests were served better by large-scale emigration of the poor, which relieved land pressure in Ireland. Famine emigrants, therefore, coming primarily from the landless lower classes, were resentful of both British and Irish middle-class power but transformed this resentment by projecting their confusions onto the process of emigration itself. As a result, they interpreted themselves as exiled victims of British oppression, and as outsiders in a strange new land. Once an Irish middle class had emerged in America, it had similar problems initially in exerting hegemony over the lower classes.[5] Third, certain premigration factors, including lack of economic freedom and property ownership in their native country, lack of industrial skills, and a disproportionate ratio of female to male immigrants, complicated Irish males' economic rise. Boston's unique history of anti-Catholic origins formed an additional religious barrier to economic integration. Yet, despite unpreparedness for urban and industrial life, the Irish achieved (with the Jews) the highest rate of permanent immigration to America. Massachusetts became a national exception, however, because the percentage of its unskilled Irish labor actually increased over time.

Elsewhere the growth of skilled Irish laborers enabled the Irish to dominate the craft unions of the American Federation of Labor. Even though each immigrant nationality developed classes with conflicting interests, ethnicity tended to defeat class consciousness and to keep cities divided by nationality and race. Boston's Irish-controlled dock and construction unions, for example, effectively shut out the Italians, who responded by relying on their own ethnic organizations and labor racketeers whose protection further fragmented the working class.[6] Boston, consequently, never became a center of labor radicalism, and Irish Americans, although rising to leadership in many federation unions, tended to uphold the conservative outlook of craft unionism and to support their ethnic bloc against attempts to forge an all-inclusive labor movement. The Church's strategy of constructive conservatism toward ethnic and class issues is described below, as it nurtured particular attitudes that point to its growing absorption of the hegemonic values of the American ruling classes.

The Boston Catholic Elite

Even with several American-born generations behind them, the Irish Americans were overrepresented in unskilled labor and lagged behind other ethnic groups in upward mobility. As William Shannon observed, by 1900 "the Irish were therefore the group closest to being 'in' while still being 'out.'"[7] Undeniably, lack of economic autonomy and land ownership under eight centuries of foreign rule in Ireland, combined with ethnic and religious discrimination in America, slowed Irish Catholic entry into professional schools and white-collar jobs through the end of the First World War. Like landless African American slaves after emancipation, Irish Americans had no autonomous past to look back on. Recognizing the persistence of economic and cultural barriers that arrested social mobility among Irish Americans, it is still possible to locate a body of Boston Catholics who attained middle-class status, as defined by the dominant culture's standards. They became civil servants, self-employed businessmen, and white-collar professionals, but the lack of a common thread uniting the careers of the Catholic elites of Boston as well as their lack of a "distinctive business style" may account for their relative invisibility in American corporate history.[8]

Irish entrepreneurs and professionals who succeeded in Boston did so primarily in the fields of grocery and liquor retail, contracting, undertaking, law, politics, and journalism. The priesthood, the major vocational choice of men, was not a paying career, yet it offered the alluring compensations of social mobility and prestige. In a study of Irish Americans who appear in the *Dictionary of National Biography,* Dorothy Ross found that the priesthood claimed about 33 percent of the males profiled, followed by careers in business at 27.1 percent. Law finished a distant third at 14 percent.[9] Although Irish

Americans comprised more than half of Boston's population, and while about 20 percent of the city's lawyers were Irish in 1900, only about 3 percent of the Bar Association's 811 members were of Irish descent.[10] Since a successful law practice often became a stepping stone to political office, many elected Catholic officials had legal training. About 16 percent of Boston's physicians were Irish, but less than 5 percent of the city's total were civil engineers and surveyors.[11] More than 20 percent of Boston's journalists were Irish by 1905, although this percentage may seem less significant when one realizes that the career had a high dropout rate because of its demanding pace.[12]

Among the cohort of Catholic men born around the end of the Civil War and dying before World War II, or having a lifespan of approximately 1870 to 1935, the highest stratum achieved affluence by making links with the economic power of the Anglo-Saxon elites, not through business ventures with recent Catholic immigrants. Affiliation with the dominant culture overwhelmed religious solidarity as a determinant of economic success. Nonetheless, there was a tradition of cross-class mutuality since the Irish American bourgeoisie and small businessmen relied on the working-class Irish for their clientele. Groups like the men's fraternal organizations usefully enhanced these existing cross-class relationships among Catholics.[13] Moreover, the rhetoric of "race uplift" among Irish Catholics exhorted young men to use their "blood and brawn" to "put some of our energy now given to politics into business and industry."[14] Among the Irish Catholic entrepreneurs and professionals of Boston, a sample of six, drawn from two overlapping cohorts of pre– and post–Civil War births, will represent the diverse professional pursuits of a middle-class elite, as well as men's enduring ties to the Catholic Church, excluding the most obvious bond represented by the priesthood.

Thomas Bernard Fitzpatrick (1844–1919), arguably the best-known Catholic philanthropist and businessman in late nineteenth-century Boston, was a manager of a dry goods business. In 1905 he received the Laetare Medal, awarded by Notre Dame University to eminent laymen who serve the cause of "religion, education, and morality." Born in Grafton, Massachusetts, of immigrant parents, he had a high school education in Hopkinton and went to work for a dry goods firm. After the Boston fire of 1872, he became junior partner of the firm's reorganized successor, the Brown-Durrell Company, which became the largest dry goods house in the East. He served as director of several trust companies and banks and was treasurer of the United Irish League. Two governors appointed him to the state board of education, and he served as a member of the school committee of Brookline. Married in 1874, he had four sons and two daughters. He owned property throughout the state and became one of the first Catholics to have a summer home in Swampscott, a traditionally Protestant haven.[15] Fitzpatrick generously gave time and money to various Catholic charitable institutions through his involvements with the Working Girls' Home, Working Boys' Home, and St. Mary's Infant Asylum. He delivered the laity address at Archbishop Williams's golden jubilee. In addition, his donations helped found three Catholic orphanages, build the Catholic Union of Boston, and fund the Boston Cottage at the Catholic Summer School, for which he donated the site as well.

James J. Phelan (1871–1934), born in Toronto, entered the Boston stock exchange as a page in 1887. In 1888 he was hired by Hornblower & Weeks as its only staff member and was promoted to the partnership in 1900. In 1909, with several Irish Catholic partners, he established the Federal Trust Company and became its vice-president, the youngest bank officer in Boston at the time, at the age of thirty-eight. A member of the Charlestown Catholic Literary Union, and its president, he received the Laetare award in 1931 from Notre Dame. He earned an LL.D. from Boston College and became a lay trustee at Notre Dame University. He also received numerous papal decorations: Pius XI named him the first American to receive the rank of knight commander; he was a Knight of St. Gregory as well, and master of the American chapter of the Knights of Malta, of which he was named its first knight in 1927. In 1921, however, Phelan was drawn into a court case involving $250,000, brought by "one of the blackguard Catholic lawyers who is now up for disbarment," according to his wife, Helen Phelan. Angry that her husband's legal defense caused the couple to cancel a trip to Rome, she commented to Archbishop O'Connell's secretary, "It involves 250 thousand. At least half of our possessions, and so it is up to us to protect it. When the K of C and the Catholic Church are rid of a few of these crooks every one will stand a better chance to live."[16] Helen Phelan's reference is probably to the badger game played by attorney Daniel Coakley for some years with the complicity of several district attorneys, of extorting money from entrapped victims. Her vehemence suggests that Catholic elites had become as property- and image-conscious as any Brahmins reacting to threats to their property and reputation.

Voluntarism and entrepreneurship were combined in the career of James M. Prendergast (1851–1920), a director of the Boston Elevated Railroad and the New England Trust. Active in the Knights of Columbus, he was a self-appointed informant to William O'Connell, updating the archbishop on the local activities of "dangerous" groups such as the American Protective Association, the IWW, and the Socialist party by enclosing newspaper clippings and extracts from inflammatory pamphlets in his letters. Prendergast made large donations to many Catholic causes and handled the arrangements for the reception for O'Connell's elevation to the cardinalate in 1911. He typifies the kind of arriviste layman O'Connell collected in his inner circle and re-

warded for providing useful information about radical movements the archbishop considered to be foes of Catholicism.

Charles A. DeCourcy (1857–1925) of Lawrence was one of several leading
Massachusetts laymen who attended Georgetown University in Washington,
D.C. He graduated in 1878, received an M.A. in 1889 and an LL.D. in 1904,
and served as president of the alumni association. Admitted to the Massachusetts Bar in 1881, and a student in Oliver Wendell Holmes's office, he was
appointed an assistant district attorney in Boston from 1884 to 1890. He
became associate judge of the superior court from 1902 to 1911 and supreme
court justice from 1911 to 1924. He was also president of the State Conference of Charities. His commercial interests included directorships for the Mer-
chant's National Bank, the Gas Company, and the Lumber Company of
Lawrence. One of his two sons attended Georgetown; the other went to Harvard and Harvard Law School. An obituary reported that DeCourcy was "religious by nature, a faithful attendant upon public worship, strictly observant
of all the rites of his church."

Born in Ireland, Daniel P. Toomey (1862–1916) emigrated with his parents
in 1873 and became apprenticed to a printer. He pursued a successful journalism career in Boston, purchasing the *Columbiad* in 1898 and managing it
until 1916. Previously, from 1893, he had been publisher of *Donahoe's Magazine* until it merged with *Catholic World* in 1908. Toomey served on the
Boston City Council (1890–91) and was twice a member of the Massachusetts legislature. In Catholic activities, he was president of the Young Men's
Catholic Association and grand knight of the Boston chapter of the Knights
of Columbus. When the K of C made the *Columbiad* its official organ and
moved its headquarters to New Jersey, he followed, organizing a new Knights
chapter there, and joined the Elks as well. He died in New Jersey in 1916.

Corporate expert William Francis Fitzgerald (1869–1937) of Fitzgerald,
Hubbard, & Company made a fortune in diversified interests as a financier
of copper mines, electric companies, and shoe manufacturers. From Charlestown, Massachusetts, Fitzgerald attended public school and became an office
boy with a stockbrokerage firm, later renamed Towle & Fitzgerald. He became president of Turner Tanning Machinery Company in 1906 after heading
a syndicate that took over the business. There he installed life insurance and
workmen's compensation policies that had been pioneered in the German
branches of his company's factories. He served as a director of the port of
Boston (1912–17) and as director of the Boston Opera Company. He was a
Republican until 1912, when he switched support to Woodrow Wilson (as
did many Irish Americans despite Wilson's rejection of Irish nationalism).
Fitzgerald served as president of the Catholic Union from 1907 to 1908. He
donated a reference library to Boston College and was recognized as an out-

standing supporter of Catholic charities. He had three children and owned a summer vacation estate in New Hampshire.

Far from showing that Irish Americans were "allergic to success," as has been charged against their peasant farmer ancestors, these stories of achievement portray men who did not see themselves as victims lacking control of their own destinies, or as exiles in America. Whether born in Ireland, Canada, or Massachusetts, they built, with support from Democratic (and sometimes Republican) political and social ties, a male Catholic organizational network, an image of the Irish Catholic businessman as ambitious and prosperous but loyal to family, community, and church. Only one of the six attended college, but this pattern would soon change as more Catholics attended public colleges, trade schools, and evening courses, as well as the Catholic colleges and universities that flourished a few decades later. Catholic entrepreneurs' consumption patterns in sports, real estate, and cultural events reflected the tastes and leisure habits of the American middle class. As the layman improved his financial status, he fulfilled his filial duty toward Catholicism by financing the Church's growing network of parishes, seminaries, schools, convents, hospitals, monasteries, and colleges. Although the Church frowned on the pursuit of excessive wealth, the bourgeois Catholic was not discouraged from enjoying the fruits of success in his lifestyle and leisure pursuits.

Although one result of the Church's activities was to stabilize the assimilating Catholic community by mediating between communalism and selfish individualism, the primary concern of churchmen was institutional preservation, a charge that clergy passed on to lay voluntary groups. Hence men's clubs were praised as proof of the "wonderful organization of the Roman Catholic Church . . . which bind their members to the Church."[17] The new Catholic middle class and its ethnoreligious bureaucracy became the Church's necessary allies to provide steady income that helped O'Connell protect the financial security of the archdiocese. James Prendergast and many laymen like him delivered talks to Catholic audiences on topics such as the relationship between fraternal organizations and civic life, and job opportunities for young men, which affirmed Catholic attempts to influence secular involvements. For their generosity, exemplary businessmen were rewarded by the papacy with medals and membership in the elite lay orders such as the Order of the Holy Sepulchre, the Knights of Malta, and the Knights of the Order of St. Gregory. John R. Slattery (1867–1922), for example, who served as Archbishop O'Connell's personal physician and was fundraiser and superintendent for profitable St. Elizabeth's Hospital from 1912 to 1922, was named a Knight of the Holy Sepulchre. These honors in recognition of a social elite who served the goals of the hierarchy symbolized a meritocracy among lay Catholics that mirrored the Church's hierarchical paradigm of society. The connotations of feudal knighthood attached to the papal orders exploited the medieval chivalric code to define the obligations of the laity as brave defenders of the Church's interests. The lay elite had no reason to challenge the Church's assumptions about the naturalness of this social order.

The hierarchy and clergy, therefore, promoted a standard of masculinity and of material success conducive to the health of the institutional church and to the emerging middle class. Rather than following Protestant preoccupations about how feminization was enervating masculine vigor and sapping men's economic drive, the Catholic Church expressed its anxieties in terms of losing control of the laity. The Church, therefore, sought to produce young men who could compete economically with Yankees without losing their religious loyalty.

Some historians have claimed that certain popular ethnoreligious customs such as wakes, festivals, St. Patrick's Day parades, saloons, street gangs, and secret societies constituted threats to clerical control, yet there is no decisive evidence of this in Boston. Irish and Catholic societies seemed to coexist amicably, probably due to the close integration of religion and ethnicity as a premigration feature of Irish culture. One Irish society that was initially hostile to the Church, the Ancient Order of Hibernians, voluntarily became more closely tied to it after about 1890, thereby securing greater hierarchical approval.[18] Cardinal O'Connell was even a national officer of the order in the 1910s. All in all, the Irish clergy and laity were more likely to unite in mutual suspicion of societies formed by other Catholic immigrants (hence what became known as "the Italian problem," for example) or against Protestant missionary workers. The Church's support for attitudes and activities that would foster both the faith and the economic assimilation of laymen was an improbable and unstable mixture of feudal social principles and orthodox capitalism. Nonetheless, the Church helped members make a social transition from outsider to insider by supporting personal moral habits that promoted a middle-class ethic and that purported to be uplifting models for the working class as well. Consequently, the archdiocese of Boston did not act upon the critiques of capitalism implied in Catholic social teaching, because of its own growing relationship to capitalism. Despite the hierarchy's warnings against the secularizing danger of assimilation, the identity of an Irish American elite and its religious leaders could not escape association with the values of the host culture and its economic structures.

As a Catholic subculture emerged containing both planned and unintended aspects, its institutions adapted to the hegemonic demands of American society, and especially to the conditions of Irish American bourgeois life. Historically, Catholicism had stressed the communal interdependence of social relations, rooted in the family, against the demands of selfish individualism, which it associated with secularism and materialist philosophy. On the other hand, the Church had firmly defended private property as a natural right and thus aligned itself with central creeds of liberalism and individualism that have defined post-Enlightenment philosophy and society. Nonetheless, the Catholic perception of individualism in the early twentieth century was generally pejorative, synonymous with egoism, hedonism, or disintegration. As expressed by a Boston pastor, "We have seen the destructive effects of individualism run mad. Individualism in religion has bred religious disruption, and individualism in the social order breeds selfishness. The natural training school of character is the family, the home. There one lives not for himself alone, and in the continual giving and taking one is trained to the spirit of unselfishness."[19]

While thus rejecting the crassest forms of individualism, the Church's leadership adopted a vision of America as a land uniquely blessed by divine providence. Doing so enabled the hierarchy to equate national destiny with the Church's agenda of preservation of the family and Catholic identity, by entrusting the Church with the nation's future. A Catholic subculture, as distinct from an ethnic subculture, never fully resolved its outlook on American individualism. It mediated between insiderness and outsiderness and represented an exaggerated loyalty to both ethnic and American identity, to Catholic unity and to American pluralism. Thus the subculture addressed Catholic integration while keeping its inherently contradictory and polarizing qualities in tension.

By 1900 Boston's Catholic middle class had some elements of an "Irishtocracy." While sharing the Church's suspicion of selfish individualism, some Irish Catholics noted that their growing prosperity and social mobility were causing some of their cohort to denigrate ethnic identity and religious pride. No contemporary commentator has so bluntly stated the problem of Irish assimilation as a source of division within the Catholic community as Daniel Coakley, who later was exposed as one of the most unsavory lawyers in Boston:

> The real problem as I see it spending much time necessarily in company with non-Catholics is to get our fellows to view themselves and their race and religion in as good a light as biased historians have ever taken. The kow-towing of our own, chiefly those who have gotten together a few dollars or had handed to them some honors, is from a layman's point of view our present chief hardship here in Boston. To be classed as "a bit different from the rest of the Irish" is the ambition of some of our "prominent" men, prominent, I feel, only in that they have corralled some money or achieved political success.[20]

The Church answered Coakley's lament that the prominent Catholic valued Yankee approval above loyalty to his own kind, by flatly denying the existence of class antagonism and by interposing Roman Catholicism as the universal bond linking all races.[21] Following the lead of papal statements from the late nineteenth century, which defended common interests between capital and labor and which also upheld private ownership and the need for social hierarchies, Boston's archbishop refused to acknowledge class interests among Church members and eschewed any language recognizing class conflict. Having repressed the existence of class tensions, in rebuttal against the basic premise of Marxist materialism, how did the Church react to wealthy Catholics who were abandoning their ethnic and religious roots by siding with their former oppressors?

One action taken by the archdiocese was the sponsorship of propaganda measures to fight for the loyalty of Catholics and, indeed, to define a "good Catholic." Lay organizations met the needs of the expanding Catholic population by creating a sense of shared identity that promoted conservative social reform without stirring up class hostilities. They adopted a paternalist attitude toward Catholic success, and they participated in rewriting American history to include the contributions of Catholics.

To impress Bostonians with the vigor of Catholicism, the hierarchy defined Catholicism against a narrative of Protestant decline.[22] Despite the alleged waning of WASP hegemony and of Boston's economic importance, the urban population increased from 595,380 in 1905 to 748,060 in 1920. The Catholic population of the archdiocese, which extended beyond the city's corporate limits, was estimated at 610,000 in 1900 and 1,039,000 in 1930, the era of its most dramatic increase.[23] Census reports and church records show that Roman Catholics in Boston outnumbered all other groups of citizens and churchgoers in the city by 1905. In 1906 they numbered 72.3 percent of all church members in Boston's churchgoing population of 422,423; in 1916, they made up 73.5 percent of that total. A Boston College student voiced the hope of local Catholics that their numerical dominance would translate into social status: "To those who can recall the Boston of thirty or forty years ago, and the Catholic numerical strength then as it compared with the balance of the city's population, the showing of the present is one of exceeding gratification, while as a taste of what is to come, the possibilities seem simply stupendous, and radiant with the brightest hope for Boston and Catholic interests."[24]

While diocesan population totals cannot be correlated exactly with city censuses because the archdiocese exceeded the city's geographic limits and because pastors notoriously misreported parish sizes, there can be no doubt that Massachusetts had become more Irish and that the bulk of Boston's Catholics were of Irish descent. The hierarchy, priests, sisters and nuns were overwhelmingly of Irish descent. A sharp 34 percent increase in numbers of

ordained priests in the diocese between 1915 and 1925 had even created a
local clergy surplus.[25] As the ratio of priests to parishioners rose dramatically,
some pastors reported being hard pressed to find useful activities for their
junior assistants.[26] Even while the number of Boston's parishes increased from
194 in 1907, to 256 in 1920, and to 289 in 1930, due in part to the influx
of non-Irish Catholic immigrants to the city, most pastors were Irish priests.[27]
While Yankee Protestant birth rates and social control appeared to be diminishing, Catholics advanced in every category: fertility, immigration, and numbers of churches, parishes and missions, religious vocations, converts, lay
associations, parish and diocesan expenditures, parochial schools, colleges,
teachers and students, and professionals and businessmen. As if to capitalize
on demographic data that seemed to predict a limitless future for Catholics,
the Church presented itself as guardian of the integration of its members.
Continuing a symbolic usage formulated in nineteenth-century Europe,
O'Connell represented the pope as Holy Father and the Church as Holy
Mother, who defended their children from the evil world. Paradoxically, the
Church assisted the assimilation process by taking an increasingly active role
in fighting anti-Catholic prejudice that created a barrier to integration in New
England.

Nativist attacks on Roman Catholics tended to increase in response to perceived economic threats to the commercial interests of the Yankee elites. In
the 1860s and 1870s, for instance, Catholics had been relatively unperse-
cuted. To a certain extent the American Irish were even in an enviable position
among all immigrant groups during the Gilded Age because their enemies
began to abandon antebellum "racial" images of the Irish as indolent, violent,
and irresponsible. Intermittent spats with Protestants during the 1880s and
1890s about alleged bigotry by the president of Harvard University; anti-
Catholic remarks from outspoken Protestant ministers; the intense but brief
parochial school debate of 1888–89; the American Protective Association riot
of July 4, 1895; and the anti-Catholic leagues and anti-Catholic press later
gave way to more sustained anti-Catholicism, which became widespread in
Boston after 1900. This was mitigated by some influential Brahmins who favored the Irish, stressing their participation in British culture and arguing that
Irish Catholics were preferable to more recent arrivals from southeastern Europe, Russia, and Asia. For example, in 1901 the *Boston Herald* asserted:
"The vigor of Ireland has been driven from it. America has profited incal-
culably by the exodus, and the record of the Irish race in this country affords
a demonstration that cannot be gainsaid that the native forces of the race are
not decadent when they have favorable opportunities for development."[28] An
opposing segment of New Englanders began to challenge Catholic immigrants
by using political muscle to impose literacy tests, poll taxes, and immigration

restrictions.[29] In contrast to the Reconstruction decades, which had been a time of cordial relations between enlightened Protestant politicians and Irish Catholic liberals, the era between the American Protective Association riot of 1895 and the Johnson-Reed Immigration Act of 1924 saw the revival of old prejudices, suggesting that both nativism and anti-Catholicism were renewed in response to a more aggressive Catholic economic presence as well as in a backlash to the second immigrant wave of the second decade of the century. As the contemporary accounts below indicate, nativists tried once again to represent Irish Catholics as political, economic, and psychological misfits, to which the Irish could respond by retreating into a subculture dominated by its identification with the Catholic Church.

Until about 1905, the Irish had fared well with the Yankee elites in contrast to attacks on the "new immigration." After that time, Yankees coordinated attacks on Irish control of urban politics, which was never as complete as Protestants feared, nor ever sufficient to capture the state government. Boston Catholics of all ethnicities also felt the ripples from the rebirth of a rural anti-Catholic press in the southern and western states after 1910. Tom Watson's magazine in Georgia and Wilbur Phelps's *Menace* from Missouri are two such examples; less well known but equally offensive was the monthly *Anti-Catholic Crusade* from Iola, Kansas, whose masthead stated, "If you are a Jesuit run for your life, we are after you." During the drive for "100 percent Americanism" following World War I, antialien groups nationwide generally focused their attacks on German Americans, but in Boston such pieces as *The Whole D Family* appeared. This vitriolic pamphlet listed all the Irish surnames of city employees beginning with *D* and disclosed their salaries. It declared fearfully, "of the 12,000 people employed by the city of Boston, more than 11,000 are Irish Roman Catholics." To show how Irish Catholics had monopolized the city budget, the pamphlet listed the horrifying fact that there were 43 Donovans earning more than a total of $52,000; 47 Dohertys securing over $38,000; 36 Dolans totaling more than $31,000; and 26 Driscolls receiving over $24,000 per year.[30] In contrast to English Victorian caricatures of the simian, low-browed Irishman and to the alcoholic loafer given to "Rum, Romanism and Rebellion" satirized in American political cartoons of the Gilded Age, this scapegoating tactic did not even try to mask the economic root of the racial and religious prejudice against Irish Catholics.[31]

In addition to classifying the Celt as a political and economic threat, Anglo-Americans enlisted the popular pseudoscience of racial typing. The benevolent character traits identified with the Irish became clichés reproduced in popular fiction and theater and in British Victorian and Edwardian literature, as in Bostonian Henry Childs Merwin's composite portrait of the Irishman as a "passionate, impulsive, kindly, unreflecting, brave, nimble-witted man; but he lacks the solidity, the balance, the judgment, the moral staying power of the Anglo-Saxon."[32] Some of these tributes became, even for Brahmin stalwarts such as Henry Cabot Lodge, ways to diffuse fears about Irish success. Ingratiating articles with titles such as "The Irish-American as Citizen" appealed to New England readers to welcome the Irishman for "what gifts and graces, what virtues and values, he brings to American democracy, and what contributions of soul and spirit, character and conduct he has made to the composite human document we call the American."[33] In addition to this "melting pot" approach, the New England press published biographical sketches of leading Irish American professionals, labor aristocrats, and politicians in order to "prove" that, as politicians, the Irish possessed quicker wits and were better organizers; as business managers, they were endowed with the gift of managing men; as factory workers, they were too imaginative to endure the monotony; as citizens, they were combative and public spirited.[34] Local socialists like Vida Scudder used her novels as forums to discuss the urgent need for the "poetic sensitiveness" of the Irish working girls to enrich the "arid, hardened, materialized, nervous" English stock.[35] Thus, liberal Brahmins recognized non-threatening, often childlike or mystical traits of the Irish as proof of assimilability, which justified the toleration of a limited Irish Catholic elite in their midst.

Irish Americans, meanwhile, had begun to revise their own public representation. They began to see Yankee society as synonymous with respectability rather than hostility. This concession toward English-defined culture contrasted strongly with firm resistance against anglicization in Ireland, where the native peasantry, lacking a native rural middle class, rejected English Protestantism and found an alternative path to solidarity and social organization among their own educated Catholic priests and nuns. From the mid-1800s, because the Catholic Church became the sole agent of the civilizing process, "the Irish avoided becoming Protestant and fully anglicized."[36] In America, by contrast, the postimmigrant Irish were able to "kow-tow" their way to success by affiliation with Anglo culture in ways not possible in Ireland, because their class identity in the United States was not uniformly established by ethnicity. Nonetheless, religious and ethnic consciousness in America remained subordinate to the nation's class structure; therefore it is more meaningful to speak of the functions of religion and ethnicity within a classed society rather than debating their relationship to each other.[37]

For the American Irish, a Catholic subculture became a way to contain the contradictions between resentment of Yankee Protestant power and the allure of bourgeois values. By 1900 many Irish Americans were "blacklegs" of the second or even third generation, and fully two-thirds had been born in the United States. They were indebted to the public leaders of the 1880s and 1890s who had managed to unite politics and culture without the aid of the Church. Hugh O'Brien, who became the city's first Catholic mayor in 1884, and leaders Patrick Collins (mayor in 1901), John Boyle O'Reilly, Charles Donnelly, Patrick Maguire, James Jeffrey Roche, Thomas Dwight, Thomas Galvin, and Thomas J. Gargan helped upgrade the image of the Irish American through their displays of patriotism and their reception into the Protestant social elite. These politicians were also well-known poets and orators and capitalized on the use of humor, folklore, and literature to express a generation's nationalist hopes. Nonetheless, they expressed ambivalent separatist and integrationist attitudes toward America. The separatists remained nostalgic for Ireland, as in immigrant author Mary Elizabeth Blake's praise for Irish Americans as "Sons of the dear old mother that waits beyond the sea[,] . . . Proud that fruit of her womb can stand where the provident be."[38] But Blake's contemporaries, including poet Mary Anne Conroy (fl. 1880s) and reformer John Boyle O'Reilly, also addressed the intermingling of Protestants and Catholics in American history. Conroy's verses pictured a peaceable nation of every race and creed united in common thanksgiving for the blessings of liberty, as in her commemoration of the 250th anniversary of Sandwich, Massachusetts, in 1889, a town noted for its anti-Catholicism. O'Reilly, unquestionably the leading figure of his generation, appeared before all sorts of audiences. He suggested to his countrymen that "we can do Ireland more good by our Americanism than by our Irishism."[39] O'Reilly's historical poems, such as "The Pilgrim Fathers," "Mayflower," and "Crispus Attucks," which extolled Americans who fought for freedom and republicanism, imputed these same ideals to the Irish: "No treason we bring from Erin—nor bring we shame nor guilt!"[40] Yet it seems that no matter how Americanized the Irish became in Boston, guilt about forgetting Ireland constantly surfaced as a melancholy motif, as in Denis McCarthy's poem to America:

> We've thought for thee, we've wrought for thee—we've fought for thee
>   as well;
> We've helped to bear thy banner through the battle's blazing hell—
> We love thee as our peerless queen, O gracious land and glad;
> But ah, the dear old mother land so lowly and so sad![41]

Though McCarthy cast a nostalgic gaze at Ireland, he was still endorsed as a public speaker by the New England Congress of Forums and was advertised as "poet and preacher of patriotism." Even the jocular O'Reilly, an exemplary Americanizer, has been described in a revisionist study as a divided personality, tortured by insomnia and possibly driven to suicide by his inability to reconcile ethnicity with the assimilative pressures of America.[42] Where the turn-of-the-century Irish leaders had tried to keep alive their oral tradition of legends and ballads, the succeeding generation preserved Irishness with greater difficulty and changed tactics somewhat to launch an offensive against the Brahmin aristocracy's delusion that "the one thing that saves us yet is the thin stream of Puritan blood in the foreign ocean."[43]

Before the twentieth century, American Catholics met anti-Catholicism in the only way they knew: with defensive hostility and from a position of withdrawn entrenchment. The problem of loss of Irishness led to a rechanneling of Catholic identity in the early 1900s, compounded by the victory of conservative Church politics over short-lived liberal initiatives. After 1907 the Romanizing policies of Archbishop O'Connell directed Boston Catholics to the formation of a triumphalist, separatist Catholic subculture, with cooperation from the successful laity. Lay leaders began to join their defensiveness and isolationism to a new style of political and cultural aggression. Their willingness to represent themselves as acculturated succeeded by the 1920s, as one writer stated: "Even here in Massachusetts, we Catholics are out of the catacombs."[44] Based on their numbers and a growing institutional network, Catholics' new civic assertiveness now assigned Catholics an active, insider role in American history.

Irish American cultural leaders began to construct a "usable" past for Catholic Americans by integrating the Irish into the colonial, revolutionary, and Civil War narratives in order to unearth a history unknown to many Catholics. The historical societies and journals that sprang up in the United States in the 1890s mark the growing historical consciousness of the Irish American elite, especially against the current popularity of "patriotic" WASP fraternal organizations. The era between the founding of the American Irish Historical Society in 1897 and the Gaelic League, which nationalized in 1898, and the establishment of the American Catholic Historical Association in 1919 encapsulated two decades of identity formation that often merged ethnic with religious identification. The American Irish Historical Society was housed in Boston until 1922, where by 1900 the venerable Charitable Irish Society, founded originally by and for the Scotch-Irish in 1737, had also become an Irish Catholic stronghold where the likes of Denis McCarthy wrote its anniversary verses. Irish American historical journals laboriously depicted the Catholic contributions to colonial settlement, the American Revolution, the antislavery movement, and the Civil War.[45] Catholic women also participated in this revisionism by founding an equivalent to the Daughters of the American Revolution (1890) in 1903 called the Catholic Daughters of America. Irish Americanism sometimes went overboard in claiming Irish origins for everything American, including credit for the tunes to the "Star Spangled Banner" and "Yankee Doodle."[46]

On the other hand, in locations where anti-Irish feeling had softened, im-

James Jeffrey Roche. He and John Boyle O'Reilly dominated Irish Catholic public life in the 1880s. Roche was a collaborator with Douglas Hyde and Lady Gregory on the ten-volume series *Irish Literature* and editor of the Boston *Pilot* after O'Reilly's death. (From Winslow, *Literary Boston of To-Day*)

migrant institutions began to adopt American habits. As early as the 1870s, numerous clubs organized around the Church began to emerge alongside the Gaelic leagues and secret Hibernian societies. The Boston Catholic paper, the *Pilot,* which was coopted as the official diocesan organ in 1908 after going bankrupt as a privately run newspaper, dropped its Irish county news and Gaelic lessons by about 1909, substituting extensive coverage of Catholic diocesan and parish social and religious events at the archbishop's mandate. These components of a religious bureaucracy supplemented the ethnic bureaucracy already existing among its emergent urban bourgeoisie and helped to consolidate Irish Catholic elites. But against this process of class identification, Church authorities, pursuing a separatist agenda, had to make certain that nationalism would not overwhelm Catholicism as the laity's primary source of identity and unity.

The Church's effectiveness in demonstrating that Catholics could out-Yankee the Yankees was assisted in part by the decline of Yankee genteel culture and the fragmentation of a unified Protestant identity.[47] From the 1880s, Yankees bemoaned the collapse of their characteristic social conservatism and the decay of two centuries of cultural and economic supremacy. "We are vanishing into provincial obscurity," wrote a Harvard professor. "American has been swept from our grasp. . . . I feel that we Yankees are as much a thing of the past as any race can be."[48] American Protestantism had splintered as well, its many denominations spanning a wide range from the social reformism of Social Gospel liberals to the reactionary antimodernism of fundamentalism. Catholic Americans interpreted these constantly subdividing denominations and schismatic sects as proof of Protestant disunity and falsehood. They appropriated Yankee Protestant chauvinism into their own narrative of American history in order to present Catholics as the real agents and saviors of national destiny. Archbishop O'Connell personified Catholic confidence through his public self-image of an arrogant prince of the Church who brooked no condescension from Yankees. In a terse obituary for Brahmin culture, the Catholic diocesan paper staked his claim to ascendancy over Boston's WASP elites: "About the only representatives of the Old Back Bay aristocracy left in public life are Henry Cabot Lodge, Winthrop Murray Crane, Augustus Peabody Gardner and Butler Ames and the tenure of every one of them is threatened with an untimely end."[49] Ideally, the erosion of a WASP elite could have paved the way for the emergence of a more representative, pluralist culture in Boston. However, through its militant triumphalism, the Catholic Church seemed less committed to pluralism or as fond of democracy as its leaders professed in public. Privately, etiquette cues from the archbishop earned the gratitude of Irish Catholic climbers, as one layman stated to O'Connell: "We are all learning from you how to kindly treat and mildly patronize the non-Catholic acquaintance and express the hope that sometime he may see the light religiously though he may never have an Irish lineage."[50]

District Attorney Pelletier

As Catholics amalgamated into city and county politics in Massachusetts, they remained vulnerable to criticism from the Protestant establishment. One area that became particularly volatile was the office of district attorney, which regulated the prosecution of criminal activity. A Catholic of French-Irish heritage, Joseph C. Pelletier, held that post in Boston from 1906 to 1922. In 1921 he was brought to trial for illegal activities after being observed carefully for some years by the Watch & Ward Society, a citizens' para-police group dedicated to exposing promiscuity and related vices in Boston. Born in Boston in 1872, the son of a successful French American banker and an Irish mother, Pelletier attended public schools before attending Boston College. After attaining his B.A. in 1891, he received an M.A. in 1893. From Boston University he gained his LL.D. in 1895 and passed the Suffolk County Bar the next year. He opened his legal practice with Irish Catholic partners who were, like himself, active in Massachusetts's new Knights of Columbus chapters. When a Boston chapter opened in 1902, Pelletier moved up the ranks in the Knights and was elected as Massachusetts state deputy for a remarkable five successive terms, from 1901 to 1906. Professionally, in 1906 he became the district attorney for Suffolk County, with jurisdiction over the city of Boston. In 1912 he delivered Boston's Fourth of July oration, "Respect for the Law," which would prove ironic in hindsight. Described as a typical Catholic family man, Pelletier reportedly never traveled on Sundays or holy days because he refused to miss Mass, and he kept a correspondence file of hundreds of letters he had written in response to anti-Catholic remarks or to correct misinformation about Catholicism.[51] Between 1907 and 1922 Pelletier served as the supreme advocate to the Knights of Columbus, a national position that he had to relinquish in June 1922, four months after his conviction for malfeasance while district attorney. His subsequent bid for reelection in November was unsuccessful, although he was nominated by an "overwhelming plurality."[52]

A campaign to force Pelletier from public office had begun in 1917, led by the Watch & Ward Society.[53] The Watch & Ward had old scores to settle with Pelletier, who had derided its use of harsh tactics against the citizens of Boston in the past decade. In 1917 the society lodged formal complaints against Pelletier for his failure to close down numerous Boston hotels that were rumored to be brothels. The timing of these charges clearly reflected the status anxiety of Republican social elites, who wished to curtail Irish Catholic Democratic control of the city government. Not finding their civil service reforms to be

Joseph Pelletier, district attorney of Suffolk County and supreme advocate for the Knights of Columbus, prior to the scandals that removed him from office in 1922. (*Extension Magazine,* February 1921)

effective enough, Republicans often turned to groups like Watch & Ward. Throughout the year, Watch & Ward officials filled the Boston press, primarily the Brahmin-controlled *Boston Evening Transcript,* with letters urging that district attorneys be appointed by the governor rather than elected.[54] Watch & Ward further accused Pelletier of conspiring to extract fees from defendants awaiting trial in Boston by promising to drop charges or by entrapping innocent citizens with groundless threats of criminal prosecution. The society hired a detective to keep Pelletier under surveillance and in November secretly installed dictagraphs in Pelletier's office and the office of the ex–assistant district attorney. Pelletier learned of the espionage the following spring from an informant, and the watch-sized machine was discovered by professional inspectors in July 1918 and removed in August.[55]

In a December 14 petition to the Massachusetts Supreme Court, Watch & Ward leaders Godfrey Cabot, Frederick Allen, and John H. Storer charged Pelletier with blackmail and racketeering. The appearance of the charge during the height of the mayoral campaign between incumbent James Curley and his Democratic and Republican challengers suggests that anti-Catholicism became an expedient spark to ignite political prejudices.[56]

While serving as a member of the Knights of Columbus national Committee on Religious Prejudice from 1914 to 1917, Pelletier had acquired firsthand knowledge of anticlerical atrocities in Mexico and of the anti-Catholic societies that had resurfaced in America.[57] A midwestern group, the American Purity League, based in La Crosse, Wisconsin, also distributed virulent anti-Catholic material in Boston, although the group had no recorded members in Massachusetts. The Pelletier case fanned Catholic sensitivity to religious bigotry, even though the district attorney's character was not that of a true son of the Church. A supporter in the Knights of Columbus who decided that the best defense was a good offense attacked Pelletier's enemies as a cohort that included a convicted felon, an "avowed atheist," a "notorious Anglophile," and a "renegade Catholic and Mason."[58] Pelletier's trial of December 1921 focused on the question of whether or not he had abused his elected office. He was found guilty in a civil suit of ten charges of blackmail and extortion (numerous other charges were dropped) and was removed from office in March 1922. Criminal charges were never brought forward, after a grand jury dismissed evidence against him as insufficient. Pelletier's death in Boston two years later was rumored to be suicide.

Pelletier's Catholic credentials, having peaked in 1921 when the pope named him a commander of the Knights of the Order of St. Gregory, crumbled after his conviction and his resignation from public and religious offices. The Knights of Columbus neither exonerated nor condemned him, although several Knights had quixotically risen to his defense, including the supreme knight, his friend James A. Flaherty. A tribute to Pelletier in the Catholic *Extension Magazine* of February 1921 incredibly gave no hint of scandal and lavishly praised Pelletier for keeping Boston free from vice and hypocrisy and for guiding the Knights with a policy of "progressive conservatism."[59] The Hartford *Catholic Transcript,* however, reported that "Mr. Flaherty's defense of his partner in Supremacy might have been begotten of the knightly instinct, but it was not begotten of wisdom." Flaherty created further dissension among the K of C by allegedly questioning the integrity of the Massachusetts Supreme Court for its conviction of Pelletier. Anti-Flaherty and anti-Pelletier factions in the Knights emerged, incensed by this threat to their pro-American reputation. Following Pelletier's resignation as supreme advocate, the divided Knights had the "stormiest" national convention in their forty-year history, during which members demanded a thorough housecleaning of the executive staff.[60]

Pelletier's supporters and detractors divided the Catholic community of Boston and the nation. The trial and conviction was even compared hyperbolically to the Alfred Dreyfus affair in France, suggesting the presence of a persecution complex among Catholics that is a common enough feature of an insider-outsider mentality.[61] During Pelletier's trial, some Knights of Columbus maintained that the case was biased by Protestant prejudice and therefore could not hope for a favorable verdict. Other Knights claimed that Pelletier's silence in his own defense proved his guilt and that his criminal activity deserved punishment.[62]

Pelletier's fall can be viewed in several contexts relating to Catholic identity.[63] First, it symbolized how politicized anti-Catholicism tried to discredit the patriotism of Catholics. As legal counsel to the leading organization of Catholic professional men, Pelletier had once before protected the reputation of the Knights of Columbus against the publication of a bogus oath in 1912.[64] Anti-Catholicism gained further fuel from the Mexican constitution of 1917, which institutionalized anticlericalism, confiscation of Church property, and prohibition of religious services. The Knights of Columbus embarked on an extensive publicity campaign in the United States, directed largely against Mexican Masons. To the frustration of the Knights, the American government refused to intervene in Mexico, allowing anti-Catholic events to continue unchecked. Although the Knights had a just cause, they followed a poor strategy in the Mexican situation. The Pelletier case, therefore, seemingly put Catholic civic responsibility on trial in Massachusetts at a time when Catholic loyalty was being tested in both American domestic and foreign affairs.

Second, Pelletier's prominence in the leading Catholic fraternal organization struck at Catholics' national image and the assimilationist hopes of the laity. The choice between redeeming Pelletier's reputation or expelling him from the Knights created a dilemma for Boston Catholics anxious to verify their own Americanism. The Massachusetts Knights, for example, had been instrumental leaders in campaigns against un-American activities. In 1914 they had initiated an antisocialist campaign by hiring David Goldstein of Boston and Peter Collins as itinerant lecturers "to present the Catholic views on social issues in general and socialism in particular."[65] The Knights' carefully crafted patriotic image was in danger of being undone by the Watch & Ward Society's hounding and by Pelletier's refusal to defend himself, which exposed Catholic insecurities about being seen as outsiders, frauds, corrupt politicians, and even blackmailers. Watch & Ward prosecutors, themselves protecting the power of a diminishing tribe of Protestant insiders, capitalized on this chance to destroy Catholic civic credibility and to divide the Catholic community and Democratic party internally.

Pelletier did not evoke sympathy from Church leaders in Boston. O'Connell and his chancery made no public pronouncements, though in the past the archbishop had not hesitated to express his opinion on contemporary issues. One clue to the cardinal's silence is a letter from Bernard Rothwell of Boston, anonymous author of an anti-Pelletier pamphlet, to the papal apostolic delegate to the United States. Rothwell criticized the Church's failure to offer moral guidance: "The continued silence of our spiritual leaders—interpreted by many of our own Communion, and by the majority of those outside the Faith as tacit approval—has long been deplored by a large number of loyal, conscientious, thoughtful Catholics in this section."[66] Archbishop Bonzano, who had no love for O'Connell, had recently begun an investigation of the Boston archbishop. O'Connell's disregard for Pelletier thus became explicable in relation to two scandals within his own administration, which, while remaining unreported locally (possibly because of O'Connell's pressure on newspaper reporters), were known to Pelletier. In the wake of a first episode that exposed the marriage of Father David Toomey, O'Connell acted to suppress information about his nephew. Apparently Joseph Pelletier had learned about James O'Connell's marriage and escapades from investigative sources in New York City long before their exposure, and he had revealed his knowledge to Cardinal O'Connell as early as 1918. When O'Connell denied everything, Pelletier's office joined the investigation of O'Connell, and in April 1920 Pelletier told Bonzano about his conversations with the cardinal.[67] In the following month O'Connell was humiliated in Rome by the pope, following the revelation of his nephew's secret marriage and his embezzlement of funds from the archdiocese. After the bishops of New England had become aware of this second scandal and denounced O'Connell in April 1921 for his poor example of moral leadership, O'Connell could hardly be expected to assist the man who had been an informant to the Vatican. O'Connell received some relief from Vatican scrutiny when Benedict XV died suddenly in 1922, but his Curial influence had ended.

The Pelletier affair indicated that while anti-Catholic prejudices persisted in Boston through the 1920s and were projected into debates over political control, they touched many deeply rooted problems in Boston. As "civic catechists," Catholics seemed unsophisticated compared with the WASP establishment, who resentfully recalled brighter days when "literature was the town's chief product—not Ponzis, Pelletiers and Curleys, as is the case now."[68] O'Connell's fear of exposure may explain his detachment from the Pelletier scandal, but Pelletier's guilt meant that the Catholic community could not portray Pelletier as an innocent victim of anti-Catholicism, although the technique worked often enough for James Curley.

The Church's nonintervention in the Pelletier affair also suggests its conflicted political involvement in the United States in general. The Catholic hierarchy maintained that religion should have a role in determining moral standards, yet the archbishop failed to live what he preached. As the O'Connell administration disgraced itself, it lost credibility as a moral beacon. In party politics as well, the Church mirrored the weaknesses and strengths of Irish Catholics' varied outlooks. It tried to balance conflicting interests by identifying Catholicism with an unassailable ethical realm, but the hierarchy's disengaged stance, by and large, proved to be more theoretical than actual.

Police Commissioner O'Meara

At the opposite pole from Joseph Pelletier, Stephen O'Meara (1854–1918) did much to strengthen the reputation of local Catholics as leaders in the arena of law enforcement. Catholics admired O'Meara, the police commissioner of Boston from 1906 to 1918, because of his moral reform of the police force and strict enforcement of Boston's Sunday closing laws and blue laws, which soothed Protestant fears of Irish drunkenness and disorderliness on the Sabbath.[69] The impact of Catholic principles upon Police Commissioner O'Meara's thought is revealed in his personal correspondence as well as in his public actions. In O'Meara's letters to his wife, sister, and daughters, Catholicism was a frequent and unself-conscious subject. In his "first serious letter" to his daughter Frances, for example, he stated, "We believe that religion and morality are linked together and cannot be separated; that morality turns naturally towards religion and that religion strengthens and makes clear the course of morality."[70] Another daughter, Alice, summarized her parents' priorities thus: "They were generous in giving their children an active Roman-Catholic heritage, a liberal arts education, foreign travel and strong affection."[71]

Born on Prince Edward Island in 1854, O'Meara was raised in the Irish ghetto of Charlestown, Massachusetts. He came to know Boston intimately as a *Boston Globe* reporter in 1872, moving to the *Journal* two years later, where he served successively as reporter, city editor, news editor, and general manager. In 1896 he became editor in chief and publisher of the Republican *Journal,* which he sold in 1902. He had received an honorary A.M. from Dartmouth in 1888, and in 1898 he had been the New England speaker at the Atlanta, Georgia, International Peace Celebration. In 1900 the Boston City Council chose O'Meara as orator for the Fourth of July celebration, one of the first Catholics to be so honored, in a tradition of distinguished speakers that included John Hancock, John Quincy Adams, Horace Mann, Charles Sumner and Oliver Wendell Holmes. In 1906 Governor Curtis Guild of Massachusetts recalled O'Meara from a year-long vacation in Europe to become Boston's commissioner of police. Reappointed to that office twice by Republican governors in 1911 and in 1916, O'Meara served until his death in 1918.

Using his ties to the civil service, municipal politics, and the media, O'Meara ran for nomination for several political offices, but never successfully: as Republican congressman for the Eleventh District in 1904 and 1910, and as a nominee for mayor for the Citizen's Municipal League in 1908. Finally, the Good Government Association appealed unsuccessfully to him to run for mayor as head of a third, independent, citizen's party, a cause with which he sympathized.[72] O'Meara was president of the Boston Press Club for several years, and from 1911 to 1914 he was appointed lecturer on municipal government at Harvard University. His membership in the Algonquin, Exchange, St. Botolph, and Union Clubs was no mean feat for an Irish Catholic immigrant from Canada. O'Meara's lifestyle reflected the refinement of Brahmin tastes, such as his extensive library collections in European and American history and English literature, which rivaled those of his friend and fellow bibliophile Philip Hale, the music and arts critic for several Boston newspapers. In occasional columns in the *Herald,* Hale commended O'Meara's speaking skill as a model for after-dinner oratory.[73] O'Meara was fond of the theater and held a Boston Symphony subscription. As a member of the social elite, he evinced concern for the vitality of the arts in Boston, the quality of the school system, and the prestige of the press. His reputation was so secure that J. J. Roche once even considered the heretical move of entrusting the fate of the long-Democratic *Pilot* to the Republican O'Meara by proposing him as a buyer for the paper in 1904.[74] O'Meara also spoke frequently at Catholic events, such as the Harvard Catholic Club, the Catholic Literary Union of Charlestown, and the John Boyle O'Reilly Club. He received an honorary LL.D. from Boston College in 1908. Yet his daughters attended Smith College, not a Catholic institution, suggesting that religion buttressed O'Meara's ambition for social mobility without dominating it. His class status served to protect him from complete conformity to the Church's moral control and parochialism.

As police commissioner, O'Meara improved the reputation of the force through his policy of discouraging acceptance of bribes for routine favors, of enforcing uniform codes, and by overseeing promotions for merit. As an occupational choice for the Irish, police work had gradually emerged as "the most practically attainable of the three P's—priest, politician, policeman."[75] By 1900 Boston's police force saw itself primarily as a defender of the peace. Formerly run by the city of Boston, control of the force was transferred in

1885 to the state, primarily as a Republican reaction against Irish Democratic power, which also buttressed Yankee plans to regulate Irish drinking habits by giving the state the authority to issue liquor licenses. State governance of the Boston police endured until the 1960s, when racial strife precipitated another major internal crisis.[76] While O'Meara was commissioner, the police force increased in size from 1,358 to 1,877 officers. This represented more than a 200 percent increase over the 789 officers on the force in 1885 and established Irish control of law enforcement.[77] Salaries rose as well, as an 1898 pay scale proposal was finally implemented in 1913: a patrolman earned $1,200 per year; captains, $2,500.[78] O'Meara, however, continued to regard the enlarged force as a small, familial unit. In consonance with the familism of the Irish politician and the paternalist style of the archbishop, he mistrusted the "impersonality" of a police union, preferring his own counsel and centralized authority. His personal style of promotion review based on subjective analysis of character did not appeal to the entire force and in fact led to undesirable comparisons with ward bosses, yet O'Meara maintained devotion of officers by acquiring smart new uniforms and by increasing salary security by eliminating the former policy of fines and suspensions that, he realized, posed unnecessary hardships for officers' families.[79] Cardinal O'Connell commended him frequently for the efficiency of police service during the centenary celebration in 1908 and for monitoring official visits of Catholic dignitaries. O'Meara's exemplary career record and his prudent reticence about discussing personal views or police business with journalists enabled him to foster a moral atmosphere in the workplace without seeming excessively rigid, and to maintain friendly relations with the press.

O'Meara died before the police strike of 1919; thus he missed both the strike and the Sacco-Vanzetti trial of 1926, the most difficult challenges in Boston police history prior to the civil rights struggles of the 1960s. Francis Russell has claimed that if O'Meara had lived to serve a third term, the strike probably would not have occurred. He characterized O'Meara's successor, fifty-seven-year-old Edwin Upton Curtis, as "an uncompromising martinet with no previous experience in police administration and no great affection for the Boston Irish."[80] Curtis, no fan of Catholicism, had been a sponsor of the sectarian amendment at the 1917 Massachusetts constitutional convention that rejected authorization of aid to Catholic parochial schools. Even though O'Meara was a Republican conservative, and in many ways the docile tool of Yankee aspirations, his death was a blow to the police force, which mourned the loss of a chief who had held off tensions by using Irish clannishness to his advantage. To his family, his life had successfully balanced the tensions between Catholicism and social esteem, as his sister reminded him: "I shall close by telling you, dear Steve, that I feel more happiness in the knowledge that you are a practical Catholic, living in the friendship of God, than if you were as eloquent as Demosthenes, as wealthy as Vanderbilt, or as exalted as Hendricks the former vice president; for I have the hope of meeting you now, some day in a land where it will be always a Happy Christmas and a Happy New Year."[81]

Although O'Meara was a rags-to-respectability Catholic, applauded as a model citizen and parent, he was an anomaly among Boston's Irish Catholics in several significant ways. First, he was a Republican. Second, his substantial income and political connections permitted him to provide a broad range of cultural opportunities and material advantages for his family and secured him a wide circle of Protestant and Catholic friends who acknowledged his decency and sense of duty.[82] Finally, O'Meara was unusual because his social status allowed him to diverge in some ways from the expectations of the Catholic subculture, because his conservative strategies were approved by the Church.

O'Meara and Joseph Pelletier represented extremes of Catholic public presence in Boston. Where Pelletier's usefulness to Protestants had stemmed from his flaws as an ethnic political leader, O'Meara's success derived from his incorruptibility and his denial of the necessity of the political patronage game, which frustrated Democrats and Republicans alike. On the other hand, O'Meara was never elected to office by a party constituency, having received his commissioner's appointment from Republicans in the statehouse who saw him as a stable influence for the city. O'Meara served the Republican party's conservative interests, but he served his ethnic group as well by striving to overcome the unruly image of the Irish through forging an exemplary police force, by living as a respectable gentleman, and by his refusal to give political favors. In his twelve years in office he provided new jobs for over 500 Irishmen, indicating a strong sense of ethnic solidarity.

Coming from a Catholic family of mixed ethnicity and comfortable income, Pelletier had been born with certain advantages of wealth unknown to O'Meara, but he was unable to escape from the system of corruption, bribery, and cronyism that disgraced the Irish machines. In brief, he remained unassimilated to a non–Irish Catholic milieu. Opponents of Pelletier were able to exploit him by proving that he lacked integrity, certainly a disappointment to advocates of the moral superiority of the Catholic college education that Pelletier had received. Pelletier's downfall, while it embarrassed many Catholics, was supported by insiders close to the hierarchy who wanted to punish him for defecting from the Church's subculture. As a Catholic wrote to Bernard Rothwell, commending Rothwell's condemnation of Pelletier, "The younger generation and the group of so-called high-brows who are pointed out with pride by our orators and writers are not so proud of their religion under these circumstances so that cases of this kind are likewise a contributary cause of the 'leakage' from our Church."[83] O'Meara, an immigrant, climbed up the ranks of journalism and then into a political appointment to the police force. O'Meara was above suspicion as a cause of Catholic leakage, but he also seemed to be a bit above his own people, toadying to the Republicans and distancing himself from the rowdy Irish. In emulating Brahmin culture, he joined the lace curtain phalanx who acculturated by copying New England's notion of social stability and who married material success to political conservatism. His loyalty to the Church never in question, O'Meara nonetheless stood for a type of Irish Catholic layman emerging in the early twentieth century whose absorption of the lifestyle of Yankee elites and his achievement of affluence protected him from making decisions that were uniformly governed by and conforming to the limits of the Catholic subculture. He was both within and without the boundaries of an ethnic middle class.

"Ishmaelites in America": Defining Catholic Manhood

The Church played an important role in the formation of ideals of Catholic manhood, which in turn converged with attitudes about class status, social duty, and material success. Following one interpretation, in the final third of the nineteenth century a "loose coalition of Catholic clergy, fiction writers and social critics sought to define and promote Catholic notions of masculinity."[84] Of these three groups, which overlapped considerably, priests, as seminarians and as pastors, were subject to many of the same contradictory pressures affecting laymen.

In 1911 O'Connell dismissed the Sulpicians, the French order of priests teaching at St. John's Seminary in Brighton. He installed in their place a Roman-trained faculty of his own choosing, thereby ending any possibility of liberal seminary reforms.[85] Since 1908, O'Connell had made the Sulpicians unwelcome by subjecting them to a variety of petty harassments.[86] Subsequently, O'Connell refused admission to St. John's to students from outside his archdiocese. Between 1904 and 1923 St. John's ordained about 314 priests for Boston. As local pastors died, O'Connell replaced them with personal favorites. The Pilot reported that by 1922, seven-eighths of the pastors in Boston were O'Connell appointees.[87] He also created new parishes to fill with pastors of his choosing. As early as 1911 O'Connell may have accomplished a conservative overhaul of the Boston clergy.[88] O'Connell likened his takeover of St. John's to Rome's victory over dangerous Gallican controversialists. In reality, the removal of the Sulpicians had more impact on the tone than on the content of seminary education.[89] Through his control of priestly formation via seminary faculty appointments and his pastoral assignments,

O'Connell strengthened the potential for diocesan uniformity. Still, O'Connell's punishment of nonconformity among his priests and his standardization of what seminarians learned did not make him all-powerful. Robert Sullivan has observed that "the life of even strictly hierarchical organizations usually owes more to the society and culture that support them than to the aspirations and directives of any leader, no matter how forceful. The collective biography of Boston's priests conforms to this generalization. The governance of their church . . . was marked by the attenuation of feudalism."[90] The actions of diocesan priests and the religious orders of men and women, therefore, hardly represent total subservience. Those who needed to outwit the archbishop usually could, by appealing to the papacy as the ultimate sanction for their actions. To thwart insubordination, O'Connell desired "hard-working, devoted, docile, obedient" priests—a list that resembled his litany of female virtues.[91]

Although Bishop Bernard McQuaid of Rochester had called seminaries "nurseries of heaven," in 1900 they more nearly resembled military academies. To foster obedience and to maintain a controlled atmosphere, clerical training throughout the United States emphasized military style discipline joined to an antiquated theological curriculum. They did approximate nurseries to the degree that the protectively male and clerical environment prevented much encounter with the laity beyond family visits. Traditional gender roles were reinforced by seminary life, since the only women seen there were likely to be sisters hired to cook and clean. Spiritual growth of seminarians was not fostered by the ethnic predisposition of the students against self-reflection. Faculty reports about the students noted that Irish Americans were unusually "reticent" about discussing their spiritual lives.[92]

In 1907 *Pascendi domenici gregis* condemned Modernism as a heresy, and the appended syllabus listing sixty-five errors of Modernism appeared, having a chilling impact on American Catholic intellectual life. As such, "the post-Pascendi years in American Catholicism were marked by intellectual retreat and theological sterility. Cultivation of the life of the mind became suspect. A thoroughgoing and immensely effective educational police action isolated the theological reaches of the Catholic community from the contemporary world with which tentative contact had so recently been established."[93] Boston seminary life suffered from this intellectual drought. O'Connell had become archbishop a mere week before the anti-Modernist encyclical appeared. Predictably, his first official pronouncement, a pastoral letter dated November 30, endorsed the pope: "More quickly than others can he detect the menacing dangers disguised in attractive array," wrote O'Connell. "It is such a danger that the Pontiff sees in Modernism. It is of such a danger and of its far reaching evil that we, inspired by his zeal, would warn our beloved faithful. Our words are but the echo of the Holy Father's voice."[94]

Seminarians at St. John's, class of 1922–23. (Archives of the Archdiocese of Boston)

American seminaries did not lack reformers altogether. Rev. John Talbot Smith (1855–1923) of New York, no stranger to Boston audiences, had investigated American seminaries in the 1890s.[95] His call for a thorough restructuring of every aspect of a seminarian's life, from exercise and diet to reading and curriculum, was heeded somewhat at St. John's, where improvements were made to the physical facilities and the curriculum. Yet even Smith, an outspoken crusader for reform of seminary education, initiated no discussion about the noncelibate world among seminarians, maintaining the strict division between clergy and laity.

In the absence of a diocesan minor seminary, nearly all of Boston's seminarians attended (but not necessarily completed) Boston College or Holy Cross College before entering St. John's. Catholic higher education contributed to male character formation by reinforcing Church paternalism and clerical power. The relationship between these two Jesuit colleges, therefore, and St. John's was crucial, since so many of its students became priests. Class size at St. John's increased from 60 seminarians in 1907 to 159 in 1916, rising to a peak of 253 in 1930. For men who chose religious orders, such as the Jesuits, one recent critic has stated that the Jesuit version of Catholic piety "eventually displaced the pietism itself," producing an "oblique" piety in a boy "whose acquaintance with Cicero or Shakespeare gave him just the coin to provide him with cultural affluence."[96] Nonetheless, it was precisely their superficial sophistication that made the Jesuits ideal spokesmen for the social aspirations of O'Connell for his priests.

One source about Jesuit formation is Michael Earls, who attended Holy Cross for three years, graduated in 1896, and then went to Woodstock Seminary in Maryland, after deciding to leave the Sulpician seminary in Montreal for the Jesuit order. Earls's diary of his experiences in Maryland in 1899–1900 when he was twenty-seven unwittingly reveals how novices developed prejudices about clergy superiority and about the mechanics of liturgical propriety. In several passages he reported assisting at Mass for Irish indigents in a county poorhouse: "It was like an old chapel on the frontier in pioneer days; when the hardy men of the settlement differed as much in toilet niceties from the fastidious churchgoers of our fashionable times." Earls remarked with surprise that the men crawled up the narrow aisle on their knees for communion but returned by jumping over the benches. When he saw his first corpse at the poorhouse, Earls commented that "one could not see a more powerful sermon on the rottenness of the human body." Living in even humbler dormitories beneath the Irish floor, according to Earls, were blacks, "sane and insane, and a place of sights and smells and sounds."

Earls's attempt to impose spiritual meaning on these events led him to hope that a fellow priest's talk to a dying man had saved his soul; after baptizing several candidates who were totally ignorant of their faith, he concluded that "book-learning and eloquent reasonings may help, but it is the Good Shepherd who turns these lost sheep into the safe pasture again." Although he credited God's grace for these conversions, he also believed in the role of the priest to administer discipline and the sacraments: "Now I see that we should drill these women and whatever men we can find in several practices of devotion— the Rosary, the Morning Offering and the like . . . and we can teach the prayers and catechism to a little child there, and to some negroes." Nor was Earls above employing a little sentimental persuasion: "To catch the heart of an Irishman one had but to mention something about old Ireland, or the Soggarth Aroon."[97]

Earls lamented that "sameness is the principal dish on the bill-of-fare of a novice's life."[98] He intended the diary in which he confided these private thoughts to become a gift to his sister Bess several years later. Although afraid to sound complaining, he wrote, "Yes, it is pretty heavy here, at times, and the eternal sameness of the life is a hard load, and the moping about the same old walks and halls makes it a little heavier. I will not mention the various bits of the harness that is about us."[99] At the diocesan seminary, O'Connell harnessed young men by limiting their access to newspapers and periodicals, continuing and heightening a precedent from the previous century.[100] He reversed the lenient policy of the former Sulpician director, Charles Rex, who subscribed to numerous secular and religious journals for the seminary reading room.[101] O'Connell's decision seemed to run against the aim of seminary reformers such as Father Smith, who had suggested that "the priest who is to enjoy the fullest influence over all classes of citizens must have the manners, habits, and appearance of a gentleman."[102] O'Connell's policies at St. John's vacillated between two contrasting ideals of the priesthood: first, a Counter-Reformation understanding of the priest as the sacred incarnation of Christ, which justified the extreme isolation of the seminarians from worldly temptation, similar to Christ's isolation in the desert prior to his crucifixion. Alternately, from his own Roman training and comfortably appointed household, O'Connell admired a cosmopolitan clergyman who was at ease in cultured society, suggesting the need for a sophisticated seminary atmosphere.

Whatever O'Connell's view of the priesthood, it never challenged the ethnic dominance of Irish Americans in the clergy. Curiously, O'Connell never arranged for the Irish American priests or seminarians to learn foreign languages, which might have helped serve the non-English speaking Catholics of Boston, and which might have diffused tensions between national parishes and Irish priests.[103] Generally, O'Connell's concerns for the purity and social elevation of priests mirrored the concerns of his contemporary churchmen and reflected the larger process of middle-class formation and a growing reaction against secularism among Catholic bishops. Attempting to mold the ideal priest from a seminary population drawn from the Irish lower middle class, O'Connell had limited success at polishing their sophistication. Boston's priests matured in an atmosphere of reverence for Roman ecclesiology and of unquestioning loyalty to Church dogma, underscored by the limitations of St. John's curriculum. A clergy vocation virtually guaranteed young men upward mobility and respect in the Catholic community, but seminarians' segregation from the world offered them little savoir faire, less sympathy for lay experience, and scant preparation for assessing the administrative complexities of twentieth-century parish life.

Laymen, on the other hand, lived in the midst of the world's temptations. Among Irish Catholics, one of those evils was spending too much time with other men, which was apparently only suitable among priests and seminarians. Thus, one part of the Church's self-designated role regarding male identity seems to have been to erase the tendency in Irish society that privileged male friendships and socializing over family unity and male-female intimacy. The Catholic press printed frequent warnings that "to the world outside, that man is a good fellow who spends several nights a week in company with boon companions at some club or society meeting. The wife and children see the other side of good fellowship of that kind, and they are not impressed with it."[104] The relationship between an ethic of success and an ideal of Catholic masculinity shows, once again, the contradictions of the insider-outsider mentality and the tensions created within American Catholicism in response to

Michael Earls as a Jesuit novice. (Holy Cross College Archives)

the economic pressures of competitive capitalism. Male companionship was worthwhile, so long as it did not threaten the family, which was still viewed as the basic productive unit of American society.

A second concern of the Church for men was the temptation to greed and avarice. During the Gilded Age, Protestants commonly expressed the fear that the accumulation of wealth and luxury were creating effeminate and indolent young men, thereby undermining the masculine image and the creed of individualism at the heart of Americanism and Protestantism. Hence, liberal Protestant theology took a dynamic turn in the Social Gospel movement, whose Salvation Army and settlement houses expressed a muscular, activist piety that, in a nice paradox, often emulated Catholic mendicant orders.[105] The more feminized side of liberal Protestantism was perhaps expressed as an aestheticized interest in the Gothic Revival and in exploration of medieval mystical piety.

The Catholic Church expressed a muted and less articulated resentment of a "feminization" of culture and, prior to the 1920s, did not spawn an equivalent branch of Boston social Catholicism as proof of its virility. When Catholic Action did emerge in the 1930s, it was based largely on English or continental models and was doctrinally quite conservative. There were isolated remarks like Archbishop O'Connell's about the need for a more assertive manhood to check the growth of feminism, but these were offset by calls for men to become more deeply involved in the emotional and nurturing aspects of domesticity. In 1909 a Boston Irish newspaper reported that "fathers are wont to throw the burden of religious training on the school, if it be a private school, or on the already overburdened mother. How many fathers take thought during that precious time when their own son would be flattered beyond words at their notice to win the boy's confidence, and sound certain moral and spiritual depths which are beyond the mother's reach!"[106] To become good models for their sons and brothers, adult males were enjoined to attend Mass regularly, but material rewards were also implied. According to an 1897 parish calendar, a churchgoing man earns "the good word and good will of others and that helps him, too, materially in his life work, whatever it may be."[107]

In domestic relations and in the workplace, Catholic men were sometimes encouraged to imitate the diligence and reliability of Catholic working women.[108] The Church, then, deviated from certain features of Victorian America's strict division between domestic/feminine values and economic/ masculine values. If Catholic men were supposed to copy female work habits as well as feminine maternal instincts, it was because these behaviors were meant to stabilize the Catholic family by redefining manhood as family oriented. The Church's formula fit the needs of a growing Catholic middle class by trying to overcome Irish society's "unnatural" tendency toward all-male bonding. In doing so, Catholic teaching employed the central assumption of the Protestant version of domesticity, that women were religious and pure by nature, whereas men needed to be transformed to be so through the acquisition of particular habits.[109] In part, the Church's fear of women in the marketplace was a sexual anxiety, that by being in daily contact with the "unrestrained animalism" of men, and their social Darwinist values, women would become desexed and turn into voracious, profit-driven beings. In part, also, the Church's denial of women's careers stemmed from the belief that if women went to work, the building blocks of Catholic culture—the family, motherhood, patriarchy—would topple and men's status, including that of the clergy, would invariably decline as women's improved. Thus, despite a few instances where the Church encouraged men to imitate the economic self-sufficiency of Irish domestics, and a few examples of iconoclastic journalism by Catholic women defending the superiority of women in business, women functioned primarily in a Catholic subculture as symbols of antimaterialism and anticompetition, immune to (but also excluded from) the perils of the marketplace.[110] The Church fully supported feminine privatization and deplored industrial conditions that made working mothers necessary. The proper task of mothers, stated by *Ave Maria,* was to "come forward and check the advance of materialism that is demoralizing their sons."[111]

The Church's view that gender spheres corresponded to division of labor represented a sectarian Catholic bias against working women as well as a reflection of the dominant economic relations in Boston. Yet, occasionally among the monotonous commentaries to women were suggestions that Catholics must teach their daughters to be competitive. A columnist in the Boston *Republic* questioned "if the diminution of competitions in our high class schools for girls is a good thing. All life is a fierce competition, whether the girl go forth from high school or college to a home of affluence, or to seek a means of maintaining herself until the natural settlement in life is due. . . . Yet, what meets even the daughter of a wealthy home at the outset of her social career? Competition." Though these voices were a minority in the Catholic press, they do suggest that the laity saw gender definitions in somewhat less rigid terms than the official Church, and that it had internalized the necessity of survival through competition. Nonetheless, the lay press felt obliged to reassure readers that bracing girls for a competitive world could be accomplished "without destroying their innocent happiness."[112]

In the 1890s, Protestant America had replaced an ethic of male success traditionally defined in terms of personal character with one that described manliness through monetary achievement, making pursuit of wealth a crucial part of masculinity. This change drove a wedge into middle-class culture between the Protestant stress on the independent individualist and the obligation to seek a productive worldly vocation. "The crisis," claims James Fisher, "was neither felt by nor relevant to the masses of Catholics, but after 1930 the *idea* of Catholicism as a potential antidote to bourgeois sterility and weightlessness became suddenly attractive to those, like Dorothy Day, seeking a way out of the gilded cage."[113] In this interpretation, Catholicism served as the virtuous Other against which Protestant Americans, jaded by the pressures of bourgeois conformity, measured themselves. The Gothic Revival spearheaded by the elitist elements in certain Protestant denominations expressed this romantic idealization of Catholic unity, hierarchy, and aestheticism.

Between the 1890s and World War I, and before the Catholic lay countercultural movements of the 1930s, Catholics had protested the unlimited pursuit of wealth. Despite its growing role as an agent of economic assimilation, the Church had condemned the rapacious greed of industrial capitalists. But due to the uneven pace of the arrival and assimilation of Catholic immigrants over the course of a century, a Catholic work ethic in America represented an amalgam of several past social formations. It contained an ascetic sense of the "calling" reminiscent of Max Weber's description of the Reformation Protestant, and it echoed the attitudes of preindustrial America, rather than "the lust for wealth of the late Victorian."[114] The "Calvinist" features of the work ethic that the Catholic Church professed in 1900 had been forsaken by liberal Protestants, who had replaced self-denial with a "wealth ethic." The Episcopal bishop of Massachusetts, for example, became widely quoted for his startling claim that "Godliness is in league with riches."[115] He meant that it was impossible to achieve great wealth without acting morally, thereby interpreting wealth not as a corrupting force but as an assurance of God's blessing. As Bishop Lawrence wrote, "To seek for and earn wealth is a sign of a natural, vigorous, and strong character."[116]

Boston Catholicism, at an earlier stage in the formation of its own middle class, professed a different view of wealth that, in the words of *Rerum Novarum,* was intended to "keep down the pride of those who are well off, and to cheer the spirit of the afflicted; to incline the former to generosity and the latter to tranquil resignation."[117] Addressing itself to the haves and the have-nots, the Catholic Church was unlikely to bless the separation of economics from morality or to recommend a man's pursuit of a career at the expense of his soul and his family. The incongruity between Catholic economic principles and capitalism's expansion were shaped by many contemporary phenomena. First, the European Church's inability to come to terms with the irreversible realities of industrial capitalism and the rival authority of the liberal state conflicted with American Catholic perceptions. It was difficult for the American Church to maintain constant enmity toward liberal democracy when it guaranteed the separation of church and state that enabled Catholics to freely practice their faith.

Second, the American Church's desire to associate itself with the ideals of republican democracy, associated roughly with the decades of 1790 to 1830, reflected the uniqueness of American Catholicism in relation to Rome. Living in a democratic culture that promoted and valued individualism, how could American Catholics avoid being influenced by the gospel of individualism? The Church's promotion of a work ethic suited to the preindustrial era produced an American Catholic subculture that was an unstable blend of resistance and accommodation to a middle-class sensibility and to political ideals that were themselves in a period of flux and uncertainty. Thus, although the famine generation of Irish immigrants did not achieve widespread rapid success owing to their lack of industrial skills and their colonized status that may have predisposed them against bourgeois culture, their descendants had thoroughly embraced the capitalist ethic, supported (at least tacitly) by Catholicism. The Church, in fact, was likely to support elements of a capitalist social structure that maintained a social hierarchy. This perhaps indicates why the Church's record on labor disputes in Massachusetts during this era consistently supported social order against the demands of workers and unions, and the use of strikes or violence. In the city of Lawrence, in both the 1912 "Bread and Roses" strike and the 1919 strike, the Church acted as a conservative arbitrator, concerned primarily with getting children of Italian strikers' families to safe temporary homes and with saturating the community with anti-socialist leaflets after the strikes had ended.

As expected, elements of the Catholic subculture were marshaled in support of the Church's ethos of success, attitudes about work, and definitions of manhood. In literature, Catholic novelists created a genre of success stories which suggested that "wealth and virtue were almost mutually exclusive." As opposed to Protestants' gospel of success, Catholics even produced a variety of "downward mobility" tales, about how the single-minded pursuit of wealth would destroy happiness and virtue.[118] Thus, Horatio Alger–type stories (or at least the inaccurate reputation of these tales as rags-to-riches myths) were deemed unsuitable for Catholic boys because they prized individualism at the expense of family life.[119] Catholic writers, and especially priest-authors, clung to preindustrial views on labor, social order, and the transience of worldly goods, ostensibly to keep boys and men from forgetting their faith and their families. The *Pilot*'s seventieth anniversary edition of 1907, for example, published a lengthy article on the keys to advancement, stating, "Each boy can cultivate his desire to succeed by emulating those whom he instinctively believes to be his superiors." Added to this was the naive remark that "boys must not think that it is necessary to take money away from anyone in order to make money."[120] In sum, the Church advised boys to be responsible about their own success but to cultivate precapitalist devices of imitating their betters and relying on the wisdom of adults such as priests. Whereas the laity perhaps needed practical advice about living as Christians in the world of economic competition, the clergy focused on protecting the Church's belief in organic social hierarchy and imitation of social superiors. Lay writers, however, seemed equally uncertain about the promises of wealth if it jeopardized friends, family, and salvation.

The Church's ethic of moderation was an attempted compromise between ruthless competition and moderate accumulation. Moderation would prevent men from forsaking family and religious duties for all-male bonding, drinking, gambling, or other antifamily activity. Moderation also permitted the Church to reaffirm its commitment to the protection of private property without placing undue emphasis on excessive acquisition of goods. Evidence of this attitude emerges vividly in Archbishop O'Connell's letter to entrepreneur James Prendergast: "I have always prayed that God would prosper you in every way—even financially. Usually I often feel like asking Him to prevent SOME of our good people from getting MUCH money. But you have never been either soiled or spoiled by it and you have always done good with it."[121] O'Connell reasoned that a few Catholics who used wealth virtuously should be rewarded, as Prendergast was by being named knight commander in a papal order, but for the vast majority, it was better to remain unsoiled by the temptations of success.[122] Roman Catholic tradition had always esteemed a life of poverty above excessive wealth, but here an archbishop justified a go-getter attitude among a favored minority of Catholic businessmen because their success assured the Church's financial stability. Lay Catholics were thus enabled to justify both worldly success and spiritual health despite the seeming contradictions of this union. A local Catholic newspaper asserted with confidence that "worldly success is, of course, not a test of a man's success in spiritual things. . . . But a high-toned Catholic life is in no way inconsistent with success in any reputable business or profession."[123]

Without attacking wealthy individuals directly, the Church attempted to regulate the selfishness and indulgence associated with surplus income by emphasizing the moral demands of philanthropy and stewardship of the poor. Patrick Donahoe stands out as the philanthropic saint of nineteenth-century Boston. An immigrant in 1825 who founded *Donahoe's Magazine* and the Boston *Pilot*, Donahoe was editor and publisher of the latter from 1839 to 1875. He earned an annual salary in excess of $40,000 but reportedly said to his friends, "I have enough. It is time to give to the poor." Subsequently, Donahoe founded the Home for Destitute Children in Boston and gave generously to the Church. The Donahoe story, which idealized a less competitive and allegedly more communal era in American history, was a cautionary tale for Catholics making the transition to competitive capitalism not to lose sight of their moral obligations to the needy. The archaic and nostalgic aspects of this work ethic not only reflected Catholic ambivalence about the impact of capitalism and class stratification, but also the self-serving position of the hierarchy and of the clergy, who knew that their own economic security rested on the growing affluence of their parishioners. It is not surprising, therefore, that priests supported the prosperity that came from individual enterprise and rarely criticized the wealthiest Catholics. The leading Catholic families of Boston—Fitzgeralds, Kennedys, Cunninghams, Pelletiers, Prendergasts, Slatterys, and others—have survived a century of family scandals, political corruption, unscrupulous financial machinations, and ruthless business dealings without Church condemnation.

Irvin Wyllie once described the American Protestant success ethic as follows: "The greater the poverty out of which a man climbed, the greater the testimony to the force of his character."[124] By contrast, Catholic success literature minimized the dramatic acquisition of wealth and instead judged a man's character by how he used his money to help his family or the less fortunate. The range of advice to Catholic men on what and how to achieve oscillated between uplift and chastisement. On one hand, there were counsels against seeking too high a professional specialization. Edward McSweeney warned that "the Irish should not put all their hope in law and medicine; humanity takes neither with pleasure, and only under compulsion. Go into trade and industry."[125] Catholic advocates of industrial training emphasized knowledge of machinery and of production as a key to success, obviously preparing Catholics for a future tied to the industrial sector.[126] On the other hand, Catholics were encouraged to surmount genuine obstacles and their own self-defeating outsider attitudes in order to get out of the underclass. Laymen exhorted fellow Catholics to demand more for and from themselves: "Too many of our Catholic men and women are ready to give up at the first rebuff. They have had it so dinned into their ears from their earliest years that they were Ishmaelites in the social life of America. . . . They are satisfied with second places and second-class effort when they possess native ability that should it be properly directed place them in the first rank."[127] In this context, Catholic teaching about work and success was meant to help Catholics overcome the stigma of being "Ishmaelites."

The first rank of success, however, was not without its burdens. The hierarchy and clergy perennially complained that successful Catholics no longer gave enough to the poor. The laity responded with attempts to understand its own alleged indifference. "Perhaps the secret," wrote a woman journalist, "is that the parish church is looked upon as a distributing agency to care for the needs of the poor of that particular parish, and that parishioners in comfortable circumstances content themselves with giving to the collections taken up at stated periods, or responding to calls made upon them privately for special cases."[128] This Catholic muckraker saw the inertia that resulted from the increased rationalization and bureaucratization of Church philanthropic activities in the early 1900s. While Catholics continued to tithe at the parish level, support for the plethora of new extra-parish groups became a voluntarist option. Moreover, parishioners seemed more willing and likely to support neighborhood programs rather than submit their funds to a diocesan pool for use at the archbishop's discretion. However, the Church benefited indirectly from the growth of voluntarism, which provided large sums for religious charities that supplemented the amounts derived from parish collections.

Joining the hierarchy and clergy were leading laymen who reminded successful Catholics about the obligation to use their wealth to help others. James J. Phelan told the Catholic Literary Union of Charlestown that "there is no reason why we should not succeed to a far greater extent. There is more room at the top than at the bottom. . . . No matter what your salary or position is, don't be satisfied; try for a higher position." He also warned laymen, "Don't let success influence the size of your head. Remember that there are a lot of unfortunates in this world whom we can help. Let us be charitable."[129] Archbishop O'Connell likewise advised affluent Catholics to empathize with the less fortunate: "I would sum it all up in one word: If you are well up the ladder, turn and give a hand as you rest a moment to those below you; and if you have your feet as yet only on the lower rungs, take the hand offered to you, but do not pull those above you down."[130] A laywoman took an "ends justifies means" perspective that resolved a potential contradiction in the Church's position. She reasoned that wealth is virtuous when it is used for good works, which thereby transformed money into a means to personal salvation: "Our prosperity is meant to be, in moderation, for ourselves, in exuberance of substantial help and sympathy and personal service for our fellows. This is making for ourselves friends of the mammon of iniquity, but purchasing it with a right to everlasting dwellings."[131] Here, "saving" took on two connotations: saving income, and spiritual salvation. As these examples show, the Church confronted the basic premises of capitalism—self-interest and the profit motive—in its own spirituality by continuing to stress the laity's obligation to voluntary good works as a way to mitigate the selfishness associated with competition, and as a means to gain heaven.

The Church's discussion of charity to the poor, as with its remarks on the responsibilities of wealth, had a large audience in the Irish Americans who swelled the ranks of its clergy and its lay societies. But urban pauperism, as a significant problem in the archdiocese, was not confined to the Irish community. Poor relief for non-Irish immigrants was unfortunately marred by traces of Irish Catholic nativism. Archbishop O'Connell, for example, gave condescending advice to the largest group of recent arrivals, the Italians: "Alas, I fear that a strange phenomenon shows itself in many Italians as soon as they land in this country. . . . Many of you lose your individualism and become, like the other inhabitants of this continent, avaricious of the material things of this world, even at the loss of what is more noble in your souls."[132] Somewhat inconsistently, O'Connell challenged Italians to leaven American culture with their venerable civilization, in apparent disregard for the fact that most of Boston's immigrants were southern Italians and Sicilians, while the Italian high culture he revered was embodied by Counter-Reformation Rome or by opulent Renaissance Florence. Italians, although apathetic about parish schools, energetically founded Catholic clubs and nonreligious benevolent social societies, which proliferated to such as degree that a prominent Italian lawyer counted 107 Italian associations in Boston in 1911.[133] Nonetheless, among Catholics there remained a gulf between those providing and those receiving charity, and a lurking fear that academics and social workers from Harvard and Simmons College, or the Protestant missions, were always ready to pounce on Catholic immigrants. Hence, a competitive spirit was fostered among lay Catholics in order to preserve the Church's power over all national groups, resulting in the formation of groups like the Catholic Italian Civic League in 1919 and the Catholic Immigration Bureau in 1921, which emphasized religion above ethnic particularism.[134]

A negative result of the Church's constant harping on the duties of charity was to place a financial burden on the "high-tone" Catholic, whose formerly active role in community "works of mercy" was being transformed into that of anonymous donor to a diocesan poor fund or benefactor of the St. Vincent de Paul Society. The Church disapproved of secular charities precisely because their "dry monetary offering" paled against the kindly word of advice and the personalized approach of Catholic agencies. But the Church's own increasing use of impersonal giving was a concession to a new trend in philanthropy as well as a potential strain on the finances of the limited affluent Catholic population. A Boston layman in a position to assess the limits of lay charity noted that for a fundraiser to build a prep school for Georgetown University, only a dozen New England men "can afford to contribute $1000 or more each."[135] Still, generosity to the Church remained a significant part of the Church's definition of manliness.

It seems clear that Catholics accommodated certain dominant American values. Already in the mid-1800s Catholic acculturation to a capitalist economy was well under way, although never explicitly addressed by Church leaders.[136] Seventy years later, a Catholic ethos of work and of worldly success retained an organicist base, modified accordingly to affirm the creed of hard work that suffused preindustrial America. Because Catholics believed that their notion of good works as communal endeavors would conquer egoist individualism, they accepted the Church's role in disposing of surplus income and caring for the needy. Charity was highlighted as the organizing principle of Christian manhood, which in the Church's eyes would overcome social and economic inequality by moral rather than revolutionary transformation.

Catholic Education and Material Success

Lay Catholics promoted the Church's advocacy of a separate but equal sub-culture by helping to establish Catholic higher education. The advent of Catholic colleges and universities in Massachusetts represented a decisive step in middle-class formation and consolidation. Two of the state's Catholic schools, the College of the Holy Cross in Worcester (1843) and Boston College (1863), were Jesuit schools for men. Each expanded significantly in the early 1900s. In 1907 Boston College moved from a small, downtown building to its present spacious, scenic, Gothic Revival campus in Chestnut Hill across the street from St. John's Seminary, where many of its graduates continued their studies as candidates for the priesthood. The stated goal of Jesuit higher education was to mold students into "whole men" serving the entire community. Consequently, publicists for Boston College advised a young man "to equip himself morally and intellectually, to fill his place in the city's life and honor to himself, and win credit to the Church, who through him, emphasizes its power in moulding the ideal man and citizen."[137] As educators, the Jesuits saw their mission as the transmission of a communal consciousness and in-stitutional loyalty that derived from the whole man philosophy but that had to be tailored to the economic needs of a generation of assimilating Catholics. Catholics professed no less suspicion toward public education at the grammar school level, although in the 1890s they could not build parochial schools fast enough in Boston to absorb the more than 50,000 pupils in the public system. Nonetheless, Katherine Conway expressed popular sentiment in suggesting that if children "can get half a loaf of religion, isn't it better than the 'no bread' regimen of our poor little ones in the public schools!"[138]

Catholic claims about the uniqueness of their institutions, however, mani-fest a sectarian spirit that ran counter to their desire to show that Catholic schools were no different from public institutions. A system of Catholic pa-rochial schools, mandated by the Third Plenary Council of Baltimore in 1884 and governed under the auspices of the Catholic Education Association since 1898, upheld the notion of Catholic distinctiveness. A national association of

Walnut Park, the Newton estate of Joseph Flanagan, a banker, was willed to the Sisters of St. Joseph in 1922 and was renamed St. Agnes School for girls by Cardinal O'Connell. The cardinal's nephew attended when it subsequently became a boys' school. Here, pupils process in front of the carriage house, which was used for classes, swimming lessons, and extracurricular activities. (Sisters of St. Joseph, Brighton)

Catholic colleges was also founded in 1898. Catholic educators were determined to prove that they were not antithetical to American principles, but there remained an implicit sense that Catholic education was morally superior to public instruction. A good example comes from the family of Stephen O'Meara, a public school graduate and supporter. His sister maintained that he had managed to absorb Catholic values from his Catholic-educated siblings despite attending public school: "Judge by yourself—would you be a practical Catholic now, but for your early training at the college, and the Catholic atmosphere of our home, caused by the fact that the rest of us were pupils of Catholic schools? A Catholic atmosphere is what all children should breathe, both at home and in school; and how many have miserable homes in which they remain as short a time as possible. Where can they imbibe Catholicity if they attend non-Catholic schools?"[139]

This belief in Catholic atmosphere explains why the Church expanded its system of parochial schools in response to the Plenary Council decrees of 1884. The religious orders of women, notably the Sisters of St. Joseph, were largely responsible for the growth of elementary education in Boston, running seventeen of forty-seven schools opened between 1907 and 1923. Additionally, these sisters held the first teachers' institute for the diocese in 1908, which became an annual affair in 1910 and which soon developed to include all religious and lay teachers of the archdiocese. Religious women's important role in children's education did not reflect a softening of Church patriarchy, however. Between 1870 and 1940, the growing numbers of teaching sisters resulted from the fact that the hierarchy had narrowed options for women religious by displacing them from former strongholds in hospital and social service work.[140]

Brahmin elites took a dim view of the growth of Catholic higher education in the 1890s. Harvard president Charles Eliot made some widely publicized hostile remarks on Jesuit schools, which he later retracted. Father John O'Brien, then a pastor in Cambridge, praised Eliot's apology: "Such service on your part will tend to cement still more closely the friendly feelings now existing between Harvard's sons and the many graduates of Holy Cross and Boston College now associated together in professional or business life. In the city of Boston, for instance, in its hospitals, its asylums and its public institutions of all kinds, graduates of these institutions are found working side by side."[141] As O'Brien saw it, between 1880 and 1900 a Catholic-educated professional class had matured, with the potential to share the professional rewards of Ivy League Yankees. The number of degrees awarded at Boston College grew between 1872 and 1923 from 30 to 400 bachelors of arts per year. The ethnic hegemony of the graduates is indicated by the fact that in a total of 3,457 alumni during those 51 years, only about 30 graduates, less than 1 percent, had non-Irish surnames. Occupational listings for these graduates show that the highest percentage became clergymen, clerks, salesmen, teachers, and journalists, respectively. Lawyers and physicians were represented, but the majority of graduates occupied positions of lesser social and economic status.[142]

The Church no doubt exaggerated the successes of Catholic college graduates as propaganda to reinforce claims of Catholic educational superiority. Secular colleges were criticized for permitting "atheistic professors" to make "weaklings of some men intended for nobler spheres of usefulness." Catholics implied that pagan educators would in fact emasculate young men by preventing them from filling "the niche that God intended they should fill" by wasting their time in "striving to solve the problem of class consciousness or the worship of the ego."[143] But once tacit religious and racial quotas and overt anti-Catholic measures had begun to disappear from local colleges, Catholic leaders began to channel their hostility toward the Ivy League universities, because they were the Church's major potential rivals for ambitious Catholic students. Church propaganda notwithstanding, approximately 12 percent of Harvard's total enrollment in 1904 was Catholic.[144] As in the case of parochial schools, Catholic colleges relied on a rhetoric of ethical hauteur to attract students but lost students to public and non-Catholic colleges nonetheless. Father Thomas Gasson, while president of Boston College, made a typical boast that the college surpassed Harvard because of its moral training in ethics and knowledge of natural law: "When I compare my training with that received at Harvard, I find that I reason where they quote; I can use intellectual weapons with more or less ease, while they can only cite the facts of the past. . . . As to moral training, they have received none; all have lost their faith, and each one has a public record which casts a deep shadow over his home."[145] Gasson's righteousness was echoed by an exasperated editorialist in *America*: "And yet, we dare say, there will be infatuated Catholics who will continue to send their children to these [Harvard and Yale] and other similar universities."[146]

The intentions of the clergy and hierarchy appeared to clash with the desires of the laity. In protest against the trend among Catholic students to attend business colleges, Archbishop O'Connell almost surely fabricated the following "Short Dialog Overheard by the Listener" for publication in the *Pilot*: "The whole atmosphere [of non-Catholic schools] is against Faith: the teachings, the talk, the clubs. He lives entirely in it—no antidotes, no moral restraints, no Catholic influences, no Catholic books. The whole trend is away from faith and religion. Do you expect flowers to bloom in winter?"[147] In addition to denigrating secular colleges for their irreligion, churchmen rejected the materialist utilitarianism of business colleges. In 1898 a priest active at several midwestern Jesuit colleges read a paper at the first conference of the Association of Catholic Colleges entitled, "The Catholic College as a Preparation for a Business Career," which upheld the idealist goals of Catholic education: "Collegiate studies should be pursued, not because they form a ready means for money making, but because they elevate the character, ennoble the ideas, secure higher enjoyments to those who are successful, and enable men of culture to exercise a stronger influence on their fellow-men." In a superior tone he suggested that educators (meaning priests like himself) knew better than parents, who "in many cases . . . are far from being competent judges of the studies to which their children should apply themselves."[148] Despite this rhetoric, by the late 1920s, business colleges had the highest enrollments among Catholic professional schools in America.[149]

In offering moral restraints and spiritual uplift to students, Catholic colleges meant to secure lay consensus on the value of Catholic education as a character builder and as a stepping stone to respectability: "To make youth religious and conscientious; to teach the duty of self-control, self-respect, and

Acting out gender switches was standard fare in student dramatics and a regular
feature of more frivolous productions, such as Harvard's Hasty Pudding Club theatricals. Here, a male student as Hecuba in an outdoor performance of Euripides' play
in 1926 at Holy Cross. The freshman class performed in Greek and in English on
the Fitton athletic field. (Holy Cross College Archives)

rational independence; to show the beauty of virtue, the nobility of labor, man's mission to battle and struggle and act through principle and duty; and since character is made up of habits and principles, education is the formation of good habits and inculcation of sound principles."[150] Thus, clerical educators prided themselves on forming young men's characters for the mutual benefit of the entire society, while the economic advantages of diplomas were not lost on the laity. By 1920 Cardinal O'Connell extended the mission of Catholic education from the private subculture to the public sphere. He named the Catholic school as the defender of the rights of individual citizens and as the stronghold of parental influence against the tyranny of the state.[151] As in his defense of Catholic charities against state welfare, O'Connell asserted that Catholic institutions protected individuals against the coercive state at the same time they were training pupils for integration into civil society.

Despite the enormous effort by the Church to establish a lofty spiritual purpose for Catholic education, a split between the Church's attacks on secularism and the practical interests of the laity is evident. Nationwide, first of all, in 1907 two-thirds of all Catholic college students were attending non-Catholic schools. Some products of the Catholic system, such as Dr. James J. Walsh, when asked to describe what Catholic education had meant to them, dutifully pointed out the great traditions of the medieval universities and the moral bent of Catholic education toward "old-fashioned charity."[152] Yet Walsh's view competed with the pragmatic laymen of Boston's Catholic community, who showed increasing interest in linking the business community with Catholic education, thereby making technical training the most desired instrument of career aspirations of the middle class. As Edward McSweeney predicted, "In the coming century one school of technology, and a good textile school in Fall River or Lowell will make more breadwinners than a half-dozen colleges; and one man who learns how to build a locomotive will do more to advance his race than a hundred cooling their heels in a law office."[153] Catholic parents, too, seemed inclined to associate college education with providing trade skills and professional certification for their offspring, somewhat undercutting the purely religious standards and the philosophical and classical curriculum that the hierarchy associated with a Catholic liberal arts education. Furthermore, economic ambitions of Catholic parents seemed to overcome any moral qualms about sending their children to secular schools. Irish Catholics in Boston eagerly took advantage of the opportunities afforded by trade schools and evening schools run by the city. The Church responded in 1910 by sponsoring evening classes for the Young Men's Catholic Association, whose curriculum included accounting, ethics, and philosophy.[154] But even when both public and parochial schools emphasized risk taking and self-help, educators could not overcome parental pressure on Catholic children to take union jobs or to choose the safety of the city payroll.[155] It must be noted that Boston's public and parochial systems were unusually closely entwined because of the ethnoreligious unity provided by Irish Catholic women, who as sisters dominated parochial education and as laywomen constituted 20 percent of the public school teachers, as they did in many large American cities.[156] Public and parochial systems probably encouraged similar outlooks on achievement, which may have been subject to family pressures for job security. The pre–World War I era, when Catholic schools suffered chronic under-enrollments, represents a transition to a period of dramatic gains in students attending Catholic colleges and professional schools that followed both World Wars.

Although a majority of Catholic students did not attend Catholic colleges, middle-class alumni and priests jointly attempted to convince potential students of the unique sacred purpose of Catholic education. The laity, however, mediated this religious idealism with its pragmatic view of higher education as an assimilative tool that provided professional training and expertise. They proposed to include in the general curriculum lectures to college men from captains of industry. In contrast, the clergy and hierarchy seemed more inclined to identify formal education with the unified Christian culture of the Middle Ages. The Catholic middle class had thus begun to make its own interests felt against the dominant priorities of the hierarchy, while still participating in the overall aims of the subculture.

Lay Associations and Fraternalism

The unitive intentions of Catholic higher education were enhanced by laymen's clubs and associations, which imitated the structure and format of secular fraternal orders and service clubs while remaining distinct from them. O'Connell's overhaul of the archdiocese consolidated piecemeal and overlapping parish programs into new structures that superseded the formerly autonomous parish and ethnic neighborhood. The Church supervised clubs for men that emphasized family duties and nurtured Catholic solidarity, but these associations were already beginning to reflect the external influences of "social scientific" approaches to social problems and philanthropy. Catholic orphanages and asylums, for example, began to classify their residents into categories, such as the Children of Preservation, Penitents, and Magdalens of the House of the Good Shepherd. In short, the Catholic Church adopted certain features of the bureaucratized state in order to define differentiated functions for the hierarchy and laity; at the same time it justified the need for a Catholic subculture based on suspicion of those very philosophies of rationalism and efficiency. By rationalized behavior on the part of the Church I mean that it instituted changes, channeled from the hierarchy and clergy to the laity, required to bring about its continued growth and success. The analogy between the rationalization of the behavior of religious institutions and the expansion of capitalism in the American economy becomes apparent when we see how, in both cases, former systems of mutual support among individuals had given way to systems of competition, with the goal of increasing the total supply of services available in the marketplace. The Catholic Church, no longer absorbed with immigrant survival, was now in a position of having to compete with other religious denominations, mainly by providing certain "goods" to its members, namely social services, without losing the communal ethic it had espoused.

Catholic colleges and male social bonding played a central role in forging both class and religious identification and in associating the Church's goals with those of the ethnic middle class. Men's clubs, alumni associations, and business histories demonstrate how the Church and laity cooperated to promote a work ethic that incorporated definitions of Christian manliness and attitudes toward material success that ultimately sustained men's loyalty to the Church. The Church attempted to remain competitive with other religious groups through its network of lay associations whose middle-class leaders were intended to "downwardly diffuse" Catholic values to the working class.[157] Guidelines for correct behavior in the workplace were reinforced through religious rituals and in sermons and pious literature as well as through the meetings and ceremonies of businessmen's clubs. Catholic magazines that often grew out of lay associations helped fashion a work ethic by their advice columns devoted to getting ahead and in interviews with successful Catholics in "People in Print" in *Donahoe's Magazine,* "Seen and Heard in Knightdom" in *Columbiad,* and "In Society and Clubdom," in the *Republic.* Notably, these Irish Catholic journals played down rags-to-riches tales in favor of less spectacular stories emphasizing moderation.

For Catholics who attended college as well as those with little formal education, men's clubs and fraternal organizations both reaffirmed members' economic status and manifested the Church's separatist intentions. While this process of class and sectarian differentiation had already begun in the late nineteenth century, a hierarchy of clubs soon appeared, which acknowledged some as more exclusive than others. Over time, Catholic men's associations served the needs of various social strata: they reflected the presence of an Irishtocracy, fostered the growth of joint business ventures among Catholics, and assisted the petit bourgeois to secure Catholic clients. Society membership brochures, for example, always listed the occupation and Catholic professional associations of members and often advertised special rates for services to fellow Catholics. J. Edward Barry of Cambridge, a Knight of Columbus and New England tourist agent for the Wabash Railroad, was one of many who noted that he would be "pleased to have any brother call on him in regard to rates."[158] By these means, clubs assembled a cohort of Catholic professional and business men who were able to trade career insights, form business part-nerships, and extend the web of social, charitable and cultural ties among Catholics. They produced an alternative system to the economic and cultural imperialism of the Boston Brahmins. Rituals such as Mass and Communion breakfasts for men's clubs confirmed their sacramental distinctiveness without threatening family unity or the communal outlook associated with Catholi-cism. In fact, as the Knights of Columbus magazine hastened to reassure, "the inherent attractiveness of fraternalism is the fact that its central purpose is protection for home and home interests."[159]

Support for family unity became yet another area in which Catholic or-ganizations attempted to reassure the public of their Americanism. The Church's policy of safeguarding the family reflected a broad American con-sensus on the family's importance as the building block of ethical community life. The Church's concern for men to participate more actively in child nur-ture and familial duties suggests that among Catholics, as well as among middle-class Progressives of this era, a form of "male domesticity" flourished for a time. Upward mobility of Catholic men did not exclude the working class from religious societies. Although class differences were present, a wide distribution of interests prevented the middle class from completely suppress-ing proletarian concerns, as did the rhetoric of brotherliness and noncom-petitiveness.[160] On the other hand, the cross-class character of Catholic men's societies discouraged formation of separate working-class institutions and en-couraged a consensus based on middle-class values. The long-term impact of this phenomenon in Massachusetts may have been to inhibit the possibility of working-class unity among Catholics.

The extensive network of Catholic clubs for professional, skilled, and semi-skilled workers served both integrative (economic) and separatist (religious) functions, in the clubs' appeal for a Catholic defense of American idealism. Men's societies can be grouped in four general categories: beneficial societies, of which the Knights of Columbus represents the largest body; social/edu-cational; devotional; and charitable. The Knights of Columbus had been founded in neighboring Connecticut in 1882 to sell affordable life insurance for Catholics, but "with higher motives in view." A Bostonian, Thomas Cum-mings, became its first paid national organizer. In 1902 a Boston chapter opened with about 7,000 members. By 1919 there were 43,015 members in Massachusetts and by 1920, over 47,000, making it the fastest growing state in the nation for the Knights. The Knights were phenomenally successful in expanding to all 50 states, Canada, Mexico, and the Philippines. Prior to 1901 the organization's insurance rates had not been based on actuarial tables of mortality; hence the premiums paid by a member were set at a fixed rate when he joined. A committee to revise this potentially insolvent system determined that a step-rate plan would align the Knights with other commercial companies. The new rates for monthly premiums were scaled to reflect age and actuarial data, with increases every five years rather than at each annual policy renewal. The cost of term insurance ranged from $.70 per month for an eighteen-year-old, to $2.40 for a fifty-nine-year-old.

While the Knights' insurance rates were reconciled to prevailing business practices, their code of Christian manhood derived its language and symbols from feudal chivalry ostensibly represented by Christopher Columbus. The Catholic Church provided the Knights with rituals and symbols that deepened male bonding, already well established through the Irish ancestry shared by nearly all the members. Under the leadership of Edward Hearn of Massachusetts, the Knights established its highest honor in 1899, the Fourth Degree, for members who embodied extraordinary patriotic, religious, and community service. The K of C's history demonstrates the class stratification that quickly accompanied the emergence of a Catholic middle class: the Sir Knights of the Fourth Degree eventually began to meet separately, despite complaints that the costs of its special uniform set up unwelcome class distinctions. For regular members, the Knights continued to shape gentlemanliness and group mission, forging loyalty to the nation and to Christian knighthood. The ideals of knighthood became pragmatically associated with an ardent Americanism (especially in the Fourth Degree), which implied allegiance to the egalitarian economic presumptions of American society rather than to the ancient social hierarchies of Europe. Accordingly, the feudal ceremonies, uniforms, and customs of the Knights were grafted onto capitalist, patriotic propaganda.[161]

Edward Hearn, the supreme knight from 1897 to 1909, responded to the question "Of what advantage to a business man is membership in the Knights of Columbus?" thus: "The idea that a businessman would deliberately join the Knights of Columbus to advance his business interests is not to be entertained, but that our Order has for its object the advancement of the social and business interests of its members is true, for we are a body of Catholic men associated for our common good."[162] In pursuit of their common good, the Knights ran an employment bureau for members and endowed a free bed at Carney Hospital and a scholarship at Boston College. Their programs copied existing philanthropic models just as their rituals mimicked the fraternal orders that were prevalent in late nineteenth-century America. Knights referred to fellow Knights as "brothers," for example. By their upright image and insurance rate revisions, the Knights hoped to establish the reputation of the Catholic elite of Boston as dedicated to sound business principles and managerial expertise and as incomparable fundraisers for Catholic colleges, civic art, and worthy charities. Other beneficial societies included the International Catholic Benevolent Union, the Ancient Order of Hibernians, and the Massachusetts Catholic Order of Foresters, which likewise paid sick and death benefits to members and donated money for service and education.[163]

Only slightly preceding the formation of Catholic beneficial organizations were male social clubs such as the Catholic Union of Boston, incorporated in 1877 with approval of Archbishop Williams, to unite the "elite of the manhood of Boston and vicinity" in loyalty to the pope and the interests of the Church in Boston.[164] The union, from its handsome headquarters on Worcester Square, enrolled about 500 Catholic members during the Gilded Age. By 1910 it could skim its membership from the rolls of the larger Catholic clubs. The union's activities included educational, religious, and charitable projects. Related choices for men included antidrinking societies such as the Catholic Total Abstinence Union, more popular with women and the clergy than with laymen; self-development groups such as the Catholic Reading Circles; and ethnic groups such as the Friendly Sons of St. Patrick and the Society of the Knights of St. Brendan, which promoted interest in Irish history, language, and culture. Like the fraternal society pledgers, these groups proclaimed the values of charity, industry, and communalism. Many later established ladies' auxiliaries. The guiding ethic of these laymen's organizations blended early nineteenth-century American ideologies of the self-made man who triumphed through character and hard work with notions of the twentieth-century bureaucrat and manager who succeeded by acquiring the symbolic capital necessary for success, namely educational training, occupational expertise, and social status.

More religious advice about material success was generated for Catholic men than for women. Clergy and laymen together upheld the doctrine of separate spheres, even in lay societies with mixed membership. In the Catholic Reading Circles, for example, men were exhorted to educate themselves for success, women to increase their piety. The *Reading Circle Manual* asked about successful men, "How did they rise? . . . These men read. Their fund of information was not gathered at the corner grocery, but from the great books of the world."[165] Catholic women, by contrast, were steered toward marriage and motherhood, even though ideologically they represented the culture that reading implied and, numerically, constituted a significant portion of Boston's labor force. Nonetheless, O'Connell customarily warned women, as in his commencement speech at Emmanuel College in 1927: "Do not let your heads be turned by money. . . . Money can do nothing for you but spoil you."[166] Likewise, working-class women were subject to Church paternalism because of their presumed extra vulnerability to sin.[167] By discouraging women from aspirations to wealth or profitable careers, the Church gained their voluntary service as workers in its many charitable and educational institutions. Whereas laymen's societies supported a wage-earning prerogative, women's groups supported the Church's definition of appropriate roles for women as volunteers. Since there were few barriers to female benevolence, it was deemed natural that girls would willingly substitute a life of religious activism for entrepreneurship. When women did have jobs, as did Mary Scanlon of Roxbury, who worked for many years for an accountant, it was reported that "her religion in no way interfered with her business." Intended as advice about how to apply religion in the workplace, Scanlon's obituary made her an example "to young Catholic girls who are now just beginning a business career" because "she was always more mindful of the pleasures and comforts of others than her own."[168]

In its promotion of new lay associations, the Church often joined the rhetoric of the medieval guilds to institutional precedents of the nineteenth century. The religious core underlying the lay societies of the early 1900s prepared the way for the activist lay apostolate that peaked in the 1940s and 1950s. The term *lay apostolate* came into use in the 1930s ostensibly to describe a new role for the laity, while in reality it represented no more than a reactivation of papal and clerical control. The revival of the sodality movement anticipated this phenomenon of lay activism fully two decades prior to the advent of the lay apostolate.

Founded in 1563 by a Jesuit for the spiritual formation of the upper classes of Europe, by the late nineteenth century the sodality was in use as a parish organization for girls and young women. Male participation in sodalities was revived in the early 1900s by an international movement known as the Queen's Work, also the title of its monthly magazine. Led by a Jesuit, a Boston chapter grew and flourished after its establishment there in 1914. Under the direction of Father P. J. Halloran, the Queen's Work supported special filial devotions of members to the Virgin Mary as well as securing pledges from sodalists to defend the Church from hostile criticism.[169] Another national organization popular in Boston was a longtime project of the Dominicans called the Holy Name Society. It was an antiblasphemy league for men, who pledged to avoid swearing or profaning the names of sacred figures. At one point, the Holy Name men literally took to the streets of Boston by posting signs stating, "Profanity is no sign of intelligence." The purely sacramental origins of these devotional associations evolved into units of the subculture aimed at disciplining the individual Catholic and defending the corporate body of the Church.

While few Irish Catholics left personal documents such as diaries discussing the impact of these activities on their piety, their organizational histories relate

Cardinal O'Connell, scowling, at Holy Name Society convention in Baltimore, 1924. Rev. Michael Splaine is at his side. (Archives of the Archdiocese of Boston)

that men felt a sense of solidarity and purpose from belonging, which enhanced their religious pride. The behaviors that sodalities regulated, such as swearing, drinking, and irreligion, were part of the Church's totalizing approach to molding the daily habits of individuals (as did parochial schools) in such a way as to support their upward mobility based on exemplary conduct without jeopardizing their loyalty to Catholicism. We might see Catholic preoccupation with regulating the human body in its smallest details, such as posture, gestures, speech, and dress, as symbols of the Church's role in rendering the body invulnerable to loss of control and in giving its members the necessary attributes for social mobility by instilling socially acceptable habits. In a larger context, each individual body represented the integrity of the Church's corporate body, and each rule of manners and discipline became part of the middle class's identification of propriety with pleasure.

Like the lay organizations, even individual pious practices such as prayer and meditation became institutionalized. Group retreats emerged, devoted to traditional exploration of the interior spiritual life, now conducted with a group of individuals of the same social status. In Boston, this process led to establishment of the laymen's retreat leagues, such as those run by the Passionist Fathers at Saint Gabriel's Monastery, Brighton.[170] The Passionists came to Boston in 1905 at the invitation of the archdiocese and offered their first laymen's group retreat in 1911. Businessmen especially were encouraged, in metaphors appropriate to their work, to take spiritual inventory of themselves. Groups of forty could attend the contemplative retreats from Friday evening to Monday morning and, without missing any workdays, retire from "the hurly-burly of everyday struggle" to reflect upon their sins.[171] Saturdays and Sundays were devoted to prayer, spiritual reading, recreation, and "heart to heart talks" on the "dangers of the world with its alluring pleasures, its enticing riches, its empty honors."[172] The retreat director suggested that reflection on the suffering and solitude of Christ would fire men's souls to go forth in battle "against that malignant enemy, Materialism." In 1927 the popularity of these retreats warranted building a separate retreat house on the monastery grounds. According to reports, many retreatants willingly followed the monastic schedule of the Passionists, rising at 2 A.M. for matins. "This," according to O'Connell, "is the regime that makes men." The adaptation of monastic practice and values to lay work schedules typified the Church's method of training laymen to combat materialism, fortified by contemplating the suffering Savior. Catholic manhood was to be formed according to standards of semimonastic self-discipline and holy suffering, nonetheless responsive to the time demands of the workweek.

A final type of laymen's society was the charitable institution, the majority of which were founded as protection for the first wave of poor, unskilled Catholic immigrants to Boston. By the early twentieth century, the best-known and largest of these was the St. Vincent de Paul Society. Established in Boston in 1861, it had 61 parish conferences in 1910 and 115 in 1923, a remarkable increase of nearly 90 percent in 13 years. Originally a parish institution dedicated to caring for abandoned children, in the 1880s the society had expanded its work to include the instruction of Catholic children in charitable and penal institutions, establishment of employment bureaus, placement of Catholic children in suitable foster homes, and after 1895, special work with immigrants, paid for by the Charitable Irish Society.[173] As happened with many lay charitable groups, the lay autonomy of the Vincentians declined when it was subsumed into the clergy-dominated CCB in 1910. By that time, however, significant problems stemming from its aging membership, dwindling leadership, and the temperance orientation of the society had limited the Vincentians' ability to reach the poor. The emergence of wealthier Catholic enclaves and suburban parishes also took its toll on charity conducted by door-to-door visitation in downtown Boston.[174]

The Church's rejection of the theory of class conflict was mirrored in the attempts of men's clubs to teach notions of Christian manliness that transcended class distinctions. Through their sermons and speeches, priests who served as spiritual directors and chaplains taught spiritual and economic principles that combined paternalism, self-help, and charity. The clergy encouraged men to apply their talents and income to philanthropy, which helped build character, as well as calling upon them to acquire the "four keys to success"—ambition, industry, intelligence, and integrity.[175] As revenue-generating entities, Catholic men's associations sold insurance and sick benefits; funded burials; sponsored relief to paupers, orphans, widows, and immigrants; raised funds for church charities; and sponsored philanthropic projects such as college scholarships. Their social events, dances, minstrel shows, theatricals, and spiritual retreats absorbed the leisure time of professionals, businessmen, the labor aristocracy, and wage workers. In sum, they provided the Catholic subculture with access to social improvement. As they regulated the economic and social lives of men and families, Catholic voluntary associations also pointed toward religion as the ultimate source of human identity.

Catholic men of this generation were encouraged to be club joiners, to acquire habits of social duty and of charitable giving. The Church strongly disapproved of the laity using wealth as an end in itself. "Unfortunately there are many disloyal Catholics," commented a priest in O'Connell's inner circle, "who are willing to enjoy whatever benefits the name of Catholic can bring them, but who for convenience and self-interest put aside the duties and responsibilities of a Catholic."[176] The withering critique of social climbers who shirked their duty to the Church's institutional interests did not stop laymen from joining non-Catholic organizations, just as clergy criticism of atheism could not stem the tide of students entering secular universities. Mayor John Fitzgerald, for example, was initiated as an Elk in 1907, and Catholic publisher Daniel Toomey was a member as well.[177] Since the Church did not strictly forbid its laymen from joining secular associations, it often opted for hopeful resignation. For example, at Daniel Toomey's funeral Father Bogan stated delicately that "to the societies not necessarily claiming membership within the Faith he brought the wealth of his moral worth that showed itself not more in his loyalty to their constitutions than in his devotion to the intimate interests of the individual members."[178] The mere fact of Catholic membership in the Ancient Order United Workmen, Odd Fellows, and Elks suggests that laymen did not make choices according to a religious bias, despite admonitions from the hierarchy and clergy. Yet laymen expressed the same outsider anxieties as the clergy in their defense of Catholic organizations against attacks in the secular press. The Knights of Columbus responded forcefully to the vicious anti-Catholicism, for example, that appeared in Upton Sinclair's *The Profits of Religion* in 1918. Conversely, journalists who reported favorably on Catholic societies, like Henry Hyde of the *Chicago Tribune,* who characterized the Knights as "greater Philanthropists than Rockefeller," were widely reprinted in Catholic newspapers and magazines.[179]

In evaluating those lay groups that functioned as part of a religious system of separatist integration, we find that Catholic voluntary associations helped the Church impose a unified morality on all social classes, utilizing the middle class as a model of virtuous industry and as the charitable agent for the working class. The devotional core and sacramental rituals of laymen's associations enhanced spiritual bonds among the expanding Irish Catholic business community. Simultaneously, they offered essential employment and educational and language services for the working class and more recent immigrants. Those societies that were primarily charitable were, over time, subjected to the centralizing pressures of O'Connell's administration, suggesting that lay initiatives were always regarded by the Church as supplemental efforts to those of the clergy.

A Catholic Critique of Individualism

A Catholic critique of individualism has only haltingly emerged in the twentieth century. Liberal observers claim that it is a logical extension of a coherent corpus of Catholic social teaching; conservatives interpret social Catholicism as a way to preserve social order without making any demands for radical change in political and economic structures. In Boston the Church's animus against secularism reflected Catholicism's conflicted attitude toward individualism. As Catholic entrepreneurs and professionals established themselves, the Church gave a two-tiered message of thrift and honesty for the working man and moderate living based on stewardship of the poor for the successful one. Archbishop O'Connell agreed that "the growth of industry is a blessing," but he also maintained that "there must be a higher ideal than the mill or a commercial industry" and "something more than material prosperity and the home," by which he meant the Church and its principles.[180]

Boston Catholicism's relationship with acquisitive capitalism and the so-called Protestant work ethic remained logically unstable because the Church simultaneously attacked and defended individualism. The Church had condemned the excesses of both collectivism and economic individualism but had muted its criticisms of capitalism for the reasons demonstrated above. Further, the Church's promotion of preindustrial communalism was altogether different from the cooperative commonwealth sought by contemporary populists and socialists. What the Church called its third way between socialism and capitalism represented in fact its gradual accommodation to neoclassical economics. According to Church leaders, selfish individualism produced contempt for authority, custom, and tradition. The middle class was admonished, therefore, to find a divine purpose in economics and to moderate their personal demands. Some Catholic laymen obliged: "How can labor be made happy?" asked James Carroll, president of the Industrial Accident Board of Massachusetts. "Not the selfish and narrow philosophy of individualism and liberalism, nor the airship philosophy of socialism. . . . In other words, if we would hope to succeed, God must reign not merely in the world of nature where He directs the rise and fall of the tides, but in the world of industry, where He directs the actions and hopes of men."[181] Thus mindful of a supernatural benign "invisible hand" directing industry, successful Catholics were also expected to seek the common good. When this meant sizable financial contributions to the Church, individuals were rewarded with papal honors. When this led to plans to re-Christianize the professions, Catholics revived the idea of guild organizations to "offer some sort of a remedy to the paganism of the times."[182]

The Church's fear of betrayal (by the rich) and of violence (by the poor) was revealed through its strategies of class containment, even while it claimed that classes did not really exist. Nonetheless, middle-class associations such as the AFCS were formed precisely to protect America from "the vices of wealth and the violence to which evil leaders try to stimulate poor wage-earners."[183] The devout entrepreneur or professional who belonged to Catholic clubs supporting professional development absorbed the Catholic work ethic and, implicitly, the Church's compliance with capitalism. By the beginning of World War I, Cardinal O'Connell felt confident that Catholic anti-socialist programs among the working class had prevented a crisis in the social order, arguing that "in this city the Catholic Church is doing a wonderful work for moral order. Is it appreciated? How long would order exist without the Church? Look at Europe. It is not the loss of the home and the mills that is tearing the hearts of the people so much as it is the destruction of the beautiful churches raised by enormous sacrifices."[184]

The Church's position on material opportunities and individualism sheds light on the broader phenomenon of its vacillation regarding liberalism. In 1900, social Catholicism was caught between its traditional rejection of classical liberalism (defined by limited government, laissez-faire economics, and maximum individual freedom) and its accommodation to the progressive liberalism of the late nineteenth century, which allowed government a right and even a duty to intervene in the economic and social life of a nation.[185] Lacking the feudal aristocratic heritage that led the European Catholic leaders to oppose republican governments, labor unions, and anticlericalists, American Catholic Church leaders nonetheless fell back upon a paternalist and organicist model of feudal social relations, as seen in their rejection of secularization, materialist philosophy, positivism, and class strife. This may in part have been a result of a worldwide attempt by the papacy to deprive bishops of their autonomy and render them Vatican functionaries.

The postwar era brought dramatic changes in the character of American philanthropy and of Catholic social reform. Cardinal O'Connell expressed the view of many religious leaders that the war itself was proof of the barbarism caused by irreligion. But he was not a fan of the postwar passion for centralization and bureaucratization in government and the proliferation of state and federal commissions, "each one of which means a restriction upon the sphere of independent individual activity."[186] In addition to what he saw as encroaching Bolshevism, O'Connell disapproved of the changes in American philanthropy that linked large-scale giving more closely to American corporations as they began to receive tax breaks for corporate contributions.[187] He began to fear that, consequently, poor relief and Americanization programs affecting immigrants would fall into the hands of Protestants or the encroaching state, who would come to manipulate the Catholic poor. O'Connell confided to the St. Vincent de Paul Society in 1922 that the apathy of wealthy Catholics exacerbated this trend: "To tell the truth, it is universally acknowledged and deplored that most of our Catholics of wealth do practically nothing for anything or anybody but themselves. Their Protestant neighbors might well teach them a lesson. There are comparatively few wealthy Protestants who do as little in these matters as the great majority of our wealthy Catholics. . . . The rich Protestants and the poor Catholics seem to be blood-brothers in generosity and charity. Bolshevism can never grow out of that relationship."[188] A Catholic work ethic, therefore, applauded individual industry and perseverance, but never at the expense of the common good. Accordingly members of Catholic professional associations were encouraged to advance communal rather than private business interests. While it is hard to draw precise conclusions about the impact of Catholic doctrines about work and success on the lay community in this era, some speculations emerge, following recent scholarly interpretations of Catholic integration in politics, education, and labor.

Archbishop O'Connell presented himself as a bulwark against Yankee bigotry. His plea for Catholics to be "patriotic not political" alternated with his insistence that "the child of the immigrant is called to fill the place which the Puritan has left."[189] He thus implied that Catholics were not only loyal Americans but were taking control. To avoid Protestant charges of a Catholic conspiracy, he "strictly prohibited" diocesan priests from mixing in politics and stated that the bishop alone had the responsibility to speak for the religious rights of Catholics.[190] Whereas he believed priests' political remarks would be "distorted to merely partisan ends," he also felt that politics could polarize

Catholic lay organizations and lead to accusations that the Church resembled New York's Tammany Hall: "We want no machine tactics. . . . We have no favors to ask; we shall not go to city hall or Beacon Hill with cringing petitions."[191] Concerning his own role in politics, he reassured Catholic elected officials that he would not meddle in their work, though he was not a stranger to pressure strategies. By dissociating Catholicism from the corrupt machines and from party endorsements, O'Connell hoped to assure Protestants that Catholic religious orders and lay societies would not align themselves with political parties and that private Catholic schools would not undermine democratic principles. But within the Catholic community he was also furnishing a way to protect Catholic manhood from impure associations with machine politics and from secular schooling.

Stephen Erie has suggested that the Irish political spoils system hampered Irish integration by putting a low ceiling on advancement and that the lure of financial security kept men in low status civil service jobs.[192] Presumably, a "preoccupation with security" prevented Irish Americans as a unit from reaching higher levels and greater diversity of white-collar occupations. Despite the presence of an Irish radical political and labor minority in parts of the United States, revisionist historians like Erie and pluralist historians both agree that the Irish urban machines retarded the development of labor parties in America by providing many services independently of unions, but from within the parameters of an existing political party. Further, the Irish machines helped individual politicians and contractors but did not advance the Irish as a group, as Rose Fitzgerald Kennedy herself has noted from firsthand knowledge of her father. Hence, some Irish Americans made mistakes with long-term consequences by relying too heavily on "boodle" and by opting for secure jobs in the public sector that were ultimately dead ends. Individuals like Joseph Kennedy succeeded by their thoroughly ruthless approach to capitalism and competition, not by their piety or communal spirit. To some degree political machines reflected Catholic religious identity because they duplicated the conservative outlook held by its elite patrons, and they were, like the Church, forms of sectarian institutions. Like the Church, machines angled for financial security that could purchase the good life as defined by capitalism. In obvious contrast to the Church's advocacy of the common good, however, the greed and graft of individual politicians undermined the public reputation of Irish Catholics. However, as the ward bosses expanded their influence in the twentieth century, the spoils system fostered a kind of "mass conservatism" that coincided with both the Church's moral puritanism and the social attitudes of the Catholic bourgeoisie.

4 | THE FUNCTIONS OF CATHOLIC ARCHITECTURE

Catholic art must have its roots deep in the past, though there need
be much trimming of its dead branches.—Charles Maginnis, "The
Movement for a Vital Christian Architecture"

The Middle Ages are a load which we have no disposition to carry.
—Orestes Brownson, "The Church in the Dark Ages"

And why this strange resurrection of Catholic art and architecture in
non-Catholic temples and in our public buildings?—William
O'Connell, "The Knights' Work"

It is no less than Christian civilization we have to restore, and we
may find one road to our goal by the way of a Christianized art that
leads us to beauty, that in its turn serves as one of the channels of the
grace of God. So there is no unreason in our effort to build Gothic
churches today, for this particular art we try to recover is the title-
deed to our inheritance. Every stone that we cut and lay, however
clumsily and by inadequate modern methods, is so much added to
the new fabric of a restored civilization.—Ralph Adams Cram,
"Restore Civilization through Art"

A Catholic Antiurban Tradition

Just as a daily newspaper derives its existence from the presence
of a city, so was the archdiocese of Boston defined by an urban core. By the
1920s, more than half of American Catholics lived in cities, and yet the
Church had become critical of urban life.[1] Catholic hostility toward the modern city encompassed traditional fears about poverty and criminality as well
as the topics of overcrowded, high-density tenement housing and ghetto land-
lessness. These concerns reflected several roots within Catholicism, among
them papal-inspired concern for the urban poor expressed in the social encyclicals, and Church-inspired nostalgia for the communal medieval village.
Social transformations outside religion also affected Catholicism: the upward
mobility of Catholics led to suburban enclaves that contrasted with the living
conditions of a large Catholic urban underclass in the metropolis.

In Boston, Catholic immigrants had little choice about where they lived,
and the bulk of the Irish Catholic working class remained urban, ghettoized,
and propertyless from the initial famine generation of 1845 through the
1920s. Perhaps because of the lack of an urban tradition in Ireland, most
immigrants to the United States found that city living required major psychic

and cultural adjustments. By about 1900, it was the strategy of upwardly mobile Catholics to escape the center city for the suburbs springing up around the new streetcar lines in Roxbury, Dorchester, Jamaica Plain, Brookline, and Newton, epitomized by the purchase of a single-family house. As Sam Bass Warner had concluded in his study of Boston's suburbs: "Above all else the streetcar suburbs stand as a monument to a society which wished to keep the rewards of capitalist competition open to all its citizens. Despite ignorance and prejudice, during this period of mass immigration, the suburbs remained open to all who could meet the price."[2] That price, namely the ability to buy a house, represented the pinnacle of success and pervaded contemporary Irish American novels as the dominant metaphor for achievement. Home ownership and title to a plot of ground itself promoted conservative attitudes, since it was dependent upon considerable planning and initiative by the purchaser, in addition to being an expression of his class status. The nesting instinct was evident also among Catholic lay societies, as in the Knights of Columbus's "permanent home" campaign, a national fund drive begun in 1910 to house all local chapters in their own buildings.

With Boston's emerging suburbs and rail system acting as an escape valve to diffuse religious and ethnic tensions somewhat, the growth of the Catholic middle class and the process of suburban retreat meant that class and geography began to distance more affluent Catholics from direct contact with urban poverty. The suburbs created new possibilities for Catholics, which in turn led the Church to fear a declining interest among the affluent to assume responsibility for the poor, except through parish tithing and periodic special collections at Mass. Therefore the benefits of Catholic middle-class respectability were offset by a potential loss of financial aid to the needy. Suburban life may have been promoted as a way to foster togetherness of the nuclear family by preserving it from urban evils, but it may have challenged and even contradicted Catholic rhetoric about the importance of community.

The Church responded to this social stratification by calling on rich and poor alike to acknowledge the virtue of Christian organicism and the noncompetitive paternalist relations of preindustrial society. Rather than developing economic critiques of the structures causing urban problems, the Church continued to practice its individualized forms of poor relief. Ministering to persons and families on a case-by-case basis, Catholics condemned radical reformers and statist centralizers for seeking to overthrow the harmony of organic society. Catholics located the causes of material and spiritual squalor in human sinfulness resulting from materialism and hedonism bred in the cities. This connection between virtue and rural life perhaps explains an investigative article on pauper children in *Donahoe's Magazine* of 1903. Illustrated with photographs of pathetic children who had become wards of the state, the report is concluded with a line drawing of what is obviously a white-washed, thatch-roofed Irish country cottage. Catholic distaste for the modern city implied a nostalgia for medieval Europe that might have seemed anachronistic to American values, yet it corresponded closely enough with the Jeffersonian pastoral ideology of American republicanism. Indeed, Catholic fascination with a "rural myth," as Jay Dolan has called it, had led the Church to numerous ill-fated rural colonization projects in the 1880s.[3]

Because the United States lacked a medieval past, it may seem surprising that American Catholics turned to the Middle Ages for inspiration. Nonetheless, it seems the dominant factor behind popularized medievalism was its nostalgia for an "imagined community." As the late Raymond Williams has noted, "The only sure fact about the organic society . . . is that it has always gone."[4] As a Catholic middle class strove to represent itself as a model citizenry, the rhetoric of Jeffersonian individualism—America's equivalent of feudal pastoralism—converged with Catholic medievalism. This was well illustrated by a Boston *Pilot* editorial about how the modern city reflected both the "materialism and confusion of American life" and man's loss of "the charms of individual life, and a house of his own, air sunlight and green grass."[5]

Regret about the loss of community, property, and the virtue that Jefferson had associated with debtlessness pervaded many of Cardinal O'Connell's speeches, notably an address to the Knights of Columbus in 1912 called "The Country Boy."[6] In it, O'Connell described the city's malevolent power to corrupt, to alter value systems, to make "purely accidental" differences seem "essential." In the city's demoralizing atmosphere, youth lost its rural innocence and became "the victim of the vulgar materialism of the city atmosphere, in which the talk is only money and the language is dollar signs. It would be a miracle if something of this innovating, enervating germ did not get into his moral system and rob him of its honest manliness." In addition to these striking images of the city as contagion and disease, O'Connell claimed that American cities would be even worse if they did not constantly recruit strong-hearted men and women "from the sturdy homes of the country," whose earnest labor made the city prosper. Perhaps identifying himself with the upright "rural town" boy, the archbishop speculated: "The chase for silly social pleasures, the ceaseless haunting of the theater and ballroom sap unconsciously the sturdiness of a boy's character. . . . The boy of the small center of the rural town is spared much of this. And as a consequence, he retains greater powers of concentration, greater resistance to fatigue, a clearer head to plan, and a steadier hand to accomplish. The city too often destroys,—the country has the secret of building up."

O'Connell's pastoral reveries were not unique, and in fact constituted part of a recognizable antiurban tradition among American bishops, activated by John Spalding, bishop of Peoria, Illinois. Spalding's negative views of urban life stemmed from his pastorate in the 1870s in New York City and his role as cofounder of the unsuccessful Irish Catholic Colonization Society (1879–1884).[7] Four decades later, Massachusetts priest Michael Earls, ordained in 1912, described the occasions of his annual Jesuit retreats as a "fine distance from all the cheap things of the city—and so near to a ground that reflects our Lord's Heaven."[8] O'Connell's speeches and sermons echoed this antiurban tradition that linked the nineteenth and twentieth centuries, even though most of his flock had always been nonagricultural, landless city-dwellers. He also seemed to ignore the undeniable fact that the direction of Catholic migration was not of poor farmers to Boston but of successful Catholics hoping to flee the city's aggravations, not for farms, but for suburbs, an entity still undefined. Nonetheless, O'Connell persisted in preaching a gospel of rural goodness that justified Catholic antimodernism: "The backbone of the Church is not that portion of her children who have been bitten by the contagion of vulgar show and silly ambitions for a semi-pagan social life. It is the sturdy home life of the simple, God-loving people such as our fathers, whether in heart or in distance from the artificial standards which too often constitute the city atmosphere and environments." O'Connell led the clergy in a conservative crusade to cultivate orderly habits and moral behavior among the urban laity based on rural virtues, which he believed were achieved in the Middle Ages through the organic unity of art, architecture, and the leadership of the parish priest. By striving to restore medieval organicism to the city, Catholics presumably could conquer the "contagion of a thousand sophistries" associated with urban capitalism, and the even more dangerous individual sins of "pride of life and the corruption of luxury."[9] In doing so, O'Connell reiterated, without being dogmatic about it, the pervasive anti-industrial themes of the neo-Gothicists, who argued that "strength comes from the earth, weakness from the machine."[10]

The religious focal point in the urban Catholic experience was the parish, which represented a miniature form of the medieval pastoral world by creating an enclosed haven from the city streets. Surprisingly, there has been little research on the modern parish as a focus of Catholic lay experience and as a visual, geographical, or spiritual center until recently, when a growing body of quantitative and social historical studies have addressed it as a distinct topic in Catholic scholarship.[11] We can imagine an inclusive definition of sacred space here, because the collection of buildings that comprise a parish is not limited to the church itself.

Catholic parishes served a local community, provided dozens of social and charitable services, and remained to a large degree the focus and initiator of these activities. In Boston, as in all Catholic dioceses, the parish administered the sacraments and presided over feast days, provided poor relief, and hosted plays, picnics, games, bazaars, dances, and dinners that encompassed the ritual cycle of birth, courtship, marriage, child rearing, death, and burial. Its cluster of church, rectory, convent, school, and meeting halls was relatively unchanged since the Middle Ages. These buildings hosted both spiritual and social activities that allowed the Catholic parish to function both as a mini-city and as a macro-family. In the early 1900s even a biased Yankee sociologist noted in his studies of Boston neighborhoods how the Catholic parish was instrumental in "neighborhood and nation-building" by creating close-knit communities and organizing activities in a tangible place for shared intangible goals.[12]

As Boston's hundreds of thousands of Catholics worshiped in their Gothic, Norman, Romanesque, and even Spanish Mission style churches, they remained spatially and emotionally close to their relatives and friends, which permitted parochial and neighborhood affiliation to complement their sense of connection to the universal Church. As interpreted by Cardinal O'Connell, "Mere material prosperity is inadequate. Busy shops and fine houses and all the comforts of life do not satisfy. And that is why the Catholic people take such delight in building churches."[13] His first decade as archbishop marked a peak in Catholic parish involvement and growth, despite the Catholic press's monotonous alarms to the contrary about the bane of secularization. Diocesan priests were obliged to keep hectic schedules in order to stir up competition between the parish lay associations, as attested in a note from Father Anderson to O'Connell: "You will excuse this hastily written letter as I am going crazy over the charities and the Bazaar. However everything is forming. Both meetings of the ladies at the Somerset [Hotel] and the men yesterday at the Lenox were great successes and the indications are most favorable and encouraging. I have the Hibernians, Foresters and the Knights also stirred up and the rivalry to outdo each other is beginning already to manifest itself."[14]

Through their extrasacramental activities, such as dances, dinners, bingo, and bazaars, Catholic parishes helped Americanize Catholics. Further, the parish represented a macro-family, within which the family unit served as a mini-church, giving parents authority analogous to that of the clergy. As we have seen, the Church's defensive posture toward anything that appeared to threaten family integrity further contributed to Catholic antiurbanism. While immigrant historians have claimed that the family unit was emphasized more among Italian, Slovak, and Polish Catholics than among the Irish, the Irish family nonetheless doubled as a model for ecclesiology and for political cliques in Boston. The parish and the family, led by authoritarian Irish American priests and fathers, had equivalents in the ward and the spoils system, where

Irish ward bosses and mayors operated as though dispensing favors to favorite obedient children.[15] Catholic lay elites nonetheless found themselves poised between two choices: proving Catholicism compatible with American democratic principles or risking association with left-wing and unassimilated immigrants who were suspected of undermining the American way of life. The Church's outlook on the city, therefore, and its involvement in the daily life of Boston became a crucial test of the ability of the Church to preserve future generations of Catholics from encroaching secularism and from the errors of both partisan machines and political radicalism that threatened images of Catholic patriotism.

What relationship existed between the urban parish as a physical space and the Catholic Church's defenses of pastoralism and medievalism? It was the Church, after all, that elided these two distinct discourses of geography and theology in its use of medieval Christianity to represent the image of a harmonious social ideal against the corruptions of the urban environment. Nationally, though, aside from one book by a layman, American Catholics contributed little to the passion for medievalism that had swept up Episcopalians and the high-church wings of other Protestant denominations.[16] This neo-Gothic revival represented a third and final phase of Gothicism in America, ended by the 1929 stock market crash and Great Depression. It was led by upper middle-class WASPs such as Henry Adams and was particularly associated with Anglo-Catholics such as Ralph Adams Cram. Architects and artists foregrounded the iconography, arts, and organic unity of the medieval Christian world, while the Gothic revival inspired some utopian romantics to attempt to apply them to the environment of urban industrial America. The "discovery" of social problems and of scientific social engineering during this era were likewise coopted to produce utopian plans for redesigning model cities rooted in localized craftsmen's guilds. American Catholics, rather than ridiculing Protestants' escapism as a symptom of an identity crisis, pointed to these trends as signs of the revitalization of Catholic ideals against ebbing Protestantism and bankrupt secularism. Few Catholics were as blunt as John Talbot Smith, however, in noting the woeful inadequacies of seminaries in preparing priests for the "kaleidoscopic misery of the metropolis": "The student should be prepared for the work, should study methods, read the special books on the subject, and learn what he has to face. It will take from his confidence to read such a book as Riis' 'How the Other Half Lives.'"[17]

The urban parish, therefore, assigned a social function to church architecture and design, in addition to its sacred role. At the heart of the parish was the church building itself, whose design style symbolized political as well as theological attachments. Although architecture is a static art, it does depend on the active engagement of its users and viewers to grasp, even unconsciously, its meaning. The theories and designs of Boston's Catholic architects can be viewed in part as an apologetic, an aesthetic, and a social critique of urbanism.

Architecture as Apologetic

The phenomenon of Catholic antimodernism, especially its nostalgia for feudal, Christian Europe, established a triangular relationship between the Catholic hierarchy, the liturgical arts, and a lay elite. Despite the fact that American Church leaders were sponsoring efforts to promote Catholic integration, they also criticized modern culture based on their preference for hierarchical social relations within a feudal economic model that was pastoral, production oriented, and village centered. The major virtue of the Middle Ages, from the Church's viewpoint, was the naturalness of its social entities—families, villages, and craft guilds—superior to the atomized environment of the modern city, the "artificiality" of social classes, and the encroachments of the centralized, bureaucratic state. It was a simple step for the Church to associate its medieval past with the discipline of architecture not only because of architecture's significance in translating God's creation into church building and decoration, but also because a particular aesthetic—Gothic—could be used to convey the link between Catholicism and social conservatism.

As architecture became a more regulated and specialized occupation, precisely to distinguish itself as a form of high culture, the rising Modernist movement also reflected the concern of architects to protect style itself from the taint of mass production. Thus, reactionary elements often underlay modernist architecture, articulated by non-Catholics such as Louis Sullivan and his student Frank Lloyd Wright, who espoused a kind of neofeudalism. Gothic residues can be seen primarily in their idiosyncratic forms of applied decoration, which ran counter to their stated intention to eliminate superfluity in design.[18] At the moment of American architecture's transition to modernist style, church architecture, which by its very nature is not a popular art, exhibited affinities to high modernism's determination to remain aloof from the crassness of mass-produced objects and from mass culture. In a parallel fashion, the profession of architecture became more exclusive. Since the process of becoming an architect involved an advanced level of social certification, those Catholics who were actually trained as architects prior to about 1930 represented an extremely small percentage of the lay population. The anonymity of the teams of craftsmen who erected the medieval cathedrals had given way by 1910 to an array of specialists: architect, engineer, landscape architect, interior designer, carpenter, and so forth. The vast majority of the professional cohort of Catholic architects in Boston, predictably, came from Irish backgrounds.

Given the Brahmin pedigrees of Bostonians who traditionally had become architects, the arrival of Roman Catholics to the profession represented an ethnic, if not class, change. A modus vivendi was achieved between Catholic architects and the Church hierarchy: architects prospered because of Church commissions and patronage, thereby circumventing social obstacles to gaining clients in the polarized society of New England. In return, the Church benefited from the construction of structures—churches, convents, schools, hospitals, and monasteries—which furnished its "cultural capital" in Boston. Catholic architects might therefore be seen as allies in the Church's aggressive policy of separatist integration. Catholic lay professionals perhaps recognized this situation as necessary because it helped them to overcome obstacles to their professional development and upward mobility. By exploring relationships between the Catholic Church's view of church building and the urban environment, and by studying discussions among Catholics about what churches ought to be and do, we realize three things: First, the architect, as a lay patrician, served the institutional Church's strategy of antimodernism and cultural triumphalism. Second, the Catholic Church played a unique but not monolithic role in the aesthetic debates over neo-Gothicism. Finally, the mere presence of Catholic architects demonstrated the class fissures that complicated Catholic social mobility into the Yankee elite. As Catholic architects delineated themselves from a lower strata of builders, and from the new professional class of civil engineers, they contributed to Catholic middle-class integration.

In ecclesiastical architecture, traditionalism and triumphalism governed the outlook of the archbishop. O'Connell was keenly aware of the constant physical reminder of Boston's many Protestant and Unitarian churches and hoped that Catholics, too, would command the urban environment "from pinnacle to pavement."[19] Nonetheless, he never mandated Gothic as the only acceptable style for archdiocesan buildings. Rather, O'Connell claimed that he would approve construction projects based on their quality rather than their quantity. Yet he could barely conceal his pride in the rising numbers of new Catholic structures: "Nearly every hilltop is now crowned with a new architectural glory,—Boston College, the Passionist Monastery, the Cenacle Convent,—all proclaim life, energy, and unceasing activity, and there are others yet to come."[20] When he was under Vatican investigation in the early 1920s, O'Connell pointed to his architectural contributions as one defense against his opponents that was perhaps irrefutable: after completing a survey of his accomplishments, he presented the Vatican with an impressive tally of "eighty-one new parishes, 25 missions, two colleges, two retreat houses, all debt-free."[21] Nothing succeeds like success, he grandly implied.

In addition to the archbishop's use of the built environment to aggrandize or defend his reputation, architects, mayors, and city managers found economic opportunities in Boston's expanding commercial and ecclesiastical architecture. As Boston's limits pressed outward to form a sprawling metropolitan area, planners and designers found a market for Catholic churches and schools that corresponded to O'Connell's desire for growth. Yankee architects had enjoyed a long monopoly over church building, but as a Catholic professional class emerged, so did an equivalent market. Though the Catholic hierarchy and clergy severely criticized the moral bankruptcy of most forms of popular culture, the Church continued to assign great moral weight to the literary arts and to architecture.[22] In fact, in the original edition of the *Catholic Encyclopedia* (1907), the one-line entry for "Architecture" states, "see Christian Architecture."

Christian architectural design was an apt medium for the Church's aesthetic idealism and elitism. The practice of architecture represented the opportunity to draw inspiration from the physical world to construct an ideal world and to unite the via contemplativa with the via activa. Bishop Spalding of Peoria, who, despite his antiurbanism, was among the most liberal and popular of the episcopal contemporaries of Archbishop O'Connell, expressed an unbreakable correspondence between the real and the ideal in his preface to a book on Christian art: "Art, like religion, looks not so much at what is, as at what should be. It draws its inspiration from a world of ideals, because it can discover nothing in the real world which is in complete harmony with its dream of beauty."[23] Gothic enthusiast Ralph Adams Cram proclaimed a similar theme: "Beauty must be linked again with life, and art given back its true service. I know of no place where this can better begin than in the case of religion."[24] Thus, Catholic architects, who shared some of the intellectual and spiritual stirrings of Protestant churchmen and artists, saw themselves pursuing a restorationist aesthetic, majestically indifferent to the innovations of the avant-garde emerging in the plastic arts, while sharing the distaste of high modernism for mass culture. In many ways, Catholic aesthetics duplicated the conservative bias of the architectural academy against radical change. In other ways, it was decidedly opposed to the modernists. In resisting the surrender of the urban skyline to modernist skyscrapers and unadorned boxes, the Church preferred architectural ideals that valued the past. The neo-Gothicists thus dissociated themselves from modernism, as in Cram's remark that "the modernist style used of late, and most unaccountably, for certain Catholic churches in France, and sporadically in the United States, must absolutely be eschewed."[25]

Yet the major problem facing potential Catholic architects was social and class bias rather than aesthetic difference. Catholics remained largely excluded from the architecture schools and accrediting institutions and had to overcome formidable obstacles in order to break into the profession of architecture. It was only since 1867 that MIT began the first four-year architecture curriculum in the nation and that the Boston Society of Architects was founded. In the preceding decades, an architect functioned mostly as a "purveyor of taste" in residential construction for his clients, learning technical drafting by apprenticeship, and practical experience by informal means.[26] By the turn of the century, however, the architectural profession was erecting social and educational barriers to distinguish gentlemen-architects from mere speculative builders. The influence of European building styles and the importance of European travel as a direct source of knowledge of historical styles began to be felt, along with certain religious overtones. Architecture schools pictured themselves as molding ministers for the moral mission of architecture in the new century. In 1899 the *Architectural Review* declared, for example, that the architect was rapidly becoming "in the eyes of the public both a censor of what we may call 'aesthetic morals' and also a kind of public instructor therein."[27] That combination of didacticism and moral authority appealed to a Catholic sensitivity toward keeping religion in the public realm. Through their church designs, Catholic builders were charged with being vital, visionary, and virtuous. In philosophic terms, they hoped to embody a Catholic aesthetic, uniting the human seer, who remains transfixed by the ultimate dream of beauty, with the doer, who helps realize it. In pragmatic terms, lay Catholics needed to find ways to enter the professional schools and get academic certification from this bastion of the WASP elite or else remain contented with the technical and construction jobs associated with mere tradesmen, builders, and architecture book copyists.

Articulation of a Catholic aesthetic surfaced by the late 1890s, stimulated by the growth of a professional class. Expression of an aggressive Catholic presence in Boston through architecture was aided by the expansion of Catholic education, which provided architects not only with college degrees in preparation for advanced training but also with steady commissions to build Catholic schools and colleges. Although dozens of Catholic churches dating from the 1850s already filled Boston's center, attesting to the vitality of urban, immigrant Catholicism, it was after 1900 that a special self-consciousness about a visible presence emerged, made possible by the presence of a small middle class and of stable parish financial bases. Monetary resources and the desire to be noticed and esteemed led Catholics to an unparalleled burst of construction.[28] In the previous century, Catholic immigrants had often taken over Protestant and even Unitarian church buildings for their own worship, as in the case of St. Stephen's, Hanover Street, in the North End. Designed by Charles Bulfinch in 1802, it was originally the North Meeting House ("New North") of the Episcopalians before it became the Catholic church of

St. John the Baptist in 1842, renamed St. Stephen's in 1862. As Catholics needed more parishes and schools, Catholic firms emerged that specialized in ecclesiastical commissions, such as the 1909–28 construction at Boston College, designed by Maginnis and Walsh for this proposed Catholic "Oxford of America."[29] Closer to downtown, on prime property in the fashionable Fenway, the Notre Dame Convent Academy built by Charles Maginnis in 1916 reopened in 1919 as Emmanuel College for women. In 1915 St. Paul's Church was erected near Harvard Square to serve the Catholic population of Harvard College and central Cambridge, long dominated by Protestant and Unitarian steeples.

O'Connell promoted parish building at a steady pace in the archdiocese by creating 121 new parishes and building 32 new parochial schools between 1907 and 1930, in contrast to the modest building accomplishments of his predecessor.[30] He raised funds for the architectural restoration of San Clemente, his own titular church in Rome, and its catacombs, which had recurring problems with flooding and decay. In personal real estate matters, he acquired family residences in Lowell and a choice waterfront mansion in Marblehead in 1911, which he "Romanesqued" by adding decorative shrubs and cherub motifs.[31] O'Connell also made purchases on the North Shore in 1930 and shrewdly exploited the investment possibilities of property.

O'Connell hoped that his building boom would express Catholic social arrival, complementing assimilationist achievements in politics, literature, and journalism. Yet architecture also recalled Catholics to a separatist heritage linked to feudalism. Catholic architects were engaged to try to represent both a recovery of tradition and a blueprint for a utopian future. But the application of the "Gothic spirit" to modern society often confused the categories of aesthetics and action, leading some Catholics to blur the boundaries between Gothic as an artistic style and as a program for reforming society.

It is not always clear whether Church leaders and builders differentiated between Gothic as an expression of a historical past and as a tool to restore it. Although Catholics feared "the capacity of the Gothic spirit to resist the challenge of modernism," they also asserted hopefully that "the traditional is slowly gaining ground."[32] Thus, a dual stream of aggression and insecurity, of antimodernism and world transformation permeated Catholic aesthetic principles, reflecting also the competing elements of an insider-outsider mentality at work within the hierarchy and among its allies.

Gothic design was not the only archetype available to architects. The growing numbers of Catholic architects and firms with Catholic partners in Boston could select from a range of historical styles, which was reflected in their choice of various models and materials for schools, churches, chapels, convents, and monasteries at the opening of the twentieth century. College cam-

Neo-Gothic at Boston College: four buildings designed by Maginnis and Walsh. (John J. Burns Library, Boston College)

puses became a particular outlet for Catholic social and religious ideologies. In 1907 Rev. Thomas Gasson revealed a plan to expand Boston College from its facilities in one building in Boston's South End, to a complex of new buildings on thirty pastoral acres at Chestnut Hill, formerly owned by Yankee Amos A. Lawrence.[33] Conveniently, the farmland lay opposite the Catholic diocesan seminary. The neo-Gothic buildings of puddingstone, limestone, granite, slate, and stained glass erected between 1909 and 1928 by Maginnis and Walsh earned the admiration of Catholic and non-Catholic architectural critics alike. The partners displayed their designs through a stereopticon to a "crowded meeting" in May 1909, after winning the competition against thirteen other firms.[34]

The construction of a Catholic campus to rival Harvard received "pride of place" among Catholic students and became a first step toward economic integration. Father Gasson predicted, "It will be the beginning of a great movement for the Church."[35] Some sixty years later, historian William Shannon aptly described the evolution of the Irish middle class in Boston as the struggle of Boston College graduates to make a dent in Harvard's hegemony in the financial, legal, and judicial worlds.[36] At the time, O'Connell opposed Gasson's plan because he was scheming to gain control over the college, but in general, other commentators praised the project. The *Pilot* asserted that "the Catholics of New England are forging to the front, and a great future can be established especially in the intellectual side."[37] Felix McGettrick told the Knights of Columbus in Brookline that "the establishment of a great Cath-

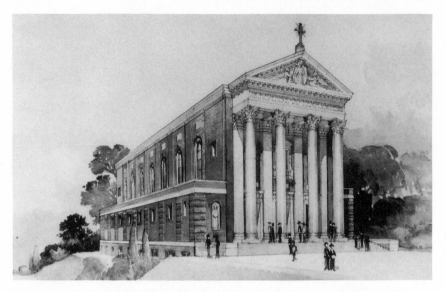

The design for St. Joseph's Chapel at Holy Cross College shows Maginnis and Walsh in a neoclassical mood. (Holy Cross College Archives)

olic college here in Boston means much to Catholics and to the country. An institution where coming generations may have all the advantages obtainable at Harvard or Yale, a course of higher education free from the modern tendency toward secularism that gets impulsion from a superficial and false conception of the fundamental principles that underlie the relations of the creature and the Creator, is the crying demand of Christianity today."[38] Offering his architectural judgment, Cram stated that after a precedent like Boston College, "there is no excuse for organized education or organized religion to revert to the bad old ways of cheap, ugly and ignominious architecture."[39] Clearly, Boston College Gothic served more than a decorative purpose: it was a denouncement of secular education of young men, and it signaled the Catholic Church's identification with a restorationist outlook, which at the same time served the assimilationist needs of Catholic students.

The Gothic Ideal

"One looks naturally for a larger meaning in this triumphant twentieth-century Medievalism centered in once-Puritan Boston," comments one modern architectural historian.[40] Indeed, one wonders why Gothic designs became fashionable in Protestant Christianity at a time when Protestants and Catholics had made only token gestures toward ecumenism, and when unresolved sectarian conflicts left them divided on liturgical standards governing church design as well as the controversial presence and even naming of altars or tables, sanctuaries, baptismal fonts, and pulpits, and on the uses of clerical vestments, altar cloths, and statuary. Some answers surely lie in the connection between Gothic design and the ideology of social order.

Among Catholics, Charles Maginnis (1867–1955) championed Gothicism in American Church architecture, beginning with his earliest commissions in Massachusetts.[41] Maginnis, born in Londonderry, Ireland, in 1867, migrated via Canada to Boston in 1888, where he came up through the ranks of promising students until he reached the position of head draftsman in the city architect's office, which he entered in 1891. Through his success as a partner in Maginnis, Walsh and Sullivan from 1898 to 1907 and in Maginnis and Walsh (1908–54), his reputation spread nationwide.[42] Though lacking formal architectural training, Maginnis went on to gain extensive professional honors and recognition, even delivering the commencement address to the class of 1938 at MIT, the mecca for budding architects. He died in Boston in 1955.

Although Maginnis has been variously labeled a "late Victorian eclectic," a neo-Gothicist who "was most persuasive as a Classicist," and a self-professed "conservative," he first received attention as a designer of Gothic churches in the early English Perpendicular style and in the regional simplicity of Lombard and Tuscan Italianate. His task was aided in Massachusetts by the ready availability of puddingstone in local quarries. In the early 1900s Maginnis published numerous criticisms of contemporary church architecture that brought him professional and religious recognition, stemming from his first independent commission in 1899, a small Catholic church in Whitinsville, built to the specifications of one of his own magazine pieces.[43]

Among architecture historians, Ralph Adams Cram (1863–1942) has usually been credited for single-handedly transforming the visual aesthetic of the New England churches through his ecclesiastical designs. Douglass Tucci, for example, has claimed that Cram persuaded "almost everyone in America in the early twentieth century to a common Christian architecture," which Cram referred to as "prophecy of the Great Recovery" of Christian ideals.[44] As the architect for projects as immense and diverse as the Cathedral of St. John the Divine; the Swedenborgian Church of Newton, Massachusetts; West Point; and Princeton University, Cram wanted to perfect American society by imposing Gothic on a grandiose scale. His towering presence has generally overwhelmed the contribution of Maginnis. Yet the two architects were acquaintances, members and officers of the same professional and, often, the same social clubs, with striking career parallels. For example, while Maginnis was architect for Boston College, perhaps the finest example of his Gothicism, Cram had been appointed supervising architect by President Wilson at Princeton University from 1909 to 1931. Cram founded the Medieval Academy in 1925; Maginnis was one of the founders of the Liturgical Arts Society (LAS) in 1928. Maginnis wrote the introduction to *The Work of Cram and Ferguson,* and Cram favorably reviewed Maginnis's Boston College buildings for the press. Cram highly praised Maginnis's design for St. Paul's, Dorchester, as "undoubtedly one of the really fine Catholic Churches in the United States. So far as its exterior is concerned it is a notable model of what Catholic architecture should be. Of course nothing else was to be expected from Maginnis & Walsh."[45]

Maginnis and Cram shared the belief that a building's artistic form must be united with the spiritual ideals underlying the form. We find echoes of Cram, who called "the Gothic spirit" the driving force behind his work, in Maginnis, who stated, "I hold no brief for a modern Gothic architecture. . . . What we do want is the *spirit of Gothic* if we are to give the Church in America responsible standards of art."[46] Maginnis said that Cram "never for a moment ceased to be heart and soul a medievalist. The Gothic idea is the very core of his philosophy."[47] In fact, there were many Crams, as Richard Wilson has noted, among which Cram the knight errant played an integrating role.[48] Cram's own Gothicism was shaped by his love of pre-Tudor England, mediated by the influences of Henry Adams and English architect Henry Vaughan (who practiced in a Boston firm), by a tour of Italy, and by his own conversion to Anglo-Catholicism in 1887.[49] Cram's romance with Gothic art underlay his aestheticism: like Ruskin and Morris, he associated medieval art with perfection and the Industrial Age with profanity. Catholics shared Cram's reverence for the Middle Ages, basking in his praise of the superiority of parochial schools and his fervent desire for the reunion of church and art in America. Through "social and economic reform," Cram said, the Church could reverse the damage done by the European Reformation, to "make art once more universal and omnipresent, the property of all men."[50] Cram's interpretation of the philosophy embodied in Gothic, his admiration for the High Mass as the supreme manifestation of Christian art, and his appreciation of monastic ideals, confirmed a desired self-image of Roman Catholics.[51]

Among Protestants, Cram appealed primarily to the most ritualist segment, High Anglicans, and despite his expressed desire to make art accessible to all people, his "dyspeptic" antimodernism was notably antidemocratic and monarchical. Cram blamed American democracy for lowering standards and for creating a generation of mediocre men for whom Protestant and Catholic religion "is now, and has been for a long time, a negligible factor."[52] Cram's highbrow elitism had been reinforced by his youthful experiences with the bohemian Decadents and the genteel guild-based socialism of William Morris and the Arts and Crafts movement. Thus, while Cram cannot be labeled solely

Charles Maginnis. (John J. Burns Library, Boston College)

a medieval revivalist, given the complex mixture of his artistic influences (he had his Japanese phase, for example, like painter James Whistler), his specific link to Catholic aesthetics lay in his conviction that Christianity could unite life and art, and in his love of a hierarchical culture in which Church reigned supreme. The inconsistency between his aristocratic elitism and democratic principles was endemic also to Catholic discourse.[53]

Catholic elites mirrored Cram's fear of the leveling impact of mass culture, the degradation of marketplace competition, and the costs of modernization.

Yet despite the Catholic Church's affinities with the elitism of the aesthetes and the antimodernism of the Gothic revivalists, the designers and decorators of Boston's Catholic churches did not lionize Cram. Perhaps priests found his association with High Church Anglicanism, which cultivated the theatrical in Roman Catholicism and worshiped medieval unity as an antidote to the chaos of industrial society, to be a disguise for latent anti-Catholicism. There is evidence that Catholic tribalism went so far as to keep Cram from too close association with Catholic professional organizations: in the case of the LAS, a mere draftsman at Maginnis and Walsh strongly opposed Cram's member-ship on the grounds of his non-Catholicism. This move may have been "more a mask for professional jealousy than an expression of ecclesiastical purism," but despite Cram's goodwill and financial gift to the LAS, he was placed in a reduced membership category.[54] In this instance, Catholic separatism seemed irrational, except as an expression of group insecurity, since Cram had been an avid and early supporter of the LAS. Otherwise, Catholic artists may have tired of Cram's insistence upon Gothic. Nevertheless, his outlook expressed the insoluble paradoxes at the heart of all branches of the Gothic revival in America: How could medieval style express the twentieth century? How could feudal hierarchalism be reconciled with democratic egalitarian-ism? How could Gothicism initiate a full-scale transformation of the world?

While Charles Maginnis offered Catholics a vital interpretation of Gothi-cism for modern society without rejecting eclectic possibilities, another Cath-olic member of Cram's circle, whom he called "the most vital and creative personal influence in the lives of all of us who gathered together at this time," lived in the past. Louise Guiney shared Cram's love for the Middle Ages but found little to admire in contemporary culture.[55] The "assemblage of ardent youth" in the Boston circle of Cram and Guiney represented a mandarin elite—art connoisseurs, architects, and aesthetes—most with Ivy League edu-cations, who had the wealth, worldliness, and leisure to appreciate the stone vaulting of an English country chapel, the delicate wood tracery of an altar screen, and the merits of fine bookbinding. Their rarefied interests did not reflect those of the average Catholic, for whom construction of American par-ish churches had a more pressing function of providing social services to their parish and neighborhood. Lacking a genuine bohemian clique, the fledgling Catholic literary elite looked to architecture as one realm in which Catholic motifs and subjects linked Catholics to Brahmin high culture. Catholics cele-brated, for example, the medieval elements in McKim, Mead and White's otherwise Renaissance Revival Boston Public Library. They rejoiced that John Singer Sargent's interior murals there included a Madonna and concluded that Edward Austin Abbey's Holy Grail paintings, "utterly out of harmony with Boston's Protestant traditions," signified a benediction for Catholicism.[56] For the educated laity, Catholic Reading Circles and the League of Catholic Women (LCW) offered public lectures on the meaning of Christian architecture to publicize this trend. In 1912, for example, Rev. Francis Kenzel delivered an address entitled "Symbolism in Church Architecture" to the LCW. At another such event, Katherine Conway reported that "Frank Fitzpatrick finished out the John Boyle O'Reilly Circle lecture course this evening, with his 'Side-Lights in Church Architecture of the Middle Ages'—most interesting to those who, like myself, have a feeling for construction right in the blood, and who have seen many of the great European churches. I wish he had said more of the inspiration of them."[57]

Compared with Cram and Guiney, Charles Maginnis was neither polemical nor elitist in his politics, although he shared Cram's prejudice that "except for St. Patrick's New York City, there is no worthy Gothic Catholic architecture in the United States. The most available and beautiful style for the Catholic Church in America is English perpendicular, while early round-arched style of Lombardy and Sicily are also nice. In light of this Byzantine tradition, we ought not to patiently tolerate the gaudily tinted walls and the parti-colored statuary which distinguishes so many of our American churches."[58] Maginnis acknowledged the unlikelihood that polyglot America would soon produce a national architectural vocabulary. If "to Gothic designers their style was once a living language and an inherited vernacular," Maginnis asked, "what, then is meant here in America by the jumble and conflict of styles which are not of us? Have we no language of our own? We seldom ask ourselves the question."[59] Drawing his artistic inspiration from abroad, Maginnis itemized the superiority of English church architecture: "In the first place their art is far more thoughtful, more scholarly; and in the second, their point of view is more ethical. . . . The ethical view is evident in the integrity of structural appearances. Masonry enters into the architecture of the interior, giving the vital look which nothing else can give. We can feel stone acting against stone. There is blood and muscle and power. And there is fine symbolism of the Church founded upon a rock."[60] Like Cram's, this language pays homage to virility, force, and honesty of materials—the ethical and symbolic roots that must be joined to produce authentic architecture; but here Maginnis's technical expertise, his fondness for genuine masonry and stone construction, and his aesthetic sensitivity hardly reflect the voice of the average Catholic churchgoer. He was not a social snob, but he was not far from Cram's patrician outlook that the appeal of English Catholicism lay in its affluence as well as in its aesthetic vocabulary. According to Cram,

> English Roman Catholics have been, and are still claimed to be, the flower of the nation; belonging chiefly to the aristocratic classes, they have al-

ways had influence, culture, and wealth, in striking disproportion to their limited number. They are an illustrious and successful household, whose methods, perfected by long thought and in peace, are superior at every point to those here, interrupted perforce by the crying problems of ignorance and poverty, and hampered by the difficulty of welding together the heterogeneous immigrated flock of the present century. Why would not American Catholicism be willing at last to admit all this, and following the classic axiom, think it expedient to learn something from an enemy?[61]

In short, Cram preferred the aristocratic heritage of English Catholics to the immigrant masses in America because he believed that nurturing an upper class produced a more highly civilized culture. Maginnis, as a successful immigrant Catholic, represented the Boston Irishtocracy; he had achieved success denied to many men of his ethnic and religious background, but he had absorbed much of the elitism of the dominant upper class without distinguishing how those arguments had been used to prevent the advancement of his own kind.

The emergence of Catholic consciousness about architectural styles emerged only with its middle class and with the firmer financial footing of the second and third generation removed from immigrant status. Cram had bluntly called the progress of Catholic architecture in America "a carnival of horror."[62] Louise Guiney stated that the worst defects of the "vulgarian horrors" of American churches were overcrowding and faulty ventilation.[63] Maginnis generously "was at pains to be constructive" in his first published article on Catholic architecture by objecting gently to a polyglot abuse of architectural tradition. He recognized that "until we become racially homogeneous, it is clear that Catholic architecture in America must be largely and variously reminiscent of Europe. . . . Catholic art must have its roots deep in the past, though there need be much trimming of its dead branches."[64] Thus Maginnis, like Cram, used European historical models but avoided imposing exact imitations on American churches. Unlike Cram, he did not persist in pushing Gothic as the only style appropriate to religious and, particularly, Catholic architecture. "Indeed," Maginnis observed, "it is an obligation upon the Church to be more intelligently eclectic in the development of a vital architecture."[65] He recognized that technology, namely, "the camera and the steamboat made it possible to canvass the historic panorama of architecture," enabling designers to choose among a wide range of historical styles for church designs.[66] In fact, at least one architectural critic has found Maginnis most persuasive as a classicist.[67] Espousing an educated eclecticism for Catholic architecture, Maginnis ridiculed the tendency of other denominations to draw indiscriminately from the styles associated with the Roman tradition: "Congregationalism looking as though it had fond memories of mediaeval Italy, Baptistism of an Italy still more benighted. Episcopalianism has, for once, forsaken Canterbury for Arles and Salamanca. Here is Mrs. Eddy running the entire gamut of the Renaissance and Baptistism again—amazing ineptitude!—in the atmosphere of the terrible Inquisition!"[68]

Maginnis's suggestion to prevent Catholics from succumbing to a random potpourri was for "each archdiocese to elect a particular historic style, to which the designs of its subsequent constructions would consistently conform." He promised that "it would make for a coherency of expression, an organic orderliness within the precise geographical limits of each ecclesiastical district, which would be edifying to a degree."[69] Maginnis's hopes were never realized in Boston, and his proposal probably derived from an 1894 article by Cram in *Catholic World,* which attributed the superior appearance, quality, and comfort of English parish churches to admirable cooperation between pastor, people, and architect.[70] Cram recognized the incongruity of Anglo-American Protestants worshiping beneath medieval vaulted naves or attending school in the shadow of Italianate campaniles, so he originally encouraged his clients to choose Georgian and Colonial designs. He also cited "Parisian Renaissance [as] expressive of our secular life."[71] However, the Gothic revival he had inaugurated as a repudiation of New England's Puritan-Transcendentalist-Unitarian heritage was so successful that "Protestant congregations declined pretty generally to admit our Colonial premises, and increasingly demanded good Catholic art, refusing to accept any substitute, so we had very promptly to abandon our original position and do just as good Gothic as we possibly could for Presbyterians, Congregationalists, Baptists, and even Unitarians."[72] In November and December 1916, Cram's address to the venerable audience of Boston's Lowell Institute, *The Substance of Gothic,* outlined his perspective on Christian architecture from Charlemagne to Henry VIII. He concluded that the false humanism of the Renaissance had usurped the authentic humanism of the Middle Ages and of the Catholic religion.[73] *The Substance of Gothic* represented the climax to the Gothic revival that had begun in the 1890s. While Maginnis seemed content to limit his Gothic visions to blueprints for churches, Cram, encouraged by the success of prewar Gothic revivalism, proposed plans to rebuild American life by reconstructing entire cityscapes. For Boston, his city planning work led to a comprehensive plan for renovating East Boston in 1915 and a report for the Boston North End Planning Commission in 1919.

Cram's estrangement from reality was apparent in the self-indulgent and impractical nostalgia of his post–World War I reflections. The Great War diminished the optimism of many Americans and took a toll on utopians, architects, and planners as well. Nonetheless, in *Walled Towns* (1919), Cram recommended returning to the medieval practice of enclosed cities, drawing a metaphorical parallel between the city as refuge and that of the church as sanctuary. His fervent desire for escape emerged in his half-jesting remarks to friend Louise Guiney: "My solemn conviction is that the great demand of the present century is for a monastic order which will take in married men with their wives and children!"[74] He thought that walled towns, organized under the guild system of production for use, would redeem war-weary society and spread by imitation. Although the Catholic press reviewed *Walled Towns* favorably, Maginnis and his Catholic colleagues never seriously advanced anything similar, nor did Catholic Gothicism use antimodernism as sheer escapism. Related suggestions for restructuring the economy through guild socialism were too foreign to the experience of American Catholics to have much impact on laborers, although they briefly excited a clerical and lay elite.[75] Maginnis expressed his devotion to hand craftsmanship inspired by Gustav Stickley and the Arts and Crafts movement and perhaps found some thera- peutic psychic link between their disarming simplicity and medieval designs, but he was not dedicated to re-creating the entire social fabric of the Middle Ages via cottage industries. Maginnis, working from within the Catholic faith, and Cram, an Anglo-Catholic eccentric, represent slightly varied at- tempts to revive the Gothic spirit for Americans, reflecting their personal differences regarding its historical associations with feudalism, and its asso- ciation with a social formation of a Christendom based on aristocratic patronage.

The Financing of Churches

Maginnis recognized the market forces governing his profession and the Church's treasury, and he seemed sensitive to the financial constraints im- posed by the budgets or more pressing needs of "immigrated" parishes. Gov- erning his view of the building market, perhaps, was his dislike of the commercialization of sacred art, where "the factory, not the artist, is the unit of production, and sacred objects may be bought from counters as we buy groceries." In Maginnis's judgment, capitalism's worst faults were its power to compete with the Church itself and its potential to destroy Christian belief in the virtue of poverty: "Need it be said that no art worthy of the name— and verily no Christian art—can develop from so unhealthy and degenerate a system of production as this,—a system which grows rich on the poverty of the Church by making its poverty ridiculous?"[76] Other than these few re- marks, however, Maginnis left scant record of his opinions about the impact of technology, the factory system, and mass production on his vocation. Maginnis realistically assessed the financial factors involved in constructing parish churches but concluded that lower budgets did not have to compromise artistic merit. In an article published early in his career, he made his peace with the status quo: "Our Catholic architecture might have been twice as costly without being in the least better. Standards of good taste are not at all affected by the element of cost, nor is the real value of a work of art dependent on it."[77] In 1917, as an established architect, he argued the same, adding a warning against the greed and extravagance of many architects: "To be really artistic, churches need be neither costly nor elaborate. They should be, on the contrary, more simple, if only they be more thoughtful also. If good art is to be had, the lesson architects must learn from the modest means at their disposal is to make their churches modest, too!"[78]

The generally low profit for architects from church commissions seems to have been a justifiable complaint by Maginnis, who commented in a draft version of his unpublished memoirs "that churches rarely yield any profit to an architect who is dependent for his income upon the more secular side of his practice."[79] Churches did not tend to be lucrative ventures for architects because resources were dependent on what the local parish could muster. According to Maginnis, it was customary to pay architects a flat fee of 6 percent of the cost of the church, which in his opinion, barely covered a "perfunctory performance" by the architect. He grumbled that architects were treated like surveyors, rather than "musicians, authors and baseball players." It was not until several decades later that a minimum fee of 10 percent was established, with a bonus added for customized items such as sanctuary designs.[80]

Congregational tithing and building drives financed the construction of Catholic parishes. The pitfalls of relying on wealthy benefactors are illustrated in an anecdote told by Boston's police commissioner. On a visit to his birthplace on Prince Edward Island, Stephen O'Meara found a new, but unfurnished, cathedral in 1902: "Payment for the property must be a heavy task. It was supposed that Owen Connolly who died a millionaire would leave much money for the cathedral, but as a matter of fact he did not leave a cent to it. I learned that toward the close of his life he had made an offer to build the Cathedral himself on the condition that he should be permitted for a period of years to manage the business and receive the revenues. The idea was so absurd that the Bishop would have nothing to do with it."[81] Although this appears to be an isolated incident, the intrusion of the profit motive into the spiritual sphere had spawned plans to make even churches a form of private enterprise. The anecdote expresses the Church's worst fears of a world where everything is for sale.

Pastors, too, stated their concerns about the burden of church building upon parishioners, but perhaps not often enough for the overextended purses of the laity. In Pastor John Farrell's announcement to St. Paul's, Dorchester, about instituting a special "envelope system" to finance the erection of a new church, he asked parishioners to contribute their usual weekly offering of 50 cents, plus 15 additional cents, for one year. Use of envelopes, he argued, would distribute the burden equally, not just upon the 500 faithful contributors out of 1,700 families. An anonymous handwritten comment on a copy of his letter to the parish noted:

> Does not this seem to be almost a hardship on poor people who are now contributing generously? Sixty five cents every Sunday means a sacrifice to so many with living as high as it is, and this outside of the many collections during the year. It makes some of us wonder why it is necessary to build a cathedral in a district where the Catholics are to be in the minority soon. It also makes us wonder if the authorities ever consider that there is a limit—that people with small incomes have already been called on to contribute more than they can afford.[82]

This vignette encapsulates the elements that distinguish a twentieth-century archdiocese from its predecessors: building expansion on a grand scale, the professionalization and rationalization of tithing, the desire for democratic donation procedures, the anxiety about high costs to the laity, and the clerical rejoinder that "attendance at the theatres and moving pictures, membership dues in fraternal order, etc., as a rule call for as much if not more of an outlay." Lay Catholics were constantly reminded by the clergy and hierarchy that their duties included church upkeep, ostensibly because of the spiritual benefits attached, but in reality their donations meant institutional survival.

O'Connell liked to portray himself as a stern judge of the quality of church proposals, choosing only those that were simple, graceful, and no financial burden to the local parish.[83] However, pastors became subject to O'Connell's related concern to avoid staggering construction bills by being required to get his approval for all new construction and repair work. The chancery records of construction and repair costs to all parish property in the archdiocese were kept meticulously and compiled annually. A chart for 1907 to 1922 summarized a dramatic and steady increase in the numbers of new churches erected, in expenditures by the archdiocese, and in the value of church properties. Between 1907 and 1920, except for 1918 (because of World War I), about ten new churches were constructed each year. The total expenditures of the archdiocese averaged over $1 million annually between 1910 and 1917 and in 1922 had reached nearly $3 million.[84] O'Connell's policy of requiring pastors to submit requests for all proposed expenditures over $100 represented more than careful bookkeeping or aesthetic pride: it signaled his desire to control the minutest details of parish life. Archives of parish files contain

A CHURCH BUILDING FOR $8,740

THE question of building a church or a chapel for a new congregation is one that arises continually in every diocese throughout the land, and very often the buildings put up are unsatisfactory in point of durability and design on account of the lack of funds. It is questionable whether it pays to put up a temporary frame building and in the course of a few years tear it down and rebuild with a permanent structure.

It has been a growing custom in many dioceses to design buildings, or parts of buildings, that will be complete and durable as far as they will be erected, so that the money put in the same will not be lost.

In some cases combination buildings are provided, so designed that the first floor will be used for a school and the second floor for a temporary church, the building being designed as a future school building and retaining the character of a school. However, in some localities, especially in small country districts, where the school cannot be afforded, a church is built, and in some cases so designed that it can be extended at any time in the future, as demands, made by reason of the growing congregation, permit. Such was the case in the new parish established in a town in Pennsylvania. Here the rector desired to put up a building that was worthy as a Catholic church and at the same time come within the means of the new congregation. Mr. John T. Comes, the architect, therefore designed a building that at the present time seats 250 people, temporary provision for the sanctuary and sacristy being made in what will be

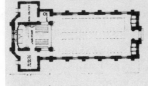

the future nave or body of the church. In the future, the sanctuary proper and the new sacristy will be built on in the rear which will then afford about 100 more seats.

The building is built of variegated color quarry stone and trimmed with concrete stone. All the window tracery instead of being made in the usual manner of wood, is cast in concrete which costs very little more than wood and is as durable as stone. The ceiling of the Church is an open timber ceiling, so common in England, a method of construction which has a beauty and stability not generally found in the regulation plaster ceiling.

The stained glass windows are of a simple geometrical design each containing a different emblem, the window over the altar being a memorial, containing the figure of St. Felix. Spaces for confessionals are provided at either side of the front entrance vestibule.

The building is heated by hot air, ventilation being afforded by the vent flue in the chimney stack. All of the furniture was designed by the architect, and is of a simple, yet ecclesiastical design, and harmonizes with the architecture of the church.

The contract for this building was $8740, exclusive of furniture and windows; the total cost of the building with furniture, etc., is about $11,000.

The exterior stone work was done by country masons and the stone was laid in a rubble fashion and quite irregular in appearance, which picturesque effect is desirable in a country church. The roof is of green slate, and altogether the color scheme is delightful.

The pastor has taken a special interest in the designing and construction of the building and has secured, with ordinary and unpromising conditions, a result which is very satisfying. If an architect is to do his best work, this co-operation by the pastor is not only desirable but necessary, if Catholic architecture is to rise above the common level in which it finds itself to-day.

Editor's Note—If any of our readers among the clergy are interested in the above building we shall be glad to give them further particulars. Plans and specifications can be had at a moderate cost by addressing a letter to The Catholic Church Extension Society, 20 Adams St., Chicago, Ill.

Advertisement for architectural designs for parishes with modest means. The trend toward church construction "by the book" paralleled the vogue for ready-made blueprints in domestic architecture. (*Extension Magazine*, September 1907) hundreds of letters to O'Connell from pastors requesting permission for all alterations and repairs, sewage, electricity, painting, roofing, and additions. Fierce individual loyalty to a pastor, if not to the hierarchy, often played a part in the generally strong support for parish funding drives, and additional bequests to the Church from the wills of priests, nuns, and laity amassed sums well beyond regular tithing obligations. Catholics often made personal financial sacrifices and attended Mass in makeshift environments until their churches were completed. In Dorchester, for example, the largest of Boston's streetcar suburbs, the parishioners awaiting the construction of St. Kevin's heard Mass inside the Strand Theater at Upham's Corner.[85]

Ultimately it must be acknowledged that the Catholic middle class as well as the working poor were the Church's true church builders, and that the success of a Catholic identity based on architecture rested on lay funding of parish building projects. It was the work of skilled Catholic laborers and the presence of lower-class Catholic clients that made possible the success of architects like Maginnis and Walsh and the careers of many others whose trades depended on Church-related construction projects.

Catholic Architects and Builders in Boston

In 1909, as ground was being broken for the new Boston College buildings, the *Republic* listed architecture as an "open profession" for Catholic men in Massachusetts.[86] Among those who were tasting the early fruits of professional success were Charles Maginnis and his partner since 1898, Timothy Francis Walsh (1868–1934). Maginnis and Walsh, in addition to expanding Boston College, also designed numerous structures in the Brighton vicinity: the cardinal's residence; and the Cenacle convent and chapel and St. Gabriel's monastery and chapel (1927–29), across Commonwealth Avenue from Boston College. They had built the chapel and seminary buildings at St. John's between 1899 and 1902 and later erected the chapel and most of the campus buildings at Holy Cross College, Worcester, Massachusetts. In contrast to Boston College's neo-Gothic, Holy Cross's chapel and campus buildings were designed along neoclassical lines.[87] Whereas Patrick Keely (1816–1896) had dominated Catholic church architecture in the nineteenth century by producing some 600 churches, so Maginnis and Walsh dominated the twentieth century, rivaled only by Cram and Ferguson in the total of local churches commissioned between 1900 and 1920. The former pair have twenty-four churches to their credit; the latter, forty-one, mostly Protestant churches, including several restorations and interior remodelings.[88] The *Architectural Record* marked Maginnis as the leader of the renaissance in American church architecture.[89] By 1922 the archdiocese of Boston had commissioned 296 projects: 259 parish churches and 37 mission churches, awarded primarily to Maginnis and Walsh.

Maginnis amassed extensive professional and religious honors: he was president of the Boston Society of Architects from 1924 to 1926, two-term president of the American Institute of Architects from 1937 to 1939, and winner of a rarely awarded gold medal from the latter organization for lifetime achievement. In Massachusetts he was a member of the Boston Arts Commission from 1909 to 1934 and a trustee of the Public Library since 1930; he was a member of the State Art Commission from 1911 to 1923 and its chairman from 1923 to 1928. With Ralph Cram he was a member of the Boston Society of Architects Committee on Municipal Improvements. Maginnis served as a master and then president of the Arts and Crafts Society and the first (and four-time) president of the LAS in the 1930s. He was member and, later, academician of the National Academy of Design. He served as president of the Charitable Irish Society in 1932 and the Catholic Alumni Sodality in 1935. He received honorary doctorates in law from Boston College and Holy Cross, in arts from Harvard, and in humane letters from Tufts College. Notre Dame awarded him its Laetare Medal in 1924. The Eire Society of Boston and the American Irish Historical Society also awarded him gold medals for his achievements. Cardinal O'Connell's successor, Cardinal Cushing, eulogized him in 1955. Maginnis's daughter recalled that Cushing's presence surprised her, since the family believed that the local Church hierarchy had snubbed Maginnis, forcing him to look outside Boston for ecclesial commissions.[90] This claim seems unwarranted, given the many projects awarded to Maginnis, including the design of two high schools and construction of his own parish church, St. Aidan's, Brookline (1911). Maginnis's relations with O'Connell may have been strained, however, by O'Connell's lack of support for the LAS in the 1930s. O'Connell's pressure to prevent two priests from St. John's Seminary faculty from accepting an invitation to the advisory board to the LAS, as well as his refusal to assign it a chaplain, led the society to relocate its headquarters to New York City.[91]

There were close connections between Catholic elites, Catholic architects, and Church-related commissions. For example, Maginnis's design for St. Catherine of Genoa, Somerville, was paid for largely by a generous subvention from its pastor, the grandson of the first Catholic mayor of Boston. Maginnis's partner, Timothy Walsh, had a brother who became the founder of the Maryknoll order of priests and brothers, and he enabled Maginnis and Walsh to get the project to build their novitiate in upstate New York. Female relatives who became sisters or nuns often provided the leverage for an architect to receive a convent or school construction project.

Certain premigration factors aided the material success of Maginnis, while Walsh, from a leading Catholic family of Cambridge, had enjoyed the benefit of European travel. He had studied in Paris ateliers and had worked in the Boston offices of Peabody and Stearns before joining Maginnis and Sullivan in 1896. He later married one of Maginnis's daughters.[92] Maginnis had won honors abroad for his drawings before coming to Toronto in 1885 and Boston in 1888. His manual, *Pen Drawing* (1898), ran to seven editions, making him well known among architectural students and practitioners. From 1891 he had been an apprentice in the office of Edmund M. Wheelwright, a highly regarded draftsman in Boston who was architect of the Boston public schools.[93] The firm of Maginnis and Walsh (renamed Maginnis, Walsh and Kennedy from 1955 to 1970) had an active practice in many states, including California, Illinois, Maine, Maryland, Massachusetts, Michigan, New Jersey, New York, Ohio, Pennsylvania, Rhode Island, and Washington, D.C.

Catholic architectural partnerships succeeded when there was a ready and expanding market among Catholics for Church-related projects and because of the building boom in Boston. Non-Catholics such as Ralph Adams Cram prospered by their Protestant and Unitarian clients but also received some Catholic commissions for new churches as well as for interior restorations. Cram's decision to specialize in church architecture in the 1890s was a deliberate one, as he explained: "If a young firm such as ours was to get anywhere we should have to find some comparatively virgin field and, if possible, make it our own. A careful survey indicated that there was such a field, and that was one of which my new interests, acquired in Rome, argued acceptance. This was the building of churches."[94]

The careers of Boston's most notable Catholic architects proved Cram's statement. Maginnis and Walsh represent a benchmark for local and national success, based on a profitable blend of contracting in both ecclesiastical and commercial buildings. Outside of Church contracts, the emergence of Irish entrenchment in City Hall from the 1880s, in combination with the expansion of Catholics into civil service jobs, created a natural connection between city managers and administrators and professional Catholics in building design and construction.[95] The penetration of Catholic architects of Maginnis's caliber into the elite realm of independent practice was far less typical than a broader diffusion of Catholic entrepreneurs into the building arts and trades in Massachusetts.[96]

Beginning in the 1880s, Catholics started to appear on the municipal payroll as builders, civil engineers, and planners, but not as professional architects. The dominant characteristics of this first generation of Catholic builders and architects were their Irish heritage, lack of professional degrees and training, technical knowledge of construction rather than artistic training in de-

St. Catherine of Genoa, Somerville (1907–16). This Italian Romanesque church is considered Maginnis's masterpiece. It was one of few church projects that had full financial backing at the outset thanks to its pastor, who was the grandson of Boston's first Catholic mayor. Maginnis engaged the best craftsmen to provide the interior woodcarving and opalescent windows. The elevated and unobstructed site was unusual for a city church, affording Maginnis a rare chance to construct a formal entrance from the street and to emphasize the basement's "equal spiritual importance with the upper church." (Maginnis, typescript of unpublished memoirs. Photo, Errico Studio, Somerville, Mass.)

sign, and a clientele of mostly fellow Irish Americans. One of the earliest practitioners, however, was exceptional because he held a college degree: Patrick J. Ford (1848–1900), who emigrated from Ireland, was a graduate of Queen's College, Cork. Active in Boston from the 1870s, he built the House of the Good Shepherd for the Catholic Church, Mt. St. Joseph's Academy in Brighton, and triple-decker housing in the Irish wards. Through the 1890s, Irish Catholics such as Ford and Daniel O'Connell made careers primarily as builders of these wooden triple-decker tenements.[97] Irish names regularly appeared in competition rosters for inexpensive house designs, such as one sponsored by the Wells Workingmen's Institute of Boston.[98]

Charles J. Bateman of Cambridge had a more diversified career. In 1883 he became the city architect and served for four administrations. He built St.

Cecilia's Church in Back Bay, one of Boston's most affluent parishes, especially after Archbishop O'Connell became its rector; the Working Boys Home,
Bennet Street; the reconstruction of Carney Hospital; and St. Vincent's Hospital, Worcester. In the 1880s and 1890s Bateman's designs for churches,
apartments, tenements, and public and parochial schools, according to his
amazed clients, never exceeded the price of his initial estimates.[99] Charles
Damrell's *A Half Century of Boston Building* (1895), which traces the prominence of the Irish in residential construction, design, and materials from
about the 1880s, provides evidence that Bateman and his peers followed the
wealthier Catholics to the streetcar suburbs. Bateman was architect and
builder, for example, of two very costly houses for J. Duncan in an upper
middle-class residential area of Dorchester in 1890 and 1897. Furthermore,
it seems to be a discernible pattern that Irish Catholic domestic architects
profited from their creations in numerous ways, sometimes intending them
for relatives and sometimes for renting. T. F. Kearney of Dorchester is listed
as architect, builder, and owner of four $4,000 houses, which were probably
given to family members or sublet. T. Edward Sheehan (1866–1922) of
Dorchester practiced in the east for forty-five years, where he designed buildings ranging from St. William's, Dorchester, to Regis College, Troy, New
York. He also designed numerous houses for clients with Irish surnames in
Dorchester, from the 1890s. For a time in the 1920s he formed a partnership
with William B. Colleary, one of several ephemeral Irish collaborations.

M. W. Fitzsimmons of Boston found another lucrative option, that of merging architectural training with a position in city administration: in 1878 he
became assistant inspector of buildings, then deputy inspector and supervisor
of plans. Patrick A. Tracy served ten years in Boston architecture offices before
studying draftsmanship in New York in 1891. In 1892 he took the civil service
exam, returned to Boston, and became superintendent of construction for
United States Public Buildings. Samuel Dudley Kelley of Boston got commissions for numerous parish reconstruction projects. His correspondence with
Rev. John O'Brien of Sacred Heart, Cambridge, concerning additions and repairs to the parish affords a rare glimpse into parish financial realities.[100] John
William Donahoe (1869–1941), who was born in Springfield and became
architect for that diocese, built additions for Our Lady of the Elms College
in Chicopee. Wendell T. Phillips (1857–1955), an Irishman, became architect
for Springfield diocese several decades later, after graduating from Notre
Dame in 1912 and working for Maginnis and Walsh until 1940. William and
John McGinty of Vermont practiced in Boston. William (d. 1922) contributed
articles to *Catholic World* and *American Architecture* on Irish and Catholic
art and architecture. Designer of numerous churches, convents, asylums, and
hospitals in New England, he is noted for the Holy Ghost Home for Incurables

in Cambridge, Massachusetts. Joseph McGinnis, who received the prestigious Rotch Scholarship from MIT in 1909, designed an addition to the Boston Public Library. Edward F. Maher (1865–1937) left Maryland to study at MIT and in Paris. In 1907 he opened a practice in Boston and earned the nickname "Dean of the Boston draftsmen" for his skillful designs. From 1913 to 1928 he had a partnership with Charles A. Winchester. The firms of Mulcahy and McLoughlin and of O'Connell and Shaw, like Maginnis and Walsh, designed many New England churches. Richard Shaw, born in Boston, graduated from the Harvard School of Design in 1912. Timothy O'Connell had previously served Chickering and O'Connell from 1904 to 1911.

One anomaly in the male-dominated field of architecture and among Catholic career women was Eleanor Manning (1884–1973) of Lynn, who has merited a listing in the *American Catholic Who's Who* but has been ignored, as women have been generally, in histories of the architecture profession.[101] "At age of nine," she said, "I had selected my profession and had begun to prepare for it."[102] After high school she went immediately to MIT, graduating in 1906 as among the first women to receive an undergraduate architecture degree, and the only female in her class.[103] At this point in architectural careerism, the academic route to success was "reestablishing the classical model of the architect as an educated, aesthetic advisor," preventing not only ethnic minorities but women from achieving academic recognition even if they were fortunate enough to gain admittance to a university program.[104] In 1907 Manning became a draftsman with Lois Howe, who had begun individual practice in Boston in 1893. During a year's leave of absence devoted to European travel, Manning cut her trip short when she was invited to become Howe's partner in 1913. Howe and Manning were later joined by Mary Almy in 1926. Howe, Manning and Almy was the first women's architecture firm in Boston, responsible for hundreds of New England house restorations and low-income housing projects.

In addition to her design career in a distinguished firm, during the next forty years Manning also served on metropolitan, regional, and state housing committees and lectured in architecture at Simmons College in Boston and Pine Manor Junior College, Wellesley (1918–36.) Supported by Yankee elites for her professional advancement, Manning was nonetheless subject to cultural gender constraints that relegated female academics to positions at women's and junior colleges. In the architectural field, in a deliberate contrast to male architects and builders who received church commissions and were encouraged in lofty ambitions for major public buildings, women usually specialized in domestic architecture because of their association with the family and housewifely duties.[105] Manning, offering a different justification for her choice of specialization, claimed that she became an expert in the restoration of colonial and Georgian houses because it provided stable income during times when architects, especially women, had difficulty getting commissions. She offered a glimpse of her place in a field dominated by men in a *Boston Globe* interview in 1934. In response to the interviewer's questions, "How about openings for women in architects' offices? Can women get the necessary practical experience before opening offices for themselves?," she replied, "In ordinary time, yes. In this fifth year of the depression, no. New York has always been more open-minded than Boston about hiring women draftsmen, and the West is, as one might suppose, unaware that discrimination, because of sex, is either wise or expedient."[106] She noted that the standard barrier to women's success in architecture was difficulty in getting practical experience as an apprentice in an architectural office. "Probably the wise young woman will start in a small community on her own and learn by doing unimportant jobs," wrote Manning.[107] In marked contrast to Manning's career choice, the expected role of women in churches focused on their domestic role in altar guilds that maintained church interiors. The Boston *Republic* described the ideal woman as "zealous for the revival of the beautiful old Catholic traditions of Church architecture. She belongs to the Tabernacle Society of her Alma Mater and to the parish Altar Society, if there is one at her church. She learns all she can about the vestments and altar linen; and gives all the time she can to preparing and renewing them."[108]

Manning's architectural specialization conformed to feminine stereotypes in that she believed women possessed a special affinity for domestic architecture, yet her choice to concentrate on home restoration was also pragmatic, given the fact that women often could not get internships and office training following completion of their professional degrees. She entered the profession at a time when women's professional presence was extremely limited but nonetheless symbolically established through the achievements of another MIT graduate and the three artists who designed the Woman's Building at the World's Columbian Exposition in Chicago in 1893.[109] Like her enterprising classmates, Manning transcended gender stereotypes by deliberately relating woman's sphere to public life through developing a political interest in government policies concerning family housing, urban planning, and the availability of quality housing for all classes, "a vertical cross section of the community."

As is the case with the handful of women architects of her generation, it is difficult to say how typical Eleanor Manning's experience was. Daughter of a building contractor in Lynn, her upbringing suggests upwardly mobile ambitions, industrious middle-class values, and certain class privileges. For instance, during a year of European travel in 1912, she wrote letters to her family revealing a sense of both religious and class identity. On her transatlantic passage on the SS *Cymric* she wrote, "The Catholic priest is an Irishman and very charming. (By the way the O'Neals are Catholics.)" In describing the players in a vaudeville troupe on board, she observed, "Socially they are not in 'our' class which is not snobbish but simply a fact. For instance we asked them to play with us one evening and I said to the one like Mary, 'What is your name?' And she answered, 'Peggy.' Can you imagine a girl of 18 answering that in our immediate family? The class feeling is evidently very strong in England."[110] Further evidence of the family's social and economic aspirations can be seen in the life of Eleanor's older sister, Edith, a Smith College alumna. After a few years as a public school teacher, Edith married Thomas Logan, a widower and wealthy Lynn shoe manufacturer who was the father of a high school friend. The Logans commissioned Eleanor to design their new home.[111]

On the other hand, Manning's career took her outside the Catholic subculture, marked by her membership in the Massachusetts Woman Suffrage Association, which the Church opposed, and during the 1940s, her chairmanship of the Housing Committee for the Massachusetts Civic League, long controlled by WASPs. Overcoming gender limitations, she was elected to the American Institute of Architects in 1923 and kept close ties to it, exhibiting no visible rancor at the gross underrepresentation of women.[112] In sum, Manning capitalized on her decision to focus on domestic building and used all the connections derived from her education and social background to further her career. The only hint that a demanding career strained her personal life comes from an undated letter from her husband, Johnson O'Connor, whom she married in 1931 when she was forty-seven: "But I think that you ought to take more of the responsibility of our affairs. I am getting awfully fed up with this never being together and I will not go on any longer in this way. There is no chance of my being in Boston again except for one day for two or three months. You will have to make some kind of a decision and do something about it."[113]

In retrospect, Manning's success was due to her professional degree combined with her opportunity for apprenticeship in a firm of women partners; her delayed marriage to a successful man; her concentration on markets ignored or avoided by men, namely restoration and low-income clients; and her acquired expertise in housing issues, which led to government appointments to local and state housing committees and planning boards.

Growth of Related Industries

In tandem with the growth of Catholic architects, builders, civil engineers, and professional firms came the expansion of industries dependent on eccle-

Eleanor Manning O'Connor. (MIT Museum Collection)

siastical architecture and decoration. These included the quarrying and cutting of granite and marble for grave memorials, altars, and baptismal fonts, and bronze smelting to produce chimes and bells. Ecclesiastical paintings, mosaics, sculptures, stained glass, organs, and so forth involved many skilled tradesmen. In addition, craftsmen, printers, and builders provided goods and furnishings for convents, monasteries, schools, and churches, including altarware, pews, candles, stearic acid, glycerin, sanctuary oil, ciboria, crucifixes, rosaries, medals, copes, albs, surplices, altar linens, religious music, and calendars. Metalsmiths were regularly needed for repair of chalices, crucifixes, and other sacred objects. An unprecedented increase in the value of this religious market occurred in the 1920s. By 1930, as calculated by the business manager for the new magazine *Liturgical Arts,* the annual market in Catholic church building and decorating was in the area of $100 million.[114]

The related business of advertising for these products and services provided a desirable source of revenue for the Catholic press at a time when secular daily newspapers derived from 50 to 75 percent of their income from advertising. In Boston, Catholic weeklies such as the *Pilot,* the *Sacred Heart Review,* the *Republic,* and even most parish bulletins began to feature increasingly ostentatious ads from Catholic firms through the 1910s and 1920s. The Catholic Church Supply House, for example, offered a special deal for Bostonians on gold chain rosaries with imitation stones, ranging from fifty-nine to ninety-eight cents.[115] The *Columbiad* advertised the Gorham Company's latest innovation: a bronze St. Christopher hood mount for automobiles. Even the front pages of Catholic magazines carried advertisements for household products, such as Lenten fish flakes, while in the inner pages could be found testimonies to the ubiquitous Catholic remedy, "Father John's Medicine." Mass culture and advertising techniques had begun to penetrate the Church's anti-commercialism and reflected its new relationship with lay entrepreneurs who were making careers in design, manufacture, advertising, and distribution.[116]

It was not long before the Church capitulated to the related tendency toward professional specialization, which isolated the field of sacred art with the founding of the LAS in 1928 and the Catholic Art Association in 1937. Although the LAS had been centered in Boston initially, certain decisions by O'Connell, combined with petty jealousies among some of its founders, ended Boston's chance to lead liturgical art renewal in the United States.

It is apparent from the career limitations facing Catholics entering the field of architecture, or who aspired to the profession by gaining experience in the construction industry, that few achieved the success of Charles Maginnis or Timothy Walsh or wrote as eloquently about the spiritual impulse underlying Christian architecture. In stating that "the Catholic imagination is vindicated or compromised by the aspect of even the humblest of Catholic structures,"

The triumph of advertising in the Catholic press: fish flakes for the observation of Lenten abstinence from meat.

Maginnis estimated his designs with an eye to aesthetic purity as well as to the financial means of the laity.[117] Most Irish Catholic professionals, however, remained outside the increasingly professionalized architecture schools while serving instead as apprentice draftsmen and builders to gain the necessary experience and clients. Few Italian Catholics or members of other ethnic groups entered these fields prior to the 1930s, judging from the architectural files of the Boston Public Library.[118] Perhaps because the American Institute of Architects was seeking to elevate architects from mere builders by "tacitly devaluing the apprenticeship system, which had its roots in the building trades," the Irish Catholic apprentice was able to enter a skilled trade by apprenticeship but rarely to become an accredited professional among the ranks of the gentleman-architect.[119]

Architecture as Tradition

Returning again to the situation of Catholic architecture and the Church's opposition to the evils of the city, one finds a polemical triumphalism suffusing Catholic art criticism in the early 1900s, supported by a particular interpretation of the Catholic artistic legacy. For some, the atrocities of World War I only reinforced the moral primacy of Gothic, as in James J. Walsh's statement "Where Catholicism dwindles, art disappears. Protestants ruined the art of Europe." The view that the war symbolized the death of medieval communalism led some Catholics to draw a parallel with the Protestant Reformation, which had despoiled Catholic art and architecture. Any perceived return of Catholic subjects and symbols to public art in Boston was therefore heralded by Catholic commentators as the just restoration of Catholicism over false religion.[120] Within this context, architecture took on a highly propagandistic role for Catholics. Charles Maginnis's architectural designs for the Catholic Church represented the elegant yet cost-conscious solutions of a self-educated and resourceful professional who wished to elevate the taste of individual clients and to guide the archdiocese to a unified historical style. Though this latter wish remained unfulfilled, his talents and the national demand for Catholic churches led Maginnis to projects in many states and to a reputation that extended beyond the archdiocese of Boston. While he provided the norm for superior architecture among Catholic church builders, lesser-known Catholic firms and practitioners in Boston also began to specialize in church commissions, which enabled them to further diversify their practices through contracts for parochial schools, religious hospitals, and seminary and college buildings. The Church's building needs created a boom in the market for Catholic architects and builders and spawned growth in fields dependent on the building trades and among Catholic liturgical suppliers. Some Catholic architects and builders followed the growing market for domestic housing, finding clients among those Catholics moving to Boston's suburbs. Within the male-dominated profession of designers and builders, Eleanor Manning served as an exception to rules ostensibly limiting Catholic women's career-ism, but her focus on domestic architecture and housing reflected gender biases governing the profession in general.

Concerning the relative prominence of architectural styles for churches in the archdiocese of Boston and in suburban Massachusetts, English and Ital-ianate Gothic dominated church designs well through the 1920s, although variants of Renaissance classicism, Byzantine, and Spanish Mission designs were also represented locally. No plan was devised or enforced to unify or restrict the styles approved for new parishes. Thus, while medievalism was readily available as a discourse that combined the Church's traditionalism and utopianism, it had begun to yield its dominance to the marketplace's variety of styles. In its cultural commentaries, the Church proposed guild handcrafts-manship as the solution to crass commodification and the profit motive. But the success of newly certified Catholic architects benefited the Church so tan-gibly that plans for reviving medieval crafts remained mostly rhetorical. Con-servative ultramontanists like William O'Connell preferred to make grand claims for Gothicism and to see in its rediscovery by other denominations proof of Roman Catholic moral superiority, as well as a cure for the pitfalls of modern materialism. For the lay Catholic elite, the revival of Gothicism in Boston was similarly interpreted as the victory of their seeming folly over decaying moral and artistic standards and a triumph for the Church's idealist principles of beauty. Sacred space became a form of propaganda describing what the Catholic Church stood for, and a form of rivalry against what Roman Catholicism rejected. Religious architecture, in both the city and the suburbs, shaped a generation's attachment to the Church and molded suggestive images of the past into physical realizations of the imagined community.

5

THE IDEOLOGY OF CATHOLIC WOMANHOOD

We need be neither prude nor Puritan to see and to realize that
something is passing in the hearts and minds of the women of today
which is leaving them hard and unwomanly, and that year by year
this transformation goes on until, if it continues, there will be neither
home, nor family, nor normal womanly nature left. If this is the new
woman, then God spare us from any further development of an
abnormal creature! Certainly this is not the Catholic woman.
—Archbishop William O'Connell, "The True Faith Undying"

Men, God bless them, are our natural guides and protectors in most
things, but in matters of morals, women should be leaders, not
merely followers. It is our particular province to stress the moral virtues, to uphold the moral standards, to develop the underlying principles, spread a knowledge of them in the public mind, and insist upon
their application to the great political and ethical issues of the
present day.—Mrs. Francis E. Slattery, "The Catholic Woman in
Modern Times"

Woman's rights? What does a woman want iv rights whin she has
priv'ledges? Rights is th' last thing we get in this wurruld. They're
th' nex' things to wrongs. They're wrongs tur-rned inside out.
—Finley Peter Dunne, "Rights and Privileges of Women"

The Church's View of Woman

As it tried to prescribe proper behavior and duties for men, so the
Catholic Church helped construct female identity. At the opening of the twentieth century, the Catholic Church and the other Christian churches supported
separate (but not exclusive) roles and functions for each sex. Suspicious of
new scientific claims in biology and psychology, and uncertain about rapid
socioeconomic change that seemed to threaten religious orthodoxies, both
Protestants and Catholics defended the fixed nature of gender roles by citing
the authority of revealed Scripture. Using interpretations of the Bible from the
book of Genesis through the Pauline corpus, Christianity had sustained a system of gender relations that assumed universal male and female traits. At least
since the Middle Ages, the contrast between Eve, originator of sin, and the
Virgin Mary, symbol of purity, described a polarity ascribed to women's essential nature. Catholic doctrine therefore encompassed the negative association of woman with the story of humanity's fall from grace, redeemed only
through Mary, the sinless Mother of God. Stereotypes about the physical and
intellectual inferiority or vulnerability of women were further biased by theo-

logians' use of erroneous assumptions of contemporary biology and ethnology about the female body. The lamentable impact upon women was that "inspired by the erroneous idea that a woman's proper attitude is that of deferential submission, many excellent women commit serious blunders whose consequences are far-reaching and deplorable."[1]

It is no secret that Irish Catholic males of Boston have received far more attention from historians, politicians, novelists, and journalists than have Catholic women. A glance at the numerous biographies of James Michael Curley, for example, suggests one reason why: a flamboyant rascal made irresistible copy. Where else but in Boston would one find the mayor calling one of his rivals "you little pisspot"? Fortunately, scholarship about women has burgeoned in the last thirty years to compensate for a male-centered historiography that has idolized Curleys as heroic individualists or as Irish chieftains. Women's representation and experience in medieval Christianity have been well served by recent studies, while the quest for a usable past for women in American religion has excluded Catholics by focusing on Protestantism, Judaism, and "radical" or fringe religious groups such as the Quakers, the Shakers, the Unitarians, and the spiritualists. One fruitful focus of research on American Protestantism has been an examination of the impact of economic modes of production on female sexuality. The emergence of capitalism in the nineteenth century erased the excessive carnality attributed to women in the seventeenth century and refashioned women into domesticated, morally pure, and self-disciplined Victorians.[2] Within capitalist economies, ancient fears of female sexual power were repressed by spiritualizing women's power in order to lessen it, and especially to protect the economic power sought by men. Divisions between public and private, production and reproduction were thus closely intertwined with religious interpretations of gender, and American churches attached a religious significance to rules governing women's behavior that reflected these economic changes. Nineteenth-century women were therefore encouraged to become perfect wives and mothers, moral guides for their children, and devotees of domesticity. As a counterweight to the individualism that was socially acceptable for males, and in fact mythologized even in ethnic climbers like Mayor Curley, women were taught to sacrifice themselves for their families. Later their role expanded to embrace responsibility for civic virtue on a national scale, yet without including demands for women's equal rights.[3]

The creation of a Catholic ideology of womanhood generally paralleled the Church's negative encounter with modernity. Internationally and in Boston, the Catholic Church responded harshly to the changes accompanying the status and roles of women, especially women's growing tendency to remain unmarried, to defer marriage, or to seek advanced education and careers.

Foremost, the Church defined womanhood within a patriarchal context. Next, it defined women relationally, that is, as responsible to and for others, rather than as autonomous individuals. Roman Catholicism reaffirmed the "primal vocation" of woman to motherhood, whether as a mother of a family or as a celibate "spiritual mother" in a women's religious order.

Any considerations of women in Roman Catholicism must begin with the concept of patriarchy, by which I mean a system of male domination that preceded capitalism (and that may have been itself a mode of production), but which is also functional for capitalism and the gender relations institutionalized in its family structures. Recognizing that there are ongoing theoretical debates about the definition and origins of patriarchy, I am not suggesting a precise or nuanced resolution. Here I am more concerned with patriarchy's residual effects on the formation of a Catholic ideology about women by its articulation of a sexual division of labor, and its control of women's sexuality and spirituality, rather than an analysis of female wage labor and the relative merits of making class or sex the primary determinants of patriarchy.[4] Guidelines for Catholics on the proper role of women in society were established by the authority vested in male leaders: popes, bishops, and priests. Pope Leo XIII supported the sexual division of labor in *Rerum Novarum* when he stated that "certain occupations likewise are less fitted for women, who are intended by nature for work of the home—work indeed which especially protects modesty in women and accords by nature with the education of children and the well-being of the family."[5] As historians have observed, this first of the social encyclicals was conservative in most respects. When it was belatedly adopted by American Church leaders, they robbed the statement of whatever reforming potential it had on social and economic issues.[6] Since the document suggested no changes in the Church's mandate for motherhood as woman's essential role, *Rerum* was a useful weapon against feminism and careerism. In its mission to consolidate hierarchical authority in the decades following Vatican I, the Church did not undertake to develop a theology that acknowledged recent social change or class diversity within laywomen's experience, nor did it ever challenge the family itself, which may be the locus of women's oppression.[7] Nor did the papal outlook on woman's role evolve between Vatican I and Vatican II, as seen in the following excerpts. Pius X, successor of Leo XIII, told the Italian Women's League in 1909 that "women in war or parliament are outside their proper sphere, and their position there would be desperation and ruin of society. Woman created as man's companion must so remain—under the power of love and affection, but always under his power."[8] Not until 1939 did a pope give official recognition to women's ministry in charitable work outside the home, even though Catholic sisters had been performing that service for centuries.[9] Pius XII's statement in 1945, "On Woman's Duties," did not alter any features of the Leonine corpus. Rather, Pius nostalgically recalled the simplicity of gender roles in preindustrial society: "We see a woman who, in order to augment her husband's earnings, betakes herself also to a factory, leaving her house abandoned during her absence. The house, untidy and small perhaps before, becomes even more miserable for lack of care. Members of the family work separately in four quarters of the city and with different working hours. Scarcely ever do they find themselves together for dinner or rest after work—still less for prayer in common. What is left of family life? And what attractions can it offer to children?"[10] In 1979, the present pope stated in a general audience that "motherhood is woman's vocation . . . yesterday . . . today . . . always; it is her eternal vocation. . . . A mother is the one who understands everything and embraces each of us with her heart. . . . Today the world is hungrier and thirstier than ever for that *motherhood* which, *physically* or *spiritually,* is woman's vocation as it was Mary's."[11] In 1991, in an address to women workers at an Italian textile factory, John Paul II stated: "Work . . . must not take away from the woman, spouse and mother, the possibility of fulfilling the social and family functions which are proper to her, because only in this manner can she fulfil her human vocation in its feminine aspect as well."[12] John Paul had summarized his outlook on women in an earlier encyclical, *Mulieris Dignitatem,* another restatement of women's universal mission and function.[13]

Despite irreversible economic, technological, and social changes in the past century, papal and pastoral counsel to girls and women has remained unalterably tied to laments about the noxious effects of industrialism on the family. The popes' exaggerated vignettes of women soldiers, politicians, or factory drudges indicated an inability to conceive of a spectrum of careers open to women and, over the past century, an ignorance of how capitalism has changed since the first stages of industrialization. The Church only grudgingly accepted woman's utility as a wage earner in times of "necessity and duty." The Church envisioned women neither as primary or equal income providers for a family nor as permanent, single wage earners. Despite women's entry into the labor force even prior to the First World War, at the close of the war priests typically maintained that "the wage-labor of countless women is to a great extent unnatural, because unnecessarily enforced upon them through capitalistic greed, through inadequate legislation and through personal habits of thriftlessness and excess."[14] Further, Church documents often denied the need for female higher education and professional careerism, while at the same time opposing women's long-term unskilled labor. Underlying this denial was anxiety about the loss of the Church's authority over laywomen, forecast by the possibility of their intellectual and economic independence, and a general fear of the decline of patriarchy, which protected the nuclear family, whose fate the clergy linked to declining birth rates and rising divorce rates.

In addition to the effects of patriarchy within a capitalist mode of production, ethnicity was a crucial determinant in the construction of Catholic female identity. The predominance of the Irish in Boston Catholicism affected women's histories as well as that of the priesthood and hierarchy. Irish American women were unique among immigrants because they gained unprecedented economic autonomy in their lives by entering the work force in large numbers. They formed strong same-sex bonds and often deferred marriage, following economically driven patterns established in response to the great famine in Ireland, yet remained aloof from organized women's rights movements.[15] Despite the bonding experience of migration and of the workplace, gender did not become a unifying factor for Irish American women.

In America, immigrants and first-generation Irish women often became the primary breadwinners for their households as domestics, laundresses, and needleworkers, jobs that enabled them to propel their daughters upward into clerical fields and positions as public school teachers and telephone operators. Thus, prior to about 1890, Irish American women's careers either actively opposed or subtly circumvented the domestic ideology that later defined Catholic women and that affirmed "the nuclear family, isolation of women in their homes, and Christian rearing of children."[16] Despite these had atypical experiences of employment, over time a conservative ideology prevailed among Irish women, supplanting their relative autonomy of 1880–1900 with a doctrine of domesticity indebted to American bourgeois ideals. Given the emphasis on habit formation in contemporary Catholic ethics, women were reconstituted from breadwinners into moral guides for men and children. In this regard Catholicism followed the path of WASP culture in valuing woman's moral influence as an integral component of the "cult of true womanhood."[17] Upwardly mobile Catholics replicated Protestant domesticity, which was a class-based ideology, while continuing to present its doctrines as unique proof of Catholic adherence to natural law.

While approving certain vocations for women, the Catholic hierarchy and clergy perceived that agitation for women's rights was gaining ground in America after 1900, and the "woman question" could not be conveniently ignored. Between 1893 and 1919 several Church documents emanating from the American hierarchy contained statements on womanhood. The Catholic Lay Congress of 1893, which convened in Chicago one week before the World's Congress of Women and the World's Parliament of Religions and in conjunction with the Columbian Exposition, seemed to inaugurate a new Catholic interest in women's issues, as attested by its numerous sessions and papers on women's situation in the past and present.[18] By contrast, it is worth noting that no women were included in the official Catholic delegation of six laymen and fourteen priests to the Parliament of Religions. However, women's addresses at the lay congress emphasized their desire for visible roles in the Church and affirmed ecumenism and modernity, whereas the male Catholic delegates attempted the opposite. Where women suggested that "marriage ought not to be the ne plus ultra," anatomist Thomas Dwight, one of the few Catholic professors at Harvard, attacked the theory of evolution, while Monsignor Robert Seton fumed against the new biblical criticism.[19]

Catholic women asserted their public presence by their participation in the exhibitions and meetings of the Columbian congress, which featured several lectures and panel discussions devoted to women's issues. Not until after World War I, however, did the American hierarchy pay increased attention to women. In 1919 the bishops published their first national pastoral letter since 1884, which included two sections about women: a paragraph on mothers and a subsection on women's influence, which enlarged women's sphere to "the learned professions, the field of industry and the forum of political life," and which reflected increased recognition of women's participation in the work force.[20] The Bishops' Program of Social Reconstruction, issued earlier in the same year, recommended that women wartime workers "disappear as quickly as possible" from arduous jobs or from those "harmful to morals," but at least it supported equal pay for equal work for women performing the same tasks as men.[21]

Archbishop O'Connell ignored the liberal potential of the opinions aired at the congress of 1893 as well as the egalitarian spirit cautiously voiced by the bishops in 1919. Suspicious of what he termed sinister feminism, O'Connell dedicated himself to "saving" marriage and motherhood, reinforced by his promotion of diocesan campaigns against birth control, divorce, "immodesty," socialism, and suffrage. O'Connell's opinions and actions reiterated European Catholics' political arguments against the onslaughts of encroaching statism and, to this extent, indicate the derivative nature of American Catholic discussion of social problems, mediated through the Romanized perspective of O'Connell.

O'Connell was not unusual among the American bishops in his static view of womanhood. James Gibbons, the leader of the American Church as cardinal archbishop of Baltimore, was already notorious for his antisuffrage position, though he remains identified as one of America's liberal bishops because of his (highly qualified) support for organized labor and for Catholic assimilation. Archbishop Sebastian Messmer of Milwaukee, taking a reactionary view of history shared by many other Catholics, blamed the excesses of the French Revolution for women's unnatural desire for equality. He concluded that "instead of saying equal rights one should say similar rights."[22] Tellingly, Messmer was more concerned with the anticlericalism generated by the events of 1789–94 than with the woman question. William Stang, the first bishop of Fall River, Massachusetts, opposed education of women with the argument, "Smartness is not becoming in women; it makes them unlovely, as it deprives them of a great deal of the characteristic modesty so desirable in woman."[23] These examples show how clerical status anxiety manifested itself as hostility to women's civil rights. Some Catholic bishops used theology to support their traditionalism about women; others argued from "science" that women should not seek to "de-sex" themselves and lose their natural (biological and spiritual) qualities; still others cited "history" to imply that violent social and political upheavals lay behind these unnatural demands of women. William O'Connell agreed with these biological and historical polemics, adding yet a third cause for anxiety: economic independence of women. "It is plain," stated the archbishop, "that any attempt to make the individual woman a unit of society by giving her the same earning capacity as a man in ignoring the differences that make them alike yet complementary to each other, is certain to bring about disaster and ruin in the present family order."[24] O'Connell's concern for preservation of the family unit repeated the most common Catholic argument made against women's rights movements and later against feminism. From among O'Connell's opponents, the liberal bishops in America, whose force was seriously diminished by the Americanist and Modernist controversies of 1899 and 1907, came no challenge to the doctrine of woman's sphere.

Thus, while the Church's rhetoric affirmed the divine origins and eternal qualities of femininity, it denied the need for women to develop social and economic existences outside the family and the faith. Churchmen maintained that female economic autonomy and expanded female education would damage the family. Clearly, the Church feared that if a cult of female individualism were to replace the cult of domesticity, the family would be the casualty, which explains its intensely protectionist posture toward family unity and its refusal to confront squarely the existence of female wage earners. In western Europe and the United States industrialization had transformed the family economy from a productive unit into a wage unit. Nonetheless, the family continued to influence the productive activities of its members, and the Church continued to confine women within a cycle of responsibility to others. Part of what may loosely be termed a Catholic critique of the growing economic freedom of women stemmed from ancient Jewish and Christian precedents that equated women with the sins of self-indulgence and wasteful squandering and that implied that women could not be trusted with personal wealth.

The Church's resolute stance against indulging female luxury may also rep-

resent a reaction against the rising bourgeoisie and its ideology of accumulation and possessiveness. While expressing misogynist attitudes deeply
rooted within religious tradition, Catholic views of female consumption habits and female value also participated in the contemporary cultural debate surrounding the waste and excess that characterized affluent America. In the
Victorian middle class, as Protestant women became consumers rather than
producers, conspicuous consumption became essential to their lives because
it preserved society's reverential and deferential attitudes toward women.[25]
Ostentatious display and luxurious possessions became signs of leisure, affluence, and culture, as noted by religious and secular critics alike. The sharpest
critic of the function of this ethic of waste in the Gilded Age was Thorstein
Veblen, whose *Theory of the Leisure Class* observed how among those corrupted by excessive wealth, the value of an object increased according to its
uselessness.[26] As applied to women, Veblen's analysis condemned the fact that
women's uselessness as producers in effect guaranteed their value. Catholic
leaders tried to discourage women from uselessness and self-indulgence by
setting limits on both male and female economic ambition. Perhaps this was
an impossible form of resistance to the dynamic of waste and efficiency generated by industrial capitalism. Catholic men, often at an earlier stage in class
integration than men in the Protestant establishment, were encouraged to succeed, but not to the degree of relieving women from their household duties.
Predictably, the Church took a dim view of modern technology that enlarged
the leisure time of mothers: "Unfortunately, very many women seem to have
lost their footing, and are striving by new departures in all directions to fill
up the gap in their lives occasioned by superfluous leisure." The fear that
women would waste their new freedom in consumer pursuits prompted the
Catholic press to revalorize female self-sacrifice: "Can she ever be titled
mother who does not devote even one fourth of her day to the care and upbringing of her offspring? What are her claims to reverence and obedience
whose life is filled with a thousand occupations in which her children have
no part?"[27] The Church therefore encouraged female productivity insofar as
it meant domestic tasks and home economics. To its credit, it protested wom-
en's involvement in the abusive sweatshop system and other exploitative forms
of in-home labor.

The immigrant character of American Catholicism clearly left a mark on
values, consumption habits, and gender ideology. Among the rising Catholic
bourgeoisie, theories of womanhood reflected an amalgam of nostalgic representations of vulnerable femininity and new middle-class assumptions. The
Church responded to the alarming materialism of Boston's Irishtocracy by
preaching moderate economic aspirations and by reclaiming domesticity as
the basic force in society: "The standard of civilization is everywhere judged

by the home, and the nucleus of the home in every race and clime is indisputably the mother." But an equal function of the mother was her assimilative role in keeping her household from wasteful practices and in guarding its tenuous income.

The Church defined acquisitive materialism as an enemy of maternalism. It also confounded materialism, meaning excessive consumption, with philosophic materialism, meaning socialism. When linked to socialism, materialism provided the Church with a means to attack the feminist movement: "With Socialism's appalling menace so close and so persistent, there is no excuse for any mother, but more particularly for the Catholic mother, to live in apathy or indifference. Hers is the greatest responsibility; for every means is within her reach to cope successfully with the enemy."[28] O'Connell, as well as nearly all the American Catholic bishops, ran vigorous diocesan antisocialist campaigns based on propaganda about the preservation of motherhood and family, which included attacks on the women's movement designed to convince Catholics that feminism was antithetical to the values of Catholic womanhood.

Home and the Moral Order

In the early years of his long tenure, Archbishop O'Connell stated that "when mothers are superficial, society will be vile." As New England's highest-ranking Catholic leader, O'Connell maintained this conservative outlook his entire life. In 1912 he told the women of Boston, "Every Christian woman ought to have two things always at heart,—first, if married, the welfare of her husband, her children, her home; if unmarried, of her immediate family; their happiness must be her most sacred duty."[29] In his 1913 pastoral letter, "The Family and the Home," he presented the Holy Family as the model for Christian living with Mary at its center: "It is her high privilege, as it is her most solemn obligation, to put a deep and tender love of God, of Jesus and His Blessed Mother into the heart of her child before it even leaves the family sheepfold for the instruction of Church and school."[30] A survey of Archbishop O'Connell's eleven volumes of published sermons reveals an unmodified view of feminine virtue. Of those sermons and addresses given between 1907 and 1922, approximately ten directly address woman's role, motherhood, or family. In them, O'Connell described mothers as "the first, the most persuasive and the most effective" teachers; nuns he defined as virgins "consecrated" to serving God and children; single women, the most volatile and vulnerable group, he warned to "cast away at once and forever the dress, dance, amusement and entertainment" that threaten the destruction of true womanhood.[31] To highlight his reverence for motherhood, O'Connell never missed a public opportunity to expose the horrors of feminism as he defined it, in florid anecdotes that increased his reputation as an antifeminist. As late as 1935 O'Connell intimated that he would not receive women at the altar rail for Communion if they were wearing lipstick.[32] Scornful of cosmetics, short skirts, dances, male "crooners," movies, and novels, O'Connell's moralism was representative of the hierarchy and clergy.[33]

Reiterating papal statements, Boston's archbishop defined women in relational and obligational terms, as part of a married couple or a family unit, and as spiritual, if not always biological, mothers. In the 1940s he still proclaimed that "the home is woman's normal sphere—maidenhood, wifehood, motherhood, and home. It is God's institution. It is the cornerstone of civilization and the foundation of social order. Upon its purity and integrity God based the stability of nations and the peace and prosperity of society." Throughout his career he praised the power of domesticity: "The home is a sanctuary where woman's functions are sacred, and in the performance of these she exercises a power that is practically unlimited. Necessity and duty may demand her work and presence elsewhere, but normally her place is at home."[34] As in all doctrinal matters, he dutifully adhered to the guidelines on female purity set by recent popes. Those documents, which included Leo XIII's "Instructions to Christian Women on Fashion" and Pius X's prohibition of *grand décolletage* at receptions where church dignitaries would be present, provided a Roman context for O'Connell's crusade for female modesty.[35]

O'Connell resembled his neighboring bishop, William Stang, who had given this advice to an audience of "mostly women" at the Boston Catholic Union Building in 1907: "In the greatest peril besetting young women religion is a safeguard. When a certain misfortune falls upon women without religion, they rush to water to end all, or resort to the poison bottle, paris green or arsenic. But the Christian woman, what is her resort? Her first thought is Christ and Calvary. She feels the pangs of sorrow, but her soul's prayer is, 'Lord, thy will be done.'"[36] Stang's melodramatic defense of the power of religion against female hysteria drew a parallel between the Christian woman's lot and the suffering of Jesus. By offering the model of divine self-sacrifice, Stang attempted to elevate the suffering of women to that of Christ, the perfect servant of God's will. In this regard, he used images well-established in Catholic didactic and sermon literature for women, which linked female suffering not only to Mary but to the Savior. Leaders like O'Connell and Stang regarded female suffering as natural to women's sphere, which enabled priests to interpret female inequality also as obedience to God's will.

Clerical teachings about home and family were intended to maintain unchanging gender roles for women, which assumed tautologically that women's responsibility for the quality of home life proved their natural inclination against public life. Laity shared in the belief that women were responsible for creating a social utopia based on virtuous homes. Yet the correspondence between Catholic and Protestant ideals of motherhood suggests a common origin in middle-class ideology, which further functioned to obliterate class distinctions by creating one role for all women. Domesticity served the emerging Catholic middle class by protecting the family basis for property and its transmission to the next generation, while its codes of modest conduct and prudent saving exhorted the working-class family to imitate their betters.

Describing the details of domesticity in the early twentieth century became a project of immense proportions, for which clergy and laity alike produced sermons and instructional manuals, supported laywomen's societies, and held public rallies and forums. One early example by a Bostonian was a three-volume publication entitled *Our Church, Her Children and Institutions,* which reflected a residual Victorian piety:

> What an earthly paradise is a refined Catholic home! The parents belonging to some of the church societies, and the elder children are members of the sodality. The sacraments keep them innocent, and the Sacrament of sacraments gives them the ineffable peace of Christ. Quiet, order, gentleness and kindness are the guardian angel of the household, and education brings in its accomplishments to add their charms to the ordinary monotony of life. The souls of all the members of the family are growing in grace; their minds are open to what is most choice in science and art; and in their material surroundings, they enjoy all the comforts and some of the luxuries of nineteenth [*sic*] century existence.[37]

Sacralizing bourgeois home life by tying it to the sacramental system of the Church was a justification used also by Catholic women. In *Girlhood's Hand-Book of Woman,* a compendium of papers delivered at the Congress of Women in 1893, editor Eleanor Donnelly of Philadelphia exhorted her readers that teaching salvation "is the primal, the most important office of the Catholic wife and mother; for what work accomplished by gifted women in art, literature, science, or statecraft, can compare with the molding of a single childish character, with the gospel of salvation engraven upon a single, childish soul?"[38] Donnelly's fin de siècle belief in the virtuous role of mothers as molders of character endured in twentieth-century ideology. The twelve essays in her volume, three by Bostonians, focused on the achievements of Catholic women through the ages. Those profiled included nuns who were missionaries, nurses, and teachers; saints, queens, and martyrs who had political influence; and laywomen who helped the poor but who did not neglect their own families. As Donnelly explained, "The average woman can have but one mission, one kingdom—that of Home." Donnelly's own phrase "the pulpit of the hearthstone" both described the spatial limits of woman's influence and linked it metaphorically with the clergy's preaching function. Consequently, Catholic women of Boston who wished to extend their sphere beyond the home began to employ the didactic and moral rhetoric that the clergy associated with motherhood and domesticity.

The Catholic doctrine of the model family relied on the privatization of women. As a Catholic delegate stated at the Congress of Women, "The work of woman radiates from that home as from its most natural as well as from its most universal center."[39] In fact, the norms governing laywomen were nearly indistinguishable from the rules for women in religious orders. The application of a quasi-monastic formula to laywomen limited the Church's vision for them. As cloistered beings, women were taught to gain satisfaction vicariously through their children by providing the nation with its next generation of patriots and priests. Yet as American women began to have public careers, the Catholic Church was challenged to reassess its understanding of demands for women to serve roles both inside and outside the family. Since the Church honored mothering above careerism, female charity work provided one acceptable outlet for women outside the home. The Church ignored the fact that poor and single women did not have the luxury of opting for service work over getting employment in order to survive. Publications by Catholic laywomen, however, rationalized work more sympathetically: "The sensible woman realizes that any sort of work is a thousand times better than an unhappy marriage, and the unselfish one often chooses to earn a living rather than to be a burden on an overtaxed father or brother. . . . The favored daughters of genius hardly count in the vast army of stenographers, cashiers, clerks, who go forth to battle for bread because they would have to do without if they did not."[40] Here, too, middle-class women developed ways to use religious doctrine about selflessness to justify getting a job.

Although Catholics blamed feminists for making an unnatural fuss about gender rights, Cardinal O'Connell intimated that motherhood was being endangered not only by feminism but by "a growing weakness of the manhood of the nation." O'Connell asserted that feminism resulted from men's abdication of their rightful authority, which gave "an undue prominence to the feminine side." In other words, feminism would not exist if men would claim their legitimate power.[41] By chastising both sexes for failing to uphold Catholic standards of womanhood and by creating a sense of crisis that demanded immediate, united Catholic action, O'Connell hoped to insure widespread interest in sustaining the status quo for women as a guarantee of secure and stable social relations. Home continued to represent for Catholics an institution of God, a sacred space, a nursery for heaven, and a building block of American patriotism. The social function of the Christian home, presided over by women, was to teach children obedience to authority and to prepare them to defend their Catholic faith in the world.

From Daughters of Eve
to Children of Mary

In contrast to the fertility goddesses of pre-Christian cults, the Virgin Mary of the early Christians was an unusual entity. Unlike Christianity, which has uniquely developed veneration for a virgin saint, pagan cults generally worshiped fecundity, making a virgin deity somewhat anomalous.[42] Recently, Christian devotions to Mary have been subjected to revisionism by feminist historians and theologians who conclude that the image of Mary has been manipulated by a male clergy and hierarchy to justify female submissiveness, an "eternal woman" mythology, and male domination, signified in the Church's substitution of one virgin saint for the plural goddesses of pre-Christian religions. Others have argued less polemically that the Virgin Mary was elevated by the Church to provide a safe object of contemplation and adoration for its celibate male clergy, as well as a model of purity and an intercessor for all Christians. While these hermeneutic questions do not particularly concern our study of Boston, such scholarship is significant because it also addresses the historical construction of gender in Catholicism, which has depended on the impossible unity of virgin and mother, and on the definition of woman as man's Other.[43]

Historians and anthropologists have recently demonstrated that the widespread revival of Marian piety in the nineteenth century was undergirded by reactionary social and political concerns. In fact, according to one interpretation of the function of Marian apparitions, "This defensive antimodernism may be the most distinct legacy of the Church-defined Marian cult of the nineteenth century."[44] Following this claim, during the past century Mary was isolated as a special symbol of Catholic antimodernism, and today's visionaries show no sign of altering the pattern. By analyzing devotional and didactic texts generated by both men and women, we can further understand the character and uses of Marian devotion in Boston. Clearly, the image of the Mother of God was employed by Church leaders to foster lay devotion to a desired definition of femaleness, but it also represented resistance to modern change. In general, pre–Vatican II Marian theology was based on scant biblical proof of Mary's life and character, relying instead on papal teaching, popular devotions, and philosophical arguments accumulated through centuries of post-biblical traditions.[45]

In Boston, Marian ideology was employed as part of the Church's construction of a separatist Catholic subculture against the Protestant tradition. Catholics might have argued that their heritage held a more positive image of the feminine qualities because of their devotion to Mary, which had been suppressed in Protestantism. Instead, Marian devotion was used primarily to justify Catholic political conservatism, papal infallibility, and irrationalist piety. Reflecting the insights of anthropologist Mary Douglas, Peter Williams has suggested that the overall increase in Catholic saints' devotions from the 1850s reflects an inward-turning trend in the institutional Church, which manipulated popular devotions in order to shield itself from external threats to its "body." The rise of Marian devotions between Vatican I and II fit this pattern of defensive piety and obsession with bodily purity by representing the Church, like Mary, as a nurturing, protecting mother.[46]

A second, more obvious use of Mary in Catholic devotions was as a gender model. In her manual for girls, Eleanor Donnelly exhorted Catholics to follow the example of Mary, who "except on two occasions" did nothing extraordinary. Even in her two unusual roles, first by requesting Jesus to transform water into wine at the wedding feast of Cana and second by blessing the unborn John the Baptist in his mother's womb, Mary "explained woman's vocation" and "showed forth woman's duty to the Christian."[47] In these two New Testament stories chosen by Donnelly, Mary acts as intercessor and prophet in situations meant to prefigure the revelation of her son's glory. By cultivating similar humility, girls were taught to imitate Mary's example of reflecting Christ's power, avoiding egotism. Donnelly's *Hand-Book* was dedicated to the Children of Mary, the convent school alumnae society that fostered imitation of this passive model of womanhood. By contrasting a negative assessment of women as descendants of Eve with that of women as children of Mary, the Church designated the strong but obedient, maternal yet virginal Mary as the model Catholic woman.

Mary's "prerogative" as the "Immaculate Conception," associated with the Lourdes apparitions of 1858, had become especially significant to American Catholics since 1865, when the American bishops had successfully petitioned the Vatican to dedicate the United States to devotion to the Blessed Virgin. By the early 1900s, Americans too were experiencing an impact from Europe's "Marian century," the revival of piety and pilgrimages following numerous reports of Marian apparitions beginning in the 1830s.[48] Pope Leo XIII issued eleven encyclicals on the rosary, the major form of Marian devotion, eight of them between 1891 and 1898.[49] Although the United States was not the site of a Marian apparition until the 1950s, its Catholics nonetheless participated in the widespread increase in Marian devotions in western Europe, particularly after the apparitions at Lourdes (1858), Pontmain (1871), and Fatima, Portugal (1917), which were publicized in America by French missionaries.[50] A copy of the Lourdes grotto was constructed for the devotions of male students at the University of Notre Dame in 1896, and grotto visits have remained a feature of campus spiritual life well into the present. Further, one can trace the Marian devotionalism behind the founding of several American Catholic journals in the late nineteenth and early twentieth century to promote a Marian ideal in literature, in vocations, in private devotions, and in parish sodalities. The Latin phrase *Tota pulchra es Maria* (here the word *pulchra* connotes Mary's complete moral perfection) became the motto of the American sodality magazine, the *Queen's Work* (St. Louis), whose title itself is a reference to Mary, Queen of Heaven. Other national publications including *Ave Maria* (Notre Dame), edited by a Bostonian; *Our Lady of Good Counsel* (Philadelphia); and *The Magnificat* (Manchester, New Hampshire) were inspired by attributes of Mary. Bishops and priests who professed special devotions to particular attributes of the Blessed Virgin urged both men and women to follow Mary's example.[51]

Unfortunately, overemphasis on Mary's biological role as mother of Jesus led the Church to equate femininity with motherhood. The objectionable 1912 *Catholic Encyclopedia* entry called "Woman" asserted that "the completely developed feminine personality is thus to be found in the mother."[52] The *Encyclopedia* had defined women as "in some respects inferior to the male sex, both as regards body and soul. On the other hand, woman has qualities which man lacks." Evidently the author, Augustine Rösler, an Austrian Scripture and Hebrew scholar, could not recollect any affirmative female traits because he enumerated none. Instead he went on to dissect the "woman question" for readers by rejecting secular feminism: "It is only by the restoration of Christianity in society that the rightful and natural relations of man and woman can become once more restored. This Christian reform of society, however, cannot be expected from the radical woman movement, notwithstanding its valuable services for social reform." Typically, Rösler did not separate the social identity of women from the family unit, and his concept of Christian restorationism echoed the Catholic neofeudalism of his contemporaries. A venerable lineage of Catholic saints, from Paul to Thomas Aquinas, and popes, from Leo XIII and Pius X, had agreed that the "natural position is assigned to woman in every form of society that springs necessarily from the family."[53] It was in part this inability to consider women as distinct from the family that defined women's selfhood through their responsibility for the physical and spiritual well-being of others.

In the early 1900s the Catholic hierarchy, clergy, and press went on to manufacture an apocalyptic crisis mentality about the decline of motherhood and of the home, intended to mobilize girls and mothers to their defense. The Boston *Pilot* reported, for example, "The pious customs of the home and its religious traditions are disappearing; parental vigilance is growing lax, and the spirit of the world is driving from the Catholic abode the signs of the Catholic faith its occupants profess."[54] Cardinal O'Connell claimed that "if ever there was a period in our country's existence when good and God-fearing women were needed, it is to-day. If ever it was necessary for the Nation's womanhood to exert themselves in the interest of virtue and religion, and to throw about the Nation's children the saving influence of a Christian home, that time is now."[55] The search for a female role model to guide the faltering family inevitably led back to the Marian virtues. "In all things, dear girls," wrote a priest in a sodality book for the Children of Mary, "you should try to resemble your Heavenly Mother."[56] O'Connell chose the Marian feast of the Immaculate Conception (which was, incidentally, his birthday) to deliver in 1913 his lengthiest statement on the Christian family.[57] O'Connell's appeals to Marian devotion became more strenuous as he aged. In the 1930s he argued, "It is through womanhood especially, that Mary's power and influence must be manifested in the world." Not only did O'Connell define true womanhood in terms of Mary's submissive suffering, but he linked her purity to the salvation of the United States. In a sermon called "Mary and Womanhood," O'Connell linked mothering to patriotism, which, like charity, began at home: "No trifling influence, then, is woman's; no unimportant mission is hers; no insignificant responsibility does she assume. She is the educator at the hearthstone where the destinies of a nation are determined, for there the character of a nation's citizenship is formed."[58] Once again, women were encouraged to subordinate their wills to the common weal. This ideology, centered on Mary, remained unchanged in Boston for the next decades and among the various ethnic groups. John Cardinal Wright, for example, advised the LCW in 1946 that Mary "should be for you a symbol of the fact that in all His plans for humanity and at every crisis in history God depends upon the cooperation of women."[59]

Numerous laywomen described Mary's role in Catholicism, usually without directly challenging the clerical interpretations. As Catholic social integration increased, some Catholic women became preoccupied with explaining the meaning of Marian devotions to non-Catholics in order to defend their Americanness. They commonly justified their devotion to Mary as a natural form of homage to a heroine. Katherine Conway delivered one such speech entitled "The Blessed among Women" to an audience that included Protestants:

> But what of the pictures and statues of the Blessed Virgin—what of the scapulars and medals? I ask with equal reason, what of the statues of Governor Winthrop, and John Quincy Adams, and Horace Mann? What of the pictures of William Lloyd Garrison and Wendell Phillips? What of the ribbon of the White Cross League; the blue ribbon of the temper-

ance cause; the red, white and blue button of the Grand Army men; the miniatures of lovers or husbands which fond women wear about them? The same principle—and it is an innocent, grateful, and honorable principle—underlies the honors which our human hearts prompt us to pay to the eminent of our kind, whether they be heroes in the natural or in the supernatural order.

In order to disarm Protestant apprehensions about Catholic "Mariolatry," Conway noted the "sympathetic understanding shown by so many New England writers, of the true meaning of Catholic devotion to the Blessed Virgin," including Longfellow, Whittier, Hawthorne, and Holmes.[60] Protestant converts to Catholicism often became strong defenders of Mary, as did Emma Forbes Cary in this self-effacing address to the 1893 World's Congress of Women: "I will not touch the dangerous ground of theology; I appeal to history to show that public opinion was so purified by the veneration felt for the Virgin Mary as to lift at once the service of women in the early church to a position of dignity."[61] Without attempting to trespass on the "male" realm of intellect, Conway, Cary, and other women argued that Mary deserved reverence from humankind because of her heroic role in uplifting women's service.

In this context, Mary the woman and Mary the mother served the Church's strategy of Catholic integration. On the other hand, we may also interpret the somewhat exaggerated attention to Marian ideology by men and women in Boston as further evidence of Catholic sectarianism—attempts to locate a distinctive outsider identity apart from Protestantism or secularism. Appeals to virgin-mothers and virgin-warriors were used to rally Catholics to the cause of saving the family and society and to enhance the community's sense of relationship to a legion of saints battling the corrupt world.

Female saints, therefore, also contributed to women's spiritual and social formation. It seems that female saints who had active, "masculine" lives were usually interpreted as exceptional, not "normative."[62] As a rule, girls and women were steered toward the contemplative rather than the active virtues of saints and were actually counseled to avoid unsupervised reading of the writings of mystics like Teresa of Avila, whose erotic mystical images were deemed too dangerous for the untutored female imagination.[63] We have seen that Mary the Virgin Mother was the most common example offered to women and girls. But women's interpretations of the Virgin suggested that all women were not thereby obliged to be limited to the vocation of motherhood. A proponent of "The Public Rights of Women" in *Catholic World* noted that "the same reasoning would force all good men to be artisans because our Saviour was a carpenter." She concluded that "we cannot absolutely draw the line separating the domestic from the public life. The boundary of woman's sphere is constantly shifting, and no two of our opponents themselves will exactly agree as to its proper position."[64] Thus women defended a range of vocations for themselves in public life by arguing that saints had set the pattern of following unique calls, not merely copying the life of Mary.

In Europe and America the symbol of Joan of Arc had experienced a revival that peaked in the years around World War I. Examples of her popularity in the Boston area include a Harvard student performance of Johann Schiller's play *The Maid of Orleans* in the Harvard stadium in 1909.[65] Sarah Bernhardt, who spoke only French, was just one of a series of continental actresses to portray her. In 1916 Cecil B. DeMille completed a film of Joan's life, adapted from Schiller's play, which he modernized by adding trench scenes from the world war and monumentalized by the addition of a coronation scene involving a a crowd of thousands. While the commercial value of St. Joan was exploited by the entertainment industry, Catholic devotions to her (and to other saints) nonetheless express related political underpinnings to the popular piety of this era. Joan's appeal reflected a cross-cultural and cross-denominational interest in medieval mystics and in nationalism, perhaps as cultural attempts to resolve social and political concerns as well as individual psychological preoccupations.

While this is not the place to discuss the role of religious symbols in the evolution of European statehood, it is significant that Joan of Arc was admired by Catholics and Protestants. For Catholics, she played a central role in nationalist propaganda in France. English and American Catholic writers such as Agnes Sadlier, Robert Hugh Benson, and Bernard Vaughan dedicated plays, sermons, poems, and stories to the Maid of Orleans that were popular in the United States.[66] For middle-class Protestants, Catholic saints may have offered models of self-control as well as means to an emotional catharsis preparing them for an authentic experience of faith.[67] Writers as diverse as Henry Adams, Mark Twain, Francis Cabot Lowell, Andrew Lang, Anatole France, Albert Bigelow Paine, and George Bernard Shaw wrote about St. Joan. Lowell delivered the Lowell Institute Lectures in Boston about Joan in 1895 at the opening of the revival of interest in her; Shaw's *St. Joan* was first produced in 1923 shortly after her canonization.

Devotions to Joan of Arc and to other female saints, notably Mary, Monica, Ann, Catherine of Siena, and even Teresa of Avila, were usually invoked by the hierarchy and clergy in support of female dependence and submission. It is not surprising that Mary was used to defend motherhood, but it is somewhat remarkable that Joan's striking military and political career was transformed, as in Archbishop O'Connell's interpretation, into a patriotic blow against socialism's "damnable negations."[68] St. Joan also was translated into

a symbol of female subordination, as a "Virgin-Warrior who aids men to fulfill men's goals."[69] Bernard Vaughan, an outspoken Jesuit who was chaplain
to the Catholic Women's League in Great Britain, argued as much when he
wrote that women could learn from Joan how to exercise "that refining and
spiritualizing influence which is her special charm as well as her principal
prerogative and primal duty."[70] His Joan was a combination of political traditionalism and self-sacrificing femininity. As man's visionary inspiration, Joan
confirmed patriarchy rather than female initiative or female exceptionalism.

    Interpretations of St. Joan by laywomen both supported and revised those
of the clergy. Two Massachusetts Catholics, Louise Guiney and Susan Emery,
were among a group of writers and poets who praised the active virtues of
the female saints. According to Guiney's niece, Louise's "affection for the
active saints rather than the contemplative[,] . . . not least, the tardily can-
onized Jeanne d'Arc,—saints who were not just edifying names to her but
perpetual 'fire and wings' to cheer and to inspirit,—was typical of one who
never forgot she was a soldier's daughter."[71] Guiney's affinity for Joan, partly
explicable by her strong psychological identification with her father's military
career, was therefore not for "feminist" reasons, since Guiney used Joan primarily to justify traditional notions of female virtue. Nonetheless, more nuanced interpretations of Joan did emerge among women. Poet and essayist
Katherine Brégy, for example, stated that Joan's beatification was never "more
timely in our own professedly feminist age! Only, it does seem superficially a
little curious that Jeanne should not be even more confidently, more universally, exploited by women, both within and without the Church." Because
Joan of Arc perfectly blended the virtues of mother and father, she was the
ideal symbol for the modern woman, Brégy concluded.[72] Brégy's subversion
of the Church's distinctions between separate masculine and feminine spheres,
and her vision of an ideal human who united male and female traits, offered
an alternative to the Church's view of eternal gender separation. Instead of
picturing gender relations as a binary opposition, Brégy and others undermined sexual division in order to make female saints into symbols of all humanity. While these interpretations did not amount to a revisionist feminine
spirituality, they do indicate that women generated their own interpretations
within the Church's official representations of women.

    The politics of Joan's canonization between the presentation of her case for
sainthood in 1888 to her canonization in 1920 contributed to her revival in
American piety. The French bishop of Orleans, Monsignor Dupanloup, had
urged Joan's case largely to oppose socialist threats to the Church. By 1894
Leo XIII, mindful of socialist electoral gains in France, declared Joan venerable, locating her as a symbol of faith and patriotism against atheism and
socialism. In 1909 the succeeding pope, Pius X, declared her blessed. Joan's

canonization in 1920 by Benedict XV reflected successful continued pressure in France from Action Française. Throughout Europe, Joan was manipulated by both the political right and left. The official Church position tended to be reactionary, emphasizing her symbolic role in defending Roman Catholicism against political radicalism.[73] Joan of Arc rose in prominence in Catholic devotions, and in the Boston hierarchy she came to hold a special place.[74] In "Mary and Womanhood," Cardinal O'Connell modified the Church's usual distinction between the passive Mary and the active Joan. By reinvesting Mary with the traits of Joan he re-invented the role of Christian housewife as an activist vocation. He made motherhood itself into an act of heroism. But when discussing the lives of female saints other than Mary and Joan, O'Connell conspicuously toned down the radical or extraordinary features of their lives by accenting instead their exemplary holiness and their advisory roles. Saints Theresa and Catherine of Siena, for example, "though both . . . models of extraordinary piety and devotion, . . . were conspicuous for their exceptional common sense. St. Theresa gave advice to the great men of her day. St. Catherine, the daughter of a wool-dyer, directed the affairs of Popes and Kings. It was their womanly fineness of perception, plus their great holiness, that enabled them to accomplish so much."[75] Like the hierarchy, laymen argued that the Church had never restricted women's opportunities for holiness, such as those inherent in the vocations of nun and sister. In an address to women college graduates, James J. Walsh stated, "Our mother Church, far from wanting to keep women in the background, has always accorded them full and equal rights in their own domains and, above all, has given them absolute independence in the religious organizations as far as that is compatible with effective co-operation in good work."[76]

By interpreting the Church as egalitarian, men could present Joan, a soldier and martyr, to women as an exception to the norm for ideal womanhood established by the docile Mary, but still well within the tradition of female chastity and obedience to rightful authority.[77] Still, Joan's peculiarities were formidable: she dressed like a man, heard voices like a prophet, persuaded hesitant kings to act boldly, and suffered a violent fiery death. However, in Catholic devotions, her active traits were presented as proof that Joan, made exceptional by God's grace, possessed traits transcending gender altogether. Traditionally, this strategy has allowed Church spokesmen to place Joan within an "androgynous zone" that, Marina Warner has claimed, has become synonymous with asexual angelic purity in Catholic sainthood. Simultaneously, the Church has retained its traditional contrast of Joan and Mary as emblems of the active (masculine) and passive (feminine) components of womanhood. The view that women should exert influence in the world indirectly through moral example was not solely an invention of priests and laymen. It was seconded by a chorus of women, who took their models from the saints of early Christianity. Mary Maher, for example, gave an address at the World's Congress of Women in 1893 in which she speculated, "Would John Chrysostom have been 'the golden mouthed' without his mother-educator? Left a widow in her twentieth year, she gave her life and labor for the culture of her boy. Augustine, too, was not indebted wholly to the 'Hortensius' of Cicero for his searching after truth, nor to the pleadings of Saint Ambrose to renounce his sinful life. His sainted mother Monica's entreaties, supplementing his prayers, aroused his sluggish will at last, and through her brave, uplifting love her son was raised to the church's calendar of saints."[78] Maher's focus on the mothers of saints supported the idea that mothers held power that was primarily moral, and goals that were vicarious. Her interpretation was echoed by Cardinal O'Connell: "I have the fullest confidence in the sturdy faith of the men of this great Diocese. And my chief reason for confidence is that they are the sons of such saintly Catholic mothers. Those noble women have known what sacrifices loyal Catholicity requires. They have met the rigid demands of unswerving faith nobly, and without compromise. The sons of such mothers will surely never falter."[79]

Aside from perpetuating the doctrine of separate spheres, at least two other results stemmed from official attitudes toward female saints in the early twentieth century. The first, as I have implied, was a sentimentalization of home as a sacred space, presided over by a pious mother, modeled on Mary, and permanently consecrated by God in the Holy Family. A Boston mother of eleven described the ideal Christian home: "There is the honor and purity of the fireside respected; the overpowering sweetness and strength of family ties acknowledged; the reverential home that awaits upon the father and mother shown. There are sensitive and refined women bearing sorrow with resignation and hardship without rebellion; combating pain with patience and fulfilling harsh duty without complaint."[80] In this utopia, children never challenge the authority of parents, and mothers never question their harsh duties. Laywomen seemed to acquiesce in this view because the positive images that Mary evoked reinforced already powerful cultural norms of womanhood in America and sanctified the sorrow and suffering associated with womanhood. A wife of a Catholic journalist was inspired by this challenge to be humble and self-denying: "We feel that the ideal of purity which is held before our eyes from childhood, the ideal that points to the Virgin Mother as the supreme achievement of human virtue is the greatest tribute that any church could pay to woman."[81] The self-denial of Catholic women was further made into a mark of their superiority to their non-Catholic sisters, "who buy the right to idleness and personal adorning at the expense of the childless homes which are a disgrace and menace to the nation."[82] By portraying Roman Catholicism as the agent responsible for elevating their sexual identity through motherhood, women were directed to see themselves as the religious leaders of America, comparable to St. Joan and Queen Isabella in Christian Europe. Americans seemed unconcerned to question the relevance of this feudal, aristocratic model from an earlier social formation for their own democratic culture; hence Catholic piety contained and perpetuated highly conflicted notions of womanhood.

A second Church use of the female saints went beyond reassuring women, as O'Connell and Walsh attempted, that Catholicism's historical record was "pro-woman," to invoking female saints in defense of the Church. The Church's claim that it encouraged accomplished, active women not only ignored very real constraints on women set by canon law, but also selected a handful of exceptional female saints to represent the masses of women. To further underscore the elevated status of womanhood, devotional literature represented the Church as a hospitable mother and as a home for all believers, as in O'Connell's tribute to "the fruitful mother of many children, she gives of her endless bounty to all who live within her house."[83] The parish, the unit of Catholicism with which most members formed intimate contact, had become a "household of faith" in the nineteenth century.[84] O'Connell told the AFCS that all races "own the Catholic Church as their spiritual mother, she becomes the great unifier, the strong but gentle eradicator of narrowness and jealousy, the supreme teacher of human brotherhood which transcends all nationalism."[85] He invoked the metaphor of Mother Church as a universal nurturer as frequently as his image of the Church Militant battling all threats to civilization.[86] O'Connell again chose maternal imagery to contrast the motherly warmth of Catholic charity with the cold calculation of secular philanthropy: "The Church is a mother. She consequently knows and sympathizes with her family and keeps her eye on the pedagogue with his myopic vision, rigid face, and his hand on the ruler. When, as often happens, he attempts to make round plugs fit square holes, she reminds him that the world is not a little red schoolhouse, and that humanity is a family, not a formula."[87] The Church, like the ideal woman, united the omniscient mother and the vanquishing warrior. Hence, the laity were encouraged to regard the Church both as a protector and as a body vulnerable to attack. Revivals of devotions to the saints and to the Church's image of Holy Mother (the Church) joined with Holy Father (the pope) projected a familial model of the institution, in which lay children were harbored from the evil world by loving parents. This domestic scenario provided a further rationale for the laity to defend the autonomy of a Catholic subculture.

Backyard theatricals at Guiney's Longwall Cottage, Oxford, England, September 1918. Dressed up as Catholic monarchs of Europe are Grace Guiney as Queen Blanche of Castile and her niece Loulie as the young King Louis IX of France. (Guiney Room, Holy Cross College Rare Books and Special Collections)

Women and Education

While Catholic women were excluded from institutional sources of power, namely the priesthood and theological instruction, the Church elevated compensatory didactic roles for them in teaching and literary vocations, which allowed women to fulfill their "natural" role as moral guides. Single women became writers, performed voluntary charity work, and taught in primary schools. In fact, the teaching profession was becoming dominated by women in Boston. The relationship between parochial school systems, with very few lay teachers (only forty-six in 1920 because of the large number of teaching sisters in the archdiocese), and the public system, whose instructors were mostly unmarried Irish Catholic women, became a distinctive feature of Boston life. The relatively low percentage of parochial schools for Boston, in 55 percent of its parishes during O'Connell's tenure, contrasted with Chicago's national high of 80 percent, signified that Boston was a laggard in parochial schooling prior to the 1930s.[88] However, this situation may have been tolerated by the Church because Irish Catholic women dominated both public and private elementary education. There is evidence that an overlap existed between teacher training programs for both systems as well as in ethnoreligious domination by Irish Catholics in school administration by the 1920s.[89]

Cardinal O'Connell himself was not above pressuring the superintendent of public schools to follow Church guidance, as in this communication of 1922: "His Eminence says that he hopes that the Catholic teachers will take a firm stand against the Turner-Sterling Bill which is opposed by most of the best educators in the country today as this measure tends to socialism and tyranny of the State in education."[90] Given the hegemony of the Irish in Boston public education, and the tepid support for parochial schools, gender became an important factor in education of young children since women came to dominate this profession that the Church regarded as an essential female function.

Despite the negative connotations attached to their intellects in some contexts, women, and especially women religious, were expected to be educators of the young in the Catholic subculture, guided by the clergy. Priests exerted influence disproportionate to the number of women religious in Boston. In 1907 when O'Connell arrived there were 598 active priests in the city. In 1910 a total of 654 priests were stationed in Boston; 517 were diocesan, and 137 were in religious orders. In 1920, 804 priests were active in Boston, an increase of nearly 16 percent in 10 years. Despite the availability of clergy, in 1923 there were 1,984 women religious in Boston, more than twice the number of priests. While the most promising diocesan priests were sent to advanced studies in Rome, most nuns and sisters who entered novitiates in their teens had difficulty obtaining permission to pursue academic degrees or advanced professional training. In comparing priestly training with the educational opportunities of women religious, we find that the Church welcomed women's religious vocations but restricted the autonomy of individuals and of the order. Advantages resulting from a religious vocation differed for each sex as well. Women were called upon to express altruism and submission, while Catholic men could at least expect to enhance their social status by joining the priesthood and, once within that vocation, to be upwardly mobile through educational opportunities or parish appointments.

Children were entrusted to the care of women religious because of the association between female purity and childhood innocence, whereas the intellectual training of adult men was reserved for celibate clerics. In 1908 O'Connell required pastors to appoint a parish priest as director of each parish school, further cementing his episcopal power and male dominance in Catholic education.[91] O'Connell summarized the value of the teaching sisters as consisting "mainly of two things—obedience to the law of God and to the civil laws, and the conformation of their lives to God's will." According to him, children learned from the regulated lives of the sisters that "every day and every hour of that life is regulated by a law, by rule. Their whole life is made to conform to God's will in every way."[92] The ideological function of

Sisters of St. Joseph in the St. Regis Orchestra, formed in 1913 for the golden jubilee of their superior, Mother Mary Regis. (Congregation of Sisters of St. Joseph)

religious women teachers, therefore, was to mold a conformist, rules-abiding Catholic child.

Girls consistently outnumbered boys in Boston's parochial grammar schools by 6,000 students in a total of 50,000, while teaching sisters outnumbered teaching brothers 906 to 77.[93] By 1920 girls in parochial elementary and high school in Boston numbered 40,510, while the total number of male students was only 31,836.[94] In higher education, however, men continually surpassed women in opportunities and numbers. Katherine Conway, first woman editor of the Boston *Pilot,* found a mistrust of educated women built into the attitudes of male religious orders, such as the Jesuits: "Now, I humbly hold it against St. Ignatius Loyola that he was so inflexibly a man's man; and I have known certain of his sons whose spirit to the devout sex might be aptly summed up as 'Tolerari potest.'"[95]

It is useful to consider how seminary formation represented women. In general, the training of male candidates for the priesthood ignored many dimensions of lay experience and instead focused on the traditional study of Scripture, moral and dogmatic theology, homiletics, church history, philosophy, canon law, and liturgy. Seminarians' spiritual literature remained Eurocentric and derivative.[96] Standard theology texts used at the Brighton seminary since its founding in 1884 probably included the works of two French theologians. The first, Gallican Louis Bailly, had been placed on the Index of Censored Books in 1852. His work was subsequently replaced by the texts of Adolph Tanquerey, author of *The Spiritual Life* (1930), which was used in many American seminaries until Vatican II. A textbook by Bishop Stang, *Pastoral Theology* (1896), also had influence in Boston. This is not surprising, since Stang had been vice-rector of the North American College in Rome and professor of pastoral theology at the time O'Connell was attending. Stang revived the Italian strain in American piety that followed the eighteenth-century writings of St. Alphonsus de Liguori, founder of the Redemptorists and a staunch defender of the Jesuits. Liguori's influential book, *The Glories of Mary* (1750), starkly divided women into two categories: nuns, who were revered, and laywomen, who were dangerous. Clerical fears of laywomen were epitomized by the fact that the most frequent warning issued to seminarians about the temptations facing them in the priesthood was that of hearing female confessions.[97] Intent on isolating a clerical elite, college professors and the faculty at St. John's Seminary paid scant attention to women and consequently were puzzled by and hostile to the "new woman."

It would be anachronistic to suggest that Boston seminarians would have studied the woman question, but it is significant to discover that the modern woman was blamed for all the sins associated with modernity: socialism, race suicide, juvenile delinquency, divorce, and the self-indulgence of dances, movies, dime novels, clothes, and cosmetics. Since these latter items were directed at the consumption habits of a female audience, they afforded the Church the opportunity of continuing an ancient theological tradition admonishing luxury and selfish behavior in women, to which they added modern complaints against consumption for purely personal gratification.

Gender distinctions were institutionalized in education by the less academic orientation of the curriculum of girls' academies. Since there were no Catholic colleges for women prior to 1896, the closest approximation of higher education or seminary training for women was the convent school, which in no way equaled an advanced academic curriculum.[98] *The Christian Maiden* proposed this course of study for girls: "You may study music and painting and the like; but the careful nurturing of the qualities of the heart must always be your chief endeavor. Be loyal to the interests of your home and family, and practice the virtue of domesticity."[99] Women's reproduction of the cult of true womanhood in education scarcely changed through World War I, which modified the curriculum only slightly to encourage girls' patriotic duty, and even these tasks were invested with sacred glamour. Blanche Murphy, a schoolteacher from Maine completing a master's thesis at Clark University about convent education, stated in 1918 that a convent student "must share the soldier's sacrifice in numberless ways, she should be encouraged to make sacrifices which the present war requires, she should do without luxuries; economize in preparation of food and prevent all household waste; repress the instinct to conform to fashion and wear a suit or garment of a few months' previous style; to substitute simple home affairs for elaborate receptions, teas, dinner and theater parties."[100] Self-denial, after all, was not a new facet of the convent curriculum. For Agnes Repplier of Pennsylvania, "the habit of self-restraint induced by this gentle inflexibility of discipline, this exquisite sense of method and proportion, was the most valuable by-product of our education. There was an element of dignity in being even an insignificant part of a harmonious whole."[101] Unlike most Catholic women, who attached significance to being a small part of a larger unity and who saw nothing extraordinary in being asked to suppress personal desires, Repplier later sharply attacked the Church's inability to support any role for women except virgin or mother. In a remarkably modern essay of 1904 entitled "The Spinster," she argued that single women could be as devout as married or religious women: "That self-dependence might degenerate into loneliness we can understand; but how or why should loneliness degenerate into self-dependence, and what has either loneliness or self-dependence to do with 'the disappearance of religious devoutness'? May we not be devout in solitude?"[102]

Daughters of affluent and middle-class families generally attended convent boarding schools or religious day academies, the relative merits of which were weighed in Katherine Conway's guide, *Bettering Ourselves,* and in Lelia Hardin Bugg's novel, *The People of Our Parish.* Both texts show convent schools as finishing schools that fit a girl for her proper station but that also expose the tensions of upward mobility created by education. Conway's book contains a fictional monologue by an eighteen-year-old girl dissatisfied with her home life, longing for the benefits promised by a convent school:

> We are not rich; but we are prospering people; and my parents have been able to give me better chances than they had themselves. There is nothing even now to hinder me from keeping up my music and reading and even having more or less company. But the truth is, I am not in the right environment. I have gone forward, and my parents have stood still. Our house is awfully old-fashioned, and our way of living is not up-to-date. I would make no additional expense to have things and to do things a little differently, so that I could feel more at ease with my friends.[103]

Conway's character felt the tension between the hardships of her parents' generation and her own desire for social improvement.

In Bugg's novel, two Catholic women debated the role of girls' schools in preserving class distinctions in American society. The first speaker wondered, "When Mary Brown, whose parents can just read and write, returns from boarding-school to a stuffy flat over her father's carpenter-shop, of what service would be her training in the arts of refined society? She was sent to school to get the rudiments of an education, and to be taught her religion,—how to be a good true woman in her own sphere, and not to be fitted for a society which she may not enter." A companion responds, "Good manners belong to a woman's training, no matter what her sphere. And in this country, a girl's sphere is just as exalted as she can attain, either through marriage, or through her father's success in business."[104] These examples illustrate the Catholic adoption of values that emphasized privatization of women and their vicarious achievement of social status, which was itself a fixed category. The concern for Mary Brown's overeducation suggests that Catholics' belief in fixed gender and class spheres conflicted with their own assimilative aspirations. Women's advice to women suggests also that they had internalized the Church's outlook on female subservience and embraced its obsession with bodily disciplines, contenting themselves with self-renunciation in order to achieve some higher, communal goal. Catholic ideals of womanhood were in many ways indistinguishable from Protestant counterparts, whether emulated consciously or unconsciously. Above all, the Catholic construction of femininity showed how the Church became a center of regulative practices that absorbed American bourgeois ideals into a system of gender attitudes.

Convent schools, the most elite style of education for young women, were of two types: finishing schools, described above, and college preparatory. Boston girls from affluent Catholic and Protestant backgrounds attended convent schools, which typically offered a choice of five different courses of study: general, classical, scientific, household arts, and English.[105] A Massachusetts bishop maintained that above all else, convent students should master the Catholic catechism, the ceremonies of the Mass and administration of the sacraments, the gospels for Sundays and holy days, and Bible history. His vision in effect duplicated seminary education for girls, training them to defend the rituals and history of their faith as though they were preparing for the priesthood.[106] In the Boston area, the Sacred Heart Academy and the Academy of Notre Dame were the most select of the eight academies, and the Sacred Heart nuns of the former generated more convent academy graduates than any other religious order.[107] The Sacred Heart Academies at Manhattanville, New York, and Elmhurst, Rhode Island, were also popular with successful Bostonians. John Boyle O'Reilly and Denis McCarthy sent their daughters to Elmhurst, while Cardinal O'Connell paid for his great-nieces' education at Manhattanville. Mayor John Fitzgerald's youngest daughter, Eunice, attended all three Sacred Heart schools in the course of her high school education. In the early 1900s, however, far more Catholic girls attended parochial or public schools than the elite convent schools, which were not necessarily the only avenue to a college education. In fact, of the Catholics who graduated in the first classes of Radcliffe College, all were graduates of public schools.[108]

By imposing strict discipline on girls, parents and teachers reflected the concern for developing virtuous habits that flavored Catholic doctrine. Convent students wore severe black merino uniforms, undistinguished except for colored merit ribbons awarded by the sisters. Girls kept silence in their hallways and stairs, observed scheduled hours for sewing, and were discouraged from lending clothes, wearing jewelry, and forming "particular friendships." Books, periodicals, and letters were subject to inspection by the superior, as at a seminary. Convent educators stated that these norms reflected permanent religious truths, not just arbitrary whims. The relationship between rules and faith is suggested by the report of Sacred Heart Academy in Boston that Catholic pedagogy offered "the happiness of knowing that one's life is governed by convictions and not merely by custom."[109] Despite the disciplinary role of nuns and sisters, girls turned to them for personal advice and friendship. Denis McCarthy wrote to his daughter at Elmhurst Academy: "So far as your studies are concerned, I need to say nothing about them. Knowing how well you did in the past I am confident of your future progress. One thing I would say: Don't hesitate to ask your teachers about anything you do not understand. Go to them in your difficulties and they will be glad to help you. And I would say the same with regard to other matters not connected with your lessons."[110] The characteristic feature of convent schooling may have been its contradictory ethic: on one hand, it tried to be egalitarian, discouraging any outward signs of exceptionalism or competition among the students. On the other, it tried to efface individualism by insisting on group conformity to a disciplined regime tailored to serve a paternalist notion of womanhood and a bourgeois social structure.

Further proof that middle-class norms governed Catholic educational practice comes from the daily schedule itself, whose hourly units monitored the convent regimen. "Woman must be educated to make systematic use of her leisure, and to do this she must first of all know how to organize her leisure," suggested Denis McCarthy, who reminded his daughter, with a touch of humor, not to waste time even while ill. "Now that you have the whooping cough, you will have time enough on your hands to write something fine—a story or a play or a poem or sumpin. Lacking inspiration to do any of these things, you may write letters describing the feelings of a whooping cougher isolated from all contact with the rest of the world."[111] To break bad habits such as procrastination, convent education clearly distinguished rest from idleness, and demanded obedience to external strictures. On one occasion, Rufina McCarthy's father praised her conformity as a virtue: "You said yesterday, speaking of the rules of the school, that they were just common sense. That is an excellent way to look at them. They were made for the good of the pupils. They can be irksome only to those who have not sense and balance enough to know what is good for them. I think you will be all right on this score."[112]

The gravity of the academic report card as a monitor of how successfully girls became diligent students and dutiful Catholics is suggested by McCarthy's comments on his daughter's first evaluation:

> If there is not a rule against your seeing your report, I am sending it herewith in order that you may know your strengths and your weaknesses, and so may be able to strengthen the weak spots. "Diligence in studies" and "French" might be bettered, I think. So with "Order," "Penmanship," and "Needlework." You've had good needleworkers on both sides of the family, so it must be in the blood somewhere, if you will give it a chance to come out. Penmanship also. As to "order" and "diligence in study," you'll have to develop them without much help from heredity.[113]

While primary and secondary education for girls emphasized regulation of the body and of time as ways of converting the girl's body into a productive unit within the Catholic subculture, members of the American hierarchy offered varying degrees of support for secondary education for women and very little approval of female higher education. While Bishop John Spalding of Peoria was a rare episcopal supporter of advanced education for women,[114] among the laity, there is evidence of stronger support for women's education. Denis McCarthy was certain that his daughter deserved a college education, as he wrote his wife from Washington, D.C.:

> Today I was at Howard University at the graduation exercises on the Campus, and I marched as a guest with the faculty, black and white. And when I saw all these black fellows with the gowns and hoods of college doctors, I had a sort of sorrow that there was something my life had missed. And when I saw the crowd of negro boys and girls in caps and gowns, it seemed to me that we must strain every effort to send Rufina through college. If these sons and grandsons, daughters and granddaughters of *slaves* realize the importance of it, surely we ought to make every sacrifice for the same end.[115]

Archbishop O'Connell, however, took Christian motherhood as the ultimate female achievement, surpassing academic degrees and professional expertise. In the case of women determined to go to college, such as Rose Kennedy, O'Connell was able to convince her father to send her to a Catholic school instead of to Wellesley, but there were also several notable exceptions of women from the Catholic elite who attended non-Catholic colleges.[116] Women's college attendance was justifiable in the eyes of the Church when it led to the award of normal school diplomas and librarians' certificates, which would expand the infrastructure of Catholic women working in Catholic schools. From the Church's perspective, the goal of a Christian gentlewoman's education was to prepare the soul before the intellect. If she must be educated, her learning should to support the Catholic subculture, as Bishop Spalding explained: "The Catholic girl who is to become a social leader needs to be especially well grounded in her faith, its history as well as its dogmas, and she needs to be shown the things that tend for culture *from the Catholic point of view.*"[117]

Despite the intellectual and physical limitations of the convent academy regime, many Catholic women recorded that they derived a positive sense of self-worth from the self-denial and leveling tendencies of its atmosphere. The hoped-for impact of the convent school environment was suggested by the bishop of Fall River: "She knows that in a large piece of mechanism the smallest wheel is as important as the largest."[118] It is possible that the convent school system allowed nuns to ennoble the concept of self-sacrificing womanhood through the building of virtuous daily habits. By such reasoning, girls were persuaded by female teachers that their futures represented a solemn contract of lifetime service and that conformity to a higher will and a loftier purpose made their sacrifices worthwhile. On the other hand, there is enough evidence to suggest that products of convent education could also grow to challenge the subordinate status of women within the Church and that the very values inculcated by the nuns and sisters led Catholic women to challenge traditional restraints.[119] Further, new pressure on schools from the Catholic press argued for training young women to survive a competitive world, or in other words, to treat girls like boys.[120]

After they completed high school, Catholic women had limited opportunities for pursuing formal advanced education. Informal avenues of self-development came from the spiritual and quasi-educational activities of the archdiocese, including the lecture courses and spiritual retreats held at the Cenacle Convent in Brighton and at Notre Dame Convent in the Fenway. Priests presided over most of these occasions and at women's club events, reading circles, and lectures sponsored by parish and diocesan organizations. After about 1910 the archdiocese sponsored evening lecture courses for women, regulated by the clergy. Through one such program, about 600 women took the evening classes at "the people's university" of the Young Men's Catholic Association, which permitted women to attend after 1911.[121] Between 1896 and the end of World War I, when several women's colleges were founded, two of them in Boston, women's educational options expanded, yet control of college curricula remained in the hands of the clergy. St. John's Seminary professors, for example, taught at Emmanuel College for women when it opened in Boston in 1919.[122] Prior to 1920, self-development through higher education was not widely encouraged for women. Existing opportunities were mediated by the clergy and aimed at teaching women to defend the faith, not to pursue a career, a trade, or an advanced degree at a secular institution. Few Catholic leaders were ready to take up Bishop Spalding's challenge to the Church: "We degrade her when we consider her as little else than a candidate for matrimony. A man may remain single and become the noblest of his kind, and so may a woman."[123]

"A Properly Guarded Youth": Female Advice Literature

The condescending perception that women needed moral instruction because they were only capable of imitative behavior, combined with the conflicting bourgeois assertion of the natural moral superiority of women, produced a distinctive Catholic didactic literature for women and girls. Many of these behavior guides were written by male authors (often priests) in the decades following the Civil War, including Rev. George Deshon's *Guide for Catholic Young Women* and Bernard O'Reilly's *Mirror of True Womanhood*.[124] Deshon stated that "books are, next to sermons, next to the living voice of the preacher, the most powerful means to excite us to virtue."[125] Rev. Francis Lasance published *The Catholic Girl's Guide* in 1906, and T. E. Shields's *The Education of Our Girls* appeared one year later. These manuals provide representative sources of advice to Boston girls.

Generally, advice literature for women was based on the unequal but supposedly normative social relationship between men and women that followed the model of teacher and pupil. Women, it seems, could copy moral behavior when provided with good models. Whether a woman chose celibacy or marriage, she remained answerable to the superior wisdom of the divine mouthpiece—the priest—as Archbishop O'Connell explained to women at Mt. St. Joseph's Academy, Brighton: "Be a teacher six days of the week, and a pupil on the seventh. On that day sit under the pulpit and be a pupil of God. Regardless of the gifts of the preacher, consider that God is talking to your soul."[126] Even the *Republic,* Boston's lively Democratic weekly, showed how ubiquitous patriarchy was among Catholics, in this example from its advice column for wives: "Unless he asks your opinion, don't put your hypothesis of this or that public matter before him. Perhaps it pleases him to be the first to set you right on it. You haven't the chance of studying the matter. Let him instruct you."[127]

As the Catholic publishing industry grew, a second source of advice to women, imported manuals, became increasingly available in Boston. Bishop

Stang commented that "the book market has lately been flooded with translations from the French and German." These inexpensive, pocket-sized translations of the works of European priests directed young women away from "the allurements of the world and the seduction and fascinations of an outwardly refined, but inwardly corrupted society."[128] Foreign manuals no doubt were encouraged in Boston because of their ultraconservative piety. The particular manual to which the German-born Stang prefaced the remarks above became a translation project for the sodality at Holy Trinity, Boston's German parish. Its chapters included instructions on veneration of the Virgin, fidelity to parents, industry, and being the "perfect sodalist." As a blend of doctrinal and familial advice, The Christian Maiden's lecture on chastity provides the most memorable imagery: "Human bodies are like glasses which cannot be carried when they touch one another, without the danger of their being broken; or like tender fruits, which, by too close a contact, are easily impaired. . . . Never allow anybody to touch you, even in jest."[129] The passage underscores how the clergy represented women as tender fruits, easily bruised or broken, and yet also saw them as capable of dangerous sensual desires that they must repress to make certain that "Eve withdraws."[130]

Protectionist attitudes about women also mirrored the institutional Church's fear of violation of its own purity and innocence, indicating how representations of women's bodies linked them symbolically to the Church's "body," to be protected by the laity in its loyal defense of a separatist subculture. Advice for women transcended ethnic boundaries, as demonstrated in the overriding sameness of books produced by and for German, Italian, Polish, and Irish Catholics. Clergy books and newspaper advice columns repeatedly stated the need for girlish innocence toward authority, adulthood, and life: "There are facts which she must face eventually. Don't break them to her roughly. God safeguards innocence by allowing certain necessary knowledge to come to us in a properly guarded youth very gradually."[131]

Perhaps the most significant fact about this new literature directed at women was that it announced the appearance of a middle-class audience among Boston Catholics. Father Lasance's counsel, for example, eschewed "anything which would not apply to girls of the middle class."[132] Deshon's Guide encouraged the restraint and modesty associated with bourgeois propriety: "Simplicity and economy in your dress, for these things are suitable to your condition and station in life, and are pleasing to God. Avoid setting your heart on dress and fashion, for they will produce in your heart vanity and self-love, that destroy the love of God."[133]

The task of training Catholic girls in self-discipline was also taken up by women, who authored a third category of women's literature: fiction and non-fiction by a predominantly eastern establishment of middle-class women such as Katherine Conway, Eleanor Donnelly, Mary Elizabeth Blake, and Lelia Hardin Bugg. They portrayed Catholics of their own class background, but they encouraged working girls to emulate middle-class gentility without expressing dissatisfaction with their "station in life." Bugg's popular *The Correct Thing for Catholics,* which has been called a bourgeois bible of etiquette, provided instruction to fellow Catholics interested in fitting in American society. Its preoccupation with how to behave properly appeared in fiction as well, where characters explored the correct response to their improved social status. In short, women's manuals and novels epitomized the concern for self-representation inherent in the logic of class formation. Standards of female etiquette also served the Church's role in controlling the behavior of the increasing female population in the city. While the Church applauded the presence of an assimilated male Catholic, who was expected to have transcended the Old Country traditions of his ancestors without losing his religion, it remained ambivalent about where women belonged in the intellectual life of the Church and in American society. Were women spiritually superior and mentally inferior to men? Were women morally deficient because they were less educated? Did women even need education? While the Church affirmed women's inherent moral sensibility, it also recognized the importance of subordinating women to the supremacy of the male intellect. What, then, does literature for and by Catholic women reveal? Surely it is more than a collection of repetitive examples of sexism. As we recognize that mere exposure of sexism does not constitute criticism, we need to place Catholic biases against women's intellectual abilities and economic independence in historical perspective, such as that provided by the fastest-growing medium, the press.

If advice manuals, sermons, novels, and schooling established the boundaries of Catholic feminine identity, a final mode of communication that conveyed notions of womanhood was the Catholic press. Generally speaking, Catholic journalism between 1865 and 1914 sustained static notions of femininity against rapid social change. Further, against the middle-class canons of behavior reinforced in Catholic publications, an even more conservative ideal of womanhood was being advanced at this time by immigrants from southern and eastern Europe.[134] While these ethnic communities achieved a minimal journalistic presence in Boston, affirmation of the subordinate role of women and the teaching authority of the Church was otherwise easy to find in the pages of the *Pilot.* Although the diocesan weekly featured a column entitled "Talks to Young Men" and addressed its articles on education to "Our Catholic Manhood," on two occasions in 1911 "Talks to Young Women" appeared. Generally, though, women's advice was incorporated in the family life column, "In the Family Sitting Room." A typical editorial bit, reprinted from a distant foreign source, suggested that "girls who are straining their eyes over the recipes in the 'Hints to Beauty' columns of the daily press will be certain of keeping their hands soft and white if they follow this advice from the Bombay Examiner: 'Soak your hands three times a day in dishwater while your mother rests.'"[135] While daughters were washing dishes, mothers were advised to avoid wasting their time trying to keep up with their Protestant neighbors. The *Pilot* warned that "this pathetic household drama is more evident in New England than elsewhere. It is a relic of that chill Puritanism that yet lingers among us here and there."[136]

Catholic journalism provides further evidence of the fear that competitiveness and acquisitiveness was affecting women as well as men, even though women were presumed to be immunized against the struggle for possessions by their marriages. The *Republic* stated, "All life is a fierce competition, whether the girl go forth from high school or college to a home of affluence, or to seek a means of maintaining herself until the natural settlement in life is due."[137] Although a minority of Catholics had acknowledged the economic advantages of educating girls, women were generally expected to succeed indirectly through the careers of their fathers, husbands, and brothers. Because of this inequity, a Catholic woman journalist noted that working women were all the more to be admired "because they have not the incentive of gaining the highest places and largest salaries. These are the perquisites of their brothers, and no amount of fitness will qualify a woman for such positions."[138] Women rarely expressed any bitterness about the situation of male economic dominance. In fact, women seemed to agree that "no woman goes out into the downtown business world simply because she wants to be there. The normal woman loves her home, and her social pleasures, and her clubs for intellectual improvement, too well to exchange them voluntarily for the industrial bondage of a salaried person."[139] For women who did hold paying jobs, men seized the opportunity to offset the presumed brutalizing effects of work to encourage them not to "only make it a lucrative thing; but get it also to help your character."[140]

The *Pilot*'s advice columns to women can be summarized as anonymous sermons against luxury, frivolity, and the ultimate evil—betrayal of the faith. They were scornful of women who did not live their faith, such as the young lady "who married a non-Catholic, a Presbyterian minister officiating, [who] may have been educated in a convent as the dailies state, but evidently she did not bring her convent education out into the world."[141] By chastising women for being lazy, materialistic, or irreligious, the *Pilot* confirmed the ideological biases of Catholic journalism, which maintained an image of women as maidservants of the clergy and of men in general. This view was underscored visually by frequent photographs in the Catholic press of women garlanding the archbishop's residence for his return from visits to Rome, by reports of women's theatrical and musical programs for Catholic meetings, and by society gossip columns describing the fashionable (but not immodest) attire of prominent women at parish dances and dinners. By decorating banquet halls, churches, and rectories and in providing food, music, and light entertainment for parish events, women shared in producing and reproducing a gender ideology that consigned them to decorative and service roles. The sheer abundance of Catholic parish events for women to attend underscores the importance of parish-centered Catholicism in these decades, yet it also signals the all-encompassing and insular nature of ghetto Catholicism. In all activities of daily life, a Catholic woman could be segregated from any extramural influences to preserve her innocence and her separate sphere.

Female Converts to Catholicism

"'Another story of a conversion! The same old tale probably!' I seem to hear these words as I begin to write."[142] Although Julia Robins feared that her story was commonplace, historians have overlooked a striking phenomenon in Boston Catholicism of the abundance of female converts in the period 1890–1920. The four volumes of *Notable American Women*, for example, identify only thirty Catholic convert women in three centuries, including several persons who are incorrectly identified as Catholics. The abundant histories of Boston and environs written by Brahmin matrons and literary salongoers at the turn of the century suppress nearly all mention of Roman Catholic women. Even the names of Emma Cary, sister of Elizabeth Cary Agassiz, and of Rose Hawthorne Lathrop, daughter of Nathaniel and Sophia Hawthorne, rarely appear. Among Catholic reference sources, statistics on female conversions are hard to find while names of male converts are readily available, especially of those who subsequently became Catholic priests.[143] The Massachusetts women whom I have identified as converts were educated, middle-class to upper middle-class Episcopalians or Unitarians who subsequently became active leaders in the Catholic community. Boston's LCW owed its existence to two former Protestants, Bostonian Pauline Willis and Briton Margaret Fletcher. Louise Guiney noticed that among her British friends, the most active Catholics were the converts. The premier example, perhaps, was Monsignor Robert Hugh Benson, the convert son of the archbishop of Canterbury. In the American Catholic population, many leading novelists, journalists, and poets were converts, suggesting a need to explore the meaning of these conversions in an era of separatist integration.

Bostonians of 1900 could choose from an extensive menu of alternative religions that flourished in its bohemian quarter, ranging from stargazers, "psycho-physicists," orientalists, and vibrationists to "daughters of the Druids."[144] So what did Roman Catholicism offer, especially to New England women? One often proposed answer is that Catholicism's "richness and complexity" drew converts who were disenchanted with the literalness of Protestantism. Among New Englanders this aesthetic discrimination flourished: many were attracted to Roman Catholicism and flirted with conversion but generally went no further than Anglo-Catholicism. Of the Boston set, which included Mrs. Jack Gardner, Ralph Adams Cram, Henry Adams, George Santayana, and Bernard Berenson, only Berenson was baptized. Under the influence of two Catholic artists, John La Farge and Augustus Saint-Gaudens, Henry Adams rediscovered Gothic cathedrals for American audiences, convinced that art and religion had formed a perfect unity in the Middle Ages. But like Adams, certain Protestants were content to find in Catholicism a safe haven against the uncertainty of the future or the novelty religions of the trendy set. Some upper-class Brahmins journeyed toward the Roman Church as pilgrims in search of something picturesque, exotic, and vital, an escape from their own religious pasts or melancholia, or even as an antidote to the drabness of urban industrial society.

Judging from conversion accounts of women in my sample, however, doctrinal principles and the Church's attitude of confident righteousness were the persuasive factors, not an aesthetic experience of religion. Of the six New England women profiled below, all became published apologists for Roman Catholicism, had literary careers, and came from old New England Protestant families. Two were widowed, four remained single, and one of the widows founded an order of women religious. Their high socioeconomic status was typical of national conversion patterns: the Catholic Church always gained more converts from Episcopal and Unitarian congregations than from the evangelical Protestant churches.[145] The Massachusetts women evaluated here shared certain biographical traits that make them a logical cohort: they were born in the late 1840s to 1860s and converted as adults, despite often hostile reactions from their families. Engaged in a quest for "truth," they were often challenged spiritually by a priest or an acquaintance. Nonetheless, personal contact with a Catholic, often an Irish domestic or a priest, seemed to be a less effective means of conversion than Catholic literature, which women frequently cited as a decisive factor.

The wave of Protestant converts to Catholicism after 1875 was at least the second such influx of the century. In the marked increase of antebellum conversions, the American Protestant exodus corresponded roughly to the conversions of the Oxford Movement apostates in England. In the United States, the current brought Orestes Brownson and Isaac Hecker to Catholicism as well as numerous women in the Hawthorne, Ripley, Lathrop, and Dana families. A second wave of conversions continued into the twentieth century.[146]

Of my sample, five women published accounts of their conversions, and one left no record. A conversion narrative represents a unique literary genre whose style is often formulaic and restricted, since its goal is to provide religious propaganda. The narratives of convert women reflect common concerns: dissatisfaction with previously held beliefs and opinions, resolution of anti-Catholic biases, and experience of emotional release following the acceptance of Roman Catholicism. The choice of vocations by these women suggests that conversion opened up a life of Christian activism, not confinement to passivity. In fact, as autobiographical documents, we may consider their spiritual autobiographies to be marks of their individualism rather than of their invisibility.

Martha Moore Avery (1851–1929), a convert who became arguably the most public Catholic laywoman in New England, came from an elite Unitarian background in Maine, from which she became a Bellamy nationalist and then a member of the Socialist Labor party before joining the Socialist party in 1901. Her exchange of socialism for Catholicism in 1904 had profound effects on the public character of Boston Catholicism, because of her part in defining the role of women and her antisocialist work as a street evangelist. At least two events, by her account, led her to Catholicism. First, while visiting friends in Toronto she was impressed by the convent education of their daughter and decided to put her own daughter in a convent school.[147] Second, Avery's faith in socialism was shaken by the divorce case of socialist minister George Herron in 1903.[148] Her belief that the Socialist party supported free sexual liaisons at the expense of family responsibility chilled Avery's enthusiasm for socialist views on morality and religion. In May 1903, as socialist power peaked in Massachusetts, Avery became disillusioned with the party. Encouraged by her daughter's reports of her newfound serenity, Avery herself became a "convert from Marx to Christ." In reaction to the Herron divorce, David Goldstein, Avery's colleague at the Boston Karl Marx Class, also converted, noting, "There was developing in me, at the time I left socialism a conviction that is stronger now than ever that religion is the basis of individual and social morality which alone leads to happiness."[149] Developing a program based on the social encyclicals of Leo XIII, the pair became the leading lay Catholic evangelists of Boston and gained national fame during the next three decades.

American Catholics deduced socialist ideas about gender primarily from *Woman under Socialism*, published by German socialist August Bebel in 1879. Bebel's book revolutionized German socialism by challenging its sexist prej-

Martha Moore Avery: convert from Marx to Christ. (John J. Burns Library, Boston College)

udices against working women. Bebel accepted female wage labor and gave a new materialist analysis of the woman question that made socialism the means to woman's emancipation.[150] Catholics were unaware of Bebel's theoretical revolution within socialism, which heretofore had failed to address the oppression of women, and reviews in the most influential Catholic serials and newspapers in Boston, including the *American Catholic Quarterly Review, Ave Maria, Benziger's Monthly, Catholic Mind, Catholic World,* the *Pilot,* the *Republic,* and the *Sacred Heart Review,* indicate that Bebel's popularity led Catholics to vigorously refute his book. As David Goldstein asserted, "The entire Socialist movement shall be held responsible for Bebel's work."[151] Translated into fourteen languages and printed in fifty editions between 1879 and 1910, Bebel's book was cited frequently by American-born socialists such as Kate Richards O'Hare. Guilt by association was enough to turn Catholic opinion against it, since Catholics blamed socialism for allowing the state to compromise women and families.[152] In other words, a socialist state would prevent women from following their primal vocation to motherhood by destroying the sanctity of marriage, by sanctioning birth control, and by usurping the child-rearing duties of parents, especially the socializing function of mothers. It was Christianity, particularly veneration of the Virgin, Catholics contended, that had elevated woman from the oppression and inequality of paganism.[153] Rejecting socialism as the new paganism, the Church was unwilling to let socialists topple the Christian woman from her pedestal, so it demonized socialism as a monolithic heresy. Avery and Goldstein's first collaborative book, *Socialism: The Nation of Fatherless Children* (1903) dramatized the evils of socialism and illustrated the contrast between Avery's postconversion ideas and Socialist party beliefs.[154]

Exceptional among Boston laity because of her high visibility as a female orator and because of her outspoken stands on topics usually reserved to the clergy for public commentary, Avery held a charmed position in O'Connell's Boston.[155] The archbishop promoted her because of her flamboyance and charisma: as a convert from a wealthy family and from a political heresy, she became a valuable asset to Roman Catholicism. Just as the archbishop got clerical solidarity by filling local pastorates with his own choices, so he promoted lay conformity by giving Catholics what he wanted them to hear. A significant body of scholarship has already detailed Avery's work with David Goldstein in the Catholic Truth Guild, established in 1917 as a national lay evangelization movement, and her work with the Common Cause Society, which she helped found in 1912.[156] Her unconventional involvement in lay preaching nonetheless confirmed the Church's prescribed role for women.

Avery's postconversion conservatism pitted womanhood against socialism. "The man's part is the positive, the projective force in life, and the woman's the receptive, the conservative force," she wrote in 1915.[157] To her, the Catholic Church represented stability, as she revealed to an audience of Catholic women in 1910: "Certainly, as Catholic women, our case is simple. No need have we to cry: 'Lo, here! Lo, there!' For there is only one Authority."[158] Avery was a maverick in developing and exploiting the street apostolate to Catholics but soon became a familiar sight in Boston, speaking on the Common in the summer and in lyceum halls in winter. She issued flamboyant challenges to socialists whenever possible, as in this report of a confrontation with a local minister: "Last night at the Christian Socialist meeting, Rev. Willis Cooke as speaker, I got into a good row. Cooke had said that Father Gasson, who spoke at Ford Hall a week ago, wanted to keep women in servile slavery to men. My *not so,* struck every body there like a shot. After the meeting adjourned I was asked if I would debate with Cooke? Indeed, yes. 'Where? here?,' the Secretary, a woman, asked. I said when any Socialist gets ready to debate with Mrs. MMA Tremont Temple will not be too large a hall to accomidate [*sic*] the audience."[159] Avery's zeal and unflagging self-assurance enhanced her platform appearances. However, her disregard for separation of church and state due to her enthusiasm to infuse American government with Catholic principles led to conflicts in her political friendships. For example, when Avery advised the National Civic Foundation and its leader, Ralph Easley, how to wage war on socialism, he frequently had to remind her that the foundation was not in the business of making theological statements against the socialists.[160] Avery's political involvement included appearances at the Lawrence textile strike of 1912, where she delivered an address entitled "Socialism as Assault on the Nation" immediately after the strike had ended in March. Soon after Avery's appearance, the LCW bought and distributed some 5,000 antisocialist pamphlets throughout the community, signaling Avery's successful diffusion of the Church's ethic of constructive conservatism among Catholic women. In economic debate, her past participation in the Karl Marx Class in Boston enabled her to anticipate and rebut socialist arguments. Her numerous talks to women's groups on socialism versus the home were attempts to persuade middle-class audiences that they must save the working class from socialism. Avery explained that the trade unions and the socialists had antagonistic goals, particularly about marriage: the socialist wife, she claimed, was "only a comrade—no longer the other half of 'these twain made one flesh,' but a hail fellow well met upon the highway of life's journey, so long as sex fondness lasts, or for the stated period of limited marriage."[161]

Avery did believe that women should contribute to political and industrial life: "When we pass from the sphere of philosophy where the blind lead the blind to the uproar of the industrial world there is plenty of work which Catholics may do to reconcile man to man and class to class," she claimed.[162] On the subject of professions for women, however, she said unequivocally that women were not intended for lifetime jobs. Speeches like one delivered to a Cenacle Convent guild refuted feminism. For the Boston *Pilot,* Avery wrote that "only one woman in a 100,000 attains to merited fame equal to the fame of men in the professions, in art, in science. The reason for this is not lack of ability on the part of women but that she is designed for a higher sphere of accomplishment. God intended women for domestic and social functions and not for the professions."[163] Her message to Catholic women reflected the doctrine of separate spheres in which the higher sphere of morality belonged to women. Avery warned Catholics to be grateful for their Church's absolute truth and the security conferred by sacramental marriage bonds. "Let me assure you," she wrote, "that it is not so easy for one born into an environment where the Christian Faith was repudiated, unknown, where confusion of thought reigns supreme; where even the instinct to prayer is chilled."[164]

Avery abandoned two prior ideological affiliations before becoming a Catholic: Unitarianism and Marxian socialism. She was not alone in being a New England nonconformist who felt that Catholicism offered a secure haven. The antebellum converts, including Sophia Ripley, Charlotte Dana, and Margaret Fuller Ossoli represented the leading families of Boston and Cambridge—the Bancrofts, Danas, Hawthornes, Jameses, Websters, Peabodys, and Whittiers.[165] Two Brahmin converts of that generation, Emma Forbes Cary (1833–1918) and Rose Hawthorne Lathrop (1851–1926), provided a bridge from that generation to the present.

"We stand at the threshold of the twentieth century," stated Cary, "and muse on the future that it holds for spiritual and intellectual women. Does the church ask less of them than of their ancestors in the faith?"[166] Cary, from Cambridge, converted in 1855 through the influence of her mother's Irish hairdresser, Harriet Ryan, with whom she visited the poor and ill.[167] Baptized by Bishop Fitzpatrick, she was also friend to Archbishop Williams and later to Archbishop O'Connell, who delivered her eulogy in 1918. Her sister, Elizabeth Cabot Cary, married Louis Agassiz, later president of Harvard. Emma and Elizabeth became interested in founding Radcliffe College for women. As Elizabeth concerned herself with the academic details of transforming the "Harvard Annex" into Radcliffe College, eventually becoming its president, Emma tended to young women's spiritual concerns and founded the Radcliffe Catholic Club in 1906, which met regularly at her Brattle Street home.[168] Before the first Catholic women's college was founded in 1896, Catholics were supposed to avoid schools such as Wellesley, Vassar, and Radcliffe, although there were at least three to five Catholics from the Boston and Cambridge area in every Radcliffe class between 1900 and 1910, and there was evidence of Catholic women attending other area colleges.

Because of her interest in helping the poor, Emma Cary became an advocate of prison reform through her work as a member of the prison commission of Massachusetts from 1867 to 1892, where she befriended Katherine Conway. Like Conway and Avery, Cary had a literary career, although a more modest one: she edited a devotional diary called *The Day-Spring from on High* and wrote for the Paulist monthly, *Catholic World,* and its juvenile publication, *The Leader.*[169] Cary was devoted to helping "fallen" women at the House of the Good Shepherd and in assisting the Children of Mary, the sodality for girls at the Notre Dame Academy. In contrast to her sister, she remained single. Her address at the 1893 World's Congress of Women marked her rupture with a Protestant upbringing. In "The Elevation of Womanhood Wrought through the Veneration of the Blessed Virgin," Cary based her vision of woman's active role in the Catholic Church on Mary, whom she interpreted as the woman uniting women through the centuries. In Cary's view, women had more responsibilities in the twentieth century because of the effects of democratization and education: "The privileges which formerly belonged only to a few are now generally diffused. . . . We claim all that is highest in modern education, in modern ingenuity, and unite ourselves to the traditions of the past, going back nineteen hundred years to the household of Nazareth, to study the spirit which should animate domestic life, life in communities, and that complex existence led by those who have not the protection of either the one or the other."[170] Cary subtly used her wealthy connections to make a Catholic presence felt in Cambridge, in the most self-effacing manner possible. Because she was raised in a time that saw repeated outbreaks of anti-Catholicism in Massachusetts, Cary's view of Protestant-Catholic relations seemed now to support the O'Connell administration's strategy of separatist integration. Consequently, her advice to Protestant and Catholic social reformers was to pursue the same goals but to maintain an amicable segregation: "It is easy to work with Protestants if one stands squarely as a Catholic. The hierarchy in Holland say to those Dutch Catholics who unite their forces to those of the Anti-Revolutionary Protestants, 'March separately, but fight shoulder to shoulder,' advice which applies to such social work in this country as demands combined action of Protestants and Catholics."[171]

In her twenty-five-year career in prison reform Cary fought anti-Catholic and antiimmigrant prejudice that led officials to give overly harsh sentences to juvenile offenders, most of whom were Irish. Cary tried to persuade state prison officials to distinguish between hardened criminals and minor offenders and to avoid inhumane overcrowding of state jails.[172] In old age, Cary was cared for by a community of Catholic sisters, spending the summers of her last years at the Cenacle Convent in Brighton, where she died at age eighty-five. Her success at converting others reportedly resulted from her humility,

188 CATHOLIC WOMANHOOD

in contrast to the confrontational style of Martha Avery. Further, as Cardinal O'Connell remembered Cary, "There was no trace of luxury about her, she was too genuinely refined for that."[173] A biographer offered a descriptive epitaph: "Miss Cary in religion was neither erratic, nor ecstatic, nor fanatic, but full to the brim of common sense."[174] Her usefulness to the Boston Catholic community derived from the prestige lent by her blueblood background, her obedience to episcopal authority, her financial patronage of priests such as Daniel Hudson, her devotional publications, and her attempts to end nativism.

Rose Hawthorne Lathrop's lifetime spanned the epoch of nativist rejection of Irish immigrants to Progressivism's emphasis on absorption of immigrants through Americanization. The spiritual journey of Nathaniel Hawthorne's daughter from Puritan roots and her family's Unitarianism to Catholicism has been documented, but her interest in Roman Catholicism has never been definitively explained by her or her biographers. She apparently never completed an explanation of her conversion, as evidenced by the blank slip of paper among her manuscripts headed, "The Way as I Found It—a book upon my experience during and after conversion."[175] By some accounts, Rose was drawn to Catholicism through immersion in Christian art and the exoticism of Italian culture during her family's sojourns in Europe; in other versions, she was influenced by the faith of her family's domestic, Nellie Sullivan.

As a young woman Rose wanted to excel in literature, although she seems to have felt eclipsed by her father and older brother, Julian. Even her husband, George, who received the commission to edit the Riverside edition of Nathaniel Hawthorne's works, was better known in literary circles than she. In 1888 Rose did publish her own poems in a volume called *Along the Shore*, which received mixed reviews for its often pessimistic tone, and she later edited some of her father's works. In her compilation, *Memories of Hawthorne* (1897), are hints about her former prejudices against Roman Catholicism among her comments on her mother's diary entries and correspondence. As a child, Rose noted from hindsight, she had often misjudged Catholicism. On eating some Lenten pancakes in Rome, she was disappointed by their ordinariness: "If they had been appetizing I should have been sharply interested in the idea of becoming a Catholic, but the entire absence of which convinced me that the Italians lacked mental grasp and salvation at a single swoop."[176] Rose implied that thirty years later her conversion enabled her to find the wisdom of Catholicism in the sights and practices that she had misread in Italy, including "the unexplained catacombs"; the "unlovely" monks; the "child's play, useless and fascinating" of funeral procession chants; and the holy relics, "forms of folly."

Against the wishes of her family Rose married George Parsons Lathrop in

Rose Hawthorne Lathrop left her New England family and Unitarian roots to be-come Mother Mary Alphonsa, foundress of a Dominican religious order for the care of cancer patients among the poor. (Holy Cross College Rare Books and Special Collections)

1871 in an Anglican church in London. Her sister, Una, refused to attend their wedding, perhaps out of jealousy, and subsequently suffered a mental breakdown. Brother Julian, formerly on good terms with George, now shunned him. Rose's mother had just died prior to the wedding, leaving Rose feeling alone and estranged from her remaining relatives. After the death of her first child in 1876, she was partially reconciled to Julian, but at that point she and her husband developed a pattern of long periods of separation, begun while they were in Europe. In 1883 Rose apparently even planned to leave George and made financial arrangements to make that possible.[177] She and George tried a separation but then resumed living together in New York City from 1884 to 1887.

Rose's decision, therefore, to leave her husband, several years after their equally surprising joint conversions to Catholicism in 1891, becomes part of the complicated narrative of her adult life.[178] In the early 1890s, it appears that the couple's growing acquaintance with priests and nuns had a profoundly positive impact on Rose's images of femininity and of the Catholic Church. She and George, with support from Paulist priests, became founders of the Catholic Summer School in 1892. For the next year they traveled frequently to Washington, D.C., to research their coauthored history of the Visitation Order of nuns, founded in France in the sixteenth century by Jane de Chantal.[179] Rose's observations of the nuns' history of altruistic service and the way in which their convent community functioned as an extension of the family unit gave her a sense of the possibilities for women in Catholicism as yet unavailable to her. In the self-sacrificing behavior of the nuns on behalf of all humanity she saw an alternative to the stifling demands of motherhood as defined by her own family and by the possessive individualism at the heart of the religious culture of the bourgeois nuclear family. In the eyes of her family and friends, she feared, it was heretical for a woman to look beyond motherhood and family for her fulfillment. Rose's obvious sympathy with the personality and achievements of Jane de Chantal, revealed in her observations on the Visitation nuns, suggests that the idea of sisterhood provided her with a way to combine her nascent feminism with Catholicism, and a means to reconcile the opposition between communitarian feminism and individualism.

From about 1892, Rose's poetry manifested an observable new interest in topics relating to the realm of social reform and Christian praxis. During a period of acute financial crisis, due to George's gastric illness and inability to work, she provided their sole income.[180] During the next few years they became estranged, and Rose eventually left him. George experienced increasing health problems due to a kidney ailment, and by the date of his death from chronic nephritis in 1898 (possibly related to alcoholism), Rose had already decisively placed Catholicism at the center of her life by living the ascetic life of a lay sister. As Sister Mary Alphonsa, she devoted herself to the care of the terminally ill in the poorest slums of New York City, living the words she had written in *A Story of Courage*: "We ought really, all of us, to regard the great human family with the same tenderness we have been in the habit of bestowing upon the single private family. Christ taught us that we should not restrict our love and interest to the narrow limits of the threshold of the home."[181] Upon being widowed, she and two friends persevered in their care for persons in the last stages of cancer, despite the frustration of being refused the official sanction of the archbishop, Michael Corrigan. In 1899 she was able to purchase a building that became St. Rose's Free Home for Incurable Cancer (named for St. Rose of Lima) and petitioned the archdiocese to affiliate her group with the Third Order of St. Dominic. Finally partially acknowledged by Corrigan, she took the name of Mother Mary Alphonsa and led a small band of women called the Servants for Relief of Incurable Cancer, which soon expanded to open a second home in Westchester County, New York.[182]

Between 1901 and 1904 Mother Alphonsa published and wrote *Christ's Poor,* a unique subscription magazine that publicized the problem of urban poverty and dramatized the plight of the outcast cancer patient. The articles and regular columns reveal Rose's growing understanding of a relationship between care of the poor and dying, and God's demands for a society based on the destruction of class and sex differences. The editorials and articles contained in this unusual publication also adumbrate those of a later development in American Catholicism, the radical Catholic Worker movement of the 1930s and its weekly newspaper. Anticipating the demanding outlook of Dorothy Day, Rose Lathrop expressed an uncompromising ethic of unrelenting Christian labor associated with her conversion: "I have been indolent, self-indulgent, cowardly for many years," she stated, "then, one day, I awoke." Contrasting the "charms of recreation" of her careless youth with her moral progress away from "selfish ease," she reached a sense of purpose and peace in her vocation and encouraged others to do likewise: "No matter how selfish we are, let us learn the art of generous activity. It is ever so much more absorbing than china-painting, or a boat-race. But it takes more than four years to graduate from its schools. Yet remember this: what it is hardest to do, it is sweetest to see done!"[183] Evidently Lathrop's conversion and new vocation conquered a sense of lassitude, ennui, and guilt felt by many Anglo-Saxon elites, which was resolved by her new spiritual focus and through strenuous service to humanity. In military metaphors similar to those used by Louise Guiney and a surprising number of contemporary women, Lathrop compared a society run by women to a strong army, and related the supervision of charity to the training and discipline forged by army officers.[184] "Work is our honored patron," declared Mother Alphonsa, at the same time minimizing her own significance as foundress of a religious order. "Forgive me for grappling with questions that are undoubtedly beyond any handling of mine. For if a woman desires a hearing for her thoughts at all, I think she may as well speak of the dearest interest woman has in this world. Now, I hope I shall never cease to believe that, as it was in the time of the three Marys, the chief interest of woman is to follow Christ,—and lead the children to Him."[185] Here she honored the traditional pattern of maternal service, but her work among the marginalized urban poor in America also adumbrates the countercultural critiques of American capitalism made later by convert Dorothy Day. In locating women's work among the unwanted and outside her immediate family, Lathrop may be interpreted as a radical, with parallels to Day further suggested by the monasticism that governed the community of sisters founded by Lathrop and the austere quality of life that was the core of Catholic Worker communities. Yet, the fact that Lathrop's work among social outcasts had precedents among earlier converts, such as Sophia Ripley, suggests a pattern that evolved among convert women of identifying themselves, as women and as converts, with the marginal elements of American society—the poor, the imprisoned, the disfigured, and the dying—and which allowed them to critique the limits imposed upon them by the "obligations of blood relationship."

Rose Lathrop died in 1926, having been a wife and a nun for twenty-seven years each. In converting to Catholicism, leaving her husband, joining a sisterhood, and founding a new religious order for women she broke images of feminine passivity. By severing ties with her quarrelsome family and leaving few clues regarding her decisions, she challenged the central canons of domesticity. Based on archival materials and biographies, we can speculate that Catholicism became the centering, energizing, ordering principle of her existence that allowed her to develop a social ministry of active care for the sick and destitute, and that, in fact, permitted her to overcome the guilt she felt about her privileged background, the "trivialities" of her carefree youth, the loss of a child, and the stigma of a failed marriage. Rose combined paternal and maternal identities within herself as a way to resolve familial and social anxieties: her determination to help the unwanted may have been based on her memories of her father as Christlike, while her role as a spiritual mother to young women entering her Dominican sisterhood united the nurturing role expected of women with an activist spirituality that was shared among women. Rose Lathrop's conversion and new vocation released enormous energies on behalf of others, a common enough psychic phenomenon, as noted by William James and later by Sigmund Freud, which was manifested in her wide-ranging plans for reforming the lives of sisterhoods and of Catholic charities. While her strenuous work ethic recalls ascetic Calvinism, her ameliorative programs gave Catholicism a model of radical and compassionate social reform.

Unlike the personal cues that drew Rose Lathrop to Catholicism, an entirely academic approach to religion led Julia Gorham Robins (1846–1918) to convert. A descendant of Colonel Thomas Crafts, who read the Declaration of Independence from the Massachusetts statehouse balcony in 1776, and of patriot Samuel Parkman, Robins remarked that she was "born and bred in Boston in the center of Unitarianism of the conservative type, sometimes spoken of as Channing Unitarianism." Gorham was educated in private schools in Boston, and her conversion filled her with zeal to correct popular prejudices about Catholics. Accordingly, she always carried a "huge telescope suit-case fairly crammed with Catholic reading matter" to distribute at any opportunity. The experience of a convent retreat during Passion Week in 1899 convinced her that she "did not wish to run the chance of dying outside the Catholic Church."[186] After seven weeks of religious instruction she was baptized. Robins became a contributor to the *Sacred Heart Review,* to the *Catholic Encyclopedia,* and to *America* magazine. As she recounted her intellectual quest in *A New England Conversion,* her transformation was a mental process of breaking down former doctrinal prejudices against Catholicism. Her acceptance of Catholicism's claim to be the one true church, its unified interpretation of Scripture, and its doctrine of the real presence of Christ in the Eucharist indicated that her spiritual journey became a laborious point-by-point refutation of her former Protestant beliefs. In effect, Robins conceived of her spiritual growth as an intellectual pilgrimage, which ultimately convinced her that she had been a Catholic prior to her announced conversion, a claim that perhaps eased the psychic trauma associated with conversion.

Like Julia Robins, Susan Lyman Emery (1846–1923) was a convert from a similarly Yankee family and conservative Protestant background who became notable for her editing and publishing career. From Dorchester, "of a highly intellectual and religious family, real New England stock, and all ardent believers in the Episcopal religion," Emery's High Church affinities led her to a position as assistant editor of the Episcopal church's missionary magazine, *The Young Christian Soldier,* from 1871 to 1874.[187] But she resigned in that year, tormented by new religious doubts. By chance, she read a book of sermons by an Irish Dominican priest left in her house by "one of those Irish maidens who have done so much towards spreading the faith in New England," which convinced her that the Catholic Church was the one true church. Two months later, at age twenty-nine, she was baptized a Catholic in Boston, made a secret vow of virginity, and afterward dressed always in black.[188] Her distraught family claimed that she had publicly disgraced them.

Emery delved into parish work at nearby St. Peter's, Dorchester, serving as as sacristan, catechism teacher, and later, parish historian.[189] Turning her editorial talents to her new religion, in 1891 Emery became assistant editor of the *Sacred Heart Review.* There Emery promoted the literary talents of local Catholics, especially Hugh Blunt, then a curate in her parish.[190] She was a gentle literary editor, penciling in corrections "very light, so they could be easily erased." Her own poems, stories, and nonfiction were widely published in the *Review, American Catholic Quarterly Review, Catholic World, Columbiad, Harper's,* and *Irish Monthly.* She is best remembered for a devotional guide, *The Inner Life of the Soul,* which offered meditations on the liturgical calendar from Advent through Pentecost.[191] In another work, an essay on her conversion, she employed the common image of conversion as a path to security: "The roads that lead souls into the Catholic Church are many and various. Rome rhymes with home, and indeed all roads lead there."[192]

Like Emery, Alice Hayes (1855–1920), a matron at the Woman's Reformatory Institution in Sherborn, "came as far as the portals of the Church with no human help other than that obtained from the printed page" but then needed personal inspiration for the final step.[193] While employed as the censor for inmates' books and papers at Sherborn prison, Hayes thumbed through the *Sacred Heart Review,* the first Catholic publication she had seen. From its pages she gained a favorable impression of Catholicism and soon embarked on a pamphlet-reading program. Hearing a Catholic Mass for the inmates caused her to wonder about a Church that acknowledged its members to be both sinful and faithful. Hayes reported that she gradually overcame this seeming paradox and the two intellectual stumbling blocks of her Protestant upbringing—the doctrines of papal infallibility and Marian devotion—by reading the Catechism. She was also instructed by a pastor in Amesbury and was tutored by Father (later Bishop) John Nilan of Hartford and the editors of the *Sacred Heart Review,* Father John O'Brien and convert Susan Emery. Her own spiritual progress was halting, as she anxiously reported to Father Nilan: "I must have made some serious mistakes since I took the first step towards the Church last Winter, for I began sanely enough. I had promised myself for a longtime that when certain hinderences [*sic*] ceased to exist I would become a Catholic—provided the Church would receive me. I had no Catholic friends but having taken the 'Review' for many years I finally wrote Father O'Brien, asking him where I belonged."[194]

The contrasting spiritual styles of Emery ("something of a mystic") and the prosaic O'Brien confused her in her spiritual quest, for she wanted unity and certainty from Catholicism, not controversy. "One thing that frightens me," she wrote, "if I do not believe the Catholic Church then I believe nothing at all. But what I *want* is not only an intellectual belief, but a motive strong enough to control the thoughts and acts of every day."[195] Like many female converts, she identified Catholicism with a convincing design for living. She converted in 1905, explaining her choice in *A Convert's Reason Why.* The book followed the format of the Baltimore catechism and illustrated each answer by one or more extracts from various authors, including converts and non-Catholics. After favorable reviews she revised the book in 1913 and sought wider distribution for it through an international publisher such as Longmans, Green of London, as she confided to Bishop Nilan.[196] Hayes's conversion narrative is significant as an attempt to distinguish true Catholic conversion, a process combining instruction of mind and heart, from the climactic emotional "saving change" sought by Protestants. Hayes's interest in aiding imprisoned women and supporting the women's movement in her later life is suggested by her work for prison reform in Massachusetts and by her articles for the *Sacred Heart Review* and the *Catholic Charities Review.* Further, the bibliographies she published on woman suffrage and related subjects attest to her familiarity with the works of Jane Addams, Edith Abbott, Charlotte Perkins Gilman, Florence Kelly, John Stuart Mill, Olive Schreiner, Elizabeth Cady Stanton, and Thorstein Veblen.[197] She did not find her knowledge of feminist writers at odds with her faith, nor did she express fear that Catholicism would limit her occupational choices.

The conversions of these six women and their subsequent contributions to Catholicism in the fields of devotional literature, evangelization, and social service demonstrated how they found doctrinal certainty, infallible authority, and inner peace within the Catholic Church. As believers, like Julia Robins, they admired Catholicism's "lofty moral standards" and found in it "the best credentials for an interpretation of the Bible."[198] As women they accepted papal infallibility, clerical leadership, and the Church's view of women. They deferred to priestly advice: "For these grand priests, thank God!," wrote Susan Emery in one of her poems; and they praised domesticity: "God intended women for domestic and social functions and not for the professions," claimed Martha Moore Avery. Convert women satisfied their spiritual and career longings but did not regard themselves as radicals. This self-image of conventionality allowed women to represent their faith as the factor that made their lives exceptional. Alice Hayes, for example, received this severe advice from Bishop Nilan that compared the discipline of prison inmates to the self-sacrifice inherent in women's service to the Church: "Kindness does not consist in showering favors or in raining sympathy but in consistent acts of justice, and in severe words of correction for those who have gone the way of the transgressors. Just as force must be used and pain be caused before the disjointed limb is in place again so the wayward woman must feel the weight of authority and know the value of sacrifice before getting started on the way to reform."[199]

Female converts cited similar emotional and spiritual benefits resulting from their conversions: a sense of security and tranquility and a feeling of faith deepening with intellectual inquiry and practice. The "weight of authority" and "the value of sacrifice" coupled with the ritual, aesthetic, and doctrinal appeal of Catholicism attracted those who felt that theological rigor had evaporated from their liberal churches. Convert women seem to have been attracted to Catholicism for its paradoxical embrace of mysticism and rationalism, its sacramental rituals, and its assertion that self-denial leads to true freedom. Some convert women felt, as did male contemporaries, that Catholicism answered the confusion and subjectivity of modern thought. Furthermore, their energetic contributions in charitable and social service are reminders that the institutional Church's strongest defenders of its social conscience were not necessarily Irish Americans or "cradle Catholics." The publication of converts' narratives potentially heightened Catholic cultural isolation by emphasizing the ways in which Catholic doctrine was superior to Protestantism, atheism, and other "false" worldviews forsaken by the converts. Accordingly, conversion accounts that stressed the intellectual choices leading to an acceptance of Catholicism became important propaganda that highlighted the importance of the mind in acts of faith, as contrasted with evangelical Protestant appeals to the emotions. Yet, against overly rational Unitarianism, Catholics stressed the need for a heartfelt experience that was genuine and enduring. Finally, some women converts provided the Church with the symbolic capital of representation among the Boston elites, who utilized the familiar devices of the conversion narrative and the female charitable worker. The Jesuits made numerous converts among Brahmin women at their parish, Immaculate Conception, while Cardinal O'Connell himself was decisive in the conversion of the wife of Republican governor Curtis Guild of Massachusetts. The fact that the Catholic converts evaluated here made outstanding contributions in nursing, prison reform, education, publishing, and social work suggests that Catholicism did not constrain their opportunities and achievements. They were able to make the boundaries of woman's sphere fluid.

The Ideal Catholic Woman

Several major themes have emerged in this reconstruction of a Catholic ideology of womanhood in the archdiocese of Boston. Appearing initially in the late nineteenth-century immigrant Church, Catholic domesticity absorbed various cultural influences, including European Catholic traditionalism, the cultural values of the Irish (and other ethnic groups), and norms associated with the Yankee middle class. Thus, Catholic womanhood was a hybrid of residual, imported, dominant, and emergent cultural elements, which were modified by class determinants as well. Because the Gilded Age produced an ascendant American Catholic middle class with a domestic ideology as "colorful and sentimental as any proper Victorian," it is hard to separate distinctively Catholic elements of womanhood from those produced throughout the United States by the sexual division of labor that accompanied the rise of a bourgeois class. The presence of new social relations of production in America had profoundly shaped patterns of middle-class formation based on a notion of separate gender spheres that demanded the privatization of women, while changing patterns of production and consumption simultaneously denied them an economically productive role. These processes were reflected in the rhetoric of Catholic leaders as the Church attempted to minimize the desirability of a permanent female wage earner and to maximize the value of motherhood and domestic virtues. In their protests against the dangers of modern life, churchmen and laymen alike exploited the symbol of motherhood in a conservative fashion. Allowing that economic forces contributed to the construction of Catholic womanhood, we may summarize the key elements of this ideology as it was promoted by the hierarchy, clergy, and laity.

The concept of woman's sphere, the elevation of female purity, and the cloistering of women in the home shifted women's social role from producer to domestic icon and manager of rational household consumption. This shift was reinforced by the Catholic educational system in the gender separation of the Catholic convent school, which institutionalized sex segregation, emphasized the disciplined regulation of time and the body, and sacralized home and motherhood. Well into the twentieth century, women had limited access to higher education, and measurable discrepancies existed between opportunities available to laywomen and laymen and between the status of women religious and priests. The Church's protectionist attitude toward adult women bound them to the preservation of family unity and defined antimaterialism, antisocialism, and antisuffrage as threats to the family. Later, antidivorce and anti–birth control campaigns would also become planks of the Church's "profamily" agenda. As Catholics became increasingly successful and affluent in Boston, the Church portrayed women as antidotes to the excesses of materialism. As caretakers of Catholic values, women were taught to protect the family unit by modeling themselves on those saints who were exemplary mothers and patriots. In didactic literature, virgin-mother and virgin-warrior roles ascribed to women paralleled the Church's own use of Church-mother and Church-militant metaphors. Churchmen selected holy women from Catholic history to convince laywomen that their innate, positive, feminine qualities belonged in the household, but also to show that the Church had never limited the potential of women. As the unusual degree of economic freedom of Irish Catholic immigrant women was curtailed and brought under the influence of Church conservatism in the early 1900s, Church limitations upon female behavior served the class aspirations of male Catholics on the rise. Instead of having their own careers, which threatened prevailing prejudices about the market, women were encouraged to promote the success of their husbands and sons. Or, if they must work, women were asked to regard a job as a temporary exercise in character building. Set in the larger context of American history, the Church's advice to mothers to mold future leaders for the nation gave rise to "republican motherhood" among Catholics, which repeated a historical pattern of Protestant women of the postrevolutionary generation and again in the Progressive era. This civic role, however, remained closely tied to the coercive ideology of domesticity. As one Catholic woman asserted, "The world rests upon the Christian mother. Society, the commonwealth, the church are based upon the tortoise-like keeper of her own home."[200] Catholic ambivalence about how much public presence women should have represented the Church's absorption of the conflicted elements of domesticity, as well as its conservative role in immigrant assimilation and class formation. By maintaining control over women's access to social power, the Church maintained women's dependent status.

The Catholic ideology of womanhood retained numerous vestiges of European aristocratic culture, clearly visible in the elitist tone of convent schooling and its reliance on such evidence of high culture as the study of French. The revived Marian sodalities, originally founded among European aristocratic families of the sixteenth century, also maintained many of the ceremonies of the culture of the pious elite. Thus, the tenets of noble charity to the poor were introduced to Boston's middle-class girls. Although derived from the ruling classes of feudal Europe, the traditions were adapted to a gender sensibility based on female propriety and motherhood and were tailored to serve as models for working-class girls as well in coping with the instability and uncertainty of urban life.

The Church's advice to women expressed the urgency of its crusade against the crises of modern civilization. Sermons and advice literature, which represented women in terms of binary oppositions (Eve or Mary, sinner or angel), typically alternated between criticism and praise for the feminine. Although visceral fear of female sexual power remained an undercurrent in clerical writing, the Church focused on the selflessness and chastity of women, admonishing them to purify the public domain of male competition. Women were summoned to holy habits not exclusive to women, but that were recommended to both genders: prayer, Bible and devotional reading, meditation, and exemplary living. In practice, denoting women as household queens did not deprive them of all social power, since women's alleged purity justified their entry into the public realm as "moral leaders, not followers." Herein, one might argue, was the riddle at the heart of the ideology of Catholic womanhood: how much worldliness could women experience and still safeguard their innocence and purity? The search for answers to these questions points us toward the study of women's activities outside the home.

ORGANIZING CATHOLIC WOMEN

Look out for what I call Protestant influence. I mean that rotten principle of Protestant culture which teaches people to be polite and refined exteriorly, and keep white sepulchres of foulness within. Bess, learn mother's ways, of looking at everything through the eyes of faith, of learning that the beginning of wisdom is the fear of the Lord.—Michael Earls to Bess, January 22, 1909

The Cardinal laid down the law under which a Catholic club must operate. If . . . there are women who mean to work on their own will, they are not wanted. It was said as bluntly as that.—Martha Moore Avery to David Goldstein, June 16, 1918

I have never had a complete vacation since I am in charge; for no one person would take my whole load, and I can't afford two. My pro-motion advantaged me not financially; although my old salary as as-sistant editor, was fair for that place . . . I have been fifteen months without even a partial rest. Do say a little prayer for me.—Katherine Conway to Father [Daniel] Hudson, May 5, 1907

Clubwomen and Middle-Class Formation

The archdiocese of Boston serves as an excellent case study of the contradictions inherent in the experience of American Catholic women. At the outset, we can draw parallels between Catholic women and nineteenth-century Protestant women, for whom domestic ideology became a basis and even a precondition for the emergence of secular feminism. The recent schol-arship of historians of American women outside the Catholic tradition helps contextualize the evident lack of a feminist movement or of significant feminist activity among Catholics. Histories of Protestant women and of the origins of American feminism have established that feminism has been the product of the white middle class and that it spread via women's organizations outside the home, including many moral reform or "ultraist" groups indebted to nineteenth-century evangelicalism, particularly antislavery, abolition, and temperance.[1] In the early 1900s, organizations of Catholic women also de-rived their social activism from religious doctrines, which expressed a similar confusion of motives for their social role: were women concerned primarily with securing rights (a bourgeois, individualistic preoccupation), or with pro-viding service (a pious, communitarian goal)?

The origins of this dilemma between rights and service stemmed from the dual sources of the nineteenth-century American women's rights movement:

the natural rights political theory of the Enlightenment, which insisted on the legal and political rights of all individuals in a society, regardless of gender; and domestic ideology, which highlighted the particular aspects of feminine existence shared by all women. Each of these perspectives supported female equality for a different reason: the former was political and judicial; the latter based its claim on the concept of a separate sphere for women. Each strand of thinking could also be interpreted in ways that limited women's autonomy: the concept of universal domesticity slighted the uniqueness of each woman's experience and obliterated variations among classes and ethnic groups, whereas demands for political rights mistakenly presupposed that women's structural equality had already been achieved.

More than mainline Protestantism, Roman Catholicism had been at odds with the legacy of two Enlightenment principles—separation of church and state, and republican government. Thus, the American tradition of disestablishment and demotic representation of interests conflicted, in theory at least, with the medieval Catholic ideology of hierarchy and social duty. By 1900 in the United States, the Catholic hierarchy contained some bishops who supported the Vatican's vision of a return to medieval unity, some who hoped to ultimately convert America to Catholicism, and others who strove to interpret the compatibility of Catholicism and Americanism as a continuous tradition. The power of Catholic women's associations, limited as it was by the male authority vested in bishops, clergy, politicians, and the legal system, would soon experience the same contradictory pulls of male-dominated social norms, between rights and service, individualism and communitarianism, self-sacrifice and self-assertion, conformism and reformism. In the early 1900s, women's societies became agents of Americanization, definers of social class, and extensions of ecclesiastical control over women. As bearers of the Catholic ideology of womanhood, they enabled the Church to wage a two-front "war" against feminism in the upper and middle classes, and against socialism among the lower classes and working women.

The most readily available unit for organizing Catholic laywomen was the parish. Whether defined territorially or ethnically, parishes had served as centers of lay organizations in the nineteenth century. Until the 1880s most parish societies, such as the sodalities and the confraternities, had been devotional in nature, and the highest percentage of their active membership was female.[2] The Sodality of the Children of Mary, for example, founded in 1816, held monthly meetings, an annual retreat, and performed works of charity for the poor and cared for altar linens and priests' vestments. Sodalists reassured Catholics that members were "drawn from every walk in life, all meeting on the same plane, thus avoiding un-American distinctions of class and caste."[3] By 1900 a Boston Catholic girl was enveloped from childhood to motherhood by a network of pious institutions, from the Holy Angel's Sodality for young children, to the Sodality of the Children of Mary for girls, then to a young ladies' sodality, and finally to a sodality for married women.[4]

In the organizational revolution that transformed urban Catholicism in the late nineteenth century, however, most of the independent laywomen's societies disappeared, to be replaced by ladies' auxiliaries that were affiliated with autonomous institutions, such as convent schools, hospitals, orphanages, and homes for delinquents.[5] The increase in affiliated social service groups for women after 1890 reflected a change in Catholic voluntarism: whereas men and women were about equally represented in Church work in 1870, by 1890 women predominated.[6] Groups such as the Young Ladies' Charitable Association of Boston, a general association with officers in each of twenty districts of the city, emerged to found and fund a home for consumptives and to provide care and services for the sick and impoverished without regard to creed or color. The young women who visited the home daily to read to the sick, run the kitchens, and provide burial services supplemented the care of professional nurses and the matron. They raised money by means of a monthly subscription drive and later added a children's library and working girl's club.[7] As this ambitious attempt indicates, the parish was no longer the sole locus for women's charity work, nor was the parish the nostalgically recalled welcoming and sociable community of a generation ago. As urban parishes struggled with balancing different social classes, nationalities, and community needs, women were becoming providers of a host of overlapping health and social services that they initially controlled. Concern about the unsupervised freedom of women gradually led the archdiocese to force women's groups to federate with diocesan-regulated agencies. The Church's efforts to centralize women's groups represent a form of paternalism, a further example of Catholic sectarianism, and later, a part of the Church's resistance to state-run social services.

Women, therefore, helped redesign the Catholic Church's social services in the early twentieth century in ways that both preserved traditional domesticity and that employed the Progressive era's language of professionalization and centralization. *America* magazine urged Catholics to adopt the efficiency model: "Organization is the secret of success in social service. The more complete the centralization of societies within their various provinces and under competent directorates, the more satisfactory must evidently be the results achieved."[8] The magazine also suggested that Catholic women could even learn from the tactics of socialist women, "especially in the literary propaganda and zeal for organization displayed by them."[9] From a female perspective, clubs and societies offered avenues of learning and self-culture, and altruism and spiritual development, against the religious, financial, class, and gender barriers that effectively restricted women's access to higher education and professional careers before the 1930s. The emergence of laywomen's clubs took place in conjunction with at least three national trends: restructuring of Catholic charities, expansion of women's associationism as an extension of the domestic domain, and professionalization of social work and child welfare.

Women's affiliations fit one or more categories: charitable groups federated with the League of Catholic Women or the Massachusetts Catholic Women's Guild, devotional and spiritual clubs for middle-class gentlewoman, and local chapters of national or international Catholic organizations defined by a single purpose, such as the Catholic Reading Circle movement, the Catholic Summer School, the Catholic Total Abstinence Union, the Catholic Truth Guild, and the International Federation of Catholic Alumnae. The Church could easily employ the stereotypes implied by the notion of a separate sphere for women to discourage women from public life. Further, the involvement of women in voluntarism aided the Catholic Church in its efforts to extend a uniform gender code to all classes of women. However, despite the Church's paternalism, strong bonds that were forged among middle-class women also held the potential to mitigate paternalism and to allow women to gain a sense of power based precisely on the maternalist ideology of woman's sphere and domestic feminism.

The Church's desire to protect female purity catalyzed a social conscience among Catholics that reflected religious and social attitudes about the vulnerability of the female sex. A large percentage of Boston's Catholic social agencies dating from the 1860s were intended to preserve the innocence of girls and women or to serve the needs of "penitent females." These included refuges for "fallen" women, such as the House of the Good Shepherd (1867), and infant asylums such as the Home for Destitute Catholic Children (1864), St. Anne's Infant Asylum, Dorchester, and St. Mary's Infant Asylum, Dorchester. Vocational schools for women and girls were formed, such as the Daly Industrial School (1899) and the Working Girl's Home (St. Helena's House, occupied 1893), which emphasized domestic skills of sewing, cooking, and cleaning or secretarial skills of typing and stenography rather than managerial talents. The elderly were cared for by agencies such as St. Joseph Home (originally affiliated with St. Helena's House for working girls), which became a residence for aged women in 1915.

Most charities were managed and staffed by nuns and sisters, notably the Sisters of Mercy, the Sisters of Charity, and the Grey Nuns of Montreal. In 1910 these agencies became part of the CCB founded in 1903.[10] The situation of women religious was in significant ways analogous to that of laywomen: after 1900 they were increasingly stripped of their autonomy and subordinated to episcopal power and centralization. As recent scholarship on American women religious has suggested, there is evidence that the Vatican eroded the distinctive identities of the different orders, traditionally based on special charisms and goals, and generally diminished the uniqueness of women's religious orders by subjecting them to the canon law revisions of 1917.[11] Since nuns defined themselves primarily as servants of others, they were unlikely to become radical social reformers or advocates of women's rights, working instead collectively to ease individual suffering without seeking structural change. Further, certain aspects of nuns' charity work imitated contemporary urban reformism but at the same time inhibited the growth of gender consciousness among the sisters. Although Protestants admired Catholic sisterhoods as models of cooperation and sources of essential labor, nuns were anonymous and nonpublic; next, their vows of obedience to their order and to poverty obliged them to accept low wages without complaint; and finally, their aid to the poor did not translate into gender solidarity because nuns, like most Catholics, did not mobilize responses to urban problems by personal or political appeals to moral indignation, shame, or guilt. Although they accomplished much to alleviate human misery, religious women had no basis upon which to build a critique of mass apathy toward solving poverty, overcrowding, and crime. Consequently, their homes and schools for working-class women, unmarried mothers, and orphans served as protective agencies rather than as agents of change.

While the lives of nuns were becoming more restricted by clerical authority, laywomen began creating agencies for mothers and infants. Their initially autonomous guilds were soon obliged to federate with the LCW and the CCB. Eventually the expanding voluntarism of laywomen into charity and education must have created a certain tension with nuns and sisters, who found some of their ministries being duplicated or overtaken. The increased autonomy of laywomen occurred, it seems, while nuns were being removed from some of their semipublic activities and were being returned to a stricter definition of cloister. Laywomen faced their own obstacles, however. In contradiction to the covenanted unity of the sisterhoods, laywomen were isolated by the constraints of Catholic domesticity and by the divisive effects of individualism and professionalism on their attempts to work together on behalf of their sex and on behalf of the needy.

The role of lay and religious women in Catholic philanthropy became part of the diocesan and, indeed, national effort by the Church to rationalize philanthropy. This was an unwieldy process in which the struggle for control of charities pit laywomen against women religious, and each of them against the clergy and hierarchy. Laywomen's struggles ultimately seemed to produce leaders who were more progressive about charitable reform than the laymen and clergy who held controlling positions in philanthropic work. Still, women's activism in social service did not translate into support for organized feminism. Sisters, who previously welcomed the assistance of laywomen, now opposed restructuring of charities for fear that they would lose their autonomy and their privileged role in home visitation.

Since the 1890s when the ministries of sisters and laywomen had begun to overlap, young women were no longer content to act merely as fundraisers for the sisterhoods. By the 1920s, several demographic changes converged to produce the need for a different kind of Catholic philanthropy: as the Catholic population assimilated, nuns came less frequently from working-class communities and more often from the educated middle class. As immigration peaked, however, there were more Catholics in need of charitable institutions in Boston. Middle-class matrons continued to devote their lives to the home and conservative forms of service, but as a younger generation of women entered the work force, they became less available for volunteer work. The result was that more middle-class nuns and laywomen were serving an underclass population of a different ethnic background and with which they had less and less intimate contact.[12]

Catholic Women's Societies

Three distinct kinds of laywomen's affiliations were the products of the period 1880 to 1910: educational and self-development; charitable and social; and spiritual, represented respectively by the Catholic Reading Circles, the LCW, and the Cenacle Retreat Guilds. As a rule, they attracted middle-class Catholics who generally followed the doctrines of domestic feminism. Although these groups may have mitigated against emergence of a feminist position, they may have fostered instead both female consciousness and communal consciousness. As defined by Nancy Cott, these latter two terms provide a more precise vocabulary for the range of possibilities in women's lives and thought relevant to public activism. Cott suggests that "female consciousness" signifies "a mind-set not biologically female but socially constructed from women's common tasks"; "communal consciousness" conveys solidarity with men and women of the same group, including religious identity. Both of these mindsets are distinct from "feminist consciousness," which is "clearly oppositional, reformist, or revolutionary." Female and communal consciousness seem to accurately represent the awareness of Catholic women in Boston.[13]

Catholic women had no access to the sacramental power of the Church embodied in the priesthood. Yet, by taking advantage of the lack of social barriers to their involvement in benevolence toward women, children, and the poor, Catholic women achieved a measure of autonomy by their voluntarism outside the home. To receive official Catholic status, their associations were subject to approval by the archbishop, who preferred local groups to national organizations over which he had limited or no authority. The effect of this policy was to secure large memberships for diocesan and parish organizations, which further enhanced a Catholic subculture in Boston. Only one national group, the AFCS, established in 1901, gained his approval. "Radical" Catholic labor groups, found intermittently throughout the West and Midwest and often among German communities, such as the Central Verein (1856) and the Militia of Christ for Social Service (1910–14), were not affiliated in Boston. No equivalent of Chicago's Catholic Socialists or of midwestern labor priests sprung up among the New England Irish. Women's groups, predictably, had to be properly deferential in order to succeed. O'Connell discouraged women from joining non-Catholic clubs such as Sorosis, from affiliating with labor groups such as the Women's Educational and Industrial Union, and from membership in political societies such as the New England Woman Suffrage Association. He played an infamous part in trying to destroy the founding of the National Catholic Welfare Council after World War I, which planned to include a national women's council that ultimately became the National Council of Catholic Women.

Justification for clergy supervision of women's associations emanated from Rome: Popes Leo XIII and Pius X mandated Church control of Christian lay movements.[14] In the 1890s, when attempts to organize lay initiatives were gaining momentum in the United States through the lay congress movement, Katherine Conway wrote to her local bishop in Rochester: "But why all this fuss about 'lay participation' anyhow? Any level-headed, intelligent Catholic layman—or woman for that matter—with ability and enlightened zeal to work for religion can't help but make his record in church work. And I never knew a bishop or priest who wanted to hinder him. Why talk about 'participating,' when there's nothing to do but go ahead and participate!"[15] Conway's optimism proved to be unwarranted in Boston and, indeed, nationwide. The lay congress movement was effectively killed during the 1890s, due to lack of hierarchical support.[16] In the following decades, any women's society seeking Catholic approbation in Boston was assigned a chaplain by Archbishop O'Connell. In 1910 it became his policy to assign a priest to all lay societies.[17] For women's groups, O'Connell went so far as to define the positions they should take on selected political issues and to mandate when they should remain silent. "Even at the risk of becoming tedious," he told Catholic women of greater Boston in 1918, "I wish again to impress upon you the paramount importance of that unity that is gained only by submission to authority and discipline. . . . To put this on a practical basis, every Catholic society ought to have a chaplain and heed his services."[18]

A survey of Catholic chaplaincies suggests that O'Connell handpicked priests from his inner circle for the most prominent diocesan societies. His chancellor from 1907 to 1913, Michael J. Splaine, became spiritual director of the LCW and of the Catholic Truth Guild. In 1921 Rev. Joseph Murphy, another trusted associate, succeeded Splaine as spiritual director of the Truth Guild. O'Connell appointed his auxiliary bishop, Joseph G. Anderson, to head the diocesan charitable bureau from 1908 to 1911, which worked with the eighty societies federated in the LCW.[19] Father Jones I. Corrigan, professor of ethics and jurisprudence at Boston College, also became closely affiliated with the LCW. He taught its public affairs course for seven years, becoming exactly the type of publicist O'Connell sought. Well known in New England as "a source of Catholic thought on public questions," Corrigan "fought persistently and courageously, Prohibition, Birth Control, the League of Nations, the World Court, Pacifism, the Child Labor Amendment, Mexican Anti-clericalism, Socialism, and especially Bolshevism and the Recognition of Russia."[20] O'Connell chose Rev. Patrick J. Waters, who was his trouble-shooter at the Lawrence textile strike in 1912 and ghostwriter of his economic pastoral letters, as chaplain to the Common Cause forum when it was founded in that year. Martha Moore Avery objected to the term *chaplain* since the forum was intended to be entirely secular. O'Connell agreed to call Waters a spiritual advisor, a minute victory for lay, but not specifically female, resistance.[21] Splaine, Anderson, Corrigan, Waters, and others formed a clerical cadre of club boosters who formulated the constitutions, bylaws, and official statements for women's societies on private and political issues, without soliciting female input. Not surprisingly, O'Connell did not appoint a priest to the Margaret Brent Suffrage Guild, a Massachusetts Catholic suffrage group led by Margaret Foley and named after the Catholic laywoman of colonial Maryland who was deemed the first American suffragist because she requested voting power in the assembly.[22] Opinions published in the Boston *Republic* suggested that laymen seconded the clergy's conservatism: "Personally, we think the ballot is a doubtful good for any woman, and hosts of the ablest whom we know would not have its responsibilities, no matter how easy it might be of attainment."[23]

The Catholic Summer School
and the Reading Circle Movement

Catholic associations that emerged in the late nineteenth century frequently modeled themselves on existing bourgeois institutions. The Catholic Summer School represented one such imitation of the summer encampment and self-culture experiments of Protestants. Designed along the lines of the Methodist Chautauqua movement begun in 1874, the Catholic Summer School planned to educate Catholic adults about a variety of topics in a relaxing and scenic atmosphere. The summer school derived from the two most prominent groups within the Catholic Reading Circle movement—the Columbian Reading Union (1884) and the Catholic Educational Union (1889)—which had copied the format of the Chautauqua Literary and Scientific Circle (1878).[24] The presence of significant female leadership and membership in the reading unions continued in the summer schools and the reading circles. From the reading circles had also come support for the national lay congress movement, marking its lay members as drawn from the more progressive ranks of American Catholics.

In Boston, the John Boyle O'Reilly Circle was one of the earliest reading groups. Katherine Conway described how it expanded from quarters in a dim, poorly heated room at St. Joseph's Parish, Roxbury, in 1889 to the elegant rooms of the Catholic Union in downtown Boston, where it shared meeting space with a rival circle led by Mary Elizabeth Blake. Conway's group advertised its existence by offering a public lecture course and manifested its seriousness by giving reading assignments to members: "We took up the Messianic literature[,] . . . such subjects as the Pagan Vestal and the Christian nun. All this involved considerable reading and they took their medicine."[25] The O'Reilly circle survived the death of its namesake in 1890 to become the most prestigious local circle. Under Conway's leadership, membership increased to 135 in 1902; members avidly discussed a range of biblical books, poetry, fiction, and nonfiction. They also attended a logic class and ran a public lecture series. A priest commented with approval: "Not only will the Reading Circles and the guide-lists help Catholics, but will serve our American society at large. The Public Library will learn to know us better than it does. We shall be recognized not simply as readers, but as the owners and makers of a good, honest, healthy literature—a literature characterized by a just sense of art and by a high claim."[26] This idealism was transferred to the Catholic Summer School, whose first session met at New London, Connecticut, in 1892 before moving in 1897 to a permanent location at Cliff Haven, New York, on the shores of Lake Champlain. New England gradually lost its central role in hosting the summer school, as Conway explained through allusion to the waning of Transcendentalism at Brook Farm: "The scepter passed from the hands of New England to those of New York. We had plain living and high thinking, but we hadn't the money. . . . Boston began to sit back in the shady places."[27] Within a few years a midwestern version began at Spring Bank, Wisconsin. Maryland held its own summer school at various locations between 1900 and 1905, and New Orleans attempted a winter school in 1896. Notably, it was the Catholic Summer School press in 1907 that first published James J. Walsh's influential homage to medievalism, *The Thirteenth the Greatest of Centuries.*

The Catholic Summer School was not intended to be the domain of women. Priests found women more refined and educable than men, but, paradoxically, less in need of a worldly education. Noting that most of the summer school attendance was female, an observer asked, "Why should women be so far in the majority? Because many of them have more leisure, are less preoccupied with the sterner things of life. That answer is only partly true. There is a no less obvious positive reason. Women tend more naturally to the ideal. Things spiritual and intellectual find in their more refined and sympathetic nature a closer affinity and a more spontaneous reaction."[28] While many Catholics agreed that women tended more naturally to the ideal, a second, related explanation surfaced to explain the preponderance of women: the claim that the schools served as marriage marts.[29] Katherine Conway, who "strongly opposed" coeducation in the summer school, contended that it was the presence of men that furnished an unwelcome distraction.[30] While women appeared to view the summer school as an opportunity for education for its own sake, clerical paternalism viewed it as a safeguard against female apostasy and corruption by the secular world. A clergy magazine stated, "Catholic women are reaching out for knowledge, for opinions, views, if you will; and if we do not supply the goods, these Catholic women will go elsewhere to get them. Unwittingly, too, they'll get them damaged with error and sophistry."[31] Coupled with this bias against secular liberal arts education came complaints that summer school courses failed to be rigorous enough to sustain interest, or that they were becoming too Protestant. Nonetheless, one positive effect of the movement was to encourage self-education for a generation of adult Catholics who may have completed only primary or secondary school. As an adaptation of a Protestant practice, it was perhaps the only equivalent of advanced education available to the laity of both sexes. The high attendance at the summer school sessions indicates the program's expanding popularity: 1,500 participated in 1894 and 1895; 5,281 in 1903; and 7,011 in 1905.[32] By the time the summer school jubilee was celebrated in 1916, Boston was providing a core of some 600 summer school attendees each year. Archbishop O'Connell had spoken to one of its earliest gatherings in 1895 while still a parish priest.[33] His close associate, Monsignor Michael Splaine, became its director in 1933, suggesting that although lay control may have shifted to New York, Boston clergy remained influential.

Conway and convert couple George Parsons Lathrop and Rose Hawthorne Lathrop led the Bostonians who were prime movers in the Catholic Summer School and its parent organization, suggesting a further convergence with

Cardinal Gibbons preaching outdoors at Mass during the Catholic Summer School,
Cliff Haven, New York, 1910. Note the improvised birch-tree pulpit and leaf decorations on the altar. (Knights of Columbus Supreme Council Photo Archives)

Brahmin culture.[34] Because of J. J. Roche's failing health Conway did not
attend the summer school after 1897, but her two friends Mary Elizabeth
Blake and Katherine O'Keeffe O'Mahoney,[35] who had also participated in the
inaugural meeting in 1892, continued to lecture. Other involvements by Boston women included a July 1909 series entitled "Socialism Weighed and
Found Wanting" by Martha Moore Avery, lectures on biblical parables by
Mary Boyle O'Reilly, and numerous discussions devoted to the novels of Conway herself. Reports from the O'Reilly circle praised Conway's support for
lay education as its leader for thirteen years:

> There has been no change of president from the beginning. Having cho-
> sen at the start the right one for the place of intellectual leader, the mem-
> bers have shown no desire to transfer to a new candidate the honors
> belonging to the highest office in their gift. No doubt they know . . . that
> they have a model president, who is also a worker able to plan and to
> achieve splendid results in co-operative methods for self-improvement.

This organization is a type that should be imitated, as it furnishes the best model of what a Catholic Reading Circle should be.[36]

Reading circles, such as the East Boston Literary Union, the Notre Dame Reading Circle, the St. Vincent's Reading Club, the O'Connell Reading Club, the St. Gregory's Circle (Haverhill), and the Cardinal Newman (Lawrence), spread quickly throughout Massachusetts. A national magazine, the *Catholic Reading Circle Review,* published in Worcester, Massachusetts, from 1892 to 1897, provided national coverage of the circles and published their reading lists. The national Paulist monthly magazine, *Catholic World,* also featured reading circle news in its "Columbian Reading Union" department. The column's name changed to "With Our Readers" in October 1909 as reading circle news began to appear less frequently, suggesting that the circles had outgrown the need for publicity or had passed their prime.[37]

The reading circles raised issues of clerical, class, and gender control. Humphrey Desmond, owner of a Catholic publishing chain in the Midwest, composed *A Reading Circle Manual* in 1903, which formulated guidelines for membership and conduct of the meetings, opting for greater clerical control of the movement than seen in the O'Reilly circle, whose success was "attributed to the remarkable unanimity among the members, and particularly to the able management of the president, Miss Katherine E. Conway."[38] Desmond contended that "the advice of the priest is always most desirable, both at the inception and in determining the general program of the reading circle. . . . There is no safer guide when it comes to selecting text books and sources of information on current questions of a Catholic nature, than the priest." As for female participation, he admitted that "there are Catholic women, with a convent education or high school training, who would gladly continue that culture of the mind for which they have acquired a bent." He gave precedence, however, to "the Catholic professional men in our community, our lawyers, doctors and journalists. We next think of the young women in the teaching profession. These classes are the pillars of the Catholic intellectual movement."[39] The preference for professionals implied that working women, except teachers, were not likely recruits. Conway disapproved of class condescension, as she hinted in one of her novels. In *The Way of the World and Other Ways,* Mrs. Ray "never could get used to seeing school teachers received on equal terms socially, and had wished very much for a by-law excluding them definitely from the Daughters of St. Paula," a reading circle that "wished in all things to distinguish themselves from the members of another larger and better-known literary association which met in the evening, and had many wage-earners on its register."[40] Conway's real-life circle may have tried to include all levels of the social strata, but a Catholic elite clearly presided. As her diary entry reported concerning a meeting in 1908, "The Archbishop was there, also former Mayor Fitzgerald with his wife and daughter, and in general a very cultivated and good sized audience."[41]

For women, the reading circles provided alternatives to New England Protestant women's clubs that had excluded Catholics, and offered Catholics a sense of insider affiliation. However, since the reading circle movement peaked by the late 1890s and scarcely lasted for one generation, the predominance of female leadership and membership might be explained precisely because of the movement's decline and marginalization. Nonetheless, the circles provided a form of education for women and, in keeping with canons of domesticity, usefully absorbed the leisure time of mothers. There were even do-it-yourself programs for women at home "who don't have the advantage of belonging to clubs or reading circles," suggested by Susan Emery of Cambridge. In a two-part article in *Donahoe's Magazine* in 1899 she proposed a daily half-hour self-guided reading program emphasizing religious topics and centering on literature by or about Catholic women such as Catherine of Siena, Frances de Chantal, Teresa of Avila, and Joan of Arc.[42] Emery's suggestion may have been inspired by local events in Cambridge, namely the formation of the Society to Encourage Studies at Home by Elizabeth Cary in 1873. While Cary went on to become the first president of Radcliffe, her sister Emma converted to Catholicism, no less involved in sharing a vision of higher education with Catholic women. The uniquely Catholic flavor of at-home programs implied by the advocacy of pious or hagiographical literature hoped to deter Catholic women from tasting "the deadly absinthe of the worst type of French novel."[43]

In sum, summer schools, reading circles, and home education strategies developed by laywomen served their social and intellectual needs during an era when the Catholic hierarchy welcomed female apologists but was cautious and divided about endorsing pleas for women's higher education. Expressing a view pervasive in American culture, the Church feared that advanced education outside of its control would teach women to despise motherhood, as argued by a Jesuit lecturer popular with Boston audiences: "When a dislike for family life, based on love of ease and pleasure, or on an *unregulated intellectualism* begins to show among Christian women, a dark hour for Church and State alike is at hand."[44] Working against such patriarchal biases on the part of the clergy, women made the movement a success and at least established a habit of reading and discussion of Catholic literature among a lay audience. For women, the principles guiding the Catholic Reading Circle movement also served a class function by continuing the regimentation of the convent school and its concern for using time productively, which prepared upwardly mobile Catholics to diffuse middle-class values throughout their subculture. Although histories of intellectual women in Boston have generally highlighted the leadership of Brahmin Protestants and Unitarians at Radcliffe and Harvard, the reading circle movement is a reminder that Catholic women, too, played a part in devising and adopting early prototypes for higher education of women.

The League of Catholic Women

A perceptible demand surfaced after 1900 in the Catholic press about the need for women's associationism. Appeals for women to move beyond the home stated that "Catholic women are needed to fight the growing tendency toward paganism in the home and in society."[45] Women were thus enjoined to carry Catholic values into the American mainstream in order to protect the nation from moral decay. The vehicle for Catholic women's efforts was the LCW, which soon became the largest women's agency in the archdiocese. Pauline Willis, a native of Boston residing in London, brought the plan for a league to Boston in 1910. Its history was marked by opposition between clerical control and feminine initiative, and between competing notions of femininity.[46] Willis (b. 1870), a cousin of Phillips Brooks, Episcopalian rector of Trinity Church in Copley Square, and member of an eminent family of Catholic converts, told Elizabeth Dwight about the English Catholic Women's League begun by Margaret Fletcher at Oxford in 1906.[47] According to Willis, the league intended to confront "various alien propaganda [that] find shelter under cover of the woman's movement, with which Catholics must be in direct and open conflict. And we have to recognize the fact that with the spread of education, intellectual questions confront Catholic working women which, though easily disposed of by the highly educated, are really difficulties to them."[48] To train leaders to preserve the faith of the vulnerable working class, Fletcher founded and edited a quarterly magazine advocating female higher education that gained subscribers on both sides of the Atlantic.[49] In the spring of 1910, Dwight gained Archbishop O'Connell's approval to start the Boston LCW, which convened on May 2 at the Cathedral of the Holy Cross. O'Connell presided over a program of speakers that featured Dwight; Willis, who was described by the press as "a young woman of fine presence and appealing earnestness"; and Louise Guiney, another Boston expatriate and Oxford acquaintance of Margaret Fletcher.[50] Among the 100 or so attendees were leaders such as Katherine Conway, Katherine O'Keeffe O'Mahoney, and Susan Emery. Membership grew quickly as programs expanded.[51] By 1915 the Boston LCW numbered about 1,715 women; in 1919, over 4,000, peaking in the 1940s at about 7,500. It federated more than 40 women's societies, and its membership quickly surpassed that of the premier men's clubs.[52] Elizabeth Dwight served as LCW president until about 1917, when Mrs. Michael Cunniff, a former president of the Children of Mary sodality, succeeded her. The president from 1919 to 1932 was Lillian (Mrs. Francis E.) Slattery, who was appointed by O'Connell and who was a very unpopular choice with members. She was the sister-in-law of O'Connell's personal physician, a prominent wealthy Catholic in O'Connell's inner circle, but apparently lacked any history of civic or charitable involvement. O'Connell also drew up the executive board of the league, from its initial organizers. As patron, he continued to exercise nominating authority over the LCW board into the 1920s and beyond. In 1921, in what must have been a rare refusal to one of his requests, Helen Phelan politely turned down a leadership opportunity by revealing, "I simply cannot organize with women! I am shy and afraid of them. This may sound ambiguous to you—but I never get in a crowd with them that I do not have a headache."[53]

Designed to support and coordinate available Catholic charities without establishing new ones, the LCW's objective was "to unite Catholic women for the promotion of spiritual, cultural, and educational work."[54] The English league had been inspired by a recent predecessor, the German Katolischer Frauenbund. Nearly simultaneously, LCWs were being established in Italy, Holland, Belgium, France, Switzerland, Canada, and South America, suggesting an orchestrated score for the growth of women's organizations.[55] In Europe and Latin America, the leagues were dominated by women from aristocratic Catholic families friendly with the papal court. In American cities, leaders came from the upper middle and professional classes. After one year in existence, the Boston LCW affiliated with the International Federation of the Leagues of Catholic Women at its Madrid convention. Boston did not send a delegate to an international meeting until 1913. There was no national council of Catholic women until 1920, although many city and diocesan leagues had been founded in America before then.[56]

Among its numerous programs and services, the LCW ran a successful educational lecture series, which, in its first decade, featured a cross-section of local, national, and international speakers. The LCW lecture series was held in the Notre Dame Academy, a Catholic convent school, ironically hosting more male than female speakers. According to Mrs. C. W. Macdonald of Roxbury, the LCW vice-president, "When we can secure men who are enthusiastic and who have been successful in their special line of work we feel that we will be taught and not simply entertained."[57] Her remark suggests both women's desire for educational experience and deference to male intellectual superiority. On the other hand, the league realized that it was more likely to attract new members by having a superlative roster of speakers rather than by advertising its pious activities. As Elizabeth Perkins explained to O'Connell in 1911, "If the Catholic Women's League membership is to increase from its present 600 members—to the hoped for one thousand, by next spring, the Lectures must be so interesting that many will join for them alone. (Alas! So few join simply because the work is good in itself.)"[58] In its first six seasons (1910–15), for example, the fall and spring subscription lectures sponsored talks on Christian art, Catholic missionary work, Irish poetry, Dante, educational psychology, prison reform, German politics, Italian immigration, the Spanish novel, Hungarian music, disease control, and the French Revolution ("with stereopticon"). The topics reflected a potpourri of concerns: purely Catholic issues were juxtaposed with contemporary national issues, evidenced by increasing attention to social engineering and reform of cities, schools, and institutions initiated by the Progressive movement. A dual "track" system based on dues payment evolved within the league to encourage the stability of the lecture series: regular members were permitted to attend one series; sustaining members who paid higher dues could attend an additional series.

With some notable exceptions, most of the early LCW speakers were local. Occasional European visitors, usually prominent English Catholics, boosted revenues, enabling the LCW to pursue social work in juvenile probation, classes for mothers, and a nursery program for working mothers. Bernard Vaughan (1847–1922), an English Jesuit, spoke in 1911, and popular Catholic novelist and convert Monsignor Robert Hugh Benson (1871–1914) spoke twice in 1914, prompting the LCW secretary to comment: "Apart from realizing so large a sum, we should feel much gratified to be able to bring to Boston so great an orator and scholar as Monsignor Benson."[59] Vaughan's talks were controversial: although his antisocialist sermons were popular in England, in America he was described by "many" as a "woman-hater." He made no secret of his scorn for the "New Woman," the "sort of girl found in some of our picture papers—the sea front, go-with-the-times woman—the girl with even less in her than on her. This type does not, I hope, really represent the future mothers of our race. But they are too much in evidence at prize fights, in divorce courts and massage resorts."[60] Addressing Catholic audiences in Philadelphia, New York, and Boston, Vaughan became known for using Joan of Arc as an icon of antisuffrage. According to a friend and biographer, Vaughan "arrived in America with the not quite undeserved reputation of being out of sympathy with the ambitions of so many of the finest characters among American womanhood, and his invective against suffragism, often repeated during this tour, did little to mitigate the indignation felt by many who would otherwise have been his hearers and indeed admirers."[61]

In 1913 the LCW departed from its original policy of inviting "no one but Catholics to address us." A new progressive spirit among the women suggested that "we feel we could depart from this rule twice for the sake of the special advantage offered by their subjects."[62] By 1918, the LCW lecture roster had broadened. Cardinal O'Connell appeared on the program as usual, but speakers now came from the faculty of Catholic University, Washington, D.C.; several national industrial unions; Loyola University, Chicago; Bryn Mawr College; Fordham University; and the offices of the Jesuit weekly magazine, *America,* in New York City. Lecture topics reflected an evolution from the educational and self-development themes of the early 1900s to subjects more appropriate to post–World War I America, namely, labor relations, industrial reconstruction, democracy, and peacemaking. The lecture series continued to sell out, and capacity crowds filled the Fenway auditorium each Saturday afternoon. Under the LCW's auspices appeared such well-known Catholics as Father John Ryan.[63] The presence of the Reverends Joseph Husslein, William Kerby, John Burke, Peter Guilday, and Edward A. Pace attested to the Boston LCW's sympathy with the views of Catholic social reform represented by this group, among which were the subsequent founders of the National Catholic Welfare Council. Social reformism, however, did not include a progressive agenda on gender. For example, in 1923 Common Cause sponsored Edward Joyce of Newton to address feminism and its danger to the American home; in his speech he condemned advocates of women's rights as "unnatural, un-American and ungodly."[64]

The educational component provided by the lecture series appealed to LCW members. Yet, traditional charitable work formed the bulk of its labor: an information bureau that published job openings for women; a confidential home visitation ministry to "backslidden" Catholics; a lodging referral service for Catholic women traveling alone; service projects that provided readers for the blind and medical attention to the sick and poor; and exercise classes.[65] In 1914 it took up probation work, handed over from the all-male St. Vincent de Paul Society, which had worked with the Massachusetts Juvenile Court since its founding in 1906 to place Catholic delinquents in Catholic homes.[66] In 1914, with O'Connell's permission, the league hired May Burke as a probation officer to handle this new project for the league's young charges. Assisted by women volunteers, Burke helped supervise girls who had been brought before the court, offering vocational training, job placement, and emotional and spiritual support and noting that "the care given them at such a time may well mean the salvation of their souls."[67] LCW involvement with the state penal system suggests that Catholic women were well acquainted with and surprisingly integrated into these public agencies. Several LCW leaders were also active in Massachusetts penal reform.[68] This phenomenon suggests a revision of thinking about Catholic women as isolated from the currents of social scientific reform: in Massachusetts, Catholics were involved with the major affiliates of the American Social Science Association (and its

Boston chapter), which included the National Prison Association and the National Conference of Charities.[69]

LCW members were mostly middle-class Irish Americans, who were now serving Catholics other than the Irish, including Boston's immigrant Italians, French Canadians, and Poles. However, like the clergy, LCW leadership remained overwhelmingly Irish American. Only one Italian was a member of the LCW executive committee, probably because she was related by marriage to Thomas Dwight, a leader in the St. Vincent de Paul Society, and came from a wealthy Italian family in Boston. The Committee for Italian Social Service had a staff of eighteen volunteers, a paid social worker, and an expert cloth cutter to serve its first project for the North and West Ends of Boston—sewing classes. Chairwoman Eveleen Devlin organized the Mother's Sewing Club with child care available, where mothers learned how to make and repair clothing. The class, averaging twenty-four students, made 253 articles of clothing in its first year, "as well as many pairs of stockings darned."[70] The committee also ran classes for working girls in "aesthetic, folk and social" dancing, taught by volunteer Theresa Connell. To cement ties to other social agencies, the LCW affiliated with the North American Civic League for Immigrants, another instance of Catholic linkage to secular associations in an era marked by the Church's suspicion of social engineering. During World War I the LCW ran numerous war preparedness campaigns in accord with the archbishop's flag-waving and, on its own, financed and presented a field ambulance to the Massachusetts Ninth Regiment.[71] Women's volunteer and paid services during the war were invested with a sacred mystique by laywomen and clergy, symbolizing the growing link between Catholicism and Americanism. After the war, during the flu epidemic of 1918 O'Connell permitted the league to continue its wartime nursing by allowing it to use a local convent to house children whose parents were afflicted.[72]

Some LCW members chafed under O'Connell's limitations on their autonomy. Two extended crises led to a disagreement between the league and the cardinal in the early 1920s. First, Agnes Regan, executive secretary of the new National Council of Catholic Women, publicly supported the Child Labor Amendment, against O'Connell's wishes. In Massachusetts, O'Connell was credited for the defeat of the proposed constitutional amendment against child labor in the 1924 campaign, in which he called the proposal "nefarious and bolshevik."[73] From that point on, the Boston LCW never held active leadership in the National Council of Catholic Women (NCCW), perhaps due to prior bad blood: when the founding of the NCCW as a part of the National Catholic Welfare Council was in the planning stages, lay and clergy organizers tried to prevent Boston delegate and LCW president Lillian Slattery from obtaining a national office because Slattery was a puppet of O'Connell. O'Connell's unreasonable disapproval of the formation of the National Council of Catholic Women within the newly restructured National Catholic Welfare Council may also have been a smokescreen to mask the scandals involving his nephew that threatened to become public.[74] The episode was further proof for women that ecclesiastical politics was "the murderer of so many good projects."[75]

Despite these conflicts between local and national levels of the women's organization that arose in the 1920s, within a decade of its founding, Boston's LCW was thriving in every aspect. By 1920 membership topped 10,000; its lecturers had standing-room audiences, and O'Connell boasted that it was the largest women's federation in the world. Its image was upgraded to reflect its social aspirations: the league purchased a headquarters building at 1 Arlington Street, a prestigious address opposite Boston Public Garden, which it maintained until 1968.[76] As the leading nonpolitical Catholic women's group, it channeled middle-class benevolence into the neighborhoods of Boston and its suburbs and represented a lay innovation rapidly brought under episcopal control to help strengthen and reproduce a Catholic subculture. By the 1930s the Boston LCW sought wider local audiences through radio addresses given by President Slattery during the Catholic Truth Hour. The LCW founders were converts devoted to episcopacy; some of its leaders were handpicked by the archbishop and installed as his loyal supporters; the predominantly Irish American membership seemingly deferred to priestly authority, but managed to enlarge woman's sphere by performing significant social service outside the home to immigrants, working girls, prisoners, the sick, and the poor.

Like its Protestant and secular counterparts, the LCW grew in stages characteristic of the American clubwoman: a transformation from domestic feminism to public benevolence or "municipal housekeeping."[77] The Catholic women's clubs of Boston evolved from self-culture, self-improvement societies run by a small elite in the 1880s and 1890s, into organizations that emphasized structured charity work as well as language and job training for immigrants and working women. They changed further by supporting civic programs such as Americanization classes, vocational training, and rehabilitation for underprivileged women and children. Although not explicitly using the rationalist vocabulary of the new social science associations of Boston, Catholic women nonetheless duplicated their concerns for women's involvement in "the three ameliorative fields of social science," health, education, and social economy.[78] During World War I the LCW's wartime preparedness and service committees signaled the convergence of patriotic Americanism with an assimilationist spirit, seemingly at odds with the Church's strategy of separatism. Yet, most Catholic middle-class women did not become "professional altruists," to borrow Roy Lubove's phrase, because they were segregated by the Church from professional training, were not permitted to cooperate with secular reform associations, and did not receive wages for their work.[79] Catholic women's philanthropy, then, evolved from an era in which Catholic principles were archetypically Victorian, to an era of loosely interlocking or autonomous groups that had formed before 1900, before finally forming a federation of societies overseen by the LCW and the CCB. All of these social service agencies were dependent upon the unpaid labor of laywomen and the underpaid labor of Catholic sisterhoods. In an age when American social reformers were witnessing the devaluation of voluntarism and of religious charities, and their replacement by efficiency-minded managers, the Catholic Church reaffirmed the necessity of spiritually grounded works of mercy by volunteer women. In this sense, women's organizations institutionalized the moral conscience of the Church. At the same time, however, the effect of isolating a woman's charitable sphere was in part to deter women from entering the male economic domain of competition and production. In time, Catholic women's charities would also have to face the growing conflict within professionalized social work over support for immediate material aid to families versus agitation for large-scale social reform.

Spiritual Retreats for Women

In addition to the educational and charitable projects of the LCW, the self-education strategies of the Catholic Summer School and the Catholic Reading Circles, women's societies devoted to spiritual growth and devotional practices were also thriving. In one instance, Archbishop O'Connell tried to foster women's devotion to the Holy Cross by reviving the practice of Eucharistic devotion supported by Bishop Jean-Louis Cheverus of Boston in the previous century. O'Connell stressed that "the most important thing, however, is the spiritual work of your own salvation," implying that women should keep their attention focused upon self-discipline rather than self-assertion.[80] In this regard, nuns were instrumental in fostering laywomen's spirituality. By 1911 the Cenacle Convent Retreat Guilds, run by a religious order that developed spiritual retreats for women along occupational lines, had organized meetings at the Cenacle Convent in Brighton once a month for a day of prayer and recollection and annually for a three-day retreat.[81] The Religious Order of Our Lady of the Cenacle, whose superior was a Piedmontese noblewoman, was one of three orders of nuns introduced by O'Connell into the archdiocese, although as a pontifical order they were not subject to his control. O'Connell supported their lay retreat movement, especially because it attracted the wealthier Catholic women, whom he desired to cultivate. The Cenacle nuns had a particular philosophy of evangelization, well suited to Boston's growing middle class and to Catholic ideals of domesticity. "The parlor is our mission field," said one nun to a woman who recorded her experiences at the Cenacle Convent for the diocesan newspaper.[82] The Cenacle Convent housed between ten and twenty sisters who conducted retreats for women and taught what was then called Christian doctrine. The Cenacle guilds were composed of lay-women grouped by occupational categories. In 1911 the St. Anne's Association for married women was founded; the Association of the Cenacle, for business women, and the Association of St. Regis, for teachers, were also initiated. In the next year stenographers and secretaries met in the Guild of St. Genesius; domestics formed the Guild of St. Zita. High school girls were organized into the Guild of St. Agnes in 1914; in 1919 factory girls in the Guild of St. Imelda and telephone operators in the Guild of the Presentation of the Blessed Virgin were organized.[83] The chronology of these guilds may reveal the order in which retreatants came in contact with the Cenacle: married women were organized first, then white collar professional women, next educated girls, and finally, factory workers. The fact that the sisters grouped women by occupations for their spiritual development does not imply approval of working women. Rather, the recovery of the guild system for spiritual growth signified the Church's attempt to revive medievalism, which the Church interpreted as offering a desirable solution to modern problems. In Cardinal O'Connell's view, "We are steadily going back to the practice of the early guilds of the Catholic Church. We are finding that many of the customs and practices of centuries, once regarded with scorn as old-fashioned and primitive, hold the secret of the remedy for the many ills that beset modern society."[84] Similar occupation-based guild structures had been created for Boston Catholic men, among lawyers, physicians, dentists, and so forth.[85] Some, like the Guild of St. Elizabeth, founded by Father Gasson in 1899 and incorporated in 1901, stretched the definition of guild until it virtually functioned as a settlement house: it held a nursery school six days a week for about 300 children of all "creeds, color and nationalities" and offered classes in sewing, cooking, stenography, millinery, and folk dancing; it also offered monthly talks for mothers and a lending library. As industrial capitalism was giving way to corporate capitalism, Catholic charities generated more specialized agencies such as day nurseries and industrial schools, which were nonetheless interpreted by the Church as contributions toward the restoration of guild organization of craft and artisanal labor.[86] Paradoxically, despite the sectarian biases of Catholic domestic and guild projects, they promised to provide millennial benefits to the nation.

From an ecclesial perspective, the Church welcomed the women's retreat movement, directed by a sisterhood founded in France to conduct retreats for women and girls, because it reinforced the Church's endorsement of occupational niches without having to endorse female careerism. Retreats also emphasized the individualized character of a feminine quest for prayer and holiness. They complemented the older tradition of parish missions and represented a planned alternative, since they obliged women to leave their daily occupations for a designated period of prayer and reflection. Boston women who participated in the Cenacle retreats presumably would transmit the spirituality of the Cenacle religious to immigrants to strengthen their Catholic identity and to prevent the success of Protestant evangelization among immigrants. This intention served the Church's goal of separatist integration and seemed to fit the general pattern of women's social ministry being welcomed for its role in preventing leakage of Church membership.

Professional Laywomen: Two Examples

Although laywomen who pursued careers were discouraged by the Church from entering most paying occupations, they were encouraged in a limited range of professions, notably writing and editing. In these fields, women would ideally be associated with Catholic publishers and journals, subject to clerical supervision and censorship, and express the high moral purpose associated with Christian womanhood. Literary professionals such as Katherine Conway and Louise Guiney sometimes suppressed their personal opinions to conform to Church positions on gender, class, and Catholic social integration, but they also inhabited a secular literary environment.

The life of Katherine Conway (1853–1927), journalist, novelist, poet, professor, and the first woman editor of Boston's Catholic newspaper, exemplified the contradictions of Catholic womanhood and of postimmigrant Catholicism.[87] As an unmarried careerist, she did not fulfill the traditional roles of wife and mother. Raised in Rochester, New York, Conway was convent educated by Sacred Heart nuns in Rochester and Buffalo and began writing for a Catholic monthly in 1875 under the pen name Mercedes. Her father, born in England, had been forced to emigrate because of his Chartist activities. Her mother came from a long line of well-educated women. In 1878, when her father lost his fortune, Conway joined the Buffalo *Catholic Union and Times*, becoming its assistant editor in 1880.[88] John Boyle O'Reilly invited her to join his staff in Boston in 1883. Her first major assignment was covering the Catholic Centenary Congress of 1889 in Baltimore.[89]

The 1889 Catholic congress to celebrate the centennial of the American hierarchy involved laymen but not women. Four years later, however, Conway served as a delegate to the World's Columbian Congress of Women in Chicago, which met just prior to the World's Parliament of Religions. The mere fact of Catholic participation in the Parliament of Religions was a controversy ended only when Cardinal Gibbons of Baltimore successfully pressured the Vatican for permission to attend. Conway's comments on the relationship between the women's congress and the Catholic Columbian congress revealed that she opposed segregating the women's portion of the conference as detrimental to both Catholics and to the non-Catholic public. As she wrote to William Onahan of Chicago, the conference chairman: "You will note that these 'Women's Congresses' will be done to death by the Woman's Auxiliary. I know some of the Catholics likely to figure in them, and they are not big fish. Now let these be exploited just as far as possible in the philanthropic and other Congresses of the Woman's Auxiliary—, but don't let us get it all warmed over again at the Catholic Congress. Do let us have something fine and distinctive—or exclude the women altogether."[90] The papers given in Chicago by Conway and two other delegates, Eleanor Donnelly and Alice Toomy, were published as a roundtable discussion in *Catholic World*. Later all the addresses appeared in a volume entitled *Girlhood's Hand-Book of Woman*, where Conway's address, formerly called "Woman Has No Vocation to Public Life," became "The Normal Christian Woman." It validated supernatural claims for domesticity: "The vocation of the overwhelming majority of women is to wifehood and motherhood; and their bodily and mental sensitiveness and timidity, and the fixed aversion, or at least indifference, of most of them to public work, are safeguards raised by God's own hand about the sanctuary of life."[91]

By this account, Conway stood squarely within the cult of true womanhood, which made God the benign author of women's physical inferiority and social isolation. At convent school, Conway had been taught that women's primary function was child rearing. She wrote that women, whether serving as mothers or as spiritual mothers (nuns), were intended to train "the future congenial wives of intelligent men."[92] By contrast, Conway's impassioned letters to the chair of the Catholic congress had affirmed the need for women's integration into public life as well as the need for "fine and distinctive" Catholic contributions to American culture:

> I beg to enter my humble protest against a "Woman's Day" at the Catholic Congress. I think it would be a mistake. That "Woman" business is overdue in non-Catholic circles. Don't let us take it up off their hands, and run it into the ground. Let the women's papers be few and good— and mixed up with the rest in the regular programme. This is a world of men and women working together to the fulfillment of God's plan. The work of women influences men, and the work of men is for the

race. . . . Why should there be a pale Catholic reflection of the Woman's Auxiliary and the Woman's Congresses? I've protested against a Woman's Auxiliary to the Catholic Summer School. Get the best women possible for the papers—avoiding those who are known *only* in Catholic Circles. This Congress is for America and for the world, as well as for the Church.[93]

Conway's unequivocal demands against sexist segregation of women and against an inferior and parochial Catholic subculture point to a rupture between her knowledge of women advocates of female equality and her public persona, which conformed to the Church's stereotype.

The events of 1893 strengthened Conway's conviction to improve Catholicism's role in America and to expand women's role in the Church. However, her position at the Boston *Pilot* increasingly absorbed her time. Although the assistant editor, J. J. Roche, had become editor upon O'Reilly's death in 1890, Conway did the majority of the editing and production work. Officially she did not succeed Roche until 1905 when he received a diplomatic post in Europe. Privately she confided to a priest that "on Mr. Roche's departure for his consulate, no one was put into help me out on the Pilot staff. It is true that for seven years previous to his departure, he had been a good deal of an invalid, and I had often carried the paper alone for considerable intervals."[94] By 1905, heavily burdened with work, no salary increase, and only one staff assistant, Conway went without vacations to produce "an almost incredible weekly output."

Conway's employment at the *Pilot* eventually led to a contest between gender and power. After O'Connell's accession as archbishop in 1907, Conway was reduced to a nonentity on the staff, and her salary was not increased for her service as editor in chief.[95] As she recorded in her diary after a visit to the staff offices in May: "Made my first visit to Pilot office in many months. I was a wreck and J.V. saw it, as he later told my brother."[96] When O'Connell bought the *Pilot* in 1908 and made it the official diocesan organ, he dismissed Conway entirely. Her diary of 1908 records a period of such poor health that she was relieved of Lenten fast and abstinence requirements, and that she relied on veronal powders to get to sleep. Eventually she made an extended trip to Europe.

O'Connell's attitude, which may be described as cavalier and paternalistic, was especially disappointing in light of Conway's close relationship with O'Connell's predecessor, John Williams, whom she called "my silent but effective friend and benefactor," and in light of her friendship with her hometown bishop, Bernard McQuaid.[97] O'Connell's release of Conway was not for personal or budgetary reasons. He simply wanted direct control of the paper as part of his design to manipulate all archdiocesan institutions. While he was by no means completely successful, he tried repeatedly to eliminate the *Pilot*'s most significant rival for Catholic readers, the *Sacred Heart Review* of Cambridge.[98]

O'Connell's *Pilot* takeover involved Conway in a prolonged, humiliating struggle to regain personal income that she had loaned to the paper. When the new business manager ignored Conway's requests, she wrote to O'Connell, reminding him, "I have no hope except in you, and in the good words you said to me at my outgoing in 1908. Not a thing done for me yet, and much of the money due dates back nine years, and even longer." When she was reimbursed for $1,432, a second dispute began over a lesser sum, and the matter dragged on in 1910 for several more months. A wheedling tone of flattery crept into Conway's pleas to the archbishop: "There was no thought of the poor little editor, who nearly destroyed her life in trying to hold things up until your Grace came in. Even the wages due me for the year in which I went out, 1908, might still be unpaid, had it not been for Your Grace's merciful intervention."[99] For 1911 and 1912 Conway accepted a teaching post as lecturer in English at Saint Mary's College, South Bend, Indiana, where she had a noted influence on the next generation of woman leaders. Mary Evaline Wolff, who later became well known as Sister Mary Madaleva, a leading women's educator and poet, and president of Saint Mary's, called Conway her "literary guardian angel."[100] Ill health, however, forced Conway to abandon teaching. She returned to Boston and became literary editor and then managing editor of the *Republic,* John Fitzgerald's weekly, until it folded in 1926.[101] Devoted to Fitzgerald because his charisma and kindness reminded her of O'Reilly, Conway reported to a friend that when the *Republic* ceased, she was able to return to the editorial staff of the *Pilot,* writing short pieces published anonymously.[102]

After a break in her relations with O'Connell from 1915 to 1920, Conway resumed her correspondence, sending him numerous reports of her prolonged and painful convalescence from a rare form of aggravated anemia. O'Connell sent her several checks as "back pay from the Pilot which will always remember your good work in hard times," perhaps as a belated apology for treating her so cavalierly. Conway, imagining that he had snubbed her for the last five years, responded: "I had an uncomfortable feeling that in some way I had dropped from your favor. What vast conceit on the part of a poor little patched-up 'shut in.'"[103] O'Connell's donations and promised visits comforted Conway. She joked with him that if he visited her at home, she "couldn't properly drill my good 'New-Thought' attendant" to receive the cardinal with the customary torches.[104] In 1925 Conway wrote *Pilot* columns while bedridden due to deterioration of her vision and muscle control. Having composed her final editorial only a week before her death, her prolific output is remarkable when juxtaposed with her diary entries over the course of nearly twenty years detailing her serious ongoing illnesses as well as lesser nervous afflictions endured by many prominent women of her generation.

Despite his disregard for Conway in her editorial role, O'Connell made women useful agents of his plan for increasing the circulation of the *Pilot*. Having made it mandatory for all parishes to sell the *Pilot* in 1909, in 1918 O'Connell decided to boost sales by assigning each parish a required number of subscriptions.[105] While it was reported that priests did the work of parish visitation for the campaign, a closer examination of the campaign files and clippings shows that Irish Catholic women were its backbone. The campaign has received attention primarily as the springboard for the early career of Francis Spellman, subsequently the cardinal archbishop of New York, but when studied along gender lines, the campaign takes on new meaning. Catholic women, who were supervised in each parish by the clergy, made the Literature Campaign successful. Women made visits to 210 of 265 parishes, got new subscriptions, and conducted follow-up visits after solicitations. As a result, new subscribers poured in from Massachusetts to Florida to California.[106] Building a national Catholic audience represented an important segment of O'Connell's plan for ingratiating himself at the Vatican, and at the same time was a device for monopolizing Catholic readership. Women's participation in the campaign indicated how their volunteer labor nurtured the loyalty of Boston Catholics to O'Connell and to a Catholic subculture. As the *Pilot* noted, "The duty of the Catholic author, journalist, or artist is plain. But what of the duties of the intelligent and devout Catholic who is not in any of these vocations? To train himself—or, as we are mostly concerned with the apostolate of Catholic women, let us say herself—to appreciation of the best that our own people are doing, and to give it the encouragement, not only of praising words, but of financial patronage."[107]

During her editing career, Conway made a marked contrast to her predecessor Roche, who would have instantly traded his editor's desk for the swashbuckling adventures of his idol Richard Harding Davis.[108] While visitors to the *Pilot*'s offices would find Roche entertaining some sunburned soldier of fortune in a "book-littered chaos he called his editorial room," Conway often edited newspaper copy from her home in Roxbury, Massachusetts. However, while Roche was ill, Conway often published the paper single-handedly. She expressed horror at women's "mania for being in the Public Eye" by renting an apartment or space in a hotel, and rejected such impulses as vain and self-advertising.[109] Described as "a frail delicate-looking woman" notable for her "beautiful dark eyes" and her "humility, a rare virtue among American literary women," Conway was not listed in the paper's editorial box and mast-

Katherine Conway, ca. 1907, at the time of her reception of Notre Dame's Laetare Medal. "In Miss Conway's beautiful home, filled with books, pictures and all that constitutes culture and refinement, one is apt to meet most of the Boston celebrities as well as those of the other cities who may be passing through this 'modern Athens.'" (Photo, University of Notre Dame Archives)

head.[110] Nowhere did she receive credit for her position as de facto editor while Roche was in Europe or as editor in chief.[111]

The *Pilot* has had an interesting ownership and management history. A privately run weekly until bankruptcy threatened owner/editor Patrick Donahoe, it was bought by O'Reilly and Archbishop Williams. In its heyday under O'Reilly, the *Pilot* united Irish ward politicians and local literary leaders and began to reflect the genteel norms expected of upwardly mobile Irish Catholics, as seen in its new advice columns. While Conway was ghost editor, the paper ran weekly "Talks to Young Men," a carryover from the O'Reilly years. On two occasions after Conway had left the paper, "Talks to Women" appeared, most likely composed by the archbishop or Father Hugh Blunt, the new chief editorial writer. The first of these stated darkly in 1911, "It should be clearly understood that when women enter into business affairs they must meet not only Christian gentlemen, but must also associate with men whose whole method of living is unrestrained animalism."[112] By supporting the seclusion of women instead of the reformation of men, the *Pilot* continued to keep women outside the public sphere. Conway may have written an unsigned weekly column called "In the Family Sitting Room" for the *Pilot* or the *Republic,* or both. Subject matter and stylistic evidence support the theory: the column featured titles such as "Women and the Inevitable," "War and Women," "What Shall the Home Woman Talk About?," and "Woman and Literature in Life." In these columns Conway's views on womanhood did not differ significantly from the *Pilot*'s conservative outlook.[113] Nor did the paper change its message in the decades following.[114]

Despite the ups and downs of her career, Conway enjoyed a wide involvement in public, secular life, including membership in the New England Woman's Press Club, founded in 1885, for which she served as president from 1890 to 1913.[115] In 1889 she became the first Catholic to address the Women's Educational and Industrial Union of Boston. Conway was a member of the board of trustees of the Boston Public Library and was on the board of prison commissioners of Massachusetts. In 1907 she received the University of Notre Dame's Laetare Medal for her distinguished contributions to society, making her one of its few female recipients.[116] Author of some twenty books of essays, fiction, and poetry and numerous articles and tributes, Conway also became a member of the eminent Boston Author's Club, one of the few Catholics so honored.

Conway's emancipated public life did not override her conservatism. In 1893 she had written that it was "beyond question that woman, as woman, can have no vocation to public life. . . . Woman, being after man, and from man, does not represent humanity in the full and complete sense that man does. It cannot be necessary, nor even useful, that she should try to do what she cannot do."[117] She believed that Catholic women were fulfilled through their families rather than through "selfish" careerism or in public service. Conway stressed the privatized nature of woman's vocation, and women's God-given "aversion" to public work. Notre Dame's Laetare Medal dedication of 1912 honored her for showing women how to "lead consecrated lives within the cloister of the heart, and dignify a public career by noble service." Conway had indeed referred to her own retiring lifestyle as cloistered, yet she also was an iconoclast among the laity as a champion of Catholic culture, and to women as a single wage earner who was productive despite chronic health and financial problems.

Even Conway's journalism career, however, conformed to conventional standards. The "family claim" that linked single and married women by virtue of their same domestic duties also demanded service to the Church from both. As long as a spinster's career did not reject domesticity, the ideal of Catholic womanhood would remain intact. If married women worked outside the home, they, too, were expected to choose some calling that served Catholicism and that kept them segregated from the corrosive competition of the male workplace. In 1897 Conway agreed that women should save the world through pious example, not the overthrow of domesticity: "Social regeneration must come from within—not from without. Regenerated society will draw its pure life from the guarded wellsprings of those homes whence women trained and developed on normal lines diffuse high motives, refined tastes and virtuous examples of ordinary domestic and social opportunity—where the old-fashioned Christian gentlewoman exercises the social apostolate."[118] As early as 1905 Conway cautioned women that the proliferation of women's societies could become burdensome:

> Looking abroad on the world of secular life, in which we Catholic women have to bear our part, is one not tempted sometimes to think that we are becoming over-organized? Besides our distinctly religious organizations, have we not our professional guilds, our social clubs, musical societies, art circles, literature and language clubs, associations for the patronage of every virtue and the destruction of every vice;—unions, leagues, auxiliaries, names in every language, living and dead, and in languages invented for the emergency?[119]

Her involvement in numerous women's clubs suggests that she ignored her own warning. Female fellowship and lay leadership seemed to be important to Conway, as much as her conviction that women should be judged with men by a single standard of excellence and not as "just women." Breaking new ground for laywomen, she addressed the inaugural session of the Catholic Summer School in New London, Connecticut, in 1892; attended the World's

Congress of Women as a delegate in 1893; lectured at many functions of the LCW; and served as founder and president of the O'Reilly Reading Circle. Conway made women visible while remaining true to Catholic belief in woman's sphere and female dependence. Conway's best contribution to Catholic American culture is perhaps likely to remain unexplored—her unpublished corpus of insightful literary and religious talks delivered to the reading circles, the summer school, and Catholic social clubs, which constituted the only existing forums for bluestockings like herself.[120]

As an example of the third generation among American Catholic writers, Conway wrote novels and essays on Catholic literature that seem to embody typical bourgeois morality. On the other hand, for the first time in American Catholic fiction, her novels confronted middle-class acquisitiveness, the limits of domesticity, and the cost of Catholic assimilation. In *The Way of the World*, for example, a snobbish matron recoils at the prospect of admitting schoolteachers as equals in her neighborhood reading circle. A 1901 novel, *Lalor's Maples*, discusses middle-class anxiety about upward mobility in its portrayal of Irish Catholics and Protestants in a Yankee town named Baychester, a thinly disguised Rochester. The novel enjoyed good reviews because Conway wrote well, objecting to novels that read like sermons. "Catholics may write ardent love stories," she commented dryly, "in which the love tokens exchanged need not take the form of pearl rosaries."[121] A modern literary historian has characterized *Lalor's Maples* as fiction that makes stabs at realism but ultimately lapses into sentimentality. Most likely influenced by William Dean Howells's *The Rise of Silas Lapham*, Conway, with less facility, combined his emphasis on the American quest for success with two archetypal symbols of Irish American fiction: the overbearing matriarch and the private family house, symbol of material achievement.[122]

Love, marriage, family, and success were valued in Conway's nonfiction as well. Although never married, she did not extol the joys of spinsterhood. Her publications are further evidence of the appeal of religion over gender, since Conway represented motherhood and family as normative. Further, she symbolizes how class identification superseded gender consciousness. Conway taught middle-class values to Catholics in her five volumes of essays for the Family Sitting Room Series of the Boston Pilot Publishing Company.[123] The books' titles and the genteel parlor conjured by the series title reveal how Catholics were creating a social sensibility that emphasized self-improvement and propriety. For Catholic girls and women Conway wrote a series of manuals such as *Bettering Ourselves, Making Friends and Keeping Them, The Christian Gentlewoman and the Social Apostolate,* and *Questions in Honor of the Christian Life,* describing how to become well assimilated, well liked, and well read. As with her *Pilot* work, Conway submitted these books for clerical approval, in this case to a Jesuit censor at Boston College.[124] Conway's early nonfiction indicated that woman's role in society should be guided by male models and mentors and that, in religion, women should preserve the Church's teaching. Her mature work at least hinted at economic and class roots for the emerging symbolic system of the Catholic subculture.

Besides generating novels and how-to guides for a new middle-class Catholic audience, Conway warned against the dangers of women's economic independence: selfish women, for example, wanted only to liberate themselves from the embarrassment of poor parents. "A few months of downright drudgery in shop or office," Conway wrote, "with a dingy boardinghouse to come and go from, and the effort to be well-dressed, well-fed and happy on five dollars a week, would rectify many a young woman's ideas about the joys of freedom and her power to make a career, and would teach her to appreciate as never before the blessings of a well-provided home and a loving family—even though her supply of pocket-money were slender."[125] Conway also warned against "the disposition of the better educated women to defer marriage, the vast increase in the number of self-supporting women, constitute now a grave problem in political economy."[126] This stern ethic presented Catholicism at its most convoluted, arguing that self-serving career women would strive to avoid marriage, thereby becoming a drain on the economy. Conway never systematically developed the economic implications of a large population of single working women, as indeed neither did the Church, but the moral lesson implied by each was identical: overeducation was at fault for encouraging women to prefer careers to marriage. Higher education's true mission, according to Conway, was to produce "not a more abundant yield of women publicists, but of noble, and intelligent, and virtuous women for the home and social life."[127] By supporting conservative notions of the moral potential of education, Conway refused to consider the single, working woman as a permanent fixture in the American economy. Addressing the Catholic Women's Club of South Lawrence in 1910 on the topic "Woman and a Career," she predicted that careerism was merely a phase "which will, doubtless have among other good results the raising of the standard of manhood, and the consequent multiplying of happy homes."[128]

Katherine Conway's writings helped keep Catholic women privatized, yet they encouraged women, as promoters of Catholic culture, to contribute to an American mainstream. Conway symbolized a polarity in Catholicism that required women to stay at home and give moral direction to their families at a time when Progressive women were demanding the chance to improve society through activism and feminist radicals fought for civil equality. Conway, however, remained convinced that women would be tainted by "the world," which mitigated against the development of a Catholic feminist awareness and against Church support for out-of-home careers for women. Her professional and social affiliations suggest that joining charitable and social clubs and writing apologetic literature became legitimate outlets for women's energies because those activities confirmed middle-class propriety and conformed to the designated service role for women in O'Connell's Boston. Like middle-class Protestants, Catholics protected the domestic sphere by fostering a community of like-minded women, centered on the home but presided over by male ministers. Publishing and volunteer charity work were safe choices for women because they did not interfere with family togetherness, they permitted an outlet for the expression of women's piety, and they retained male direction over women's intellectualism. In fact, the phenomenon of Catholic newspapers and magazines edited by priests but staffed by young women became a commonplace during Conway's lifetime. Although one interpreter of Catholic women writers has argued that they favorably contributed to women's autonomy and restlessness with this status quo, Conway embodied the kind of Catholic woman who pressed for the right to individual fulfillment but who remained blind to the inherent opposition between individualism and gender unity.[129] She was pleased when Catholics avoided joining groups advocating women's rights because she believed that women's causes demonstrated an unhealthy gender exclusiveness. Instead, "in good works outside the home, they had co-operated with men, and moved under the guidance of the Church." Conway was bemused by Catholic women who raised the woman question, since she could not see how Catholicism had ever oppressed them. "What doors indeed, has the Church closed on intelligence and ability as manifested by women," she asked, "but the doors of the sanctuary and the pulpit?"[130] With this query Conway exhibited a disappointing reluctance to see what doors had been closed on her own life by not regarding women as a class doubly bound by gender and religion.

Louise Guiney (1861–1920) was a contemporary of Katherine Conway who yearned for Catholicism to exert universal impact on culture, but whose personal response was to retreat from modernity altogether.[131] Born near Boston in Roxbury, Massachusetts, Guiney resisted being claimed by the Irish and by Catholics as a hyphenated American. "If I am to be hyphenated," she wrote, "I am several kinds of a hyphen, with a Scots and a French near paternal ancestor, and all my English blood on Mother's side! but plain 'American' is my due, and suits me well enough. One of the oddest of Irish qualities is this almost universal grabbism: they claim anything and everything which they think is the least creditable!"[132]

Daughter of an Irish immigrant who became a Civil War hero and one of the first Catholics to hold public office in Massachusetts, Louise Guiney was conscious of her Irish heritage but not governed by it. A graduate of the Sacred

Heart Academy at Elmhurst, Rhode Island, Guiney became an accomplished musician, studied Latin, and spoke French and Italian. Described as a tomboy who "hated clothes," "habitually broke rosaries," and was happiest when doing gymnastics or hiking, Guiney made her literary debut in the 1880s. She was welcomed into the Yankee literary circle of Annie Adams Fields, the widow of publisher and editor James Fields; her friend and housemate Sarah Orne Jewett; and Louise Chandler Moulton.[133] Moulton, as hostess to "the most inclusive and varied assembly in Boston" for her Friday receptions in Rutland Square, was nearly as famous as the literary giants of New England gathered at the Fields house at 148 Charles Street. Guiney recalled its mystique: "Though only a solid item in a red brick block, it is a very exciting doorway. . . . On that knob Emerson's hand has been, how many times; the steps keep the spirit of Longfellow's feet; Thackeray's tender voice haunts the porch[,] . . . familiar Hawthorne, who went long ago, as real there as Kipling who came yesterday, and will come again tomorrow."[134]

Guiney's Brahmin patrons, her Anglophilia, and her refusal to embody a specific ethnic identity represent an exception among most American Catholic writers. She exemplifies a uniquely assimilated American Catholic who, though both insider and outsider, evolved into an elitist and an expatriate. The role of Louise Guiney in the growth of Catholicism's public presence in Boston therefore represents both the triumph and the failure of the marriage of Catholicism and high culture. Though she appreciated her native literary heritage, Guiney preferred the seventeenth century to the twentieth, a fact recognized by her friend Ralph Adams Cram and her biographer and fellow New Englander Alice Brown. Subsequent biographers have romanticized Guiney's melancholic displacement in the twentieth century. Epithets such as Soul Ordained to Fail, Laureate of the Lost, Belated Cavalier, and Loyal Rememberer suggest Guiney as a female equivalent to Henry Adams, an American seeking the secrets of psychic and spiritual unity of the preindustrial past.[135] Richard Le Galliene, reviewing the publication of Guiney's Letters in 1925, called her "by nature, a champion of lost causes, she was, moreover, a passionate Jacobite—a sufficient incongruity in a New England girl."[136] In her anonymous autobiography in Scribner's, Guiney commented sadly: "As I have spent much of my lifetime already, so, unrepentantly, shall I spend the rest of it, with what skill I have acquired; with such motives, purely Gothic, so to speak, as I cannot now swerve from; with measured civility toward a world which does not want me, and which is old enough to know its own mind."[137] Publishing first under two pseudonyms (Roger Holden and P. O. L.), Guiney flourished under the sponsorship of Oliver Wendell Holmes and Louise Moulton. Her modest income came from occasional library jobs and small dona-

Louise Imogen Guiney with her dog, Wendell Phillips, in a photograph taken by Fred Holland Day in 1889. The portrait may have accompanied this verse in a magazine article about Guiney: "A maker of smooth verse and facile rhymes, / And lover of quaint legends from old times; / A joyous singer in New England bleak— / Her heart is Irish and her mind is Greek." (Guiney Room, Holy Cross College Rare Books and Special Collections)

tions from Moulton. A promised bequest from the will of Annie Fields never materialized, however, because Fields had overestimated her estate.[138]

A formative part of Guiney's youth derived from her association with Boston's decadents known as the Visionists—a group that included architects Ralph Adams Cram and Bertram Goodhue, photographer Fred Holland Day, art critic Bernard Berenson, and publishers Herbert Stone, Herbert Small, and Herbert Copeland. These friends were dedicated to combating the crass materialism of the industrial age and gave Guiney an aesthetic sensibility more sophisticated than most Catholic Bostonians, for whom overcivilization was hardly the problem. As she became an experienced traveler and internationally known writer, Guiney developed a cultural cliquishness that led her to hold high expectations for a Catholic cultural renaissance. Her tastes led her to overestimate Boston Catholics' readiness for projects like Cram's short-lived magazine, *Christian Art*, while her poem "Knight Errant" furnished the title for another of his ephemeral publishing forays.

Although only part of it was published, Guiney's voluminous correspondence with hundreds of authors, artists, priests, publishers, and friends reveals an energetic and buoyant woman fond of wordplay, nicknames, gushing revelations, and tendencies toward aestheticism and decadence. These latter two penchants might seem to clash with Guiney's orthodox Catholicism, but in fact her mysticism and Jacobitism provided links between her religion and the aristocratic and reactionary pretensions at the heart of the decadent movement. She shared the aesthetes' passion for appreciation of the beautiful— collecting fine books and printing, dressing up in quaint costume, performing backyard theatricals, and producing little literary magazines—as well as their delight in irrationalism and sensuality.[139] From among the Visionists she found a soulmate with whom she shared a romantic relationship for about eight years. Fred Holland Day (1864–1933) was a struggling photographer, a Unitarian, three years her junior, and like Guiney, an only child. Their romance of 1888–96 can only be reconstructed, however, from the evidence of her letters to him. His missives were burned by Guiney's biographer, who thought them too indiscreet for public readership.[140] The remaining correspondence indicates that Guiney developed a maternal yet flirtatious, platonic yet unconventional, relationship with him, in which the two flouted social conventions by traveling to Europe together. Perhaps he needed her to mother him by introducing him to polite society and potential portrait clients; indeed she called him Sonny, Sonnikins, and Me Boy in her letters. Perhaps she needed a presentable escort in London, and not a demanding lover who might challenge the perfect memory of her father, a Civil War hero. Guiney and Day were engaged in 1892 but never married. In 1893 Guiney's letters hint of a growing jealousy of the young women whom Day had taken on as wards while volunteering in a Boston settlement house.[141] Guiney's affectionate but ultimately chaste relationship with Day seemed to adumbrate a pattern for her future friendly relationships with men who were unlikely to rebuff her need to be mother and mentor, or to raise false romantic expectations, especially in her friendships with numerous clergymen. The households of her adult years would be composed of women friends and relatives.

On a visit to England between 1889 and 1892, Guiney and Day made pilgrimages to houses and places where the poet John Keats had lived and visited. Keats, the arbiter of the "cult of Beauty," was admired by Guiney and Day for different reasons, which became clearer as their tour progressed.[142] Perhaps Day's European tour encouraged his own sexual and aesthetic tendencies, which began to veer toward the extremes of androgyny admired by disciples of Keats and their current idol, Oscar Wilde. Intimations that Guiney's relationship with Day, based on companionship and shared artistic interests, would not last appeared when Day dallied too long over plans to leave England for Spain to meet the sister of John Keats, who unfortunately died before he could visit her. Guiney, angry and disappointed, left Europe but returned there as a permanent resident in 1901. Day never showed her the priceless Fanny Brawne letters he had obtained from Keats's niece in a later journey to Spain.[143]

In response to spinsterhood and the deaths of her relatives, Guiney formed a makeshift family and manufactured a maternal role for herself in the next decades by adopting two orphaned nieces as her "daughters." She brought Grace and Ruth Guiney to England when they were children, and they remained with her through poverty and her near-blindness.[144] The ineffectual and narcissistic Fred Day, meanwhile, went on to dabble in a number of ephemeral projects: the Copeland & Day publishing firm, photographic studies of nude boys he picked out of Boston's settlement houses, and a controversial photo series on the crucifixion of Christ, re-created in his backyard and featuring himself as Jesus. His photographic career ended abruptly when his studio burned down in 1904, and the last fifteen years of his life were marked by withdrawal into a secluded bohemian lifestyle in his oriental mansion in Norwood, where he was attended by a black servant. He toyed with prospective publishers and scholars who pursued his cache of Keats letters with promises of favors he rarely kept.

Guiney went on to excel at writing. The works that are most relevant to her role as a Catholic woman writer are her critical commentaries on the function of Catholic authors and Catholic literature in her day, and her mediations between Catholics in London, Oxford, Dublin, and Boston.[145] It would seem that her international connections would lead her to try and upgrade American Catholic cultural aspirations. She, however, was primarily determined to escape the memory of the confining environment of America. There, in her first job as postmistress at Auburndale from 1894 to 1897, she experienced the anti-Catholicism still pervasive in Massachusetts. Since Guiney's salary was based on a percentage of the stamps she sold, her enemies boycotted the local post office. National outcry against their bigotry brought her orders for stamps from around the country.[146] After a brief stint working in the Boston Public Library, Guiney left for England, returning to Boston only twice after 1900. The death of her mother, the last of her blood relations, in 1910 marked the end of her visits home. "Holding to the Catholic faith had a lot, almost everything, to do with our getting poorer and poorer," she recalled.[147] A fellow author noted likewise that Guiney had spoken of her Catholicism as "frightful responsibility."[148] Perhaps her bitterness over circumstances made her resentful at the demands Catholicism had exacted on her life. After her mother's death, Guiney sought "to emigrate to some hamlet that smells strong of the Middle Ages, and put cotton-wool in my ears, and swing out clear from this very smart century altogether."[149] She asked a friend "to pray without ceasing that I may remain in England. I would be built in, like mortar in a wall."[150] Despite her success as an author, Guiney's chronic poverty and painful, increasing deafness and blindness must have contributed to her interpretation of the present as an unbearable burden, although she did not choose seclusion like Fred Day.[151]

The Anglo tinge that Guiney contributed to Boston Catholicism was manifest in her rapport with the Brahmins and her suggestion of the English model for the LCW. She confidently hoped to educate a Catholic aristocratic elite, assisted by her influential clergy friends on two continents and by the cosmopolitan literary culture she could extend to American Catholic audiences. Among her literary friends—William Butler Yeats, Richard Garnett, Robert Louis Stevenson, Edmund Gosse, Lionel Johnson, Herbert Clarke, and Alice Meynell—and her clerical confidants, Bernard Vaughan and Henry Day, she gained insights into artistic and intellectual perspectives rarely encountered firsthand by Boston Catholics. Thus as an ambassador of culture and European Catholicism to Americans, Guiney had tremendous talents to offer. Her sponsorship by the New England literati had already established her credentials outside the Irish Catholic cliques that tended to confine the generation of American writers preceding and following her, while her research about the English metaphysical poets established her transatlantic reputation as a critic who anticipated the criticism of T. S. Eliot and others.[152]

The present neglect of Guiney's essays and poems is no indication of their lively impact on her contemporaries and misses the poignancy of her inability to foster a Catholic intelligentsia, as well as the personal turmoil hinted at beneath her shifting classical, gothic, and decadent influences. Her sense of

J. J. Roche drew this cartoon of himself dragging young Louise Guiney as a school-girl to meet the "lions," the celebrated Gosse family of English literary critics. In the following year, Guiney was employed by Sir Edmund Gosse to collect material in British libraries for his *Life of Jeremy Taylor*. (Guiney Room, Holy Cross College Rare Books and Special Collections)

the incommunicability of the deepest emotions and meanings attached to art made her wonder if solitude was essential to aesthetic experience: "Do we merely need more art? . . . Or is it, as I am inclined to think, that something inherent in the experience itself makes it remote, and that as we must die alone, so we must dream alone too?"[153] If aesthetic pleasure was ultimately solitary, Guiney pursued that solution to her estrangement by retreating into the world of the Middle Ages, the cavaliers, or the metaphysical and mystical poets, where she found the solace not afforded her by modernity. Nonetheless, Europeans did not necessarily respond to her as an antimodernist: an Irish author claimed that Guiney represented the New World's innocence and ingenuousness. "Those Americans take the world without a fear or a misgiving," she reported. "They are up and down the highways of the world with any sunburnt gypsy. That freedom of the road is in Miss Guiney's work, and blent delightfully with it is the student air of knowledge and contemplation. She carries her learning delicately; she wears her knowledge lightly as a flower."[154]

Despite her privileged status as an observer and participant in a transatlantic literary culture, Guiney exercised a passive role toward the American Catholic Church, remaining immersed in her literary excavations at the Bod-

A household of Guiney women in England. Left to right: Ruth, two-year-old Loulie (orphan of Grace's older sister), Louise Imogen, and Grace Guiney. (Guiney Room, Holy Cross College Rare Books and Special Collections)

leian Library at Oxford, where she studied the English recusant poets, John Keats, and Hurrell Froude.[155] Her response to cultural conflicts facing her peers in America was to flee the crassness of America and to immerse herself in British gentility. She remade herself into an English Catholic as far as she could, becoming something of a Catholic version of Bloomsbury, even to the point of being buried at Chipping Campden, which she called "a paradise of a village, all grey stone and grey Cotswold slates."[156] In 1915, and especially after the 1916 Irish Easter rising, Guiney became estranged from her best friend, Mary, the daughter of John Boyle O'Reilly. The two "instinctively avoided one another after that," suggesting the depth of pro-Irish feeling among the first-generation O'Reillys and the antipathy aroused by Guiney's love of everything English. When Mary O'Reilly was working in London in 1915, she barely made contact with Guiney, finding her "painfully self-centered and content and—the word expresses my meaning—immature. She was like a fine boy and she made me by contrast feel very old." In judging Guiney, some New England Catholics seem to have branded her a betrayer of her father's unionism and of her own Celtic roots. Mary Boyle O'Reilly, shortly after Guiney's death, went so far as to protest a Catholic firm's sponsorship of publication of the Guiney correspondence: "Louise was not loyal to the old traditions—even the country for which her father fought became to her a fading memory: Therefore, she must live as a woman of letters." In the same letter, Mary O'Reilly summed up the pathos of a generation's unfulfilled expectations of Catholic writers like herself, who served the Church unquestioningly under the banner of unclouded ethnic identity: "But while I reproach myself for a too critical attitude toward her I still feel, Father, that Louise failed to realize our justifiable hopes."[157] Mary O'Reilly could not sympathize with the benign assessment of Guiney by another Massachusetts woman, Katherine O'Mahoney: "Were she more Celtic and more avowedly Catholic in her literary work, it might not reach many who are, unconsciously, perhaps, benefitted by its sterling qualities."[158]

Toward Women's Autonomy: Suffrage, Work, and Social Feminism

In the early 1900s the topic of Catholic womanhood coincided with a historical moment in which the image of the new woman merged with the image of America, expressing precisely the desires and fears underneath the formation of that culture. There was a strong affinity between the list of desirable feminine qualities and those of the patriot. For Catholics in the process of becoming assimilated, therefore, womanhood had weighty overtones for their

Portrait of Mary Boyle O'Reilly originally published in the Boston *Herald-Traveler*, August 28, 1921. John Boyle O'Reilly's daughter had decided views on many topics that defied Catholic stereotypes. Concerning the teaching of history, for example, she said children "should be taught the development of social forces, the work of parliaments, the rise of business firms." (*Boston Globe*, May 22, 1911. Photo courtesy of the Boston Public Library, Print Dept.)

own identity as Americans. Issues involving women, such as suffrage, work, and feminism, generated controversies within the Catholic subculture.

Women and the Vote

In the same way that the Church feared unsupervised female spiritual and educational endeavors, so it described woman suffrage as an anarchical threat to femininity and family unity. Just as the Church directed Catholic mothers to oppose encroachment of the burgeoning state upon the family and to maintain communal values through their household labor and their moral purity, so it opposed women's search for economic independence, academic degrees, and the ballot. Martha Moore Avery became an outspoken antisuffrage propagandist for the Church and agreed that the basic issue in suffrage was salvation of the family. She asked, "Shall the family maintain its place as the unit of civil society, or shall the State establish the individual as its unit, without regard to sex?"[159] Perhaps it is ironic that Avery made a career of being an open air speaker, a technique finally adopted in 1909 by the Massachusetts Woman Suffrage Association after a visit from British suffragists who pioneered the tactic. What is significant about a Catholic antisuffrage position is how Church teaching, rather than attempting to acknowledge the irreversible social changes in the lives of American women, ignored the demands and achievements of the twentieth-century women's movement and instead chose to condemn suffrage by claiming that the fate of mankind and of the idealism of Western civilization rested on an apolitical role for women.

A Paulist priest rightly claimed that "there is no Catholic view of woman suffrage, because it is not a Catholic question."[160] Lacking an official Catholic position on suffrage, clergy and laity were free to express a range of opinions. However, only a handful of American bishops publicly supported woman suffrage.[161] While a few priests openly stated, as citizens, their support for the enfranchisement of women, by and large they were overwhelmed by a negative critique of female suffrage. Boston's leading layman of the 1880s, John Boyle O'Reilly, fanatically opposed suffrage, calling it "a hard, undigested, tasteless, devitalized proposition."[162] Three decades later, Cardinal O'Connell delivered a more subtle condemnation by stating, "This fight for decency and Christian ideals is woman's fight. It is woman's question. If women lose the ideal, the men are lost with them. How could man respect womankind thereafter?"[163] By placing the burden of male salvation upon women, the phenomenon of losing the ideal, commonly referred to in the Catholic press as the "decay of fixed ideals," flavored statements and sermons on womanhood with a jeremiad tone. In O'Connell's choice of biblical metaphors, "When true Christian women are gone, the salt will have lost its savor, and the world will have been lost."[164] His hyperbole uncovered an apocalyptic dread lurking beneath the Catholic hierarchy's brave rhetoric of fixed ideals and unchanging principles. O'Connell's essentialism implied that if woman's role changed, human society would dissolve, engulfing man along with woman. In the cardinal's rhetoric it is hard to distinguish between men's selfish instincts for self-preservation and their acquired chivalrous impulses to protect women. A further example illustrates this duality: when women's suffrage was legalized in the United States in August 1920, the archdiocese's tardy and unenthusiastic response, coming five weeks later in the *Pilot,* merely repeated its old refrain that the safety of the family depended on the continued privatization of women. "It cannot be gainsaid that woman's sphere is the home. There is always fear that when she leaves the family circle the veneration and respect in which she is universally held may be weakened and the ideal of Christian womanhood lost."[165]

Many Catholic laymen and -women agreed with the Church's view that it was better for women to influence political life indirectly and to remain sheltered from the public fray. Some Catholics remembered that when woman suffrage had first become a state amendment issue in the 1880s, Republicans supported votes for women as voters and members of school board committees only as a nativist reaction against the influence of Catholic immigrant and working-class males on the Massachusetts public schools. Others observed that many Catholic laymen opposed ballots for women to prevent the passage of temperance legislation.[166] The clergy, however, desired women's temperance votes. Certain Boston priests, such as Father Thomas Scully, president of the Catholic Total Abstinence Union of Boston, even cooperated with the Massachusetts Woman Suffrage Association in the early 1900s for the very purpose of getting the female vote to benefit and protect the family. James Kenneally, in the first historical investigation of Catholic suffragism in Massachusetts, noted that in light of women's wartime contributions, the Jesuit chairman of the philosophy department at Boston College opportunistically supported the Nineteenth Amendment.[167] The national suffrage amendment had passed in 1920, only five years after it had been defeated in Massachusetts. Catholic Church leaders accepted the change grudgingly and adopted a new tactic of blaming both sexes for upsetting the balance of gender power, pessimistically predicting catastrophe for the family. O'Connell chided men for allowing women to encroach on their proper sphere: "The very fact that women are so often clamoring to take all power and authority into their hands," stated O'Connell, "is certainly no compliment to the manhood of the nation. . . . After all, women expect fathers to have and to exercise the rightful authority and self-respect of fathers of families."[168] Decades before O'Connell, John Boyle O'Reilly had similarly called suffrage "a quack bolus [pill] to reduce masculinity even by the obliteration of femininity."[169] Even the undergraduates at Boston College submitted their "scientific" judgment that society had not changed as much as suffragists had claimed and that gender roles were governed by fixed laws that could not be altered by giving women the vote: "The scheme may work well for any given length of time, but it is inevitable that in time, whether it be fifty or a hundred or a thousand years, the immutable natural conditions will assert themselves. An airship may remain in the air for a hundred years, but in the end the force of gravity will bring it back to earth where it belongs."[170]

Prior to 1920 the Church's antisuffrage propaganda, resting on a tripod of natural law, family unity, and woman's higher calling, had successfully deterred most women from affiliating with pro-suffrage feminists, although in Massachusetts a maverick, Margaret Foley, had joined a suffrage league that the Church of course denounced.[171] American suffragists lost what limited Catholic support they had when they revealed that pro–birth control groups were also supporting them. Catholic immigrant women, however, were drawn to suffrage by reformers' arguments that the vote would help them obtain pure milk, food, improved schools, and sanitary conditions for their families. But once suffrage was legalized in 1920, the Catholic Church slowly modified its opposition by calling voting a patriotic duty of woman, but never her right. The Church maintained its authority to direct the electoral choices of women by enjoining them to follow the counsels of the clergy and their male kin. Father Jones Corrigan, for example, encouraged women to "remember that they are the daughters of their fathers, and the sisters of their brothers, and just as much in need of guarding their consciences and seeking divine light as any man can be."[172] Thus suffrage, once discouraged, was now presented by the Church as an aspect of women's civic duty, subject to the control of men and interpreted in the medieval sense of duty defined by one's social station. In this regard, the suffrage question became one of several issues involving the political autonomy of the laity that concluded with no official vindication for women, even after it had been resolved nationally through legislation. Few, if any, Church leaders in Boston would agree with the liberal sentiment of a Chicago priest who argued that women deserved to vote because their "contribution in cooking, sewing, washing, caring for the children, in forcing the income to go as far as possible, in making all that is meant by the word 'home' is, in the vast majority of cases, worth more than the man's contribution of daily wages."[173]

Katherine Conway, whose opinions on women and public life crystallized in the 1890s following the conservative influence of her mentor, John Boyle O'Reilly, epitomized the contradictions of middle-class Catholicism: on one hand, she admired the "old-fashioned gentlewoman" who avoided class pretensions by rejecting luxury, who preferred the haven of home's "guarded wellsprings," and whose social reform spirit was "pure," "refined," and "virtuous." These criteria no doubt confirmed her decision to join the Massachusetts Association Opposed to Woman Suffrage and the New York Society for the Political Education of Women. She insisted that causes devoted solely to women, such as suffrage, foolishly tried to change the world from without. Further, as Conway argued in an editorial in 1893, suffrage would overburden women who already had enough domestic duties.[174] A third strike against suffragettes was the fact that their cause served women only, which Conway interpreted as a "morbid consciousness of womanhood." She remarked thankfully that Catholic women "never needed to be told that isolated and independent effort on the part of women is against the laws of nature."[175] On the other hand, Conway held a view of intellectual excellence that transcended gender and rejected women's social segregation. In response to her experiences in Chicago at the World's Congress of Women of 1893, she had demanded "a truce to all this war about 'the cause of woman, the work of woman, the destiny of woman!' The cause of woman is the cause of man, also. There is but one standard of excellence in the arts and sciences. Every compilation and periodical restricted to the representation of feminine writers; every 'woman's building' or 'woman's exhibit' at an exposition, state or national; every 'woman's day' in a convention, religious or otherwise, is a distinct drawback to worthy and significant work among women."[176] Her striking plea for the unity of the sexes and the integration of women's accomplishments into public culture subverted the limited vision of women's social role held by the Church. Unlike many clergymen, Conway modified her opinion of suffrage after passage of the Nineteenth Amendment, encouraging women to register and make the most of their opportunities. She showed no sign, however, of abandoning the notion of women's moral superiority.[177]

Women and Work

"What the young girl needs on beginning a career in the working world is a wise, prudent counsellor; and what she absolutely must have, if she would not make shipwreck of her higher nature, is a strong, clear, luminous faith."[178] So advised a female novelist in a best-selling Catholic novel. Despite the demonstrable rise in women's participation in the work force in the early twentieth century, the Church judged female labor to be an option only in cases of dire necessity. Working women were closely monitored in Massachusetts, which in 1869 had founded one of the nation's first state labor bureaus to collect statistical information about wage rates and working conditions.

Rather than focus on that data, however, I limit my examination to Catholic sources that addressed the "woman labor problem."[179]

Women could not have remained unaffected by the fact that between 1880 and 1930 the number of working women in Boston aged ten and older increased 108.5 percent.[180] Nationwide, between 1900 and 1910, employed women became 21 percent of the total work force.[181] A leader in Boston's LCW claimed that in 1920, 230,000 of 719,000 wage earners in Massachusetts were women, or about 31 percent of those employed, more than the national average. The existence of a surplus of single women in America and an unprecedented increase in working women at this time created an obvious gap between economic reality and the Catholic ideology of womanhood. Most of the female work force in Boston was composed of unmarried Irish Catholics. Aside from wage employment, a young woman might choose to become a nun. Since the majority of American nuns were of Irish extraction, this fact suggests that a religious vocation became one popular outlet for the abundant population of Irish females. For women who did not enter the convent, on a national scale 60 percent of first-generation immigrants worked as domestic servants. For the second generation this figure dropped to 19 percent, suggesting that Irish American women successfully promoted their daughters into higher job aspirations.[182] Irish Catholic women of the second generation and beyond worked as public school teachers and administrators, clerical and retail workers, telephone operators, needleworkers, and writers. Deviating from the ideal of domesticity and motherhood, these single women constituted a sizable population of unskilled or low-status workers, to which were added a cohort of educated middle-class women who worked outside their homes as public school teachers, journalists, and social workers. At least one Catholic woman argued in print that "it is not profane to plan or to advance an individual career. We do not insult Providence by endeavoring to provide for ourselves. And if the restlessness of modern life impels women of independent fortune to enter congenial fields of work, the freedom to do this thing is their birthright and prerogative."[183]

The American hierarchy, by contrast, was uneasy about the working woman, rationalizing her as a passing stage, grudgingly acknowledging her as an evil born of economic privation, which would disappear as immigrant women were absorbed into the economic dependency of marriage and assimilated into American culture. These religious concerns coincided with a widely held economic theory that the American economy could not absorb a population of unmarried working women. For the Church, economics was secondary to papal paternalism. As Pope Benedict XV had stated, "It may be said that in our day the demon levels his shafts especially at the working class, nor indeed is it to be wondered at that his emissaries labor to instill into the heart of working girls the poison of false teachings and the most nefarious incitements to vice."[184] As long the Church held that it protected class interests by preserving women from wage labor, women would be content to remain loyal to a subculture that nonetheless restricted their social roles outside their working day. Middle-class women, too, taught themselves to believe that there was something abnormal about trading their meaningful lives for jobs. A popular novel proclaimed: "No woman goes out into the downtown business world simply because she wants to be there. The normal woman loves her home, and her social pleasures, and her clubs for intellectual improvement, too well to exchange them voluntarily for the industrial bondage of a salaried person."[185] A convulsive reaction against female autonomy appeared in priests' sermons about the working girl. A Jesuit described an ideal girl worker as one who "feels no envy for 'the idle rich,' nor aspires to the emptiness of the life they lead. She feels no pain when she reads of their doings, nor regret when she sees them rush past like the pleasures they pursue." Inevitably, he argued, even a working girl's thoughts must turn to marriage: "No matter how good and kind her employer is, the day dawns when she thinks of leaving him. She begins to think of working in some sweet little home of her own. So she looks around for the man who will make that home and keep it and guard it for her."[186]

In its sporadic attempts to explain the existence of unmarried working women, the Church represented them as individuals answering extreme economic need, which fell into the moral category of self-sacrifice for their families. In other words, wage work legitimized spinsterhood when it was holy and self-denying, like the vocation of being a nun. Taken as an entity, however, the Church saw working women as an opportunity for middle-class beneficence. As Archbishop O'Connell advised the women in the Lowell LCW: "There are hundreds of women and girls working in these mills who need a helping hand, who need encouragement and Christian friendship."[187] Hence, the archdiocese formed dozens of working women's clubs to instill Christianity and prevent labor radicalization. These clubs, in effect, served the same purposes as the Protestant-inspired settlement houses and offered places for young women to escape their tenement apartments to read, study, exercise, perform music, and take classes in a protected environment. The major distinction between them and Protestant settlements was the absence of a residential staff.

Boston produced several Catholic women journalists who wrote about working women, among them Mary Blanche O'Sullivan and Agnes McNamara. O'Sullivan (fl. 1890–1920), was born in St. John's, New Brunswick, and was convent educated. With a normal school diploma she taught in public schools before moving to Boston around 1888, where she contributed to Donahoe's Magazine before going into an unspecified business.[188] Like Conway,

Emery, Blake, and Guiney, she pursued an editing and writing career, which included publications in the *Boston Globe* as well as numerous Catholic journals. She was a respondent in a *Globe* editorial debate, "Are Women in Business More Faithful than Men?"[189] Her investigations, "Women and Wages" and "The Sacrifice of the Shop Girl," among others, evince a greater awareness of labor and commercial issues than that of most Catholic journalists, who were not noted for their social awareness and case-study method of reporting. Reflecting the influence of contemporary Progressivism, O'Sullivan's "Phases of Charitable Work among Children" (1903) is by far the most factual and detailed reporting to a Catholic audience to appear in the early 1900s. Given the hegemonic character of Catholic education, which discouraged women from attending programs such as the new Boston School for Social Workers, begun by Simmons College and Harvard University in 1904, it is not surprising that O'Sullivan represented a minority and that most women were content to accept the Church's traditional interpretations of social problems. Agnes McNamara was one such leader, a member of the LCW whose 1920 speech to the league, "The Woman Worker," was reprinted in the *Pilot,* no doubt because she recommended returning to feudal models: "Why cannot the spirit of the medieval guilds be revived and modernized in the League of Catholic Women?"[190]

Catholic working women's leagues exhibited a conflicting mixture of traditional and modern social theories. On the political left, not typical of this generation but nevertheless present, was a persistent strain of Irish female labor radicalism in America, which produced such memorable figures as Mary Harris "Mother" Jones, Leonara O'Reilly, Mary Kenney O'Sullivan, and Elizabeth Gurley Flynn. Although many Catholics headed Catholic trade union leagues throughout the country, as women they were not allowed to speak at national labor conventions. In general, Catholic women who were involved in the labor movement in Boston, such as Mary Kenney O'Sullivan, were most likely to be affiliated with the National Women's Trade Union League, which was deemed a radical group at the time of its founding in 1903 but is now seen as an ineffective cross-class agency that failed to organize working women. Given O'Connell's opposition to settlement houses, the archdiocese probably offered little support for Catholic ties to the trade union league, whose first chapters in Boston were located within the settlement house that had helped establish it.[191]

On the whole, it seems that Catholic laywomen who had personal contact with the workplace evinced more practical awareness of the needs of working women, such as the need for day nurseries and health care, which put them at odds with the dogmatism of the clergy and hierarchy. Catholic women reported pragmatically that the chief problem for a working woman was getting "education that relates to her work, and which will give her a better understanding of industrial management and the technicalities of her job." From the Church's point of view, Catholic agencies could provide essential industrial or secretarial training for single women without recourse to the public sector while it continued to preach against working mothers. For example, Bishop Stang had stated that "married women should not be permitted—a case of extreme necessity excepted—to work in factories. A married woman has entered into a solemn contract with man, before God, to fulfill her duties as wife, mother and housekeeper. This contract cannot be broken, even with her own consent."[192] Thus, attacks on working mothers by the Church perhaps overshadowed women's attempts to improve the situation of working women. The Church was able to use domesticity in this way as a weapon against its fears of female anarchy and class strife. Despite the Church's disfavor, women's organizations developed programs for day care, health care, and probation care for women and mothers who worked. The foundation they established prior to 1920 would endure as the model for Catholic female activism (and, indeed, for American women in general) for decades to come. After World War I, however, bishops' documents encouraged women to return to their prewar status as homemakers and mothers; hence the Church's advocacy of a living wage for men rather than support for continued employment for women. By 1920, therefore, clerical views of woman's mission had scarcely advanced since the 1893 Catholic congress, where women argued that their duty was toward man, not themselves, "to elevate his materialism into a spiritual atmosphere, where his soul would grow and expand into something fit for heaven and the company of angels."[193]

Women and Social Feminism

The origins and activities of Catholic organizations for women in Boston define them as types of social feminism. Catholic literary circles, devotional societies, and charitable clubs were designed to occupy the leisure time of the middle-class woman in order to prevent the loss of the bourgeoisie to radical feminism, a strand of activism that had emerged around 1910 out of earlier women's rights movements. The Church attempted to persuade women that feminism did not offer them anything they did not already possess within Catholicism, a task made easier in Boston by the fact that Irish American women, despite their unusual economic autonomy, were not attracted to feminist activism.[194] Corresponding activities for working women and immigrants, including vocational training, neighborhood clubs, civics classes, and antisocialist propaganda, were developed for similar reasons—to save them from apostasy and political extremism. How much of this process of diverting women's activity away from self-interest was deliberate strategy by the Church is hard to assess. Bishops and priests were often victims of their own idealized expectations of womanhood and dutifully parroted papal warnings that the numerous "isms" generated by secularization posed threats to woman's place and the family unit. In Massachusetts, the hierarchy greatly exaggerated the threats of both feminism and socialism. In fact, the Church's propaganda seemed largely unnecessary: in Boston, no Catholic women demanded such innovations as a salary for household labor, sexual emancipation, or cooperative kitchens, nurseries, and shopping. Many women accepted the Church's official position and seemed satisfied with their limited sphere of activity because it was defined honorably as a "higher sphere of accomplishment," encompassing domestic and social, but not economic and professional, concerns. After all, the Church had entrusted them with an urgent mission to save a world teetering on the brink of doom: "It rests with you, Catholic women," said Cardinal O'Connell, "to stand by one another and uphold true dignity in the virtue of your Christian lives. The only thing that will help you to do this is your Catholic faith."[195] Cardinal O'Connell preserved his control over women's groups as one hallmark of Catholicism's retrenchment against rapid social change that threatened existing gender roles and social structures.

For the time being, Catholic women apparently resolved the contradictions between the tenets of domestic feminism and those of public social reform by using the former as the basis for the latter. In doing so, they repeated the pattern of American clubwomen in the Progressive era, who moved from being "domestic angels" for the family to become "civic mothers" for the nation. Catholic women used the separate sphere of womanhood to create new expertise for themselves to aid the groups for which their "natural" inclinations were intended: children, women, and the poor. When compared to other white middle-class women, Catholic women had fairly similar educational and career paths: they received normal or vocational school certificates; were employed in public school teaching, administration, or clerical service; volunteered in social work; and dedicated themselves to immigrant uplift and Americanization.

The twentieth century saw the emergence of these new types of Catholic women's organizations that joined domestic rhetoric to municipal and national goals. The pious and benevolent associations developed in the nineteenth century continued, as did the charity work of nuns and sisters, now augmented by societies dedicated to laywomen's social service outside the home. Lay associations were supervised by clergy chaplains and spiritual advisors who preserved the Church's power. Boston's formation of the LCW corresponded to an international pattern of enlisting female support for the Church's antimodernist outlook. The LCW nonetheless departed from O'Connell's advice on several crucial occasions by opening its lecture series to non-Catholics and by developing links with public immigration and secular charitable agencies. The LCW also established a precedent for paying women as social workers when it hired a probation officer. The national outgrowth of local LCWs, the National Council of Catholic Women, established in 1920, went on to further institutionalize the training of women through the National Catholic Service School, which offered for the first time a graduate curriculum for women in social work at Catholic University.[196] Cardinal O'Connell continued to oppose its "radical" efforts, as he had maligned women leaders in the suffrage and Progressive reform movements.

The LCW and its federated organizations shaped roles for middle-class women as builders of a Catholic subculture and as Church apologists. Groups such as the summer schools and reading circles had successfully converted a Protestant model of self-culture to Catholic uses. The high percentage of female summer school regulars suggests that Catholics continued to associate women with a superior aesthetic sensibility and the custodianship of culture. It also expressed Catholic ambivalence about the Church's commitment to permanent institutions of female higher education and the Church's willingness to allow women to lead organizations deemed harmless. As middle-class leisure time grew and educated women began to read more extensively, the Church soon devised ways to regulate their intellectual progress, short of endorsing long-term educational goals. The Church's tutelary presence was highly visible in efforts to shape a canon of devotional and literary classics for women. The reading circles therefore reinforced Church paternalism and its precepts of feminine piety and the virtuous use of leisure. Literary movements among the laity drew upon this image of femininity in their attempts to create a Catholic intelligentsia, to cultivate Catholic authorship and readership, and to enhance the insider identity of the subculture. The Catholic Summer School peaked around 1910, then declined as public secondary education became more universal, as the Catholic publishing industry advanced, and as mass media techniques were adopted in proselytizing. The eclipse of these nineteenth-century models generated a need for new ways to coordinate women's activities, answered by the LCW, which federated a wide range of devotional societies, parish societies, and social reformers.

The backbone of laywomen's associations was, of course, the middle class. As bourgeois institutions, Catholic women's groups were not immune to the influence of national clubwoman culture, transforming themselves from emphasizing the cult of domesticity to stressing a cult of civic maternalism, which extended woman's sphere to the public realm without losing its conventional appearance. Like Protestants, Catholic women reformers produced a version of the Victorian domesticity of Catherine Beecher and, later, equivalents of Jane Addams, who espoused Progressivism with a Christian base. Catholic clubwomen were likewise torn between the tradition of female self-sacrifice and the modern concept of self-assertion. Church leaders generally opposed the suffragism and scientific approach attributed to the Progressives. The isolation of Catholic women in their religious subculture, whose organizations paralleled secular and denominational prototypes, was sometimes regretted by Catholic observers. By and large, considering the Church's antipathy toward most women's rights movements, dramatic increases in the independence of a Catholic middle-class woman was more likely to come from her exposure to higher education and to a career than from contact with organized feminism.

This narrative of Catholic women in one archdiocese suggests a paradigm for their national history through placing gender experience in the contexts of class, urban, and religious development. The example of Catholic Boston has shown that middle-class women were encouraged to uphold the social structure and values of an older social formation based on a reciprocity of duties and responsibilities between the genteel and lower classes. The Church's piecemeal attempts to revive medievalism conflicted with its support for American individualist values and patriotism, and its incorporation of some aspects of the bureaucratic style of American managerial culture. Like contemporary women's organizations, Catholic women experienced the tensions between empathy with the poor and the need for efficiency in reform efforts. The Church's solution to the "new woman" was to reaffirm motherhood and domesticity as divinely mandated and to foster those women's organizations that promoted domesticity. Just as the nineteenth-century hierarchy had used popular devotions and saints' cults to channel female piety and suppress political radicalism, so did clerical control regulate the expansion of women's groups. Women's club membership and piety served not only the interests of middle-class solidarity, but also the Church's rising plan for Catholic separatism.

As part of its outsider defensiveness, the Church organized women to channel their efforts into service work that served the needy and preserved the faith of immigrants and the working class. Indeed, the laywomen's organizations became centers of denominational loyalty. But the effect of the Church's policies was partial and contradictory, particularly when it came to the areas of female education, careerism, and suffrage. As individuals and as clubwomen, Catholic women proved to be remarkably progressive in certain areas, such as identifying social problems through journalistic investigation, by seeking greater coordination of charitable agencies, by requesting day care for children of working mothers, and by opting for paid social workers. However, although these activities benefited the immigrant population, they inculcated middle-class aspirations more widely and thereby solidified Catholic identification with bourgeois values. Further, despite their innovative and subtle subversions of authority, and evidence of conflicts preserved in the minutes of their association meetings, women were still primarily understood by the institutional Church as molders of men. Women themselves seem to have developed, by 1920, a communal ethic based on a reformism generated by female consciousness, and a spiritual justification for charity derived from their Catholic faith.

7 THE CONTROL OF CULTURE

Catholicity, in the order of ideas or principles, is the truth and the whole truth, whether the truth evident to natural reason, or the truth revealed and affirmed to us by supernatural authority. It therefore necessarily extends to every department of human thought, feeling and action. Nothing, then in any order, or under any relation, is really separable from it, exempted from its law, or commendable save as inspired by it and as it conforms to it.—Orestes A. Brownson, "Dana's Poems and Prose Writing"

Boston presents a terrible, terrifying unanimity of aesthetic discriminations. There broods over the real Boston an immense sense of finality. One feels in Boston, as one feels in no other part of the States, that the intellectual movement has ceased. Boston is now producing no literature except a little criticism. Contemporary Boston art is imitative art, its writers are correct and imitative writers.
—H. G. Wells, *The Future in America*

But the mere list of those enumerated is an encouraging sign of the fact that the Catholic people are becoming more and more inclined to read real Catholic literature, when its authors give to their work the qualities of genius, study, learning and infinite pains. We are only at the beginning. It is the generation that is coming which will complete the work inaugurated and give to the world a Catholic literature that shall be not only sound and interesting, but popular.
—Rev. Francis Cunningham, "Catholic Novelists of Today"

Situating Catholic Culture

In an address to the Charitable Irish Society in 1912, Mayor John Fitzgerald toasted local heroes "like John Boyle O'Reilly, James Jeffrey Roche, Robert Dwyer Joyce and Henry Bernard Carpenter, the brilliant poets of the last generation."[1] Within a decade after their deaths, the writers and orators he named had secured the status of cultural idols among Irish Catholics. Prophets of a cultural renaissance that never fully materialized in the 1880s and 1890s, they presided over a localized circle of poets, writers, and journalists that also included Denis McCarthy, James Riley, Louise Guiney, Mary Agnes Tincker, Mary Elizabeth McGrath Blake, Mary Catherine Crowley, and Katherine Conway.[2] These Catholics produced literature and criticism attentive to Catholic themes but not exclusively for Catholic readers. Their literary productions became a litmus test for Catholic acceptance within a high culture still controlled by Yankee Protestants and epitomized national Catholic ambivalence about Catholic identity and cultural trusteeship.

The presence of the Irish and Irish Americans listed above made Boston a potential site of Catholic cultural ferment. Of the group, O'Reilly was an adopted Bostonian by way of heroic escape from penal exile in Australia; Guiney hailed from Worcester; Roche, born in Ireland, moved to Boston in 1866 from Prince Edward Island; McCarthy and Riley emigrated from Ireland; and Conway came to Boston from Rochester in 1883.[3] Tincker, who wrote for the general public, was considered "neutral religiously" yet still "unobjectionable" for Catholic readers.[4] Crowley, born in Boston, was a convert who wrote poems, stories, juvenile fiction, and freelance magazine articles. Blake, born Mary McGrath in Ireland, emigrated to Quincy about 1850, married a Boston physician, and bore eleven children. In addition to her literary career, she was a member of the Boston Public School Association as well as an advocate of women's education. As a group, these Catholic authors had but sketchy formal education. The convent schooling of the women was characteristic; McCarthy lamented his lack of college experience; and the rest were largely self-taught.

The first sign of Catholics' integration into Brahmin culture was their acceptance into the Anglo-Protestant literary establishment. The Charitable Irish Society where Fitzgerald spoke in 1912, for example, had been founded in 1737 by the Protestant Irish of Boston and had admitted no Catholics until 1804. By the 1880s, however, Irish Catholics were well blended into its leadership. O'Reilly and Roche enjoyed personal friendships with the social elites of Boston and gained memberships in such exclusive gentlemen's clubs as St. Botolph and Round Table. O'Reilly established the Papyrus Club for journalists and writers in 1879, and Roche became its president in 1890.[5] O'Reilly also was elected president of the Boston Press Club in 1879.[6]

In an era when Irish men became "compulsive club joiners," they did not lag behind as club founders. J. J. Roche, although invited to join the twelve-member Brahmin Jury Club, was mindful of his ethnic roots and joined numerous Irish associations. With Thomas Gargan, he founded and served as an officer of the American Irish Historical Society.[7] O'Reilly found time for many Catholic affiliations, including membership in the Catholic Union of Boston, which he had helped found in 1873, and as a participant in various Irish American fraternals. The success of O'Reilly and Roche was demonstrated further by invitations from the Yankee politicians of Boston and Cambridge (John F. Andrew, Josiah Quincy, William Russell, and Nathan Mathews) to speak at civic ceremonies and patriotic events, such as their commissioning of O'Reilly to dedicate in verse the Crispus Attucks Memorial, and of Roche to compose a poem commemorating the General Butler Memorial in Tremont Temple in 1893.[8]

Some Catholic women, too, enjoyed the patronage of the Brahmin establishment. The city of Boston commissioned Mary Elizabeth McGrath Blake to write memorial verses for Wendell Phillips; Oliver Wendell Holmes complimented her; Theodore Roosevelt admired her; and the *Congregationalist* solicited her articles. Authors Conway and Crawford were among the few Catholics in the Boston Author's Club, but they also devoted considerable time to Catholic associations, especially the Reading Circle movement. In contrast, Louise Guiney, the "golden guinea" of Wendell Holmes, recalled that her circle was "never a predominantly Catholic one in the U.S.A."[9]

Having ingratiated themselves with the local arbiters of high culture, Catholics eagerly anticipated an artistic revival centered in Boston. An atmosphere of benign assimilation and cultural goodwill nourished by the universally popular O'Reilly was assisted by the episcopal style of Archbishop John Williams. Williams's unassuming personality nurtured lay cultural activity without threat of heavy-handed Church interference but stopped well short of organizing Catholic intellectuals and artists into a movement. In the O'Connell era, the individual diversity of the writers of the 1890s was minimized by certain critics in order to present them as a homogeneous group united by the Church's stamp of approval. One agent of this revisionism was Father Michael Earls, a protégé of the nineties generation, who in the 1920s and 1930s as professor of rhetoric at Holy Cross College created in his literary essays the image of his predecessors as a coherent Catholic front. For the Church, the religious orthodoxy of writers began to mean more than their writing talents. Even Earls admitted as much in 1931 when he complained that "poetry does not find more than a crutch support in a Catholic atmosphere."

Perhaps expectations of a Boston literary renaissance were unwarranted. In fact, no compelling reasons led the Catholic literati of the 1890s to organize as Catholics because their recognition as Americans was their prized distinction. Williams set the tone of quiet integration that was repeated by the Catholic lay leaders of the day. On the other hand, some ethnic stirrings were felt by Irish Americans attuned to the Celtic literary revival begun in the 1870s that popularized ancient Irish legends and settings and produced such notable poets and playwrights as William Butler Yeats, John Synge, Lady Augusta Gregory, Douglas Hyde, and George Russell ("A.E.").[10] J. J. Roche, for example, collaborated as an associate editor with Lady Gregory and Douglas Hyde to produce *Irish Literature,* a mammoth ten-volume set published in 1904.[11] John Boyle O'Reilly published scores of poems on Irish subjects and frequently joked that "it's better to be Irish than to be right." Michael Earls collected but never published a volume of Irish ballads, which Mary Boyle O'Reilly had painstakingly transcribed by hand from the collection of the Boston Public Library. Earls, the first of ten children of Irish immigrant parents, developed the theme that Catholicity forged an important bond between Irish Americans and the Irish. By 1922, as American Catholic critic and editor George Shuster suggested, ethnic and religious identifications had become inseparable: "The Catholic Spirit in Ireland has meant as much as even the national impulse. . . . That the Irish are primarily a nation of peasants, that they lack the artistic sensibility of the modern aesthete and cherish poetic stories about the pagan gods, surely does not diminish the power of the spirit of belief within them." Shuster concluded grandiosely: "Thus, with a background that is Gaelic, national, partisan, and uniquely Catholic, the Irish literary movement has attained the proportions of a renaissance which impresses the reader by its young robustness, which seems to have linked hands with the morning of the world."[12]

Shuster was too generous in his assessment. Taken on the whole, contemporary response to the literary renaissance in Ireland and in Boston was neither tolerant nor laudatory. One obvious irritation of the Irish revival was the attempt by its Anglo-Protestant writers to use the English language to colonize and retell the old Gaelic legends. Whereas the Irish struggle to preserve cultural autonomy against English conquest had ties to political nationalism, in Boston it manifested itself as a somewhat diluted form of sentimental Irishism, devoid of much of the anticolonial violence and linguistic focus that accompanied nationalism in Ireland. After 1910, the American Irish did not join the movement to revive Gaelic, nor had the majority of them ever lived in the homeland for which they were presumably fighting. While a minute Irish Catholic elite admired the works of Yeats and his circle and attempted to draw similar creative inspiration from Irish legends, the popular response to the Irish revival both in Ireland and America was unsympathetic. Irish Catholics conditioned to see art as the realization of divine ideals demonstrated by their harsh reviews that they rallied to the Catholic Church's representation of the cultural battle as one of Christian Ireland against mythical pagan characters, and especially against the unbelief of the Gaelic revivalists themselves. Irish-born poet Denis McCarthy of Boston summed up local feeling in a face-to-face confrontation with Yeats in 1911: "I don't understand many of the things that Yeats says, and there are many things in his school of playwrighting that I cannot stand for. . . . The pagan poses that most of these people assume in the plays gets on my nerves."[13]

The Catholic Church, therefore, inserted itself into this debate about the different forms of Irishness (Anglo elite versus Irish popular), which themselves reflected class-based struggles already in process between highbrow and lowbrow culture. The emergence of a high Irish and a low Irish sensibility from the late 1890s generated tensions inevitable within a postimmigrant community in the process of stratification. The new Catholic elites joined the dominant culture's literary power base, notably *Atlantic Monthly* magazine, and they also formed cultural institutions based on Brahmin models, such as those discussed in Chapters 2 and 3. Where Protestants sponsored the Ford Hall Forum and the Junior League, for example, Catholics founded the Common Cause and the Cecilian Guild. The young Rose Fitzgerald founded her own Ace of Clubs for Irish girls who could, like cultured Protestants, speak French.[14]

In 1900, Boston Catholics had not excelled in any of the fine arts, such as music performance, composition, sculpture, or painting. With the exception of architecture, by which one might make a lucrative career based on either apprenticeship or a professional degree, Catholics lacked the patronage networks necessary for producing virtuosos dedicated to single-minded pursuit of the arts. In the *Pilot*'s opinion, "The artistic quality in large degree is developed chiefly by cultivation and by association with artists, and the opportunity to see and compare their productions. The Irish emigrant had no such cultivation or opportunity in the land of his birth, where his chief occupation was turning up the soil. . . . It is not to be wondered at, therefore, that fifty years ago, about twenty-eight years after Catholics were emancipated, that Irish-American artists were as scarce as the snakes in Ireland."[15] The function of this rhetorical "poor mouthing" was to help Catholics justify their own lack of achievement as a consequence of colonial oppression by the English. Into this creative void the Church was able to represent itself as a patron and employer of artists and writers and did in fact hire performing artists to serve as church musicians and choir directors. John Augustine O'Shea of Milford (1864–1939), to cite one example, became renowned as a church organist. His Cork ancestors came to Boston soon after the American Revolution, making him a descendant of socially established, prefamine immigrants. He graduated from the New England Conservatory in 1886 and the Boston University college of music in 1887. While organist at St. Joseph's, Boston, from 1883 to 1902, he conducted a recital at the Pan-American Exposition and directed the "famous John Boyle O'Reilly concert." Subsequently he became organist at one of Boston's wealthiest parishes, St. Cecilia's, Back Bay, from 1902 until his death. Simultaneously, O'Shea was director of music for the Boston public schools from 1901 to 1934 and gave many local recitals.[16] Mary A. Dierkes (1870–1950), a native of South Boston and resident of Dorchester, sang at Holy Trinity Church, Boston's German parish. Having studied voice in Boston and at Leipzig Conservatory, she also served as a member of the Boston school board, where she worked to improve the quality of music teaching for children. Boston-born and Italian-trained opera singers such as Eliza Leveroni always received enthusiastic public welcomes when they performed at home, yet still dutifully requested permission from Archbishop O'Connell to perform concerts in churches other than their home parishes. Most women musicians, unlike Leveroni, worked for a parish in a part-time capacity, in conjunction with charitable work. Such was the case of Sarah Hayden, who was convent-educated in Boston, served as music teacher and organist for St. Joseph's, West End, and ran Catholic girls' and boys' clubs in her home while writing for the *Sacred Heart Review*.[17] Hugh Cairns, commissioned to do a bust of Archbishop O'Connell, was one of a few Catholics mentioned in local histories as a trained sculptor.[18]

The most notable achievements in Catholic art therefore came not from performing and creative artists but from poets, essayists, and novelists. Oral and written literary culture, not the visual arts or the classical musical or dance repertoires, emerged as a source of pride and of identity for the second and third generation. Literature, therefore, became an ideological weapon (as well as an ideological production) and a tool of ethnoreligious competition within the Boston establishment. Journalism, pedagogy, poetry, prose, and criticism helped to define Catholic identity and display Catholics as saviors of Boston's cultural reputation. That Protestant New Englanders had achieved a literary renaissance that made Boston the Athens of America, Catholics fully recognized. Now they demanded their own turn. Both factions, however, were to be disappointed by 1920 and were blamed by national commentators for the decline of high culture in Boston: the Protestant establishment for losing its genteel heritage, the Irish Catholic segment for never rising above prudishness and censoriousness.

What went wrong for the Catholic renaissance of the 1890s? In part, deaths and departures fragmented it. Its catalyst John Boyle O'Reilly died in 1890, perhaps by suicide; none of his daughters had children; Louise Guiney went to live in England in 1900; and Mary Elizabeth Blake, Mary Agnes Tincker, and Mary Conroy died in 1907, followed by J. J. Roche in 1908. The remnant seemed to concentrate its efforts on the local Catholic press rather than on championing a literary movement. For Katherine Conway at the *Pilot* and, later, the *Republic*, Mary O'Sullivan at *Donahoe's*, and Susan Emery and Denis McCarthy at the *Sacred Heart Review*, editing and publishing for a weekly paper competed with their personal endeavors and their economic needs.

The lack of a genuine Catholic artistic revival has also been attributed to contrasting hierarchical styles. In her study of Boston priests, Donna Merwick cast Archbishop O'Connell as a villain who "choked out" the pluralistic potential of the 1890s generation in favor of a "more dominant and—for the general Catholic populace—a more satisfying cultural strain."[19] However, the strict, two-level model she ascribed to O'Connell—elite culture on a Roman clerical/aristocratic model, supported by Boston's wealthy Catholics, versus low culture, namely sentimental devotion to Ireland—fails to explain the widening gap between elite and popular sensibilities, the significance of the Catholic middle class, and the undeniable impact of mass culture on urban Catholics.

The presence of highbrow and lowbrow outlooks in Boston Catholicism were affected by the Catholic middle class precisely because it absorbed the extremes of elite and popular culture and experienced the contradictions of its own assimilation and the Church's separatist aims. Middle-class Catholics were drawn by the hierarchy and clergy toward identification with an Arnoldian style of elitism and an aristocratic view of culture, with an explicit Christian base, however. They were exhorted by the Church to uplift the working classes whom they proselytized through control of the artistic professions and through a literary nexus of Catholic editors, reviewers, and publishers. One early attempt to edify the masses came from John Boyle O'Reilly. Upon returning from a speaking tour of Connecticut mill towns, O'Reilly complained about the muteness of his audiences to a friend, who responded:

> Your audience and your hosts were plain, unlettered men and women, who labored with their hands for their daily bread; and yet under all this there was a passion in their hearts to hear the voice of a poet. Tell me, John, did you ever hear of English mill operatives sending for Tennyson or Browning to speak them? [sic] Do you recall that American working men send for American poets to address them? Isn't there something worth while, some pearl of great price, hidden under the dross and dirt, the dullness and dumbness of those Irish mill workers? As long as a man listens to the voice of the singer his soul is not dead; when he sends a call for the singer to come to him, John, his soul is immortal.[20]

Thus, Roche reminded Reilly, poetry can save the soul, even though its workings might be as invisible as those of divine grace. Despite his momentary impatience with the millhands, O'Reilly's usually engaging style, which "charmed the humblest errand boy or the crudest laborer, as it did the choicest circle of Boston society," was symbolic of his generation.[21] The common touch was not characteristic of his successors, whose growing distance from the unlettered poor became more apparent. As Catholic elitism grew, it advocated the inseparability of art and religion. How, then, could a Catholic literature create social harmony between the social classes? Further, was ethnic solidarity enough to overcome class differences between generations?

In response, Catholics poised themselves to become cultural insiders. They hoped to accomplish this, first, by convincing liberal Yankee reformers as well as the conservative Brahmin establishment that their cultural vitality threatened neither desirable social reforms nor the Brahmin status quo. Next, they intended to use Catholic literature to bridge class differences by joining Catholic virtues, Irish identity, and typically American concerns. Catholic intellectuals were experiencing on a smaller scale what American Progressivism was undergoing: a changing conception of the role of elites. As Irish American writers struggled to define themselves, the Church—or at least the new archbishop—worked hard to present itself as a cultured and cosmopolitan institution. John Williams and William O'Connell differed not only in their degree of public visibility to Boston society but also in their vision of Catholic cultural achievement. Where Williams was unobtrusive and taciturn, O'Connell was ubiquitous and outspoken. Among the laity of Williams's generation, figures like O'Reilly became ambassadors to the Protestant world, "idol of Catholics and Puritans, interpreter of each to the other."[22] O'Connell pointed Catholics to a new resistance against Yankee Protestant culture, in contrast to Williams's attempts to blend in by minimizing sectarian differences. In many regards, genteel Catholicism and Brahmin culture shared many aesthetic presuppositions and interests, as in their idealism; the rediscovery of Francis of Assisi, Dante, and Joan of Arc; and their appreciation of America's nineteenth-century novelists and poets. Between the time of O'Reilly and that of O'Connell an important change had occurred, however, namely the emergence of a Catholic middle class to complement or challenge the Church's former intellectual caste—the clergy.

The duality of Archbishop O'Connell's self-image contributed to the uneven formation of Catholic attitudes about culture. His aggressive pursuit of status for himself, his family, and his coreligionists led him to publicize his working-class Lowell roots as an indication of how far he had journeyed toward social acceptance among Protestant politicians, socialites, churchmen, and college presidents.[23] O'Connell's class insecurities contributed to his assertions of Catholicism's cultural superiority to Puritanism, and so he implied that for Catholics to become plain Americans was a comedown; yet at the same time he was anxious to claim that Boston's luminous cultural history provided the background for Catholic greatness. When he received the red hat in 1911, he described his own cardinalate as a link between New England's glorious past and a future Catholic potency. In his first sermon in Boston after returning from Rome, he stated: "The names of Longfellow and Hawthorne and Lowell are written in gold in the tablets of this nation's story. In a large sense these were all Boston's pride. Painting and architecture and history have all been cultivated here as in no other community of this nation."[24] The Catholic contribution to America, O'Connell implied, would embrace and continue this cultural legacy. O'Connell's aggressive civic pride never hinted that Boston was in the midst of commercial and perhaps cultural decline. Instead, at his silver jubilee celebration in 1909, O'Connell had praised the cultural status quo: "Let others claim the primacy of commerce, but no one can deny that even to-day, all over Europe, the American primacy of art and intellect is still conceded to the Hub."[25]

The Celtic cast of the Roche-O'Reilly generation in Boston was Catholicism's dominant, but by no means its only, cultural hue. Some Irish Americans grew estranged from their ethnic heritage even though in 1890 Boston offered few alternatives to ethnicity as a form of personal and of group or class identity. O'Reilly's despairing, class-conscious remarks about the millhands convey a mildly anti-Irish melancholy at odds with his buoyant public persona. Guiney and Conway have been described as "alternately passive or hostile to Boston's Irish Catholics."[26] Still, Catholic writers returned to the mythology of Irish difference, as in this paean to J. J. Roche by a contemporary: "Opinions may differ as to Jeffrey Roche's place in American literature, for his work was essentially American in theme adorned by Celtic grace, inspired by the Celtic spirit and dominated by Celtic ideal, but there will be no two opinions as to his honesty, sincerity, loyalty, humanity and artistry."[27] Isolated Anglophiles such as Louise Guiney were not attempting to erase Irishness from Boston Catholicism, though she seemed aware that an overemphasis on Irishness prevented the Irish from accommodating themselves to America. They were assaulted with guilty memories of the Old Country induced by their relatives and friends remaining behind.[28] Third-generation Irish American fiction internalized this nostalgia for Mother Ireland and merged it with American authorial debates presently under way between sentimental fiction and the new realism.[29]

Thus, the strands mingling to produce a Catholic literature came from several sources, of which forms of Irish identity—popular sentimentalism and elitist Gaelic revivalism—were but two. In the cultural battles being waged between the genteel tradition and the modernist camps of realism and naturalism, Catholic idealism supported the genteel tradition. Catholic literary life was coalescing, however, as genteel culture was under attack, forcing Catholic literature to confront critical scorn for the anemic "pale decadence of New England" implied in western novels such as Owen Wister's *The Virginian*.[30] As Boston's half-century golden age came to a close, Brahmin authors saw their cultural hegemony and numbers ebbing, and the tide of American regional culture flowing toward the frontier. This "Boston Twilight" was mocked by Charles Angoff of the *American Mercury*: "But where is Boston now? In literature it is as dead as the Hittite Empire, nothing respectable in *belles lettres* has come from it in a generation. There is hardly a class of Bos-

tonians left that is unquestionably literate."[31] Angoff scathingly classed the
Yankees into two groups: the radicals who supported the contemptible
masses, and the "advanced Rotarians," composed of "Nordics" and some
Americanized Jews. But even more contemptible to Angoff were the "Irish-
Catholic anthropoids," who "don't belong even to these two pitiable classes.
They have no more interest in ideas than a guinea-pig has in Kant's 'Critique
of Pure Reason' or a donkey in Goethe's 'Faust.'"[32] Angoff ended his bilious
remarks by concluding that "these Gaels" hastened the collapse of Boston
culture by reducing it to the lowest common denominator.

While most of Boston's Yankee establishment probably did not think of the
Irish in such withering terms, Angoff exposed the raw sores that Archbishop
O'Connell was trying to heal. Fearful of being blamed for national degeneration, Catholics compensated by mythologizing their recent literary past as
heroic, even as early as 1910. In that year, celebrations commemorating the
twentieth anniversary of the death of John Boyle O'Reilly illustrated this phenomenon. Denis McCarthy composed a poem for the O'Reilly Club that sanctified O'Reilly in the minds of his contemporaries:

> And so for the debt I forever shall owe him—
> The courage he lent me when weary and faint—
> I'm fain to the world as I knew him to show him;
> My poet, my master, my hero, my saint![33]

Thus, the "failed 90s" provided Catholics with a sense of melancholic loss
that actually proved inspirational for the next two decades. The negative side
of nostalgia was an inevitable distortion of the "golden age" and the introduction of parochial standards of fiction among Catholics.[34] That is, Catholics' first literary lions were subsumed in a parochial narrative that identified
them explicitly as Catholic authors. Eventually, Massachusetts's Catholic
elites linked this parochialism to the genteel standards of highbrow culture,
so that by the 1920s, Catholics began to rival the state's Puritan ancestors as
protectors and censors of conservative taste. Most Boston Catholics probably
remained oblivious to the unfortunate side of the cultural transitions taking
place, enjoying instead the triumphalism of the archbishop and Mayor Honey
Fitz's cheerful vision of Irish Catholic potential in New England, which "pur-
posely struck the note of optimism rather than of protest and lamentation."[35]

The Anti-Ugly Crusade
in Catholic Aesthetics

The optimistic notes preferred by prelates and politicians were also characteristic of Catholic aesthetic thought. Most Boston Catholics were probably

unconscious of how deeply their worldview was structured by and derived from the Aristotelian and Thomist categories combined and embedded in Catholic theology. These traditions placed binary pairs of entities within hierarchies of moral reasoning and ethical discrimination: Reason over Body, priesthood over laity, man over woman, and parent over child. The Aristotelianism that Aquinas had adopted was affirmed as the Church's official theological method in *Aeterni Patris,* the papal encyclical of 1879.[36] The Boston *Pilot* saluted Thomism in an editorial: "The intellectual grasp of St. Thomas Aquinas and his power as an expert reasoner in things requiring the most acute intelligence might well become an exemplar for men of the modern world to study."[37] The Aristotelian-Thomist synthesis employed reason to support and explain faith. Through the centuries, it had come to associate the virtues with the rational and the vices with the emotional, creating an enduring tension between faith (reason) and the arts (sensation). Admittedly, this dynamic had undergone further modifications by medieval scholastic commentators, who often misread Aquinas. In any event, by the late 1800s, what had once been a healthy respect for human knowledge gained through sense experience now seemed to become in Catholic moral theology an almost morbid fear of corruption entering the human mind like a thief, through the "windows of the senses."[38] A theological viewpoint based on mistrust of unmediated sensual experience was resolved in the essentialist philosophy that underlay Catholic aesthetics in the previous two centuries, which explains the necessity for Catholic aesthetic teaching to affirm an indivisible link between morality and the aesthetic experience of art.[39] There were very few original statements by Catholic philosophers or theologians about Catholic aesthetics in the early 1900s, which was subsumed under the rubric of moral theology. One frequently cited Italian source was Vicenzo Gioberti's *Essay on the Beautiful,* which stated: "The contemplation of the Beautiful implies the superiority of the idea over the sensation."[40] Art, as the product of intellect and senses combined, presented a particular dilemma to the Church hierarchy: how to govern the Catholic's taste against bad art, whether in the fine arts or the new forms of mass culture, while maintaining the Church's authority as judge in these matters. At the heart of the debate, predictably, was the Church's ideological concern to protect the sanctity of the Christian home. As the *Sacred Heart Review* noted:

> The atmosphere of a home is indicated as surely by the pictures on the walls, the books on the shelves, the papers and magazines on the table, as by the conversation of the master and mistress and the deportment of the children. The Catholic home should have a Catholic atmosphere. Gaudy, flashy, pictures whose subjects are of the earth, and books and

papers that are not only trashy but positively evil are to be found in too many Catholic homes. Everybody to-day recognizes the formative value of environment on children's characters. God gave us all a free will, but we are influenced powerfully in the use of that will by the people who are our companions; by the things we see, and the things we read when we acquire the power of reading.[41]

Belief in the effect of environment on character formation continued to guide thinking in the next decades, as evidenced by a *Pilot* editorial of 1919 that suggested that even the presence of cheap reproductions of sacred art in the Catholic home could uplift the viewer: "To gaze daily upon Fra Angelico's angels is to be permeated with the spirit of that holy Dominican."[42] A similar belief in the spiritual essence of art came from John Boyle O'Reilly, who wrote to his daughters on seeing Millet's *L'Angelus* displayed in New York: "It is not a man and woman praying—it is a painted prayer. You can hear the Angelus bell filling the beautiful air; you can see the woman's lips moving; you pray with her. One looks at the lovely picture with parted lips and hushed breath. And so great is art that *all* who see it feel the same sweet influence."[43] Clearly, Catholics equated experiencing beautiful objects with receiving divine grace and acquiring virtuous standards of moral discrimination and behavior. The aesthetic experience, therefore, inherently combined edification and spirituality because it expressed a relationship with the divine. The idealist-moralist perspective on art defined an American Catholic subculture between Vatican I and Vatican II that was sustained by Irish Americans and the Irish-dominated clergy. As recently as the 1940s, for example, Catholic commentators continued to claim that art should not "stir up the silt in our natures."[44] The Church's distaste for the world as a social reality, its nostalgia for the world prior to industrialization, and its certainty of a fixed essence at the core of literature gave Catholic aesthetics a strong resemblance to liberal humanism, which, allowing for the difference in religious outlooks, would generate in the 1920s and 1930s many affinities between Catholic Neo-Scholastics and the New Humanists, Southern Agrarians, and other anti-modernists.

In the Church's view, civilization was in crisis because it no longer appealed to the best and the highest in human nature. Ideologically, Church leaders were lamenting the loss of the integrated system that it equated with Thomism and the Middle Ages. Especially since the papacy's rehabilitation of Thomism, the Middle Ages became a model for how to see (a guide to aesthetics) and how to live (a guide to action). Just as the home ought to reinforce moral values, so the urban environment, Catholic commentators argued, should support virtuous character formation by presenting opportunities for moral-aesthetic appreciation. At the opening of the twentieth century, even as Archbishop O'Connell was making bombastic pronouncements for the city's future glory, a parallel rhetoric of decline haunted Catholic journalism and homiletics in Boston. The tendency of Catholics to interpret aesthetic decay as a sign of a crisis in American civilization enabled them to seek a Catholic response against that which was "earthy," "trashy," and "evil." O'Connell preferred to blame the crisis on the decline of manners and culture: "The play, the magazine, the ballroom, all give evidence of an ever increasing disregard of even the rudiments of common decency of dress, of deportment, of conversation and of conduct."[45] The rhetoric of crisis generated by the hierarchy inspired Catholics to provide their own literary heroes and thus create a Catholic canon. A Boston priest remarked, "We are only at the beginning. It is the generation that is coming which will complete the work inaugurated and give to the world a Catholic literature that shall be not only sound and interesting, but popular."[46] Because Catholic literature would uphold noble and universal standards of art, there evolved a Catholic campaign against "the school of the ugly," which demanded that art represent only the good, the uplifting, the wholesome, the redemptive, and the universal.[47] These constituted, in the Catholic view, a "realistic" notion of life. Because Catholics affirmed the impact of sense experience on the moral imagination, they desired artists and audiences to experience the sensate only in a context that would enhance the human person. "It is worthwhile to appeal steadfastly to the best in human nature," said Katherine Conway. "Our ideal selves are after all, our true selves, and he is the truest realist who keeps constantly before humanity its highest character-types and noblest achievements."[48] Acknowledging the power of art, the Church further believed that the wayward human will, although free, required aesthetic guidance. Consequently, preservation of the Christian Church and home and individual conscience described in the remarks above was essential. Given that Catholics did espouse a kind of moral environmentalism (despite the Church's profession of universal standards of beauty), let us examine how aesthetic values were reproduced in the subculture.

It is difficult to assess whether the Boston Church's understanding of culture and aesthetics was more successfully advanced by the clergy or by the laity. American Catholicism gained some of its most comprehensive aesthetic guidelines from Orestes A. Brownson (1803–1876), a lay convert from Unitarianism and Transcendentalism. Through the essays and book reviews published in the two journals he founded, the *Boston Quarterly Review* (1838–42) and *Brownson's Quarterly Review* (1844–64; 1873–75), Brownson left American Catholics a clearly articulated moral-aesthetic formula: "Our theology determines our ethics, and our ethics determines our aesthetics."[49] After trying Transcendentalism at Brook Farm, Brownson became a Catholic. Following his conversion in 1844, he tackled in detail (but with true Emersonian inconsistency) the issues of religious versus secular art, Catholic versus secular novels, and American versus European literature. Because Brownson's idiosyncratic Church politics veered between support for religious liberals and conservatives, it is impossible to categorize linear coherence in his thought. From 1865 until his death, however, his writings reflected an extreme pro-Roman conservatism based on his absolute support for the 1864 papal encyclical *Quanta Cura* and its appended Syllabus of Errors, whereby Brownson "recognized" the faults of his previous writings and atoned for them by repudiating his former views.

Brownson lived in Chelsea, Massachusetts, from 1836 to 1855, moving to New York in that year following disagreements with Bishop Fitzpatrick of Boston, who had received him into the Church. Despite his departure, Brownson's influence in Boston was significant and enduring. Unfortunately, since he did not choose to join a faction that might have sheltered him, he often alienated Protestants by the militancy of his Catholicism, which he willingly allowed to inform all of his opinions. Influences on his aesthetic thinking, as revealed through his essays and footnotes, included Vicenzo Gioberti's *Essay on the Beautiful* and the writings of St. Alphonsus Liguori (1696–1787), who warned not only against obscene books but also against those which profaned love by treating it as obscene.[50] Brownson gained the ear of the editor of the Boston *Pilot,* thereby securing his influence in almost every Catholic publication in Boston as well as in the New York press. One historian, however, has judged Brownson as one of the great disasters to befall Boston Catholicism because of his "bitter apologetics." However, Brownson's preeminence among both Protestants and Catholics made him a model of astringent, assertive criticism unsurpassed by the 1890s generation.[51] George Parsons Lathrop stated that "because of his pugnacious quality, Catholic Americans to this day are divided in their estimate of him. Those of vigorous mind, large perceptions, and self-reliant character give him the tribute of unbounded enthusiasm, while others who imagine that faith depends on timidity and colorlessness shake the head or shrug the shoulder, half sadly, half cynically. They regard vigor and independence as 'dangerous,' but are indifferent to the greater danger of stagnation."[52]

Between 1900 and 1920 Brownson was still fashionable to quote when his advocacy was needed, but Catholic critics did not go out of their way to claim him as their ancestor, possibly because he had aggravated the Yankee Protestant audience whom they were trying to appease. It is more likely that his example of lay authority was unacceptable to O'Connell's repressive clericalism. Brownson's ideas lived on in some form among the Paulists, the religious order founded by his disciple Isaac Hecker. Lay Catholics, however, chided themselves for losing Brownson's intellectual vitality. Louise Guiney measured the mental apathy of modern Catholics against Brownson's profundity: "Dr. Brownson's own star looks dim along the modern horizon not because he was a Catholic, but because he wrote on the deepest subjects which can, but do not, engage the mind of lazy man."[53] Rev. John Talbot Smith attributed Brownson's anonymity to "the tacit scorn of the average Catholic for his own writers." "Thus passed away the great Brownson, living on his little annuity," he mourned.[54] Brownson's son, Henry, who graduated from Holy Cross College in 1852, who helped plan the 1889 lay Catholic congress, and who was himself called "the most intelligent man in America," tried to sustain his father's reputation by editing the twenty volumes of his writings. Nonetheless, Brownson's reception in America was largely overshadowed by an Englishman who converted a year after he did, John Cardinal Newman.[55] To the dismay of Catholic lay leaders, American Catholics customarily deferred to foreign commentators on religion and morals. As George Lathrop observed, "To whatever cause it be owing, Brownson is omitted from our manuals and histories of literature, or figures but slightly in them[,] . . . ignoring that fact that it [the Catholic Church] has found here one of the most virile and accomplished exponents it possesses in any part of the world."[56]

Despite Brownson's invisibility, the aesthetic principles that he represented endured in the Catholic institutions which regulated doctrinal orthodoxy. The archdiocese of Boston did not produce original theologians or philosophers under Williams or O'Connell. Instead, for guidance on moral theology, which incorporated the realm of aesthetics, the clergy relied on received tradition from medieval sources and from the few eighteenth- and nineteenth-century commentators excerpted for seminary textbooks. Boston's priests learned what they knew about appreciation of the beautiful from their lectures and manuals at St. John's, which were themselves derivative condensations or pastiches of Aristotle and Aquinas. The Catholic understanding of the relationship between ethics (the Good) and art (the Beautiful) was summarized by Jesuit Michael Earls: "Ethics is the elder sister in the household of art. Aesthetics, meaning sensation as the basis for the beautiful, must remain a modest serving girl."[57] His statement echoes and modifies Gioberti's: "Thus, philosophy and religion are sisters of the aesthetic, which is a kind of apprenticeship which intitiates the moral to the truth and to the supreme good, in the same manner that beauty is the expression, the physiognomy, and the outward part, so to speak, the vestibule or porch, of virtue and science."[58] This formula illustrates the prevalent hierarchical mentality in Roman Catholicism that placed ethics (denoting reason) above aesthetics (denoting sensation). The laity assimilated this aesthetic norm of the Good and the Beautiful from the clergy through sermons, Church pronouncements, and catechetical manuals, which they reiterated in the Catholic press, and which served many novelists and poets as the premise for their writing. Catholic poet Joyce Kilmer, for example, summarized this sense of a dynamic relationship between art and virtue: "For literature is a branch of art, and art, we know, is on the side of the angels."[59] The desire to promote moral reasoning and, thus, the moral meaning of art above sensual appreciation of the beautiful had specific ramifications in Catholic discussions of novel-writing and novel-reading.

Against Modernism

Discussion about writing and reading novels accounted for the bulk of the editorials, book reviews, and literary columns in the Catholic press in Massachusetts. "What we want today is an amusing of the Catholic conscience in this regard, the cultivation of Catholic instincts, and the acquiring of Catholic habits of thought," the *Pilot* asserted.[60] The Catholic novel had been a proving ground for cultural and moral force at least since the 1850s, when Orestes Brownson had predicted "that the novel may not be absolutely the best literary form, but it is here and now the best literary vehicle, after the newspaper and the review, that we can adopt."[61]

In 1900, the literary enemies of Catholics were the modernists, "an irregular school of arts and literateurs whose aim is the substitution of the grotesque and the horrible for the beautiful."[62] As "modernists," Catholics mistakenly equated realists and naturalists as writers who deliberately "seek not merely for the sordidness of low motive and mean aim, but even for the horror of ugliness, of parasitical abomination, and seek to palm off upon us the result of such looking as a study of human nature! Away with such!"[63] Realism, instead of representing the divinely inspired creation of an author with pure intentions, was condemned as a "callous dissection" of life. Among the realists, the muckrakers were particularly offensive to codes of Catholic fiction. Muckrakers churned out what Catholics called "the novel of exposure": "If the scene is set in Chicago we have filth and entrails galore, for 500 pages; if it is set in Pittsburgh, there the glare of furnaces lighting up stalwart victims and high in the gaudy club is heard the popping of champagne corks to a chorus girl accompaniment. The recipe seems to be: no matter about the ingredients of the brew, but make it strong. The society romancer she lays on the red and yellow with a large brush." The editorial writer concluded judgmentally, "It is a Walpurgis Night of vulgarity and mendacity."[64] An undergraduate at Boston College condemned realism with similar alacrity: "There is a certain smack of absurdity underlying the whole contention of the realist. While disclaiming allegiance to any accepted code, he is, strangely enough, the zealot and bond-slave of his masters. In his mission of interpreting 'life as it really is' his note-book is widest open when recording the sordid and the ugly. Here he finds a more congenial field. Other impressions—the beauty and the joy of life—having been frequently treated, appear to him trite and stagey."[65] Thus, the realist movement in literature, which was attempting to apply the scientific method of Darwin and Comteian positivism to fiction, was untenable to Catholic idealism because it exaggerated the sordid aspects of its subject matter, "excluding all those emotional and imaginative elements that constitute its greatest part."[66] The American naturalists, a distinguishable faction among the realists, seemed to revel in the determinism and violence that underlay European naturalist philosophy. Catholics were not only unsympathetic to this dog-eat-dog worldview but also remained aloof from naturalism's egalitarian social impulse: the desire to produce literature that was close to the masses, thus making life, not literature, the subject of art.

Catholic journalists commonly listed three faults of modern fiction: it ignored universal law, glamorized evil, and ultimately, perverted truth. Concealed under the facade of "brilliant style," "the atmosphere which these books brings is so murky and unsettled that it is difficult to see clearly the great moral issues which are brought into question," claimed the *Pilot*.[67] These comments point to the fact that Catholics could not envision novels that were not vehicles for the presentation and resolution of some moral and even explicitly doctrinal dilemma. Orestes Brownson had once observed that Catholics could object on grounds of taste to "those petty Catholic tales which mix up a poorly managed story with a dull, commonplace, and superficial discussion," but not "on the score of morals, and we would never discourage their production."[68] The tradition of the moralizing Catholic novel endured among Brownson's Catholic descendants. Father Michael Earls, for example, in *Marie of the House d'Anters* (1916) "proved" Christ's divinity through his prophecies; in *Melchior of Boston* (1910) described the conversion of a husband in a mixed marriage through a spiritual awakening during his child's school play; and in *The Wedding Bells of Glendalough* (1913) explored the topic of religious vocations.[69] Father Hugh Blunt's novels and plays followed a similar apologetic approach. Katherine Conway's fiction was somewhat more realistic, offering nearly autobiographical accounts of the prejudice encountered in daily life by Catholics in urban America. A review of her *The Way of the World* even observed approvingly that the topic was treated "with much humor, and we imagine with but little caricature."[70] Still, truth always triumphed in Catholic novels, often through the favorite contrivance of the deathbed conversion. Mrs. Hartley, a character in *The People of Our Parish*, humorously cataloged these "well-worn situations": "Lovers who separate because of a difference of religion, only to come together after years of suffering have brought to the unbeliever the gift of faith, stand easily first; the superhumanly good governess or saleswoman who inherits a fortune, forgives her rich and vulgar persecutors, and married the heir to a great house, makes a good second. Saving a train from destruction by discovering a boulder across the track, and walking miles in the snow to warn somebody, is not an unpopular device."[71] It seems that the authors of travel literature or adventure stories, such as J. J. Roche's tales of the Spanish filibusters and James Connolly's stories of Gloucester fishermen, escaped the clichés and demands of apologetics. John Boyle O'Reilly's first published poems in *Songs from the Southern Seas* (1873) also fit this mold.[72] While most of Roche's writing echoes his peer John Boyle O'Reilly, both Roche and Connolly imitated the brand of American manly adventure fiction popularized by Richard Harding Davis, who expressed the confident and imperialist mood of the 1890s. Just as Davis glibly reported foreign wars to eager American audiences without probing beneath the complacency and imperialism of the Gilded Age, so Catholic counterparts of Davis remained unawakened to the possibilities of a realist fiction that attacked social inequality and exposed the excesses of industrial capitalism. It is not surprising that Theodore Roosevelt, despite his association with Progressivism, preferred the Kiplingesque fiction of Davis and Connolly to that of the muckrakers, whom he denounced. Catholics, likewise, by finding a moral neutrality in moderate doses of adventure fiction, thus allied Catholic authors with the ahistorical idealism of the bourgeoisie.

After condemning the secular novelist on moral grounds, Catholics objected to the cultivated individualism of modern prose and poetry. Catholics further rejected the claims of modernists that art need not have a "true" ontological basis before becoming art; that an artist need not formulate or embody a metaphysics or a code of ethics; and that art is essentially subjective, and not an objective emanation from God. In this contest over aesthetic philosophy, Catholics saw their novels as antidotes to gross individualism, moral relativism, subjectivism, and anti-Catholicism. Modern Catholic writers accepted what Brownson had stated: "A novel or a poem, such as we can conceive it, would, in the present state of the reading world, do more to enable our religion to assume its proper place in American life, than the theological treatise or the polemical tract, however able or learned."[73] Katherine Conway, for example, affirmed in "The Literature of Moral Loveliness" that "half the civilized world takes its religion, morals, social theories and practice from popular literature."[74] As American Catholics began to observe popular culture, perhaps somewhat more openly than European Catholics, they at least recognized its potential power over mass audiences in their efforts to protect readers from its corrupting influences, at the same time when they struggled to define themselves culturally.

What Catholics deplored as realism meant something different to its practitioners. Even harsher than attacks on realism was Catholic hostility to naturalism. Although Catholic writers had expressed doubts about the "ultra-romantic school of fiction of the past generation" that "gave false views of life,"[75] their own fiction resembled those Victorian sentimental romances whose stock in trade included exotic foreign locales, ages past, pious gentility, and formulaic happy endings. What Catholics denounced as naturalism were extreme examples of sensationalist journalism, many of which were condemned by respectable non-Catholic critics as well.[76] To a large degree, Catholic criticism reflected a surrounding climate of aesthetic opinion. In fact, the American reading public's support for a revival of romantic fiction represented a reaction against realism, and an ideological product of periods of American economic prosperity. Because Catholics also disliked the excesses of the popular romance, it seems that they should have applauded the American realists' desire to make fiction more congruent with real life[77] and to rescue public taste from its foolish preference for romance and fantasy that was exploited by greedy and unscrupulous publishers.

However, Catholics preferred the morality tale to realism because they believed in the direct relationship of art and action articulated in the formulas of Gioberti, Brownson, Earls, and all adherents to neoscholastic principles. Because Catholicism defended the contingent relationship of art and morality, and of truth and beauty, it failed to develop a vital realist tradition and resorted to defending the purity of a Catholic subculture against the evil potential of mass secular culture. Unfortunately, none of the American literary giants of the 1920s or 1930s who were Catholics, whether converts or lapsed, fit comfortably within the bounds of Catholic tradition. Theodore Dreiser, F. Scott Fitzgerald, Eugene O'Neill, and James T. Farrell either rejected the Church's influence or continued to be obsessed by it from a negative viewpoint. "True" Catholics possessed none of the cynicism present in Fitzgerald, a disenchanted Catholic, whose Nick Carraway returns to the unspoiled Midwest at the conclusion of *The Great Gatsby,* but only as an ironic salute to a past that can never exist again. For Catholics, to make an analogy, the image of America's evergreen, ahistorical moral landscape had not yet soured into Fitzgerald's sense of the loss of a fresh, uncommon New World. Clearly, Catholic emphasis on avoiding the "grotesque and the horrible" through "acquiring Catholic habits of thought" limited the subject matter of novels acceptable to a Catholic audience, but discussions generally ignored the parochial limits that such a Catholic novel would impose on its projected public. The Boston Catholic press and its writers appeared to mistrust the moral judgment of the lay masses and therefore expected the Catholic subculture to function as a haven from the profane world and a shelter from dreary realism or malcontent naturalism.

Father Daniel Hudson, who was converted to Catholicism by Emma Cary, became editor of *Ave Maria* at Notre Dame, Indiana, and was instrumental in providing national artistic guidelines for Catholics. With a wider lay readership than arid publications such as the *American Ecclesiastical Review, Ave Maria* represented the constancy of Catholic principles on the "apostolate of print." It stated that "most of us will agree that a story which presents the facts and relations of Catholic life truthfully, adequately, and without distortion, is desirable, if it have no bad qualities to overbalance its good ones." Accordingly, the magazine sought inspirational fiction to counteract Horatio Alger–style children's tales: "[Wealth's] desirability is sufficiently emphasized by a child's ordinary experience. There is no necessity to make it a prominent feature of his literature, of which the most important service should be to supply him with ideals of a spiritual type."[78] Catholic magazines attacked the dime novel and its appeal to young readers. Dozens of editorials condemning it appeared in the *Pilot* between 1907 and 1920. "This is an age of ephemeral literature," the paper complained in a typical diatribe. "No one doubts that most of this stuff that appeals to boys and then perverts them ought to be suppressed."[79] "No sensible person criticizes novel-reading itself," wrote Katherine Conway; yet the implication remained that one must choose between good and bad novels.[80] The Catholic press found that by consuming tawdry pulp fiction, the public was losing its taste for good literature: "An evil mind cannot appreciate the pure, the correct and the wholesome. The Catholic paper and the Catholic book thus becomes a bore."[81] Fearing the loss of Catholic readership to racier serials and tabloids, Catholic writers chastised the yellow press for printing lurid stories that had "adultery as their underlying motive, with inane advice to young women; with special articles from notorious actresses as to how men may be charmed; with 'poems of passion'; with essays on the new thought that are nothing but attacks upon the fundamental principles of Christianity."[82] Girls were warned about the dangers of becoming "as gross a novel-drunkard as that pale faced, furtive-eyed lad next door who devours bad books about gamblers and interesting Western desperadoes, or finders of treasure in lonely islands, and whose 'dreams' are fast fitting him for the reformatory."[83] Catholic nostalgia for the fixed ideals of the past, coupled with the belief that ethical/aesthetic principles were molded permanently in the human mind during childhood, soon inspired the extension of the criticism of the dime novel to all forms of mass or popular culture, including newspaper comics and movies. The *Pilot* protested: "The dime novel of other days was a real danger, but some of the moving pictures of today are a positive menace."[84] Letting a mere comic strip spark an angry editorial, the Catholic press commented that "the American mind is gradually drifting away from that sense of beauty in things artistic which was so well cultivated by the generation that is past. This sense of artistic beauty is implanted in the mind in childhood."[85]

While Catholicism's opposition to literature that appealed to the "basest senses and lowest minds" seems overstated and strident, it followed exactly from the Church's expectation of permanence, emotional uplift, and moral standards in art, encompassing pulp fiction as well as genteel writing and lofty religious tracts. As a contributor to the *Pilot* explained, "We expect the author to give us ideals, and with his skill in words transport us into happier moods."[86] A successful resistance to popular culture required the presence of three elements in a Catholic subculture: clericalism, lay deference in matters of moral purity, and shared concepts of human moral development. The hierarchy, supported by the clergy, reserved the right to govern a Catholic reader's taste: "Even his reading should be governed by religion," stated the *Pilot*.[87] While priests guarded the Church's body from pollution, within the family, parents were held responsible for determining the moral values of their children by providing suitable plastic, pictorial, and literary art at home. "A moment's reflection," Alice Hayes wrote, "is sufficient to show how tremendous is the influence of the printed page; and yet, young children are now allowed to select their own reading matter—their guardians appearing to think this of small importance so long as the child is absorbed in his book and doing no mischief. In a few years the result of this policy will become apparent; but the cause of the youth's downfall is far too often not even suspected."[88] The *Ave Maria* reported, "The impressions gained in childhood are those which last. . . . It is of the first importance that they should not be wrong impressions."[89] Advice to parents therefore included warnings against the newspaper comic supplements, which the press claimed gave children "a very exaggerated idea of the importance of a child in relation to grown people."[90] Catholics feared the vulnerability of children to films, dime novels, and comic strips, arguing that although taste could be educated, "not so the moral void that often finds its origins in these supplements." The encouragement of degeneracy in children, therefore, was an expression of a "lack of respect for age and authority, irreverence for traditions and institutions, and an absence of awe for anything sacred."[91] Judging by this commentary, the Church dismissed the emerging forms of mass entertainment with the claim that they corrupted innocence and undermined traditional hierarchies of moral authority. The Church also resisted the growing culture industry because it disrupted the Church's own control over a tradition of communal entertainments shared by families and parishes and following a liturgical calendar of festival and penitential days and seasons.

The virtues of preserving Church authority, clerical and parental power, innocence, idealism, and tradition ultimately guided a Catholic perspective about all cultural products. Literary modernism, as understood by Catholics, threatened a Catholic worldview by implying that nothing is sacred. By contrast, Catholics cherished the notion that everything is sacred. As the above quotation indicates, the Church resisted a world in which its authorities lost control of art: priests should direct the laity; parents should guide their families; children should respect their elders. A desire to preserve hierarchical religious and social relations and the genteel literary codes that corresponded to them was revealed in Catholics' nostalgia for premodern values: "What a glorious task for our Catholic writers, to create a new standard, or rather win back to the old standard that maintained ere tawdry materialism gained ascendancy!"[92] The medieval theological roots to the antimodern sentiments expressed in Catholic literary criticism help explain why the Catholic literary forms scarcely evolved from the safe sentimentalism and moral certitude of the previous century. They also suggest why middle-class Catholics opposed Progressive innovations such as muckraking journalism and naturalist fiction, which disclosed information about life's terrifying injustices, which might further stir up revolutionary feeling among the populace, and which made the unwelcome claim that the petit bourgeois businessman was about to be stymied by the forces of monopoly capital.

Production of a Catholic Subculture

Boston Catholics relied heavily on bourgeois institutions to sustain a Catholic aesthetic. As Catholics enjoyed greater economic success, they gained more control of civic institutions long dominated by Protestants, including the press and publishing. In the first instance, Catholics participated in the secular press, produced their own journalism, and contributed to the Irish American press, each element playing a part in monitoring a Catholic subculture.

Catholic reading circles and the summer school movement were perhaps the earliest institutions to reflect Catholic aesthetic sensibilities and to demarcate a Catholic middle class by regulating its reading habits. The reading groups became dominated by middle-class professional men and women teachers, "the pillars of the Catholic intellectual movement," and by merchants and convent-trained women "who would gladly continue that culture of mind for which they have acquired a bent."[93] Convert Alice Hayes gave her reading circle these typical suggestions: "I am not warning you against what is called light reading; for we all need this mental relaxation once in a while. Much wisdom may be wrapped in a story. But our bodies can not be nourished with bon-bons; and unless carefully watched, the reading habit become a dissipation merely. Neither is it necessary to warn any of this Circle against what are known as 'bad books;'—none of us would dream of touching one of these."[94] Humphrey Desmond's *Reading Circle Manual,* the first publication of the movement, recommended twelve salutary novels for Catholic readers, including *The Way of the World and Other Ways* by Katherine Conway.[95] Of the dozen, probably only *Callista* by Cardinal Newman is even marginally remembered. His nonfiction choices for the "Minimum Catholic Library" of twenty books for $25 listed almost entirely Catholic, Irish, and religious histories. In fiction, Desmond praised the leading British and American novelists, from Jane Austen to William Dean Howells, but concluded that "when we come to consider the shortness of life and the large number of good Catholic stories available, we are inclined to think that the craving for fiction can be almost supplied within the fold."[96] The *Pilot* stated the case more bluntly: "The Catholic author, though he be a very Shakespeare, will die if the Catholic people abandon him; he has no other audience."[97] By waging war on the social realism of the modern novel, and on the market they blamed for the tasteless extremes of modern journalism, the Church created its own rationale for a Catholic press. Nonetheless, debates about the parochialism of the Catholic novel and novelists and about the production of fiction for readers "within the fold" attest that Catholic separatism was not uniformly desired by Boston's Catholic authors.

The Catholic press debated the meaning of the Catholic component in artistic production. Some writers maintained that divine inspiration alone guided the writer, not market forces that reduced writers to professionals who sold their technical skills for a price. While this Catholic definition of literary endeavor served the economic function of isolating a religious stronghold against capitalism, Catholic journalism also served a class purpose of diffusing middle-class cultural norms to a wide audience. If not in absolute agreement on the artistic principles governing them, Catholics did defend the moral mission of the press to stand as a bulwark against political radicalism, as expressed by Walter Lecky in an 1895 essay, "Catholic Literature and Our Catholic Poor." After praising the Boston *Pilot* as an exemplary Catholic paper, he remarked, "Let us remember in these days, when socialism claims the poor, that our own Church is not alone for the cultured, it is pre-eminently her duty to lead and guide the masses. This, to a great extent, must be done by the newspaper and book stall."[98] By attempting to lead the masses, the Church did not have in mind the production of a populist literature; rather, it sought to indoctrinate the socially vulnerable with Catholic (and middle-class) principles of social harmony and good taste.

Boston's Catholic weekly press included two newspapers, the *Pilot,* founded in 1843, and the *Sacred Heart Review* (1888–1918). The *Republic* (1882–1926), the lively Democratic weekly owned by John Fitzgerald, was operated and staffed by Catholic laity. A monthly magazine, *Donahoe's* (1878–1908), hoped to provide "reading that will elevate and instruct the present and rising generations." The Knights of Columbus publication, *Columbiad*, was edited from Boston between 1882 and 1892. Catholic college magazines of Massachusetts, such as the Boston College *Stylus* and the Holy Cross *Purple*, molded Catholic opinion on art and literature for the upcoming generation. For young children, the Church had supported several ephemeral publications, such as the *Weekly Bouquet*, which folded for want of funds. All Catholic newspapers had advice columns aimed at different age groups: boys and girls, men and women. A remarkable unanimity governed the Catholic press because its staffs and contributors were almost identical: O'Reilly, Roche, Conway, Blake, Crowley, O'Sullivan, Emery, McCarthy, Riley, Toomey, Blunt, and Earls served as editors and sometime magazine publishers as well as freelance authors. Because of financial necessity and the often ephemeral duration of Catholic magazines, journalists were typically associated with several publications in their careers. This overlap also made possible a strong sense of religious unity and communal consciousness.

One the whole, Catholic periodicals were strongest on doctrinal detail and weakest on current events and news analysis. As a notice in the *Sacred Heart Review* stated, "A Catholic journal is something more than a newspaper. It is first and before all an exponent of Catholic truth."[99] There was no daily Catholic press, and some Catholics complained that "the religious weeklies have practically no local secular news."[100] This lack of coverage is hardly surprising, given the Church's dim view of the daily news and its coverage of "murder after murder, one more odious crime succeeding another."[101] Attacks on the dailies had appeared as early as the 1880s, often in manuals for men, advising them what their wives and children should not read.

The local Catholic press was supplemented by national periodicals such as Notre Dame's *Ave Maria*, the Paulists' *Catholic World, American Catholic Quarterly Review, Magnificat, Messenger of the Sacred Heart, Queen's Work,* and *Benziger's Weekly.* These publications reinforced ethical opinion in cultural matters through their literary columns and critical essays; through book, theater, and film reviews; and through their editorial choices of serial fiction, short plays, and poems.[102] Magazines clearly served as vehicles of religious identity. Where *Brownson's Quarterly Review* had legitimated book reviews for which the books themselves served "as little more than an occasion or a text for an original discussion of some question which the author wishes to treat," new departments in newspapers helped Catholics construct a sense of peoplehood through identification with a Catholic literary heritage.[103] Beginning in 1893 Conway's *Pilot* column introduced readers to Catholic authors, as did her subsequent contributions to the *Republic* for its "Chats about Some Books and Authors."[104] The *Pilot*'s transition from an immigrant paper to one serving Catholic America is revealed by the fact that it ceased its Irish county-by-county news reports and Gaelic language department after about 1909 and focused more exclusively on diocesan religious affairs. The *Sacred Heart Review* Gaelic column survived until somewhat later. As Irish journalism crossed into some vaguely defined new territory of Catholic journalism, it began to differentiate new functions for Catholics as cultural critics and censors as well as creators of a canon. Poet Joyce Kilmer, for example, claimed that "when a magazine that has a good reputation prints an article in which some accomplished writer advocates free love or turns his scorn on law and religion, or a story in which Christianity and morality are attacked, then trained critics writing for our Catholic press should warn their readers that this particular issue of the magazine is one to avoid. This sort of criticism would eventually have a beneficial effect on the magazines criticized, and it would at once prevent Catholic readers from innocently spending their money for attacks on the things most dear to them."[105] American Catholic publishers, however, struggling for enough copy to fill their issues, were forced to reprint heavily from English and Irish Catholic journals, notably the *Month,* the *Tablet,* and the *Dublin Review,* all published in London; *Irish Monthly* (Dublin); and the *Irish Review.* As recently as the 1880s, American weeklies like *Ave Maria* had been composed "almost entirely of translations from the French."[106] By one calculation, approximately one-third of American Catholic fiction prior to 1895 first appeared in serial form, before Catholic papers were able to supply short fiction regularly.[107] Reliant upon imported content, the American Catholic press was obliged to respond to events affecting European Catholics. Some of these issues were alien to the daily lives of Americans but served nonetheless to increase the impression of the universal Church's battle for moral artistic standards. Through its editorials about foreign and local events and publications, the Catholic press of Boston acted paternalistically "to aid their charges in cultivating a correct ethical taste in reference to works of art, either of pictorial or plastic character."[108]

College literary magazines were sponsored and supervised by the Jesuits at Boston College and Holy Cross. The contents of the Boston College *Stylus,* founded in 1883, illustrate how Catholic young men were imbued with the ethical bases of artistic perception and criticism. For example, the front page editorial for the twenty-fifth anniversary issue asserted:

In college life the magazine has come to be a great factor and can be an influence for good or evil according to the ideals which it holds. In literature, as in all things else, there must be logic. Beauty and moral good must go together, beauty and moral evil can never consort. The end of poetry is the portrayal of the beautiful, and hence if moral evil be praised in any poem, or inculcated in the least by any story or essay, just in so far as they do this so they fall away from that ideal which every writer should hold before his eyes.[109]

Published from October to July, each monthly issue of the *Stylus* featured essays, reviews, and poems by students, faculty, and alumni, which reproduced Catholic aesthetic opinion. In one example, a student's review of George Bernard Shaw's *Mrs. Warren's Profession* condemned the play for focusing on the "melancholy and morose" aspects of life.[110] A review of a Catholic novel praised an author for offsetting, "in a Catholic way, the false picturing of the Gospel narrative."[111] The *Stylus* was optimistic about the arrival of a demotic Catholic writer: "It is the generation that is coming which will complete the work inaugurated and give to the world a Catholic literature that shall be not only sound and interesting, but popular."[112]

The Holy Cross *Purple,* moderated by Father Michael Earls from 1913 to 1932, indicated that students in Worcester likewise approved of the marriage of morality and aesthetics and mastered the discourse of Catholic optimism and triumphalism. Earls had also been a student editor of the *Purple* during the 1890s. According to its masthead, the *Purple* sought "to cultivate a high literary spirit among the students by exercising them in both critical and creative composition." Like the *Stylus,* its pages were full of earnest editorials, pious poems, detailed athletic summaries, and hyperbolic commentary on the importance of the college literary magazine. Undergraduate James A. Crotty claimed that "the college paper is as important a cog in the complex mechanism of college life as even athletics, and there is probably no student activity which bestows more direct rewards upon its pursuer in immediate afterlife than this primary training in the rudiments of literature."[113] Although the historians of Holy Cross College defended Earls's character against charges of Catholic ghettoism, his contribution as the son of Irish immigrants bore the marks of sentimentalism and insiderism. Although he brought prominent guests to the college, such as Irish tenor John McCormick and English apologist G. K. Chesterton, his rambling essays predictably attacked the "glib cleverness" and puerile parodies of modern journalism, literature, and vaudeville.[114] As a self-proclaimed intellectual, Earls seemed to aspire to the status of Canon Sheehan in Ireland. But was there a similar niche for an educated, freethinking priest in the United States?

With a readership of clergy, alumni, and students, literary magazines served the dual function of forging a Catholic readership and of training morally responsible Catholic men.[115] Since the future of Catholic literature required a healthy relationship between writers and readers, the Catholic college was seen as the means to create "the intelligent and educated Catholics whom we

Poet-priest Michael Earls, right, shows off his guest, G. K. Chesterton, at Holy
Cross College. "And what other poet have you ever known whose practical sense of
values would keep photographs of Chesterton at Holy Cross running for seven con-
secutive Sundays in the rotogravure section of the New York *Times*?" (Obituary for
Earls in *The Holy Cross Alumnus*, February–March 1937, Holy Cross College
Archives)

The senior debating team, Holy Cross College, 1907–8, posed formally to affect the proper scholarly and gentlemanly tone. (Holy Cross College Archives)

would call the intellectual aristocracy among our people."[116] Through the *Stylus* and the *Purple,* colleges worked to build an educated aristocracy of Catholic writers and poets. Catholic students attending local non-Catholic colleges like Harvard, Tufts, and MIT were not ignored. They founded Catholic clubs that sponsored lectures and socials as substitutes for the literary magazine. Rev. William Byrne, for example, addressed Harvard students in 1892 on authority as a medium of religious knowledge.[117] The Technology Catholic Club at MIT, founded in 1906, secured "speakers of prominence" on "subjects of current interest which may or may not have reference to religion."[118] The reports of Catholic lay associations expressed concern that Catholic education transmit stable values to students: "Look to it, you fathers of American college boys. Insist that the minds of your sons be not debased. Steer clear of the school that tolerate within its precincts the pagan idea of the materialistic conception of history, either through addle-brained professors or the Socialistic chapter. It is up to you to demand that Marxism, immorality and disloyalty to the religion of your fathers, or to your country, shall not be tolerated in any form."[119]

Joyce Kilmer, the convert poet who died in World War I combat, claimed in one of numerous articles about becoming a writer that "the Catholic young man who attends a non-Catholic college is deliberately ignoring his prospects as a writer."[120] In reality, the college literary societies were less successful at generating a Catholic literary establishment than Kilmer's remark suggests. Only a small percentage of Boston College and Holy Cross graduates pursued literary careers. Alumni who became clergy, lawyers, and physicians far outnumbered the authors, poets, and journalists combined, suggesting once again a split between the Church's ideals and lay experience.[121] Between 1880 and 1900 the percentage of Irish Americans who achieved success in letters was only 5.7 percent. In journalism the percentage was 10 percent, compared with 27.1 percent in business and 14 percent in law.[122] Of course, some of the 33 percent who became priests published essays, fiction, and poetry, but these were not subject to competitive review. Further, the college magazines, under Jesuit guidance, fostered a conformist literary-aesthetic code among its writers and readers, which attempted to mold its graduates' lifetime standards for reading and interpretation, and which was more pervasive than graduates' career choices indicate. A student's query epitomized the success of the Church's efforts: "What is the norm according to which we measure literary effort? It is the great and unchanging norm of the Catholic Church."[123] Maintaining moral standards and universal ideals was essential to the Catholic view of writing, because if art was reinterpreted as morally neutral, it would no longer fall under the Church's teaching authority and the purview of moral theology.

While college magazines reproduced devotional poetry and idealist prose for captive audiences for generations to come, other Catholic projects overestimated the bullishness of the Catholic market. One casualty was initiated by Ralph Adams Cram, who in 1907 inaugurated *Christian Art* through the Gorham Press of Boston. Inspired, perhaps, by the quality of the publications of the Kelmscott Press of the English Arts and Crafts movement, the magazine was lavishly illustrated with photographs, prints, and architectural renderings of churches, altar screens, and baptismal fonts and with drawings and photographs of vestments, tapestries, reredos, and stained glass. Cram and his contributors believed in the "ministry of art" wherein "as all art must serve some teaching purpose, for good or evil, it is an error in Church architecture to neglect its high purpose as an instrument of teaching the faith."[124] *Christian Art* featured articles by two Boston Catholic friends of Cram: essayist Louise Guiney and architect Charles Maginnis, who built collegiate Gothic at Boston College while Cram was Gothicizing Princeton University. Cram and Guiney agreed that Catholics should own and publish the magazine. "It is time we controlled a thing of this sort, and it would be simply an inspiration to the Church in America," Guiney wrote.[125] The magazine never flourished, however. Two years later, when it was "doomed to die unless somebody buys it for $5000," Guiney suggested the leading Anglo-Catholic matron of Boston, Isabella Stewart Gardner, as a purchaser. Guiney also begged her friend Frank Fitzpatrick to buy it and make his son the editor.[126] Presumably because the magazine had less than 1,000 subscribers, high production costs, and profits of less than $100 per month, Fitzpatrick declined. The original publisher even reduced subscription rates from $5 to $3 per year and increased the advertisements in order to boost sales. When Cardinal O'Connell gave a gift subscription to a local architect, the recipient was grateful and admitted the prohibitive cost of ordering the magazine for himself.[127] Nothing apparently came of Guiney's rescue efforts, and the magazine folded in December 1908.[128] Thus Boston's attempt to support a journal aimed at Catholic connoisseurs, Protestant ritualists, and amateur architectural historians was met with little interest and departed unremarked, except by Cram and Guiney, who "lamented the deceased immoderately."[129] Aside from its class limitations, Christian Art may have failed in part because of Catholics' campaign to protect the sanctity of the printed and spoken word (seen in their crusades against literary obscenity). The power of words, expressed ritually in liturgy and prayer, and in journalism, poetry, and fiction, may have lowered attention to the visual arts, especially in a journal of high price and limited appeal. The fate of Christian Art was repeated in the failure of a second publication, the Dolphin, suggesting that Catholics nationwide had only a fledgling "intellectual aristocracy." The Dolphin, a lay version of the erudite but tedious American Ecclesiastical Review, had been initiated in Philadelphia in 1901 by the editors of the Review. In 1905 the staff decided to suspend the Dolphin in order to devote full attention to a new journal, Church Music, created to promote the liturgical reforms recently suggested by Pius X. Church Music also failed, in 1909. Louise Guiney hoped that the Dolphin would then be revived, since in her opinion it was the best of the American Catholic publications. Nonetheless, the Dolphin became extinct.[130]

The Catholic Writer and Publisher

Always alert for signs of anti-Catholicism in print, Catholics debated another criterion for a canon of acceptable literature: it must be written by Catholics. Catholics looked for sympathetic portrayals of Catholics in secular novels, but rarely found them; in response they overpraised their own writers. The Reading Circle Manual explained the dangers of secular fiction: "Why of course the Catholic reader may go outside the list of purely Catholic novelists; moreover, hundreds do so, and it is to be regretted that they wander towards muddy brooks instead of towards clear and limpid waters."[131] The Boston Pilot advanced its opinion of the superiority of Catholic fiction: "For our historical novels we do not have to depend on Scott or the bigoted Kingsley. The period with which they so frequently dealt has been covered by [Robert Hugh] Benson, who grows more wonderful each day since his premature death."[132] Thus, particular English, Irish, and American Catholic writers began to acquire a reputation greater than their individual talents and were vigorously promoted by the Church, which carefully avoided problematic texts not fitting the orthodox mold.

Catholics did not ignore the American literary canon altogether. Certain authors who appeared to express a Catholic spirit fared well with critics. For example, Katherine Conway claimed that Nathaniel Hawthorne's *Scarlet Letter* was "the greatest religious novel thus far produced in America," but only because "you can see his sympathy with Catholic ideals, which flowered out later so splendidly in the Marble Faun, and which let us hope, won for him through God's mercy what his convert Catholic daughter and her convert husband would most desire for him."[133] Hawthorne's critical view of Puritanism and his curiosity about Catholic rituals and traditions allowed Catholics to welcome him as a fellow traveler. The novels of Henry James and William Dean Howells were also recommended, with some exceptions. Hawthorne, Howells, and James fared better than Edith Wharton and Mark Twain, who were criticized for their anti-Catholic characters or sentiments. The Catholic press often denounced Twain for his admission that he was "educated to enmity toward everything Catholic."[134] A critic for the *Pilot* agreed that "a Catholic will always admire Mark Twain with reservations." A reviewer stated that Twain's *Joan of Arc* was well intentioned but poorly executed; the same commentator remarked cryptically that *Innocents Abroad* "reeked of Missouri mud."[135]

The bulk of contemporary fiction, Catholic critics contended, was not of high caliber. Though fiction represented only 10 percent of the total number of books published in the United States in 1911, the *Pilot* lamented that "the pity is then that of the fiction there should be so much that is irretrievably worthless."[136] Boston's Catholic newspaper created a memorable metaphor in referring to "the fiction faucet, the pouring out of a flood of insipid, muddy stuff, because a public will drink from that reservoir alone." The Catholic press was not wholly clear where to lay the blame—with the public for drinking from the faucet or with the publishers for producing a steady stream of junk fiction—but they concurred that one antidote was more Catholic novels and Catholic publishers. As one author asked, "If Protestants can make cheap books, thereby creating the market, why not Catholics?"[137]

Boston did not become the home for Catholic firms that would become leaders in Catholic publishing, which is not surprising given the Anglophilic, aristocratic, and regional orientation of the American literary establishment and publishing network.[138] Catholic enterprises eventually centered in New York City and the Midwest. In New York, for example, were concentrated P. J. Kenedy, Paulist Press, Benziger Brothers, Devin-Adair, D. & J. Sadlier, W. J. Sadlier, and Sheed and Ward. In Milwaukee there was Bruce Publishing Company; in Detroit, Walter Romig; in St. Louis, Herder and Herder. Boston could boast only several vanity presses that served the Catholic community: the Pilot Publishing Company, Thomas J. Flynn, George Ellis, and the Angel Guardian Press. Increasingly in the early 1900s, however, Catholics observed that prestigious Boston publishers like Houghton Mifflin, Ticknor, and Little, Brown "have shown a willingness to accept good Catholic manuscripts."[139] The Boston *Republic* listed Longmans, Green of London and New York and Dodd, Mead as "glad to give their imprint to the work of a well known Catholic author, whether it be a novel, a book of travels, or even now and then, of devotion."[140] Catholic poet Denis McCarthy secured an important position as an editor for Ginn and Company in Boston in 1923 and in 1926 became head of its new Catholic book division.[141] Three years later, Mary Boyle O'Reilly went so far as to consider selling her latest book via the mass-marketing techniques of her friend department store entrepreneur Edward Filene, "who will be much interested in the theme. And the idea of getting books out through the department stores, the Five & Ten, etc., is a thing he is deeply interested in."[142] In general, however, O'Reilly's aggressive merchandising strategy was the exception. New national emphasis on the sale of best-sellers in the publishing industry did not seem to have benefited Irish American (or Catholic) authors.[143]

As the rise of a culture industry gave birth to mass-marketed literature of all types, Catholics searched for alternatives to the fiction faucet by promoting their own novelists and publishers. The quest inspired a spirited three-way debate in 1909 on the relationship of the Catholic writer to the Catholic press. Should Catholic writers patronize it exclusively, or should they follow the market and publish wherever they could? Similar positions were taken by Louise Guiney and Agnes Repplier in response to Rev. John Talbot Smith's astringent article, "The Young Catholic Writer; What Shall He Do?"[144] For Catholics anticipating the ascent of the Catholic novelist, Talbot's remarks were a blow. Used to seeing themselves as possessing eternal truths that justified their hierarchical moral standards of literary criticism, Catholics were affronted by reprimands from within the faith. It was the secular writer who was commonly condemned as "a faddist," who "eagerly grasps and fondles each new idea, theme, fancy, or what-not and shouts: Here is Salvation!" The dutiful Catholic, on the contrary, believed that "a sane choice will surely end with the exaltation of the Catholic novelist because he has been humble and truthful, and the rejection of the secular novelist because he has been arrogant and unreliable."[145]

Father Smith took a dimmer view. He denied not only the existence of an American Catholic press but even its potential to emerge, based on the dismal state of Catholic publishing: "The weekly journals of the United States vary from simply respectable to mere rot. They pay no contributors. All the work is done by one or two poorly paid editors. The news is clipped and, occasionally, but not often, rearranged from the secular press; their departments are also clipped; they print very little original matter, none of them asks for it, and none of them pays for contributions."[146] The perhaps 10 million reading Catholics in the United States, of a total 18 million, Smith calculated, could easily sustain a large corps of Catholic writers and magazines. Instead, he claimed that there were really only six decent magazines for Catholics, which fifty writers kept in business. As a result, would-be Catholic writers turned to the secular press, which promised payment, circulation, and esteem while the Catholic press and publishers failed to induce contributors to stay with them. "The Catholic writers of the past are forgotten, and those of the present are without honor or income," he stated. But the Catholic writer also suffered prejudice from the secular publishers, who "refuse recognition to Catholic writers by instinct." Paradoxically, it was in the secular realm that the Catholic writer had to gain recognition before a Catholic audience would read him or her. Therefore, Smith advised, "let our young writer conceal his faith for a time from publishers and public, shut off all expression of it in his books, and win his place as a 'nothingarian'."[147]

Smith was known and admired in Boston, numbering Katherine Conway among his friends from the founding days of the reading circles and summer school. Expatriate Louise Guiney, however, was angered by Smith's callous "acrobatic ethics." Her response to him, published four months later in *Catholic World,* charged that it was a myth to assume that 18 (or even 10) million Catholics thought, or ought to think, as a unit. According to Guiney, a Catholic, like "the vast bulk of his Protestant compatriots," was affected by the accelerating pace of American existence and lived "in a chronic tearing hurry. People read, if they read at all, only light magazines and vapid novels: and he—well, he is people! He fails to read Catholic books, not because these are Catholic, but because they are likely to stir up serious thoughts, and are by that token a bore. We are all external, superficial, in this brilliant semi-civilization of ours: we fight shy of solid religious literature, not as Catholics but as Americans."[148] Guiney charged that Smith's imaginary Young Writer would gain nothing from sojourning with nonbelievers and that he would have betrayed his soul by concealing his faith. She therefore dismissed Smith's subterfuge as a Faustian compromise. Repplier agreed, noting that "opportunism is not the noblest force in life, nor is it the lesson of all others which Americans need most to learn."[149]

Guiney's proposal, reflecting her own experience, was "to amalgamate organically and commercially, with those brethren of ours over seas whose language and laws we share: the Catholics of Great Britain." She found the English to be "a more spiritual society," less superficial than Americans, and braver about living their faith. Yet, because the public consumed fiction indiscriminately, she claimed that the Young Writer must "quite accept, as part of his future campaign, the ultimate and essential estrangement between the faith and the world."[150] Although a recent interpreter has singled out Guiney as the purest example of literary Celticism in America, here her Anglophilia seems to predominate.[151] Guiney's yearning to import the "elevated" taste of British Catholicism to the United States was already more of a fact than she admitted. Despite ethnocentrism among Boston's Irish Catholics and the beloved status of Irish canon Patrick Sheehan's novel *My New Curate* (1899), the American Irish were already reading and reprinting numerous English authors. One confirmation of their Anglophilia is the comparative fates of the literary reputations of Cardinal Newman and Orestes Brownson. Brownson, who converted a year before Newman, received far less attention from his native country. Instead, Americans devoured the writings of Cardinals Newman and Wiseman, poets Gerard Manley Hopkins and Aubrey de Vere, Monsignor Robert Hugh Benson, Wilfrid Ward and Josephine Ward, Alice Meynell, Coventry Patmore, Father Bernard Vaughan, and somewhat later, G. K. Chesterton and Hillaire Belloc, nearly all acquaintances of Guiney while she lived in England. A young Catholic writer from San Francisco agreed with Guiney that "even today, in comparatively non-Catholic England, they are much more courageous than ourselves" in confronting a nonsectarian audience.[152] Similarly, the *Republic* reported that "English Catholics are far ahead of us as yet, in the production of a literature, while Catholic in expression, is yet so excellent from the purely literary standpoint as to command the attention of the general public."[153] The American image of British Catholics as heroically triumphing over religious and social oppression was borne out by enthusiastic welcomes in Boston for the lecture tours of Monsignor Benson in 1913, Wilfrid Ward in 1914, and Cardinal Bernard Vaughan from 1911 to 1913. Additionally, American Catholic publishers began to imitate the format of English catechetical question-and-answer texts on Catholicism employed by the Catholic Truth Society of Great Britain, as well as the device of publishing inexpensive series of books on Catholic history and doctrine. In 1911 publication of the *American Catholic Who's Who* followed its English prototype of 1908.

While expressing envy at the success of English Catholic sectarianism, and despite complaints about anti-Catholic bias in the American press, many of Boston's Catholics found employment there, and perhaps greater economic security. The percentage of Boston Catholic writers and poets who established reputations in both Catholic and secular markets was high, suggesting that prejudice was more imagined than real. In fact, Katherine Conway insisted, by the mid-1920s Catholics had made their mark in "high class periodical literature."[154] Louise Guiney, for example, had published articles in *Atlantic Monthly, Blackwood's, Harper's, Living Age, Month, Nation, Notes and Queries,* and *Scribner's.* Her poetry appeared in *Atlantic Monthly, Century, Current Literature, Harper's, Independent, Lippincott's, McClure's, Nation, Poetry,* and *Scribner's.* Mary Elizabeth Blake was a columnist for the *Boston Journal* and the *Boston Gazette* and contributed to the *North American Review* and *Scribner's.* Mary Conroy published her poems in Boston's most Brahmin paper, the *Evening Transcript.* Thomas Ackland, an assistant editor of the *Pilot* under Roche and Conway, wrote on Catholicism and Irish Americans for the Sunday and weekly daily newspapers. Michael J. Dwyer, a district attorney for Suffolk County by 1911, had been a reporter for the Boston *Herald* as well as editor of *Donahoe's Magazine.*[155] Boston's police commissioner, Stephen O'Meara, had begun his career climb as a cub reporter before becoming editor in chief of the *Boston Journal,* and his brother worked for the *Boston Herald.*[156] Denis McCarthy had contributed poems to *Life* and the *New York Sun.* James Riley wrote for the *Transcript, Independent* and *McClure's* as well as serving as a coeditor of a Catholic children's magazine. Mary Catherine Crowley published in the *Boston Globe* as Janet Grant and wrote for the *Ladies' Home Journal.*

The Massachusetts Catholic who probably had the widest public readership was James Brendan Connolly (1868–1957), born in South Boston of immigrant parents and known for his traveling correspondent assignments and adventure stories. Demonstrating youthful athletic prowess in winning gold and silver medals at the Olympic Games of 1896 and 1900, Connolly subsequently served as a correspondent for *Scribner's* in Europe in 1901, for *Harper's* in the Arctic Ocean in 1902, for *Collier's* in Mexico in 1914, and in European waters during World War I. His short story "The Trawler" won *Collier's* competition in 1914, selected by Theodore Roosevelt, one of the competition's judges, because of its "elevation of sentiment, rugged knowledge of rugged men, strength and finish of writing."[157] Connolly later wrote for *Harper's, Outlook,* and the *Saturday Evening Post,* but he is best remembered for his tales of the hardy Gloucester fishermen and sailors who were his father's friends. Ironically, Connolly's work had wide popular appeal due to its subject matter, which reflected rising naturalist values of virility, physical challenge, and competition rather than the perspectives of sentimentalism or ethnicity.

It also reflected a growing market for escapist romances projected onto sea-faring ancestors whose world was far simpler than the urban ghetto of Connolly's background. In sum, Connolly's writing reflected the contradictions in the social philosophy of naturalism rather than the dilemmas of Catholic separatism. Though the child of Irish immigrants, Connolly set his novels in locales that were neither ethnic nor even very precisely detailed.[158] One wonders if fellow Catholic writers envied his success and tacitly agreed that all genres of fiction did not have to defend Catholic truth and the Irish.

By 1925, challenges from Catholics who questioned the faith of those who wrote for any paying press were few but persistent. Some Catholic critics sniped that convert Charles Warren Stoddard wrote for *Ave Maria* with one hand and for *Atlantic Monthly* with the other.[159] Denis McCarthy admitted in an interview in 1929 that as a struggling immigrant, "Writing came to me haphazard. It was largely an economic urge."[160] Mary Boyle O'Reilly, on the other hand, resented Louise Guiney's turning away from her Irish heritage and at her most spiteful had accused President Lowell of Harvard of being a British spy.[161] However, these claims of apostasy were generally not serious: the real differences between Catholic and non-Catholic markets for literature seem to have been slight, except where doctrinal issues were at stake. Encouraging signs that the secular press was softening its anti-Catholic, anti-Irish attitude led Katherine Conway to state, "If I could have only one monthly magazine, I would take the Atlantic Monthly. For one reason its intellectual hospitality is broader. Moreover there have been fair and excellent articles on the Sinn Fein Movement, the founding of the Irish Free State, and notable individuals as Arthur Griffith, De Valera and Michael Collins."[162] Among the educated Catholics of the archdiocese there was a sense that their submissions could be accepted without discrimination for the most genteel magazines, which in turn served as the stepping stone to publication of a novel. In Boston, lay Catholics could justly boast that much of the daily press was in their control. Even Archbishop O'Connell had a "kept reporter" at the *Boston Globe*.[163] Although many Irish Americans preferred the tabloid dailies, the *Globe*'s editorial staff was dominated by Irish Catholics from the 1890s onward: William D. Sullivan was the city editor from 1889 to 1926; William F. Kenney, the day editor from 1888 to 1918; and Agnes Mahan, the women's editor from 1908 to 1953. Tim Murnane and James O'Leary covered baseball, and John O'Callaghan, former publisher of the *Bunker Hill Times*, became the chief writer on Irish affairs.[164]

Having gained some footholds in New England's secular journals, Catholics were still combating a nativist and explicitly anti-Catholic press that had emerged in the South and Midwest in the 1910s. Publications such as Tom Watson's *The Menace* led Catholics to launch national campaigns to remove it from circulation. In Boston, several anti-Catholic publications were circulated, one by the Protestant Education League, a nativist group active around 1910, which in part provoked the Knights of Columbus to launch a national campaign to eradicate bigotry in the press. The Knights reported in 1915 that most decent magazines that published Catholic contributors had likewise "become interested in the movement to eliminate religious prejudice."[165]

As Catholic higher education specialized, it provided a professional means to increase Catholic representation in journalism. By 1919, Catholics were promoting new journalism schools at their own universities, namely Marquette and Notre Dame.[166] The Boston *Republic* reported: "Some may say: 'Why the need of distinctly Catholic journalists in the secular press? Isn't the daily press representing Catholic interests fairly?' Whereto, we answer with all respect: 'We believe in the good intentions of the secular press towards Catholics, but there are certain matters of great interest to Catholics which only well equipped Catholics can properly present.'"[167] Thus, Catholics of this generation who felt that they had won significant battles against exclusion from mainstream journals now demanded contradictorily that the uniqueness of their beliefs affirmed their right to special treatment by sympathetic insiders.

Catholic Books and the Market

In theological discourse, these debates about Catholic writers and publishers demonstrated that the Church wanted members to subsume every aspect of life within the realm of the sacred in order to properly glorify God. In economic discourse, Catholic publishers already seem to have conceded to the theory that supply creates demand. Catholic authors therefore began to respect the wishes of their growing audience, who wanted something more than pious claptrap and who exerted a degree of market pressure. Catholic journalism, as we have seen, expanded the audience for the lay-led discussions of art and literature begun by the reading circles in the 1890s, without necessarily improving the quality of Catholic literature. Moreover, although American Catholic authors and publishers had succeeded in making a market for themselves, they were still heavily reliant on foreign contributors.

In discussing the relationship of the Church to literature, one Boston convert conceived a fruitful simile of the Church as text: "The Church itself is a great book—or rather, a library—of art, history, law, biography; why need her children shut themselves between the covers of a volume?"[168] This attitude inspired attempts to get Catholics to buy and read the literature of their own faith, whether devotional classics or fiction. Despite variations among Catholic elites, most American Catholics were accustomed to reading stories that functioned as sermons, and thus conformed to behavior expected of a cultural minority that used art as a branch of piety in order to maintain its distinctive identity.[169]

The Catholic literary generation coming of age at the turn of the century made the significant discovery of an audience—a new, middle-class Catholic reading public—that could choose to use literature for integrationist purposes, to accommodate Catholics to American culture, or to segregate Catholics from barbaric secular influences. The arguments against secular novelists and leisure amusements suggest that middle-class literary Catholics favored a genteel style that found a via media between romanticism and naturalism but that also indulged almost millennial speculations about how the fixed ideals of Catholicism could salvage an endangered American civilization. In their steadfast idealism, however, Catholic literary standards did not differ significantly from the "defenders of ideality" (in H. L. Mencken's pejorative phrase) found in numerous Boston-based periodicals such as *Atlantic Monthly, North American Review,* and *Century.*[170] Thus, even as Catholics professed the uniqueness of their idealism, their attempts at parochial isolation actually aligned them with the genteel segment of the literary mainstream that also opposed the subjective irrationalism of modernist art and literature. The publication of Catholic authors George Lathrop, Agnes Repplier, and Louise Guiney in magazines such as *Atlantic Monthly* suggests that their fiction reproduced the canons of middle-class taste. Unfortunately, the features of Catholic fiction that made it ethnic fiction as well were of short-lived interest to conservative publishers in the 1880s and 1890s, so that Irish writers received little support from their own establishment or from the non-Catholic market to develop a distinctive Irish American style of writing. When that did happen, in the late 1920s and 1930s, the trend was led by a generation of Irish American authors indifferent or hostile to Catholicism.

Some Catholics did make a surprisingly frank assessment of what Catholic literature offered to its readers, compared with mass-produced fiction. Until recently, the primary consumers of Catholic books in America had been the teaching orders of sisters and brothers, who gave them as gifts to pupils and used them to stock school libraries. "If it were not for these two sources of support, the situation of the Catholic book trade would be exceedingly precarious," stated one writer.[171] Though Catholic juvenile literature remained formulaic and didactic at this time, a growing awareness of the audience and the dynamics of market relations led lay Catholics to demonstrate market intuition and to employ mass-marketing techniques to sell religious fiction and poetry and to expand Catholic adult readership. But it appeared that the debate had reached an impasse on the question of who should initiate the process, the publisher or the reader. According to a Catholic layman, "Supply should precede to effect demand. It is thus with everything high and good. The missionary does not wait till there is a demand from the heathen before he goes with the Gospel."[172] Drawing a stark dichotomy between the stability of the Church's eternal artistic principles and the faddishness and ugliness of modern philosophies and writers, Catholics hoped that publishers would "leaven the American mass" by supplying Catholic publications even to Catholics accustomed to "too much tribal seclusion."[173] Boston Catholic opinions on the Catholic press included claims that it did not even exist (as Father Smith charged) or that it was not highbrow enough (as Ralph Adams Cram and Louise Guiney believed). Criticisms ranged from contentions that it did not feature enough secular news to complaints that it was wholly trivial;[174] from praise that it was trying to promote universal standards of excellence to allegations that it was becoming tediously apologetic. A fairly common complaint was that the Catholic press expended too much of its energy rebutting perceived enemies, based on the assumption that "anti-Catholicism of to-day means only too often atheism to-morrow."[175]

Prior to the 1920s, Boston Catholics remained divided on the best strategy toward the secular press. They seemed to veer between integrationism, which saw Catholics as leavening agents in the secular system, and separatism, demonstrated by the expansion of a Catholic network of local and national magazines.[176] But Catholics warned each other about the monotony of sectarian and overly pious literature: "It would be well, also, in certain cases, if our novelists and historians were less given to moralizing on every occasion. They can do immense good without laying bare on every page the innermost recesses of their souls."[177] Another columnist agreed: "Catholic fiction need not be a framework for the explanation of dogma or doctrine. I think the quotation, 'Live your religion and you need not preach it,' can well be applied to the Catholic novel."[178] James Connolly explained his simple authorial code in a novel of 1920: "The first thing in telling a story is to tell it, not to stop to preach a sermon."[179]

In sum, the insecurities of Boston authors were not local ones, but national Catholic dilemmas. The failure to sustain a Boston literary renaissance in the 1890s was followed by a short-lived interest in Irish ethnic subject matter, perhaps in response to the strength of the Irish nationalist movement in the 1910s, ultimately paving the way for the creation of an identity based on a religious subculture by the 1920s. Certain Boston Catholics were conscious of being part of a transitional generation linking American Catholics of the nineteenth and twentieth centuries. Katherine Conway thought of herself, and described her friend Maurice Egan, professor of English at Notre Dame and son of an immigrant, as "among the foremost of those who eased the transition from the immigrant population of Mrs. Sadlier's day to the settled

American citizenship, prosperity and justified self-esteem of our own time."[180] Indeed, Egan was perhaps the first Irish American writer to trade his ethnic identity for a Catholic middle-class one, and to place distance between his origins and his accommodation of bourgeois elitism. However, the gradual loosening of Catholic aesthetic standards against the pressures of mass culture, coupled with the growth of an assimilated middle class, eventually led to an integrationist cultural trend in the late 1920s that lasted through the 1950s.[181] This tendency was barely apparent in 1926 when Catholic writers and critics joined a symposium in New York City sponsored by Francis Talbot, S.J., literary editor of *America* magazine, which culminated in publication of *Fiction by Its Makers*, essays by Catholics about writing.[182] The goal was to provide wholesome authors for Catholic consumption, indicating that Catholics continued to regard art as moral propaganda. Kathleen Norris's essay ended, for example, with the plea that "if our Faith is the most important influence in our lives, it should have its place in our books. And conversely, if our books are to be true, they cannot live without it."[183] But the 1920s generation brought new voices, Catholic spokesmen such as Frank Spearman, and the liberal editors of the new lay journal *Commonweal*, George Shuster and Michael Williams, who commanded an authoritative voice not possible a decade earlier. The new generation of Catholic critics was even able to suggest flaws in the prevailing passion for medievalism. Shuster named Henry Adams, Ralph Cram, and Louise Guiney as examples that "perhaps there is danger in too strong an affection for medievalism."[184] Yet, though Shuster represented a step forward in advancing a more complex view of religion and culture and a less intransigent brand of Catholic optimism and innocence, he still believed that Christianity represented the world's highest culture. In his view, Americans could view their own literary renaissance as an extension of Christianity's civilizing role in European culture.[185] Catholic intellectual life in the 1920s still suffered from the antirealist/pro-idealist standards of earlier decades. Boston Catholic writers less secure or less talented than Shuster and Williams navigated between the Anglo sentimental conventions and the immigrant ghetto outsider mentality of the prior century, and no notable realist fiction by Catholics about Catholics appeared in the United States until the Studs Lonigan trilogy of James Farrell in the 1930s.

Boston produced no thinkers like Shuster who typified the uncertainties and paradoxes of assimilation among American Catholics and who were also bold enough to exploit them. Nor did it produce a viable tradition of realist fiction, because its writers remained preoccupied with defending the reputation of the Irish and of Catholics against Yankee detractors. At first, Irish Catholic leaders asserted their equality to Anglo-Saxons and their possession of democratic traditions. Catholic integration into middle-class professions allowed

Irish Catholics with enhanced social status to confidently celebrate their Irish American heritage in art and literature. However, as a middle-class grew, Irish Americans tended to lose their ethnic center, leaving the Church to celebrate religion as the core of identity by publicizing the legacy of Catholic art in architecture and literature. A comprehensive Irish Catholic cultural renaissance failed to emerge precisely because of the growth of an Americanized middle class: paradoxically, it was the ethnic forms of piety and community that had given birth to the middle class who subsequently undermined them.

The remarkable conformity of views of art in Catholic writing was undeniably due to the fact that literary conventions were constantly reproduced by the principles and formulas of religious advice books, catechisms, and conversion narratives. The static models and aesthetic limits that were defined by religion suggests that Catholic authors intended their art to serve as moral propaganda. The duties of a new kind of American Catholic were being defined by its third generation, who reflected the conflicts between old and new generated by changing class and ethnic identity. The writers who spanned both centuries had a unique, although fading, bond to their Irish heritage; the elites looked for security and good taste among their Anglo-Yankee equivalents. Those born in the United States had begun to explore problems unique to the American scene, no longer focused on survival but on bourgeois propriety. A Catholic aesthetic proposed that art should serve humans' highest interests; therefore, "art for art's sake" was unsatisfactory. "Art for man's sake" was partially accurate, while "art for God's sake" was the ideal. Since only the beautiful could be worthy subject matter for art, Catholics opposed the subjective, realist, or irrationalist tendencies in modern art and literature. The lofty standards of Catholic aesthetics were dutifully applied not only to literary culture but to popular entertainments as well, with remarkable continuity. Louise Guiney's view of the illiterate masses during the 1890s still resounded for Catholics of the 1920s: "How can the poor be reached and uplifted . . . with all the art, breeding and culture in the world, unless they are taught Christ Our Lord?"[186]

Babylon or Israel?: The Politics of Popular Entertainment

Since the mid-nineteenth century, Boston had been designated "Athens of America." Later it became known as "the paradise of prigs."[187] Local Catholics seemed torn between these conflicting images of Boston as the promised land of Israel and as a prison for the chosen people devised by the barbaric Babylonians. The intersection of Catholic moral-aesthetic codes with repressive tendencies in Yankee morality in this era explains how the Church took up the mantle of defender of public decency. By the 1920s, Catholics were to become associated with those making Boston a prigs' paradise, although they saw themselves in a more saintly light. Catholic reactions to high culture, such as drama and literature, and to sensational culture, such as pulp fiction, burlesque, vaudeville, and film, verify the Church's attempt to shape attitudes toward leisure and entertainment. Further, Catholics' role in censorship reflects a part of their history that has been commonly associated with Boston in the 1930s but that actually emerged in earlier decades. Religious commentaries on popular culture describe the Church's resistance to massification and reinforce the presence of class distinctions among Catholics.

A Catholic siege mentality, manifested metaphorically as the defense of Israel against Babylon, defined the Church's critique of popular entertainment and its instructions for the proper use of leisure time. In an effort to promote Christian art and to control the very experience of art, the Church enlisted the Christian home and the parish to strengthen Christian habits in a secular culture. In municipal life, Irish Catholics who gained positions of authority likewise began attempts to arbitrate the moral standards of the community, particularly through the offices of the mayor, the district attorney, the police commissioner, and licensing.[188]

Catholic commentaries on popular entertainment attacked burlesque, vaudeville, and motion pictures. Already by the 1890s, theatrical-musical shows had gained a reputation for lewdness and for corruptive power over youth, among Catholic and non-Catholic critics alike.[189] By 1925 the *American Mercury* could state bluntly, "Boston culture has collapsed. In literature, where it once held hegemony, it is now a Sahara; theatrically it is the paradise of the cheapest leg shows; musically it is sinking daily."[190] But perhaps this obituary was premature. A priest wisely asked Catholics to recall "the attitude of good Christians to the stage and the novel fifty years ago. The tremendous force of public opinion has changed it favorably in our time, but the staid and respectable minority still abhor the stage and are forever tinkering with futile schemes to improve its morality."[191] As theater evolved between 1880 and 1920, so did the professionalization of acting and stage management, which increased the respectability for actors. Mass consumer culture turned actors into celebrities, and the erosion of Victorian morality was ending the stigma of theatergoing. As in most American cities, Boston's entertainment industries grew rapidly from the 1880s, indicated by the numerous new theaters, vaudeville palaces, nickelodeons, and finally, movie houses that sprung up. Although theater had been virtually taboo for the laity, and absolutely off-limits to the clergy in the 1800s, Catholics now flocked to shows, as did the general public. In 1909 and 1910 the Drama Committee of Boston's Twentieth Century Club calculated the potential weekly audiences for shows in Boston and environs, based on the seating capacity and number of weekly performances of theater houses. The figures indicated that between 10,000 and 30,000 attendees per week per theater was average, depending on the size of the house. Most theaters held continuous showings from 10 A.M. to 10 P.M., a policy initiated by local entrepreneur Benjamin Franklin Keith. Extended hours, combined with the access to downtown Boston provided by streetcars and railways, contributed to the potential for even larger, more transient audiences.[192] By 1920, bank investors like Joseph Kennedy, who understood the economic eclipse of vaudeville by movies, were buying out the smaller chains to pave the way for the movie house monopolies that soon would rule the industry by controlling all three aspects of motion pictures—production, distribution, and exhibition. Against these economic forces of mass culture, the Catholic Church attempted its strategy of separatist integration.

American society was on the verge of a revolution in popular culture due to the rise of mass entertainment, which capitalized on the increase in leisure time for workers, who had only recently secured a forty-hour workweek. A Catholic response to a culture of consumption based on leisure time, though not an organized movement within Catholicism, illustrates how mass culture, a product of capitalist entrepreneurship, lay beyond the Church's control but was not immune to its moral criticism. Within the dramatic professions, the Church launched a three-pronged attack: on the immoral impact of economic forces on theater; on the poor quality of popular drama; and finally, on the lack of spiritual guidance for actors. The Catholic Theatre Movement, the Catholic press, and the Catholic Actors' Guild helped institutionalize the Church's campaign for moral theater and decent treatment of actors and established Catholic attitudes about popular culture that provided the basis for Catholic support for the censorship of motion pictures from the 1930s on. Beginning as a noncommercial form of coercion over culture, the Church ended up being represented in powerful state-sponsored forms of censorship.

Catholics generally distinguished between serious drama and the transient fluff of the variety shows that represented "the rise of commercial drama due to capitalism," but only a few isolated commentators astutely recognized that mass leisure and mass consumption were transforming the American public. In cities with large theatrical sectors, the Church's critique remained at the level of condemning the commercialization of theater in vaudeville burlesque shows. Fashioning a united Catholic front in Boston was a difficult task, however, in a community continually torn between the demands of ethnic nationalism, Catholic morality, and economic integration.

Moral concern for the conditions of stage acting, actors, and unions and even, if Catholic readers were attentive, for the impact of capitalism on the theater filtered into the Catholic press after 1889. In that year, the first theater column appeared in an American Catholic journal.[193] There was some delay in founding organizations to protect drama and actors: the Catholic Theatre Movement appeared in 1912, led by Eliza O'Brien Lummis in New York City, while in 1914 Rev. John Talbot Smith established the Catholic Actors' Guild.[194] Smith warned: "See what consequences have followed the invasion of Capitalism into the amusement field: the motion-picture mania, the rise of commercial drama, the death of criticism, and the labor union for actors. There are a thousand others, and more coming."[195] Smith echoed the Church's fears that mass culture would lead to manic crowd behavior, the loss of standards, and the mercenary demands of organized labor. As a self-designated "custodian of culture," the Catholic Church allied itself with high art as a guardian against mass culture, symbolizing its suspicions about the irrational forces and escapist illusions unleashed upon an untutored populace. Besides being forcefully opinionated on the subjects of Catholic writers and readers and of lay and clergy education, Father Smith devoted much of his career to drama. His book *The Parish Theatre* was meant to redress the deficiencies of secular newspapers' drama reviews.[196] Due to the "death of criticism," insisted Smith, reviews were no longer "a proper guardian or informant of the public."[197] As he had done in his jeremiad on the state of the literary world, here Smith offered a stark view of the American citizen being fooled by both theater owners and theater critics, who, as tools of the owners, rendered audiences powerless to effect legislative change. The fear of plutocracy implied in his work makes him not so different from many other populists of his day who claimed to be defending the average American from predatory capitalists.

Even though Smith was a highly iconoclastic priest among the American clergy, and the author most oriented toward realism among Irish American novelists, the kinds of plays he recommended corresponded to conservative canons of Irish Catholic propriety and tastefulness. For example, 10 percent of his recommendations were for Irish comedies. He stated that *Shawn Aroon* "portrays simple Irish life of today, without allusion to the political troubles. It lacks the emphatic Irish feeling, and gets colorless here and there, but a good company will correct the deficiencies and make it successful."[198] Yet even acceptable plays could be marred by ethnic stereotyping. Smith warned that actors who performed *Brian O'Linn*, a more "genuine Irish farce," "will have to be careful not to offend modern Irish sentiments which in many places rejects the wild fun of writers like Lover and Lever, on the grounds that it misrepresents the Irish."[199] The Hannigans in *A Very Good Young Man* proved an unsatisfactory stage family because "they talk of their parish priest and of going to Mass but they give no other healthy sign of their faith."[200]

Smith's influence on Catholic dramatic opinion reached nationwide through his almost monthly columns in the *Columbiad*.

The Catholic Theatre Movement opened a Boston chapter in 1915. There, Father Francis Donnelly, in a talk to the Boston committee of the movement, summarized the Catholic position that representational art was tantamount to virtue: "History shows that responsibility, including religious responsibility, has elevated art, has been an inspiration. . . . Reproducing an immoral thing is bad art, just as painting a cow with six legs would be; either pictures the abnormal rather than the truth."[201] Like the Catholic Theatre Movement, Smith's Catholic Actors' Guild of New York had episcopal approval (from John Cardinal Farley) and attempted to offset the disadvantages of actors' transient lifestyles though a program of spiritual support. I have been unable to determine if Boston had an active chapter of the guild. Actors there, predominantly Irish Catholics, remained at the mercy of Boston's largest employer of entertainers, the Keith Circuit, which seemed to care more about not jeopardizing its ticket sales by offensive vulgarity rather than enhancing the spiritual and material welfare of its players. While Boston was second to New York as heart of the theatrical world, its acting community was keenly aware of the value of maintaining Catholic Church support. Even though actors were not necessarily churchgoers, theater owners and managers often were.

The profession of acting gained increasing respectability for various reasons. On one hand, the entertainment media were quickly replacing traditional arbiters of public taste—churches and genteel society—through a leveling influence on public consumption habits. Further, actors who had formerly been associated with a social underworld now gained legitimacy precisely by appealing to middle-class audiences.[202] Contrary to the laity's enjoyment of variety shows and actors' notoriety, the Catholic Church feared the diffusion of mass culture because it threatened to marginalize religion as one of many options in an individual's life. Instead of developing a convincing critique of mass entertainment, the Church simply deplored the loss of moral standards that it associated with all antihierarchical trends.

Determining the role Catholics played in the transformation of Victorian America into modern society lies beyond the scope of this chapter. However, in its attempts to regulate dramatic standards and theatergoing, the Church ostensibly tried to protect actors (and would-be actresses) from abuses of the industry, while extending its paternalism to sustain its own aesthetic standards on drama. Lay Catholics were caught in a dual cultural transformation, of a recently immigrant culture now facing secularization and of rapidly changing rules of American society. Boston Irish Catholics evolved concepts of proper theater conditioned by ethnic cues, which combined Catholicism and Irish pride, and by contemporary values, which idealized the family, motherhood, and female purity. For its part, the clergy was paternalistic toward the lay theatergoer. Stage-struck girls, for example, were warned against men who preyed on the innocent: "Beware of such fellows," wrote one priest. "Their intentions are bad and their morals are worse."[203] Father Smith believed that "as a rule the Catholic people know next to nothing about the modern drama, except the notable instances which illustrate their favorite prejudice against its very existence. The pious regard the play as our fathers regarded the novel half a century ago, an immoral instrument for the degradation of mankind."[204] Smith's indictment of this misled piety echoed the scorn he had heaped on the ignorance of the Catholic reading public in his essay "The Young Catholic Writer." Yet, his comparison of the realist novel's "style-and-stench" to the theater's "flood of filth" indicates the Church's negative outlook on both. Smith compared the relative faults of drama and the press: "The worst features of the stage are apparent in some of our present day musical entertainments; they are all emphatic arguments for a censorship of the drama and the stage, but let it not be forgotten that as compared with the filth of the daily press they are as pure as angels."[205] In making the tabloid press and the playwright natural foes of censorship, Smith argued that Catholics had gained an undeserved reputation for repression, even though his strident complaints against the media seem to justify it. On the other hand, Smith's recognition of the humane potential of drama, like the equanimity of the O'Reilly-Roche literary generation, placed him in a Catholic minority whose education allowed it to at least recognize its redeeming features. His Actors' Guild was described as "the wedge opening the way to a broader and more charitable interpretation of stage life."[206] The guild, the Catholic Theatre Movement, and the Catholic press urged Catholics to exert self-censorship by signing pledges supporting their published recommendations. This ethic of self-control seems more appropriate to an immigrant generation, here strikingly revived among the third-generation Irish Americans against new forms of leisure commodities that threatened Catholic moral-aesthetic standards.

Censorship and Culture

In the Progressive decades, statistics became useful for everyone involved in urban surveillance, especially censors. Boston's Good Government advocates such as the Twentieth Century Club monitored audiences to assess the business potential of plays and vaudeville; antivice societies like the Watch & Ward Society snooped on the theater and red-light districts to uncover criminal activity. Municipal planners like "Boston, 1915" downplayed crime statistics to sell Boston's cultural vitality to new businesses. But real power of censorship rested in the office of the mayor, which regulated the city's theater industry through its licensing authority. Boston had only two non–Irish Catholic mayors between 1900 and 1918, Thomas Hart (1900–1901) and George A. Hibbard (1908–9). Catholics Patrick Collins (1902–5), John F. Fitzgerald (1906–7 and 1910–13), and James M. Curley (1914–17) were elected by large Irish constituencies. Curley was ousted by Andrew Peters (1918–21), a Yankee Democrat educated at St. Paul's and Harvard, whose honorable reputation turned out to be only a veneer.[207] After 1918 an Irish Catholic constituency grew divided between the emergent bourgeoisie who preferred the seeming respectability of someone like Peters, and an ethnic bloc devoted to the spoils system embodied by Curley.

Until 1908 the mayor of Boston held the unique power to judge the immorality of a theater performance and to revoke theater licenses through his licensing division. Thereafter, reacting against Honey Fitz's administration, his Republican successor reformed the city's governing codes to make the police commissioner responsible for theater censorship in conjunction with the mayor and his licensing officer. This 1908 act did not appeal to Catholic Republican Stephen O'Meara. In lieu of the ponderous checks and balances of the licensing committee trio, O'Meara preferred to remove himself from the licensing process: "The police commissioner was included without my knowledge, and if I been aware of the intention to produce so absurd a complication, I should have protested. The full power should be with the licensing authority."[208] From 1904 to 1932 one man, John M. Casey, served as chief of the licensing division, although he never held the formal title of censor. He had formerly worked as a trap-drummer in a vaudeville orchestra. His successor, Stanton R. White, was a son-in-law of Mayor Curley's brother.[209] The appointments of Casey and White indicate that expert knowledge of theater and public entertainment was no prerequisite. The final actor in this cast of Catholic censors was Joseph Pelletier, the shifty district attorney.[210] None of these Catholics had ideal relationships with fellow Irish Catholic mayors, which meant that Democratic party and Catholic interests were often divided. Further, partisan differences between Catholic individuals, such as the Democratic mayor and the Republican police commissioner, also led to dissent.

From a position of relatively new power in City Hall and in the Suffolk County courts, Irish Catholics were caught between two opposing factions on issues of public morality: those who considered urban Irish Catholics to be morally lax and thus incapable of performing their work satisfactorily, and those who thought Catholic influence even more "bitter-pure" than that of the Brahmins or Methodists.[211] Occasionally, as in the case of the opposition to the Boston premiere of John Synge's *Playboy of the Western World* in 1911,

The consolidation of Irish nationalism and Catholic education in this ceremony at Holy Cross College: Father Carlin, S.J., presents an honorary degree to Eamon De Valera, president of the Irish Free State, February 1920. Note the pointed banner reading "Ireland" above them. (Holy Cross College Archives)

ethnic power driven by Irish nationalism heightened existing American political or religious debates.[212] Clearly, the regulation of public entertainments involved complex ethnic and political interests. Nonetheless, the combination of Irish, Democratic, and Catholic did not necessarily establish uniform and predictable patterns of behavior. Boston Catholics proved to be less solidly ethnic than expected, for example, when the Irish Democratic mayor and the Irish Republican police commissioner supported the Boston production of Synge's play against its Irish American critics; less malleable than hoped for when Republican Commissioner O'Meara tried to moderate the extremist views of para-police groups like the New England Watch & Ward Society, but without compromising his impartiality; and less puritan than desired in Catholic protests against the prohibition amendment in 1918.

Stage and book censorship became a battleground for political as well as moral control in Boston. Catholic views overflowed from the pulpit into the statements of the lay associations, and especially into the press. As with the moral-aesthetic of the anti-ugly crusade in literature, a Catholic critique of popular entertainment defended universal standards of morality that made it possible to describe what constituted proper amusement.

James J. Walsh, a lecturer popular with local Catholic audiences, regretted the "social evils" of burlesque shows. According to Walsh, burlesque appealed to the basest aspects of human sexual desire. The puerile lyrics offended standards of taste, and their general immorality especially endangered youth by glamorizing the sordid aspects of life.[213] The first complaint received detailed attention in the Catholic press. From the luridly colored posters that aroused "young men's animal passions" to complaints about the sexual innuendo of the dialogue and the vulgar display of ladies' legs, Catholic critics made it clear that unregulated lust was unacceptable. By doing so, however, the Church at least indicated that it took seriously the power of theater to affect human behavior, which was one justification for its attempts to moderate the vulgarity of popular drama. As a Knight of Columbus commented, "The stage is to-day, and has been in every age, a powerful mold of public opinion and a mighty effective instrument, either for good or bad, in forming the morals, tastes and manners of a nation. Unfortunately, in these early years of the twentieth century, the drama of beauty, poetry and nobility has given way almost entirely to obscene spectacles and tainted plays in which virtue and vice are made to exchange parts."[214] James Walsh added, "Bad taste is the rule in everything connected with them, but that is a minor objection compared to their positive immorality."[215]

In an urban setting, stage immorality disturbed Catholic critics because large audiences witnessed how "conjugal infidelity can be plausibly justified, or perhaps, may be edified by witnessing a raid on a disreputable house, or, perhaps, may have the pleasure of seeing a realistic representation of a Parisian thieves' den, with all its accompanying under-world origins."[216] In other words, modern plays began to depict the most distressing (and realistic) aspects of modern urban life to an ever-increasing number of patrons. That theater palaces were filling up with audiences that averaged at least 40 percent women probably alarmed the Church even more. As early as 1910 the AFCS addressed an open letter to theater producers stating that "there are thousands—nay, millions—of American people who are disgusted with these putrid exhibitions. We most emphatically assert that themes of divorce, adultery, seduction, double life, conjugal infidelity, free-love, and other worse performances exhibiting sexual perversity, are not what the decent people want."[217] Members of the AFCS wanted to follow up its letter with active protests to theater managers. Female audiences, meanwhile, appeared to be drawn to these melodramas that portrayed their own enslavement to men, in plots that treated white slavery, venereal disease, and even woman suffrage.

The Catholic Theatre Movement developed standards for judging a play's morality. Its biweekly *White List Bulletin* condemned a play if it was "concerned principally with sexual immorality; matters that violate the Sixth Commandment; personal purity; the sanctity of marriage; the sacredness of womanhood; the dignity of childbearing; the worth of family and of children."[218] Fear of general moral decline resulting from playgoing led similar national associations such as the LCW to adopt, among its seven annual resolutions of 1920, a blanket statement "against the folly of self-indulgence, immoral plays, indecent dances and the dissipation of moral force."[219]

Women responded to the Church's paternalist appeals to moral responsibility of the laity and for censorship that would protect the innocence of women and children. But with the Church's polemics came a call to revive Catholicism's own dramatic heritage of medieval mystery plays. Recognizing that drama had a history intimately connected with the Church, a Catholic layman recalled that "long before the age of the myriad-minded Shakespeare, the drama in the years of its struggling infancy was being nurtured in churches, convents and monasteries, and was fostered by priests, nuns and the much maligned monks. Is it any wonder, then that we, upon whose altar steps the cradle of the drama once rested, now protest when we see it being made an instrument of evil?"[220] The Church guarded children against morally objectionable plays through controlling their experience of drama in Catholic schools. As Agnes Repplier recalled of her experiences in the 1860s and 1870s at Eden Hall, a convent academy near Philadelphia, "Plays were the great diversions of our school life. We had two or three of them every winter, presented, it seemed to me, with dazzling splendor, and acted with passionate fire." Two kinds of drama were permissible in convent school. The first, expurgated by the nuns, was classic drama, whose "salient feature was the absence of courtship and of love. It was part of the convent system to ignore the master passion, to assume that it did not exist, to banish from our work and from our play any reference to the power that moves the world." The second customary fare was drama written by the nuns themselves, "as a rule, tragic in character, and devout in sentiment,—sometimes so exceedingly devout as to resemble religious homilies rather than the legitimate drama."[221]

The dramas performed at Boston's convent academies and parochial schools followed a similar model of passion-free, moral-laden theater, in consonance with Archbishop O'Connell's frequent reminder that "innocence is the strongest armor for your children. Protect that at all costs."[222] Although the curriculum of the academies was tailored to suit a wealthier Catholic clientele, the working-class parochial school likewise avoided studying anything that smacked of physicality.[223] The Catholic Theatre Movement published annotated lists of plays suitable for children's performance, "plays from which young people may learn something, and which they will enjoy seeing and performing."[224] Paralleling its attempt to publish wholesome Christian children's literature, the Church asked the Catholic community to provide its own dramatists or to revise the extant dramatic repertoire by deleting offensive passages.

Censorship and abridgement of drama for children by Church educators was one effective way of curtailing youths' exposure to "immoral" art. It fostered a subservient attitude among students, for few Catholics protested as sharply as Agnes Repplier, and even she conformed to the Catholic genteel tradition's desire for literature that demonstrated "light in the darkness and some reassuring traits."[225] Censorship in Catholic schools raises a larger issue of the Church's role in public censorship in Boston, whereby the Church extended its authority and duty to the entire community. Whether control would be exercised through the Church hierarchy, the "professional Irishmen" of City Hall, or by the decisions of local capitalists was another question.

The Catholic Church found an unusual ally in one Boston entrepreneur, Benjamin Franklin Keith (1846–1914), who made the palatial opulence of the grand opera houses available to the vaudeville audience. His didactic attitude toward variety show patrons coincided with the Church's paternalism. Keith believed "the public had to be educated in these matters and it is only because of the merit of the entertainment and attractiveness of the surroundings that people can be induced to attend."[226] Keith was not a Catholic, but his wife's pious devotion influenced his outlook to the point that his family bequeathed a large sum to Archbishop O'Connell. A native of Hillsborough, New Hampshire, Keith came to Boston in 1882 and began "educating" the public through a storefront curiosity show on the model of P. T. Barnum's Gaiety Museum in New York City.[227] The first exhibit was "Baby Alice," a three-week-old infant weighing under two pounds. Keith's Irish-born wife, Mary Catherine Brawley Keith (1851–1910), ran the boarding house for the museum performers and cleaned the museum. In about 1885 Keith bought the Bijou Theatre and dedicated his shows to "continuous" and "clean vaudeville in luxurious surroundings," provoked by his wife's desire to improve the quality of variety shows and by his own profit-seeking plan for nonstop acts from morning until night. His "amusement temples" were closed on the sabbath, leading actors to dub their work "the Sunday School Circuit."[228] Fred Allen, a vaudeville star on the Keith circuit and well known to Dorchester audiences before he became a radio personality, recalled the performance rules that Keith posted in all his theaters:

> Don't say "slob" or "son-of-a-gun" or "hully gee" on this stage unless you want to be canceled peremptorily. Do not address anyone in the audience in any manner. If you have not the ability to entertain Mr. Keith's

audiences without risk of offending them, do the best you can. Lack of talent will be less open to censure than would be an insult to a patron. If you are in doubt as to the character of your act, consult the local manager before you go on the stage, for if you are guilty of uttering anything sacrilegious or even suggestive, you will be immediately closed and will never again be allowed in a theatre where Mr. Keith is in authority.[229]

Between 1891 and 1894 Keith erected a theater next to the old Boston Theatre, his major rival, which he then undercut by offering similar shows at lower prices.[230] In the 1890s the Keith four-in-hand, an electrified wagon, roamed the city streets advertising his shows. Keith soon acquired profitable theaters in New York, Philadelphia, and Providence, which eventually evolved into the more than 400 Keith theaters of the RKO chain. A writer in *Scribner's* estimated in 1899 that more than 5 million people attended his 4 theaters annually, and that his circuit supported 300 workers and over 3,500 actors each earning at least $13,500 per week.[231] Upon his death in 1914, Keith owned 31 theaters, and his partner since 1885, Edward Franklin Albee (1857–1930), ran 2 others. Ironically, in 1928 Albee was bought out and forced out of his proprietorship by an upcoming Boston Irishman, Joseph Kennedy.

The Keiths' entertainment dynasty had a considerable economic impact on the archdiocese of Boston: their estate left about $3 million to the personal disposition of Archbishop O'Connell (a crucial legal distinction from the corporation sole of the archdiocese). O'Connell used it to finance numerous construction projects, including the cluster of Catholic buildings at Boston College and St. John's Seminary at Brighton. B. F. Keith's son, Andrew Paul Keith, who was not a religious man, donated funds for several buildings to the memory of his mother, including the archbishop's residence at St. John's Seminary, Brighton; the gymnasium there; a chapel at St. Elizabeth's Hospital; and in Lowell, Keith Academy and Keith Hall.

A portrait of B. F. Keith as a wholesome family entertainer turned church philanthropist, however, is unreliable. Clever enough to stitch two-bit variety acts into seamless vaudeville, as a businessman he was competitive, exploitative, antiunion, and intent on monopolizing the industry. His employees were never unionized because his partner forestalled any outside competition by running a "company union" called National Vaudeville Artists.[232] Yet Keith boasted of his cooperation with those existing unions essential to his shows and his more than 10,000 vaudeville artists, including the American Federation of Musicians and the International Alliance of Theatrical Stage Employees. This cooperation was undercut by the United Booking Office, founded by Albee and Keith in 1900 to book acts. This booking office kept

5 percent of the performer's salary and chiseled another 2½ percent of the 5 percent usually going to the booking agents.[233]

Publicly, Keith and Albee were honored as model managers. For example, the 1927 laying of the cornerstone of the Keith Memorial Theatre thirteen years after Keith's death brought tributes from the mayor of Boston and from the president and secretary of the National United Artists' Association, Keith's own creation. Both the city and the actors' agency thanked him for giving actors a secure salaried income rather than daily wages and praised his impeccable taste in entertainment.[234] By then, Joseph Kennedy had become chairman of the board of the Keith "successor firm" and was building his fortune as an investor. Before Keith's death, Albee was seen as the more aggressive moneyseeker, while the aging Keith spent his fortune on yachts, travel, and fine furnishings. Keith's spotless image became tarnished, however. Sine Silverman's columns in *Variety* and reviews by Joe Laurie and Bernard Sobel pictured him as a tyrannical representative of big money and credited Albee with doing all the work.[235] Keith's practice of trimming acts from his shows to suit his notions of propriety began to catch up with him.[236] Even Keith's account of his own life reveals a personality divided between love of vaudeville and lust for money and, beneath it all, a contempt for his patrons. When Keith saw his theater full of highbrow audiences of "our most prominent lawyers, judges of the Supreme Court, ministers, Governors, representative men in all walks of life," he found that he "would actually feel ashamed of them—it seemed so absurd—and I would have to get up and go out."[237] Nonetheless, his prudish moral standards for vaudeville, his manipulative plans to reform audience manners, and his financial generosity to the Catholic Church made him a powerful ally in the Church's crusade for wholesome entertainment. If the Church had moral reservations about his cutthroat competitive capitalism and authoritarian control of his employees, it remained silent.

In 1916 the *Pilot* reported: "In Boston . . . the Mayor drove from the city a foul and evil play. The Puritan, with all his narrowness, and the Irish immigrant helped to sustain a Christian standard of public opinion now being swept aside by alien and un-American elements in our national life."[238] By suppressing *Marie Odile,* a work by Harvard-educated playwright Edward Knoblock, Mayor James Curley earned the *Pilot*'s approval and a rare blessing from the AFCS, which commented, "They need a Curley in Brooklyn."[239] Negative reactions to modern plays came from Protestant and Catholic churches alike, and theater censorship was often conducted according to the dictates of their bishops and elders, who always refused any plays that mentioned abortion, illegitimacy, or extramarital sex. As Catholics increasingly identified religion with patriotism, they grew willing to join with their traditional Puritan rivals to oppose "un-American elements" in public entertainment. Previously, a relationship between Roman Catholicism and the extremist Protestant antivice association, the New England Watch & Ward Society, would have seemed impossible. Although no archival records from the archdiocese of Boston or from Watch & Ward explicitly link the two institutions, their styles of watchdog vigilance had many similarities. While the Protestant group dated from the 1870s, the Catholic mode, I argue, co-alesced with the emergence of a Catholic middle class and the rigid moralism that typified Archbishop O'Connell's leadership.

Watch & Ward, made infamous for its several failed attempts to suppress H. L. Mencken's *American Mercury,* had descended from the Committee for the Suppression of Vice, originally founded in New York City as a YMCA offshoot. A New England branch of the committee had existed until 1890, but a tradition of local antivice societies had been well entrenched since the time of Puritan colonization. It was Anthony Comstock (1844–1915) who made his reputation as a vice hunter while serving as the agent of the Committee for the Suppression of Vice, later reorganized as the Society for the Suppression of Vice.[240] American Catholics had sympathized with Comstock's protective attitudes toward children and his program of mail censorship at a time when much of the literature under his surveillance was anti-Catholic propaganda. When Comstock died, the leading federation of Catholic societies called him "a brave and unselfish fighter against impurity" and declared its pleasure that his successor, John Sumner, "expressed a willingness to cooperate with Federation in up-holding public morality, as did our old friend Anthony Comstock."[241]

Since its founding in 1876 in Boston (the date is sometimes given as 1878), Watch & Ward was led by a Brahmin board of directors, mostly preachers and politicians who were descendants of New England's first families. Its 1878 charter stated that it was founded "to remove commercialized temptations to vice and crime" in Boston and was led by men of "courageous and aggressive righteousness." These upper-class reformers decided to enforce the stringent laws passed by their ancestors against prostitution, white slavery, gambling, drugs, alcohol, and obscene literature. The society's annual reports are studded with self-congratulatory accounts of how "we had to go far back into the common law this year to find a form of complaint against an amusement nuisance in order to prosecute."[242]

The annual reports also reveal that many directors were not active participants but merely names that lent luster to the membership rolls. Rev. William Lawrence, for example, Episcopal Bishop of Massachusetts from 1893 to 1925, served as president from 1902 to 1904 and, later, as a board member, but without spending too much time pursuing the society's agenda.[243] Samuel B. Capen (1842–1914), a prominent Congregationalist who served as president of the American Board of Commissioners for Foreign Missions and on the Boston School Committee, was president from 1904 to 1908. The election of G. Stanley Hall, Clark University president and former Ph.D. student of William James at Harvard, as Capen's successor in 1909 indicated Watch & Ward's increasing interest in the social applications of moral hygiene. Hall's own record in supporting regulation of working-class leisure time in Worcester, Massachusetts, for example, and his temperance activism fitted him well for the Watch & Ward's Boston agenda.[244]

The mainstays of the society were Frederick B. Allen; Jason Franklin Chase, secretary from 1907 until his death in 1926; and Godfrey Lowell Cabot, treasurer and, later, secretary. The trio of Allen, Chase, and Cabot gave the Watch & Ward its reputation as a zealous para-police force, epitomized by the Joseph Pelletier case.[245] Watch & Ward members were also likely to be affiliated with groups such as the Immigration Restriction League, the anti-Catholic Loyal Coalition, and the Purity Federation during World War I, and to support literacy tests and poll taxes for immigrants.

The society overlapped with Catholic interests in the areas of book and play censorship, although its methods differed by being primarily punitive. Although Chase claimed that "the Irish make notable Puritans," when Catholics removed books from sale they replaced them with alternative, namely Catholic, literature and, in the case of theater, offered a white list of decent plays alongside black lists of objectionable ones. Additionally, groups such as the Catholic Theatre Movement asked members to sign pledge cards against unapproved plays, a forerunner of the Legion of Decency pledges against objectionable motion pictures in subsequent decades.[246] The Watch & Ward Society, by contrast, saw itself as a policing agent to smash vice by suppressing books and closing theaters. In the political climate of the early 1900s, however, Catholics did not need to be this aggressive. They could rely on the more subtle tactic of intimidating book dealers to remove certain books from their shelves, knowing that cases would be brought before Suffolk County's district attorneys and lower court judges, most of whom were Irish Catholics.[247]

In 1915 J. F. Chase, an ex-minister, established the Boston Book Dealers Association through Watch & Ward, which enabled him to procure information about forthcoming books to be sold in Boston without drawing unwanted publicity. Of the six-member committee, three were Watch & Ward directors, and three were booksellers.[248] As the society reported, "The Committee of the Boston Book Dealers has been most careful and helpful in calling our attention at the earliest possible moment to any book offered for sale that might by its error of taste and its insidious and false portrayal of human life overstep the proper boundaries which our State laws impose. Thus much good has been accomplished without publicity."[249] Chase claimed responsibility for having banned sales of over twenty-two books in Boston, including novels by Sherwood Anderson, Floyd Dell, Aldous Huxley, and John Dos Passos.[250] In 1922 alone the committee suppressed fourteen books. The booksellers' committee flourished between 1918 and 1927, but the climate for its work was prepared earlier by parallel efforts of Protestants and Catholics. Book suppression was less widely opposed by the public than one might suppose, since many Bostonians did not consider it an act of censorship but, rather, a legitimate form of economic protectionism for the book trade.[251]

By prosecuting Pelletier, Watch & Ward demonstrated that it had no love for Roman Catholics, whom they blamed for much illegal activity in Boston. Yet, they needed Catholics as accomplices in censorship, since Irish Catholics now virtually controlled City Hall and the lower courts. Catholics became useful to the society's Committee on Public Amusements, which thanked John Casey, the mayor's licensing secretary, for his congenial assistance.[252] Direct correspondence between Casey and the booksellers' committee cannot be definitively established, however, and the society's records reveal only a few instances where Catholics were invited to attend Watch & Ward meetings.[253] Notably, in 1914, District Attorney Pelletier was a guest of the Watch & Ward. Later he charged the society with "50 or 60" instances of hiring college men to solicit prostitutes and then testify against them.[254] Once exposed, reports of Watch & Ward's activities became an embarrassment in New England. In retaliation, the society went after Pelletier, wiretapping his office to gather evidence for its claims that Pelletier was too lax in his functions as district attorney and that he was involved in bribery and extortion rackets.[255]

Watch & Ward was guilty as well of unsavory voyeurism and lack of scruples about covert (although not illegal) means of gathering information.[256] The 1922 conviction of Pelletier had shown further that Watch & Ward befriended Catholics for political expediency but had no qualms about bringing them to trial. Frederick Allen explained the need for cooperative Roman Catholics: "I had a very interesting interview, the other day, with Mr. Wise. You know he is practically under Pelletier and he feels he must resign as our director, as it might cost him his position to remain. He did not say just this but expressed his great regret. I am very anxious to get some other R.C. in his place. He suggested Bernard Rothwell. Rothwell has been very helpful, going with us at times to the Licensing Committee."[257]

Obviously not all the exchanges between Catholics and Watch & Ward members were hostile. When stated without context, the moral outlook of each group seems identical. For example, in 1916 Rev. Michael J. Scanlan, director of the CCB and chaplain of the MIT Catholic Club, addressed the thirty-eighth annual meeting of the Watch & Ward. He told an audience of about 200 that it was time to return to the old-fashioned notion of "the objective reality of evil" and the belief that humans are still fighting "the great triple alliance" of "the world, the flesh and the devil." Despite Scanlan's mild caveats against allowing a private society to mind public morals, he "was very much in sympathy with the cause which this society represents."[258] After all, in Scanlan's opinion, the society used noble means to achieve its goals: a few generous leaders sacrificed themselves for the common good, confronted evil with moral rigor, and embodied the spirit of democracy in their use of local initiative. "I should loathe the day when the care of the community would be an official act," Father Scanlan stated, reiterating the Catholic Church's anti-statist view, which echoed a Brahmin outlook on privately sponsored benevolence as well. Finally, Scanlan related that even the persistence of evil, such as he had witnessed as chaplain for four years at the state prison, should be tempered by the optimistic Christian certainty that man basically seeks to do good.[259]

Thus, direct Catholic intervention in prohibiting book sales and play productions seems to have been slight, possibly because the Watch & Ward booksellers' committee already performed that role. Alternatively, the Church may have been unwilling to jeopardize its fledgling insider status by an alliance with the most anti-Catholic segment of Boston's elite. Nonetheless, through judicial pressure and clerical watchfulness, Catholic influence generated a public perception of Catholics as a "moral people" to counter Protestant images of their perversity. Finally, the hierarchical structure of Catholicism permitted religious regulation of books, theater, and movies through a double threat of personal sin and collective Catholic boycotts of booksellers and entertainment entrepreneurs, without the need to involve public institutions. As Catholics became more secure as citizens, they used the stricter antiobscenity laws as means to remove anti-Catholic literature from mail circulation, anticipating their attacks on Boston booksellers and theaters that characterized the 1910s. To some degree, Catholic complicity in the principles, if not the actual methods, of groups like Watch & Ward paved the way for the more repressive municipal backlash of the 1920s against the general permissiveness of that decade, and united a triangle of the Catholic hierarchy, ethnopolitical leadership, and state censorship under the slogan Banned in Boston.

In actually entering the film industry, the Catholic Church tried producing its own version of popular entertainment. Religious subjects had in fact been part of the first, flickering motion pictures almost since their birth in 1897. In 1898 Boston's Keith Theatre showed a successful eight-week run of W. K. L. Dickson's twelve scenes of Pope Leo XIII in Rome; Leo's cooperation had been secured with the argument that he could thereby convey his papal blessing to thousands of Americans. These scenes were accompanied by a lecture from a priest. Keith maximized his profits among Boston's Irish Catholics by using his large theater for Sunday showings and his smaller Bijou Opera House on weekdays. Because these early films were so brief, they were always accompanied by another offering such as a lantern slide show or an illustrated travel lecture. The papal films, for instance, were preceded by a narrated stereopticon lecture on the history of Rome.[260]

By 1917, when the Catholic Church entered film production, Charlie Chaplin's *The Tramp* and D. W. Griffith's *Birth of a Nation* had already appeared. Motion pictures had evolved from "chasers" for vaudeville acts, or fillers during intermissions, into full-length feature films. The Church's endeavor was called Catholic Truth Films, produced by the Unique Film Corporation. Boston's Auxiliary Bishop Joseph Anderson wrote the scenario for the first film, "A Dream of Empire," based on the relationship of Napoleon Bonaparte and Pius VII. A film version of the life of Christ was planned, as were several others with grandiose religious themes, meant to present a heroic vision of Catholic history.[261] According to a news report of the production company, Church authorities approved the projects for use in evangelization on the American frontier as well as in Catholic foreign missions.

A related venture by the Catholic Art Association produced copyrights and scripts for other religious titles such as *The Transgressor* (1918), *The Burning Question* and *The Eternal Light* (1919), and *Luring Shadows* and *The Victim* (1920).[262] The Catholic Art Association, based in New York City, advertised the availability of religious photoplays under the motto When Art Is True Art, Art to God Is True.[263] Little evidence can be found about these five films: only one has a surviving print, and there are few reviews of official releases, suggesting that production never advanced further than the copyrighted scenario. One commonality of these films is the screenplay writers, the team of Condé Pallen and Otto Goebel.[264] The plots included such contemporary elements as labor riots, Bolshevist plots, drug addicts, spiritualists, and the Knights of Columbus. One news item concerning *The Eternal Light* indicated that it was shown in May 1919 at a temple in Boston. Even though it dramatized the life of Christ, the state police chief banned it from being shown on Sunday nights because of the violence in it, suggesting that even religious films were subject to community standards and that they did not differ significantly from secular fare.[265] Despite an unspectacular beginning in film production, Catholics maintained the conception of art as a manifestation of the divine essence. Yet the irrelevance of the Church's moral and religious themes to the financial side of this new industry is perhaps suggested by the conference on the film industry held at the Harvard Business School in 1927. As invited by conference planner Joseph Kennedy, Harvard class of 1912, fourteen speakers addressed the present and future possibilities of film production. None of the speakers, who included Adolph Zukor, Cecil B. DeMille, Marcus Loew, and Harry

Warner, was Catholic, nor did anyone speak of a moral purpose in motion pictures.[266]

Commercial nickelodeons and secular full-length feature motion pictures were likely to be called subversive by the Church because, like theater, they reached the consumer through the marketplace without involving regulatory agencies like church, school, and family. On the other hand, movies offered the Church a potent technology for reproducing religious ideology. David Goldstein, for example, approved a photoplay shown at Boston's Majestic Theatre about the evils of birth control: "The pictures show the delight in the innocence and beauty of children and, by a terrible contrast, the barrenness of the home in which the hearts of women are given to cats and dogs, because of indecent practices. . . . The lesson ends with the sinner on her knees, asking Almighty God for forgiveness."[267] The moral and didactic possibilities of the new medium were appreciated immediately by John Talbot Smith, who wrote in 1913 that "before these wonderful, almost miraculous achievements of the motion-picture machine, the attitude of the hostile looks supremely ridiculous. In the domain of religion and religious teaching the motion picture is bound to be of tremendous service."[268] As an enhancement to Catholic journalism, Smith suggested, the impact of the motion picture would be unsurpassed: "Before magic like this, before enchantment so true and convincing, the carping of the respectable minority, the suspicions of the eminently pious, give one the sensation of disgust."[269] Smith even predicted that drama and film were destined to embody Catholic excellence in American art: "It is a sorrowful fact that the beautiful Catholic life on American soil for three centuries has only slight record in history, and none at all in the arts; no painters, poets, novelists, sculptors, essayists, musicians, record even a few fleeting glimpses of its achievement for the next generation. It must be the task of the drama and the photo-drama to revive the age of heroism, when the missionaries overran this continent side by side with the explorers and the traders."[270]

Smith encouraged American Catholics to exploit all communications technologies in the service of religion. Boston entered American radio broadcasting in 1929 when Cardinal O'Connell authorized Michael Ahern, S.J., to direct the Catholic Radio Hour, which continued until 1951.[271] Boston's role in Catholic film production, however, as in Catholic book publishing and theater, remained small in scale. The Catholic "age of heroism" was not revived, and neither Catholic plays nor films emerged as superior alternatives to secular products. The Church continued to protest the general content of films as immoral, even though this may not have been the case for the majority of productions.

Nonetheless, Catholic critics saw an ominous pattern emerge in the film industry in a shift from entertainment to sensationalism. The *Sacred Heart Review* condemned the trend: "With the exhaustion of legitimate subjects, or rather with the development of the moving picture show into a craze, came the exhibition of pictures and scenes which were enacted specially for the moving picture machine—sensational scenes, murders, robberies, lynchings, and so on, mingled with pictures of amorous adventures decidedly vulgar and suggestive if not positively indecent."[272] As the result of pressure from local communities, several cities such as Chicago voluntarily began local film censorship boards as early as 1907. The National Board of Censorship of Motion Pictures was established in March 1909.[273] Somewhat later the Catholic Church centralized and institutionalized its own film censorship and rating system in its National Legion of Decency, established in Brooklyn in 1922. By the 1930s Boston had formed a chapter of the Motion Picture Research Council, a secular organization with a rating program similar to that of the Legion of Decency, which Cardinal O'Connell thoroughly approved. On the national level, a Jesuit priest from St. Louis, Daniel Lord, who had been editor of *Queen's Work*, drafted the moral code with a committee in 1929, which was adopted by the industry's governing body in 1930. In the 1930s and 1940s an Irish Catholic layman, Joseph Ignatius Breen, served as chief censor of the Production Code Administration of the Motion Picture Producers and Distributors Association.[274] The presence of these postimmigrant Irish Catholics in key censorship roles suggests that ethnicity reinforced religious beliefs, while the hierarchical structure of Catholicism lent itself to top-down control of its members' behavior based on a close relationship between clergy and lay professionals. By the 1930s the Church took its part in state-run censorship by having clergymen as key advisors to film review boards. What seems clear is that the Catholic Church, like some local Protestant churches and quasi-religious organizations such as the YMCA and the Ford Hall Forum, wanted to seize the opportunity to exhibit films suited to its definition of wholesome family entertainment and to have a hand in the rating process.

Catholics criticized not only film content but also the emerging social patterns of film attendance. The Boston Federation of Catholic Societies, for example, found the freedom of children, and especially of females, alarming: "To these shows flock young girls who ought to be home with their fathers and mothers. These are seen in these places without escort, or in groups of two or three, at all hours of the night."[275] There was a strong correlation between the Church's disapproval of the liberty of unchaperoned girls and its criticisms of stage and screen actresses, who symbolized the "new woman"— young, single, emancipated—to impressionable audiences. The young sister of Father Michael Earls got a job playing piano at the silent movies in Southbridge, and even if she agreed that "playing for the pictures is not a very healthful job," her situation shows that even girls took advantage of the employment opportunities generated by moviegoing.[276] Perhaps practical compromising of this sort led the diocesan paper to mistrust the moral discrimination of the laity, whether children or adults, and therefore it hoped to eliminate even the chance of contagion from the "glamor of evil." According to the *Pilot*, " 'To the pure all things are pure' is no longer considered good discipline. It is a good thing to have confidence, but it is also well to remove temptations."[277]

The Church never attempted to remove entertainment from Catholic life altogether. Instead, the local parish remained a crucial link between popular culture and the leisure habits of the laity. Catholics were often introduced to the latest fads at parish functions, albeit under the Church's vigilant eye. The weekly reports in the *Pilot* of parish socials, slide shows, plays, tableaux, and minstrel shows indicate that pre– and post–World War I parishes served as mediators between Catholics and modern America, constituting yet another factor making the Catholic parish "one of the greatest social service centers in the country."[278] Parish organizations quickly adopted stereopticon shows and films for religious education, to explain the meaning of religious practices and to teach about the lives of the saints, but they did not neglect pure entertainment. For example, while the *Pilot* reported that on one occasion the president of the Laymen's Retreat Guild "exhibited some interesting stereopticon views and told of the many advantages of laymen's retreats," parish shows also featured documentaries, comedies, and travelogues.[279] In addition, Catholic lay societies were gradually incorporating stages and even athletic facilities into their meeting places and headquarters, and several of Boston's wealthier Catholics built theaters in their homes. Finally, the hundreds of parish theatricals, school plays, and minstrel shows enthusiastically produced in the diocese each year provided alternatives to Boston's vaudeville revues or playhouses. The Church thus perpetuated its moral judgments about stage and screen by holding parallel entertainments that drew large audiences among the faithful and that socialized Catholics in the protected environment of the subculture. It did not prevent Catholics from also attending the theater and movies. By the 1940s, Hollywood's recognition of the box office potential of Catholics as the subject of screenplays—notably parish dramas and convent melodramas—surely demonstrates the swift assimilation and marketability of Catholics into the popular culture the Church had so recently condemned.

8

THE ACHIEVEMENT OF SEPARATIST INTEGRATION

It is natural, when we tell the story of the Church in Boston, to lay
stress on its dramatic phases,—not only its prodigious growth in
numbers and influence, but its struggle with fanaticism and its glorious victory.—John F. Fitzgerald, "Boston Catholics"

The sanctity of the home is assailed, and divorce stalking abroad saps
at the very vitals of our national life, begetting a race of foundlings
in the subversion of moral law. The wild pursuit of worldly gain and
the fraudulent accumulation of riches have engendered hatreds which
at times threaten to rend asunder the social fabric of our communities and to endanger the security of our social institutions. The
various organizations, industrial and civil, which flourish in our communities express man's distrust of man, and the complaint of class
against class grows stronger with each recurring year.
—Thomas H. Dowd, "The Ideals of Holy Cross"

The civilization characteristic of Christendom has not disappeared,
yet another civilization has begun to take its place.—George
Santayana, *Winds of Doctrine*

"The Puritan has passed; the Catholic remains"

In 1917 a religious campaign begun in Boston splendidly illustrates the volatile nature of Catholic identity on the verge of the 1920s. Converts Martha Moore Avery and David Goldstein were preparing a national
evangelization tour as a new phase of work for the Catholic Truth Guild. They
secured approval from Archbishop O'Connell for Goldstein and a colleague,
Arthur B. Corbett, to make a cross-country trip in a customized Ford Model
T van and to hold outdoor meetings throughout the United States. Painted in
the papal colors of yellow and white, the vehicle was decorated with crosses
and American flags and carried a message emblazoned on each side. On one
door was stenciled the refrain from the cardinal's "Holy Name Hymn":
"Fierce is the Fight, for God and the Right, Sweet name of Jesus, In thee is
our might." On the opposite panel was a quotation from George Washington's "Farewell Address": "Reason and experience forbid us to believe that
national morality can prevail where religious principles are excluded."[1] Beginning in Boston on July 4, Goldstein and Corbett held eighty outdoor meetings in New England over three months while the van was shipped to the West
Coast. They began their evangelical crusade in California and worked their
way back to the East Coast. The trip lasted eight months and covered some

13,000 miles.[2] On the California leg, Archbishop Edward J. Hanna of San Francisco donated a Cadillac to Goldstein, paid for by the laity, so the campaigners could travel in style. Goldstein noted that his enemies would seize this event as proof of his insincerity, but he drove the Cadillac nonetheless. Enduring earthquake, poor roads, fundamentalist hecklers, heat, and exhaustion, the van entourage returned to Boston dust-covered but jubilant.

This missionary effort reveals several paradoxes at the heart of the Church's understanding of the role of the laity, its manipulation of insider and outsider discourse, and its alleged antimodernism. First, the commissioning of lay converts to educate and preach is striking, as is the presence of a female initiator, even though she remained in Boston. Second, the tour's purpose—public exposition of Catholic doctrine—signaled an outward-directed undertaking typical not of an immigrant Church but of one that had learned something from the methods of mass advertising as well as from Protestant tent revivals and street missions. The purchase of a special car with an angled sounding board to serve as a speaker and a portable podium, plus the sale of apologetic and informational leaflets during the tour, suggests that the Church endorsed the latest innovations in print media and marketing for self-promotion. Finally, while the van's colors signaled allegiance to the papacy, the use of two sacred symbols of American "civil religion"—the nation's first president and its flag—reassured Americans that Catholics were devoted to faith *and* fatherland. Catholics could be model citizens fully committed to the United States because the nation, as Washington had stated, needed religious principles.

The transcontinental tour of the Catholic Truth Guild represents how the automobile transformed the concept of religious space for Catholics, resulting in a unique venture that took evangelization beyond the confines of the parish mission. Superficially, it seemed that Catholicism had capitulated to the methods of mass advertising and publicity, which it scorned in other denominations. But the analysis of Boston Catholicism presented in this study suggests that Catholics frequently gave an appearance of accommodation to a shared national culture while retaining a very bounded sense of separation from it. Indeed, further exploration of the Truth Guild's missionary trip summarizes this related theme of Catholic separatism. Perhaps it is more than ironic that the Truth Guild mission began at the symbolic end of the American frontier and worked its way back toward Europe.

The archbishop of Boston's approval of Avery, Goldstein, and Corbett was a calculated bet. From Cardinal O'Connell's perspective, a former Jew and an ex-Unitarian were ideal proselytizers for the Church. As intelligent, articulate ex-socialists, Avery and Goldstein also won approval for having replaced their atheistic materialism with Catholic supernaturalism. Arthur Corbett

Martha Moore Avery inside and David Goldstein beside the customized Model T van of the Catholic Truth Guild. Quotation from George Washington appears on the side panel. (John J. Burns Library, Boston College)

rounded out the plan as a representative of the local Irish Catholic community. The trio would not have been sanctioned as lay speakers, however, if their views had not agreed with O'Connell's triumphalism, his loyalty to the papacy, and his antisocialism. Avery and Goldstein's first creation, the Common Cause forum, would not have been possible without episcopal approval and supervision, despite rumblings from its lay leaders about the heavy-handedness of clerical interference.

One goal of the Catholic Truth Guild tour was to fight socialism, proof of Catholic participation in the campaign for "100 percent Americanism" surrounding World War I. But even more, the Truth Guild wanted to demonstrate the superiority of Roman Catholicism. In the preceding decades, although they constituted a religious majority in Boston, Catholics had not easily integrated into the Protestant power structure. Lacking full social and economic integration for his flock, the archbishop now seemed determined to wring concessions from non-Catholics that "the Church is the only moral body in the whole world which has remained consistent and sternly logical."[3] Exaggerating Church claims to moral consistency, Church leaders cautioned the laity to maintain a distance from projects not directly under Catholic control, for fear of exposing the eternal truths of Catholicism to contamination and dilution. The warm reception of the Catholic van tour by numerous bishops across the nation showed it to be the model of lay social action preferred by the Church over secular, or even nondenominational Protestant, groups. The many similar lay organizations that were spawned in this era represented Catholic structures that stood apart from non-Catholic institutions, but without threatening Catholic commitment to democratic principles and to an American liberal consensus.

The national focus of the Truth Guild tour implied that Boston Catholics had lost the blindered focus of immigrants and were trying to establish Catholicism's national presence, as did other Catholic programs that flourished during the Progressive era. The postimmigrant laity supported the hierarchy's aggressive style in part because uniting behind the Church's claims to insider status supported and furthered their own socioeconomic aspirations within the Yankee Protestant establishment. Boston was somewhat unique among American cities in that Catholic-Protestant tensions also represented enduring ethnic polarizations. Catholic propaganda, therefore, typically praised the laity for their progress toward the insider status of WASPs, which the Church fostered by supporting the production of symbolic capital (college degrees, fraternal organizations, life insurance, and so forth) for Catholics. Catholic outsider consciousness was preserved to some degree, however, in both the racialism and the piety of Boston's Irish, who largely defined the character of Catholicism against the demands of other national groups. Father Earls, for example, observed little difference between Boston's Irish Catholics of 1920 and "a scene like some in Canon Sheehan's books—as they say their beads and answer to the long prayers."[4] Ethnic nationalisms continued to threaten to subdivide the Boston Church into competing factions, which chafed under Irish control of the hierarchy, clergy, pastorships, and religious rituals.

The Church's manipulation of new technology for publicity, such as the automobile, loudspeaker, pamphlets and subscription sales, and the use of stereopticon, lantern slides, and movies by parishes were embraced without question when supervised for apologetic purposes or for morally wholesome entertainment. Pioneers such as Goldstein were careful to assure skeptical Catholics that his cross-country tour was not stooping to the level of a Salvation Army "tambourine campaign."[5] When Goldstein began a second nationwide tour in 1931, his equipment kept abreast of technology. His new larger open car was fitted with an amplifier, microphone, three horns, and a mechanism to broadcast Catholic hymns through built-in loudspeakers.[6] In this fashion, the Church modernized its missionary practice. At the same time it also claimed its traditional prerogative to mediate lay access to culture. Over time, its preference for European, aristocratic high culture experienced conflict with the expanding and leveling forms of American mass culture. Arch-

David Goldstein, speaking from the autovan in front of the cathedral in San Francisco at the beginning of the cross-country tour in 1917. (John J. Burns Library,
Boston College)

bishop O'Connell was quick to point out that "the Church blesses every one
and every thing which lends itself to the glorious service of spreading the
truth," but his view of culture was decidedly elitist, even if the Church itself
sometimes became a very eclectic and undiscriminating consumer.[7]

Based on its belief that all true art emanates from divinity and must reflect the glory of God, the Church continued to define the function of art as apologetic; thus the literature and art produced by Boston's Catholics in these years was more catechetical than memorable. A Catholic sense of identity was guarded through the Church's attempts to guide aesthetic judgments by keeping a firm grip on moral standards and by using the new middle class to assimilate and defend Catholic ideals and even censorship. Catholic bravado was therefore often overstated, as in this comment reprinted for American Catholics from the London *Tablet*: "The more one thinks, the more does Catholicism prove to hold a monopoly of the means of culture. . . . Although there is civilization outside the pale of Catholicism, it is an overflow from the riches of her treasure-house."[8] Boston Catholics were thus encouraged to believe that Catholicism monopolized the world's cultural treasury. Any surplus treasure was dispensed generously to civilize the world and in defense of Catholic notions of "sublime subjects." At the same time, fear of external attacks from subjectivism, empiricism, and hedonism persisted in the Catholic subculture in its rejection of the immorality associated with the effects of philosophic materialism. The Church's hostility to modernist movements in art and literature, its anxiety about the ephemeral quality of entertainment fads, and its growing support for theater and film censorship can be read as manifestations of this identity crisis.

The presence of a Catholic middle class that emerged and expanded in Boston between 1890 and 1920 created the means by which the Church resisted secularism while trying to preserve its claim for the distinctiveness of Catholic identity. The Church's alliance with the Catholic bourgeoisie was in fact based on acceptance of the dominant culture's values. This compromise helped the laity to reconcile the contradictions between waning communal immigrant values and the capitalist individualism of America. The Church, however, never fully acknowledged its own relationship to the forces of modernization, centralization, and standardization. The Boston archdiocese had become modernized to the extent that it had rationalized a course of action for maximum benefits and had evolved a complex ethnoreligious bureaucracy to pursue its goals. Catholic ideology remained traditional, however, in that it corresponded to patterns of feudal clerical paternalism and to renewed papal demands for loyalty to Rome. The hierarchy and clergy depended on lay support to justify their own status and looked to the middle class to become their allies in an intellectual aristocracy that would uplift the masses. Lay organizations fostered Americanization at the group level, but they also tied Catholics to a subculture of resistance defined by religion. Catholics thus linked the moral idealism derived from their religion to a mission that was both parochial and patriotic: only Catholicism, with its permanent and true ideals, could save the nation from decline. The full-blown nationalist rhetoric of these years stimulated the laity to respond to the crisis atmosphere fostered by the Church in their efforts to preserve faith and fatherland.

The Catholic community of Boston absorbed prevailing assumptions about gender roles that reflected a culture in transition from Victorian to modern, and an economy being transformed from industrial capitalism to monopoly capitalism. As male success came to be equated with competitive occupational and business achievement in industry and commerce, the Church tried to moderate uncontrolled avarice by emphasizing the charitable obligations for both men and women that accompanied financial security. Catholic colleges, Catholic journalism, and men's associations became tools to diffuse a message of manly duty toward faith, fraternalism, and family. They relied largely on an anachronistic ethic akin to antebellum American society in whose open-ended capitalist economy there was room (in theory) for everyone who developed the appropriate character traits. In this regard, Catholics also shared the optimistic assumption of American liberalism that the middle class was infinitely expandable. Ambitious Catholic men were further bonded to the Church through the rituals, social events, and philanthropy of these Catholic associations. The Church, in turn, fostered the transition of members from outsiders to insiders in America by supporting habits that promoted bourgeois values and that offered nonviolent models of survival for the working class. Programs to develop Catholic reading habits, art appreciation, journalism, novels, and so forth were all part of this confirmation of middle-class values. Consequently, the archdiocese of Boston did not launch a systematic attack on capitalism because of its own growing relationship to the very economic system that enabled its quest for entitlement. Instead the Church substituted its moral ideals for social struggle.

Within the Church's idealistic representation of womanhood, Catholic laywomen and nuns functioned as symbols on various levels. Collectively, women embodied the Church's purity and innocence against the world's chaos. Between 1890 and 1920, Americans commonly identified womanhood with America, hence the strong feminine overtones in contemporary descriptions of patriotism. Catholics, too, used womanhood to symbolize the object of their loyalty—Mother Church. Individually, Catholic women confronted Boston's most extreme social problems face to face: prostitution, poverty, incurable illness, child abandonment and delinquency, malnutrition, illiteracy, and sectarian hostilities. The value of women's service in numerous charitable and educational organizations is beyond calculation, although it has remained largely anonymous in historical accounts. Female labor was characteristically unpaid, but as a form of social feminism it was justified by appeals to the assumptions of the cult of domesticity. Thus women were permitted to move into public work, especially concerns that seemed to derive from women's natural domain: children, "fallen" women, health, and education. The establishment of social work as a profession posed a dilemma for Catholic women who wished to receive certification for work in this area. The Church's conservative outlook on female education and careerism, as well as its animus against social scientific reform, worked against women who wished to become professionals in most disciplines. While men were encouraged to Christianize capitalism by penetrating the professions and imbuing them with Catholic principles, women were to exist in segregation from the workplace. However, there were exceptional women who succeeded in journalism, literature, editing, publishing, prison reform, social work, and architecture. Future research on Catholic women will undoubtedly continue to place these particular instances in a more generalized theoretical framework.

Convert women had a special role in New England Catholicism, which suggests that Catholicism answered a crisis of authority felt by women in the social elite by channeling their energies into meaningful service to humanity and by providing a lay version of monastic self-sacrifice. The Church advertised its successful conversions as rational, logical processes, superior to the unstable emotionalism of evangelical Protestantism or the hyperrationalism of the Unitarian church. Whereas a loss of social status had generally accompanied nineteenth-century male conversions to Catholicism, some female converts of the nineteenth and twentieth centuries who came from elite Yankee backgrounds were able to use their social connections to broaden the links between Catholic women's activism and progressive goals and secular agencies. For the converts of Massachusetts, conversion provided the driving force behind a growing social conscience that owed something to Brahmin reformism as well as to the expansion and growth of social Catholicism in the early twentieth century. This has been suggested by the strong relationship between converts and social service to prisoners, the ill, the homeless, and the aged. Not all converts became liberal social reformers, however. As Boston's most public female convert, Martha Moore Avery served the archdiocese by defending women's basic role in traditional ways. Her stump speaking was a milestone for women but was built on granite-solid orthodoxy.

In more private fashion, other women, excluded from the Church's tool of theological education (the seminary) and its source of authority (the priesthood), nonetheless exercised considerable influence on the Catholic community. As the archdiocese consolidated a multitude of nineteenth-century service, educational, and social organizations, lay and religious women met the transition by federating with the CCB of Boston, by occasionally resisting absorption by the chancery, and by serving diocesan and parochial charities. The Church elevated women's service roles by depicting them as a crucial part of a middle-class apostolate in a world shattered by the decline of religion. The crises of modern civilization were overwhelmingly represented by the Church as threats to women, children, and the masses due to their alleged moral and intellectual vulnerability; yet few women gained public recognition or financial compensation from the Church for their hard voluntary labor. Social, devotional, and educational clubs such as the LCW helped extend woman's sphere beyond the home, but not at the expense of motherhood and housewifery. While there were Catholic advocates for suffrage even in the priesthood, the Church did not support female careerism, unless it was dedicated, like Martha Avery's, to full-time Church service. Hence, writing, editing, and journalism serving the faith became permissible careers for Catholic women. Despite the limitations imposed by Church definitions of gender roles, women did seem to profess more farsighted views about the professionalization of charity and the need for salaried, professional social workers, to name two issues, than did the hierarchy and the clergy. While women theoretically supported the Church's antisuffragism and gender conservatism, the lives and writings of Catholic women repudiate stereotypes of themselves as weak, uncompetitive, and unfit for public activity.

Many of the tensions in Boston Catholicism amounted to debates over who should control culture in the democratic, nonhierarchical society of the United States. At the turn of the century, it had seemed that a like-minded group of liberal clergy, bishops, and laity would succeed in democratizing the Church somewhat by recognizing an active lay component. But lay initiatives, such as the national lay congresses, Boston's literary circle of the 1890s, and the Catholic Summer School, soon disappeared, submerged in Boston by the archdiocese's deliberate strategy of bringing all lay organizations under official Church direction.

To foster group commitment to Catholic values, the Church emphasized moral consensus, derived from habits of self-discipline developed by individuals through lifetime contact with a host of Catholic institutions: schools, colleges, seminaries, retreats, parish clubs, men's and women's associations, public forums, and art and literary clubs. Together these ingredients of a localized Catholic subculture, enduring through the 1950s, could nurture a genuine faith, but they also potentially insulated Boston Catholics from personal moral reflection and initiative. The Church failed to encourage a tradition of lay moral reasoning derived from individual experience because the Church mistrusted lay initiatives that might challenge the Church's magisterial and clerical teaching authority. The moral flaws of priests and politicians did not promote frank discussion, while the scandals of the O'Connell episcopacy were hushed up entirely. Instead, the Church stepped up its efforts to monitor lay opinion and behavior on issues ranging from socialism and suffrage to philanthropy and censorship. As late as 1946 a lay Boston Catholic lamented, "Lay leaders are not to be looked for in a regimented society where every Catholic association is ruled over and lectured to by a priest." "Without these monitors," she hinted, "we might learn to use our own mental and moral muscles."[9]

In their use of a rhetoric of cultural disease and decay, Boston's Catholics shared links to other protest movements and antimodernist tendencies in American culture, especially to Protestant fundamentalism and to the Populist movement, which in their own ways also struggled to restore traditional values and social relationships by imposing strict moralism and by idealizing some lost past. But despite its limitations, convolutions, and absurdities, the Catholic subculture was not solely a rigid system engineered by the clergy to manipulate the laity. As the Catholic Church's outsider response to Yankee Protestant insiders, the subculture performed a positive morale-raising function that helped Catholics define themselves according to the distinctiveness of their religious tradition in a period of rapid social change. Viewing the society surrounding them as flawed, Catholics could feel morally superior and optimistic about their role in the nation's future. Clergy and laity together generated "enabling fictions" that empowered Catholics to interpret their heritage in a particular way. By sacralizing their personal lives as cultural models, Catholics hoped to unite their private and public aspirations. The values the Church integrated into its subculture represented the conservative piety and reflexive morality frequently associated with an immigrant poor, together with the rational planning and security-consciousness of the middle class. The Catholic subculture depended on the infusion of the ethic of dutiful work and devotion into the middle class laity who would forge the Church's intellectual nobility and, in turn, edify the masses by their example. Catholic versions of middle-class obsessions with self-discipline and deferred gratification were reinforced within the family, the parish, and Catholic associations. Catholics' conformity to fixed values was stressed in a combination of celebratory and disciplinary practices in schools and recreation, in gender roles, in the home, and in the professions. Although the vibrancy of a religion stems partly from how it reflects its surrounding culture, Boston Catholics were not encouraged to believe that much in the secular world was worth emulating. Faced with elements that appeared to defy Catholic unity and doctrine, Catholics were encouraged to reject secular America and to withdraw into the security and coherence of their own subculture. That womblike space allowed middle-class Catholics to become Catholic Americans without assessing the compromises they had already made with the individualism and competition inherent in capitalism.

The Boston Catholic community experienced certain situations unique to

New England, but like other religious traditions, it was forced to respond to the disruptive impact of industrial (and, subsequently, corporate) capitalism upon America, and to anxieties typically associated with secularization. Expanding industrialization of Europe and America increased the strength and scope of capitalism, whose impact on religion and the self was increasingly to privatize social institutions that had formerly held more power within the state. If religion became more marginalized from the public realm, it also reproduced the bureaucratic institutions of the public realm in order to meet new needs of members and to centralize financial and personnel resources. Thus, in ways representative of many American archdioceses of this era, Boston Catholicism became more bureaucratic, juridical, and self-seeking. No longer able to depend on its historical European role as coequal with the state, the Boston Catholic Church sought to position itself as autonomous mediator between the state and the people, yet without conceding the privatization of religion. In its institutionalism, however, the Church expressed a hostility toward modernity, namely secular democratic government, based on a distorted nostalgia for the Thomist foundations of Christian medieval unity. The Church's triumphalism and techniques for forestalling dialogue would overwhelm any internal democratizing tendencies for the next decades as well as any ecumenical overtures. A strong Catholic subculture was gradually being constructed in Boston to respond to secularization by creating and maintaining the social practices that governed the everyday lives of Catholic individuals and groups—sacred but equal, separated but integrated.

NOTES

Abbreviations

The following abbreviations identify the locations of archival materials cited in the notes.

AABo   Archives of the Archdiocese of Boston, Brighton, Mass.
AAH   Archives of the Archdiocese of Hartford, Hartford, Conn.
ASV   Archivio Segreto Vaticano (Vatican Archives), Vatican City
BCA   Boston College Archives, Chestnut Hill, Mass.
BCSp   Boston College Special Collections, Chestnut Hill, Mass.
BPL   Boston Public Library, Rare Books and Manuscripts, Boston, Mass.
BPLf   Boston Public Library, Fine Arts Department, Boston, Mass.
CUA   Catholic University Archives, Washington, D.C.
GUA   Georgetown University Archives, Washington, D.C.
GUW   Woodstock Archives, Georgetown University, Washington, D.C.
HCA   Holy Cross College Archives, Worcester, Mass.
HCR   Holy Cross College Rare Books and Special Collections, Worcester, Mass.
HTC   Harvard University Theatre Collection, Cambridge, Mass.
HUA   Harvard University Archives, Cambridge, Mass.
KCA   Knights of Columbus National Archives, New Haven, Conn.
LCM   Library of Congress, Manuscripts Division, Washington, D.C.
MHS   Massachusetts Historical Society, Boston, Mass.
MITa   Massachusetts Institute of Technology, Institute Archives and Special Collections, Cambridge, Mass.
NDA   University of Notre Dame Archives, South Bend, Ind.
RUA   Radcliffe University Archives, Cambridge, Mass.
SCA   Simmons College Archives, Boston, Mass.
YBR   Beinecke Rare Book Library, Yale University, New Haven, Conn.

Chapter 1

1. Katherine Conway, "Personal Reminiscences of Typical Latter Day Boston Man," Box 4, BCSp. Conway refers to herself in the third person. This typescript may have been part of her intended biography of Mayor John Fitzgerald.

2. Kerby Miller, "Irish-American Ethnicity," 114.

3. As R. Laurence Moore has suggested, "A narrative focus on contests between insiders and outsiders remains one of the best ways to analyze America's past." I support, with some modifications, Moore's definition of the paradigm in his "Insiders and Outsiders," 407, 408.

4. As Moore states, "An outsider identification pursued by a group over time can provide the group with well-recognized social status within the structure of existing social arrangements" (ibid., 404).

5. Boston's high culture institutions resisted the decline of WASP dominance by rigorously excluding outsiders. See Dimaggio, "Cultural Entrepreneurship."

6. A fourth category, interethnic tensions, I have omitted in order to emphasize the broader phenomenon of Catholic separatism. Consequently, I refer only briefly to conflicts between the Irish and other nationalities as relevant to my discussion of cultural assimilation and of ethnic parishes.

7. I focus solely on the early years of O'Connell's career. James O'Toole's superb biography, *Militant and Triumphant*, supersedes Dorothy Wayman's *Cardinal O'Connell of Boston*.

8. See Merwick, *Boston Priests*.

9. O'Connell, *Sermons and Addresses*, 3:82–83. Hereafter cited as *S&A*.

10. O'Connell's policies appear in his sermon and his list of decrees to clergy at the Fourth Diocesan Synod of 1909 in *S&A*, 3:170–74.

11. O'Toole's biography suggests that O'Connell's absolutism has been overstated, and Robert Sullivan has argued that a sample based on the careers of 1,600 Boston priests "fails to reveal the easy triumph of [O'Connell's] fundamental change." See Robert E. Sullivan, "Beneficial Relations," 203.

12. Because the historiography of the Boston Irish is familiar by now, the focus of this study is not upon Irish political or clerical elites, and I do not offer an analysis of the best-known Catholic causes during the Progressive era, such as temperance or antisuffrage. Neither do I review the long history of anti-Catholic prejudice or summarize the revival of American racialism after World War I. Instead, I approach the interpretation of ethnicity via religion, mindful of the overarching influence of class identification.

13. John Talbot Smith, *History of the Catholic Church in New York*, 2:447. Irish dominance in the Catholic press is illustrated by the history of the Boston *Pilot*, a nationally circulated weekly paper, which had served as an agent of Irish assimilation since its founding in 1829. In the 1900s it continued to be dominated by the Irish, even after abandoning a long-standing tradition of publishing detailed news reports from the Irish counties. See Francis R. Walsh, "The Boston *Pilot*," 280.

14. Larkin, "The Devotional Revolution in Ireland."

15. Census card, December 31, 1909, Sacred Heart Parish, Cambridge files, Box 1, AABo.

16. Casino, "History of the Catholic Parish," 40.

17. Sanders, "Catholics and the School Question in Boston," 165.

18. Thomas H. O'Connor, *Bibles, Brahmins, and Bosses*, 132.

19. Halsey, *Survival of American Innocence*, 15.

20. See Greene, "Catholic Committee," 249–50.

21. Hall, "Cultural Studies," 33–48. Hall concludes that "though neither structuralism nor culturalism will do, as self-sufficient paradigms of study, they have a centrality to the field which all the other contenders lack because, between them (in their divergences as well as their convergences) they address what must be the *core problem* of Cultural Studies" (48).

22. Peter Williams, *Popular Religion in America*, 242.

23. Philip Gleason, "Immigrant Assimilation and the Crisis of Americanization," reprinted in Gleason, *Keeping the Faith*, 60.

24. Kerby Miller, "Irish-American Ethnicity," 113.

25. See quotation from Maisie Ward at the beginning of this chapter.

26. Avery Dulles has identified the "Church as institution" among the five ecclesiological typologies that he has named in Roman Catholic history, in *Models of the Church*. He analyzes the institutional model in chap. 2, 32–46. On p. 39 he cites Bishop Emile DeSmedt of Bruges for this summation of pre–Vatican II ecclesiology.

27. Hobgood, *Catholic Social Teaching*, 104. This is a superb analysis of Catholic statements on economics and society from 1891 to the present.

28. Campbell, "Catholicism from Independence to World War I," 1:369.

29. Timothy Smith, "Religion and Ethnicity in America."

30. Cross, "Changing Image of the City," 33–52, esp. 38.

31. Ellis, *Catholic Bishops*; Merwick, *Boston Priests*, 181.

32. These figures are from Sanders, "Catholics and the School Question in Boston," 133.

33. Ibid., 134. O'Connell's power struggles have been documented by James O'Toole, Robert Sullivan, and William Wolkovich-Valkavicius.

34. O'Toole, *Militant and Triumphant*, 221–25.

35. O'Toole documents the James O'Connell and David Toomey affairs in *Militant and Triumphant*, 176–97. A summary also appears in Slawson, *Foundation*.

36. O'Toole, *Militant and Triumphant*, 195–202.

37. *Boston Globe*, March 31, 1908. McGettrick's address seconded O'Connell's plea for a Catholic college in Boston, "for the battle against evil forces that are menacing a Christian civilization."

38. Kerby Miller, *Emigrants and Exiles*, 537.

39. Preston Noah Williams, "Religious Response to the New Deal," 51. O'Connell and Waters suffered an unexplained rupture in their friendship in later years.

40. Shenton, "Coughlin Movement," 367; Charles Coughlin, *Series of Lectures*, 70, quoted in Fisher, *Catholic Counterculture*, 78. See also Bennett, *Party of Fear*, 258.

41. The letters, handwritten and appearing together on the same yellow legal pad, are available at AABo.

42. Peter Williams, "Catholicism since World War I," 1:385. Ironically, Spellman (1889–1967), nicknamed "the American pope," rose to power despite O'Connell's attempts to sabotage his advancement by placing him in obscure positions. See Cooney, *American Pope*.

43. According to Robert Sullivan, Boston remained more decentralized than other major archdioceses, at least until the 1960s. See Robert E. Sullivan, "Beneficial Relations," 238.

Chapter 2

1. Accounts of the centenary include Kenney, *Centenary*; Langtry, *Metropolitan Boston*, 3:94; and reports in the Boston *Pilot*, *Boston Globe*, and *Boston Herald*.

2. *S&A*, 3:121–39.

3. O'Connell encouraged the Holy Name Society, which was originally founded to end profanation of the Lord's name, to open a chapter in every parish. See Wangler, "Religious Life," 255. Its prominence in this celebration marked its continued strength in Boston as a premier men's society, as it was in many dioceses. Since its mission was

a public one, there was no female equivalent, except perhaps the female membership of the Catholic Total Abstinence Union.

4. Daniel Coakley to O'Connell, February 17, 1917, O'Connell Correspondence, RGI.7, 3:12, AABo.

5. The Marian procession tally comes from an event reported in the *Boston Globe,* May 21, 29, 1911.

6. Byrne, *Glories of Mary,* 156–58.

7. Frank Jones to O'Connell, November 3, 1908, Chancery Central Subject File, M-1503, AABo.

8. Boston *Republic,* October 31, 1908, quoted in Kenney, *Centenary,* 235.

9. *S&A,* 3:32, and numerous editorials in the Catholic press.

10. *S&A,* 3:149.

11. For discussion of *Rerum Novarum,* see Curran "Confronting 'The Social Question.'" Also see two issues of *U.S. Catholic Historian,* vol. 9, devoted to "Labor and Lay Movements." For the impact of *Rerum* in Belgium, which played a leading role in developing Christian democratic groups, see Misner, *Social Catholicism in Europe,* chap. 11.

12. O'Sullivan, "Phases of Charitable Work," 40. See also Henry Spalding, "Should Catholic Associations of Charity Cooperate with Other Similar Institutions?," *Queen's Work,* October 1914, 282.

13. Cross, *Emergence of Liberal Catholicism,* 39.

14. Boston *Pilot,* July 14, 1917, 4.

15. *S&A,* 3:150.

16. Boston *Pilot,* October 14, 1916, 4.

17. Boston *Republic,* December 23, 1916.

18. O'Connell's view is outlined in his address "The Reasonable Limits of State Activity," in *S&A,* 7:14–33, and is discussed further in Chapter 3.

19. The Catholic Church did cooperate successfully with the Massachusetts state board of charities. See Philpott, "Catholicism in Boston," 240. For a summary of Catholic charities, see Walton, "To Preserve the Faith" (1985), 67–120.

20. Chancery Central Subject File, M-899, October 29, 1909, AABo.

21. Boston *Republic,* October 15, 1910, 21.

22. For information on other Catholic settlements, see Campbell, "Reformers and Activists," 170–72; and McGuinness, "Puzzle with Missing Pieces."

23. Philpott, "Catholicism in Boston," 238–47.

24. *S&A,* 3:33.

25. Boston *Republic,* December 23, 1916, 1.

26. *Boston Globe,* August 10, 1908, 2. The AFCS, founded in 1901, exemplifies the American Church's organizational revolution of the early twentieth century. Although the AFCS did not form a social service committee until 1911, whose effectiveness may have been a case of "too little too late," the federation still reflected the centralizing tendency of American life in the Progressive era. "This is the age of consolidation," a Catholic journalist reported, "in labor, in capital, even in literature" (from Chicago's *New World,* quoted in Ede, "Lay Crusade," 189). The AFCS was launched by the bishops of Trenton and Green Bay but was effectively dead by 1919 due to lack of support from the hierarchy.

27. As observed by member Hugh Farrell of Salem, in a speech of February 26, 1916. See typescript, Chancery Central Subject File, M-906, AABo.

28. However, by avoiding merging religious and patriotic symbols on such occasions, O'Connell may have deliberately kept a separation to prevent religion from seeming subordinate to nationalism. See Wangler, "Religious Life," 272.

29. *S&A*, 3:41.

30. Kelley, *Great American Catholic Missionary Congresses*, 364–65.

31. Kelley, *Great American Catholic Missionary Congresses*, contains accounts of both congresses. O'Connell's hymnal, whether or not actually his own compositions, "dominated the hymnal scene" in Boston according to Wangler, "Religious Life," 260.

32. Kelley, *Great American Catholic Missionary Congresses*, 19.

33. Lord et al., *History*, 3:552–71.

34. O'Brien, *Public Catholicism*. Of the three styles of public Catholicism that O'Brien identifies (republican, immigrant, and evangelical), the republican was the most secular, produced strong lay leadership, and recognized the healthy tensions between the religious and secular realms.

35. Orsi, *Madonna of 115th Street*.

36. Boston *Pilot*, January 16, 1915.

37. Louis A. Brandeis and Edward Filene, well known in legal and business circles, were Jewish exceptions to this Protestant list.

38. Herlihy, *Fifty Years of Boston*, 554. For an evaluation of the movement from the perspective of city planning, see Scott, *American City Planning*.

39. A. E. Gilman to Maginnis and Walsh, September 25, 1909, Maginnis Papers, Archives of American Art, microfilm, Smithsonian Institution.

40. Scott, *American City Planning*, 114–16.

41. Hentoff, *Boston Boy*, 81.

42. Boston *Republic*, March 21, 1914. He jokingly referred to his penitentiary stay as "the University of Danbury."

43. Boston *Republic* editorial of February 24, 1917, citing an article in the Boston *Traveler*.

44. For a more detailed examination of the conflicts between WASPs and other ethnic groups, see Solomon, *Ancestors and Immigrants*.

45. James O'Connell, Secretary, to M. J. Splaine, October 19, 1909, Chancery Central Subject File, M-2738, AABo.

46. Boston *Pilot*, April 23, 1910, 4.

47. *S&A*, 3:102, 105. His audience was the AFCS, meeting in Boston in October 1908, just prior to the centenary celebration.

48. Coleman, *Democracy in the Making*. Coleman's history covers 1908 to 1915. See also Lurie, *Challenge of the Forum*. The Ford Hall Forum Papers, supposedly held at the Boston Public Library, cannot be located.

49. Roberts, "Range of Speakers and Topics," 35–49. The following statistics are based on his article.

50. Ibid., 36.

51. Lurie, *Challenge of the Forum*, 105.

52. Other well-known non-Catholic speakers at Ford Hall included Ellen Richards, Norman Hapgood, Stanton Coit, Louis Brandeis, Charlotte Perkins Gilman, and Harry Emerson Fosdick. In addition to being reviewed in the local papers, forum addresses were published in the monthly *Ford Hall Folks*, subsequently titled *The Community Forum* and *Open Forum*.

53. Roberts, "Range of Speakers and Topics," 47.

54. Boston *Pilot*, January 15, 1910, 4.

55. Ryan interview in Coleman, *Democracy in the Making,* 118–23.

56. Ibid., 123.

57. Biographers of Ryan have strenuously tried to claim him as a Catholic liberal, and in doing so have overlooked or minimized the less attractive features of his extreme conservativism, epitomized in his publication *The State and the Church* (1922). A recent appraiser of his career acknowledges, however, that "the terms liberal and conservative might not be that revealing when applied to the career of John A. Ryan, for he combined something from both agendas to create his own view." See Sorvillo, "John A. Ryan," 356–64.

58. Ahern to Father Provincial, October 12, 1925, GUW.

59. Ford Hall Forum file, O'Meara Papers, BPL.

60. Lord et al., *History,* 3:548, and annual reports of the NACLI, 1908–1915.

61. Gleason, "American Identity and Americanization," 40.

62. The city of Lawrence, in Essex County, is part of the archdiocese of Boston, which includes the counties of Essex, Middlesex, Suffolk, Norfolk, and Plymouth.

63. Exchange of letters between George Dunklee and C. J. Sullivan, Secretary to O'Connell, September 12, 13, 1912, Chancery Central Subject File, M-1442, AABo.

64. Anderson, St. Paul's Dorchester, [1907–18], RG5.3, AABo.

65. Joseph Lee to Mr. Ward, December 29, 1906, Joseph Lee Papers, MHS.

66. Lee to James H. Patten, January 20, 1910, IRL Papers, in Joseph Lee Papers, MHS.

67. Daniel Chauncey Brewer, *Conquest of New England,* 186.

68. Lee to Rev D. McMahon, Dec. 14, 1905, Joseph Lee Papers, MS Collection N-14, Box 1, Immigration Restriction League, 1905–12, MHS.

69. Joseph Lee to "Dan," December 18, 1919, IRL Papers, in Joseph Lee Papers, 2:25, MHS.

70. Lee to Ward, November 27, 1920, IRL Papers, in Joseph Lee Papers, Box 3, folder 5, MHS.

71. Edward McSweeney, "The Absurdities and Dangers of Socialism," *Sacred Heart Review,* April 20, 1912.

72. Common Cause Society to Rev. John A. Ryan, November 2, 1914, CCS Papers, AABo.

73. Histories of Common Cause appear in Campbell, "David Goldstein and the Lay Catholic Street Apostolate," and Carrigan, "Martha Moore Avery." For the broader relationship between Catholic public evangelization efforts in the United States, notably the Catholic Church Extension Society, see Kelley, *Story of Extension.* Also see Charles E. Fay, "The Catholic Immigrant," extracts from a speech to the AFCS convention, Toledo, Ohio, August 17, 1915, in *Catholic Mind,* September 8, 1915, 504–5.

74. Fay, "Catholic Immigrant," 505 (emphasis added).

75. Common Cause Society Papers, notebook, January 5, 1914, p. 15, BCSp.

76. CCS Correspondence, esp. Charles E. Fay to O'Connell, April 7, 1914; C. J. Sullivan to Rev. Patrick Waters, April 8, 1914; Patrick Waters to O'Connell, November 6, 1914, O'Connell Correspondence, AABo.

77. Common Cause Society Papers, 1913–1921, notebook, esp. July 18, 1914, p. 57, BCSp.

78. C. J. Sullivan (secretary to O'Connell) to Father John B. Peterson, February 2, 1914, Chancery, St. John's Seminary file, AABo. Waters's meddling was apparent in

a letter to O'Connell requesting the society to warn John Ryan, speaker at Ford Hall, about how Ford Hall endangered Catholics. See P. J. Waters to O'Connell, November 11, 1914, O'Connell Correspondence, AABo.

79. C. J. Sullivan to Martha Moore Avery, February 4, 1914, and to Rev. Patrick J. Waters, February 10, 1914, CCS Correspondence, AABo.

80. Charles Fay to Rev. Charles J. Sullivan, March 6, 1913, CCS Correspondence, AABo.

81. Martha Moore Avery to O'Connell, February 3, 1914, BCSp. A photograph of local members shows only men. See Arthur B. Corbett, "The Common Cause Society," *Queen's Work*, March 1915, 147–48.

82. Boston *Pilot*, April 16, 1910, 1.

83. Corbett, "Common Cause Society," 148.

84. O'Connell, "The Church's Stand," in *S&A*, 3:230.

85. Rosenblum, *Immigrant Workers*, 153.

86. Folder, Archbishop and Chancery, 1913–1914, AABo.

87. John A. Ryan, *Church and Socialism*, 244.

88. Edward Feeney, *Boston Globe*, August 10, 1908.

89. Michael Earls, "Linden Lane at Holy Cross," Holy Cross *Purple*, June 1917, HCA.

Chapter 3

1. Kerby Miller, *Emigrants and Exiles*, 327. See also Kerby Miller, "Irish-American Ethnicity," 98–99, a condensed version of the thesis of his 1985 book.

2. Kerby Miller, "Irish-American Ethnicity," 124.

3. Wagner, *Addresses at Civic Occasions*, 2:251.

4. Kolko, *Main Currents*, 83.

5. Kerby Miller, "Irish-American Ethnicity," 106.

6. Green and Donahue, *Boston's Workers*, 70.

7. William V. Shannon, *American Irish*, 132.

8. William V. Shannon, "Lasting Hurrah," 177.

9. Dorothy Ross, cited in O'Brien, *Public Catholicism*, 100.

10. Dennis Ryan, *Beyond the Ballot Box*, 109 n. 23.

11. McSweeney, "Irish Immigrants in America," 559.

12. Dennis Ryan, *Beyond the Ballot Box*, 101; Stephen O'Meara, quoted in Wilson, *Labor of Words*, 209 n. 25.

13. Kerby Miller, *Emigrants and Exiles*, 534–35.

14. McSweeney, "Irish Immigrants in America," 562.

15. See Anderson, *Era of the Summer Estates*, 125, for a list of occupations of Swampscott summer residents. Fitzpatrick and Mulloney are the only identifiably Irish names.

16. Helen Phelan to Father Haberlin, 1922, O'Connell Correspondence, 9:1, AABo.

17. Henry Hyde, quoted in *Columbiad*, August 1910, 10.

18. Kerby Miller, *Emigrants and Exiles*, 534. The militant Irish nationalist movement of the 1910s also experienced conflicts with the Church.

19. Patrick J. Supple, in Wagner, *Addresses at Civic Occasions*, 2:172.

20. Daniel Coakley to Archbishop O'Connell, February 17, 1917, O'Connell Cor-

respondence, RGI.7, 3:12, AABo. Coakley was prompted to write to O'Connell in response to an editorial in the Boston *Pilot.*

21. While it may be true, as Jay Dolan has argued in his study of antebellum New York City Catholics, that ethnic identity and conflict overwhelmed class issues, the same does not hold for the early twentieth century. See Dolan, *Immigrant Church.*

22. The Catholic press ostentatiously marked the deaths of leading philanthropists and writers in the Yankee establishment not to praise them but as further proof of WASP decay. A partial obituary list includes Thomas Bailey Aldrich (d. 1907), Edward Everett Hale (d. 1909), Robert Treat Paine (d. 1910), Julia Ward Howe (d. 1910), Thomas Wentworth Higginson (d. 1911), Charles Francis Adams II (d. 1915), Henry Adams (d. 1918), and William Dean Howells (d. 1920).

23. Statistics about the Catholic population of Boston are from Casino, "History of the Catholic Parish," 107.

24. *Brochure of Boston College,* 25–26.

25. Robert E. Sullivan, "Beneficial Relations," 212.

26. See sources cited in ibid., 212 n. 21.

27. The fact that the new parishes created between 1900 and 1920 were named mostly for ethnic saints indicates pressure on Irish Americans to recognize the presence of other nationalities, notably French Canadians, Italians, Lithuanians, Poles, and Armenians. Examples of national parishes founded in this era include St. Adalbert (Polish), Hyde Park, 1913; Our Lady of Mt. Carmel (Italian), East Boston, 1905; St. Peter (Lithuanian), South Boston, 1904; St. Anthony (Portuguese), Cambridge, 1902; St. Francis of Assisi (Italian), Cambridge, 1917; and Holy Cross (Armenian), Cambridge, 1920.

28. *Boston Herald,* May 24, 1901.

29. See Bennett, *Party of Fear;* Higham, *Strangers in the Land;* and Solomon, *Ancestors and Immigrants.*

30. *The Whole D Family.* The authors chose the letter *D* "because 'Jim' Donovan is said to be, under John F. Fitzgerald, the 'boss of the city.'"

31. See Lewis Curtis, *Apes & Angels.* On American images of the nineteenth-century Irish, see Knobel, *Paddy and the Republic.* Brahmin nativist strategies are detailed in Solomon, *Ancestors and Immigrants.*

32. Henry Childs Merwin, "The Irish in American Life," *Atlantic Monthly,* May 1896, 289. American commentaries on the Irish closely mimicked the literary catalogs made by nineteenth-century English commentators such as Charles Swinburne who associated Irish writers with "capacity," "fever," "fancy," "mock-mystical babble," and innocence of "reason," "imagination," and "serious workmanship." In brief, the Irish remained, as they had since English colonization of their country in the 1550s, exotic primitives to the English. See the *Times* (London), quoted in the *Times* (London), *The Ireland of To-day* (Boston: Small, Maynard, 1915), 121.

33. Joseph Smith, "The Irish-American as Citizen," *New England Magazine,* July 1912, 257–73.

34. Ibid.

35. Scudder, *Listener in Babel,* 80–81.

36. Inglis, *Moral Monopoly,* 138–39.

37. Kolko, *Main Currents,* esp. 83–84; Kerby Miller, *Emigrants and Exiles.*

38. Living in Boston as an adult, Mary Elizabeth McGrath (1840–1907) was the daughter of parents who emigrated to Quincy around 1850. She married John Blake,

a leading physician in Boston, and became an advocate of both domesticity and women's education. Her poetry, newspaper columns, and stories were admired by Oliver Wendell Homes and Theodore Roosevelt. See Mainiero, *American Women Writers,* 1:173, and Kenneally, *History of American Catholic Women,* 135.

39. Katherine E. Conway, *Watchwords of John Boyle O'Reilly,* 7.

40. John Boyle O'Reilly, "The Exile of the Gael," 416.

41. McCarthy, *A Round of Rimes,* 26. Kerby Miller in *Emigrants and Exiles* has effectively suggested how guilt strengthened an exile mentality in the lives of Irish emigrants.

42. O'Reilly's sudden death, perhaps suicide from an overdose of chloral hydrate, suggests the pathological effects of such dissatisfaction. See Ibson, "Will the World Break Your Heart?" The morbid side of the Irish American personality, explored in further detail by Kerby Miller in *Emigrants and Exiles,* is confirmed by more than one case in Boston.

43. Boston *Pilot,* June 1, 1907, 3.

44. Katherine E. Conway, "Why Always Catholic?," 31.

45. Catholic scholars compiled rosters of Catholic patriots and heroes, including the Calverts and Carrolls of Maryland; Generals Lafayette and Rochambeau during the American Revolution; Thomas Fitzsimons, the only Catholic signer of the Constitution; John Hughes, archbishop of New York during the early national era, who fought for tax-supported parochial schools; Civil War generals, including Sheridan, Meade, Meagher, Moore, and Rosecrans; World War I servicemen and chaplains; and President Taft's chief justice, Edward White.

46. *Ave Maria,* July 6, 1912, 19–20. Rising Irish identification with Irish nationalist struggles during and after World War I irritated local Catholics from different ethnic backgrounds. Some complained that Irish Americans inflicted their struggles even upon Sunday Mass. An irate Boston Catholic sent the following complaint to the pope's apostolic delegate in 1920: "Irish Catholics, the militant ones, have brought the Holy Church to the depths of blood and crime. Their religion comes after their politics, they are the ones who talk in Church during Mass, who leave it before it is over. I am American, and as good and practical Catholic as I can be." See R. Toope to John Bonzano, August 28, 1920, Del. Ap., USA, V, file 83, ASV.

47. See Hutchinson, *Modernist Impulse.*

48. Barrett Wendell, 1893, quoted in Peterson, *New England College.*

49. Boston *Pilot,* February 10, 1912, 4.

50. Daniel Coakley to Archbishop O'Connell, February 17, 1917, O'Connell Correspondence, RGI.7, 3:12, AABo.

51. John B. Kennedy, "Joseph C. Pelletier—Knight," *Extension Magazine,* February 1921, 10.

52. Sargent, "Catholicism in Massachusetts," 740.

53. Boston *Republic,* November 2, 1919, 1. See Frank W. Chase on white slavery, prostitution, and drugs in his "White Slave Traffic in Boston," 531–39.

54. Leon Harris, *Only to God,* 222–23. Despite Boston's numerous Catholic Democratic mayors and city politicians at the state level, six of the nine governors in office between 1900 and 1920 were Republican.

55. *Boston Herald,* November 15, 1919, Reconstruction, Topic 10, Pelletier Case, November 1919, file SC-16-2-184, KCA.

56. J. Joseph Huthmacher described how the case divided Massachusetts Demo-

crats. One of Pelletier's shady friends, lawyer Daniel A. Coakley, named in several of the extortion charges, was a perennial nuisance to and sometime election opponent of Curley. Coakley, who acquired the nickname "Knave of Boston," was later disbarred from practicing law in Massachusetts for eleven years. See Huthmacher, *Massachusetts People and Politics*, 35. Correspondence between Coakley and O'Connell suggests that the archbishop privately sympathized with Coakley's plight. See Coakley to O'Connell, May 8, 1933, O'Connell Correspondence, 3:12, AABo. For details about Coakley, see Beatty, *Rascal King*.

57. One such group, the Loyal Coalition, was composed of old-stock Bostonians who opposed a free Irish republic, especially in the wake of Eamon De Valera's tour of the United States in 1920. Demarest Lloyd was its president. See Huthmacher, *Massachusetts People and Politics*, 26–27, 34, 36.

58. "Memo for Mr. McGinley," March 29, 1922, Reconstruction, Topic 10, Pelletier case, file SC-16-2-192, n.p., KCA. The statement read, in part: "Cabot and Allen may be judged from the foregoing and what follows. Weston and Holmes stand convicted of a felony as related below. Henry F. Hurlburt, President of the Bar Association, is a renegade Catholic lately become an avowed atheist. Francis Peabody is an active member of the Loyal Coalition and publicly cheered before that body after his attack on Cardinal O'Connell. Moorfield Storey is a notorious Anglophile and detests everybody Catholic or Irish. William G. Thompson was surprised when told that a Catholic could wish a blessing for a Protestant! James D. Colt describes a crook as a man with a mean face like a Jesuit! John E. Hannigan is a renegade Catholic and Mason (picked out by the Bar Association to represent the Catholics!)."

59. *Extension Magazine*, February 1921, 10.

60. Kauffman, *Faith and Fraternalism*, 247.

61. James A. Flaherty's remarks supporting Pelletier appeared in the *New York Times* in 1922. He later apologized to the Knights for having defended Pelletier; see another defense of Pelletier by John B. Kennedy, a Knights of Columbus historian, published in the *Nation*, April 12, 1922, in response to its anti-Pelletier editorial of March 8, 1922.

62. Pelletier had refused the opportunity to speak on his own behalf, claiming that he did not have adequate time to prepare his defense during an election year. See editorial "The Knights of Columbus," *Catholic Transcript* (Hartford), August 3, 1922, 4.

63. There were also implications for the court system, namely the legal questions of admitting covertly gathered evidence in court and of entrapment of defendants.

64. The bogus oath first appeared in Seattle, September 1, 1912. It charged Knights with pledging to overthrow the American government by waging "relentless war on all heretics, Protestants, and Masons" in defense of the pope. See Kauffman, *Faith and Fraternalism*, 169–72.

65. Ibid., 178.

66. February 13, 1922, Del. Ap., USA, IX, Boston, file 106, ASV. Bernard Rothwell, born in Dublin in 1859, came to the United States in 1869. Educated in public schools, he became chairman of the board of Boston Elevated Railroad, president of the Boston Chamber of Commerce (1908–10) during the ill-fated "Boston, 1915" campaign, and chairman of the Massachusetts Bureau of Immigration (1913–14 and 1917–19). He was approached by the Watch & Ward Society as a likely candidate to replace Pelletier as district attorney in 1917. His Anglo-sounding name and his puritanical nature seem

to have made him a target of anti-Catholic instigators seeking a useful ally, which suggests that he played a divisive role in the Catholic community.

67. Slawson, *Foundation*, 125.

68. Angoff, "Boston Twilight," 439.

69. On the history of partisan politics and the police, see Lane, *Policing the City*.

70. O'Meara to "Fan," October 30, 1895, Family Correspondence, O'Meara Papers, BPL. The O'Meara Papers reveal an affectionate Irish Catholic family life. In a typical letter to his wife, for example, O'Meara declared, "Believe me fully when I say that I love you more than all the world and would give my life for you and to you cheerfully" (O'Meara to Isabella Squire O'Meara, October 11, 1876). The following biography is based on O'Meara's personal papers at the BPL and information in Russell, *City in Terror*, 38–43, 48, 51–53, 84, 198.

71. Will dated August 17, 1953, addressed to William E. Dwyer, Attorney at Law, Alice O'Meara Correspondence, 1895–1960, O'Meara Papers, BPL.

72. Russell, *City in Terror*, 41. James Curley was the frequent target of the Good Government's criticisms. He scornfully dismissed them as the "Goo-Goos."

73. *Boston Herald*, October 22, 1911.

74. J. J. Roche to O'Meara, December 11, 1904, O'Meara Papers, Roche file, Rare Book and Manuscripts, BPL. Many of Roche's friends derided him as a turncoat when he reversed the paper's Democratic heritage in supporting the Republican Roosevelt for president in 1904. See Earls, *Manuscripts and Memories*, 104, and Lane, "James Jeffrey Roche and the Boston *Pilot*," 361.

75. Russell, *City in Terror*, 35.

76. Ibid., 52.

77. Lane, *Policing the City*, from *Annual Police Report* (1885), 3.

78. Russell, *City in Terror*, 47. O'Meara's annual salary of $6,000 in 1913 was considerable in an age when the average day laborer earned under $500 per year.

79. Ibid., 39, 40, 53, 84, 198. O'Meara did encourage the existence of a police social club, as long as it was not federated with a larger group such as a national union.

80. Ibid., 43.

81. Lucy (Sister Leocadia) O'Meara to Stephen O'Meara, December 20, 1885, O'Meara Papers, BPL.

82. The pallbearers at his funeral included Theodore Roosevelt, Senator Henry Cabot Lodge, Governor Eugene Foss, and Mayor Andrew Peters as well as Catholic leaders, policemen, and journalists. See report of O'Meara funeral in the Boston *Republic*, December 21, 1918, 8.

83. P. H. Callahan to Rothwell, Del. Ap., USA, file 106, folder 2, ASV.

84. Some of my interpretation of laymen follows McDannell, "True Men," 19.

85. For a history of the Sulpicians in the United States, see Kauffman, *Tradition and Transformation*. On American seminaries, see Joseph M. White, *Diocesan Seminary*, which contains numerous references to St. John's.

86. O'Connell's resentment of the Sulpicians even led him to exhume Sulpician corpses in the seminary graveyard in 1928 and ship them to their Maryland headquarters. See Joseph M. White, *Diocesan Seminary*, 261.

87. Boston *Pilot, Brief Historical Review*, 169.

88. Merwick, *Boston Priests*, 193–96. On the whole, I find Merwick's judgment of O'Connell too harsh and one-sided, while I agree with her characterization of the stifling lifestyle of priests. For criticism of her superficial treatment of a complex issue,

see Robert E. Sullivan, "Beneficial Relations," 201–38. On O'Connell's record, see O'Toole, *Militant and Triumphant*. For O'Connell's discussion of the need for a "Romanized" perspective, see O'Connell, "L'Influenza di Roma nella Formazione del Clero Americano," in *S&A*, 3:412–29.

89. St. John's Seminary faculty lacked academic specialization well into the 1930s, which meant that a single professor, like John B. Peterson, taught everything from church history to moral theology to canon law, gave talks on pastoral life without ever having lived in a parish, and became head of St. John's in 1911. See Robert E. Sullivan, "Beneficial Relations," 220–21, 216. For a sympathetic treatment of the Sulpicians' distinctiveness as teachers, see Kauffman, *Tradition and Transformation*, 229–38.

90. Robert E. Sullivan, "Beneficial Relations," 203.

91. O'Connell, "A Faithful Priesthood," in *S&A*, 8:120. This is O'Connell's funeral eulogy for a diocesan priest.

92. Joseph M. White, *Diocesan Seminary*, 227.

93. James Hennessey, *American Catholics*, 217. On the sterile intellectual atmosphere of priestly life after the papal condemnation of Modernism in 1907, the best treatment is Gannon, "Before and After Modernism," 293–383.

94. *S&A*, 3:73.

95. John Talbot Smith, *Our Seminaries*, 16–23. A later, revised and enlarged version was printed in 1908 as *The Training of a Priest: An Essay on Clerical Education with a Reply to the Critics* (London: Longmans, Green). Smith had harsh words for Catholic intellectual life in general. See his "Young Catholic Writer." The career of this energetic priest included involvement in the Catholic summer school, the Catholic theater guild, and the Catholic press.

96. Merwick, *Boston Priests*, 126.

97. Earls Diary, June 16, [1900], HCR.

98. Ibid., April 12, 1900.

99. Ibid., May 25, [1900].

100. Robert E. Sullivan, "Beneficial Relations," 221.

101. Joseph M. White, *Diocesan Seminary*, 231.

102. Quoted in ibid., 218.

103. O'Toole, *Militant and Triumphant*, 156.

104. *Sacred Heart Review*, September 30, 1911.

105. Among many accounts of the Social Gospel, see Hutchinson, *Modernist Impulse*; Magnuson, *Salvation in the Slums*; Gilbert, *Work without Salvation*; and Welch, *Protestant Thought in the Nineteenth Century*, 2:238–39, 255–65.

106. *Catholic Transcript* (Hartford), quoting the Boston *Republic*, April 8, 1909.

107. Parish calendar for January 1897, Sts. Peter and Paul, cited by McDannell, "True Men," 22 n. 8.

108. McDannell, "True Men," 33.

109. Ibid.

110. For examples of women's opinions, see the *Boston Globe* editorial debate, "Are Women in Business More Faithful than Men?," March 6, 1910.

111. *Ave Maria*, June 22, 1912, 788.

112. Boston *Republic*, May 16, 1914.

113. Fisher, *Catholic Counterculture*, xiv.

114. McDannell, "True Men," 34.

115. Lawrence, "Relation of Wealth to Morals," 287–88.

116. Ibid.

117. *Rerum Novarum,* 20.

118. McDannell, "True Men," 31.

119. Horatio Alger died in 1899 and achieved his greatest success posthumously through persistent misreadings of his stories. As Michael Moon and others have pointed out, "Alger's tales hold out a considerably less grandiose prospect for boy readers; that any boy who is reasonably willing to please his potential employers can attain a life of modest comfort" (Moon, " 'Gentle Boy,' " 262).

120. Boston *Pilot,* July 27, 1907.

121. O'Connell Correspondence, 9:3, [March 1916], AABo.

122. For evidence of how O'Connell and his wily nephew conveniently ignored this policy in the case of their own family, see O'Toole, *Militant and Triumphant,* 32, 180.

123. "Why Catholics Fail," *Sacred Heart Review,* January 13, 1912.

124. Wyllie, *Self-Made Man,* 22.

125. McSweeney, "Irish Immigrants in America," 562.

126. See, for example, Thomas O'Brien, *Columbiad,* January 1911.

127. *Sacred Heart Review,* January 13, 1912, 6.

128. O'Sullivan, "Phases of Charitable Work," 35.

129. *Boston Globe,* January 9, 1907.

130. *S&A,* 3:399.

131. Katherine E. Conway, *Christian Gentlewoman,* 98.

132. O'Connell, "The Italian in America," July 25, 1914, in *S&A,* 4:181. On the experience of Italians in Boston, see Anna Martellone, *Una Little Italy Nell'Atene d'America. La comunita italiana di Boston dal 1880 al 1920* (Naples: Guida, 1973).

133. Frank Leveroni to O'Connell, August 11, 1911, O'Connell Correspondence, RG I.7, 6:5, AABo. Leveroni was a judge of the juvenile court (1913).

134. Boston *Republic,* February 8, 1919. Catholic fear of a WASP monopoly on charity work is analyzed in Walton, "To Preserve the Faith" (1985).

135. Charles De Courcy to Fr. Donlon, April 13, 1916, GUA.

136. See Chinnici, "Spiritual Capitalism."

137. *Brochure of Boston College,* 26.

138. Conway to Bishop McQuaid, June 29, 1892, Archives of the Diocese of Rochester.

139. Lucy (Sister Leocadia) O'Meara to Stephen O'Meara, December 20, 1885, O'Meara Papers, BPL.

140. Oates, "Organized Voluntarism," 655.

141. O'Brien to Eliot, February 12, 1900, Charles William Eliot Papers, Correspondence 1892–1903, HUA. Eliot's detractions had appeared in *Atlantic Monthly* in October 1896.

142. *Boston College Alumni Directory, 1872–1923* (Chestnut Hill, Mass.: June 1924), 7–46, BCSp.

143. "Report of Committee on Public Morals," AFCS Convention, New York, August 1916, p. 19, Chancery Central Subject File, M-906, AABo.

144. William P. Leahy, *Adapting to America,* 3.

145. *Woodstock Letters* 34 (1905), 430.

146. *America,* June 21, 1917.

147. Boston *Pilot* Correspondence, RG III, 14.D, AABo. In a similar vein, O'Connell addressed Boston College seniors on retreat in 1923 and repeated the claim that

Catholic education provided essential "fixed principles" to students by placing spiritual goals above all else, even medicine and law. See O'Connell, "The Goal of Life," in *S&A*, 8:80.

148. Michael P. Dowling, S.J.,"The Catholic College as a Preparation for a Business Career," reprint of paper read, 1898, pp. 5, 7, HCA.

149. William P. Leahy, *Adapting to America*, 35.

150. Dowling, "Catholic College," 7.

151. See his address to the Catholic Education Association, April 24, 1919, "Reasonable Limits of State Activity," in *S&A*, 7:14–33.

152. James J. Walsh, *Education*.

153. McSweeney, "Irish Immigrants in America," 562.

154. Philpott, "Catholicism in Boston," 250. Reportedly, over 2,000 pupils were enrolled by 1922.

155. Dennis Ryan, *Beyond the Ballot Box*, 106. Differing from Ryan, Kerby Miller has argued that ambitious Irish American parents insisted that parochial schools provide the same opportunities for upward mobility as public education. See *Emigrants and Exiles*, 531.

156. Leahy, *Adapting to America*, 3.

157. I have borrowed the phrase from Inglis, *Moral Monopoly*, 134.

158. Boston Chapter, Knights of Columbus, *Souvenir of the First Grand Ball*, 31.

159. *Columbiad*, April 1907.

160. Kerby Miller supports the contention that Irish American organizations were not wholly bourgeois and assimilationist, but that proletarian concerns were represented by large numbers of unskilled and semiskilled laborers. See *Emigrants and Exiles*, 534.

161. Information on the founding of the Fourth Degree comes from Kauffman, *Faith and Fraternalism*, 137–43.

162. *Columbiad*, October 1898, 6.

163. The Massachusetts Catholic Order of Foresters was somewhat unusual in admitting women as equal beneficiaries. The Knights did not agree to do so; hence the formation of the ladies' auxiliary known as the Daughters of Isabella.

164. An account of the union's founding appears in Eulalie Tuckerman, "Life of Williams" (1907), typescript, esp. 292, AABo. See also Henry Coyle, "Catholic Societies and Clubs of Greater Boston," in Coyle, *Our Church*; and *Notable Catholic Institutions*, which lists members.

165. Desmond, *Reading Circle Manual*, 77.

166. *S&A*, 9:174.

167. O'Connell's remarks to them echoed statements of the papacy, such as this speech delivered by the pope to the Organization for Retreats for Working Girls: "It may be said that in our day the demon levels his shafts especially at the working class, nor indeed is it to be wondered at that his emissaries labor to instill into the heart of working girls the poison of false teachings and the most nefarious incitements to vice." Quoted in the Boston *Republic*, April 1, 1916, 8.

168. *Sacred Heart Review*, December 2, 1911.

169. Edward F. Garesché, S.J., editor of *Queen's Work* in St. Louis, frequently sought O'Connell's approval, citing encouraging letters from the Vatican, Cardinal Gibbons, and John Cardinal Farley about his work. He wrote admiringly of the growth of the Boston chapter. See Chancery Central Subject File, M-1812, AABo.

170. Similar retreats, for much larger numbers, were run by the Young Men's Catholic Association.

171. Boston *Pilot,* January 3, 1920.

172. "Laymen's Retreat Movement in the Boston Archdiocese," Boston *Pilot,* March 8, 1930.

173. Philpott, "Catholicism in Boston," 245–46. Susan Walton, in "To Preserve the Faith" (1983), uses the St. Vincent de Paul Society as one of three case studies of Boston Catholic charities.

174. Walton, "To Preserve the Faith" (1983), 179–80.

175. Boston *Pilot,* July 27, 1907.

176. Rev. David J. Toomey, *Boston Globe,* May 9, 1910. Toomey, a diocesan priest, became notorious for numerous sexual liaisons. While serving as editor of the *Pilot,* he concealed his identity as a priest to marry a woman in New York and also lived with his secretary in Cambridge, Massachusetts. See O'Toole, *Militant and Triumphant,* 184–87.

177. *Boston Globe,* January 7, 1907, 2. Daniel P. Toomey is not to be confused here with Father David J. Toomey.

178. *Columbiad,* June 1916, 12.

179. Henry Hyde, quoted in *Columbiad,* August 1910, 10.

180. O'Connell, "True Prosperity," in *S&A,* 4:220.

181. Boston *Republic,* April 18, 1914.

182. *Boston Globe,* May 15, 1910.

183. *S&A,* 3:33.

184. O'Connell, "True Prosperity," on laying a cornerstone of a new church in Brockton, in *S&A,* 4:220–21.

185. See O'Connell's "The Reasonable Limits of State Activity," written by P. J. Waters of St. John's and delivered to the Catholic Educational Association, June 24, 1919, in *S&A,* 7:14–33.

186. Ibid., 7:18.

187. Aileen Ross, "Philanthropy," 12:77.

188. *S&A,* 8:7.

189. *S&A,* 3:137.

190. O'Connell, "Address to Clergy in the Fourth Diocesan Synod" (1909), in *S&A,* 3:173.

191. O'Connell, "Address at Annual Convention of Archdiocesan Federations," (1910), in *S&A,* 3:378.

192. Erie, *Rainbow's End,* 57–72.

Chapter 4

1. Cross, "Changing Image of the City," 37.

2. Sam Bass Warner, *Streetcar Suburbs* (1962), 160. Besides real estate, the cost of suburban living included tolls at each entrance to Boston proper.

3. See James P. Shannon, *Catholic Colonization of the Western Frontier.*

4. Terry Eagleton, paraphrasing Raymond Williams in *Literary Theory: An Introduction* (Minneapolis: University of Minnesota Press, 1983), 36. Benedict Anderson has written about the mobilization of images in nationalist discourse in *Imagined*

Communities: Reflections on the Origin and Spread of Nationalism (London: Verso, 1983).

5. Boston *Pilot,* August 6, 1914, 4.

6. *S&A,* 4:105–12. Passages cited below are from this address. O'Connell's rural idyll is ironic in light of his own childhood in industrialized Lowell, Massachusetts, where he worked only one day as a millhand. He also completely ignores the phenomenon of the working girl, who operated Lowell's textile mills for decades.

7. Cross, "Changing Image of the City," 34.

8. Father Michael Earls to Bess, July 9, 1922, HCR.

9. O'Connell, "In the Beginning," in *S&A,* 3:137.

10. Cram, *My Life,* 230.

11. David O'Brien provided one example of this trend in his study of the diocese of Syracuse, New York, *Faith and Friendship.* In 1975, Jay Dolan's pioneering study of lay culture from the bottom up, *Immigrant Church,* had suggested a model for research based on parish records. Dolan has recently edited a three-volume series, *The American Catholic Parish,* which is primarily a collection of essays on regional differences, supported by quantitative data.

12. Woods, *Americans in Process,* and *Neighborhood in Nation-Building.* Woods made this point, of course, with a reason other than religion in mind. Progressive (and often nativist) reformers of the generation of Woods and his coauthor, A. J. Kennedy, were primarily interested in verifying the Americanizing role of the Catholic parish as an agent of assimilation. Green criticizes Woods's naiveté in Green and Donahue, *Boston's Workers,* 68–69.

13. *S&A,* 4:219.

14. Anderson to O'Connell [1908], Parish Files, RG5.3, AABo.

15. Recently, the alleged benefit of Irish political machines has been questioned by those who argue that they were detrimental to economic success. One such revisionist account of urban machines appears in Erie, *Rainbow's End.*

16. Gleason, "Mass and Maypole Revisited," 261–62, 271.

17. John Talbot Smith, *Our Seminaries,* 222.

18. See, for example, Narciso G. Menocal, "Louis Sullivan's Use of the Gothic: From Skyscrapers to Banks," in Rosenthal and Szarmach, *Medievalism in American Culture,* 214–50.

19. The phrase comes from O'Connell's description of a church (most likely Trinity) in Copley Square. See *S&A,* 3:397. In the same passage, he observed that the use of Roman and Italian models for public building in Boston, such as the Public Library, also paid tribute to the Catholic tradition.

20. O'Connell, "The Independence of the Holy See," in *S&A,* 4:95, an address at a Catholic Union reception, November 18, 1912.

21. Slawson, *Foundation,* 214.

22. The arts and architecture have received only slight attention from Lord et al. in their three-volume *History.* Similarly, art historians have neglected Catholic participation in America's three Gothic revivals of the 1820s, 1880s, and 1910s/1920s. One essay that considers the visual impact of statuary in some Massachusetts churches is Wangler, "Religious Life," 239–72. Peter Williams has provided a general study, "Religious Architecture and Landscape," 3:1325–39.

23. John Lancaster Spalding, preface to Healy, *On Christian Art,* 6.

24. Ralph Adams Cram, Phi Beta Kappa address, Harvard University, June 20,

1921, *Harvard Graduates' Magazine*, September 1921, p. 19, HUA. Cram had been a Harvard professor from 1903 to 1908.

25. Cram, *My Life*, 278. He also commented that had his former partner, Bertram Goodhue (1869–1924), survived another decade, his personality and designs might have "averted the debacle of contemporary modernistic art" (17).

26. Bunting, *Houses of Boston's Back Bay*, 160–63.

27. *Architectural Review*, December 1899, 146.

28. For example, see Neill, "Achievements in Architecture," 209–19: "Thus with the multiplication of churches have come the other institutions of the Church that safeguards every interest" (217). He listed schools among them.

29. While Boston College's buildings were financed through a $2 million fund drive, much of the neighboring seminary, monastery, and convent buildings were funded by the B. F. Keith estate, left as a personal bequest to O'Connell of about $3 million in 1918. See Wayman, *Cardinal O'Connell of Boston*, 187–95; O'Toole, " 'That Fabulous Churchman,' " 44; O'Toole, *Militant and Triumphant*, 210–11.

30. Sanders, "Catholics and the School Question in Boston," 121–70.

31. O'Leary, "William Henry Cardinal O'Connell," 111.

32. Charles Maginnis, foreword to Connick, *Adventures in Light and Color*.

33. Whitehill, *Boston in the Age of John F. Kennedy*, 40.

34. Boston College *Stylus* 23 (December 1909): 105–6; letter, January 27, 1909, Maginnis and Walsh file, 11.13 A9, BCA. President Gasson did not remain at Boston College to see the plan completed. He was transferred to Woodstock College, Maryland, in 1914.

35. Gasson to Messrs. Maginnis and Walsh, January 28, 1909, Maginnis Papers, BCA.

36. William V. Shannon, *American Irish*, 217.

37. Boston *Pilot*, June 1, 1907, 1.

38. *Boston Globe*, undated clipping ca. March 30, 1908, BCSp.

39. Cram, "As Ralph Adams Cram Sees the New Boston College," *Boston Evening Transcript*, April 30, 1921.

40. Douglass Shand Tucci, *Built in Boston*, 180.

41. I rely on information about Maginnis's life from the following: Emerson, "Charles Maginnis"; Shanley, "Charles Donagh Maginnis," 152–55; Douglass Shand Tucci, *Built in Boston*, and *Church Building in Boston*; materials in the vertical files at BPL, Fine Arts Division; articles in the *Boston Globe* for 1935 and 1937; and Maginnis's articles in numerous architectural journals, including *Christian Art, Brickbuilder*, and its successor, *Architectural Forum*. I also interviewed his daughter, Alice Maginnis Walsh (d. 1992), on several occasions.

42. Matthew Sullivan (1868–1948), born and educated in Boston, had met Maginnis in Edmund M. Wheelwright's office. He withdrew from Maginnis and Walsh in 1930 to open his own office.

43. Maginnis's articles that express his opinions on architectural styles and principles include "Catholic Church Architecture," *Brickbuilder* 15 (1906): 25–28, 46–52; "Movement for a Vital Christian Architecture"; "Recent Roman Catholic Architecture," an address to the Boston Society of Architects in 1909; "A Century's Progress in Catholic Architecture," *Columbiad*, June 1911, 5; "Catholic Church Architecture" (1917), 33–38, plates 17–48; and "Architecture and Religious Tradition," *Architectural Record* 96 (September 1944): 89–91.

44. Douglass Shand Tucci, *Built in Boston*, 180; Ralph Adams Cram, Phi Beta Kappa address, Harvard University, June 20, 1921, *Harvard Graduates' Magazine*, September 1921, p. 19, HUA.

45. Cram to Right Rev. R. J. Haberlin, December 11, 1924, St. Paul's, Dorchester, RG5.3, folder 4, AABo.

46. Maginnis, "Recent Roman Catholic Architecture," 9. Cram complimented Maginnis by choosing his Church of St. Catherine of Genoa, Somerville, to illustrate his architecture article for the *Encyclopedia Britannica*. See Baxter, "Selection from the Works," 103. Cram does not mention Maginnis in his autobiography, nor does Maginnis mention Cram's support for the LAS in his obituary of Cram in *Liturgical Arts* (November 1942). See Susan J. White, *Art, Architecture, and Liturgical Reform*, 19. Rather, in his unpublished memoirs, Maginnis describes his "cordial rivalry" with Roman Catholic architect John T. Comes (1873–1922) of Pittsburgh.

47. Maginnis, introduction to Cram and Ferguson, *Work of Cram and Ferguson*.

48. Cram's mystical, scholarly, and cynical personae are explored in Richard Guy Wilson's fine essay "Ralph Adams Cram: Dreamer of the Medieval," in Rosenthal and Szarmach, *Medievalism in American Culture*, 193–214, esp. 196.

49. On Cram's theory of architectural history, see his autobiography, *My Life*, 72–73, 95–97. He so admired Henry Adams that he wrote an introduction to the 1913 edition of Adams's *Mont-Saint-Michel and Chartres*.

50. Cram, *Gothic Quest*, 258.

51. In his Harvard Phi Beta Kappa lecture, Cram asked: "What was the greatest synthesis of beauty, made operative through art, that man has ever achieved? The answer is very simple; it was a Gothic cathedral of the thirteenth century during a Pontifical High Mass, and somewhere about the middle of the fourteenth century in England, or the fifteenth century in France." He expounded this theme in several books, including *The Gothic Quest, The Substance of Gothic,* and *The Catholic Church and Art*.

52. Cram, *Nemesis of Democracy*, 35.

53. Peter Conn offers an interesting recent treatment of Cram's complexities in *Divided Mind*, 203–14. He argues that Cram's defiant reactionism was redeemed from absurdity by its grand scope and lifelong consistency.

54. Susan J. White, *Art, Architecture, and Liturgical Reform*, 20.

55. Cram, *My Life*, 14. Guiney introduced Cram to Bernard Berenson, who defended classicism against Cram's Gothic taste.

56. On Abbey's murals, see Baxter, *Legend of the Holy Grail*, 1904.

57. Conway, Diary, February 20, 1908, Conway Papers, BCSp.

58. "Expression of Church through Modern Architecture," Boston *Pilot*, June 1, 1907, 4. This is an unsigned article that I have attributed to Maginnis because of the close similarities to his other publications of the same year.

59. Maginnis, "Catholic Church Architecture," 36.

60. Maginnis, "Recent Roman Catholic Architecture," 9.

61. Cram, "The Roman Catholic Church and Art," in Cram, *Gothic Quest*, 253.

62. Cram, "University Architecture," in Cram, *Ministry of Art*, 202.

63. Guiney, quoted in the *Catholic Transcript* (Hartford), January 14, 1909. Also see Lucey, "Louise Imogen Guiney," 368.

64. Maginnis, "Movement for a Vital Christian Architecture," 25.

65. Ibid.

66. [Maginnis?], "Expression of Church through Modern Architecture," Boston *Pilot*, June 1, 1907, 4.

67. Douglass Shand Tucci, *Built in Boston*, 176.

68. Ibid., 23. The mention of Mary Baker Eddy's Mother Church of Christian Science refers to the astonishingly eclectic building dedicated in Boston in 1895 and expanded between 1903 and 1906.

69. Maginnis, "Movement for a Vital Christian Architecture," 25–26.

70. Cram, "Roman Catholic Church and Art," 255–56.

71. Cram, "Good and Bad Modern Gothic," 115–19.

72. Cram, *My Life*, 96–97. In 1913 Cram's High Church chancel design for the Second Unitarian Church of Boston horrified President Eliot of Harvard, but by the 1930s its ornate altar had become the fashion in Protestant churches. See Douglass Shand Tucci, *Built in Boston*, 176. Other Cram churches in the Boston area include Ruggles Street Church, Audubon Circle; All Saints', Dorchester; Christ Church, Hyde Park; and churches in Brookline, Cambridge, Arlington, Somerville, West Newton, Milton, and Sudbury.

73. Cram, *Substance of Gothic*, 132.

74. Cram to "Lou" [Guiney], April 1, 1907, Guiney Collection, HCR.

75. One example is Rev. Jeremiah Harrington's *Catholicism, Capitalism, or Communism*. The introduction was written by Cram, in support of *Rerum Novarum* and the Bishop's Program for Social Reconstruction of 1919.

76. Maginnis, "Movement for a Vital Christian Architecture," 26.

77. Maginnis, "Recent Roman Catholic Architecture," 10. Mail-order designs for economical churches began appearing in Catholic magazines around 1907.

78. Maginnis, "Catholic Church Architecture" (1917), 34.

79. Charles Maginnis, typescript, pp. 69–70, microfilm of Maginnis Papers, Archives of American Art, Smithsonian Institution.

80. Ibid., p. 70.

81. O'Meara to his sister, July 31, 1902, file 1899–1915. Stephen O'Meara Papers, BPL.

82. "To the Parishioners of St. Paul's Parish, Dorchester, an Important Announcement," St. Paul's, Dorchester, RG 5.3, folder 1, AABo.

83. O'Connell, *Recollections of Seventy Years*, 289–90.

84. This chart is in the Chancery Central Subject File, AABo. It may have been part of O'Connell's report to the Vatican in 1923 when he was trying to weather several diocesan scandals.

85. Douglass Shand Tucci, *Second Settlement*, 82.

86. Boston *Republic*, May 1, 1909, 5; letter, January 27, 1909, Maginnis and Walsh file, 11.13 A9, BCA.

87. Some buildings at Holy Cross were completed by Maginnis, Walsh, and Sullivan. See information available at HCA.

88. For chronological and geographical listings of Maginnis and Walsh's commissions, refer to files at BPLf.

89. Baxter, "Selection from the Works," 93–115.

90. Telephone interview with Alice Maginnis Walsh, February 1987. Maginnis had another daughter, Elizabeth, and two sons.

91. Susan J. White, *Art, Architecture, and Liturgical Reform*, 13.

92. Timothy Walsh's brother, James (1867–1936), a priest, was director of the So-

ciety for the Propagation of the Faith in Boston (1903–11), and his interest in missionary work led him to found the Maryknoll order of priests and brothers (the Catholic Foreign Mission Society). Matthew Sullivan designed their headquarters at Ossining, New York. Maginnis and Walsh also built other Maryknoll projects at the novitiate in Bedford, Massachusetts, and the seminary in Los Gatos, California.

93. Maginnis's wife, Amy Brooks, a convert to Catholicism from an established Boston Episcopal family, was a poet who was sixteen years younger than her husband and who described their marriage thus: "My husband is the star of our partnership . . . so I hold my place modestly in the background." See Amy Brooks Maginnis, 25th Reunion Report, Radcliffe University, 1930, p. 21, RUA.

94. Cram, *My Life*, 72.

95. For example, Joseph J. Reilly (1881–1951) from Springfield served as chief of the Massachusetts Civil Service Commission from 1909 to 1921. See Reilly Papers and *Alumnus* obituary, 1951, HCR.

96. Excluding persons who identified themselves as masons, I have identified Catholic architects and firms from assorted Catholic sources and compared my list against Nancy Shrock, *Architectural Records,* and the *Directory of Boston Architects,* which is drawn from Boston city directories. Also helpful are H. F. and E. R. Withey, *Biographical Dictionary,* and Herndon, *Boston of Today.*

97. Daniel O'Connell, Architects card file, BPLf.

98. The organizer and president of the institute from 1879 to 1910 was Robert Treat Paine II, Episcopalian and Brahmin philanthropist.

99. *Brochure of the Young Men's Catholic Association,* 22, which incorrectly credits him with designing Boston College. Subsequent names and career information from this pamphlet are cited with caution. Other more accurate sources of biographical information on Irish Catholic architects include Kervick's *Architects in America.*

100. See his letters to Rev. John O'Brien, Sacred Heart, Cambridge, Box 4, folder 1, AABo.

101. On the invisibility of women architects and their work, see Bliznakov, "Women Architects."

102. Howe, Manning and Almy Papers, MC 9, Box 19, folder 871, MITa.

103. Earlier woman "graduates" of MIT in the 1890s, such as Frances Mahony of Chicago, had finished a special two-year course in architecture. The first four-year graduate was Sophia Hayden, according to Weimann, *Fair Women,* 145.

104. Bliznakov, "Women Architects," 123.

105. Elizabeth Grossman and Lisa Reitzes, "Caught in the Crossfire: Women and Architectural Education, 1880–1910," in Berkeley, *Architecture,* 35–36.

106. *Technology Review,* January 1935, xiii, citing the *Simmons Review,* April 1934. Additional biographical information about Manning comes from *American Catholic Who's Who, 1934–1935,* 292; vertical file, "Eleanor Manning O'Connor," SCA; and her personal papers within the Howe, Manning and Almy collection, MITa.

107. Howe, Manning and Almy Papers, MC9, Box 19, folder 871, MITa. The selection is from Manning's typed responses to interview questions.

108. Boston *Republic,* February 6, 1915, 5.

109. Bliznakov, "Women Architects," 123.

110. Howe, Manning and Almy Papers, Manning Correspondence, MC 9, Box 14, August 21, 1912, MITa.

111. *Boston Herald,* September 8, 1911.

112. In 1929 Manning was one of six women in the American Institute of Architects, which had over 3,000 members. See *Boston Herald,* July 9, 1929.

113. Howe, Manning and Almy Papers, Manning Correspondence, MC9, Box 14, undated, MITa. She was O'Connor's second wife. He was six years her junior.

114. Henry Binsse, cited in Susan J. White, *Art, Architecture, and Liturgical Reform,* 28.

115. *Sacred Heart Review,* December 17, 1910.

116. *The Catholic Year Book of New England* (1929) amply illustrates the point.

117. Maginnis, "Catholic Church Architecture" (1917), 38.

118. One exception was Charles Greco of Boston, architect of Church of the Blessed Sacrament, Roxbury, and the Hibernian Society's building in Jamaica Plain.

119. The devaluation of apprenticeship is described in Grossman and Reitzes, "Caught in the Crossfire," 27–39.

120. James J. Walsh, "Boston's Art and Catholicism," *America,* February 10, 1917, 415–16.

Chapter 5

1. Mary A. Spellissy, in "The Public Rights of Women," *Catholic World,* June 1894, 305.

2. See Karlsen, *Devil in the Shape of a Woman,* and Cott, *Bonds of Womanhood.*

3. Mrs. Mary Curley, incidentally, favored woman suffrage.

4. For an excellent survey of theoretical debates surrounding patriarchy, reproduction, and ideology, see Barrett, *Women's Oppression Today.*

5. Cronin, *Catholic Social Principles,* 305.

6. Abell, "Reception of Leo XIII's Labor Encyclical."

7. Barrett, *Women's Oppression Today,* 152. See also Chapter 6 of this book.

8. "The Pope on Equal Suffrage," *Harper's Weekly,* May 10, 1909, 5.

9. Mary Ewens, "Political Activity of American Sisters before 1970," in Kolbenschlag, *Between God and Caesar,* 44.

10. Cronin, *Catholic Social Principles,* 306.

11. The pope's remarks are cited approvingly by Joyce Little, "Mary and Feminist Theology," *Thought,* December 1987, 355.

12. *The Pope Teaches,* no. 4, 1991 (London: Catholic Truth Society), 109.

13. In the last nine years in the United States, signs that patriarchal values are finally being recognized as socially constructed emerged in criticisms of a planned pastoral letter on women by the American Catholic bishops. The choice of that topic was seen as condescending by critics because it skirted the real issue, which was not femininity or women but sexism within the Church. The bishops' decision to scuttle the pastoral letter in November 1992 reflected, perhaps, their growing awareness of women's legitimate opposition.

14. Husslein, *World Problem,* 250.

15. McDannell, "Catholic Domesticity," 51. On pre- and postfamine marriage customs, see K. H. Connell, "Catholicism and Marriage in the Century after the Famine," in Connell, *Irish Peasant Society,* 113–61.

16. McDannell, "Catholic Domesticity," 52.

17. The phrase and its four elements (piety, purity, submissiveness, and domesticity) were first described by Barbara Welter in 1965 and have been articulated further

by numerous case studies with little attention to Catholicism. See "The Cult of True Womanhood, 1820–1860," *American Quarterly* 18 (Summer 1966): 151–74.

18. William J. Onahan, "Columbian Catholic Congress at Chicago," *Catholic World,* August 1893, 606; Toomy, "There Is a Public Sphere for Catholic Women," 674–75.

19. Seager, "Pluralism and the American Mainstream," 313.

20. "The Pastoral Letter of 1919," in Guilday, *The National Pastorals of the American Hierarchy,* 314.

21. "Program of Social Reconstruction," (February 12, 1919), in Nolan, *Pastoral Letters,* 1:261–62.

22. Boston *Pilot,* July 23, 1910, 3.

23. William Stang, *Boston Globe,* January 5, 1907, 9. Stang was bishop from 1904 until his death in 1907. He had received degrees in philosophy and theology at Louvain, came to the United States, and returned to Rome to teach pastoral theology at the North American College. See *Dictionary of American Biography,* vol. 9, pt. 1, 506.

24. O'Connell, Boston *Pilot,* May 2, 1910, 9. O'Connell's remarks were delivered in an antisocialist lecture sponsored by the Church.

25. Douglas, *Feminization of American Culture.*

26. Veblen, *Theory of the Leisure Class,* 118–31.

27. "The Mission of Catholic Motherhood," *Ave Maria,* June 22, 1912, 788.

28. Ibid.

29. O'Connell, "Opportunities for Service," Address to the Ladies of Boston, Hotel Somerset, February 17, 1912, in *S&A,* 4:57.

30. O'Connell, "The Family and the Home," in *S&A,* 4:163.

31. Ibid., 4:163–64.

32. *Boston Globe,* June 17, 1935. Report of a sermon at the Cathedral of the Holy Cross for the confirmation of 500 converts.

33. The Jesuit magazine, *America,* for example, editorialized that "the feminist movement, the 'repeal of reticence,' immodest fashions, shameless plays, and in particular the indecent dances that 'everybody is dancing,' morning, noon and midnight, and during meals especially, are without question making it much harder for 'the girl of today' to be modest and lady-like, and to keep good and pure, than it was for the girls of thirty years ago" (May 9, 1914, 87).

34. Blunt, *Readings,* 35.

35. Mary O'Nolan, "Modesty in Dress," *Catholic Monthly,* June 8, 1917, 265, reprinted from the *Irish Monthly.* O'Connell was extremely devoted to Pope Leo XIII.

36. *Boston Globe,* January 5, 1907, 9.

37. Coyle, *Our Church,* 1:239. Coyle probably selected this unattributed source from a late nineteenth-century periodical.

38. Eleanor C. Donnelly, *Girlhood's Hand-Book,* 112–13. Donnelly was a Philadelphia poet, born in 1848 of an Irish father and an Irish American mother. Influenced by Father Edward Sorin, C.S.C., editor of *Ave Maria,* to begin a journalism career, Donnelly enlisted contributors and helped edit the *Messenger of the Sacred Heart,* and *Nova et Vetera.* For a time she was editor in chief of *Our Lady of Good Counsel,* the Augustinian magazine, and associate editor of the Philadelphia *Catholic Standard and Times.* See Thomas M. Schwertner, "Eleanor Donnelly—The Singer of Pure Religion," *Catholic World,* June 1917, 352–60. Her brother, Ignatius, shared none of his sister's pious interests. He severed his ties with the Church, moving to Minnesota, where he

NOTES TO PAGES 156–60

became famous as a Populist leader and author of the dystopian novel *Caesar's Column* (1890).

39. Onahan, "Catholic Women's Part in Philanthropy," 820.

40. Bugg, *People of Our Parish*, 101, 102.

41. O'Connell, "The Evils of Modern Society," in *S&A*, 7:138–39.

42. Whitmont, *Return of the Goddess*, 184. Otherwise, the author follows a Jungian interpretation of female deities, which I do not share.

43. Recent literature on Mariology includes Marina Warner, *Alone of All Her Sex*; Preston, *Mother Worship*; Tambasco, *What Are They Saying about Mary?*; essays by Victor and Edith Turner, including "Postindustrial Marian Pilgrimage"; Fiorenza, *In Memory of Her*; Pagels, *Adam, Eve and the Serpent*; Pope, "Immaculate and Powerful," 173–200. On veneration of the Virgin, see portions of Bynum, *Holy Feast, Holy Fast*, and some of the essays collected in *Fragmentation and Redemption*. In the past twenty-five years, reexamination of Christian attitudes toward women has been indebted to Mary Daly's *The Church and the Second Sex*, itself inspired by Simone de Beauvoir's *The Second Sex* (Knopf, 1st American ed., 1953).

44. Pope, "Immaculate and Powerful," 195.

45. For an excellent concise survey of the history of Marian theology, see Tambasco, *What Are They Saying about Mary?*, 4–8.

46. While this provocative insight is aligned with recent theoretical trends in the study of the body, we may alternatively trace the origins of this metaphor describing the Church as a human body to early Christianity's appropriation of the organicism of Aristotle.

47. Eleanor C. Donnelly, *Girlhood's Hand-Book*, 115.

48. Pope, "Immaculate and Powerful."

49. Joseph M. White, *Diocesan Seminary*, 224.

50. American apparitions were included in the 100+ sightings reported during the 1940s and 1950s in the United States, Europe, and Mexico, usually associated with anticommunist messages. See Kselman and Avella, "Marian Piety," esp. 407.

51. Somewhat later, Monsignor Fulton Sheen, for example, professed special devotions to Our Lady of Lourdes and Fatima and reportedly visited Lourdes thirty times and Fatima ten times. See Kselman and Avella, "Marian Piety," 411.

52. Rösler, "Woman," 15:687–94, esp. 688. The appearance of the *Catholic Encyclopedia* between 1907 and 1912 was considered to be a milestone in Catholic publishing and the most authoritative statement of Catholic attitudes. Women who were incensed by the sexism in the definition were successful in persuading the editors to change it in a later edition of 1921. An American contributor, William H. W. Fanning, wrote related articles, "Women in English-Speaking Countries" and "In Canon Law," (15:694–98), which did not challenge Rösler's conservatism. See Kenneally, *History of American Catholic Women*, 199 n. 1. Rösler also authored the entry "Nuns."

53. Rösler, "Woman," 15:687, 693, 688.

54. Boston *Pilot*, January 13, 1917, 4. Another typical example of crisis rhetoric written by a layman comes from an essay in the Holy Cross *Purple*: "The sanctity of the home is assailed, and divorce stalking abroad saps at the very vitals of our national life, begetting a race of foundlings in the subversion of moral law" (Hon. Thomas H. Dowd, '94, "The Ideals of Holy Cross," 1898, 242).

55. Blunt, *Readings*, 36. O'Connell's remarks anticipate the uses of Marian ideology during the Cold War era. See Kselman and Avella, "Marian Piety."

56. Kuehnel, *Conferences for Young Women*, 6.

57. O'Connell, "The Family and the Home," in *S&A*, 4:159–69. The iconographic decoration of local churches built in this era likewise reflected Mary's importance in contemporary devotions. She figured prominently in statuary and stained glass as Mother of Jesus and among the saints as Queen of Heaven. See Wangler, "Religious Life," 239–72.

58. Blunt, *Readings*, 35.

59. Wright, in Almagno, *Resonare Christum*, 1:85.

60. Katherine Conway, "The Blessed among Women," manuscript, pp. 41–42, 45–46, Box 4, BCSp.

61. Cary, "Elevation of Womanhood," 299.

62. Eleanor C. Donnelly, "Wife and Mother," in Eleanor C. Donnelly, *Girlhood's Hand-Book*, 113.

63. McDannell, "Catholic Domesticity," 59, citing a 1913 Catholic mother's advice manual.

64. Mary Dowd, "The Public Rights of Women," a roundtable discussion in *Catholic World*, June 1894, 317–18.

65. *Harper's Weekly*, July 3, 1909.

66. For example, Sadlier, *Jeanne d'Arc*, and Vaughan, *Life Lessons from Joan of Arc*.

67. This is the controversial but insightful interpretation of Lears, *No Place of Grace*.

68. *S&A*, 3:254.

69. Daly, *The Church and The Second Sex*, 46.

70. Vaughan, *Life Lessons from Joan of Arc*.

71. Alice Brown files, typewritten essay on Guiney by Eva Mabel Tenison, YBR.

72. "Jeanne d'Arc," *Catholic World*, February 1912, 657.

73. Information on Joan's canonization follows Marina Warner, *Joan of Arc*, 225–26, 263–64.

74. The Joan of Arc Collection at the Boston Public Library, for example, contains 4,000 titles and boxes of memorabilia collected by John Cardinal Wright (1909–1979), auxiliary bishop of Boston, 1947–50.

75. O'Connell, "Dignity of Catholic Womanhood," in *S&A*, 7:123.

76. James J. Walsh, "The Church and Feminine Education," in James J. Walsh, *Education*, 295.

77. Some Catholic colleges formed Jeanne D'Arc clubs, which promoted an activist interpretation of Joan's career. The clubs were not for social service but for evangelizing by students, who used speech, drama, lantern slide shows, and film to portray Catholicism accurately to audiences throughout America. A report of the club's activities appeared in *Queen's Work*, December 1915, 265–68. I have been unable to verify the presence of a club in the Boston area.

78. Maher, "Catholic Woman as Educator," 134.

79. O'Connell, "Catholic Mothers," in *S&A*, 4:83.

80. Mary Elizabeth McGrath Blake, quoted by Walter Lecky [William McDermott] in *Down at Caxton's*, 161. For a biography of Blake (1840–1907), see Kenneally, "Catholic and Feminist." See also Mainiero, *American Writers*, 173–74.

81. Grace Hausmann Sherwood, "Catholic Laywoman's Point of View," *Scribner's*, March 1927, 238.

82. Blake, in Lecky, *Down at Caxton's*, 161.
83. *S&A*, 3:46. See also the Boston *Republic*, December 23, 1916, 1.
84. See Taves, *Household of Faith*.
85. *S&A*, 3:33.
86. Dulles, in *Models of the Church*, 39–40, has noted that the predominant features of Church Militant imagery are inherent in the institutional model of ecclesiology cited in Chapter 1.
87. Boston *Republic*, December 23, 1916.
88. Dennis Ryan, *Beyond the Ballot Box*, 75; Sanders, "Boston Catholics and the School Question," 151–83.
89. Sanders, "Boston Catholics and the School Question," 144–45; 147. Most public school teachers were graduates of Massachusetts normal schools, but all of the first Catholic women graduates of Radcliffe, unless they married, also became public school teachers.
90. R. J. Haberlin (Secretary) to Jeremiah E. Burke, July 5, 1922, O'Connell Correspondence, 3:7, AABo.
91. George A. Lyons to "Rev. Dear Sir," September 10, 1908, Department of Education Papers, RG 3, D.11, folder 1, AABo. Before that time, parochial education had received slight attention from Archbishop Williams.
92. O'Connell, "A Practical Exemplification of True Principles," in *S&A*, 8:197; address given on the seventy-fifth anniversary of the arrival of the Sisters of Notre Dame at Boston, November 16, 1924.
93. Scanlan, *Brief History of the Archdiocese*, 60.
94. Statistics from *Official Catholic Directory* (1920), "Archdiocese of Boston," 41.
95. Katherine E. Conway, *New Footsteps in Well-Trodden Ways*, 225. "She can be endured."
96. Joseph M. White, *Diocesan Seminary*, 223.
97. Kennelly, "Ideals of American Catholic Womanhood," in Kennelly, *American Catholic Women*, 13–14.
98. See Eileen Mary Brewer, *Nuns and the Education of American Catholic Women*.
99. *Christian Maiden*, 82.
100. B. L. Murphy, "Convent Education," 79. Murphy was a fellow in psychology at Clark and was advised by William H. Burnham. See Files, Clark University Archives. My thanks to archivist Stuart Campbell for locating this biographical material.
101. Repplier, quoted in the *Dolphin* (London), August 1905, 94–96.
102. Repplier, "The Spinster," 181.
103. Katherine E. Conway, *Bettering Ourselves*, 26–27.
104. Bugg, *People of Our Parish*, 203.
105. This particular example comes from the Academy of St. Elizabeth, Convent Station, New Jersey. See B. L. Murphy, "Convent Education," 40.
106. Stang, *Socialism and Christianity*, 179.
107. Eileen Mary Brewer, *Nuns and the Education of American Catholic Women*, 192 n. 43.
108. Information provided to author by Jeffrey Wills, from research for a history of St. Paul's Parish, Cambridge, which served Catholics at Radcliffe and Harvard. These statistics cover the years 1888 to about 1915.
109. See also "Concerning Convent Schools," *Ave Maria*, April 11, 1907, 593–94.

110. Denis McCarthy to Rufina, September 24, 1917, BCSp.

111. Ibid., February 12, 1918, BCSp. I discovered the McCarthy family correspondence misfiled in another collection at Boston College. Donated by McCarthy's
daughter in 1984, the collection (still uncataloged) provides insights about one of Boston's leading lay orators and poets and about his family relationships, sources often
lacking for Irish Americans.

112. Ibid., September 24, 1917, BCSp.

113. Ibid., November 7, 1917, BCSp.

114. Spalding warned: "Let us not be so dull as to ignore the gifts of woman. . . .
If in the past she has been mentally inferior, is it not because the incentives, means,
and opportunities of intellectual growth were denied her? If her capacity has seemed
to be chiefly that of a domestic, is it not because she was refused admission to wider
fields?" See Spalding, "Woman and the Higher Education," in Spalding, *Opportunity
and Other Essays and Addresses*, 64–65.

115. Denis McCarthy to Rufine, June 4, 1919, BCSp.

116. Kenneally, *History of American Catholic Women*, 164 n. 256.

117. Spalding, "Woman and the Higher Education," 205 (emphasis added).

118. Stang, *Socialism and Christianity*, 182.

119. Kenneally, *History of American Catholic Women*, 57–59. Future scholarship
will hopefully detail the role of nuns and sisters in the transmission of Catholic intellectual life.

120. See, for example, Boston *Republic*, May 16, 1914.

121. Lord et al., *History*, 3:573. The courses were directed by the diocesan CCB.

122. Sexton and Riley, *History of St. John's Seminary*, 177.

123. Spalding, *Means and Ends of Education*, 106.

124. The former reached its thirty-third edition by 1900, was translated into German, and was published in Europe. Deshon was a convert who became a Paulist priest
and, eventually, superior of the order. Bernard O'Reilly, whose manual appeared in
1876, also wrote a companion volume, *True Men as We Need Them*.

125. Deshon, *Guide*, 43.

126. O'Connell, "Benefits of a Devout Retreat: Humility the Only Safeguard of
Knowledge," August 7, 1908, in *S&A*, 3:117.

127. Boston *Republic*, January 24, 1917, 7.

128. William Stang, March 23, 1903, preface to *Christian Maiden*.

129. *Christian Maiden*, 62–63.

130. On the polarity of Eve and Mary in American Catholicism, see James Kenneally, "Eve, Mary and the Historians," 187–202.

131. Boston *Republic*, May 16, 1914, 6.

132. Lasance, *Girl's Guide*, 10.

133. Deshon, *Guide*, 251.

134. Thomas, "Catholic Journalists and the Ideal Woman," 98.

135. Boston *Pilot*, January 20, 1912, 4.

136. Ibid., January 9, 1909, 4.

137. Boston *Republic*, May 16, 1914.

138. Mary Blanche O'Sullivan, *Boston Globe*, March 6, 1910, 42.

139. Bugg, *People of Our Parish*, 101.

140. Michael Earls, S.J., to Bess, May 24, 1910, HCR.

141. Boston *Pilot*, January 13, 1912, 4.

142. Robins, *New England Conversion*, 1.

143. A recent example, Menendez, *Religious Conflict in America*, lists few women converts, 1880–1930, and of the women I profile below, only Alice Hayes gained a listing for her book (p. 70).

144. See the description of Boston's religious eccentrics in Whiting, *Boston Days*, 352–54.

145. A German Protestant historian observed that aside from its expected appeal to the immigrant poor, the Catholic Church drew "a larger or smaller number of influential families of the higher and educated order, including many converts from the different Protestant denominations, especially the Episcopalians." (Cited in Abell, *American Catholics and Social Action*, 13.)

146. Ironically, Episcopalian converts in Boston were leaving their church just at the time when its appeal, under the charismatic ministry of Phillips Brooks at Trinity Church, was experiencing a peak. Brooks, best remembered as the author of the Christmas hymn "O Little Town of Bethlehem," was a well-liked preacher. He died in 1893, having served for only fifteen months as Episcopal bishop of Massachusetts.

147. Katherine Avery had converted in 1900 and became Sister St. Mary Martha.

148. Dr. George Herron, a Congregationalist, left his wife and four children to marry Carrie Rand, the daughter of his benefactress, Elizabeth D. Rand, who had established a professorship for him at Grinnell College, Iowa. Elizabeth Rand later founded the Rand School of Social Science. The Congregationalist Church dismissed Herron from the ministry, and Herron's behavior divided the socialists among themselves. Yet Herron's advancement within the party to its highest position, American Secretary of the International Socialist Bureau, and to chairman of the national convention in 1904, seemed like signs of party approval. The only protest by socialists against Herron came from Martha Moore Avery and David Goldstein in Boston, who both soon became Catholics. See Goldstein, *Autobiography*, 29–34; Avery and Goldstein, *Socialism*, 255–96. Hillquit, *History of Socialism* (1910), 292, 293, 355.

149. Goldstein, *Autobiography*, 94.

150. Buhle, *Women and American Socialism*, 29.

151. Goldstein, *Socialist Bubble Punctured*, 5.

152. In fact, O'Hare argued the opposite, that "Socialism is needed to restore the home," and appealed to "love, home, and babies," but Catholics never considered the possibility of conservative intersections between socialist arguments and Catholic views. See *Progressive Woman*, August 1910, 2. Nor did the Church acknowledge divisions in the Socialist party itself on the correct role of woman and family. On Bebel's positive influence on German and American socialism, see Buhle, *Women and American Socialism*, esp. 26–29.

153. "This extraordinary elevation of woman in Mary by Christ is in sharp contrast to the extraordinary degradation of female dignity before Christianity," stated the *Catholic Encyclopedia*, 690. See also 691–92. The entry described motherhood and voluntary religious celibacy as "the greatest possibilities for development" of women.

154. For Avery's socialist views, see Avery, *Woman*.

155. Katherine O'Keeffe O'Mahoney of Lawrence has also been identified as one of the first New England Catholic women to speak in public. See Georgina Pell Curtis, *American Catholic Who's Who*, 492.

156. In addition to information in Chapter 2, see Campbell, "David Goldstein and the Lay Catholic Street Apostolate," "I Can't Imagine Our Lady," and "David Gold-

stein and the Foundation of the Catholic Campaigners for Christ"; Carrigan, "Martha Moore Avery"; O'Leary, "William Henry Cardinal O'Connell," 240.

157. "Woman Suffrage, Six Papers," *Catholic Mind,* December 8, 1915, 629.

158. Boston *Pilot,* April 16, 1910, 1.

159. Martha Moore Avery to David Goldstein, February 13, 1911, Goldstein and Avery Papers, BCSp.

160. The National Civic Foundation had enlisted Avery in 1906 to campaign against woman suffrage. See O'Brien, *Public Catholicism,* 141.

161. *New York Herald Tribune,* January 7, 1909, 14.

162. "The Relation of Catholic Women to the Body Politic," Boston *Pilot,* April 16, 1910, 1.

163. "Portia: The Ideal Wife," Boston *Pilot,* May 5, 1923, 12.

164. Boston *Pilot,* April 16, 1910, 1.

165. For a list of over 700 nineteenth-century converts, see Richard Clarke, "Our Converts," (July 1893). David, *American Catholic Convert Authors,* contains several errors.

166. Cary, "Elevation of Womanhood," 302.

167. Driscoll, *Literary Convert Women,* 54.

168. In tribute to Cary, the Catholic alumnae of Radcliffe called themselves the Emma Forbes Cary Guild. Another Bostonian, Mary Josephine Rogers, later Mother Mary Joseph (1882–1955) of the Maryknoll Sisters, founded a Catholic club at Smith College.

169. Cary, *Day-Spring from on High.* The experience of women converts with literary careers was replicated by many others besides those discussed here. The following five examples suggest a pattern typical of female converts. Mary Agnes Tincker (1831–1907), a convert and author from Maine, spent most of her life in Boston. Marion Ames Taggart (1866?–1945) of Haverhill, Massachusetts, an invalid and author of children's books, was converted by the Jesuits at the Church of the Immaculate Conception, Boston. Elizabeth Russell Dewart, wife of Rev. William Herbert Dewart, the associate rector of Trinity Church, Boston, left the Episcopal church. Amy Brooks Maginnis also broke with her staunchly Episcopalian family to convert. She then married Charles Maginnis, the Catholic architect, who was sixteen years her senior. Mary Elizabeth McGrath was a convert author who married John Blake, a prominent physician in Boston. Mary Catherine Chase (1835–ca. 1905) of Pepperell, a schoolteacher, converted from Episcopalianism in 1854 to a cloistered existence from which she published children's travel books under the pseudonym Winnie Rover. In 1892 she adopted the name F. M. Edselas (a deliberate inversion of Saint Francis de Sales, who was named the patron saint of writers) and wrote articles for *Catholic World* on women, education, Boston history, and social problems "with such force and clearness as to attract much attention, giving the general impression that a masculine mind guided the pen" (Ursulines of New York, *Immortelles,* 180–81). Chase advocated the founding of professional schools to train women.

170. Cary, "Elevation of Womanhood," 302–3.

171. Georgiana Pell Curtis, *Beyond the Road to Rome,* 82.

172. Emma Cary, "Who Should Go to Prison?," *Catholic World,* April 1889, 68–74.

173. Driscoll, *Literary Convert Women,* 58.

174. Ibid., 58.

175. As noted in Maynard, *A Fire Was Lighted*, 240. Rose Lathrop's other biographies include James J. Walsh, *Mother Alphonsa*; Burton, *Sorrow Built a Bridge*; Kuhn, *Watching at My Gates*; Vance, *On Wings of Fire*; and Sheehan, *Rose Hawthorne*. Lathrop's brother Julian contributed "A Daughter of Hawthorne" to the *Atlantic Monthly*, September 1928. Her papers and correspondence are scattered among many collections, including the Essex Institute (Hawthorne-Manning Collection) in Salem, Mass.; Middlebury College (Abernathy Collection) in Middlebury, Vt.; and Dukes County Historical Society (May Abigail Dodge and Gail Hamilton Papers) in Edgartown, Mass. The first study to make extensive use of archival materials is Valenti, *To Myself a Stranger*, which should supplant all former biographies. Although I was able to see this study only at the conclusion of my work, I thank the author for sharing some issues of *Christ's Poor*.

176. Hawthorne, *Memories of Hawthorne*, 387.

177. Valenti, *To Myself a Stranger*, 67, 69.

178. Many American newspapers reported George's conversion with consternation or incredulity. See Maynard, *A Fire Was Lighted*, 228, and Valenti, *To Myself a Stranger*, 100–106.

179. Lathrop and Lathrop, *A Story of Courage*.

180. Valenti, *To Myself a Stranger*, 118.

181. Lathrop and Lathrop, *A Story of Courage*, 373.

182. Valenti, *To Myself a Stranger*, 150–56.

183. "The Life in Effort," *Christ's Poor*, March 1902, 5–18.

184. *Christ's Poor*, June 1902, 10, and January 1902, 40, cited in Valenti, *To Myself a Stranger*, 167.

185. *Christ's Poor*, March 1902, 11.

186. Driscoll, *Literary Convert Women*, 128; Robins, *New England Conversion*, 27–28. Robins's book was later published in London in 1904 by the Catholic Truth Guild.

187. Driscoll, *Literary Convert Women*, 80. Emery's conversion account appears on pp. 78–90. See also Blunt, "Susan L. Emery," and Georgina Pell Curtis, *Some Roads to Rome*.

188. Driscoll, *Literary Convert Women*, 88.

189. Emery, *Catholic Stronghold*.

190. Hugh Blunt (1877–1957) attended Boston College and St. John's Seminary. He became assistant at St. Peter's, Dorchester (1902–11); pastor of St. Francis, South Braintree (1914–17); pastor of Sacred Heart, Cambridge (1917); editor of the *Sacred Heart Review*; pastor at St. John the Evangelist (1929); and monsignor in 1944. His papers and extensive Newman collection are at Regis College, Weston, Mass. Emery's friend Mary Blanche O'Sullivan, an editor of *Donahoe's Magazine*, also promoted Blunt.

191. Emergy, *Inner Life of the Soul*.

192. Emery, in Georgina Pell Curtis, *Some Roads to Rome*.

193. Hayes, *A Convert's Reason Why*, 1.

194. Hayes to Nilan, May 16, 1905, AAH.

195. Ibid.

196. Hayes to Nilan, July 23, 1913, AAH.

197. *Bulletin of Bibliography* 8 (October 1915): 220–21, and (July 1915): 194–95.

198. Robins, *New England Conversion,* 23.

199. Nilan to Hayes, June 28, 1918, AAH.

200. Toomy, "There Is a Public Sphere for Catholic Women," 678.

Chapter 6

1. Historical studies from the past twenty years that reflect the overwhelming emphasis on non-Catholic women include Douglas, *Feminization of American Culture;* Mary Ryan, *Cradle of the Middle Class,* and *Empire of the Mother;* Epstein, *Politics of Domesticity;* Smith-Rosenberg, *Disorderly Conduct;* and McDannell, *Christian Home in Victorian America;* Ginzberg, *Women and the Work of Benevolence;* Hewitt, *Women's Activism and Social Change.* For the post–Civil War era, Leach, *True Love and Perfect Union,* provides excellent coverage of the influence of social scientific rationalism on organized feminism, which attracted women from the liberal Protestant, Unitarian, and Quaker traditions.

2. Campbell, "Struggle to Serve," 210.

3. O'Sullivan, "Phases of Charitable Work," 40.

4. Emery, *Catholic Stronghold,* 51-52.

5. Oates, "Women's Role in Catholic Charity," 667.

6. Oates, "Organized Voluntarism." Oates points out that the membership of the largest men's charity, the St. Vincent de Paul Society, peaked in the 1870s and declined thereafter.

7. As reported by L. A. Toomy in "Some Noble Work of Catholic Women," *Catholic World,* May 1893, 241-42.

8. *America,* May 18, 1912.

9. Joseph Husslein, S.J., "Social Mission of Catholic Women," *America,* June 1, 1912.

10. For a history of the CCB, see Walton, "To Preserve the Faith" (1983).

11. Detailed comment on Massachusetts sisterhoods is beyond the scope of this study. For information concerning lifestyles, salaries, and teaching activities of sisters, see Oates, "Learning to Teach"; Ewens, "Leadership of Nuns"; Mary Ewens, "Women in the Convent," in Kennelly, *American Catholic Women,* 17-47; and Dries, "Americanization of Religious Life."

12. My discussion follows Oates, "Women's Role in Catholic Charity," 667-72.

13. Cott, "Limits of Social Feminism," esp. 827-28.

14. Leo XIII spelled out these rules in *Quod apostolici muneris* (1878), *Rerum Novarum* (1891), and *Graves de communi* (1901).

15. Katherine Conway, Boston, to Bishop Bernard McQuaid, Rochester, March 9, 1892, Archives, Archdiocese of Rochester. I am indebted to R. Emmett Curran, S.J., Georgetown University, for this letter.

16. Campbell, "Struggle to Serve," 211.

17. Lord et al., *History,* 3:545. Chaplaincy appointments to men's societies were just as carefully monitored.

18. Boston *Pilot,* June 22, 1918, 2.

19. Anderson's detractors included the often indignant Father John T. Mullen of Hudson, Massachusetts, who wrote to the apostolic delegate: "And these are the men who administer the Boston diocese, even in the most secret and sacred matters. Bishop Anderson exercises no jurisdiction whatever, is a mere figurehead, or Confirmation

machine, as devoid of spirit as a piece of stone" (Mullen to Your Excellency, December 6, 1918, Del. Ap., USA, IX, Boston, file 93, ASV).

20. Obituary, Jones Corrigan, *Woodstock Letters* 66, 294–95. Katherine Conway called Corrigan's work "a wonderful course and [it] will be good for our minds and will clear the minds of our non-Catholic friends on the controverted points" (Katherine Conway, "Vital Problems—continued," typescript of address, p. 4, Conway Papers, BCSp).

21. Common Cause Forum Papers, Notebook, p. 42, BCSp. See discussion of Common Cause in Chapter 2.

22. Kenneally, *History of American Catholic Women,* 90; Kennelly, *American Catholic Women,* 1–2.

23. Boston *Republic,* December 3, 1910, 4.

24. James A. White, *Founding of Cliff Haven,* 56, 16–17. A complete history of the movement appears in White.

25. Typescript (untitled), p. 5, Conway Papers (1908–9?), BCSp. Conway reported: "I gave everything I could to the Circle" (p. 6). The Catholic Union offered space to Conway at the outset, but the chaplain demurred, calling the union "too worldly" (p. 2).

26. Rev. Thomas McMillan, "The Growth of Catholic Reading Circles," *Catholic World,* August 1895, 711.

27. Typescript, pp. 7–8, Conway Papers (1908–9?), BCSp.

28. *American Ecclesiastical Review* 54 (June 1916): 681.

29. James A. White, *Founding of Cliff Haven,* 88–90.

30. Desmond, *Reading Circle Manual,* 10–11.

31. *American Ecclesiastical Review* 54 (June 1916): 681.

32. James A. White, *Founding of Cliff Haven,* 43–45. In 1901 the Knights of Columbus Special Council even met at Cliff Haven to rewrite their insurance policies.

33. Boston *Republic,* March 18, 1916, 5, 8, 11.

34. See James A. White, *Founding of Cliff Haven,* 28–33; Lord et al., *History,* 3:412–13; and discussion of George Parsons Lathrop and Rose Hawthorne Lathrop in Chapter 5.

35. James A. White, *Founding of Cliff Haven,* 31.

36. *Catholic World,* September 1902, 851.

37. Also, Warren Mosher, editor of the *Reading Circle Review* had died in 1906, ending his detailed coverage.

38. *Catholic World,* June 1905, 567. Desmond was a thoughtful lay editor who was refreshingly iconoclastic on topics relating to social reformism and Church management of funds.

39. Desmond, *Reading Circle Manual,* 14, 8.

40. Katherine E. Conway, *Way of the World,* 7.

41. Conway, Diary, February 20, 1908, Conway Papers, BCSp.

42. "A Half Hour Club and the Public Library," *Donahoe's Magazine,* December 1899, 619. An invaluable source for the kinds of literature read by circle women are the compilations by the Ursulines of New York, *Immortelles.*

43. Katherine E. Conway, *Christian Gentlewoman,* 58.

44. William Pardow, S.J., quoted in the Boston *Republic,* January 23, 1909, 3 (emphasis added).

45. Boston *Republic,* January 23, 1915.

46. There is no published history of the league. My early investigations were presented as "Some Connections in Anglo-American Feminism," American Historical Association paper (December 1986).

47. Pauline Willis wrote a family genealogy entitled *Willis Records*. She grew up in the sheltered and exclusive atmosphere of Louisburg Square in Boston before moving to London with her mother and brother in 1884. The trio had converted to Catholicism in 1883. See *Willis Records*, 88–93. A history of the English Catholic Women's League appears in Kane, "'Willing Captive of Home'?" For more information, see McEntee, *Social Catholic Movement in Great Britain*, 237–40, and Martindale, *Bernard Vaughan*, 113–15.

48. *Boston Globe*, May 3, 1910, 6.

49. See the review of the initial issue of the *Crucible*, June 20, 1905, in the *Dolphin* (London), August 1905, 241–43.

50. Boston *Republic*, May 7, 1910, 5.

51. Dues remained affordable at $1 per year until 1930.

52. Lord et al., *History*, 3:546; *Boston Globe*, May 3, 1910, 6; Boston *Pilot*, May 7, 1910, and March 23, 1912; Annual Meeting Reports, RG VI.4, Box 1, folders 3–6, LCW Files, AABo. O'Connell generally received credit for establishing the league, as in the article written by his chancellor for a national Catholic magazine: "In looking over the acts of his administration we find that one of his earliest works was to found the League of Catholic Women" (M. J. Splaine, "League of Catholic Women in the Archdiocese of Boston," *Queen's Work*, June 1916, 262). Splaine reported that "the thanks of the Catholic women of the diocese are generously poured out to His Eminence, the Cardinal, for furnishing them this opportunity of speaking as one, under his authority and direction" (264).

53. Helen Phelan to O'Connell, [December 1921], O'Connell Papers, Correspondence, 9:1, AABo.

54. First Annual Report, 1911, RGVI.4, Box 1, folder 1, LCW Papers, AABo; Boston *Pilot*, November 29, 1919, 4. The constitution, drawn up by Splaine, closely copied the English league's charter that Willis had described to the Boston audience, and resembled LCW charters in other American dioceses. See Elizabeth Dwight to O'Connell, November 13, 1910, RG III E.10, Box 1, folder 1, LCW Papers, AABo; Catholic Women's League brochure, 1910.

55. Materials scattered throughout the Secretary of State and Apostolic Delegate collections in the Vatican Archives, Rome, chart the formation of this international network of women's groups in the early twentieth century. Italy's Unione fra le Donne Cattoliche was established in 1909. In 1920, Canadian Catholic women organized according to the Boston model, as reported in the Boston *Pilot*, October 30, 1920, 1.

56. Second Report of the LCW, May 1, 1912–May 1, 1913, p. 5, Box 1, folder 4, LCW Papers, AABo. After her success in Boston, Willis tried to organize Catholic women in New York City and requested a letter of introduction to Archbishop Farley from Archbishop O'Connell. See Letter from O'Connell, May 6, 1910, RG III E.10, Box 1, folder 1, LCW Papers, AABo.

57. Macdonald to O'Connell, January 15, 1913, Box 1, folder 2, LCW Papers, AABo.

58. Perkins to O'Connell, August 5, 1911, O'Connell Correspondence, RGI.7, Box 8, file 16, AABo.

59. Typescript of Annual Report, April 26, 1914, RGVI.4, Box 1, folder 6, LCW Papers, AABo.

60. Bernard Vaughan, in a letter to the *Daily Telegraph,* cited in the *Tablet* (London), 1921.

61. Martindale, *Bernard Vaughan,* 166–67.

62. Macdonald to O'Connell, January 15, 1913, Box 1, folder 2, LCW Papers, AABo.

63. O'Connell disapproved of Ryan, believing him to be a radical socialist, but Ryan actually shared O'Connell's conservative view of feminism, equating it with "female anarchism." Ryan published nothing in favor of woman suffrage prior to 1917, although he claimed that he lectured on female equality at seminaries early in his career.

64. *Boston Post,* November 19, 1923.

65. First Report of the LCW, 1910–1912, LCW Papers, AABo.

66. Philpott, "Catholicism in Boston," 246.

67. Third Report of the LCW, 1914–1915, typescript, LCW Papers, AABo.

68. These included Mary Boyle O'Reilly, who had a position with the state regulating commission; Emma Cary; Alice Hayes; Katherine Conway; and Katherine O'Mahoney. The Catholic chaplain to state prisons was Father Joseph Anderson, head of the CCB.

69. Leach, *True Love and Perfect Union,* 297, 315. Also see annual reports of Boston social service agencies at SCA.

70. Second Report of the LCW, 1912–1913, p. 10, LCW Papers, AABo. The most successful events offered by women's groups featured attended nurseries.

71. Boston *Pilot,* July 14, 1917, 1.

72. Ibid., March 8, 1930.

73. Broderick, *Right Reverend New Dealer,* 98–99. On the national impact of O'Connell's opposition from 1924 on, see Greene, "Catholic Committee," 249–50. For a brief account of Regan's career, see Kenneally, *History of American Catholic Women,* 143.

74. The Slattery-NCCW/NCWC episode is recounted in Slawson, *Foundation,* chap. 9.

75. J. M. Cooper to Mary Barr, [November, 1920], John Cooper Papers, CUA. Elizabeth McKeown kindly shared relevant letters from the Cooper collection about laywomen's disappointment at O'Connell's scheming tactics and their complaints about the unfitness of Lillian Slattery.

76. Cardinal Cushing sold the building then, and the league has since operated from several locations, including Emmanuel College. The luxurious appointments of 1 Arlington Street, formerly the home of William Weld, are described and photographed in Bunting, *Houses of Boston's Back Bay,* 96–97, 142–43, 148–53.

77. Blair, *Clubwoman as Feminist.* Although Blair discusses no Catholic clubs, her paradigm for secular women's clubs has informed my analysis.

78. Leach, *True Love and Perfect Union,* 319.

79. Lubove, *Professional Altruist.*

80. O'Connell, Lenten message to LCW, 1914, in *S&A,* 4:187.

81. Lord et al., *History,* 3:543. The Cenacle nuns were not vulnerable to O'Connell's interference because they were a pontifical order. A history of the order appears in Lynch, *In the Shadow of Our Lady.*

82. "The Spirit and Work of the Cenacle," Boston *Pilot,* March 8, 1930.

83. James J. Walsh, *Our American Cardinals,* 203; Lord et al., *History,* 3:542–43.

84. O'Connell, "The Guild of St. Apollonia," Address at Forsyth Dental Infirmary to Guild of St. Apollonia, August 26, 1920, in *S&A,* 7:154.

85. Boston *Pilot*, January 1 and 8, 1910.

86. In the pre–World War I era, with Boston's Ralph Adams Cram as one of its prime exponents, Catholic support for the medieval idealism that underlay the guild revival attracted numerous Catholic elites. For another assessment of the importance of the medieval ideal in American Catholicism, see Gleason, "Mass and Maypole Revisited."

87. An earlier version of this research was published as "The Pulpit of Hearthstone: Katherine Conway and Boston Catholic Women, 1900–1920," *U.S. Catholic Historian* 5 (Summer/Fall 1986), 355–70. Conway's journalism experience was more typical than has been noted in the history of Catholic women. Numerous female editors served the Massachusetts Catholic press: Susan L. Emery of the *Sacred Heart Review* in Cambridge; Mary B. O'Sullivan, editor of *Donahoe's Magazine*; Katherine O'Keeffe O'Mahoney of Lawrence founded, published, and edited the *Catholic Register* from 1892 to 1896 and contributed to the *Pilot*, the *Sacred Heart Review*, and *Donahoe's*. Mary Josephine Rogers (1882–1955), known as Mother Mary Joseph, coedited the Maryknoll magazine, *Field Afar* (Boston), with Maryknoll founder Rev. James Anthony Walsh from 1907 to 1930. In addition, many Irish surnames appear in the listing of women reporters in the *New England Woman's Press Association Handbook* (Cambridge, Mass.: Cambridge Chronicle, 1908).

88. Her sister had an equally enterprising career: she went to Buenos Aires and founded the American College there. Her sudden death in 1898 deeply depressed Conway, whose parents had died six years earlier.

89. "The Cultured Catholic Woman and Her Political Duty," typescript, n.d., BCSp. During reorganization of the Burns Library at Boston College, which housed the Conway papers in its Special Collections, the four boxes of her papers and diaries, which date from 1906 to 1926, had been temporarily numbered. Rather than using temporary designations, I identify documents and diary entries by title (if available) and year.

90. Conway to Onahan, February 19, 1893, Conway files, NDA.

91. Katherine E. Conway, "Normal Christian Woman," 149–50.

92. Ibid., 152–53.

93. Conway to Onahan, February 12, 1893, Conway-Onahan Correspondence, NDA. Her language closely resembles statements of Mrs. Schulyer Van Rensselaer about the necessity for art not limited by gender segregation. Van Rensselaer's essays in art criticism, and her appreciation of the Woman's Building at the Columbian Exposition, were probably known to Conway. See Weimann, *Fair Women*, 280–81.

94. Conway to Father Daniel Hudson, May 5, 1907, Conway files, NDA. *American Catholic Who's Who* lists Thomas Ackland as assistant editor under both Roche and Conway. The *Pilot* files at AABo do not mention him. For a brief biography of Ackland, see Georgina Pell Curtis, *American Catholic Who's Who*, 2.

95. Conway had occasionally used her own salary to meet expenses. Ironically, she delivered spirited testimony before a national press convention that the success of the Catholic press depended on "sound business principles." See Reilly, *History of the Catholic Press Association*, 20.

96. Conway, "Book of Days," May 21, 1907, BCSp.

97. Conway, Diary, August 30, 1907 [the date of Williams's death], Conway Papers, BCSp. Williams had honored her by naming her the second woman member of the Boston Catholic Union and never attempted to make the *Pilot* into the Church's

mouthpiece, even when he became co-proprietor with John Boyle O'Reilly in 1886. On the ownership and editorship of the paper from Patrick Donahoe to O'Reilly to O'Connell, see James A. White, "Era of Good Intentions," and the *Pilot* files, RG V.2 and RG III.D, AABo.

98. For the story of that contest, see *Sacred Heart Review* and Sacred Heart Parish files, and correspondence between Monsignor John O'Brien and O'Connell, AABo. O'Connell exaggerated O'Brien's insubordination by calling him "the only trouble-some one in the clergy in the Archdiocese" (Chancellor, for O'Connell, to Right Rev. Msgr. Sante Tampieri, January 31, 1913, *Sacred Heart Review,* Chancery Central Subject File, M-1693, AABo).

99. Conway to O'Connell, January 31, 1910, O'Connell Papers, 3:15, AABo.

100. Obituary for Madaleva (1887–1964), *Boston Sunday Globe,* July 26, 1964.

101. Georgina Pell Curtis, *American Catholic Who's Who,* 115. Conway's *Republic* coeditor for 1914–26 was Irene Kennedy, who is briefly mentioned in George E. Ryan, "Irish Press of Boston."

102. Conway's pitiable last years can be pieced together from her diaries and comments to friends in personal correspondence, as above, and in a letter to Denis McCarthy (December 4, 1926), which reported, "My work would not be apparent to anyone not very familiar with my style" (Conway Papers, BCSp).

103. Conway to O'Connell, August 13 or 18, 1920, O'Connell Correspondence, 3:15, AABo.

104. Conway to O'Connell, August 25, 1920, ibid.

105. In 1912, for example, the stated circulation of the paper was 85,000; by comparison, the daily *Boston Globe* sold 184,270 copies. The campaign was led by Rev. David Toomey, the appointed editor of the *Pilot* since O'Connell's takeover in 1908, and conducted by Rev. Francis J. Spellman from 1918 to 1922 and by Rev. William E. Conroy in 1920.

106. Boston *Pilot,* March 15, 1919, 8, and January 10, 1920, 8. In a memo to Father O'Brien, O'Connell stated: "Of course, very many families in this parish are now taking the Sacred Heart Review and I trust they shall continue taking it; but they can, or at least many can, and they ought also, take the Pilot. They will find in the Pilot very much more than they can find in the Review" ("Announcement about the Pilot," Sacred Heart, Cambridge, Box 1, folder 4, AABo).

107. Boston *Pilot,* February 6, 1915.

108. Roche's editorship is discussed in Francis R. Walsh, "The Boston *Pilot.*" Walsh calls the *Pilot* under Roche a "highly significant failure," because he steered it away from a ghetto Irish perspective and an artificial gentility. See also Francis R. Walsh, "James Jeffrey Roche," and the bibliography contained in *Pilot at One-Fifty,* the 150th anniversary edition of the *Pilot.*

109. Katherine E. Conway, *Christian Gentlewoman,* 18.

110. Annette S. Driscoll, "In Memoriam—Katherine E. Conway" *Catholic World,* February 1928, 487; Lecky, *Down at Caxton's,* 127. In photographs Conway appears robust, despite her anemia. A description of her in *Dominicana* confirms a healthy appearance: "Instead of tall and angular, she is graciously rounded and not above medium height" (Gilmore, "Katherine E. Conway," 466).

111. *Boston Evening Transcript,* January 23, 1927, 6. The few recognitions Conway received include a biographical sketch in O'Mahoney, *Famous Irishwomen.* More recent tributes include George E. Ryan, "PILOT's Only Woman Editor Fought for

Dignity," Boston *Pilot*, August 5, 1961, and Pam Abbene, "Katherine E. Conway remains the Pilot's only female editor," in *Pilot at One-Fifty*, 63.

112. Boston *Pilot*, September 23, 1911, 4.

113. O'Reilly, for example, had believed that "women have all the necessary qualities to make good men, but they must give their time and attention to it while the men are boys" (Katherine E. Conway, *Watchwords of John Boyle O'Reilly*, 16).

114. Conway's successor as chief editorial writer from 1911 to 1919 was Father Hugh Blunt, a local minor author who maintained a pious traditionalism. See George E. Ryan, *Figures in Our Catholic History*, 55.

115. In 1888 she delivered an address to the press club, "Some Obstacles to the success of women in journalism."

116. The report of the ceremony appeared in the Boston *Pilot*, May 25, 1907. While teaching in 1912 at Saint Mary's College in South Bend, Indiana, she received the Pro Ecclesia et Pontificio Cross from Pius X. While in Indiana she still returned to Boston for about four months each year and submitted a weekly item to the *Republic*. See Georgina Pell Curtis, *American Catholic Who's Who*, 115, and "John F. Fitzgerald in Other Aspects," typescript, p. 121, BCSp.

117. Katherine E. Conway, "Normal Christian Woman," 149.

118. Katherine E. Conway, *Christian Gentlewoman*, 21. She originally presented this as a paper to the Catholic Reading Circle of Haverhill, Massachusetts, in 1897, as reported in the *Catholic Reading Circle Review*, July 1897, 302.

119. Katherine E. Conway, *Christian Gentlewoman*, 19. The passage continues, "She is nobody, who does not belong to five or six of these, who is not the president, or secretary, or treasurer of something, and who has not been described in the newspapers after some club meeting and banquet as expert in parliamentary law, an admirable chairman, or the best of toastmasters."

120. I read notes and typescripts of her lectures in the uncataloged Conway papers at BCSp.

121. Annette S. Driscoll, "In Memoriam—Katherine E. Conway," *Catholic World*, February 1928, 487.

122. Charles Fanning, *Exiles of Erin*, 242.

123. The *Pilot* also ran a column entitled "In the Family Sitting Room," which gave advice based on situations and dialogue improvised by the editor.

124. Significantly, her nonfiction publications were biographies of local Catholic heroes John Boyle O'Reilly and Charles Francis Donnelly rather than her personal heroines. See Katherine E. Conway, *Watchwords of John Boyle O'Reilly*, and, with Mabel Cameron, *Charles Francis Donnelly*. She also compiled the biography of a dying child from his diaries, expressing a favorite Victorian theme of meaningful death. Colleen McDannell has also associated this theme with Conway's poetry.

125. Katherine E. Conway, *Bettering Ourselves*, 26.

126. Ibid., 72.

127. Katherine E. Conway, "Normal Christian Woman," 154–55.

128. Boston *Republic*, November 26, 1910, 5.

129. This favorable view of women authors is from Kenneally, *History of American Catholic Women*, 62.

130. Katherine E. Conway, "Normal Christian Woman," 151.

131. I have used Guiney papers, photographs, and drawings located at four archives: YBR, LCM, BPL, and HCR. The most comprehensive study is Fairbanks, *Guiney*.

132. Grace Guiney, *Letters of Louise Imogen Guiney*, 2:234.

133. Brégy, *Poets and Pilgrims*, 188–89. The quotation about Moulton comes from Whiting, *Boston Days*, 302.

134. Quoted in Tenison, *Guiney*, 64.

135. Sister Mary Adorita Hart, *Soul Ordained to Fail*; Fairbanks, *Guiney*; Lecky, *Down at Caxton's*; Jessie B. Rittenhouse, "Louise Imogen Guiney, Loyal Rememberer," in Rittenhouse, *My House of Life*.

136. *New York Times*, undated clipping, Guiney letter file, YBR.

137. Louise I. Guiney, "Point of View," 124.

138. Guiney to [F. H. Day], February 16, [1915], Guiney Correspondence, LCM. Roman, *Annie Adams Fields*, 164–65.

139. Several of her friends had joined the Order of the White Rose in Cambridge, or similar bohemian cliques that toasted themselves thus:

They formed a Cult, far subtler, brainier,
Than ordinary Anglomania,
For all as Jacobites were reckoned,
And gaily toasted Charles the Second!

See Gelett Burgess, "The Bohemians of Boston," *Enfant Terrible!*, April 1898, 4–5. Concerning Guiney herself, there is ample photographic evidence of her family and friends on both sides of the Atlantic performing plays and dressing up for tableaux vivants.

140. Jussim, *Slave to Beauty*, 30; Fairbanks, *Guiney*, 61.

141. Fairbanks, *Guiney*, 63–65.

142. On the popularity of Keats in Boston, see Rollins, *Keats and the Bostonians*.

143. Patricia J. Fanning, "Fred Holland Day," esp. 232. Some details conflict with those presented by Jussim. On Day's selfish withholding of the Fanny Brawne–Fanny Keats correspondence, see Rollins, *Keats and the Bostonians*, introduction.

144. See the personal recollections of Leonard Feeney, S.J., "The Guineys: Grace and Ruth," *Journal of the Associated Alumnae of the Sacred Heart*, October 1937, 41–46, HCR.

145. A recent overview of Guiney's prodigious periodical publications is Messbarger, "Failed Promise."

146. This anecdote was reported by her friend Sir Edmund Gosse in his *Silhouettes*, 368–70, and by Cram, *My Life in Architecture*, 15–16.

147. Nonetheless, poverty helped break her ties to the present, not to Catholicism. Guiney, quoted in typewritten manuscript of an essay about her by Eva Mabel Tenison, p. 9, Guiney file, YBR.

148. Brégy, *Poets and Pilgrims*, 189.

149. Gosse, *Silhouettes*, 370.

150. Guiney to Miss Morgan, quoted in Rittenhouse, *My House of Life*, 182.

151. Like Katherine Conway, Guiney suffered a debilitating ailment: increasing deafness due to an inoperable vascular lesion. See Jussim, *Slave to Beauty*, 30.

152. Messbarger, *Fiction with a Parochial Purpose*, 100.

153. *Scribner's*, January 1911, 124.

154. Katherine Tynan Hinkson, *Tablet* (London), November 13, 1920.

155. Guiney's interest in Hurrell Froude justifies including her with the Gothic revivalists and their admiration for medieval Christianity: in the nineteenth-century

British Catholic community, according to Cardinal Newman's *Apologia*, Froude represented a preference for medieval, rather than primitive, Christianity.

156. Handwritten postcard among Guiney photographs, HCR.
157. Mary Boyle O'Reilly to Rev. M. Earls, February 9, 1921, Guiney Collection, HCR.
158. O'Mahoney, *Famous Irishwomen*, 201.
159. Martha Moore Avery, "Woman Suffrage, Six Papers," *Catholic Mind*, December 8, 1915, 625.
160. Rev. J. Elliott Ross, "Why I Believe in Woman Suffrage," in Rorke, *Letters and Addresses on Woman Suffrage*, 10.
161. Bishops McQuaid, Spalding, Dowling, Foley, and Gallagher. See Kenneally, *History of American Catholic Women*, 139.
162. Katherine E. Conway, *Watchwords of John Boyle O'Reilly*, 20.
163. O'Connell, February 22, 1920, in *S&A*, 7:129.
164. *S&A*, 7:429.
165. Boston *Pilot*, October 9, 1920, 4.
166. Mary Dowd, "The Public Rights of Women," *Catholic World*, June 1894, 317.
167. Kenneally, "Catholicism and Woman Suffrage," 56.
168. O'Connell, "The Evils of Modern Society," in *S&A*, 7:139.
169. Katherine E. Conway, *Watchwords of John Boyle O'Reilly*, 20. In the same colorful passage O'Reilly called suffrage "a half-fledged, unmusical, Promethean abomination."
170. Boston College *Stylus* 26 (April 1913): 273.
171. For biographical information on Foley (1875–1957), see Kennelly, *American Catholic Women*, 138–39, and Kenneally, *History of American Catholic Women*, 137–38.
172. Report of Corrigan's speech in the Boston *Republic*, June 21, 1919.
173. Rev. J. Elliott Ross, "Why I Believe in Woman Suffrage," in Rorke, *Letters and Addresses on Woman Suffrage*, 13.
174. Boston *Pilot*, March 9, 1907, 2.
175. Katherine E. Conway, "Normal Christian Woman," 153.
176. Katherine E. Conway, *Bettering Ourselves*, 78.
177. "The Cultured Catholic and Her Political Duty," [1921?] BCSp. This corrects a misconception about Conway as a lifetime antisuffragist by Kennelly, "A Question of Equality," in Kennelly, *American Catholic Women*, 131.
178. Bugg, *People of Our Parish*, 115.
179. To date, there has been but one attempt to analyze data about the professional progress of Catholic laywomen in the twentieth century, and no sustained attempt to profile working-class Catholic women, except as an aspect of ethnic history. See Mary Oates, "Catholic Laywomen in the Labor Force, 1850–1950," in Kennelly, *American Catholic Women*, 81–124. On nineteenth-century Irish American women, see Diner, *Erin's Daughters*.
180. Herlihy, *Fifty Years of Boston*, 633.
181. Kenneally, "Question of Equality," in Kennelly, *American Catholic Women*, 132.
182. Katzman, *Seven Days a Week*, 70.
183. Repplier, "The Spinster," 181.
184. Boston *Republic*, April 1, 1916, 8.

185. Bugg, *People of Our Parish,* 101.
186. Patrick H. Casey, S.J., "The Catholic Working Girl," *Catholic Mind,* May 22, 1915, 286, 287.
187. Boston *Pilot,* May 25, 1918.
188. There is little information on her life, aside from a brief note in Ursulines of New York, *Immortelles,* 213, and the *Woman's Journal,* November 11, 1893.
189. *Boston Globe,* March 6, 1910.
190. Boston *Pilot,* February 14, 1920.
191. Trolander, *Settlement Houses,* 21. O'Sullivan herself had been a Hull House resident prior to the founding of the Women's Trade Union League.
192. Stang, *Socialism and Christianity,* 72.
193. Katherine Mullaney, *Catholic World,* June 1894, 312.
194. Diner, *Erin's Daughters,* 139–40.
195. O'Connell, *S&A,* 4:190.
196. Kenneally, *History of American Catholic Women,* 143.

Chapter 7

1. *Sacred Heart Review,* March 23, 1912, 4. (Carpenter was the only Protestant of the group.)
2. Lord et al., *History,* 3:404–5.
3. O'Reilly, born in Ireland, was convicted of treason against Queen Victoria and sentenced to twenty years of penal servitude in Australia. He escaped in 1869 and arrived in Boston in 1870, where he remained until his death in 1890.
4. Desmond, *Reading Circle Manual,* 52.
5. Francis Walsh, "Lace Curtain Literature," *Journal of American Culture* 2 (Spring 1979): 141.
6. Winslow, *Literary Boston,* 151. O'Reilly's publishing friends included Charles Hurd, the literary editor for the *Boston Transcript,* and Thomas Bailey Aldrich and William Dean Howells, who joined the Papyrus Club. See Schofield, *Seek for a Hero,* 232–33.
7. Joseph Smith, *James Jeffrey Roche,* 8–9, 12–13.
8. Winslow, *Literary Boston,* 150. On the group of Yankee Democrats and Mugwumps favoring cooperation with the Irish, see Geoffrey Blodgett, "Yankee Leadership in a Divided City: Boston, 1860–1910," in Formisano and Burns, *Boston,* 87–110.
9. Grace Guiney, *Letters of Louise Imogen Guiney,* 2:250.
10. Malcolm Brown has described the Irish literary movement as "a loose fraternity of Dublin and Cork writers who hoped to put their career in step with Irish history, marching, as it seemed, in full exultant surge into a resplendent future" (*Politics of Irish Literature,* 9).
11. McCarthy et al., *Irish Literature.* The most recent biography of Hyde (1860–1949), founder of the Gaelic League and first president of the Irish Free State, is Dunleavy, *Douglas Hyde,* which describes Hyde's life as divided between his private secret Irish circle and the public Anglo-Irish world of his parents.
12. Shuster, *Catholic Spirit in Modern English Literature,* 272–73.
13. *Boston Sunday Post,* October 8, 1911.
14. Stephen Birmingham, *Real Lace,* 185.
15. Boston *Pilot,* July 27, 1907, 14.

16. *National Cyclopedia of American Biography*, 29:494; *Donahoe's Magazine*, October 1901, 375–76.

17. Biography of Sarah G. (Carroll) Hayden, b. 1844, in Georgina Pell Curtis, *American Catholic Who's Who*, 280–81.

18. *Boston Globe*, May 27, 1911, 16.

19. Merwick, *Boston Priests*, 156. Merwick overstates O'Connell's "intellectual regimentation of the diocese after 1907" but correctly attributes it to his admiration for the model of the universal church symbolized by the pontificate of Leo XIII. James Gaffey suggests that O'Connell's power and influence in Rome and in Boston peaked early, before 1921. After that time, he figured as a leader "too formidable to be loved." See Gaffey, "Changing of the Guard," 244.

20. J. J. Roche, quoted by Joseph Smith, *James Jeffrey Roche*, 22.

21. Whiting, *Boston Days*, 447.

22. John Talbot Smith, "Young Catholic Writer," 180.

23. Birmingham called this Catholic attempt a "pathetic" and "thin echo" of Protestant conventions. See his *Real Lace*, 198.

24. O'Connell, February 1, 1912, in *S&A*, 4:25. His sermon at Boston's Catholic centennial celebration, October 28, 1908, also joined Catholic and national futures: "The Catholic Faith, changeless and undying, Christian Hope in the fulfillment of a great destiny for our country, charity uncooled and unquenchable for all" (*S&A*, 3:139).

25. *S&A*, 3:185.

26. Merwick, *Boston Priests*, 168.

27. Joseph Smith, *James Jeffrey Roche*, 18.

28. Kerby Miller, *Emigrants and Exiles*.

29. Charles Fanning, *Irish Voice in America*, 157.

30. Owen Wister, *The Virginian: A Horseman of the Plains* (New York: Macmillan, 1902), 250.

31. Angoff, "Boston Twilight," 441.

32. Ibid., 444.

33. *Boston Globe*, August 10, 1910, 4. Memorials to O'Reilly were erected in the Boston Public Library and the Fenway and at his parish in Charlestown, his summer home in Hull, and his birthplace in Drogheda, Ireland. Catholic University commissioned a bust; Notre Dame hung his portrait in its art gallery. J. J. Roche published *The Life of John Boyle O'Reilly* in 1891; Katherine Conway edited *Watchwords of John Boyle O'Reilly*; O'Reilly's widow, Mary, edited and published his poems and speeches in 1891. Studies of O'Reilly appear in Thomas N. Brown, "Irish Layman," 6:81–97; Mann, *Yankee Reformers in the Urban Age*; and William V. Shannon, *The American Irish*.

34. Messbarger, *Fiction with a Parochial Purpose*, 101. The author claims that the generation of 1884–1900 had great promise and commanded moral authority, but lost it. More recently, Charles Fanning has identified the decade 1900–1910 as the crucial one in Irish American writing, characterized by a decline in ethnic themes. See Charles Fanning, *Irish Voice in America*.

35. *Sacred Heart Review*, March 23, 1912, 4.

36. McCool, *Catholic Theology in the Nineteenth Century*, 2, 246. On the enduring impact of Thomistic philosophy on American Catholic higher education, see Gleason, "In Search of Unity."

37. Boston *Pilot*, January 23, 1909, 4.
38. This image was common to Catholic writers of the period and is attributed in one source to the Annals of St. Joseph. See *Sacred Heart Review,* June 8, 1918.
39. The Catholic tradition also resembled the classical concept of ethics as systematized in Plato and Aristotle, which itself was more akin to aesthetics than morality.
40. Gioberti, *Essay on the Beautiful,* 55.
41. *Sacred Heart Review,* February 1, 1913, 7.
42. Boston *Pilot,* May 31, 1919, 4.
43. O'Reilly to Bess and Agnes, November 18, 1889, quoted in Schofield, *Seek for a Hero,* 294.
44. P. J. Gannon, S.J., "Art, Morality and Censorship," reprinted in *Catholic Mind,* April 1943, from a Dublin publication, 482.
45. *Live Issue,* February 7, 1914.
46. Rev. Francis Cunningham, "Catholic Novelists of Today," Boston College *Stylus* 23 (October 1909).
47. The phrase appears in a *Pilot* editorial (June 22, 1912, 4) equating ugliness with anti-Christianity.
48. "The Literature of Moral Loveliness," in Ursulines of New York, *Immortelles,* 205.
49. Orestes A. Brownson, "Dana's Poems and Prose Writings," in Brownson, *Works,* 19:318. For his aesthetic principles, see especially vol. 19 in the Philadelphia edition of Brownson, *Works.* Another commonly cited edition was published in Detroit by T. Nourse, 1882–1906.
50. Brownson, *Works,* 19:240. On Gioberti's influence on Brownson, see Schlesinger, *Brownson,* 219–20, 280. Also see Caponigri, "European Influences," 100–124. Another essay in the same volume, "Orestes Brownson: Jacksonian Literary Critic," by C. Carroll Hollis, calls Brownson "the only sociological literary critic of his age."
51. Merwick, *Boston Priests,* 15. For other accounts of his literary criticism, see Marshall, *Brownson.*
52. Lathrop, "Orestes Brownson," 776.
53. Louise Guiney, "Catholic Writers," 206.
54. John Talbot Smith, "Young Catholic Writer," 174.
55. Monsignor Hugh Blunt, for example, donated his extensive Newman collection to Regis College, Boston. Joseph J. Reilly from Springfield, Massachusetts, became a renowned Newman scholar during his teaching career. Wilfrid Ward published a two-volume biography of Newman in 1912 and gave a popular lecture tour of the United States in 1913 and 1915, which included the Lowell Institute Lectures in Boston in the winter of 1914.
56. Lathrop, "Orestes Brownson," 780. Possibly the Church excised Brownson not because of his unorthodoxy but because of fear that his strident Catholicism would have a negative impact on a subsequent generation less persecuted.
57. Earls, *Under College Towers,* 40.
58. Gioberti, *Essay on the Beautiful,* 55.
59. "The Catholic Young Man in Literature," *Republic,* December 19, 1914, reprinted from *Queen's Work.*
60. "Modern Literature," Boston *Pilot,* May 21, 1910, 4.
61. Orestes Brownson, "Catholicity and Literature," in Brownson, *Works,* 19:460. Brownson seems to have paraphrased this comment from the *Literary World* (Boston)

of 1850, "The novel is now almost recognized with the newspaper and the pamphlet as a legitimate mode of influencing public opinion," suggesting that his influences were not exclusively Catholic.

62. Boston *Pilot,* June 22, 1912, 4.

63. Emily Hickey, "Catholic Principles and English Literature," *Catholic World,* May 1912, 150. Hickey (1845–1924) was an Irish-born Protestant who converted to Catholicism and became a friend of Louise Guiney in England. See Kane, "'Willing Captive of Home,'" 345 n. 46.

64. Boston *Pilot,* August 27, 1910, 4.

65. John R. Taylor, "The Unreality of Realism," Boston College *Stylus* 26 (April 1913): 247–50.

66. Ibid., 250.

67. Boston *Pilot,* January 16 and 23, 1909, 4.

68. Orestes Brownson, "Catholicity and Literature," in Brownson, *Works,* 19:460.

69. The most detailed biographical study of Earls is the four-part article by Lucey, "Record of an American Priest," 226. I have also used unpublished materials from Earls's diary, 1899–1900, and from his correspondence, HCR.

70. *Catholic World,* January 1901, 538–39.

71. Bugg, *People of Our Parish,* 170–71.

72. See also Roche, "The Story of the Filibusters," (1891), and any of Connolly's nautical tales, from *Out of Gloucester* (1902), to *Sea-Borne: Thirty Years Avoyaging* (1944).

73. Brownson, *Works,* 19:461.

74. "The Literature of Moral Loveliness," in Ursulines of New York, *Immortelles,* 203. Speech to the first Catholic Summer School.

75. Katherine E. Conway, *Christian Gentlewoman,* 57.

76. Halsey, *Survival of American Innocence,* 101.

77. Trachtenberg, *Incorporation of America,* 184.

78. Searman, "Apostolate of Print."

79. Boston *Pilot,* December 23, 1911, 4.

80. Katherine E. Conway, *Christian Gentlewoman,* 53.

81. Boston *Pilot,* November 5, 1910, 4.

82. "Catholics and Yellow Journals," *Sacred Heart Review,* February 3, 1912, 8.

83. Katherine E. Conway, *Christian Gentlewoman,* 52.

84. Boston *Pilot,* March 17, 1917, 4. For an excellent interpretation of the meaning of popular fiction, see Denning, *Mechanic Accents.*

85. Boston *Pilot,* April 30, 1910, 4.

86. Victor T. Noonan, "Stray Thoughts on the Novel, Past and Present," written for the Boston *Pilot,* October 26, 1907.

87. Boston *Pilot,* April 21, 1917, 4.

88. "The Value of Good Reading," *Sacred Heart Review,* December 21, 1912, 8.

89. Searman, "Apostolate of Print."

90. Boston *Pilot,* April 30, 1910, 4.

91. Ibid., April 30, 1907, 4.

92. Anna Cecila Doyle, "The Catholic Writer and Literary Ideals," Boston *Republic,* January 30, 1915, 9, reprinted from the *Magnificat.* The argument that Catholic optimism can be understood in the post–World War I era by the metaphor of innocence is the crux of Halsey's argument in *Survival of American Innocence.* I argue here

that parameters establishing the ideal of innocence were set in the decades before 1920, at least in Boston.

93. Desmond, *Reading Circle Manual,* 8.

94. Hayes, "Value of Good Reading," 8. For a more detailed examination of the gender implications of the reading circle movement and summer schools, see Chapter 6.

95. Even Desmond's choices duplicated numerous entries on a list composed thirty-one years earlier by Orestes Brownson. See his "Catholic Popular Literature," in Brownson, *Works,* 19:590; Desmond, *Reading Circle Manual,* 74–75.

96. Desmond, *Reading Circle Manual,* 52.

97. Boston *Pilot,* January 11, 1909, 1.

98. Lecky, *Down at Caxton's,* 205. Walter Lecky was the pseudonym of William McDermott.

99. From the Chicago *New World,* quoted in *Sacred Heart Review,* October 7, 1911.

100. Stephen O'Meara to Sister Leocadia O'Meara, October 10, 1911, Family Correspondence, O'Meara Papers, BPL. O'Meara believed that the Jesuit weekly, *America,* had "a splendid summary of the news of the world and able articles and literary reviews."

101. Bernard O'Reilly, *True Men as We Need Them,* 433.

102. Of these, *Catholic World,* founded by Isaac Hecker, was undoubtedly the ablest and least parochial. The *Pilot*'s quality of original fiction and poetry was indifferent; like most Catholic papers, it borrowed heavily from other Catholic magazines. *Catholic Mind* (New York), a monthly, was founded in 1903 to reprint the "best" from the Catholic press. The most technical magazine with limited popular appeal was the *American Ecclesiastical Review* (Philadelphia), aimed at the clergy.

103. "Catholicity and Literature," January 1856, in Brownson, *Works,* 19:447.

104. "Literary Workers Who Are Catholics" encouraged the evolution of a great Catholic writer in America and further underscored the importance of the 1890s as a catalyst for Catholic artistic intentions. The column examined, among others, Maurice Francis Egan, John Talbot Smith, Louise Guiney, and Mary Catherine Crowley. See James A. White, "Era of Good Intentions," 291. Crowley, born in Boston of Scotch ancestry, was editor of *Catholic Missions* magazine and edited *Catholic Missions: The Annals of the Propagation of the Faith since 1907,* indicating a strong link between the evangelical and didactic purposes of literature. See Logan, *Part Taken by Women,* 833.

105. *Columbiad,* January 1917, 1.

106. Shuster, *Catholic Spirit in America,* 119.

107. Messbarger, *Fiction with a Parochial Purpose,* 71.

108. *Boston Globe,* August 12, 1908, 4.

109. Charles A. Birmingham, Boston College *Stylus* 23 (October 1909): 1.

110. Cornelius Anthony Guiney, "George Bernard Shaw," Boston College *Stylus* 23 (October 1909): 18–20. He claimed that Shaw's "soul is not Catholic enough to note that the most beautiful lilies grow in the most dismal swamps, and so instead of letting in sunshine upon the lillies, he stirs up the mire and obscures them by the poisonous exhalations which result" (20).

111. Rev. Francis A. Cunningham, "Catholic Novelists of Today," Boston College *Stylus* 23 (October 1909): 28.

112. Ibid., 29. Cunningham was also an editorial writer at the *Pilot*, a contributor to *Donahoe's Magazine*, a pastor in Dorchester, and an intimate of Archbishop O'Connell. See Georgina Pell Curtis, *American Catholic Who's Who*, 134.

113. Holy Cross *Purple*, March 1910, 509.

114. For a positive view of Earls, see Meagher and Grattan, *Spires of Fenwick*, 266.

115. Debating societies at Catholic colleges provided a parallel opportunity. Prizes were awarded annually for best essays on religious topics such as the Eucharist, Easter, and the papacy. At Boston College, the Fulton Debating Society was for upperclassmen, the Marquette Debating Society formed in 1902 for underclassmen, and the Brosnahan Debating Society was created in 1910. At Holy Cross, the Fenwick Debating Society dated from 1846. The Philomathic Society opened soon after.

116. Boston *Pilot*, January 11, 1909, 1.

117. "A paper read at a students' conference, in Sever Hall, Harvard University, Cambridge, Massachusetts," February 23, 1892, microfilm, HUA.

118. Files, Catholic Club, MITa.

119. "Report of Committee on Public Morals," AFCS Convention, New York, August 1916, Chancery Central Subject File, M-906, AABo.

120. Boston *Republic*, December 19, 1914, 8.

121. For statistics, see the list of Boston College graduates and their reported careers in *Boston College Alumni Directory, 1872–1923* (Chestnut Hill, Mass.: June 1924), BCSp.

122. David O'Brien, *Public Catholicism*, 100, quoting Dorothy Ross's M.A. thesis, Columbia University, n.d.

123. Boston College *Stylus* 23 (October 1909): 1.

124. Bishop of Fond Du Lac, *Christian Art* 1 (April 1907): 10. Cram published a book entitled *The Ministry of Art* in 1914.

125. Guiney to Frank Fitzpatrick, Sr., n.d., uncataloged Guiney correspondence, BPL. Also see Lucey, "Louise Imogen Guiney," 364–65.

126. *Christian Art* has "run upon a reef," Guiney wrote. "Now do you agree with me that this is a most desirable chance for us Catholics? Do you think you could possibly take hold?" (Louise Guiney to Mr. Fitzpatrick, undated, uncataloged Guiney letters, BPL.

127. Charles Perkins to O'Connell, December 26, 1908, O'Connell Correspondence, 8:15, AABo.

128. Louise Guiney to "Sonny" [Fred Holland Day], February 16, 1909, Guiney Correspondence, LCM.

129. Guiney to Fitzpatrick, March 8 [1909?], uncataloged Guiney letters, BPL.

130. Lucey, "Louise Imogen Guiney," 366.

131. Desmond, *Reading Circle Manual*, 51–52.

132. Boston *Pilot*, August 25, 1917, 4.

133. Katherine Conway, "Vital Problems—continued," typescript of address, p. 9, Conway Papers, BCSp.

134. *Sacred Heart Review*, May 13, 1911, 9.

135. Boston *Pilot*, August 13, 1910, 4.

136. Ibid., January 13, 1912, 4.

137. Lecky, "Literature and Our Catholic Poor," in Lecky, *Down at Caxton's*, 197.

138. On the profession of writing and publishing, see Wilson, *Labor of Words*.

139. John Talbot Smith, "Young Catholic Writer," 178.

140. Boston *Republic*, December 13, 1919, 6.

141. Katherine Conway to McCarthy, December 4, 1926, McCarthy Papers, BCSp.

142. Paul Underwood Kellogg to Mary Boyle O'Reilly, November 18, 1929, Mary Boyle O'Reilly Papers, BPL.

143. Charles Fanning, *Irish Voice in America*, 240.

144. Guiney and Repplier (1858–1920) ignored the sexist implications of his title, which is itself a comment on the Catholic reading public's image of a novelist, even though many published Catholic writers were women.

145. Edward Francis Mohler, *America*, October 28, 1916, 65.

146. John Talbot Smith, "Young Catholic Writer," 171.

147. Ibid., 175–77.

148. Louise Guiney, "Catholic Writers," 209, 205.

149. Agnes Repplier, "Catholicism and Authorship," *Catholic World*, November 1909, 174. Agnes Repplier's rebuttal resembled Guiney's except that in her opinion, editors and the public were indifferent to an author's religious creed. She urged Catholic writers to seek a market anywhere they could find one.

150. Louise Guiney, "Catholic Writers," 213, 215.

151. Cf. Charles Fanning, *Irish Voice in America*, 167.

152. Kathleen Norris, "Religion and Popular Fiction," in Talbot, *Fiction by Its Makers*, 27. In 1909, Kathleen Thompson had married journalist Charles Norris, the younger brother of naturalist novelist Frank Norris, who had died at thirty-two in 1902. In 1909 the couple moved from San Francisco to the East Coast to become professional writers. Katherine Conway was one of Kathleen Norris's promoters.

153. Boston *Republic*, February 6, 1915.

154. Undated typescript, Conway Papers, Box 4, BCSp.

155. Georgina Pell Curtis, *American Catholic Who's Who*, 184.

156. Stephen O'Meara also contributed to the professional journal *Writer*, founded by William H. Hills, the editor of the *Boston Globe*. He reported in 1887 that only seven of forty-nine fellow reporters stayed with the profession after fifteen years, suggesting the instability of the reporter's career.

157. Miles, "James B. Connolly," 116.

158. My interpretation here follows Charles Fanning, *Irish Voice in America*, 240–41.

159. As reported by Katherine E. Conway, "Why Always Catholic?," 31.

160. *Boston Globe*, 1919, clipping, McCarthy Papers, BCSp.

161. O'Reilly's disappointment at Guiney's self-centered apoliticism and archaic scholarly pursuits is evident in her 1921 letters to Father Earls following Guiney's death. For example, O'Reilly recalled: "When the [First World] war came Louise seemed to deliberately shut herself away from human experience. Just once I saw tears in her eyes—when I told her of standing in the Grande Place of Louraine and seeing the Library in flames" (O'Reilly to Earls, January 30, [19]21), Guiney-Earls Letters, Guiney Room, HCR).

162. Katherine Conway, "Vital Problems—continued," typescript of address, p. 3, Conway Papers, BCSp.

163. O'Toole, *Militant and Triumphant*, 204.

164. Louis M. Lyons, *Newspaper Story*, 449, 450, 451, 82, 83.

165. Supreme Council, Knights of Columbus, "Report of the Commission on Re-

ligious Prejudices," August 1915, 18–19. See also Kauffman, *Faith and Fraternalism,* chap. 7.

166. In 1920, national concern for promoting the Catholic media led the pope, at the request of the National Catholic Welfare Conference Department of Publicity, to designate March as National Catholic Press Month. See *Extension Magazine,* March 1921, 1.

167. Boston *Republic,* July 26, 1919, 3.

168. Alice Hayes, "Value of Good Reading," 8.

169. Messbarger, *Fiction with a Parochial Purpose,* 64. While Messbarger's study finishes at 1900, his conclusions accurately reflect Boston through 1920, where Catholics, now a numerical majority, continued to perceive themselves as cultural outsiders, although they resembled mainstream Americans more than they would admit.

170. Halsey, *Survival of American Innocence,* 101.

171. "Who Buys Catholic Books?," *Queen's Work,* October 1914.

172. J. T. Durward, letter to the editor, *American Ecclesiastical Review* 56 (March 1917): 296.

173. Louise Guiney, "Catholic Writers," 210.

174. For example, this comment: "Would it not be better if we substituted thoughtful literary criticism for some of the vapid stuff which chokes the columns of our Catholic journals such as items witnessing to the trills of Kathleen O'Brien's voice at a Knights of Columbus smoker or that Rear Admiral Peregrine Maitland of the British fleet attended midnight Mass on Christmas Day in Rome or that a set of vestments was presented to the Rev. Timothy O'Halloran, curate of Cabirciveen, Co. Kerry, Ireland" (Thomas O'Hagan, "What Is Criticism?," *Columbiad,* April 1915, 12).

175. *Sacred Heart Review,* February 1, 1913, 7.

176. For this trickle-down view of the Catholic impact on the press, see Emma Sherwood Chester, *Catholic World,* June 1914, 337: "Such a contribution of the secular press has been known to check and even wholly eliminate some swelling tide of erroneous belief or propaganda.... His work filters and simplifies down from the learned theologians of the schools to the editor of *The Woman's Page* or the *Housekeeper's Corner.*"

177. "The Future of Catholic Literature in America," Boston *Pilot,* January 11, 1909, 1.

178. Lida L. Coghlan, "A Plea for the Catholic Novel," *Queen's Work,* July 1915.

179. Miles, "James B. Connolly," p. 116.

180. Katherine Conway, "Vital Problems—continued," typescript of address, p. 2, Conway Papers, BCSp. On Egan, see Charles Fanning, *Irish Voice in America,* 198–214, esp. 201.

181. See Sparr, *To Promote, Defend, and Redeem.*

182. James Connolly, Kathleen Norris, and Frank Spearman, a convert, were among the contributors. The symposium is described in Halsey, *Survival of American Innocence,* 108–10.

183. Kathleen Norris, "Religion and Popular Fiction," in Talbot, *Fiction by Its Makers,* 30.

184. Shuster, *Catholic Spirit in America,* 75.

185. Ibid.

186. LIG to Fred Holland Day, January 24, 1893, cited in Fairbanks, *Guiney,* 65.

187. Oscar Wilde coined the latter nickname in 1887 in an unsigned article, "The American Invasion," *Court & Society Review,* March 23, 1887, 270–71.

188. The same development occurred in Worcester, Massachusetts, where a large, established Catholic community almost as entrenched as the Yankee elites evolved its own network of censors through the police chief, local newspaper, and movie critics. See Rosenzweig, *Eight Hours*.

189. On the history of Boston theater from its first theater, Federal Street, founded in 1792, through the 1860s, see Alexander Corbett, Jr., "The Boston Theatre," *Bostonian* 1 (1894–95): 3–18. For the nineteenth and twentieth centuries, see Norton, *Broadway Down East*.

190. Angoff, "Boston Twilight," 439.

191. John Talbot Smith, "Motion Picture," 9.

192. Twentieth Century Club, Drama Committee, "The Amusement Situation in the City of Boston based on a study of the theatres for ten weeks from November 28, 1909 to February 5, 1910," 10–11, MHS.

193. Berry and Panchok, "Church and Theatre," 151–79, esp. 173.

194. Panchok, "Catholic Church and Theater," analyzes Smith's career. A more concise treatment of Catholics who tried to break down unjust prejudice against the theater appears in Berry and Panchok, "Church and Theatre." Smith's Actors' Guild was modeled on the Anglican Actors' Church Alliance of 1899, one more instance of Catholics appropriating existing models and British inspiration for their subculture. In 1919 he founded the Catholic Writers' Guild for journalists and writers.

195. "Certain Stage Conditions," *Columbiad*, February 1916, 14.

196. John Talbot Smith, *Parish Theatre*.

197. Twentieth Century Club, Drama Committee, "The Amusement Situation in the City of Boston based on a study of the theatres for ten weeks from November 28, 1909 to February 5, 1910," 24, MHS.

198. John Talbot Smith, *Parish Theatre*, 68–69. This judgment about his realism is from Charles Fanning, *Irish Voice in America*, 197.

199. John Talbot Smith, *Parish Theatre*, 80.

200. Brégy, "Catholic Theater Movement," 101.

201. Ibid.

202. On the religious habits of actors, see McArthur, *Actors and American Culture*, 132, 142, 164. For the middle class, drawn toward the increased social conformity demanded by urban-industrial society, actors often symbolized iconoclasm because of their unconventional private lives. In projecting its desires for social freedom onto the demimonde, bourgeois culture imagined actors as icons of escape.

203. Kuehnel, *Conferences for Young Women*, 160.

204. *Columbiad*, March 1916, 10.

205. John Talbot Smith, "The Censor and the Stage," *Columbiad*, November 1913, 9.

206. Rev. Martin E. Fahy, "Father Smith and the Catholic Actors' Guild of America," 1924 pamphlet commemorating Smith, author's collection, p. 8.

207. For all his upper-crust appearance, Peters had a sexually perverse history, which Curley surely would have exposed had he known about it at the time. Peters became guardian to a number of girls who were distant cousins of his wife. In 1917 he raped one of them, an eleven-year-old later known as Starr Faithfull, and continued to abuse her on out-of-town trips. When Starr's mother remarried, her stepfather later blackmailed Peters. Starr was found drowned on a Long Island beach in 1931. See Beatty, *Rascal King*, 206–7.

208. Letter of O'Meara, February 10, 1910, reprinted in Twentieth Century Club, Drama Committee, "The Amusement Situation in the City of Boston based on a study of the theatres for ten weeks from November 28, 1909 to February 5, 1910," 32–33, MHS. From 1885 to 1906, however, the governor and his council had been empowered to appoint three Boston citizens to administer the police department, so Massachusetts had a tradition of limiting the power of the mayor over the Boston police, especially when the mayor was a Catholic. See Russell, *City in Terror,* 35.

209. Charles W. Morton, "The Censor's Double Standard," *The Reporter,* March 14, 1950, 23.

210. For an account of Pelletier's scandalous career in the Knights of Columbus and as district attorney, see Chapter 3 and Kauffman, *Faith and Fraternalism,* chap. 7.

211. Charles J. V. Murphy, "Pope of New England," 285. See also A. L. S. Wood's commentary on a remark by the secretary of the New England Watch & Ward Society: "'The Irish make notable Puritans,' says the Rev. Mr. Chase. The Roman Catholic Methodists and the Methodist-Implacables have been regimented together in the service of Pure Literature—a formidable phalanx, indeed" ("Keeping the Puritans Pure," 76).

212. See Paula Kane, "'Staging a Lie': Boston Catholics and the Irish Literary Renaissance," in *Religion and Identity,* vol. 5 of *The Irish World Wide,* ed. Patrick O'Sullivan (Leicester: Leicester University Press; New York: St. Martin's Press, 1994).

213. James J. Walsh, "Burlesque Shows," 10.

214. McGinnis, "Descration of the Drama," 1.

215. James J. Walsh, "Burlesque Shows," 10.

216. McGinnis, "Desecration of the Drama," 1.

217. *Ave Maria* 72 (1911), 726.

218. Catholic Theatre Movement, *White List Bulletin,* October 15, 1917, 66.

219. Boston *Republic,* February 28, 1920, 4.

220. Ibid., 1.

221. Repplier, *Convent Days,* 42, 43, 44.

222. O'Connell, "The Family and the Home," in *S&A,* 4:167.

223. Dennis Ryan, *Beyond the Ballot Box,* 73–75.

224. Brégy, foreword to Brégy, "Catholic Theatre Movement."

225. Halsey, *Survival of American Innocence,* 109.

226. "An Interview with B. F. Keith," *Boston Herald,* December 1904 or early 1905, undated clipping in Keith file, HTC. Brief biographies of Keith appear in *National Cyclopedia of American Biography,* 15:297; *Who Was Who,* vol. 1; *Dictionary of American Biography,* 5, part 2, p. 289; and *Biographical Dictionary of American Business Leaders,* 2:695–97. His role in enforcing rules of decorum in popular entertainment is mentioned in Lawrence Levine, *Highbrow, Lowbrow: The Emergence of Cultural Hierarchy in America* (Cambridge, Mass.: Harvard University Press, 1988), 195–96.

227. Douglass Shand Tucci, *Boston Rialto,* 5; King, "Keith, Albee, et al.," 5.

228. George E. Ryan, *Figures in Our Catholic History,* 54.

229. Allen, *Much Ado about Me,* 246.

230. Three years under construction, costing $680,000, and designed by the New York architect who had remodeled the Metropolitan Opera House, the B. F. Keith Theatre was the marvel of Boston, containing cooled artesian wells, "an entirely new

system of heating and ventilation, and a double electric lighting plant that supplies the current for over 3000 incandescent and forty powerful arc lamps." See King, "Keith, Albee, et al.," 5; "B. F. Keith and His Enterprises," in *Brochure of Boston College*, 71. Keith bought out the neighboring Boston Theatre in 1909, and his partner razed it in 1926 to construct the B. F. Keith Memorial Theatre as a shrine to his dead partner. Billed as the "world's most beautiful playhouse," the gilt and ivory French Rococo palace was completed in 1928.

231. Cited in Auster, *Actresses and Suffragists*, 36.

232. King, "Keith, Albee, et al.," 3–14.

233. Most acts then sent an additional 5 or 10 percent to their agents, to compensate for this practice. King, "Keith, Albee, et al.," 5. Allen, *Much Ado about Me*, 214–25.

234. *Tribute to Benjamin Franklin Keith*, ceremonies attending the laying of the cornerstone, Keith Memorial Theatre, Boston, Massachusetts, August 25, 1927, HTC.

235. Moorehouse, "Keith," 66–67. Catholic architect Charles Maginnis who had met Keith at Lake Champlain in 1912 called him, by contrast, a charming, quiet man.

236. He lost a lawsuit filed by a performer who sued for back pay after Keith cut him. The plaintiff's counsel lampooned Keith's omnipotent control of his players: "I expect some day to see a museum in the clouds, B. F. Keith, proprietor, and, written in letters of gold above the door, I read 'None but angels admitted.'"

237. *Boston Herald* interview, n.d., clipping, Keith files, HTC.

238. Boston *Pilot*, September 16, 1916, 8. See also "Report of Committee on Public Morals," AFCS Convention, New York, August 1916, pp. 4–5, Chancery Central Subject File, M-906, AABo.

239. Knoblock (1874–1945), born in New York, became a British citizen in 1916. This play, produced in 1915, was one among his many successful creations.

240. Andrist, "Paladin of Purity," 86.

241. "Report of Committee on Public Morals," AFCS Convention, New York, August 1916, p. 7, Chancery Central Subject File, M-906, AABo.

242. *41st Annual Report (1919) of the New England Watch & Ward Society*, 11. The society's income derived from members' donations, private subscriptions, and its prudent investments in railroad and utilities stocks.

243. Leon Harris, *Only to God*, 218. As successor to the dynamic Phillips Brooks, Lawrence (1850–1941) made no pretense of being equally charismatic, contenting himself with being a successful fundraiser for Harvard and for the American Episcopal church. For a short account of Lawrence's life, see Forbes and Finley, *Saturday Club*, 81–89.

244. G. Stanley Hall received his Ph.D. from Harvard in 1878 and was president of Clark University in Worcester from 1888 to 1920. For information about his moral reform activities, see Rosenzwieg, *Eight Hours*.

245. Paul Boyer identifies Allen as an urbane Brahmin but calls his successor, Chase, "a man of limited horizons," at odds with the Back Bay elite because of his Methodist background and crude manner. For a critical judgment of Chase, see Wood, "Keeping the Puritans Pure," 72–78.

246. A sample list of some 150 plays, drawn up by the Philadelphia branch of the Catholic Theatre Movement, appeared in the *Sacred Heart Review*, April 15, 1916, 2. See also Catholic Truth Movement, *White List Bulletin*, October 15, 1917, 6. In the 1930s, Daniel Lord, S.J., leader of the sodality movement, joined with the Legion

of Decency and the National Councils of Men and Women to extend the tradition of publishing blacklists in *Queen's Work*. See Sparr, *To Promote, Defend, and Redeem*, 45–50. O'Connell's support for the Legion of Decency is documented in Chancery Central Subject Files, M-940, AABo.

247. Helena Huntington Smith, "Boston's Bogy-Man," 214. She mentions especially the work of William J. Foley, district attorney, and his assistant, William J. Sullivan. On the subject of the Catholic Church's role, she commented: "So far as I could learn, this is the first and last of the Church's influence on what Boston reads."

248. The book dealers were headed by Richard Fuller of the Old Corner Bookstore, a friend of Chase. See Helena Huntington Smith, "Boston's Bogy-Man," 215.

249. Treasurer's solicitation letter, May 17, 1935, Godfrey L. Cabot Papers, Watch & Ward Society file, MHS. See also Boyer, *Purity in Print*, 171; Louis M. Lyons, *Newspaper Story*, 248–49.

250. Wood, "Keeping the Puritans Pure," 78.

251. Boyer, *Purity in Print*, 172.

252. *41st Annual Report (1919) of the New England Watch & Ward Society*, 11. In fact, it was not Casey but Mayor Malcolm Nichols who rejected the production of Eugene O'Neill's *Strange Interlude*, in 1929, which represented the most publicized act of censorship since attempts to block the Abbey Theatre production of Synge in 1911. See Norton, *Broadway Down East*, 86.

253. Godfrey Cabot's biographer found that occasionally a rabbi or Roman Catholic joined the board but always left quickly and was hard to replace. The purpose of the society's invitations, then, may have been to solicit likely candidates for membership in Watch & Ward. See Leon Harris, *Only To God*, 227. A 1928 magazine report on Watch & Ward claimed that "two Catholics, with irreproachable Anglo-Saxon names," were board members. See Helena Huntington Smith, "Boston's Bogy-Man," 215.

254. "Memo for Mr. McGinley," March 29, 1922, Reconstruction, Topic 10, Pelletier case, file SC-16-2-192, n.p., KCA.

255. See Chapter 3. Also, Attorney General v. Joseph C. Pelletier, *Massachusetts Reports* 240, December 19, 20, 21, 1922; December 27, 1921–January 24, 1922; February 21, 1922. The accounts of the installation of the wiretap, and some dictagraph transcriptions provided by three hired operators, are preserved in Godfrey Cabot's papers on the Watch & Ward Society at the Massachusetts Historical Society.

256. Massachusetts law is exceptional in that there is no outright prohibition of wiretapping. Following the revelation of the wiretapping of Pelletier's office came a 1920 statute requiring a citizen, police officer, or detective to get the written permission of the district attorney or attorney general only if the information is to be used concerning an official matter. Thus, Watch & Ward's activities were not illegal in 1917. See Dash, *The Eavesdroppers*, 141–46. Further details of the Pelletier case are in Attorney General v. Joseph C. Pelletier, *Massachusetts Reports* 240; Kauffman, *Faith and Fraternalism*; Pelletier files, KCA; and Leon Harris, *Only to God*, chaps. 11 and 12.

257. Frederick B. Allen to Godfrey Lowell Cabot, February 24, 1917, Godfrey Cabot Papers, Watch & Ward Society file, MHS. Wise was apparently a Watch & Ward informant working in Pelletier's office. Rothwell, an Irish immigrant, was a prominent Catholic businessman who had been president of the Boston Chamber of Commerce and an active member of "Boston, 1915." In 1917 he was chairman of the Massachusetts Bureau of Immigration.

258. *38th Annual Report (1916) of the New England Watch & Ward Society*, 46.

259. Ibid., 45–47.

260. Musser, *Emergence of Cinema*, 219–20. See Musser's discussion of the popularity of passion plays and related religious subjects for American audiences, 218–21.

261. Boston *Republic*, March 24, 1917, 7. I have been unable to locate copies of the scripts, or any further information about Anderson's involvement, among his papers at the AABo. Film production seems to have been a project of the Catholic Church Extension Society of the United States, which sponsored the Second American Catholic Missionary Congress, held in Boston in October 1913. There Anderson played an important role, together with Rev. Francis C. Kelley, head of the Home Missionary section and guiding spirit behind the Extension movement. Pius X elevated the Extension Society to pontifical status in 1910. See Kelley, *Great American Catholic Missionary Congresses*.

262. Boston *Republic*, February 21, 1920, 4; see also Hanson, *American Film Institute Catalog*, vol. 1, *Feature Films, 1911–1920*.

263. Advertisement of the Catholic Art Association in the Boston *Pilot*, March 23, 1918, 8.

264. Condé Pallen (1858–1929) was a prominent layman and author who supported many lay projects, including the Catholic Art Association, Catholic Summer School, and the AFCS. He was one of five editors of the *Catholic Encyclopedia* (1907–14).

265. *Moving Picture World*, May 31, 1919, 1316, cited in Hanson, *American Film Institute Catalog*, 1:245.

266. Joseph P. Kennedy, *Story of the Films*.

267. Goldstein, *Autobiography*, 208.

268. John Talbot Smith, "Motion Picture," 9.

269. Ibid.

270. John Talbot Smith, *Parish Theatre*, 44. An example of Smith's work in this new medium was his preparation of a newsreel, "A pilgrimage to see the Holy Father [Pius X]," (New York: Underwood & Underwood, 1907). The *American Film Institute Catalog*, 1:281, also lists a 1914 title, "His Holiness, the Late Pope Pius X, and the Vatican," which may be a related production.

271. Lapomarda, *Jesuit Heritage*, 89. Bishop Fulton Sheen's radio and television broadcasts of later decades exemplified perhaps the most successful use of these media and reached the most diverse audience.

272. *Sacred Heart Review*, January 30, 1909, 85.

273. Rosenzweig, *Eight Hours*, 207, 41.

274. For a history of Breen and the production code, and links to Catholic moralism, see Leonard J. Leff and Jerold Simmons, *The Dame in the Kimono* (New York: Grove Weidenfeld, 1990). On film censorship, see Ruth Inglis, *Freedom of the Movies* (Chicago: University of Chicago Press, 1947). For other Catholics who participated in acceptance of a morality code, see Stephen Vaughan, "Morality and Entertainment: The Origins of the Motion Picture Production Code," *Journal of American History* 77 (June 1990): 39–65. He suggests that while Protestants actually criticized films more severely than Catholics, Catholics were better equipped, because of their hierarchical organization, to mobilize boycotts and exert censorship pressure, especially when the film studios had been weakened by the Depression in the early 1930s.

275. Boston *Pilot,* October 8, 1910, 2.
276. Michael Earls, S.J., to Bess, n.d. [1912], HCR.
277. Boston *Pilot,* May 1, 1918, 4.
278. Ibid., October 18, 1919, 4.
279. Ibid., July 21, 1917, 1. Ads for sales of stereopticons to parishes began to appear in Massachusetts church directories and newspapers in the 1910s.

Chapter 8

1. Goldstein, *Autobiography,* 266–96. For accounts of the van trip, see the Boston *Pilot,* July 14, 1917; September 22, October 13, and June 29, 1918; the *San Francisco Monitor,* October 6, 1917; and the David Goldstein Papers, BCSp.
2. Goldstein, *Autobiography,* 282–96.
3. O'Connell, "The Church and the Republic," in *S&A,* 3:99.
4. Michael Earls to Bess, August 17, 1916, from Long Island Hospital, Boston Harbor, HCR.
5. Goldstein, *Autobiography,* 277.
6. Ibid., 297.
7. O'Connell's blessing of the autovan, in ibid., 267.
8. Bernard Whelan, *Ave Maria,* February 15, 1913, 213.
9. Loughlin, "Boston's Political Morals."

REFERENCES

Abell, Aaron I. *American Catholicism and Social Action: A Search for Social Justice, 1865–1950.* Notre Dame, Ind.: University of Notre Dame Press, 1963.
———. *American Catholic Thought on Social Questions.* Indianapolis: Bobbs-Merrill, 1968.
———. "The Reception of Leo XIII's Labor Encyclical in America, 1891–1919." *Review of Politics* 7 (October 1945): 464–95.
Aiken, Charles. "The Doctrine of the Fathers of the Church on the Right of Private Property." *Catholic World,* May 1912.
Akenson, Donald H. *The United States and Ireland.* Cambridge, Mass.: Harvard University Press, 1973.
Alcorn, Richard S., and Peter R. Knight. "Most Uncommon Bostonians: A Critique of Stephan Thernstrom's *The Other Bostonians.*" *Historical Methods Newsletter* 8, no. 3 (June 1975): 98–114. Center for International Studies and the Dept. of History, University of Pittsburgh.
Alegi, Peter C. "Catholicism at Yale to 1942." Ph.D. dissertation, Yale University, 1956. Departmental Essay in American Studies.
Alexander, Jack. "The Cardinal and Cold Roast Boston." *Saturday Evening Post,* October 4, 1911.
Allen, Fred. *Much Ado about Me.* Boston: Little, Brown, 1956.
Almagno, Stephen. *Resonare Christum.* 2 vols. New York: Ignatius Press, 1988.
American Catholic Who's Who, 1934–1935. Detroit: Walter Romig, 1935.
American Second Catholic Missionary Congress, 1913. Boston: Catholic Extension Society, [1914?].
Anderson, Dorothy May. *The Era of the Summer Estates: Swampscott Massachusetts, 1870–1940.* Canaan, N.H.: Phoenix, 1985.
Andrist, Ralph K. "Paladin of Purity." *American Heritage,* October 1973.
Angoff, Charles. "Boston Twilight." *American Mercury,* December 1925.
Appel, John H. "The New England Origins of the American Irish Historical Society." *New England Quarterly* 33 (December 1960): 462–75.
Arnquist, James. "Images of Catholic Utopianism and Radicalism in Industrial America." Ph.D. dissertation, University of Minnesota, 1968.
Attorney General v. Joseph C. Pelletier. *Massachusetts Reports: Decisions of the Supreme Judicial Court of Massachusetts, 1922,* 240:264–350. Boston: Little, Brown, 1922.
Auster, Albert. *Actresses and Suffragists: Women in the American Theater, 1890–1920.* New York: Praeger, 1984.
Avery, Martha Moore. *Woman: Her Quality, her environment, her possibility.* Boston: Boston Socialist Press, 1901.

Avery, Martha Moore, and David Goldstein. *Socialism: The Nation of Fatherless Children.* Boston: Union League, 1903.

Avrich, Paul. *The Modern School Movement: Anarchism and Education in the United States.* Princeton, N.J: Princeton University Press, 1980.

Baker, Paula. "The Domestication of Politics: Women and American Political Society, 1780–1920." *American Historical Review* 89 (June 1984): 620–47.

Barrett, Michèle. *Women's Oppression Today: Problems in Marxist Feminist Analysis.* London: Verso, 1986.

Baxter, Sylvester. *The Legend of the Holy Grail as set forth in the frieze painted by Edwin Austin Abbey for the Boston Public Library.* Boston: Curtis & Cameron, 1904.

———. "A Selection from the Works of Maginnis & Walsh, Architects." *Architectural Record* 53 (February 1923): 93–115.

Beatty, Jack. *The Rascal King: The Life and Times of James Michael Curley, 1874–1958.* Reading, Mass.: Addison-Wesley, 1992.

Bebel, August. *Woman under Socialism.* 1904. Reprint. New York: Schocken Books, 1971.

Bedford, Henry F. *Socialism and the Workers in Massachusetts, 1886–1912.* Amherst: University of Massachusetts Press, 1966.

Beebe, Lucius. *Boston and the Boston Legend.* New York: Appleton, 1935.

Bennett, David H. *The Party of Fear: From Nativist Movements to the New Religious Right in American History.* New York: Vintage, 1990.

Berkeley, Ellen Perry, ed. *Architecture: A Place for Women.* Washington, D.C.: Smithsonian Institution, 1989.

Berry, John M., and Frances Panchok. "Church and Theater." *U.S. Catholic Historian* 6 (Spring/Summer 1987): 151–79.

Betten, Neil. *Catholic Activism and the Industrial Worker.* Gainesville: University Presses of Florida, 1976.

Birmingham, Stephen. *Real Lace: America's Irish Rich.* New York: Harper & Row, 1973.

Bixby, David Michael. "The Knights of Columbus in Boston." Ph.D. dissertation, Harvard College, 1976.

Blair, Karen J. *The Clubwoman as Feminist: True Womanhood Redefined, 1868–1914.* New York: Holmes & Meier, 1980.

Blessing, Patrick. "Irish." In *Harvard Encyclopedia of Ethnic Groups,* edited by Stephan Thernstrom. Cambridge, Mass.: Belknap Press, 1980.

Bliznakov, Milka. "Women Architects." *Structurist* 25/26 (1985/86): 121–27.

Blumin, Stuart. "The Hypothesis of Middle-Class Formation in Nineteenth-Century America: A Critique and Some Proposals." *American Historical Review* 90 (April 1985): 299–338.

Blunt, Hugh F. *Readings from Cardinal O'Connell.* New York: Appleton-Century, 1934.

———. "Susan L. Emery." *Catholic World,* December 1936.

Bochen, Christine. *The Journey to Rome: Conversion Literature by 19th-Century American Catholics.* New York: Garland, 1988.

Boston Chapter, Knights of Columbus. *November 24, 1902, issued as a Souvenir of the First Grand Ball of Boston Chapter Knights of Columbus.* Boston: Knights of Columbus, 1902.

Boston Landmarks Commission. *Report of the Boston Landmarks Commission on the Potential Designation of the St. Gabriel's Complex as a Landmark under Chapter 772 of the Acts of 1975*. Boston: Boston Landmarks Commission, 1980.

Boston *Pilot. A Brief Historical Review of the Archdiocese of Boston, 1907–1923*. Boston: Pilot, 1925.

Boyer, Paul B. *Purity in Print: The Vice-Society Movement and Book Censorship in America*. New York: Charles Scribner's Sons, 1968.

———. *Urban Masses and Moral Order in America*. Cambridge, Mass.: Harvard University Press, 1978.

Brégy, Katherine. *The Catholic Theatre Movement*. New York: John Wheeler, 1916.

———. *Poets and Pilgrims*. New York: Benziger, 1925.

Brewer, Daniel Chauncey. *Conquest of New England by the Immigrant*. New York and London: G. P. Putnam's Sons, 1926.

Brewer, Eileen Mary. *Nuns and the Education of American Catholic Women, 1860–1920*. Chicago: Loyola University Press, 1987.

Brochure of Boston College and the Young Men's Catholic Association. Boston: Cashman, O'Connor, 1894.

Brochure of the Young Men's Catholic Association of Boston. Boston: Cashman, O'Connor, 1902.

Broderick, Francis L. *Right Reverend New Dealer: John A. Ryan*. New York: Macmillan, 1963.

Brosnahan, Timothy. *The Courses Leading to the Baccalaureate in Harvard College and Boston College*. Woodstock, Md.: Woodstock College Press, [1900].

Brown, Alice. *Louise Imogen Guiney*. New York: Macmillan, 1921.

Brown, Malcolm. *The Politics of Irish Literature*. London: Allen & Unwin, 1972.

Brown, Stephen J. *Catholic Juvenile Literature: A Classified List*. London: Burnes, Oates & Washbourne, 1935.

Brown, Thomas N. "The Irish Layman: A History." In *The United States of America: The Irish Clergyman*, edited by Thomas T. McAvoy. Vol. 6, no. 2. Dublin: Gill & Macmillan, 1970.

———. "The Origin and Character of Irish-American Nationalism." *Review of Politics* 18 (1956): 327–58.

Browne, Henry J. *The Catholic Church and the Knights of Labor*. Washington, D.C.: Catholic University of America Press, 1949.

Brownson, Henry F., ed. *The Works of Orestes A. Brownson*. 20 vols. Detroit: T. Nourse, 1882–1906.

Bugg, Lelia Hardin, ed. *The People of Our Parish: Being Chronicle and Comment of Katharine Fitzgerald, Pew-Holder in the Church of St. Paul the Apostle*. Boston: Marlier, Callanan, 1900.

Buhle, Mari Jo. *Women and American Socialism, 1870–1920*. Urbana: University of Illinois Press, 1981.

Bunting, Bainbridge. *Houses of Boston's Back Bay: An Architectural History, 1840–1917*. Cambridge, Mass.: Belknap Press, 1967.

Burchell, R. A. *The San Francisco Irish, 1848–1880*. Manchester: Manchester University Press, 1980.

Burns, James Aloysius, and Bernard J. Kohlbrenner. *A History of Catholic Education in the United States: A Textbook for Normal Schools and Teachers' Colleges*. New York and Cincinnati: Benziger Bros., 1937.

Burton, Katherine. *Sorrow Built a Bridge*. New York: Green and Co., 1937.

Bynum, Caroline Walker. *Fragmentation and Redemption: Essays on Gender and the Human Body in Medieval Religion*. New York: Zone Books, 1991.

——. *Holy Feast, Holy Fast: The Religious Significance of Food to Medieval Women*. Berkeley: University of California Press, 1987.

Byrne, John F. *The Glories of Mary in Boston: A Memorial History of the Church of Our Lady of Perpetual Help (Mission Church), Roxbury, Mass., 1871–1921*. Boston: Mission Church Press, 1921.

Cadegan, Una Mary. "All Good Books Are Catholic Books: Literature, Censorship, and the Americanization of Catholics, 1920–1960." Ph.D. dissertation, University of Pennsylvania, 1987.

Camp, Richard L. *The Papal Ideology of Social Reform: A Study in Historical Development, 1878–1967*. Leiden: Brill, 1969.

Campbell, Debra. "Catholicism from Independence to World War I." In *Encyclopedia of the American Religious Experience*, vol. 1, edited by Charles Lippy and Peter Williams. New York: Scribner's, 1988.

——. "A Catholic Salvation Army: David Goldstein, Pioneer Lay Evangelist." *Church History* 52 (September 1983): 322–32.

——. "David Goldstein and the Foundation of the Catholic Campaigners for Christ." *Catholic Historical Review* 72 (1986): 33–50.

——. "David Goldstein and the Lay Catholic Street Apostolate, 1914–1941." Ph.D. dissertation, Boston University, 1982.

——. "I Can't Imagine Our Lady on an Outdoor Platform." *U.S. Catholic Historian* 3 (Spring/Summer 1983): 103–13.

——. "Reformers and Activists." In *American Catholic Women: A Historical Exploration*, edited by Karen Kennelly. New York: Macmillan, 1989.

——. "The Struggle to Serve." In *Transforming Parish Ministry: The Changing Roles of Catholic Clergy, Laity, and Women Religious*, edited by Jay R. Dolan, Scott Appleby, Patricia Byrne, and Debra Campbell. New York: Crossroad, 1989.

Caponigri, A. Robert. "European Influences on the Thought of Orestes Brownson: Pierre Leroux and Vicenzo Gioberti." In *No Divided Allegiance: Essays in Brownson's Thought*, edited by Leonard Gilhooly. New York: Fordham University Press, 1980.

Carey, James F., and Thomas Gasson. *The Menace of Socialism*. Boston: n.p., 1912.

Carey, Michael J. "Catholicism and Irish National Identity." In *Religion and Politics in the Modern World*, edited by Peter H. Merkl and Ninian Smart. New York: New York University Press, 1983.

Carlen, Claudia, ed. *The Papal Encyclicals*. Raleigh, N.C.: McGrath, 1981.

Carpenter, Henry. *Liber Amoris: Being the Book of Love of Brother Aurelius*. Boston: Ticknor, 1886.

——. *A Poet's Last Songs*. Boston: J. G. Cupples, 1891.

Carrigan, D. Owen. "Martha Moore Avery: Crusader for Social Justice." *Catholic Historical Review* 54 (April 1968): 17–38.

Cary, Emma. "The Elevation of Womanhood Wrought through the Veneration of the Blessed Virgin." In *The World's Congress of Representative Women*, edited by May Wright Sewell. Chicago: Rand, McNally, 1894.

——, ed. *The Day-Spring from on High: Selections Arranged by Emma Forbes Cary*. Boston and New York: Houghton Mifflin, 1894.

Casino, Joseph. "From Sanctuary to Involvement: A History of the Catholic Parish in the Northeast." In *The American Catholic Parish: A History from 1850 to the Present,* edited by Jay Dolan. Vol. 1 (Northeast, Southeast, South Central). New York: Paulist, 1987.

Catholic Encyclopedia: An International Work of Reference on the Constitution, Doctrine, Discipline and History of the Catholic Church. Edited by Charles Herbermann et al. New York: Appleton, 1907–12.

Chafee, Zechariah. *The Censorship in Boston.* Boston: Civil Liberties Committee of Massachusetts, 1929.

Chase, Frank W. "The White Slave Traffic in Boston." *New England Magazine,* January 1910.

Chase, J. Frank. "The New Puritanism." *Harvard Advocate,* May 1926.

Chesterton, G. K. "The Modern Surrender of Women." *Dublin Review,* July 1909.

Chinnici, Joseph. "Spiritual Capitalism and the Culture of American Catholicism." *U.S. Catholic Historian* 5, no. 2 (1986): 131–61.

The Christian Maiden. Translation from the German of Rev. Matthias von Bremscheid, O.M. Cap. [Matthias Lay], by members of the Young Ladies Sodality, Holy Trinity Church, Boston. Boston: Angel Guardian Press, 1905.

Christie, Francis A. "An Historical Footnote to Cardinal O'Connell's Recollections." *New England Quarterly* 8 (June 1935): 258–62.

Clark, Dennis. *Hibernia America: The Irish and Regional Cultures.* Westport, Conn.: Greenwood Press, 1986. Contributions in Ethnic Studies #14.

———. *The Irish in Philadelphia: Ten Generations of Urban Experience.* Philadelphia: Temple University Press, 1973.

Clarke, Richard. "Our Converts." *American Catholic Quarterly Review* 18 (July 1893): 539–61.

Clarke, Richard. "Our Converts." *American Catholic Quarterly Review* 19 (January 1894): 112–38.

Coleman, George, ed. *Democracy in the Making.* Boston: Little, Brown, 1915.

Committee for a New England Bibliography. *Massachusetts: A Bibliography of Its History.* Boston: G. K. Hall, 1976.

Commonwealth of Massachusetts. Bureau of Statistics. *Labor Bulletin #104. (Part 1 of the Annual Report on the Statistics of Labor for 1915). Handbook of the Labor Laws of Massachusetts, February, 1915.* Boston: Wright & Potter, 1915.

Conlin, Joseph R., ed. *The American Radical Press, 1880–1960.* 2 vols. Westport, Conn.: Greenwood Press, 1974.

Conn, Peter. *The Divided Mind: Ideology and Imagination in America, 1898–1917.* Cambridge: Cambridge University Press, 1983.

Connell, K. H. *Irish Peasant Society: Four Historical Essays.* London: Oxford University Press, 1968.

Connick, Charles Jay. *Adventures in Light and Color.* New York: Random House, 1937.

Conway, Jill. "Women Reformers and American Culture, 1870–1930." *Journal of Social History* 5 (1971): 164–77.

Conway, Katherine E. *Bettering Ourselves.* Boston: Pilot, 1899.

———. *The Christian Gentlewoman and the Social Apostolate.* 4th ed. Boston: Pilot, 1905.

———. *A dream of lilies.* N.p., 1893.

———. *The Good Shepherd in Boston. Silver Jubilee Memorial.* Boston: Flynn & Mahony, [1892].

———. *In the Footprints of the Good Shepherd, New York, 1857–1907.* New York: Convent of the Good Shepherd, 1907.

———. *A Lady and Her Letters.* 2d ed. Boston: Pilot, 1895.

———. *Lalor's Maples.* 4th ed. Boston: Flynn, 1909.

———. *Making Friends and Keeping Them.* Boston: Pilot, 1895.

———. *New Footsteps in Well-Trodden Ways. Sketches of Travel.* 2d ed. Boston: Pilot, 1899.

———. "Normal Christian Woman." In *Girlhood's Hand-Book of Woman,* edited by Eleanor C. Donnelly. St. Louis: B. Herder, 1898.

———. *The Story of a Beautiful Childhood, compiled from the Journals of Joseph Astley Gallagher.* Boston: C. M. Clark, 1909.

———. *The Way of the World and Other Ways, a story of our own set.* Boston: Pilot, 1900.

———. "Woman Has No Vocation to Public Life." *Catholic World,* August 1893.

———. "Why Always Catholic?" *Columbia,* May 1925.

———, ed. *Watchwords of John Boyle O'Reilly.* Boston: J. G. Cupples, 1891.

Conway, Katherine E., with Mabel Cameron. *Charles Francis Donnelly, a Memoir, With an Account of the Hearings on a Bill for the Inspection of Private Schools in Massachusetts, in 1888–89.* New York: J. T. White, 1890.

Conzen, Kathleen. "Immigrants, Immigrant Neighborhoods and Ethnic Identity: Historical Issues." *Journal of American History* 66 (December 1979): 603–15.

Cooney, John. *The American Pope: The Life and Times of Francis Cardinal Spellman.* New York: Times Books, 1984.

Corry, John. *Golden Clan: The Murrays, the McDonnells, and the Irish American Aristocracy.* New York: Grosse Point, 1977.

Cott, Nancy F. *The Bonds of Womanhood: Woman's Sphere in New England, 1780–1835.* New Haven: Yale University Press, 1977.

———. "The Limits of Social Feminism." *Journal of American History* 76 (December 1989): 809–829.

Coyle, Henry, comp. *Our Church, Her Children and Institutions.* 3 vols. Boston: n.p., 1908.

Cram, [Ralph Adams], and [Frank William] Ferguson. *The Work of Cram and Ferguson, Architects, Including Work by Cram, Goodhue, and Ferguson, with an Introduction by Charles D. Maginnis.* New York: Pencil Points Press, 1929.

Cram, Ralph Adams. *The Catholic Church and Art.* New York: Macmillan, 1929.

———. *Church Building: A Study of the Principles of Architecture in Their Relation to the Church.* Boston: Marshall Jones, 1914.

———. "Good and Bad Modern Gothic." *Architectural Review,* August 1899.

———. *The Gothic Quest.* New York: Baker & Taylor, 1907. Rev. ed. Garden City, N.Y.: Doubleday, Page, 1915.

———. *The Ministry of Art.* Houghton Mifflin, 1914.

———. *My Life in Architecture.* Boston: Little, Brown, 1936.

———. *The Nemesis of Democracy.* Boston: Marshall Jones, 1918.

———. *The North End, a Survey and a Comprehensive Plan.* Boston: City Planning Board, 1919.

———. *The Substance of Gothic.* Boston: Marshall Jones, 1917.

Cremin, Lawrence A. *The Transformation of the School: Progressivism in American Education, 1876–1957.* New York: Knopf, 1961.

Criscuola, Joseph Noel. *Business and Boston's Best after the Civil War: A Class History.* Chicago: University of Chicago Press, 1969.

Cronin, John F., ed. *Catholic Social Principles: The Social Teachings of the Catholic Church Applied to American Economic Life.* Milwaukee: Bruce, 1950.

Cross, Robert. "The Changing Image of the City among American Catholics." *Catholic Historical Review* 48 (January 1962): 33–52.

———. *The Emergence of Liberal Catholicism in America.* 1958. Reprint. Chicago: Quadrangle Books, 1968.

———, ed. *The Church and the City, 1865–1910.* Indianapolis and New York: Bobbs-Merrill, 1967.

Cullen, James Bernard, ed. *The Story of the Irish in Boston.* 1889. Rev. ed. Boston: n.p., 1893.

Curran, R. Emmett. "Confronting 'The Social Question': American Catholic Thought and the Socio-Economic Order in the Nineteenth Century." *U.S. Catholic Historian* 5, no. 2 (1986): 165–93.

Curry, Lerond. *Protestant-Catholic Relations in America: World War I through Vatican II.* Lexington: University Press of Kentucky, 1972.

Curtis, Georgina Pell, ed. *American Catholic Who's Who.* St. Louis: B. Herder, 1911.

———, comp. and ed. *Beyond the Road to Rome.* St. Louis: B. Herder, 1914.

———, ed. *Some Roads to Rome in America.* St. Louis and Freiburg: B. Herder, 1909.

Curtis, Lewis. *Apes & Angels: The Irishman in Victorian Caricature.* Washington, D.C.: Smithsonian Institution Press, 1971.

Daly, Mary. *The Church and the Second Sex.* Boston: Beacon Press, 1968.

Damrell, Charles. *A Half Century of Boston Building.* Boston: Louis P. Hager, 1895.

Dash, Samuel. *The Eavesdroppers.* New Brunswick, N.J.: Rutgers University Press, 1959.

David, Martin. *American Catholic Convert Authors: A Bio-Bibliography.* Grosse Pointe, Mich.: Walter Romig, 1944.

Day, Dorothy. *From Union Square to Rome.* [1938]. Reprint. New York: Arno, 1978.

De Marco, William M. *Ethnics and Enclaves: Boston's Italian North End.* Ann Arbor, Mich.: UMI Research Press, 1980.

Dehey, Elinor Tong. *Religious Orders of Women in the United States: Accounts of Their Origin, Words and Most Important Institutions, Interwoven with Histories of Many Famous Foundresses.* 1913. Reprint. Hammond, Ind.: W. B. Conkey, 1930.

Delaney, John J. *Dictionary of American Catholic Biography.* Garden City, N.Y.: Doubleday, 1984.

Denning, Michael. *Mechanic Accents: Dime Novels and Working-Class Culture in America.* London and New York: Verso, 1987.

Deshon, George. *Guide for Catholic Young Women.* New York: Catholic Book Exchange, 1900.

Desmond, Humphrey. *A Reading Circle Manual.* Milwaukee: Citizen, 1903.

Dimaggio, Paul. "Cultural Entrepreneurship in Nineteenth-Century Boston: The Creation of an Organizational Base for High Culture in America." *Media, Culture and Society* 4 (1982): 33–50.

Diner, Hasia R. *Erin's Daughters in America*. Baltimore and London: Johns Hopkins University Press, 1983.

Dinneen, Maurice. *The Catholic Total Abstinence Movement in the Archdiocese of Boston*. Boston: n.p., 1908.

Directory of Boston Architects, 1846–1970. Cambridge, Mass.: Massachusetts Commission for the Preservation of Architectural Records, 1984.

Dohen, Dorothy. *Nationalism and American Catholicism*. New York: Sheed and Ward, 1967.

Doherty, Robert. "The American Socialist Party and the Roman Catholic Church, 1901–1917." Ph.D. dissertation, Teachers College, Columbia University, 1959.

Dolan, Jay. *The Immigrant Church: New York's Irish and German Catholics, 1815–1865*. Baltimore: Johns Hopkins University Press, 1975.

————, ed. *The American Catholic Parish: A History from 1850 to the Present*. Vol. 1 (Northeast, Southeast, South Central). New York: Paulist, 1987.

Dolan, Jay, R. Scott Appleby, Patricia Byrne, and Debra Campbell. *Transforming Parish Ministry: The Changing Roles of Catholic Clergy, Laity, and Women Religious*. New York: Crossroad, 1989.

Donnelly, Eleanor C., ed. *Girlhood's Hand-Book of Woman*. St. Louis: B. Herder, 1898.

Donnelly, James F. "Catholic New Yorkers and New York Socialists." Ph.D. dissertation, New York University, 1982.

Douglas, Ann. *The Feminization of American Culture*. New York: Avon, 1977.

Dries, Angelyn. "The Americanization of Religious Life: Women Religious, 1872–1922." *U.S. Catholic Historian* 10, nos. 1 and 2 (1989): 13–24.

Driscoll, Annette. *Literary Convert Women*. Everett, Mass.: n.p., 1928.

Dulles, Avery. *Models of the Church*. New York: Image, 1978.

Dunigan, David Ronan. *A History of Boston College*. Chestnut Hill, Mass.: University Press of Boston College, 1947.

Dunleavy, Janet. *Douglas Hyde: A Maker of Modern Ireland*. Berkeley: University of California Press, 1991.

Dunne, Philip. *Mr. Dooley Remembers: The Informal Memoirs of Finley Peter Dunne*. Boston: Little, Brown, 1963.

Dwight, Thomas. *Thoughts of a Catholic Anatomist*. London: Longmans, Green, 1912.

Earls, Michael. *Manuscripts and Memories: Chapters in Our Literary Tradition*. Milwaukee: Bruce, 1935.

————. "Mr. Chesterton on the Irish." *American Catholic Quarterly Review* 36 (April 1911): 222–31.

————. *Under College Towers: A Book of Essays*. New York: Macmillan, 1926.

Ede, Juan Alfred. "The Lay Crusade for a Christian America: A Study of the American Federation of Catholic Societies, 1900–1919." Ph.D. dissertation, Graduate Theological Union, 1979.

Eisenmenger, Robert. *The Dynamics of Growth in the New England Economy, 1870–1964*. Middletown, Conn.: Wesleyan, 1967.

Ellis, John Tracy. *The Catholic Bishops: A Memoir*. Wilmington, Del.: Michael Glazier, 1984.

————. *The Life of James Cardinal Gibbons, Archbishop of Baltimore, 1834–1912*. 2 vols. Milwaukee: Bruce, 1952.

————, ed. *The Catholic Priest in the United States: Historical Investigations*. Collegeville, Minn.: St. John's University Press, 1971.

Emerson, William. "Charles Maginnis." *AIA Journal* 23 (May 1955): 209–19.

Emery, Susan L. *A Catholic Stronghold and Its Making: A History of St. Peter's Parish, Dorchester, Massachusetts, and of Its First Rector The Rev. Peter Ronan, P.K.* Boston: G. H. Ellis, 1910.

————. *The Inner Life of the Soul*. London: Longmans, 1903.

Epstein, Barbara. *The Politics of Domesticity: Women, Evangelism and Temperance in Nineteenth-Century America*. Middletown, Conn.: Wesleyan University Press, 1981.

Erie, Stephen P. *Rainbow's End: Irish-Americans and the Dilemmas of Urban Machine Politics, 1840–1985*. Berkeley: University of California Press, 1988.

Evans, John Whitney. *Apostles of Hope: A History of the Newman Movement, 1883–1971*. Notre Dame, Ind.: University of Notre Dame Press, 1980.

Ewens, Mary. "The Leadership of Nuns in Immigrant Catholicism." In *Woman and Religion in America*, edited by Rosemary Radford Ruether and Rosemary Skinner Keller. New York: Harper & Row, 1981.

Fairbanks, Henry G. *Louise Imogen Guiney: Laureate of the Lost*. Albany, N.Y.: Magi Books, 1972.

Fallows, Marjorie R. *Irish Americans: Identity and Assimilation*. Englewood Cliffs, N.J.: Prentice-Hall, 1979.

Fanning, Charles, ed. *The Exiles of Erin: Nineteenth Century Irish-American Fiction*. Notre Dame, Ind.: University of Notre Dame Press, 1987.

————, ed. *The Irish Voice in America*. Lexington: University Press of Kentucky, 1990.

Fanning, Patricia J. "Fred Holland Day: Eccentric Aesthete." *New England Quarterly* 53 (June 1980): 230–36.

Fenton, Edwin. *Immigrants and Unions: A Case Study of Italians and American Labor, 1870–1920*. New York: Arno, 1975. Reprint of author's 1957 thesis.

Finkelstein, Louis, ed. *American Spiritual Autobiographies*. New York: Harper, 1948.

Fiorenza, Elizabeth Schussler. *In Memory of Her: A Feminist Theological Construction of Christian Origins*. New York: Crossroad, 1983.

Fisher, James. *The Catholic Counterculture in America, 1933–1962*. Chapel Hill: University of North Carolina Press, 1989.

Fogarty, Gerald P. *The Vatican and the American Hierarchy, 1870–1965*. Vol. 21, *Papste and Papstum*. Stuttgart: Anton Hiersemann, 1982.

Forbes, Edward W., and John H. Finley, Jr., eds. *The Saturday Club: A Century Completed, 1920–1956*. Boston: Houghton Mifflin, 1958.

Formisano, Ronald P., and Constance K. Burns. *Boston, 1700–1980: The Evolution of Urban Politics*. Westport, Conn.: Greenwood Press, 1984.

Fox, Mary Harrita. *Peter Dietz, Labor Priest*. Notre Dame, Ind.: University of Notre Dame Press, 1953.

Fremantle, Anne, ed. *The Papal Encyclicals in Their Historical Context*. New York: Putnam's, 1956.

Funchion, Michael F. "Irish-America: An Essay on the Literature since 1970." *Immigrant History Newsletter*, November 1985.

Gaffey, James P. "The Changing of the Guard: The Rise of Cardinal O'Connell of Boston." *Catholic Historical Review* 59 (July 1973): 225–44.

Galvin, John T. "The Dark Ages of Boston City Politics." *Massachusetts Historical Society Proceedings* 89 (1977): 80–111.

———. *Twelve Mayors of Boston, 1900–1970.* Boston: Boston Public Library, 1970.

Gannon, Michael. "Before and After Modernism: The Intellectual Isolation of the American Priest." In *The Catholic Priest in the United States: Historical Investigations,* edited by John Tracy Ellis. Collegeville, Minn.: St. John's University Press, 1971.

Gardiner, Harold C. *The Catholic Viewpoint on Censorship.* Garden City, N.Y.: Hanover House, 1958.

Garland, Joseph E. *Boston's Gold Coast: The North Shore, 1890–1929.* Boston: Little, Brown, 1981.

———. *Boston's North Shore.* Boston: Little, Brown, 1978.

Gearty, Patrick W. *The Economic Thought of Monsignor John A. Ryan.* Washington, D.C.: Catholic University of America Press, 1953.

Gilbert, James. *Work without Salvation: America's Intellectuals and Industrial Alienation, 1880–1910.* Baltimore: Johns Hopkins University Press, 1977.

Gilmore, Mary Sarsfield. "Katherine E. Conway." *Dominicana: A Magazine of Catholic Literature* 2 (1901).

Ginzberg, Lori. *Women and the Work of Benevolence: Morality, Politics, and Class in the Nineteenth-Century United States.* New Haven: Yale University Press, 1990.

Gioberti, Vicenzo. *Essay on the Beautiful, etc., or, Elements of Aesthetic Philosophy,* translated by Edward Thomas. 2d ed., rev. London: Simkin & Marshall, 1860.

Gleason, Philip. "American Identity and Americanization." In *Harvard Encyclopedia of American Ethnic Groups,* edited by Stephan Thernstrom et al. Cambridge, Mass.: Belknap Press, 1980.

———. "Coming to Terms with American Catholic History." *Societas* 3 (Autumn 1973): 283–312.

———. "The Crisis of Americanization." In *Contemporary Catholicism in the United States.* Notre Dame, Ind.: University of Notre Dame Press, 1969. International Studies of the Committee on International Relations.

———. "Guilds and Craftsmen: Echoes of the Middle Ages in American Social Thought." *Studies in Medievalism* 1 (Spring 1982): 51–72.

———. "Immigration and American Catholic Intellectual Life." *Review of Politics* 26 (1964): 147–73.

———. "In Search of Unity: American Catholic Thought 1920–1960." *Catholic Historical Review* 65 (April 1979): 185–205.

———. *Keeping the Faith: American Catholicism Past and Present.* Notre Dame, Ind.: University of Notre Dame Press, 1987.

———. "Mass and Maypole Revisited: American Catholics and the Middle Ages." *Catholic Historical Review* 57 (July 1971): 249–74.

Gleason, Philip, and David Salvaterra. "Ethnicity, Immigration and American Catholic History." In *Harvard Encyclopedia of American Ethnic Groups,* edited by Stephan Thernstrom et al. Cambridge, Mass.: Belknap Press, 1980.

Golden Jubilee of the Society of Jesus in Boston, Massachusetts, 1847–1897, October 3, 4, 5, 6, 1897. Boston: St. Mary's Parish (North End), 1897.

Goldstein, David. *Americanism versus Communism.* Boston: n.p., 1936.

———. *Autobiography of a Campaigner for Christ.* Boston: Catholic Campaigners for Christ, 1936.

———. *Bolshevism, Its Cure.* Boston: n.p., 1919.

———. *Socialist Bubble Punctured, Carey's Sophistry Exposed.* N.p., n.d.

Gompers, Samuel. *Seventy Years of Life and Labor.* New York: 2 vols. E. P. Dutton, 1925.

Goody, Marvin E., and Robert P. Walsh. *Boston Society of Architects: The First Hundred Years, 1867–1967.* Boston: Boston Society of Architects, 1967.

Gordon, Milton M. *Assimilation in American Life: The Role of Race, Religion and National Origins.* New York: Oxford University Press, 1964.

Gosse, Edmund William. *Silhouettes.* London: William Heineman, 1925.

Greeley, Andrew M. *The Irish Americans: The Rise to Money and Power.* New York: Harper & Row, 1981.

———. *The Mary Myth: On the Femininity of God.* New York: Seabury, 1977.

Green, James R., and Hugh Carter Donahue. *Boston's Workers: A Labor History.* Boston: Trustees of the Public Library, 1984.

Green, Marguerite. *The National Civic Federation and the American Labor Movement, 1900–1925.* Washington, D.C.: Catholic University of America Press, 1956.

Green, Martin Burgess. *The Problem of Boston.* New York: Norton, 1966.

Greene, Thomas R. "The Catholic Committee for the Ratification of the Child Labor Amendment, 1935–1937: Origins and Limits." *Catholic Historical Review* 54 (April 1988): 248–69.

Guilday, Peter K., ed. *The National Pastorals of the American Hierarchy, 1792–1919.* Washington, D.C.: National Catholic Welfare Council, 1923.

Guiney, Grace, ed. *Letters of Louise Imogen Guiney.* 2 vols. New York: Harper, 1926.

Guiney, Louise. "On Catholic Writers and Their Handicaps." *Catholic World,* November 1909.

———. "The Point of View." *Scribner's,* January 1911.

Hall, Stuart. "Cultural Studies: Two Paradigms." In *Media, Culture and Society: A Critical Reader,* edited by Richard Collins et al. London: Sage, 1986.

Halsey, William M. *Survival of American Innocence: Catholicism in an Era of Disillusionment, 1920–1940.* Notre Dame, Ind.: University of Notre Dame Press, 1980.

Hanson, Patricia King, ed. *American Film Institute Catalog of Motion Pictures in the United States.* 2 vols. Berkeley: University of California Press, 1988.

Harper, Richard C. "The Catholic Church and the Democratic Party in Boston, 1924–1936." Ph.D. dissertation, Harvard College, 1975.

Harrington, Jeremiah. *Catholicism, Capitalism, or Communism.* St. Paul: E. M. Lohmann, 1926.

Harris, Leon A. *Only to God: The Extraordinary Life of Godfrey Lowell Cabot.* New York: Atheneum, 1967.

Harris, Neil. "The Gilded Age Revisited: Boston and the Museum Movement." *American Quarterly* 14 (Winter 1962): 545–66.

Hart, Albert Bushnell, ed. *Commonwealth History of Massachusetts*. 5 vols. New York: States History Co., 1927–30.

Hart, Sister Mary Adorita. *Soul Ordained to Fail: Louise Imogen Guiney, 1861–1920*. New York: Pageant Press, 1962.

Hartt, Julian. *A Christian Critique of American Culture: An Essay in Practical Theology*. New York: Harper & Row, 1967.

Hayes, A[lice] J[eannette]. *A Convert's Reason Why*. Cambridge, Mass.: Riverside Press, 1911.

Hayes, Alice J. "The Value of Good Reading." *Sacred Heart Review*, December 21, 1912.

Healy, Edith. *On Christian Art*. New York and Cincinnati: Benziger Bros., 1892.

Hennessey, James. *American Catholics: A History of the Roman Catholic Community in the United States*. New York: Oxford University Press, 1981.

Hennessy, Michael E. *Massachusetts Politics, 1890–1935*. Norwood, Mass.: n.p., 1935.

Henthorne, S. M. Evangela. *The Irish Colonization Association of the United States*. Champaign, Ill.: n.p., 1932.

Hentoff, Nat. *Boston Boy*. New York: Knopf, 1986.

Herlihy, Elizabeth M., ed. *Fifty Years of Boston, 1880–1930*. Boston: Tercentenary Committee, 1932.

Herndon, Richard. *Boston of Today: A Glance at Its History and Characteristics*. N.p.: Post Publishing Co., 1892.

Hewitt, Nancy A. *Women's Activism and Social Change: Rochester, New York, 1822–1872*. Ithaca: Cornell University Press, 1984.

Higham, John. *Strangers in the Land: Patterns in American Nativism, 1860–1925*. New York: Atheneum, 1968.

Hillquit, Morris. *History of Socialism in the United States*. New York: Russell & Russell, 1903. 5th ed. New York: Harper, 1910.

Hinding, Andrea, Ames Sheldon Bower, and Clarke A. Chambers, eds. *Women's History Sources: A Guide to Archives and Manuscript Collections in the United States*. 2 vols. New York and London: R. R. Bowker, 1979.

Hobgood, Mary L. *Catholic Social Teaching and Economic Theory: Paradigms in Conflict*. Philadelphia: Temple University Press, 1991.

Hoehn, Matthew, ed. *Catholic Authors: Contemporary Biographical Sketches, 1930–1947*. Newark, N.J.: St. Mary's Abbey, 1948.

House of the Angel Guardian. *Useful Almanac*. Boston: Angel Guardian Press, 1880.

Howard, Brett. *Boston: A Social History*. New York: Hawthorn, 1976.

Husslein, Joseph C. *The World Problem, Capital, Labor and the Church*. New York: P. J. Kenedy & Sons, 1919.

Hutchinson, William Robert. *The Modernist Impulse in American Protestantism*. New York: Oxford University Press, 1976.

Huthmacher, J. Joseph. *Massachusetts People and Politics, 1919–1933*. 1959. Reprint. Cambridge, Mass.: Belknap Press, 1969.

Ibson, John Duffy. "Will the World Break Your Heart?: A Historical Analysis of the Dimensions and Consequences of Irish-American Assimilation." Ph.D. dissertation, Brandeis University, 1976.

Inglis, Tom. *Moral Monopoly: The Catholic Church in Modern Irish Society*. New York: St. Martin's, 1987.

Jackson, Holbrook. *The Eighteen Nineties: A Review of Art and Ideas at the Close of the Nineteenth Century.* New York: A. A. Knopf, 1913.

Jussim, Estelle. *Slave to Beauty: The Eccentric Life and Controversial Career of F. Holland Day, Photographer Publisher Aesthete.* Boston: David R. Godine, 1981.

Kane, Paula. " 'The Willing Captive of Home'?: The English Catholic Women's League, 1906–1920." *Church History* 60 (September 1991): 331–55.

Karlsen, Carol. *The Devil in the Shape of a Woman.* New York: Vintage, 1989.

Karson, Marc. "Catholic Anti-Socialsm." In *Failure of a Dream?: Essays in the History of American Socialism,* edited by John Laslett and Seymour Martin Lipset. Garden City, N.Y.: Anchor Press, 1974.

Katzman, David M. *Seven Days a Week: Women and Domestic Service in Industrializing America.* New York: Oxford University Press, 1978.

Kauffman, Christopher J. *Faith and Fraternalism: The History of the Knights of Columbus, 1882–1982.* New York: Harper & Row, 1982.

———. "Supreme Knight, Edward L. Hearn: A Decade of Dynamic Growth." *Columbia,* September 1982, 36–39.

———. *Tradition and Transformation in Catholic Culture: The Priests of Saint Sulpice in the United States from 1791 to the Present.* New York: Macmillan, 1988.

Kaufman, Polly. "Boston Women and City School Politics, 1872–1905: Nurturers and Protectors in Public Education." Ph.D. dissertation, Boston University, 1978.

Kavanaugh, Peter. *The Story of the Abbey Theatre: From Its Origins in 1899 to the Present.* New York: Devin-Adair, 1950.

Keating, John S., ed. *Boston College in the World War, 1917–1918.* Chestnut Hill, Mass.: Boston College, 1922.

Keenan, Sister Angela Elizabeth. *Three against the Wind: The Founding of Trinity College, Washington, D.C.* Westminster, Md.: Christian Classics, 1973.

Kelley, Francis Clement. *The Great American Catholic Missionary Congresses.* Chicago: J. S. Hyland, 1914.

———. *The Story of Extension.* Chicago: Extension Press, 1923.

Kellogg, Gene. *The Vital Tradition: The Catholic Novel in a Period of Convergence.* Chicago: Loyola University Press, 1970.

Kenneally, James K. "Catholic and Feminist: A Biographical Approach." *U.S. Catholic Historian* 3 (Spring 1984): 229–53.

———. "Catholicism and Woman Suffrage in Massachusetts." *Catholic Historical Review* 53 (April 1967): 43–57.

———. "Eve, Mary and the Catholic Historians." *Horizons,* December 1976.

———. *The History of American Catholic Women.* New York: Crossroad, 1990.

———. *Women and American Trade Unions.* St. Alban's, Vt.: Eden Press Women's Publications, 1978.

Kennedy, Joseph P., ed. *The Story of the Films.* Chicago: A. W. Shaw, 1927. Facsimile ed. by Jerome S. Ozer, 1971.

Kennedy, Rose. *Times to Remember.* Garden City, N.Y.: Doubleday, 1974.

Kennelly, Karen. *American Catholic Women.* New York and London: Macmillan, 1989.

Kenner, Hugh. *A Colder Eye: The Modern Irish Writers.* New York: Knopf, 1983.

Kenney, William F. *Centenary of the See of Boston, a newspaper man's compilation of the leading events of the 100th anniversary of the Diocese of Boston, October, November, 1908.* Boston: J. K. Waters, 1909.

Kervick, Francis W. *Architects in America of Catholic Tradition*. Rutland, Vt.: Charles E. Tuttle, 1962.

King, Donald C. "Keith, Albee, et al." *Marquee* 7 (1975): 4–10.

Kirkland, Edward Chase. *Dream and Thought in the Business Community, 1860–1900*. Ithaca: Cornell University Press, 1956.

Kirwin, Harry W. "James J. Walsh—Medical Historian and Pathfinder." *Catholic Historical Review* 45 (January 1960): 409–35.

Knobel, Dale. *Paddy and the Republic: Ethnicity and Nationalism in Antebellum America*. Middletown, Conn.: Wesleyan University Press, 1986.

Kolbenschlag, Madonna, ed. *Between God and Caesar: Priests, Sisters and Political Office in the United States*. New York: Paulist Press, 1985.

Kolko, Gabriel. *Main Currents in Modern American History*. New York: Harper & Row, 1976.

Kornbluh, Joyce L., ed. *Rebel Voices: An I.W.W. Anthology*. Ann Arbor: University of Michigan Press, 1964.

Kselman, Thomas, and Steven Avella. "Marian Piety and the Cold War in the United States." *Catholic Historical Review* 72 (July 1986): 403–24.

Kuehnel, Reynold. *Conferences for Young Women*. New York: Joseph Wagner, 1916.

Kuhn, Anna. *Watching at My Gates*. Milwaukee: Bruce Publishing, 1948.

Laetare Medal Centennial, 1883–1983. Notre Dame, Ind.: University of Notre Dame Press, 1983.

La Farge, John. *The Manner Is Ordinary*. Garden City, N.Y.: Image Doubleday, 1954.

Lane, Roger. "James Jeffrey Roche and the Boston *Pilot*." *New England Quarterly* 33 (September 1960): 341–63.

———. *Policing the City: Boston, 1822–1885*. New York: Atheneum, 1971.

Langtry, Albert P., ed. *Metropolitan Boston: A Modern History*. 5 vols. New York: Lewis Historical Publishing, 1929.

Lapomarda, Vincent A. *The Jesuit Heritage in New England*. Worcester, Mass.: Jesuits of Holy Cross College, 1977.

Larkin, Emmet J. "The Devotional Revolution in Ireland, 1850–1875." *American Historical Review* 77 (June 1972): 625–52.

Lasance, Francis Xavier, ed. *The Catholic Girl's Guide: Counsels and Devotions for Girls in the Ordinary Walks of Life and in Particular for the Children of Mary*. New York and Cincinnati: Benziger Bros., 1906.

Lathrop, George Parsons. "Orestes Brownson." *Atlantic Monthly*, June 1896.

Lathrop, George Parsons, and Rose Hawthorne Lathrop. *A Story of Courage: Annals of the Georgetown Convent of the Visitation of the Blessed Virgin Mary*. Boston: Houghton Mifflin, 1894.

Lathrop, Rose Hawthorne. *Memories of Hawthorne*. Boston: Houghton Mifflin, 1897.

Lawrence, William. "The Relation of Wealth to Morals." *World's Work*, January 1901.

Leach, William. *True Love and Perfect Union: The Feminist Reform of Sex and Society*. New York: Basic Books, 1980.

Leahy, William A. "Archdiocese of Boston." In *History of the Catholic Church in the New England States*, edited by William Byrne et al. Boston: Hurd & Everts, 1899.

―――, comp. and ed. *The Catholic Churches of Boston and Its Vicinity and St. John's Seminary, Brighton, Massachusetts.* Boston and New York: McClellan, Hearn, 1891.

Leahy, William P. *Adapting to America: Catholics, Jesuits, and Higher Education in the Twentieth Century.* Washington, D.C.: Georgetown University Press, 1991.

Lears, T. J. Jackson. *No Place of Grace: Antimodernism and the Transformation of American Culture, 1880–1920.* New York: Pantheon, 1981.

Lecky, Walter [William A. McDermott]. *Down at Caxton's.* Baltimore: John Murphy, 1895.

Lippy, Charles, and Peter Williams, eds. *Encyclopedia of the American Religious Experience.* 3 vols. New York: Scribner's, 1988.

Liptak, Dolores. *European Immigrants and the Catholic Church in Connecticut, 1870–1920.* Staten Island, N.Y.: Center for Migration Studies, 1987.

―――. *Immigrants and Their Church.* New York and London: Macmillan, 1989.

Litt, Edgar. *The Political Culture of Massachusetts.* Cambridge, Mass.: MIT Press, 1965.

Loftus, David J. *Boston College High School, 1863–1983.* Boston: A. C. Getchell, 1984.

Logan, Mrs. John A. (May S.), ed. *The Part Taken by Women in American History.* Wilmington, Del.: Perry-Nalle, 1912. Reprint. New York: Arno, 1972.

Lord, Robert H., John E. Sexton, and Edward T. Harrington. *History of the Archdiocese of Boston in the Various Stages of Its Development, 1604 to 1940.* 3 vols. New York: Sheed and Ward, 1944.

Loughlin, Katherine. "Boston's Political Morals." *Commonweal,* March 15, 1946, 545–48.

Lubove, Roy. *The Professional Altruist: The Emergence of Social Work as a Career, 1880–1930.* Cambridge, Mass.: Harvard University Press, 1965.

Lucey, William L. "Louise Imogen Guiney and the American Ecclesiastical Review." *American Ecclesiastical Review* 136 (1957): 364–70.

―――. "The Record of an American Priest: Michael Earls, S.J., 1873–1937." *American Ecclesiastical Review* 137 (September–December 1957): 145–55, 217–29, 297–307, 414–22.

Luria, David D. "Wealth, Capital and Power: The Social Meaning of Home Ownership." *Journal of Interdisciplinary History* 7 (1976): 262–82.

Lurie, Reuben L. *The Challenge of the Forum: The Story of Ford Hall and the Open Forum Movement.* Boston: Richard G. Badger, Gorham Press, 1930.

Lynch, Sister Helen M. *In the Shadow of Our Lady of the Retreat in the Cenacle. Published in Commemoration of the First Half Century of the Cenacle in America.* New York: Paulist Press, 1941.

Lyons, Louis M. *Newspaper Story: One Hundred Years of the Boston Globe.* Cambridge, Mass.: Belknap Press, 1971.

Lyons, Sister Jeanne Marie. *Maryknoll's First Lady.* New York: Dodd, Mead, 1964.

McArthur, Benjamin. *Actors and American Culture, 1880–1920.* Philadelphia: Temple University Press, 1984.

McCaffrey, Lawrence J. *The Irish Diaspora in America.* Bloomington: Indiana University Press, 1976.

McCarthy, Denis A. *A Round of Rimes.* 2d ed., rev. and enl. Boston: Little, Brown, 1909.

McCarthy, Justin, et al., eds. *Irish Literature.* 10 vols. Philadelphia: John D. Morrison, 1904.

McCool, Gerald. *Catholic Theology in the Nineteenth Century: The Quest for a Unitary Method.* New York: Seabury Press, 1977.

McDannell, Colleen. "Catholic Domesticity, 1860–1960." In *American Catholic Women,* edited by Karen Kennelly. New York and London: Macmillan, 1989.

———. *The Christian Home in Victorian America, 1840–1900.* Bloomington: Indiana University Press, 1986.

———. "True Men as We Need Them: Catholicism and the Irish American Male." *American Studies* 27 (Fall 1986): 19–35.

McEntee, Georgiana Putnam. *The Social Catholic Movement in Great Britain.* New York: Macmillan, 1927.

McGinnis, Thomas J. "The Descration of the Drama." *Columbiad,* June 1910.

McGuinness, Margaret M. "A Puzzle with Missing Pieces: Catholic Women and the Social Settlement Movement, 1897–1915." *Working Paper Series* 22 (Spring 1990). Cushwa Center, University of Notre Dame, Notre Dame, Ind.

MacMahon, William. "Bebel's Libel on Woman." *Catholic Truth Society,* September 1911.

McSweeney, Edward F. "Irish Immigrants in America." *Donahoe's Magazine,* 1903.

Maginnis, Charles D. "Catholic Church Architecture." *Architectural Forum,* August 1917.

———. *Catholic Church Architecture.* Boston: Everett, 1906.

———. *Charles Donagh Maginnis, FAIA, 1867–1955: Selection of his Essays and Addresses.* Edited by Robert P. Walsh and Andrew W. Roberts. New Haven: Yale University Press, 1956.

———. "The Movement for a Vital Christian Architecture and the Obstacles—the Roman Catholic View." *Christian Art* 1 (April 1907): 22–26.

———. "Recent Roman Catholic Architecture." In *Proceedings of the Boston Society of Architects.* Boston: Boston Society of Architects, 1909.

Magnuson, Norris. *Salvation in the Slums: Evangelical Social Work, 1865–1920.* Metuchen, N.J.: Scarecrow Press, 1977.

Maher, Mary A. B. "The Catholic Woman as Educator." In *The World's Congress of Representative Woman,* edited by May Wright Sewell. Chicago and New York: Rand, McNally, 1894.

Mahoney, John Joseph, and Charles M. Herlihy. *First Steps in Americanization: A Handbook for Teachers.* Boston and New York: Houghton Mifflin, 1918.

Mainiero, Lina, ed. *American Women Writers: A Critical Reference Guide from Colonial Times to the Present.* 4 vols. New York: Frederick Ungar, 1979–82.

Mann, Arthur. *Yankee Reformers in the Urban Age: Social Reform in Boston, 1880–1900.* New York: Harper & Row, 1954.

Marriner, Ernest Cummings. *Jim Connolly and the Fishermen of Gloucester: An Appreciation of James Brendan Connolly at Eighty.* Waterville, Maine: Colby College Press, 1949.

Marshall, Hugh. *Orestes Brownson and the American Republic.* Washington, D.C.: Catholic University Press, 1971.

Martin, Stephanie Lang. "A Guide to the Records of Sacred Heart Parish, East Cambridge." Master's thesis, University of Massachusetts-Boston, 1980.

Martindale, C. C. *Life of Bernard Vaughan.* London: Longmans, 1923.

May, Henry F. *Protestant Churches and Industrial America*. New York: Harper, 1949.

Maynard, Theodore. *A Fire Was Lighted: The Life of Rose Hawthorne Lathrop*. Milwaukee: Bruce, 1948.

Meagher, Timothy J. "The Lord Is Not Dead: Cultural and Social Change among the Irish in Worcester, Massachusetts." Ph.D. dissertation, Brown University, 1982.

———. "Sweet Good Mothers and Young Women out in the World: The Roles of Irish American Women in Late Nineteenth and Early Twentieth Century Worcester, Massachusetts." *U.S. Catholic Historian* 5 (Summer/Fall 1986): 325–44.

———, ed. *From Paddy to Studs: Irish American Communities in the Turn of the Century Era, 1880 to 1920*. Westport, Conn.: Greenwood Press, 1986.

———, ed. *Urban American Catholicism: The Culture and Identity of the American Catholic People*. New York: Garland, 1988.

Meagher, Walter J., and William J. Grattan. *The Spires of Fenwick: A History of the College of the Holy Cross, 1843–1965*. New York: Vantage Press, 1966.

Menendez, Albert. *Religious Conflict in America: A Bibliography*. New York: Garland, 1985.

Merwick, Donna. *Boston Priests, 1848–1910: A Study of Social and Intellectual Change*. Cambridge, Mass.: Harvard University Press, 1973.

Merwin, Henry Childs. "The Irish in American Life." *Atlantic Monthly*, March 1986.

Messbarger, Paul. "American Catholic Dialog, 1884–1900: A Study of Catholic Fiction." Ph.D. dissertation, University of Minnesota, 1969.

———. "The Failed Promise of American Catholic Literature." *U.S. Catholic Historian* 4, no. 2 (1985): 143–58.

———. *Fiction with a Parochial Purpose: Social Uses of American Catholic Literature, 1884–1900*. Boston: Boston University Press, 1971.

Meyers, Donald B. *The Protestant Search for Political Realism, 1919–1941*. Berkeley: University of California Press, 1961.

Michel, Virgil. *The Critical Principles of Orestes A. Brownson*. Washington, D.C.: Catholic University of America Press, 1918.

Miles, Albert J. "James B. Connolly." In *Dictionary of Literary Biography*. Vol. 78, *American Short-Story Writers, 1880–1910*, edited by Bobby Ellen Kimbel. Detroit: Gale, 1989.

Miller, David W. *Church, State and Nation in Ireland, 1898–1921*. Dublin: Gill & Macmillan, 1973.

Miller, Kerby. "Class, Culture, and Immigrant Group Identity in the United States: The Case of Irish-American Ethnicity." In *Immigration Reconsidered: History, Sociology, and Politics*, edited by Virginia Yans-McLaughlin. New York: Oxford University Press, 1990.

———. *Emigrants and Exiles: Ireland and the Irish Exodus to North America*. New York: Oxford University Press, 1985.

Misner, Paul. *Social Catholicism in Europe from the Onset of Industrialization to the First World War*. New York: Crossroad, 1991.

Mitchell, Brian, ed. *Building the American Catholic City: Parishes and Institutions*. New York: Garland, 1988. The Heritage of American Catholicism, vol. 4.

Mofford, Juliette. *Greater Lawrence: A Bibliography*. Lawrence, Mass.: Merrimack Valley Textile Museum, 1978.

Moody, Joseph N., ed. *Church and Society: Catholic Social and Political Thought and Movements, 1789–1950.* New York: Arts, Inc., 1953.
Moon, Michael. "'The Gentle Boy from the Dangerous Classes': Pederasty, Domesticity, and Capitalism in Horatio Alger." In *The New American Studies: Essays from Representations,* edited by Philip Fisher. Berkeley: University of California Press, 1991.
Moore, R. Laurence. "Insiders and Outsiders in American Historical Narrative and American History." *American Historical Review* 87 (April 1982): 390–412.
———. *Religious Outsiders and the Making of Americans.* New York: Oxford University Press, 1986.
Moorehouse, Vera. "Benjamin Franklin Keith, Vaudeville Magnate: The First Fifty Years, 1846–1896." Master's thesis, Eastern Michigan University, 1975.
Muccigrosso, Robert. *American Gothic: The Mind and Art of Ralph Adams Cram.* Washington, D.C.: University Press of America, 1979.
———. "Ralph Adams Cram and the Modernity of Medievalism." *Studies in Medievalism* 1 (Spring 1982): 21–42.
Mullany, Katherine Frances. *Catholic Pittsfield and Berkshire.* 2 vols. Pittsfield, Mass.: Sun Printing, 1887–1924.
Murphy, B. L. "Convent Education." Master's thesis, Clark University, 1918.
Murphy, Charles J. V. "Pope of New England: A Portrait of Cardinal O'Connell." *Outlook & Independent,* October 23, 1929.
Murphy, Maureen. "Irish-American Theatre." In *Ethnic Theatre in the United States,* edited by Maxine Seller. Westport, Conn.: Greenwood Press, 1983.
Musser, Charles. *The Emergence of Cinema: The American Screen to 1907.* Vol. 1 of *History of the American Cinema,* edited by Charles Harpole. New York: Charles Scribner's Sons, 1990.
Neill, Stephen. "Achievements in Architecture." *Donahoe's Magazine,* August 1907.
Nolan, Hugh J., ed. *Pastoral Letters of the United States Catholic Bishops.* 4 vols. Washington, D.C.: NCCB/USCC, 1984.
Norton, Elliot. *Boston Down East: An Informal Account of the Plays, Players and Playhouses of Boston from Puritan Times to the Present.* Boston: Trustees of the Boston Public Library, 1978.
The Notable Catholic Institutions of Boston and Vicinity. Boston: n.p., 1897.
Oates, Mary J. *Higher Education for Catholic Women: An Historical Anthology.* New York: Garland, 1988.
———. "Learning to Teach: The Professional Preparation of Massachusetts Parochial School Faculty, 1870–1940." *Working Paper Series* 10 (Fall 1981). Cushwa Center, University of Notre Dame, Notre Dame, Ind.
———. "'Lowell': An Account of Convent Life in Lowell, Massachusetts, 1852–1890." *New England Quarterly* 61 (March 1988): 101–18.
———. "Organized Voluntarism: The Catholic Sisters in Massachusetts, 1870–1940." *American Quarterly* 30 (Winter 1978): 652–80.
———. "Women's Role in Catholic Charity, 1820–1920." In *Philanthropy and the Religious Tradition,* 1989, 663–77. Spring Research Forum Working Papers, prepared for a conference cosponsored by Independent Sector and the United Way Institute.
O'Brien, David J. "The American Priests and Social Action." In *The Catholic Priest in the United States: Historical Investigations,* edited by John Tracy Ellis. Collegeville, Minn.: St. John's University Press, 1971.

———. *Faith and Friendship: Catholicism in the Diocese of Syracuse, 1886–1986.* Syracuse, N.Y.: Catholic Diocese of Syracuse, 1987.

———. *Public Catholicism.* New York, London: Macmillan, 1989.

———. "Social Teaching, Social Action, Social Gospel." *U.S. Catholic Historian* 5, no. 2 (1986): 195–224.

O'Connell, William. *The Letters of His Eminence William Cardinal O'Connell, Archbishop of Boston.* Cambridge, Mass.: Riverside Press, 1915.

———. *Recollections of Seventy Years.* Boston and New York: Houghton Mifflin, 1934.

———. *Sermons and Addresses.* 11 vols. Boston: Pilot, 1911–38.

O'Connor, Thomas H. *Bibles, Brahmins, and Bosses: A Short History of Boston.* 1976. 2d ed., rev. Boston: Boston Public Library, 1984.

———. *Fitzpatrick's Boston, 1846–1866: John Bernard Fitzpatrick, Third Bishop of Boston.* Boston: Northeastern University Press, 1984.

O'Connor, Ulick. *All the Olympians: A Biographical Portrait of the Irish Literary Renaissance.* New York: Atheneum, 1985.

O'Dea, John. *History of the Ancient Order of Hibernians and Ladies' Auxiliary.* 3 vols. Philadelphia: Keystone, 1923.

O'Grady, John. *Catholic Charities in the United States.* 1931. Reprint. New York: Arno, 1971.

O'Leary, Robert Aidan. "William Henry Cardinal O'Connell: A Social and Intellectual Biography." Ph.D. dissertation, Tufts University, 1980.

O'Mahoney, (Mrs.) Katherine A. (O'Keeffe). *Famous Irishwomen.* Lawrence, Mass: Lawrence Publishing, 1907.

Onahan, Mary. "Catholic Women's Part in Philanthropy." In *The World's Congress of Representative Women,* edited by May Wright Sewell. Chicago: Rand, McNally, 1894.

O'Neill, James L. *Catholic Literature in Catholic Homes.* New York: P. O'Shea, 1894.

An Open Letter to the Loyal Citizens of Boston: An Appeal from the Loyal Women of American Liberty. Judge Fallon's Resignation, and a Review of his Reasons Therefor. Boston: National Association of the Loyal Women of American Liberty, 1890.

O'Reilly, Bernard. *True Men as We Need Them: A Book of Instruction for Men in the World.* 4th ed. New York: P. J. Kenedy, 1883.

O'Reilly, Elizabeth Boyle. *How France Built Her Cathedrals.* New York and London: Harper & Bros., 1921.

O'Reilly, Eliza(beth) B(oyle). *My Candles, and Other Poems.* Boston: Lee & Shepard, 1903.

O'Reilly, John Boyle. "The Exile of the Gael." In *Life of John Boyle O'Reilly, by James Jeffrey Roche. Together with his Complete Poems and Speeches,* edited by Mrs. John Boyle O'Reilly. New York: Cassell, 1891.

Orsi, Robert A. *The Madonna of 115th Street: Faith and Community in Italian Harlem, 1880–1950.* New Haven: Yale University Press, 1985.

O'Sullivan, Mary Blanche. "Phases of Charitable Work among Children." *Donahoe's Magazine,* July 1903, 25–43.

O'Toole, James M. *Guide to the Archives of the Archdiocese of Boston.* New York and London: Garland, 1982.

————. *Militant and Triumphant: William Henry O'Connell and the Catholic Church in Boston, 1859–1944*. Notre Dame, Ind.: University of Notre Dame Press, 1992.

————. "'That Fabulous Churchman': Toward a Biography of Cardinal W. O'Connell." *Catholic Historical Review* 70 (January 1984): 28–44.

Pagels, Elaine. *Adam, Eve and the Serpent*. Oxford: Oxford University Press, 1988.

Panchok, Frances. "The Catholic Church and Theatre in New York, 1890–1920." Ph.D. dissertation, Catholic University, 1976.

Pearson, Henry Greenleaf. *Son of New England: James Jackson Storrow, 1864–1926*. Boston: Thomas Todd, 1932.

Peterson, George. *The New England College in the Age of the University*. Amherst, Mass: Amherst College, 1964.

Philpott, A. J. "Catholicism in Boston." In *Catholic Builders of the Nation: A Symposium on the Catholic Contribution to the Civilization of the United States*, by A. J. Philpott. Boston: Continental Press, 1923.

The "Pilot" at One-Fifty: A Special Edition. Boston: Pilot, 1979.

"Pilot" Centenary Edition. Boston: Pilot, 1930.

Pope, Barbara Corrado. "Immaculate and Powerful: The Marian Revival in the Nineteenth Century." In *Immaculate and Powerful: The Female in Sacred Image and Social Reality*, edited by Clarissa Atkinson et al. Boston: Beacon Press, 1985.

Preston, James J., ed. *Mother Worship: Theme and Variations*. Chapel Hill: University of North Carolina Press, 1982.

Preuss, Arthur, ed. *The Fundamental Fallacy of Socialism*. St. Louis: B. Herder, 1909.

Reckitt, Maurice B. *Faith and Society: A study of the Structure, Outlook and Opportunity of the Christian Socialist Movement in Great Britain and the United States of America*. London and New York: Longmans, Green, 1932.

Reher, Margaret. "Americanism and Modernism—Continuity or Discontinuity?" *U.S. Catholic Historian* 1 (1981): 87–103.

————. *Catholic Intellectual Life in America*. New York: Macmillan, 1989.

Reilly, Mary Lonan. *A History of the Catholic Press Association, 1911–1968*. Metuchen, N.J.: Scarecrow Press, 1971.

Repplier, Agnes. *In Our Convent Days*. Boston and New York: Houghton Mifflin, 1905.

————. *Points of View*. Boston and New York: Houghton Mifflin, 1892.

————. "The Spinster." In *Compromises*, by Agnes Repplier. Boston: Houghton Mifflin, 1904.

Rhodes, Anthony. *The Power of Rome in the 20th Century: The Vatican in the Age of Liberal Democracies, 1870–1922*. New York: Franklin Watts, 1983.

Rideout, Walter B. *The Radical Novel in the United States, 1900–1954*. Cambridge, Mass.: Harvard University Press, 1956.

Riley, Arthur Joseph. "Catholicism and the New England Mind." Reprinted from the *Transactions of the Colonial Society of Massachusetts*, vol. 34. Boston: Colonial Society of Massachusetts, 1943.

Ripley, William Z. "The European Population of the United States." The Huxley Memorial Lecture for 1908, presented at the Royal Anthropological Institute of Great Britain and Ireland, London, 1908.

Rittenhouse, Jessie B. *My House of Life: An Autobiography*. Boston and New York: Houghton Mifflin, 1934.

Roberts, James P. "The Range of Speakers and Topics." In *Democracy in the Making,* edited by George Coleman. Boston: Little, Brown, 1915.

Robins, Julia Gorham. *A New England Conversion.* New York, n.p., n.d.

Robinson, Doris. *Women Novelists, 1891–1920: An Index to Biographical and Autobiographical Sources.* New York: Garland, 1984.

Robinson, Henry Moston. *The Cardinal.* New York: Simon and Schuster, 1950.

Roche, James Jeffrey, ed. *John Boyle O'Reilly: His Life, Poems and Speeches.* New York: Cassell, 1891.

Roddy, Edward G. "The Catholic Newspaper Press and the Quest for Social Justice, 1912–1920." Ph.D. dissertation, Georgetown University, 1961.

Rollins, Hyder Edward. *Keats and the Bostonians: Amy Lowell, Louise Imogen Guiney, Louis Arthur Holman and Fred Holland Day.* Cambridge, Mass.: Harvard University Press, 1951.

Roman, Judith A. *Annie Adams Fields: The Spirit of Charles Street.* Bloomington: Indiana University Press, 1990.

Romig, Walter, ed. *The Book of Catholic Authors.* Detroit: W. Romig, 1942– . First series.

Roohan, James Edmund. "American Catholics and the Social Question, 1856–1900." Ph.D. dissertation, Yale University, 1952.

Rorke, Margaret Hayden, comp. *Letters and Addresses on Woman Suffrage, by Catholic Ecclesiastics.* New York: Devin-Adair, 1914.

Rosenblum, Gerald. *Immigrant Workers: Their Impact on American Labor Radicalism.* New York: Basic Books, 1973.

Rosenthal, Bernard, and Paul E. Szarmach, ed. *Medievalism in American Culture.* Binghampton, N.Y.: Medieval and Renaissance Texts and Studies, 1989.

Rosenzweig, Roy. *Eight Hours for What We Will: Workers and Leisure in an Industrial City, 1870–1920.* Cambridge: Cambridge University Press, 1983.

Rösler, Augustine. "Woman." In *Catholic Encyclopedia: An International Work of Reference on the Constitution, Doctrine, Discipline and History of the Catholic Church,* edited by Charles Herbermann et al., 15:687–97. New York: Appleton, 1912.

Ross, Aileen. "Philanthropy." In *International Encyclopedia of the Social Sciences,* edited by David Sills. New York: Macmillan, 1968.

Ross, Edward Alsworth. *The Old World in the New: The Significance of Past and Present Immigration to the American People.* New York: Century, 1913, 1914.

Russell, Francis. *A City in Terror: 1919, the Boston Police Strike.* New York: Viking, 1975.

Ryan, Dennis. *Beyond the Ballot Box: A Social History of the Boston Irish, 1845–1917.* Rutherford, N.J.: Fairleigh Dickinson University Press, 1983.

Ryan, George E. "The Irish Press of Boston." *Bulletin* 24 (Eire Society of Boston), December 5, 1965.

———, ed. *Figures in Our Catholic History: Brief, Illustrated Biographies of Men and Women Who Helped Write the Story of Boston.* Boston: St. Paul Editions, 1979.

Ryan, John A. *The Church and Socialism, and Other Essays.* Washington, D.C.: n.p., 1919.

———. *A Living Wage.* New York: Macmillan, 1910.

Ryan, Mary. *Cradle of the Middle Class: The Family in Oneida County, New York, 1790–1865.* Cambridge: Cambridge University Press, 1981.

——. *The Empire of the Mother: American Writing about Domesticity, 1830 to 1860.* New York: Institute for Research in History and Haworth Press, 1982.

Ryan, William Patrick. *The Pope's Green Island.* Boston: Small & Maynard, 1912.

Sadlier, Agnes. *Jeanne d'Arc: The Story of Her Life and Death.* Baltimore: John Murphy, 1901.

Salvaterra, David L. *American Catholicism and the Intellectual Life, 1880–1950.* New York: Garland, 1988.

Sanders, James. "Boston Catholics and the School Question, 1825–1907." In *Building the American Catholic City: Parishes and Institutions,* edited by Brian Mitchell. New York: Garland, 1988.

——. "Catholics and the School Question in Boston: The Cardinal O'Connell Years." In *Catholic Boston: Studies in Religion and Community, 1870–1970,* edited by Robert Sullivan and James O'Toole. Boston: Roman Catholic Archbishop of Boston, 1985.

Santayana, George. *The Sense of Beauty.* New York: C. Scribner's Sons, 1896.

Sargent, Kate. "Catholicism in Massachusetts." *Forum,* May 1925.

Scanlan, Michael J. *A Brief History of the Archdiocese of Boston.* Boston: Nicholas M. Williams, 1908.

Scannell-O'Neill, Denis James, ed. *Distinguished Converts to Rome in America.* St. Louis: B. Herder, 1907.

Schlesinger, Arthur. *Orestes A. Brownson: A Pilgrim's Progress.* Boston: Little, Brown, 1939.

Schofield, William G. *Seek for a Hero: The Story of John Boyle O'Reilly.* New York: Kenedy, 1956.

Scott, Mel. *American City Planning since 1890.* Berkeley: University of California, 1971.

Scudder, Vida. *A Listener in Babel.* Boston: Houghton Mifflin, 1903.

Seager, Richard H. "Pluralism and the American Mainstream: The View from the World's Parliament of Religions." *Harvard Theological Review* 82–83 (1989): 301–24.

Searle, George M. "Why the Catholic Church Cannot Accept Socialism." *Catholic World,* July 1913, 444–53.

Searman, Inigo. "The Apostolate of Print." *Ave Maria,* November 11, 1911.

Seaton, Douglas P. *Catholics and Radicals: The Association of Catholic Trade Unionists and the American Labor Movement, from Depression to Cold War.* Lewisburg, Pa.: Bucknell University Press, 1981.

Sexton, John E. *Cardinal O'Connell: A Biographical Sketch. Souvenir of the Silver Jubilee of his Episcopate.* Boston: Pilot, 1927.

Sexton, John E., and Arthur J. Riley. *History of Saint John's Seminary, Brighton.* Boston: Archdiocese of Boston, 1945.

Shanley, J. Sanford. "Charles Donagh Maginnis, 1867–1915." *Liturgical Arts,* August 1955.

Shannon, James P. *Catholic Colonization of the Western Frontier.* New York: Arno, 1976.

Shannon, William V. *The American Irish.* New York: Macmillan, 1963.

——. "The Lasting Hurrah." In *America and the New Ethnicity,* edited by David Colburn and George Pozzetta. Port Washington, N.Y.: Kennikat Press, 1979.

Sheehan, Arthur. *Rose Hawthorne: The Pilgrimage of Hawthorne's Daughter.* New York: Vision Books, 1959.

Shenton, James P. "The Coughlin Movement and the New Deal." *Political Science Quarterly* 83 (September 1958): 352–73.

Shields, Leo W. *The History and Meaning of the Term Social Justice.* Notre Dame, Ind.: University of Notre Dame Press, 1941.

Shields, Thomas E. *The Education of Our Girls.* New York: Benziger, 1907.

Shrock, Nancy, ed. *Architectural Records in Boston: A Guide to Architectural Research in Boston, Cambridge and Vicinity.* New York: Garland, 1983.

Shuster, George N. *The Catholic Spirit in America.* New York: Dial, 1927.

———. *The Catholic Spirit in English Literature.* New York: Macmillan, 1922.

———. *The Catholic Spirit in Modern English Literature.* New York: Macmillan, 1922.

Sinclair, Upton. *The Profits of Religion: An Essay in Economic Interpretation.* New York: Vanguard, 1918.

[A Sister of St. Joseph]. *The Ideal Catholic Readers Sixth Reader.* 1916 Reprint. New York: Macmillan, 1936.

A Sister of Saint Joseph. *Just Passing Through, 1873–1943.* Boston: Sisters of St. Joseph, 1943.

Skerret, Ellen. "The Irish Parish in Chicago, 1880–1930." *Working Paper Series* 9 (Spring 1981). Cushwa Center, University of Notre Dame, Notre Dame, Ind.

Slattery, Mrs. Francis E. "The Catholic Woman in Modern Times." *Catholic Mind,* March 22, 1930. Radio address, WNAC Boston, December 29, 1929, by the president of the League of Catholic Women.

Slawson, Douglas J. *The Foundation and First Decades of the National Catholic Welfare Council.* Washington, D.C.: Catholic University of America Press, 1992.

Smith, Arthur Warren. *Baptist Situation of Boston Proper.* Boston: Griffith-Stillings, 1912.

Smith, Helena Huntington. "Boston's Bogy-Man." *Outlook,* June 1928.

Smith, John Talbot. *History of the Catholic Church in New York.* 2 vols. New York: Hall & Locke, 1905.

———. "The Motion Picture and the Drama." *Columbiad* October 1913.

———. *Our Seminaries: An Essay on Clerical Training.* New York: n.p., 1896.

———. *The Parish Theatre: A brief account of its rise, its present conditions and its prospects. To which is added a descriptive list of one hundred choice plays suitable for the parish theatre.* New York: Longmans, Green, 1917.

———. *A Pilgrimage to See the Holy Father (Pope Pius X).* New York: Underwood & Underwood, 1907.

———. *Our Seminaries: An Essay on Clerical Training.* New York, 1896.

———. "The Young Catholic Writer: What Shall He Do?" *St. John's Quarterly* 6 (July 1909): 168–80.

Smith, Joseph. *James Jeffrey Roche: A Memory and Appreciation.* Boston: n.p., 1909.

Smith, Timothy L. "Religion and Ethnicity in America." *American Historical Review* 83 (December 1978): 1155–85.

———. "Religious Denominations as Ethnic Communities." *Church History* 35 (June 1966): 207–26.

Smith-Rosenberg, Carroll. *Disorderly Conduct: Visions of Gender in Victorian America.* New York: Knopf, 1985.

Smyth, Newman. *Passing Protestantism and Coming Catholicism.* New York: Scribner's, 1908.

Solomon, Barbara. *Ancestors and Immigrants: A Changing New England Tradition.* Cambridge, Mass.: Harvard University Press, 1956.

Sorvillo, Mark. "John A. Ryan." In *Twentieth-Century Shapers of American Popular Religion,* edited by Charles Lippy. Westport, Conn.: Greenwood Press, 1989.

Spalding, John Lancaster. *Means and Ends of Education.* Chicago: A. C. McClurg, 1895.

———. *Opportunity and Other Essays and Addresses.* Chicago: A. C. McClurg, 1900.

———. *Religion and Art and Other Essays.* N.p., 1905.

Sparr, Arnold J. "From Self-Congratulation to Self-Criticism: Main Currents in American Catholic Fiction, 1900–1960." *U.S. Catholic Historian* 6 (Spring/Summer 1987): 213–30.

———. *To Promote, Defend, and Redeem: The Catholic Literary Revival and the Cultural Transformation of American Catholicism, 1920–1960.* New York: Greenwood Press, 1990.

Stack, John F. *International Conflict in an American City: Boston's Irish, Italians, and Jews.* Westport, Conn.: Greenwood Press, 1979.

Stang, William. *Socialism and Christianity.* New York: Benziger Bros., 1905.

State Street Trust Company. *Mayors of Boston.* Boston: State Street Trust Co., [1914].

Stave, Bruce M., ed. *Socialism and the Cities.* Port Washington, N.Y.: Kennikat Press, 1975.

Stone, Orra Laville. *History of Massachusetts Industries: Their Inception, Growth and Success.* 4 vols. Boston and Chicago: S. J. Clarke, 1930.

Sullivan, James Stephen. *One Hundred Years of Progress. A Graphic, Historical and Pictorial Account of the Catholic Church of New England, Embracing the Archdiocese of Boston.* Boston and Portland, Maine: Illustrated Pub. Co., 1895.

Sullivan, Robert E. "Beneficial Relations: Toward a Social History of the Diocesan Priests of Boston, 1874–1944." In *Catholic Boston: Studies in Religion and Community, 1870–1970,* edited by Robert E. Sullivan and James M. O'Toole. Boston: Roman Catholic Archbishop of Boston, 1985.

Sullivan, Robert E., and James M. O'Toole, eds. *Catholic Boston: Studies in Religion and Community, 1870–1970.* Boston: Roman Catholic Archbishop of Boston, 1985.

Sweeney, Francis. "Miss Repplier of Philadelphia." *Catholic World,* July 1951.

Talbot, Francis X., ed. *Fiction by Its Makers.* New York: America Press, 1926.

Tambasco, Anthony J. *What Are They Saying about Mary?* New York: Paulist, 1989.

Tanquerey, Adolphe. *The Spiritual Life.* Tournai: Desclée, 1930.

Taves, Ann. *The Household of Faith: Roman Catholic Devotions in Mid-Nineteenth-Century America.* Notre Dame: University of Notre Dame Press, 1986.

Tenison, Eva Mabel. *Louise Imogen Guiney: Her Life and Works, 1861–1920.* London: Macmillan, 1923.

Thernstrom, Stephan. *The Other Bostonians: Poverty and Progress in the American Metropolis, 1880–1970.* Cambridge, Mass.: Harvard University Press, 1973.

Thomas, Samuel J. "Catholic Journalists and the Ideal Woman in Late Victorian America." *International Journal of Women's Studies* 4 (1981): 89–100.

REFERENCES 401

Timberlake, James H. *Prohibition and the Progressive Movement, 1900–1920.* Cambridge, Mass.: Harvard University Press, 1963.
Toomy, Alice Timmons. "There Is a Public Sphere for Catholic Women." In "The Woman Question among Catholics: A Round Table Conference," *Catholic World,* August 1893, 674–77.
Trachtenberg, Alan. *The Incorporation of America: Culture and Society in the Gilded Age.* New York: Hill and Wang, 1982.
Tribute to Benjamin Franklin Keith, Father of Modern Vaudeville. New York: I. Goldman Co., 1927.
Trolander, Judith Ann. *Settlement Houses and the Great Depression.* Wayne State University Press, 1975.
Trout, Charles H. "Boston during the Great Depression, 1928–1940." Ph.D. dissertation, Columbia University, 1972.
Tucci, Douglass Shand. *The Boston Rialto: Playhouses, Concert Halls and Movie Palaces.* Boston: Boston Conservation League, 1977.
———. *Built in Boston: City and Suburb, 1800–1950.* Boston: New York Graphic Society, 1978.
———. *Church Building in Boston, 1720–1970, with an Introduction to the Work of Ralph Adams Cram and the Boston Gothicists.* Concord, Mass.: Rumford Press, 1974.
———. *The Second Settlement, 1875–1925: A Study of the Development of Victorian Dorchester.* Boston: Trustees in Observance of the Centennial of St. Margaret's Hospital, 1974.
Tucci, Paul Douglass Shand. *Gothic Churches of Dorchester.* N.p., 1974.
Turner, Victor, and Edith Turner. "Postindustrial Marian Pilgrimage." In *Mother Worship: Theme and Variations,* edited by James J. Preston. Chapel Hill: University of North Carolina Press, 1982.
Ursulines of New York. *Immortelles of Catholic Columbian Literature, Compiled from the Works of American Catholic Women Writers by the Ursulines of New York.* Chicago and New York: McBride, 1897.
Valenti, Patricia. *To Myself a Stranger: A Biography of Rose Hawthorne Lathrop.* Baton Rouge: Louisiana State University Press, 1991.
Vance, Marguerite. *On Wings of Fire.* New York: Dutton, 1955.
Vaughan, Bernard. *Life Lessons from Blessed Joan of Arc.* London: George Allen & Sons, 1910.
———. *Sinless Mary and Sinful Mary.* London: Burns & Oates, 1905.
———. *Socialism from the Christian Standpoint: Ten Conferences.* New York: Macmillan, 1912.
Veblen, Thorstein. *The Theory of the Leisure Class.* 1899. Reprint. New York: New American Library, 1953.
Vidler, Alexander. *The Modernist Movement in the Roman Church: Its Origins and Outcome.* New York: Gorden Press, 1976.
Vidler, Alex R. *A Variety of Catholic Modernists.* London: Cambridge University Press, 1970.
Wagner, J. F., ed. *Addresses at Patriotic and Civic Occasions by Catholic Orators.* 2 vols. New York: n.p., 1915.
Wallace, Lillian Parker. *Leo XIII and the Rise of Socialism.* Durham, N.C.: Duke University Press, 1966.

Walsh, David I. "Labor in Politics: Its Political Influence in New England." *Forum,* August 1919.

Walsh, Francis Robert. "The Boston *Pilot:* A Newspaper for the Irish Immigrant, 1829–1908." Ph.D. dissertation, Boston University, 1968.

———. "Lace Curtain Literature: Changing Perceptions of Irish American Success." *Journal of American Culture* 2 (Spring 1979): 139–46.

Walsh, James J. "Burlesque Shows—A Crying Social Evil." *Columbiad,* January 1917.

———. *Education: How Old the New.* New York: Fordham University Press, 1920.

———. *Mother Alphonsa: Rose Hawthorne Lathrop.* New York: Macmillan, 1930.

———. *Our American Cardinals.* New York: Appleton, 1926.

———. *Success in a New Era.* Hoboken, N.J.: Franklin-Webb Co., 1919.

Walton, Susan Scharlotte. "To Preserve the Faith: Catholic Charities in Boston, 1870–1930." Ph.D. dissertation, Boston University, 1983.

———. "To Preserve the Faith: Catholic Charities in Boston, 1870–1930." In *Catholic Boston: Studies in Religion and Community, 1870–1970,* edited by Robert E. Sullivan and James M. O'Toole. Boston: Roman Catholic Archbishop of Boston, 1985.

Wangler, Thomas. "Catholic Religious Life in Boston in the Era of Cardinal O'Connell." In *Catholic Boston: Studies in Religion and Community, 1870–1970,* edited by Robert E. Sullivan and James M. O'Toole. Boston: Roman Catholic Archbishop of Boston, 1985.

Ward, Maisie. *The Wilfrid Wards and the Transition.* 2 vols. New York: Sheed and Ward, 1934.

Warner, Marina. *Alone of All Her Sex: The Myth and the Cult of the Virgin Mary.* New York: Knopf, 1976.

———. *Joan of Arc: The Image of Female Heroism.* New York: Knopf, 1981.

Warner, Sam Bass. *Streetcar Suburbs: The Process of Growth in Boston, 1870–1900.* 1962. 2d ed. Cambridge, Mass.: Harvard University Press, 1978.

Warner, William Lloyd, ed. *Yankee City.* New Haven: Yale University Press, 1963.

Watkin, David. *Morality and Architecture: The Development of a Theme in Architectural History and Theory from the Gothic Revival to the Modern Movement.* Oxford: Oxford University Press, 1977.

Watkin, Edward. *Enter the Irish-American.* New York: Crowell, 1976.

Wayman, Dorothy G. *Cardinal O'Connell of Boston: A Biography of William Henry O'Connell, 1859–1944.* New York: Farrar, Straus and Young, 1955.

———. *David I. Walsh: Citizen-Patriot.* Milwaukee: Bruce, 1952.

———. "Some Unpublished Correspondence between the Bellamy Storers and Cardinal O'Connell, 1908–1929." *Catholic Historical Review* 40 (July 1954): 129–77.

Weimann, Jeanne Madeline. *The Fair Women: The Story of the World's Columbian Exposition, Chicago 1893.* Chicago: Academy Chicago, 1981.

Welch, Claude. *Protestant Thought in the Nineteenth Century.* Vol. 2, 1870–1914. New Haven: Yale University Press, 1985.

White, James A. "The Era of Good Intentions: A Survey of American Catholics' Writing between the Years 1880 and 1915." Ph.D. dissertation, University of Notre Dame, 1957.

———. *The Founding of Cliff Haven.* New York: U.S. Catholic Historical Society, 1950.

White, Joseph M. *The Diocesan Seminary in the United States: A History from the 1780s to the Present*. Notre Dame, Ind.: University of Notre Dame, 1989.

———. "Historiography of Catholic Immigrants and Religion." *Immigration History Newsletter*, November 1982.

White, Susan J. *Art, Architecture, and Liturgical Reform: The Liturgical Arts Society, 1928–1972*. New York: Pueblo Publishing, 1990.

Whitehill, Walter Muir. *Boston in the Age of John F. Kennedy*. Norman: University of Oklahoma Press, 1966.

Whiting, Lilian. *Boston Days*. Boston: Little, Brown, 1902.

Whitmont, Edward. *Return of the Goddess*. New York: Crossroad, 1982.

The Whole D Family: Just One Letter of the Alphabet, and the Lesson It Teaches. Boston: American Citizen, 1919.

Wiebe, Robert H. *The Search for Order, 1877–1920*. New York: Hill & Wang, 1967.

Williams, Michael J. *American Catholics in the War: The National Catholic War Council, 1917–1921*. New York: Macmillan, 1921.

Williams, Peter. "Catholicism since World War I." In *Encyclopedia of the American Religious Experience*, vol. 1, edited by Charles Lippy and Peter Williams. New York: Scribner's, 1988.

———. "Medievalism in American Culture." In *The Medieval Heritage in American Religious Architecture*, edited by Bernard Rosenthal and Paul E. Szarmach, 1989.

———. *Popular Religion in America*. Urbana: University of Illinois Press, 1989.

———. "Religious Architecture and Landscape." In *Encyclopedia of the American Religious Experience*, edited by Charles Lippy and Peter Williams. New York: Scribner's, 1988.

Williams, Preston Noah. "Religious Response to the New Deal: The Reactions of William Henry O'Connell, Msgr. John A. Ryan, Clarence E. McCarney, and Reinhold Niebuhr to the Economic Policies of the New Deal." Ph.D. dissertation, Harvard University, 1967.

Willis, Pauline. *Willis Records: or, Records of the Willis Family of Haverhill, Portland, and Boston*. 2d ed. London: St. Vincent's Press, 1908.

Wilson, Christopher. *Labor of Words: Literary Professionals in the Progressive Era*. Athens: University of Georgia Press, 1985.

Winslow, Helen M. *Literary Boston of To-Day*. Boston: L. C. Page, 1902.

Winsor, Justin, ed. *The Memorial History of Boston, Including Suffolk County Massachusetts, 1630–1880*. 4 vols. Boston: Ticknor, 1881.

Withey, Henry F., and Elsie Rathburn Withey. *Biographical Dictionary of American Architects (Deceased)*. Los Angeles: New Age, 1956.

Wittke, Carl. "Immigrant Theme on the American Stage." *Mississippi Valley Historical Review* 39 (September 1952): 211–32.

———. *The Irish in America*. Baton Rouge: Louisiana State University Press, 1956.

Wolkovich-Valkavicius, William. "Cardinal and Cleric: O'Connell and Mullen in Conflict." *Historical Journal of Massachusetts* 13 (1985): 129–39.

Wood, A. L. S. "Keeping the Puritans Pure." *American Mercury*, September 1925.

Woods, Robert A. *The City Wilderness*. Boston: Houghton Mifflin, 1898.

———. *The Neighborhood in Nation-building*. Boston and New York: Houghton Mifflin, 1923.

————, ed. *Americans in Process: A Settlement Study by Residents and Associates of the South End House*. Cambridge, Mass.: Riverside, 1898.

————, ed. *Americans in Progress*. Boston: Houghton Mifflin, 1902.

Worland, Carr Elizabeth. "American Catholic Women and the Church to 1920." Ph.D. dissertation, St. Louis University, 1983.

Wyllie, Irvin G. *The Self-Made Man in America: The Myth of Rags to Riches*. New Brunswick, N.J.: Rutgers University Press, 1954.

Yeomans, Henry Aaron. *Abbot Lawrence Lowell, 1856–1943*. Cambridge, Mass.: Harvard University Press, 1948.

Zaretsky, Eli. *Capitalism, the Family, and Personal Life*. Rev. and exp. ed. New York: Harper & Row, 1986.

Action Française, 164
Adams, Henry, 113, 122, 162, 181, 292
Advertising: as revenue for Catholic press, 141
Advice literature: for boys, 84–85, 99; for girls, 176–80, 197
Aesthetics: influence of Gioberti, 263, 267; Aristotelian-Thomist content of, 263–64, 267; formation of Catholic, 263–68; and affinity with liberal humanism, 264; influence of Brownson, 265–67; influence of Earls, 267; and attack on dime novels, 272; learned in childhood, 273. *See also* Architecture; Neo-Thomism
Aeterni Patris, 263
Ahern, Michael, 36, 38, 311
Albee, Edward Franklin, 304
Allen, Fred, 303
Allen, Frederick B., 68, 307, 308
American Catholic Historical Association, 63
American Federation of Catholic Societies, 12, 22, 29, 105, 206, 301, 305
American Federation of Labor, 50
American Institute of Architects, 133, 143
American Irish Historical Society, 63, 133, 254
Americanist movement: condemned, 9
Americanization. *See* Assimilation
American Protective Association, 2, 53, 59, 60
American Purity League, 68
American Social Science Association, 216

Ancient Order of Hibernians, 23, 56, 99
Anderson, Auxiliary Bishop Joseph, 33, 39, 112, 207, 310
Anglo-Saxonism, 41, 49
"Anti-Aid" amendment: failure of, 2
Anti-Catholicism. *See* Nativism
Antisuffrage: among Catholics, 6, 241–44. *See also* Woman suffrage
Anti-ugly crusade of Catholics, 262–68. *See also* Aesthetics
Archdiocese of Boston: history of, 2; population of, 2, 58–59; reflects institutional model, 4; ethnic diversity in, 5; parochial schools in, 167–68. *See also* Centenary of Archdiocese of Boston
Architecture: of Catholic churches, 113–15, 126; elitism in, 115–17; as profession, 116–17; Catholics in, 129; and women, 137–39
Arts and Crafts movement, 122, 128
Assimilation: of Catholics, 7–8
Association of Catholic Colleges, 92
Avery, Martha Moore, 43, 44, 182–86, 188, 195, 207, 314, 315, 321, 322; and antisuffrage, 241

Bateman, Charles J., 135–36
Belloc, Hillaire, 286
Benedict XV, Pope, 17, 19, 70, 164, 245
Benson, Monsignor Robert Hugh, 162; as convert, 180; and LCW, 215; literary reception of, 286
Berenson, Bernard, 181, 234

Bishops' Program of Social Reconstruction, 150
Blake, Mary Elizabeth McGrath, 62, 178, 208, 210, 253, 254, 255, 258
Blunt, Hugh, 15, 194, 227, 269
Bolshevism, 106. *See also* Socialism and historical materialism
Bonzano, Archbishop John, 17, 70
Boston, city of: economic condition of, 33, 58; politics in, 60; as theater center, 297; censorship in, 305–13
Boston Author's Club, 255
Boston College, 14, 15, 54, 89, 115, 132, 133; graduates of, 91, 119. *See also* Earls, Michael; Gasson, Thomas; Maginnis, Charles; Society of Jesus
Boston Finance Commission, 33, 39
"Boston, 1915," 22, 32–33, 298; failure of, 33; Catholic participation in, 33–34, 46
Boston Press Club, 254
Boston Public School Association, 254
Boston School for Social Workers, 247
Boston School of Political Economy, 44
Boston Society of Architects, 117, 133
Brahmins, 53; hegemony of, 33, 97, 306; decline of, 58, 65, 258, 261–62; domination of architecture profession, 115, 134; as converts, 181–82, 186, 196; and Catholic culture, 210, 232, 254, 260
Breen, Joseph Ignatius, 312
Brégy, Katherine, 163
Brewer, Daniel Chauncey, 41
Brown-Durrell Company, 33
Brownson, Henry, 267
Brownson, Orestes, 181; impact on Catholic aesthetics, 265–67, 268, 269, 270, 286
Bugg, Lelia Hardin, 171, 178
Byrne, William, 280

Cabot, Godfrey Lowell, 68, 307
Cairns, Hugh, 258
Capitalism: absence of Catholic critique of, 45, 104; and Protestant work ethic, 82–83, 86, 104; and morality,

83; and Catholic work ethic, 84–85; and religious institutions, 96, 128; and gender roles, 146–47
Cary, Emma Forbes, 161, 180, 186–88, 212
Casey, John M.: as drama censor, 299, 308
Catholic Actors' Guild, 295, 296, 297, 298
Catholic Alumni Sodality, 39
Catholic Art Association, 141, 310
Catholic Charitable Bureau, 14, 28, 39, 102, 203, 321
Catholic Church: separatist integration and, 3, 295; centenary in Boston, 22–24; nationalism and, 65; in England, 286
Catholic Columbian Congress: of 1889, 12, 221, 267; of 1893, 12, 149, 221–23
Catholic converts. *See* Converts
Catholic Daughters of America, 63
Catholic Education Association, 89
Catholic Encyclopedia, 116, 159
Catholic Evidence Guild (London), 43
Catholic Immigration Bureau, 88
Catholic Immigration Society, 39
Catholic literature: role of, 258, 268. *See also* Catholic novels and novelists
Catholic novels and novelists, 268–74; and ideology, 258, 268; conflation of realism and naturalism, 268–69; didacticism of, 269–71; opposition to individualism, 270; post-1920, 271
Catholic Order of Foresters, 23, 99
Catholic publishers, 284
Catholic Radio Hour, 311
Catholic Reading Circle movement, 99, 125, 203, 205, 219; history of, 211–13
Catholic Summer School, 203, 219, 322; history of, 53, 207–10; and women, 209, 228; decline of, 250
Catholic Theatre Movement, 295, 296, 297, 301, 302, 307
Catholic Total Abstinence Union, 203, 242

Catholic Truth Films, 310
Catholic Truth Guild, 46, 184, 203; autovan tour of, 314–17
Catholic Truth Hour, 218
Catholic Truth Society of Great Britain, 286
Catholic Union of Boston, 53, 54, 99, 208, 254
Catholic University: National Catholic School for Social Service, 250
Catholic Worker movement, 191, 192
Catholic writers. See Catholic novels and novelists
Celtic literature. See Irish literary revival
Cenacle Convent Retreat Guild, 186, 205, 219
Censorship in Boston, 262, 299, 309; of theater, 6, 294–95, 307, 309, 319; of motion pictures, 6, 294–95, 319; by Watch & Ward Society, 300, 306–8; of books, 300, 307–9
Centenary of Archdiocese of Boston, 22–24
Charitable Irish Society, 63, 253–54
Charity. See Manhood; Nuns and sisters; Philanthropy; Progressives and Progressivism
Chase, Jason Franklin, 307
Chautauqua movement, 207–8
Chesterton, G. K., 286; at Holy Cross College, 278
Child labor laws: Catholic opposition to, 6
Christian Endeavor Society, 24
Churches, Catholic: architecture of, 117, 118, 125, 127, 144; financing of, 126, 129, 130, 132. See also Architecture; Parishes
City Beautiful Movement and Boston, 33
City life. See Rural myth; Urbanism
Class (as social and economic concept): divisions among Irish, 4–5, 50, 259; Catholic Church's attitude toward working class, 8; conflict not acknowledged by Catholic Church, 13; formation of middle class, 50–

59, 260, 319; cross-class unity, 97; domesticity and, 149; and sodalities, 201; in reading circles, 211–12; characteristics of middle class, 323
Clubwomen, Catholic. See specific organizations
Coakley, Daniel, 53, 57
Coleman, George, 36
Colleary, William B., 136
Colleges and universities: founding of, 89–90; Catholic identity of, 91, 92, 94; underenrollment in, 95; for women, 174–75
Collins, Patrick, 62, 299
Collins, Peter, 69
Common Cause Society, 22, 184; history of, 42–45, 216, 316
Communism and communists. See Socialism and historical materialism
Comstock, Anthony, 306
Congregation of St. Paul (Paulists), 187, 190, 241, 266
Connolly, James, 270, 287–88, 291
Conroy, Mary, 62, 258, 287
Convent schools: and upward mobility, 171–72; curriculum in, 172; regulations in, 172–74; theater in, 302
Converts: men, 180, 303–5; women, 180–96, 321; among New England Protestants, 186
Conway, Katherine, 1, 125, 160, 169, 171, 178, 187, 206, 208, 209, 210, 213, 253, 254, 258, 285; biographical information, 221–31; description of, 225; as novelist, 229, 269, 275; literary opinions of, 265, 270, 287, 288, 291
Cooper Union (New York City), 36
Corbett, Arthur B., 314, 315
Corbett, Joe, 6
Corrigan, Jones I., 38, 207, 243
Corrigan, Archbishop Michael A., 38, 191
Coughlin, Charles, 19
Cram, Ralph Adams, 133, 134, 181, 232; influence on Gothic revival, 113, 121–28, 292; influence on Maginnis, 121–22; and aristocratic

elitism, 122, 125–26; and Visionists, 234; and *Christian Art*, 281–82
Crowley, Mary Catherine, 253, 254, 287
Cultural studies, 7
Cunniff, Mrs. Michael, 213–14
Curley, James Michael, 5, 33, 35, 71, 146, 299, 305
Curtis, Edwin Upton, 73
Cushing, Richard Cardinal, 17, 133

Day, Dorothy, 83, 191, 192
Day, Fred Holland, 234; romance with Guiney, 234–35; fascination with Keats, 235
DeCourcy, Charles A., 54
Del Val, Rafael Merry Cardinal, 15
Democratic party, 55, 70
Desmond, Humphrey, 211, 275
De Valera, Eamon, 42; and William O'Connell, 18
Dickson, W. K. L., 309
Dierkes, Mary A., 257
Domestic feminism. *See* Feminism
Domesticity. *See* Feminism
Donahoe, Patrick, 85, 227
Donahoe, William, 136
Donnelly, Charles, 62
Donnelly, Eleanor, 155–56, 158, 178, 222
Donnelly, Francis, 297
Donovan, James, 6
Dougherty, Archbishop Dennis, 20
Dreiser, Theodore, 271
Dwight, Elizabeth, 213
Dwight, Thomas, 62, 150, 217
Dwyer, Michael, 287

Earls, Michael, 78, 111, 255, 269, 317; moderator of college magazines, 278
Easter Rising (Ireland, 1916): divides Irish Americans, 239
Egan, Maurice, 291–92
Eliot, Charles, 26, 91
Emery, Susan Lyman, 193–94, 195, 212, 213, 258
Emmanuel College, 99, 118, 175
Ethnic identity: Catholic Church strat-

egy concerning, 51; of Italians, 51. *See also* Irish Americans
European Catholic Church: and influence on O'Connell, 18, 76; and feudalism, 105; influence on American Catholic culture, 236

Farley, John Cardinal, 297
Farrell, James T., 271, 292
Fay, Charles, 43
Femininity. *See* Womanhood
Feminism, 154, 200–201; eschewed by Irish women, 149; three types of, 205; and domesticity, 205, 218, 222, 248–49; social feminism, 248–49, 320
Fiction, Catholic, 268–71, 284–89, 293. *See also* Catholic novels and novelists
Fields, Annie Adams, 232
Filene, Edward A.: and "Boston, 1915," 32; and mass marketing of books, 284
Fine arts: and lack of Catholic patronage, 257
Fitzgerald, F. Scott, 271
Fitzgerald, Mayor John ("Honey Fitz"), 5, 33, 103, 172, 253, 299; as publisher of *Republic*, 224, 275
Fitzgerald, William Francis, 54
Fitzpatrick, Thomas Bernard, 33, 52–53
Fitzsimmons, M. W., 136
Flaherty, James A., 68
Fletcher, Margaret, 180, 213
Foley, Margaret, 207, 243
Ford, Patrick J., 135
Ford Hall Forum, 22, 312; Catholic participation in, 36–38; compared to Common Cause, 43, 46, 257
Foss, Eugene, 32

Gaelic League, 63
Galvin, Thomas, 62
Gardner, Isabella Stewart (Mrs. Jack), 181, 282
Gargan, Thomas J., 62, 254
Gasson, Thomas, 15, 34, 92, 119, 220

Gender roles, 180, 320. *See also* Manhood; Womanhood
Gibbons, James Cardinal, 39, 150, 222
Goebel, Otto, 310
Goldstein, David, 43, 69, 182, 184, 311, 314, 315
Good Government Association, 33, 72
Gothic Revival, 83, 89, 113
Grey Nuns of Montreal. *See* Sisters of Charity
Guild, Governor Curtis, 72, 196
Guiney, Grace, 235
Guiney, Louise I., 124, 126, 128, 180, 213, 253, 258, 261, 281–82, 287, 290; biographical information, 231–39; and debate on Catholic fiction, 284–86, 293
Guiney, Ruth, 235

Hall, G. Stanley, 307
Hanna, Archbishop Edward J., 315
Harvard University: and Catholics, 26, 59, 91–92; Business School, 310
Hawthorne, Nathaniel, 180, 188, 283
Hayden, Sarah, 258
Hayes, Alice, 194–95, 273, 274
Hearn, Edward, 98
Hecker, Isaac, 181, 266
Hegemony, 49, 50
Higher education: by Jesuits, 89, 169; and non-Catholic colleges, 91, 92, 174; and career choices of men, 91, 94, 281; and career choices of women, 167–70, 174, 175, 212
Holmes, Oliver Wendell, 54, 72; and Guiney, 232, 255
Holy Cross Cathedral, 22, 29
Holy Cross College, 77, 78, 89, 132, 133
Holy Name Society, 23, 100
Holy Trinity Parish (German), 177
Hornblower & Weeks, 53
Howe, Manning and Almy firm, 137
Howells, William Dean, 283
Hudson, Daniel, 188, 272

Immigrants, Catholic: and assimilation, 7, 48–51; third-generation novelists,

229, 261, 292, 293. *See also* Irish Americans; North American Civic League for Immigrants
Immigration Restriction League, 34, 40–42, 307. *See also* Lee, Joseph; Ward, Robert DeCourcy
Individualism, 56–57, 104–7; and women, 151–53
Industrial Workers of the World, 42, 53
Innocence: as paradigm of American Catholic history, 6
Insider-outsider mentality of Catholics, 2, 31, 48, 79; defined, 2–3, 10, 19
International Catholic Benevolent Union, 99
International Federation of Catholic Alumnae, 203
International Federation of the Leagues of Catholic Women, 214
Ireland: and Boston, 42; emergence of Irish middle class to challenge British hegemony, 50
Irish Americans: formation of "Hibernarchy," 4–5; and Irish nationalism, 18, 42; and political machines, 35; and nostalgia, 49, 62; and craft unions, 50; downward mobility of, 50, 84; and labor competition, 51; and religious vocations, 51, 79, 168; occupations of, 51–55, 167–68, 274; situation in Massachusetts, 55; upward mobility of, 56–58, 108; and American identity, 61, 63; and male bonding, 79, 82; and fraternal societies, 96, 98, 103; and political machines, 107; property ownership of, 109; in censorship roles, 312. *See also* Subculture; Suburbanization
Irish Catholic Colonization Society, 111
Irish Free State, 41, 42
Irish immigrants in Boston. *See* Insider-outsider mentality of Catholics
Irish literary revival: impact on Boston, 255–57
Irishtocracy, 57, 96, 152. *See also* Class
Italians in Boston, 56, 88, 112; in

Lawrence strike, 42, 84; in architecture, 143, 345 (n. 118)
Italian Women's League, 147

James, Henry, 283
Jesuits. *See* Society of Jesus
Joan of Arc: Catholic devotions to,
162–65, 215; and French nationalism, 163; and high culture of Boston,
260
John Paul II, Pope: on womanhood,
148
Journalism: and womanhood, 178–80;
as female career, 228–31, 246–48;
and Boston Catholics, 258, 275–82;
and sensationalism, 271; and social
control, 275; as male career, 287–88;
and high culture, 290; weaknesses of
Catholic press, 291

Katolischer Frauenbund, 214
Kearney, T. F., 136
Keely, Patrick, 132
Keith, Andrew Paul, 304
Keith, Benjamin Franklin, 295, 309;
biographical information, 303–5;
bequest to O'Connell, 304, 341
(n. 29)
Keith, Mary Catherine Brawley, 303
Kelley, Samuel Dudley, 136
Kennedy, Joseph P., 107, 295, 305, 310
Kennedy, Patrick, 6
Kennedy, Rose Fitzgerald, 48, 107,
174
Kilmer, Joyce, 268, 277, 280
Knights of Columbus, 22, 42, 66, 97,
110, 310; antisocialist campaign, 42,
69; and Pelletier scandal, 68–70; and
Mexican anti-Catholicism, 69; pro-
Americanism campaign, 69, 103;
founding and growth in Massachu-
setts, 97–98, 109; and chivalric
codes, 98; and Fourth Degree, 98
Knights of Malta, 53, 55
Knights of St. Gregory the Great, 53,
55, 68
Know-Nothingism, 2

Laetare Medal: given to Fitzpatrick,
52; given to Phelan, 53; given to
Maginnis, 133; given to Conway,
227–28
La Farge, John, 181
Lathrop, George Parsons, 188, 190,
209, 266, 267, 290
Lathrop, Rose Hawthorne, 180, 186,
188–93, 209
Lawrence, Bishop William, 37, 83,
306
Lawrence, Massachusetts, strike: of
1912, 39, 42, 84, 185; of 1919, 18,
84
Lay apostolate, 47, 100
Laymen's Retreat Guild, 313
League of Catholic Women, 125, 203,
205, 322; and settlement houses, 28;
history of, 213–19, 249–51; based
on English model, 236; resolutions
of, 302
Lee, Joseph, 40–42
Legion of Decency, 312
Leo XIII, Pope, 10, 12, 18, 44, 147,
154, 159, 163, 182, 206; in motion
pictures, 309
Leveroni, Eliza, 258
Liberalism, classical and progressive,
104, 105
Liturgical Arts Society, 122, 124, 133,
141
Lodge, Henry Cabot, 41, 61
Lomasney, Martin "Mahatma," 6
Lord, Daniel A., 312
Loyal Coalition, 307

McCarthy, Denis, 62, 63, 172–74, 253,
256, 258, 262, 284, 287, 288
McCarthy, Rufina, 173
McGettrick, Felix, 17, 119
McGinnis, Joseph, 137
McGinty, William and John, 136
McNamara, Agnes, 246–47
McNicholas, Archbishop John, 20
McQuaid, Bishop Bernard, 76, 223
McSweeney, Edward, 94
Maginnis, Amy Brooks, 344 (n. 93)
Maginnis, Charles, 118, 121–29, 132–

34, 141, 143, 281; and "Boston, 1915," 32
Maguire, Patrick, 62
Maher, Edward F., 137
Maher, Mary, 165
Manhood: defined by Catholic Church, 75–89, 103; and feminism, 81, 156; and Protestant work ethic, 83–89; and monasticism, 102
Manning, Eleanor, 137–39, 144
Margaret Brent Suffrage Guild, 207
Marianism: encouraged by sodalities, 100, 198; and female devotions, 157–62; and male devotions, 159; defended, 160–61, 187; and saints' devotions, 162–66
Marxism, 18. *See also* Socialism and historical materialism
Mary. *See* Virgin Mary
Maryknoll Missionaries, 133
Massachusetts Association Opposed to Woman Suffrage, 244
Massachusetts Catholic Women's Guild, 203
Massachusetts Civic League, 40, 139
Massachusetts Institute of Technology, 117, 121. *See also* Technology Catholic Club
Massachusetts Woman Suffrage Association, 139, 241, 242
Medievalism: and American Catholicism, 113, 114, 251, 292. *See also* Architecture; Rural myth
Mencken, H. L., 290
Messmer, Archbishop Sebastian, 150–51
Mirari Vos, 11
Modernism, social and political: Catholic opposition to, 3, 26, 146, 269, 319; as intellectual, artistic avant-garde movement, 268
Modernism, theological, 3, 11; Vatican rejects, 9, 76; impact on seminary life, 76; and women's rights, 151
Motherhood. *See* Feminism; Gender roles; Womanhood; Working women
Motion pictures: censorship of, 294–95, 312; produced by Catholics,

310; attitudes toward, 311; religious potential of, 313, 317
Moulton, Louise Chandler, 232
Muckrakers, 268, 270, 274
Mullen, John, 15, 354 (n. 19)
Mundelein, Archbishop George, 20
Murphy, Blanche, 170

National Board of Censorship of Motion Pictures, 312
National Catholic Service School, 250
National Catholic Welfare Council, 20, 206, 216, 217
National Civic Foundation, 185
National Council of Catholic Women, 206, 217
National Women's Trade Union League, 247
Nativism: in Boston, 2, 8, 59–60; before 1900, 59; in Midwest, 60, 288–89; Knights of Columbus opposition to, 68, 103, 289
Naturalist fiction, 290; and muckrakers, 274; by Catholics, 287–88. *See also* Catholic novels and novelists
Neo-Thomism: and aesthetics, 263–64
New England Congress of Forums, 36, 62
New England Speaker's Bureau, 38
New England Watch & Ward Society. *See* Watch & Ward Society
New England Woman's Press Club, 227
New England Woman Suffrage Association, 206
Newman, John Cardinal, 267, 275, 286
Nilan, Bishop John, 194, 195
Nineteenth Amendment, 6
Norris, Kathleen, 292
North American Civic League for Immigrants, 38–40, 217
North American College in Rome, 14, 15, 170
Notre Dame Convent Academy, 118, 175; and Children of Mary sodality, 187; hosts LCW lecture series, 214–16

Nuns and sisters: educational opportunities of, 168; surplus in Boston, 168; as teachers, 172–75; and communalism, 190; autonomy curtailed, 203–4; and charitable work, 203–5; and competition with laywomen, 205. *See also* Women religious *and specific orders*

O'Brien, Hugh, 5, 62
O'Brien, John, 91, 136, 194; and *Sacred Heart Review*, 15
O'Connell, Daniel, 13, 19, 135
O'Connell, James P. E., 70; marriage and scandal, 15–17; discovery by Pelletier, 70
O'Connell, Joe, 6
O'Connell, Timothy, 137
O'Connell, Archbishop William, 3, 4; early career, 13–21; and diocesan expansion, 14; education in Rome, 14, 18; control of parishes, 15, 130, 132; and scandals, 15–17, 70; opposition to liberal bishops, 18; eclipsed in 1930s, 20; opposition to participation in "Boston, 1915," 34; silence on Pelletier case, 70–71; and St. John's, 75–76; outlook on priesthood, 79, 106; attitude toward wealth, 85; and secular education, 92, 168; on antiurbanism, 110–11; property purchases of, 118; on motherhood, 150, 153–54, 160; opposition to feminism, 150, 154; and takeover of *Pilot*, 223–24; and Catholic culture, 258–59; on decay of civilization, 265
O'Mahoney, Katherine O'Keeffe, 210, 213, 239
O'Meara, Stephen, 71–75, 90, 129, 287, 299, 300
Onahan, William, 222
O'Neill, Eugene, 271
Order of the Holy Sepulchre, 55
O'Reilly, John Boyle, 62, 172, 221, 223, 227, 241, 254–55, 259, 260, 262; death of, 258, 264
O'Reilly, Mary Boyle, 36, 210, 256,

284; criticism of Louise Guiney, 239, 287
O'Shea, John Augustine (organist), 257
O'Sullivan, Mary Blanche, 246–47, 258
Oxford Movement, 181

Pallen, Condé, 310
Parishes: financial administration of, 4; and ethnic diversity, 5; and Americanization, 7; as social center, 111–12; and laywomen's clubs, 201–2, 204–5
Parochial schools. *See* Schools, parochial
Pascendi domenici gregis, 76
Pastoralism. *See* Rural myth
Patriarchy, 147–49
Paulists. *See* Congregation of St. Paul
Pelletier, Joseph C., 34, 299, 307, 308; scandal while district attorney, 66–71
Peters, Andrew, 299
Phelan, Helen, 53, 214
Phelan, James J., 53, 87
Philanthropy: Catholic outlook on, 24–28, 39, 85, 88–89; laywomen in, 25–26; changing administration of, 28
Philpott, A. J., 36, 38
Piety. *See* Marianism; Society of Jesus
Pilot (Boston): ceases Gaelic column, 65; history of, 65, 72, 227; under Conway, 223–27; evolution from immigrant paper, 276–77
Pittsburgh Survey of 1909, 32
Pius X, Pope, 12, 14, 15, 147, 154, 159, 163, 206, 282
Pius XI, Pope, 18, 53
Pius XII, Pope, 147–48
Playboy of the Western World, 299
Police in Boston: dominated by Irish, 72; under Commissioner O'Meara, 72–73
Popular culture, 270. *See also* Aesthetics; Motion pictures; Vaudeville in Boston
Prendergast, James M., 53–54, 55, 85

Priests: predominance of Irish, 5, 59;
chaplaincy assignments, 44, 206–7,
249; surplus of, 59; assignment of
pastors, 75; spiritual formation of,
76, 78; seminary training of, 76–79,
169–70; in parish organizations,
102–3, 112
Prison reform, 187, 195, 215
Progressives and Progressivism, 6, 32,
36, 38, 40, 198, 230; Catholic criticism of, 24–28, 274; Catholic simi-
larity to, 202, 215, 251, 260
Protestant-Catholic cooperation, 27
Protestants in Boston. See Brahmins

Quadragesimo Anno, 18
Quanta Cura, 266
Queen's Work sodality, 100

Radcliffe College Catholic Club. See
Cary, Emma Forbes
Regan, Agnes, 217
Religious of the Sacred Heart, 221
Repplier, Agnes, 171, 284, 290, 302,
303
Republican party: and Catholics, 54,
72, 73, 74
Rerum Novarum, 10–11, 18, 25, 83,
147
Riley, James, 253, 254, 287
Robins, Julia Gorham, 193, 195
Roche, James Jeffrey, 62, 72, 210, 223,
225, 254, 258; as Irish writer, 261;
as adventure writer, 270
Roosevelt, Theodore: as admirer of
James Connolly, 270, 287
Rösler, Augustine, 159
Rothwell, Bernard, 33, 39, 70, 74
Roxbury Mission Church (Redemp-
torist), 24
Rural myth: among Irish Americans,
109–10; in American ideology, 110
Ryan, John A., 36, 37, 38, 46, 216

Sacco-Vanzetti trial, 73
Sacred Heart Academy: at Manhattanville, 172; at Elmhurst, 172, 173,
232; at Boston, 172–73

Sacred Heart Review (Cambridge), 15,
194, 195, 224, 258, 275, 277
St. Gabriel's Monastery, 101, 115, 132
Saint-Gaudens, Augustus, 181
St. John's Seminary, 14, 75–77, 169–
70, 175, 304; O'Connell's policies
and, 79; construction of, 132
St. Vincent de Paul Society, 88, 102,
106, 217
Santayana, George, 181
Scanlan, Michael J., 308, 309
Schools, parochial: defeat of public
funding for, 2; religious instruction
in, 90, 167–68; single women as
teachers in, 167. See also Convent
schools
Schools, public, 168; and Irish teachers,
149, 168
Scudder, Vida, 61
Second Catholic Missionary Congress:
O'Connell's role in, 29–30
Seminaries, U.S., 76; and Modernist
heresy, 76; and reformers, 77
Separatist integration: as Catholic strat-
egy, 26, 47, 63, 104, 295, 324
Servants for Relief of Incurable Cancer,
191
Seton, Robert, 150
Settlement houses, 81, 246; Catholic
attitude toward, 27, 28
Shaw, Richard, 137
Sheehan, Canon Patrick, 278, 286
Sheehan, T. Edward, 136
Sheen, Fulton J., 20
Shuster, George N., 256, 292
Sinn Fein movement, 42
Sisters of Charity (Grey Nuns of Mon-
treal), 203
Sisters of Mercy, 203
Sisters of St. Joseph, 90
Sisters of the Sacred Heart. See Reli-
gious of the Sacred Heart
Slattery, Francis, 49
Slattery, John R., 55
Slattery, Lillian, 214, 217–18
Smith, John Talbot, 77, 79, 113; on
seminary reform, 77, 113; on Brown-
son, 267; on Catholic fiction, 284–

86; on drama, 296, 298; on motion pictures, 311

Social Gospel movement, 27, 36, 65, 81

Socialism and historical materialism: anti-Catholic propaganda, 6, 44, 57, 58, 153; Catholic crusade against, 18, 105–6; in Massachusetts, 26–27, 45–46; influence of Bebel on, 182–84. See also Common Cause Society

Socialist Labor party, 182

Socialist party of America, 53, 182; foreign-born members, 45; native-born members, 45; tactics useful to Catholic women, 202

Society of Jesus, 15, 38, 196; outwits O'Connell, 15; piety of, 77; role at Boston College, 77, 89

Society of St. Sulpice, 75

Society of St. Vincent de Paul. See St. Vincent de Paul Society

Sodality movement, 100, 177, 187, 198

Sodality of the Children of Mary, 201, 202, 214

Spalding, Bishop John, 111, 116, 174, 175, 176

Spearman, Frank, 292

Spellman, Francis, 20, 225

Splaine, Michael, 45, 207, 209

Stang, Bishop William, 151, 154, 170, 177

Steffens, Lincoln, 32

Storer, John H., 68

Subculture: defined, 1, 7, 9; and Irish Catholics, 61–65; and Catholic journalism, 274–82

Suburbanization, 109, 136

Success ethic. See Capitalism; Individualism; Manhood

Sullivan, Louis, 114

Sullivan, Matthew, 341 (n. 42), 344 (n. 92)

Sulpicians. See Society of St. Sulpice

Syllabus of Errors, 8, 11, 266

Talbot, Francis, 292

Technology Catholic Club, 280, 308

Temperance movement, 200, 203, 307; supported by clergy and women, 242

Third Plenary Council of Baltimore, 89

Thomism, 11, 30, 263, 264. See also Neo-Thomism

Tincker, Mary Agnes, 253, 258

Toomey, Daniel P., 54, 103

Toomey, David J.: marriage and scandal, 15–16

Toomy, Alice, 222

Towle & Fitzgerald firm, 54

Tracy, Patrick A., 136

Twain, Mark, 162, 283

Twentieth Century Club, 39, 294, 298

United Irish League, 52

Urbanism: Catholic Church outlook on, 108–11, 143; and rural myth, 110–11

Vatican I, 8, 10, 12, 46

Vatican II, 12, 20, 46

Vaudeville in Boston: and Catholic Church, 294

Vaughan, Bernard, 162, 163, 215, 236, 286

Veblen, Thorstein, 152

Virgin Mary: as symbol, 145, 157–62, 184; priests' devotion to, 159. See also Marianism

Visitation Order, 190

Walsh, David I., 5

Walsh, James J., 38, 94, 143, 164, 209; attacks burlesque shows, 301

Walsh, Bishop Louis, 17

Walsh, Timothy, 32, 132, 133, 134, 141

Ward, Robert DeCourcy, 40

Ward, Wilfrid, 286

Watch & Ward Society, 66–68, 69, 298, 306–8; establishes Boston Book Dealers Association, 307

Waters, Patrick J., 18, 43–44, 207

Wharton, Edith, 283

White, Stanton R., 299

Williams, Archbishop John, 14, 19, 99, 186, 223, 227, 255, 258
Williams, Michael, 292
Willis, Pauline, 180, 213
Wilson, Woodrow, 54, 121
Winchester, Charles A., 137
Wolff, Mary Evaline (Sister Mary Madaleva), 224
Womanhood: Catholic ideology of, 147–49, 172, 197–98; and mother-hood, 153–57
Woman suffrage: opposed by Catholic Church, 6
Women religious: as educators, 167–68; outnumbering of men, 168; charitable work of, 203–5
Women's Educational and Industrial Union, 206, 227
Women's rights: versus service orientation, 200–201. *See also* Feminism
Woods, Robert A., 32, 36

Working women, 82, 230, 244–48; Irish, 149, 198, 245
World's Columbian Exposition, 138, 149
World's Columbian Congress of Women, 149, 155, 156, 161, 187, 221, 228–29, 244
World's Parliament of Religions, 149–50, 222
World War I, 4, 6, 25, 83, 105, 127, 130, 148, 170, 175, 218
Wright, Frank Lloyd, 114
Wright, John Cardinal, 160

Young Ladies' Charitable Association, 202
Young Men's Catholic Association, 94, 175
Young Men's Christian Association, 24, 39, 312